Montmartre

Opéra
Quarter

Tuileries
Quarter

Beaubourg
and Les Halles

The Marais

N E

St-Germain-
des-Prés

Ile de la
Cité

Ile St-
Louis

Latin
Quarter

Luxembourg
Quarter

Jardin des Plantes
Quarter

Montparnasse

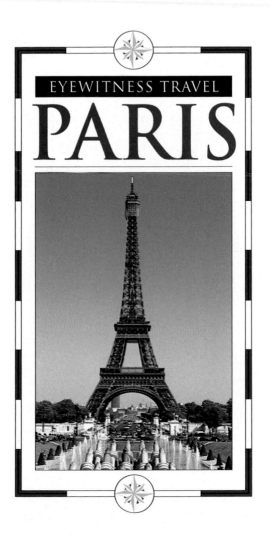

EYEWITNESS TRAVEL

PARIS

EYEWITNESS TRAVEL

PARIS

MAIN CONTRIBUTOR: ALAN TILLIER

LONDON, NEW YORK,
MELBOURNE, MUNICH AND DELHI
www.dk.com

PROJECT EDITOR Heather Jones
ART EDITOR Janis Utton
EDITOR Alex Gray
DESIGNER Vanessa Hamilton
DESIGN ASSISTANT Clare Sullivan

CONTRIBUTORS
Chris Boicos, Michael Gibson, Douglas Johnson

PHOTOGRAPHERS
Max Alexander, Neil Lukas, Robert O'Dea

ILLUSTRATORS
Stephen Conlin, Stephen Gyapay,
Maltings Partnership

This book was produced with the assistance of
Websters International Publishers.

Reproduced by Colourscan, Singapore
Printed and bound by South China Printing Co. Ltd., China

First published in Great Britain in 1993
by Dorling Kindersley Limited
80 Strand, London WC2R 0RL

12 13 14 15 10 9 8 7 6 5 4 3 2

Reprinted with revisions 1994, 1995, 1997 (twice), 1999, 2000, 2001, 2002, 2003, 2004, 2005, 2006, 2007, 2008, 2009, 2010, 2011, 2012

Copyright © 1993, 2012 Dorling Kindersley Limited, London
A Penguin Company

ISBN 978 1 4053 6873 5

FLOORS ARE REFERRED TO THROUGHOUT IN ACCORDANCE WITH FRENCH
USAGE; IE THE "FIRST FLOOR" IS THE FLOOR ABOVE GROUND LEVEL.

Front cover main image: The Louvre Museum at twilight

MIX
Paper from
responsible sources
FSC™ C018179

**The information in this DK Eyewitness Travel Guide
is checked annually.**

Every effort has been made to ensure that this book is as up-to-date
as possible at the time of going to press. Some details, however,
such as telephone numbers, opening hours, prices, gallery hanging
arrangements and travel information are liable to change. The
publishers cannot accept responsibility for any consequences arising
from the use of this book, nor for any material on third party
websites, and cannot guarantee that any website address in this
book will be a suitable source of travel information. We value the
views and suggestions of our readers very highly. Please write to:
Publisher, DK Eyewitness Travel Guides, Dorling Kindersley,
80 Strand, London, WC2R 0RL, or email: travelguides@dk.com.

◁ **Sacré-Coeur and the Butte Montmartre**

CONTENTS

Henri II (1547–59)

INTRODUCING
PARIS

Pont Alexandre III

Opéra National de Paris Bastille

The Kiss by Rodin (1886)

Sacré-Coeur in Montmartre

An island in the Bois de Boulogne

TRAVELLERS' NEEDS

Noisettes of lamb

SURVIVAL GUIDE

The Panthéon

HOW TO USE THIS GUIDE

This Eyewitness Travel Guide helps you get the most from your stay in Paris with the minimum of practical difficulty. The opening section, *Introducing Paris*, locates the city geographically, sets modern Paris in its historical context and explains how Parisian life changes through the year. *Paris at a Glance* is an overview of the city's specialities. The main sightseeing section of the book is *Paris Area by*

Area. It describes all the main sights with maps, photographs and detailed illustrations. In addition, eight planned walks take you to parts of Paris you might otherwise miss.

Carefully researched tips for hotels, shops and markets, restaurants and bars, sports and entertainment are found in *Travellers' Needs*, and the *Survival Guide* has advice on everything from posting a letter to catching the metro.

PARIS AREA BY AREA

The city has been divided into 14 sightseeing areas. Each section opens with a portrait of the area, summing up its character and history, with a list of all the sights to be covered. These are clearly located by numbers on an *Area Map*. This is followed by a large-scale *Street-by-Street Map* focusing on the most interesting part of the area. Finding your way about the section is made simple by the numbering system used throughout for the sights. This refers to the order in which they are described on the pages that complete the section.

1 Area Map *For easy reference, the sights in each area are numbered and located on an area map. To help the visitor, the map also shows metro and mainline RER stations and car parks.*

2 Street-by-Street Map *This gives a bird's-eye view of the heart of each sightseeing area. The most important buildings are picked out in stronger colour, to help you spot them as you walk around.*

A locator map shows you where you are in relation to surrounding areas. The area of the *Street-by-Street Map* is shown in red.

The Conciergerie 8 is shown on this map as well.

Colour-coding on each page makes the area easy to find in the book.

Photographs of facades and distinctive details of buildings help you to locate the sights.

Sights at a Glance lists the sights in the area by category: Historic Streets and Buildings, Churches, Museums and Galleries, Monuments, and Squares, Parks and Gardens.

The area covered in greater detail on the *Street-by-Street Map* is shaded red.

A suggested route for a walk takes in the most attractive and interesting streets in the area.

Travel tips help you reach the area quickly.

Numbered circles pinpoint all the listed sights on the area map. The Conciergerie, for example, is **8**

Stars indicate the sights that no visitor should miss.

PARIS AT A GLANCE

Each map in this section concentrates on a specific theme: *Museums and Galleries, Churches, Squares, Parks and Gardens, Remarkable Parisians*. The top sights are shown on the map; other sights are described on the following two pages.

Each sightseeing area is colour-coded.

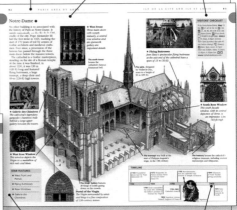

The theme is explored in greater detail on the pages following the map.

3 Detailed information on each sight
All important sights in each area are described in depth in this section. They are listed in order, following the numbering on the Area Map. *Practical information is also provided.*

PRACTICAL INFORMATION
Each entry provides all the information needed to plan a visit to the sight. The key to the symbols used is on the inside back cover.

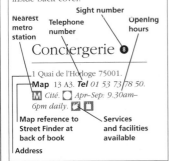

Nearest metro station

Telephone number

Sight number

Opening hours

Conciergerie **8**

1 Quai de l'Horloge 75001.
Map 13 A3. **Tel** 01 53 73 78 50.
M *Cité.* ◻ *Apr–Sep: 9.30am–6pm daily.*

Map reference to Street Finder at back of book

Services and facilities available

Address

4 Paris's major sights *These are given two or more full pages in the sightseeing area in which they are found. Historic buildings are dissected to reveal their interiors; and museums and galleries have colour-coded floor plans to help you find important exhibits.*

The Visitors' Checklist provides the practical information you will need to plan your visit.

The facade of each major sight is shown to help you spot it quickly.

Notre-Dame **0**

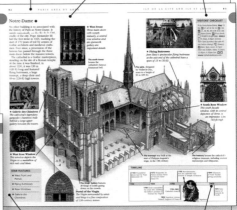

Stars indicate the most interesting architectural details of the building, and the most important works of art or exhibits on view inside.

A timeline charts the key events in the history of the sight.

INTRODUCING
PARIS

FOUR GREAT DAYS IN PARIS

Paris is a city packed with wonderful things to see and do. There may be a temptation to spend the trip in a café letting the French way of life wash over you, but it would be a shame to miss its treasures. Here are the best of the city's must-dos. Energetic sightseers

Rodin's Thinker

should manage everything on these itineraries, but this selection can also be dipped into for ideas. All are reachable by public transport. Price guides are for two adults or for a family of two adults and two children, excluding meals and transport costs.

Pyramide du Louvre, from across the fountain pools

ARTISTIC TREASURES

- Fabulous art at the Louvre
- Lunch at chic Café Marly
- A visit to the Rodin sculpture garden or take in the Pompidou Centre
- Dine at Tokyo Eat

TWO ADULTS allow at least €70

Morning
Begin with the **Musée du Louvre** *(see pp122–9)*, one of the world's most impressive museums. Beat the crowds by using the little-known entrance at the Carrousel du Louvre (99 Rue de Rivoli). Save time by getting a floorplan and working out where you want to go and sticking to it.

Lunch
There are many cheap eateries nearby, but for a great lunch experience head to smart **Café Marly** *(see p304)*. On warm days sit in the outside gallery or revel in the cozy red velvet and gilt splendour of the interior.

Afternoon
Choose from three destinations for the afternoon. The fatigued should head to the sublime **Musée Rodin** *(see p187)* for a soothing stroll in the sculpture garden and a pensive moment next to *The Thinker*. Those seeking modern masterpieces should visit the **Pompidou Centre** *(see pp110–13)*, an intriguing inside-out building housing works from 1905 to the modern day. To go even more modern, explore the crop of galleries that are known as "Louise 13", situated on the **Rue Louise Weiss** *(Map 18 E4)* in the 13th arrondissement (district). The galleries are all rather cutting-edge, but the most important (and funky) is Air de Paris.

Evening
The **Palais de Tokyo** *(see p203)* is one of Paris' most fashionable exhibition spaces, with its multimedia displays open till midnight. After a quick tour around, stop at restaurant Tokyo Eat.

RETAIL THERAPY

- Buy foody treats at Le Bon Marché
- Lunch at a top department store restaurant
- Drinks and dinner at Kong

TWO ADULTS allow at least €40

Morning
One-stop shops for gourmets and gluttons include **Fauchon, Hediard** and **La Grande Epicerie** at **Le Bon Marché** *(see pp320–21)*. In fact, anything that is edible – as long as it's delicious – can be found here. Specialist shops include **Poilâne** for bread, **Richart** for chocolate, **Legrand** for wine and **Pierre Hermé** for cakes. Or head down the Rue Mouffetard, one of the city's best market streets.

Lunch
Shopaholics can eat in one of the main department stores. The World Bar at **Au Printemps**, designed by Paul Smith, is a super-cool eatery *(see pp320–21)*, for example.

Ultra-hip interior of Kong, which also has stunning rooftop views

The surrounding area is a busy shopping and eating hub, so you can combine the two with no difficulty.

Afternoon
Either shop on till you drop, or go esoteric and visit the **Musée des Arts Décoratifs** near the Louvre *(see p121)*; a true temple to the decorative arts with a fabulous shop to pick up gifts. Boutique lovers should go to **Claudie Pierlot, Agnes B, Isabel Marant, Vanessa Bruno** *(see pp324–7)*.

Evening
Head for restorative drinks and dinner at **Kong** on top of Kenzo's flagship store and fashion shrine *(see pp317–18)*.

Reflections in La Géode, giant sphere at the Parc de la Villette

---

CHILD'S PLAY

- **Explore Parc de la Villette**
- **See animals at the zoo at Jardin des Plantes**
- **Stop for a café lunch**
- **Go up the Eiffel Tower**

FAMILY OF FOUR allow at least €190

Morning
Take receptive young minds to **Parc de la Villette**, which has an impressive children's programme. **La Cité des Sciences et de l'Industrie** (Science City) is packed with interesting interactive exhibits for budding Einsteins *(see pp236–9)*. Family fun can be found at the **Ménagerie** *(see p164)* in the Jardin des Plantes area where the zoo

is very popular. Even more exciting than the live animals for some are the skeletons and stuffed beasts in the **Muséum National d'Histoire Naturelle** *(see p167)*.

Lunch
There are lots of cafés in the Jardin des Plantes area or a more formal lunch can be had at **Mavromatis** *(see p307)*.

Afternoon
No child can resist a trip up the **Eiffel Tower**, so take them up in the afternoon for a proper view of the city, or wait until nightfall and time your trip to coincide with the changing of the hour when thousands of lights twinkle for ten minutes *(see pp194–5)*. If there's time, take a tour of the waxworks at the **Grévin** museum *(see p218)*. Most of the models are of French celebrities, but big international names in art and sport can also be spotted.

THE GREAT OUTDOORS

- **Boat trip on the Seine**
- **Lunch on the Rue de Rivoli**
- **A walk to Luxembourg Garden**
- **Take a balloon ride**

TWO ADULTS allow at least €65

Morning
For today's trip the metro is banned, so instead take the hop-on-hop-off batobus up the Seine. The first "stop" is near the **Eiffel Tower** so a quick look around the

Modern water sculpture and glasshouse, Parc André Citroën

Champ-de-Mars underneath Gustave Eiffel's monument is recommended *(see p191)*. Continue on the batobus to the Louvre stop, jump off and wander around the **Jardin des Tuileries** *(see p130)*.

Lunch
The tea salon **Angélina** *(see p318)* is a cut above other cafés on Rue de Rivoli. Leave space for the famous Mont Blanc cake of chestnut purée and cream.

Afternoon
Reboard the boat and head up to **Notre-Dame** *(see pp82–5)*, then it's a good walk down the Boulevard St Michel to the **Jardin du Luxembourg** *(see p172)*. There's lots to see – chess tables, beehives and donkey rides – and the **Musée du Luxembourg**, which hosts blockbuster exhibitions. For a final blast of fresh air, cross the city to the **Parc André Citroën** and take a tethered balloon ride *(see p247)*.

A floral display in the Jardin des Plantes

Putting Paris on the Map

Paris, the capital of France, is a city of over two million people covering 1,200 sq km (460 sq miles) of northern France. It is on the River Seine at the centre of the Ile-de-France, the region which is home to 11.5 million people, around one-fifth of the French population. An important European business and cultural centre, it is the focus of activity in the north of France.

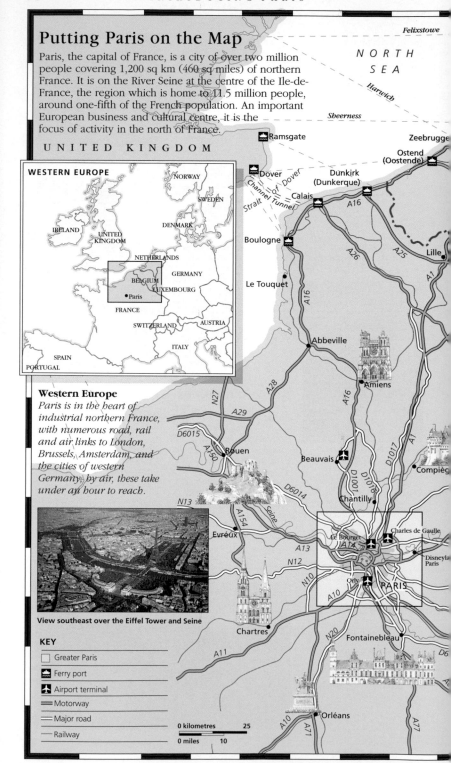

WESTERN EUROPE

NORWAY
SWEDEN
DENMARK
IRELAND
UNITED KINGDOM
NETHERLANDS
GERMANY
BELGIUM
LUXEMBOURG
• Paris
FRANCE
SWITZERLAND
AUSTRIA
ITALY
SPAIN
PORTUGAL

Western Europe

Paris is in the heart of industrial northern France, with numerous road, rail and air links to London, Brussels, Amsterdam, and the cities of western Germany; by air, these take under an hour to reach.

View southeast over the Eiffel Tower and Seine

KEY

- ☐ Greater Paris
- ⚓ Ferry port
- ✈ Airport terminal
- ═══ Motorway
- ─── Major road
- ─── Railway

0 kilometres 25
0 miles 10

NORTH SEA
Felixstowe
Harwich
Sheerness
UNITED KINGDOM
Ramsgate
Zeebrugge
Dover
Ostend (Oostende)
Channel Tunnel
Strait of Dover
Calais
Dunkirk (Dunkerque)
A16
Boulogne
A26
A25
Lille
A1
Le Touquet
A16
Abbeville
Amiens
A28
A16
N27
A29
D6015
A150
Rouen
Beauvais
A17
D1017
Compiège
D1001
D1076
Chantilly
D6014
N13
A154
Seine
Evréux
Le Bourget
Charles de Gaulle
A14
Disneyland Paris
A13
N12
Orly
PARIS
N10
A10
Chartres
N20
Fontainebleau
D6
A11
A10
A71
Orléans
A77

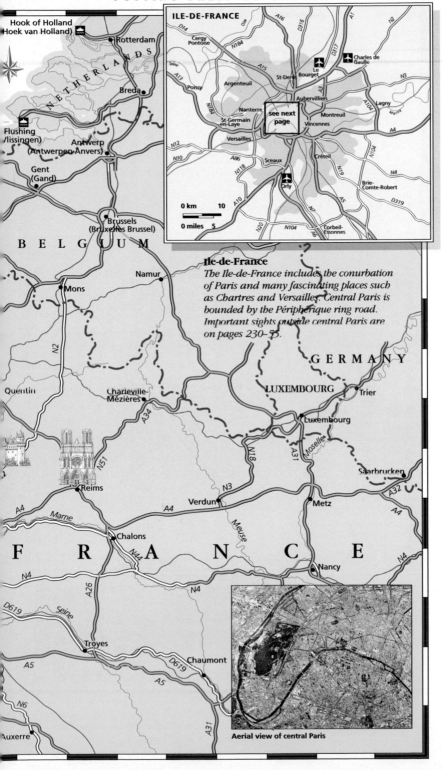

ILE-DE-FRANCE

Hook of Holland
(Hoek van Holland)
Rotterdam
NETHERLANDS
Breda
Flushing
(Vlissingen)
Antwerp
(Antwerpen-Anvers)
Gent
(Gand)
Brussels
(Bruxelles Brussel)

BELGIUM

Namur
Mons

Quentin

Charleville-
Mézières

GERMANY

LUXEMBOURG
Trier

Luxembourg

Saarbrucken

Reims
Marne
Verdun
Metz
Chalons

F   R   A   N   C   E

Nancy

N4

Troyes

Chaumont

Auxerre

Ile-de-France map inset labels:

Cergy
Pontoise
Charles de
Gaulle
Poissy
St-Denis
Le
Bourget
Argenteuil
Aubervilliers
Nanterre
St-Germain-
en-Laye
Montreuil
Lagny
Vincennes
see next
page
Versailles
Créteil
Sceaux
Brie-
Comte-Robert
Orly
Corbeil-
Essonnes

0 km   10
0 miles   5

Ile-de-France

The Ile-de-France includes the conurbation of Paris and many fascinating places such as Chartres and Versailles. Central Paris is bounded by the Périphérique ring road. Important sights outside central Paris are on pages 230–55.

Aerial view of central Paris

Central Paris

This book divides Paris into 14 areas, comprising central Paris and the nearby area of Montmartre. Most of the sights covered in the book lie within these areas, each one of which has its own chapter. Each area contains a range of sights that convey some of its history and distinctive character. The sights of

Napoleon's Arc de Triomphe

Montmartre, for example, reveal its village charm and its colourful history as a thriving artistic enclave. In contrast, Champs-Elysées is renowned for its wide avenues, expensive fashion houses and opulent mansions. Most of the city's famous sights are within reach of the heart of the city and are easy to reach on foot or by public transport.

Dôme Church
The gilded Dôme Church (see pp188–9) lies at the heart of the Invalides.

Eiffel Tower
Named after the engineer who designed and built it in 1889, the Eiffel Tower is the city's best-known land-mark (see pp194–5). It towers more than 320 m (1,050 ft) above Champ-de-Mars park.

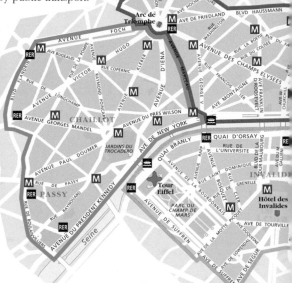

KEY

■	Star sights
Ⓜ	Metro station
🚉	SNCF (train) station
RER	RER station
⛴	Boat service boarding point
ℹ	Tourist information office

Musée du Louvre
Right in the heart of Paris, adjacent to the River Seine and the Tuileries garden, lies the city's most impressive museum, with an unrivalled collection of artifacts from around the world (see pp122–9).

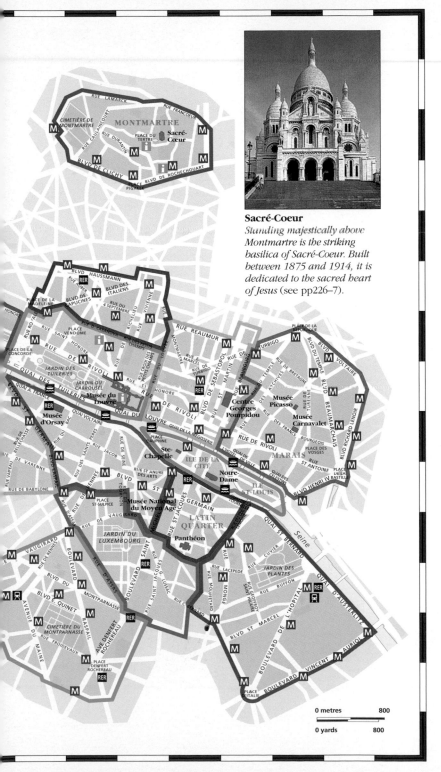

Sacré-Coeur
*Standing majestically above
Montmartre is the striking
basilica of Sacré-Coeur. Built
between 1875 and 1914, it is
dedicated to the sacred heart
of Jesus (see pp226–7).*

REPUBLIQUE FRANCAISE
LIBERTE EGALITE · FRATERNITE

THE HISTORY OF PARIS

The Paris conquered by the Romans in 55 BC was a small flood-prone fishing village on the Ile de la Cité, inhabited by the Parisii tribe. A Roman settlement soon flourished and spread on to the Left Bank of the Seine. The Franks succeeded the Romans, named the city Paris and made it the centre of their kingdom.

Fleur-de-lys, the royal emblem

During the Middle Ages the city flourished as a religious centre and architectural masterpieces such as Sainte-Chapelle were erected. It also thrived as a centre of learning, enticing European scholars to its great university, the Sorbonne.

Paris emerged during the Renaissance and the Enlightenment as a great centre of culture and ideas, and under the rule of Louis XIV it also became a city of immense wealth and power. But rule by the monarch gave way to rule by the people in the bloody Revolution of 1789. By the early years of the new century, revolutionary fervour had faded and the brilliant militarist Napoleon Bonaparte proclaimed himself Emperor of France and pursued his ambition to make Paris the centre of the world.

Soon after the Revolution of 1848 a radical transformation of the city began. Baron Haussmann's grand urban scheme replaced Paris's medieval slums with elegant avenues and boulevards. By the end of the century, the city was the driving force of Western culture. This continued well into the 20th century, interrupted only by the German military occupation of 1940–44. Since the war, the city has revived and expanded dramatically, as it strives to be at the heart of a unified Europe.

The following pages illustrate Paris's history by providing snapshots of the significant periods in the city's evolution.

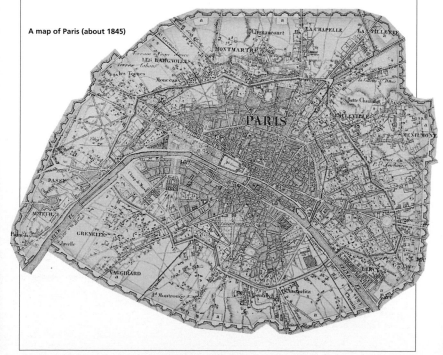

A map of Paris (about 1845)

◁ *Allegory of the Republic* (1848) by Dominique Louis Papety

Kings and Emperors in Paris

Paris became the power base for the kings of France at the beginning of the Capetian dynasty, when Hugh Capet ascended the throne. Successive kings and emperors have left their mark and many of the places mentioned in this book have royal associations: Philippe-Auguste's fortress, the Louvre Palace, is now one of the world's great museums; Henri IV's Pont Neuf bridge links the Ile de la Cité with the two banks of the Seine; and Napoleon conceived the Arc de Triomphe to celebrate his military victories. The end of the long line of kings came with the overthrow of the monarchy in 1848, during the reign of Louis-Philippe.

768–814 Charlemagne

566–584 Chilpéric I

558–562 Clotaire I

447–458 Merovich

458–482 Childéric I

695–711 Childebert II

674–691 Thierri III

655–668 Clotaire III

628–637 Dagobert I

743–751 Childéric III

716–721 Chilpéric II

954–986 Lothaire

898–929 Charles III, the Simple

884–888 Charles II, the Fat

879–882 Louis III

840–877 Charles I, the Bald

1137–80 Louis V

987–996 Hugh Capet

1031–60 Henri I

1060–1108 Philippe I

400	500	600	700	800	900	1000	110

MEROVINGIAN DYNASTY — **CAROLINGIAN DYNASTY** — **CAPETIAN DYNASTY**

400	500	600	700	800	900	1000	110

751–768 Pépin the Short

721–737 Thierri IV

711–716 Dagobert III

691–695 Clovis III

668–674 Childéric II

637–655 Clovis II

584–628 Clotaire II

562–566 Caribert

511–558 Childebert I

996–1031 Robert II, the Pious

986–987 Louis V

936–954 Louis IV, the Foreigner

888–898 Odo, Count of Paris

882–884 Carloman

877–879 Louis II, the Stammerer

814–840 Louis I, the Debonair

482–511 Clovis I

1108–37 Louis VI, the Fat

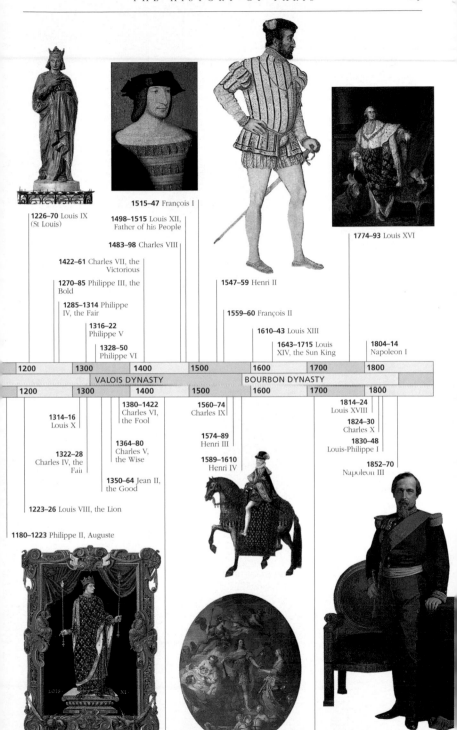

1515–47 François I

1226–70 Louis IX
(St Louis)

1498–1515 Louis XII,
Father of his People

1483–98 Charles VIII

1422–61 Charles VII, the
Victorious

1270–85 Philippe III, the
Bold

1285–1314 Philippe
IV, the Fair

1316–22
Philippe V

1328–50
Philippe VI

1774–93 Louis XVI

1547–59 Henri II

1559–60 François II

1610–43 Louis XIII

1643–1715 Louis
XIV, the Sun King

1804–14
Napoleon I

1200	1300	1400	1500	1600	1700	1800
VALOIS DYNASTY				BOURBON DYNASTY		
1200	1300	1400	1500	1600	1700	1800

1314–16
Louis X

1322–28
Charles IV, the
Fair

1380–1422
Charles VI,
the Fool

1364–80
Charles V,
the Wise

1350–64 Jean II,
the Good

1223–26 Louis VIII, the Lion

1180–1223 Philippe II, Auguste

1560–74
Charles IX

1574–89
Henri III

1589–1610
Henri IV

1814–24
Louis XVIII

1824–30
Charles X

1830–48
Louis-Philippe I

1852–70
Napoleon III

1461–83 Louis XI, the Spider

1715–74
Louis XV

Gallo-Roman Paris

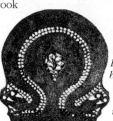

Paris would not have existed without the Seine. The river provided early peoples with the means to exploit the land, forests, marshes and islands. Recent excavations have unearthed canoes dating back to 4,500 BC, well before a Celtic tribe, known as the Parisii, settled there in the 3rd century BC, in an area known as Lutetia. From 59 BC,

Roman enamel brooch

the Romans undertook the conquest of Gaul (France). Seven years later Lutetia was sacked by the Romans. They fortified and rebuilt it, especially the main island (the Ile de la Cité) and the Left Bank of the Seine.

EXTENT OF THE CITY

| 200 BC | | Today |

Bronze-Age Harness
Everyday objects like harnesses continued to be made of bronze well into the Iron Age, which began in Gaul around 900 BC.

Iron Daggers
From the 2nd century BC, short swords of iron replaced long swords and were sometimes decorated with human and animal shapes.

Baths

Theatre

Forum

Present-day
Rue Soufflot

Glass Beads
Iron-Age glass beads and bracelets have been found on the Ile de la Cité.

Fired-Clay Vase
Pale ceramics with coloured decoration were common in Gaul.

Present-day
Rue St-Jacques

TIMELINE

Helmet worn by Gaulish warriors

4500 BC Early boatmen operate from the banks of the Seine

52 BC Labienus, Caesar's lieutenant, defeats the Gauls under Camulogenes. The Parisii destroy their own city

4500	400		200

Parisii gold coin minted on the Ile de la Cité

300 BC Parisii tribe settle on the Ile de la Cité

100 BC Romans rebuild the Ile de la Cité, and create a new town on the Left Bank

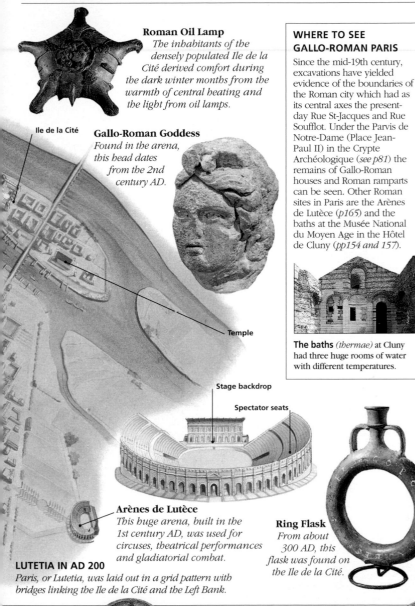

Roman Oil Lamp
The inhabitants of the densely populated Ile de la Cité derived comfort during the dark winter months from the warmth of central heating and the light from oil lamps.

Ile de la Cité

Gallo-Roman Goddess
Found in the arena, this head dates from the 2nd century AD.

Temple

WHERE TO SEE GALLO-ROMAN PARIS
Since the mid-19th century, excavations have yielded evidence of the boundaries of the Roman city which had as its central axes the present-day Rue St-Jacques and Rue Soufflot. Under the Parvis de Notre-Dame (Place Jean-Paul II) in the Crypte Archéologique (*see p81*) the remains of Gallo-Roman houses and Roman ramparts can be seen. Other Roman sites in Paris are the Arènes de Lutèce (*p165*) and the baths at the Musée National du Moyen Age in the Hôtel de Cluny (*pp154 and 157*).

The baths *(thermae)* at Cluny had three huge rooms of water with different temperatures.

Stage backdrop

Spectator seats

Arènes de Lutèce
This huge arena, built in the 1st century AD, was used for circuses, theatrical performances and gladiatorial combat.

Ring Flask
From about 300 AD, this flask was found on the Ile de la Cité.

LUTETIA IN AD 200
Paris, or Lutetia, was laid out in a grid pattern with bridges linking the Ile de la Cité and the Left Bank.

Roman floor mosaic from the Cluny baths

200 Romans add arena, baths and villas

285 Barbarians advance, Lutetia swept by fire

360 Julien, prefect of Gaul, is proclaimed Emperor. Lutetia changes its name to Paris after the Parisii

200

400

250 Early Christian martyr, St Denis, beheaded in Montmartre

451 Sainte Geneviève galvanizes the Parisians to repulse Attila the Hun

485–508 Clovis, leader of the Franks, defeats the Romans. Paris becomes Christian

Medieval Paris

Manuscript illumination

Throughout the Middle Ages, strategically placed towns like Paris, positioned at a river crossing, became important centres of political power and learning. The Church played a crucial part in intellectual and spiritual life. It provided the impetus for education and for technological advances such as the drainage of land and the digging of canals. The population was still confined mainly to the Ile de la Cité and the Left Bank. When the marshes *(marais)* were drained in the 12th century, the city was able to expand.

EXTENT OF THE CITY

■ *1300*	□ *Today*

Sainte-Chapelle
The upper chapel of this medieval masterpiece (see pp88–9) was reserved for the royal family.

The Ile de la Cité, including the towers of the Conciergerie and Sainte-Chapelle, features in the pages for June.

Octagonal Table
Medieval manor houses had wooden furniture like this trestle table.

Drainage allowed more land to be cultivated.

Weavers' Window
Medieval craftsmen formed guilds and many church windows were dedicated to their crafts.

A rural life was led by most Parisians, who worked on the land. The actual city only occupied a tiny area.

TIMELINE

512 Death of Sainte Geneviève. She is buried next to Clovis

725–732 Muslims attack Gaul

845–862 Normans attack Paris

500	700	800	900

543–556 Foundation of St-Germain-des-Prés

Golden hand reliquary of Charlemagne

800 Charlemagne crowned Emperor by the Pope

THE HISTORY OF PARIS

Notre-Dame

The great Gothic cathedrals took many years to build. Work continued on Notre-Dame from 1163 to 1334.

University Seal

The University of Paris was founded in 1215.

The Monasteries

Monks of many different orders lived in monasteries in Paris, especially on the Left Bank of the Seine.

The Louvre of Charles V with its defensive wall is seen here from the Ile de la Cité.

The Nobility

From the mid-14th century, dress was considered to be a mark of class; noble ladies wore high, pointed hats.

A MEDIEVAL ROMANCE

It was in the cloisters of Notre-Dame that the romance between the monk Pierre Abélard and the young Héloïse began. Abélard was the most original theologian of the 12th century and was hired as a tutor to the 17-year-old niece of a canon. A love affair soon developed between the teacher and his pupil. In his wrath, Héloïse's uncle had the scholar castrated; Héloïse took refuge in a convent for the rest of her life.

THE MONTHS: JUNE AND OCTOBER

This illuminated prayer book and calendar, the Très Riches Heures (left and above), was made for the Duc de Berri in 1416. It shows many Paris buildings.

1010–22 Christians burn Jews and heretics

1167 Les Halles food market created on the Right Bank of the Seine

1253 The Sorbonne opens

1380 The Bastille fortress completed

Joan of Arc

1000	1100	1200	1300	1400

1079 Birth of Pierre Abélard

1163 Work starts on Notre-Dame cathedral

1245 Work starts on Sainte-Chapelle

1430 Henry VI of England crowned King of France after Joan of Arc fails to defend Paris

1226–70 Reign of Louis IX, St Louis

1215 Paris University founded

Renaissance Paris

Couple in fine courtly dress

At the end of the Hundred Years' War with England, Paris was in a terrible state. By the time the occupying English army had left in 1453, the city lay in ruins, with many houses burned. Louis XI brought back prosperity and a new interest in art, architecture, decoration and clothes. During the course of the 16th and 17th centuries, French kings came under the spell of the Italian Renaissance. Their architects made the first attempts at town planning, creating elegant, uniform buildings and open urban spaces like the magnificent Place Royale.

EXTENT OF THE CITY

☐ 1590 ☐ Today

A Knight Preparing to Joust
The Place Royale was the setting for jousting displays well into the 17th century.

Printing Press (1470)
Religious tracts, mainly in Latin, were printed on the first press at the Sorbonne.

Jewel-Encrusted Pendant
A sign of the new prosperity, jewels became an important part of dress.

Pont Notre-Dame
This bridge with its row of houses was built at the start of the 15th century. The Pont Neuf (1589) was the first bridge without houses.

PLACE ROYALE
Built by Henri IV in 1609, with grand symmetrical houses round an open, central space, this was Paris's first square. Home to the aristocracy, it was re-named Place des Vosges in 1800 (see p94).

TIMELINE

1453 End of the Hundred Years' War with England

François I

1516 François I invites Leonardo da Vinci to France. He brings the *Mona Lisa* with him

1450	1460	1470	1480	1490	1500	1510	1520

1469 First French printing works starts operating at the Sorbonne

1528 François I takes up residence in the Louvre

16th-Century Knife and Fork Set
Ornate knife and fork sets were used in the dining rooms of the wealthy to carve joints of meat. Diners used hands or spoons for eating.

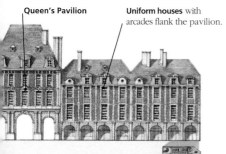

Queen's Pavilion

Uniform houses with arcades flank the pavilion.

WHERE TO SEE RENAISSANCE PARIS TODAY

Besides the Place des Vosges, there are many examples of the Renaissance in Paris. Churches include St-Etienne-du-Mont *(p153)*, St-Eustache *(p114)*, as well as the nave of St-Gervais–St-Protais *(p99)*. Mansions such as the Hôtel de Sully *(p95)* and the Hôtel Carnavalet *(pp96–7)* have been restored, and the staircases, courtyard and turrets of the Hôtel de Cluny *(pp154–5)* date from 1485–96.

The rood screen of St-Etienne-du-Mont (about 1520) is of outstanding delicacy.

PLACE ROYALE (PLACE DES VOSGES)

Walnut Dresser (about 1545)
Elegant carved wooden furniture decorated the homes of the wealthy.

Nine symmetrical houses line each side of the square.

Hyante and Climente
Toussaint Dubreuil and other artists took up Renaissance mythological themes.

King's Pavilion

Duels were fought in the centre of the square in the 17th century.

1534 Ignatius of Loyola founds the Society of Jesus

1546 Work starts on new Louvre palace; first stone quay built along Seine

1559 Primitive street lanterns introduced; Louvre completed

1572 St Bartholomew's Day massacre of Protestants

1589 Henri III assassinated at St-Cloud, near Paris

1609 Henri IV begins building Place des Vosges

1530	1540	1550	1560	1570	1580	1590	1600

1547 François I dies

1534 Founding of the Collège de France

1533 Hôtel de Ville rebuilt

1559 Henri II killed in a Paris tournament

1593 Protestant Henri of Navarre converts to Catholicism, and is crowned as Henri IV in 1594

1610 Henri IV is assassinated by Ravaillac, a religious fanatic

The assassin Ravaillac

The Sun King's Paris

Emblem of the Sun King

The 17th century in France, which became known as *Le Grand Siècle* (the great century), is epitomized by the glittering extravagance of Louis XIV (the Sun King) and his court at Versailles. In Paris, imposing buildings, squares, theatres and aristocratic *hôtels* (mansions) were built. Beneath this brilliant surface lay the absolute power of the monarch. By the end of Louis' reign the cost of his extravagance and of waging almost continuous war with France's neighbours led to a decline in the monarchy.

EXTENT OF THE CITY

☐ *1657*   ☐ *Today*

The mansard roof, with its slopes at both sides and both ends, came to typify French roofs of this period.

An open staircase rose from the internal courtyard.

Cross section of the living quarters

The Gardens of Versailles
Louis XIV devoted a lot of time to the gardens, which were designed by André Le Nôtre.

Louis XIV as Jupiter
On ascending the throne in 1661, Louis, depicted here as Jupiter triumphant, ended the civil wars that had been raging since his childhood.

The ground floor contained the servants' quarters.

Chest of Drawers
This gilded piece was made by André-Charles Boulle for the Grand Trianon at Versailles.

TIMELINE

1610 Louis XIII's accession marks the start of *Le Grand Siècle*	*Louis XIII*		*Cardinal Mazarin*	**1643** Death of Louis XIII. Regency under control of Marie de Médicis and Cardinal Mazarin	**1661** Louis XIV becomes absolute monarch. Enlargement of Château de Versailles begun
		1624 Completion of Tuileries Palace	**1631** Launch of *La Gazette*, Paris's first newspaper		
1610	**1620**	**1630**	**1640**	**1650**	**1660**
	1622 Paris becomes an episcopal see	**1629** Richelieu, Louis XIII's first minister, builds Palais Royal	**1638** Birth of Louis XIV		**1662** Colbert, Louis XIV's finance minister, founds Gobelins tapestry works
1614 Final meeting of the Estates Council (the main legislative assembly) before the Revolution		**1627** Development of the Ile St-Louis			*Weaving frame*

Ceiling by Charles Le Brun
Court painter to Louis XIV, Le Brun decorated many ceilings like this one at the Hôtel Carnavalet (see p96).

Madame de Maintenon
When the queen died in 1683, Louis married Madame de Maintenon, shown here in a framed painting by Caspar Netscher.

The Galerie d'Hercule with Le Brun ceiling

Decorated Fan
For special court fêtes, Louis XIV often stipulated that women carry fans.

Formal Classical Garden

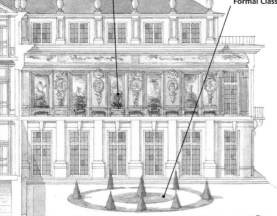

HÔTEL LAMBERT (1640)
In the 17th century, the aristocracy built luxurious town houses with grand staircases, courtyards, formal gardens, coach houses and stables.

Neptune Cup
Made from lapis lazuli with a silver Neptune on top, this cup was part of Louis' vast collection of art objects.

Dôme Church (1706)

WHERE TO SEE THE SUN KING'S PARIS

Many 17th-century mansions such as the Hôtel Lambert still exist in Paris, but not all are open to the public. However, Hôtel des Invalides *(p187)*, the Dôme Church *(pp188–9)*, the Palais du Luxembourg *(p172)* and Versailles *(pp248–53)* give a magnificent impression of the period.

1667 Louvre rebuilt and observatory established

1682 Court moves to Versailles where it stays until the Revolution

1686 Le Procope, Paris's first café

1702 Paris first divided into 20 arrondissements (districts)

1715 Louis XIV dies

| 1670 | 1680 | 1690 | 1700 | 1710 |

1692 Great famines due to bad harvests and wars

1670 Hôtel des Invalides built

1689 Pont Royal built

Statue of Louis XIV at Musée Carnavalet

Paris in the Age of Enlightenment

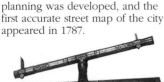

Bust of François Marie Arouet, known as Voltaire

The Enlightenment, with its emphasis on scientific reason and a critical approach to existing ideas and society, was centred on the city of Paris. In contrast, nepotism and corruption were rife at Louis XV's court at Versailles. Meanwhile the economy thrived, the arts flourished as never before and intellectuals, such as Voltaire and Rousseau, were renowned throughout Europe. In Paris, the population rose to about 650,000: town planning was developed, and the first accurate street map of the city appeared in 1787.

EXTENT OF THE CITY

☐ 1720   ☐ Today

Nautical Instruments
As the science of navigation advanced, scientists developed telescopes and trigonometric instruments (used for measuring longitude and latitude).

18th-Century Wigs
These were not only a mark of fashion but also a way of indicating the wearer's class and importance.

COMEDIE FRANÇAISE
The Age of Enlightenment saw a burst of dramatic activity, and new theatres opened. Among them was the Comédie Française (see p120), still one of the most prestigious theatres in the world.

The auditorium, with 1,913 seats, was the largest in Paris.

TIMELINE

Fireman

1722 City's first fire brigade founded

1733 Voltaire's *Lettres Philosophiques* published

1734 Fontaine des Quatre Saisons built

1748 Montesquieu's *L'Esprit des Lois* (an influential work about different forms of government) published

1751 First volume of Diderot's *Encyclopedia* published

| 1720 | 1730 | 1740 | 1750 |

Madame de Pompadour
*Although generally
remembered as the
mistress of Louis XV, she
was renowned as a patron
of the arts and had great
political influence.*

**WHERE TO SEE
ENLIGHTENMENT PARIS**
The district around the Rue
de Lille, the Rue de Varenne
and the Rue de Grenelle
(p187) has many luxurious
town houses, or *hôtels*,
which were built by the
aristocracy during the first
half of the 18th century.
Memorabilia from the lives
of the great intellectuals
Voltaire and Jean-Jacques
Rousseau is in the Musée
Carnavalet *(pp96–7)*, along
with 18th-century interior
designs and paintings.

Chocolate Pot
*By the 18th century,
bourgeois families
could afford tobacco, tea,
chocolate and coffee from Asia
and the New World.*

Vestibule with
painted ceiling

Portico with
Doric columns

Churches were built throughout
the Enlightenment. St-Sulpice
(p172) was completed in 1776.

Le Procope *(p140)* is the oldest
café in Paris. It was frequented
by Voltaire and Rousseau.

The Catacombs
*These were set up in
1785 as a more
hygienic alternative
to Paris's cemeteries
(see p179).*

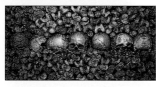

1757 First oil
street lamps

c.1760 Place de
la Concorde,
Panthéon and
Ecole Militaire
built

1760

1762
Rousseau's
Emile and
the *Social
Contract*

1764 Madame
de Pompadour
dies

*Rousseau, philosopher
and writer, believed
that humans were
naturally good
and had been
corrupted by
society.*

1770

1774 Louis XV,
great grandson of
Louis XIV, dies

1778 France supports
American independence

1780

1782 First
pavements built,
in the Place du
Théâtre Français

1783
Montgolfier
brothers make
the first hot-air
balloon ascent

1785
David paints
the *Oath of
the Horatii*

Paris During the Revolution

In 1789 most Parisians were still living in squalor and poverty, as they had since the Middle Ages. Rising inflation and opposition to Louis XVI culminated in the storming of the Bastille, the king's prison; the Republic was founded three years later. However, the Terror soon followed, when those suspected of betraying the Revolution were executed

A plate made in celebration of the Revolution

without trial: more than 60,000 people lost their lives. The bloody excesses of Robespierre, the zealous revolutionary, led to his overthrow and a new government, the Directory, was set up in 1795.

EXTENT OF THE CITY

▨ *1796*   ▢ *Today*

The prison turrets were set alight.

The French guards, who were on the side of the revolutionaries, arrived late in the afternoon with two cannons.

Declaration of the Rights of Man and the Citizen

The Enlightenment ideals of equality and human dignity were enshrined in the Declaration. This illustration is the preface to the 1791 Constitution.

REPUBLICAN CALENDAR

The revolutionaries believed that the world was starting again, so they abolished the existing church calendar and took 22 September 1792, the day the Republic was declared, as the first day of the new era. The Republican calendar had 12 equal months, each sub-divided into three ten-day periods, with the remaining five days of each year set aside for public holidays. All the months of the year were given poetic names which linked them to nature and the seasons, such as fog, snow, seed-time, flowers and harvest.

A coloured engraving by Tresca showing *Ventôse,* the windy month (19 Feb–20 Mar) from the new Republican calendar

Drawbridge

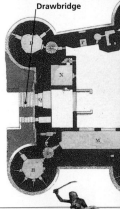

TIMELINE

14 Jul Fall of the Bastille	**4 Aug** Abolition of feudalism	
	26 Aug Declaration of the Rights of Man and the Citizen	
	17 Sep Law of Suspects passed: the Terror begins	**10 Aug** The storming of the Tuileries

1789	1790	1791	1792

Cartoon on the three Estates: the clergy, the nobility and the awakening populace

Lafayette, Commander of the National Guard, takes his oath to the Constitution

17 Jul Champ de Mars massacre

25 Apr *La Marseillaise* composed

5 May The Estates council meets

14 Jul Fête de la Fédération

Paper Money
Bonds, called assignats, *were used to fund the Revolution from 1790–93.*

La Marseillaise
The revolutionaries' marching song is now the national anthem.

The Sans Culottes
By 1792, the wearing of trousers instead of breeches (culottes) was a political symbol of Paris's artisans and shopkeepers.

"Patriotic" Chair
The back of this wooden chair is topped by red bonnets, symbol of revolutionary politics.

Wallpaper
Commemorative wallpaper was produced to celebrate the Revolution.

The dead and wounded totalled 171 by the end of the day.

 Coin tower

— Great court

— Well court

Guillotine
This was used for the first time in France in April 1792.

STORMING OF THE BASTILLE
The Bastille was overrun on 14 July 1789 and the seven prisoners held there released. The defenders (32 Swiss guards, 82 wounded soldiers and the governor) were massacred.

Jun Invasion the Tuileries	**21 Jan** Execution of Louis XVI	**16 Oct** Execution of Marie-Antoinette	**5 Apr** Execution of Danton and supporters	**22 Aug** New constitution: the Directory
10 Aug Overthrow of Louis XVI	**Autumn** Robespierre in control of Committee of Public Safety	**24 Nov** Churches closed	**19 Nov** Jacobin Club (a revolutionary pressure group) closed	
	1793		**1794**	**1795**
20 Sep Battle of Valmy	**13 Jul** Assassination of Marat, founder of *L'Ami du Peuple*, the revolutionary newspaper		*Robespierre, revolutionary and architect of the Terror*	
2–6 Sep September massacres			**27 Jul** Execution of Robespierre	

Napoleonic Paris

Napoleon Bonaparte was the most brilliant
general in the French army. The instability
of the new government after the
Revolution gave him the chance to seize
power, and in November 1799 he installed
himself in the Tuileries Palace as First
Consul. He crowned himself Emperor in
May 1804. Napoleon established a
centralized administration and a code of

**Napoleon's
imperial crown**

laws, reformed France's educational system and set out to
make Paris the most beautiful city in the world. The city
was endowed with grand monuments and embellished
with the spoils of conquest. His power was always fragile
and dependent on incessant wars. In March 1814
Prussian, Austrian and Russian armies invaded Paris and
Napoleon fled to Elba. He returned to Paris in 1815 but
was defeated at Waterloo and died in exile in 1821.

EXTENT OF THE CITY

▨ 1810   ☐ Today

Château de Malmaison
*This was the favourite
home of Josephine,
Napoleon's
first wife.*

Ladies-in-Waiting hold
Josephine's train.

Opaline-Glass Clock
*The decoration on this
clock echoed the
fashion for draperies.*

Elephant Project
*This monument
was planned
for the centre of
the Place de la
Bastille.*

Eagle's Flight
*Napoleon's flight
to Elba in 1814
was satirized in
this cartoon.*

TIMELINE

1799 Napoleon seizes power	**1800** Banque de France founded		**1812** Russian campaign ends in defeat	**1815** Waterloo; second abdication of Napoleon. Restoration of the monarchy
1797 Battle of Rivoli	**1802** Legion of Honour established			
1800	**1805**	**1810**	**1815**	**1820**
	1804 Napoleon crowned	**1806** Arc de Triomphe commissioned	**1814** Napoleon abdicates	**1821** Napoleon dies
	1800 Napoleon returns from Egypt on his ship *L'Orient*		**1809** Napoleon divorces Josephine and marries Marie-Louise	*Napoleon's death mask*

Bronze Table Top
Inlaid with Napoleon's portrait, this table marks the victory at Austerlitz.

Josephine kneels before Napoleon.

Napoleon holds the crown for his Empress, Josephine.

Russian Cossacks in the Palais Royal
After Napoleon's defeat and flight in 1814, Paris suffered the humiliation of being occupied by foreign troops, including Austrians, Prussians and Russians.

The Pope makes the sign of the cross.

The Arc de Triomphe du
Carrousel was erected in 1806
and crowned with the horses
looted from St Mark's, Venice.

WHERE TO SEE
NAPOLEONIC PARIS

Many of the grand monuments Napoleon planned for Paris were never built, but two triumphal arches, the Arc de Triomphe *(pp210–11)* and Arc de Triomphe du Carrousel *(p122)*, were a major part of his legacy. La Madeleine church *(p216)* was also inaugurated in his reign and much of the Louvre was rebuilt *(pp122–3)*. Examples of the Empire style can be seen at Malmaison *(p255)* and at the Carnavalet *(pp96–7)*.

NAPOLEON'S CORONATION
Napoleon's rather dramatic crowning took place in 1804. In this recreation by J L David, the Pope, summoned to Notre-Dame, looks on as Napoleon crowns his Empress just before crowning himself.

The Empress
Josephine was divorced by Napoleon in 1809.

1842 First railway line between Paris and St-Germain-en-Laye opens

1825	1830	1835	1840	1845

1830 Revolution in Paris and advent of constitutional monarchy

1831 Victor Hugo's *Notre-Dame de Paris* published. Cholera epidemic hits Paris

1840 Reburial of Napoleon at Les Invalides

Napoleon's tomb

The Grand Transformation

In 1848 Paris saw a second revolution which brought down the recently restored monarchy. In the uncertainties that followed, Napoleon's nephew assumed power in the same way as his uncle before him – by a *coup d'état*. He proclaimed himself Napoleon III in 1851. Under his rule Paris was transformed into the most magnificent city in Europe. He entrusted the task of modernization to Baron Haussmann. Haussmann demolished the crowded, unsanitary streets of the medieval city and created a well-ordered capital within a geometrical grid of avenues and boulevards. Neighbouring districts such as Auteuil were annexed, creating the suburbs.

EXTENT OF THE CITY

▨ *1859*   ☐ *Today*

Lamppost outside the Opéra

Arc de Triomphe

Boulevard des Italiens
This tree-lined avenue, painted by Edmond Georges Grandjean (1889), was one of the most fashionable of the new boulevards.

Twelve avenues formed a star (*étoile*).

Laying the Sewers
This engraving from 1861 shows the early work for laying the sewer system (see p190) from La Villette to Les Halles. Most was the work of the engineer Belgrand.

Circular Hoarding
Distinctive hoardings advertised opera and theatre performances.

Grand mansions were built around the Arc de Triomphe between 1860 and 1868.

TIMELINE

1851 Napoleon III declares the Second Empire

Viewing the exhibits at the World Exhibition

1852 Haussmann begins massive town-planning schemes

1855 World Exhibition

| 1850 | 1852 | 1854 | 1856 | 1858 |

1853 Baltard starts work on new Les Halles buildings

1857 The poet, Baudelaire, prosecuted for obscenity for *The Flowers of Evil*

20 centimes stamp showing Napoleon III

PLACE DE L'ETOILE

The new scheme for the centre of Paris included redesigning the area at one end of the Champs-Elysées (Elysian Fields). Haussmann created a star of 12 broad avenues around the new Arc de Triomphe. (The inset map shows the area as it was in 1790.)

Fields

Avenue des Champs-Elysées

Site of Arc de Triomphe

Drinking Fountain
In the 1870s, 50 fountains were erected in poor areas of Paris through the generosity of the English francophile, Richard Wallace.

AVE DES CHAMPS ELYSEES
AVE MARCEAU
AVE D'IENA
AVE KLEBER
DE L'ETOILE
AVE VICTOR HUGO
AVE FOCH
AVE DE LA GRANDE ARMEE

Bois de Boulogne
Given to the city in 1852 by Napoleon III, this park became a popular place for walking and riding (see pp254–5).

BARON HAUSSMANN

Lawyer by training and civil servant by profession, Georges-Eugène Haussmann (1809–91) was appointed Prefect of the Seine by Napoleon III. For 17 years he was in charge of urban planning. With the best architects and engineers of the day, he planned a new city, improved the water supply and sewerage, and created beautiful parks.

Some avenues were named after French generals.

1861 Garnier designs new Opera House

1863 The nudity in Manet's *Le Déjeuner sur l'Herbe* causes a scandal and is rejected by the Academy *(see pp144–5)*

1867 World Exhibition

1870 Napoleon's wife, Eugénie, flees Paris at threat of war

1860 | 1862 | 1864 | 1866 | 1868

1863 Crédit Lyonnais bank established

1862 Victor Hugo's epic novel of Paris's poor, *Les Misérables*, published

1868 Press censorship relaxed

1870 Start of Franco-Prussian War

The Belle Epoque

The Franco-Prussian War culminated in the terrible Siege of Paris. When peace came in 1871, it fell to the new government, the Third Republic, to bring about economic recovery. From about 1890 life was transformed: the motor-car, aeroplane, cinema, telephone and gramophone all contributed to the enjoyment of life and the *Belle Epoque* (beautiful age) was born. Paris became a glittering city where the new style, *Art Nouveau*, decorated buildings and objects. The paintings of the Impressionists, such as Renoir, reflected the *joie de vivre* of the times, while later those of Matisse, Braque and Picasso heralded the modern movement in art.

Art Nouveau pendant

EXTENT OF THE CITY

■ *1895*   □ *Today*

The interior was arranged as tiers of galleries around a central grand staircase.

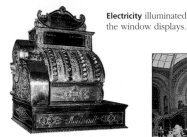

Cabaret Poster
Toulouse-Lautrec's posters immortalized the singers and dancers of the cafés and cabaret clubs of Montmartre, where artists and writers congregated in the 1890s.

Electricity illuminated the window displays.

Windows facing on to the Boulevard Haussmann displayed the goods on offer.

Art Nouveau Cash Till
Even ordinary objects like this cash till were beautified by the new style.

Central Hall of the Grand Palais
The Grand Palais (p208) *was built to house two huge exhibitions of French painting and sculpture at the World Exhibition of 1889.*

TIMELINE

1871 Third Republic established

1874 Monet paints first Impressionist picture: *Impression: Soleil levant*

Louis Pasteur

1889 Eiffel Tower built

1870	1875	1880	1885	1890

Zoo animals were shot to feed the hungry (see p226)

Entrance ticket to the exhibition

1891 First metro station opens

1870 Siege of Paris

1885 Louis Pasteur discovers rabies vaccine

1889 Great Exhibition

Citroën 5CV
France led the world in the early development of the motor-car. By 1900 the Citroën began to be seen on the streets of Paris, and long-distance motor racing was popular.

The glass dome could be seen from all parts of the store.

Moulin Rouge (1890)
The old, redundant windmills of Montmartre became nightclubs, like the world-famous Moulin Rouge (red windmill) (see p228).

GALERIES LAFAYETTE (1906)
This beautiful department store, with its dome a riot of coloured glass and wrought ironwork, was a sign of the new prosperity.

The Naughty Nineties
The Lumière brothers captured the daring negligée fashions of the 1890s in the first moving images of the cinematograph.

WHERE TO SEE THE BELLE EPOQUE
Art Nouveau can be seen in monumental buildings like the Grand Palais and Petit Palais *(p208)*, while the Galeries Lafayette *(p321)* and the Fermette Marbeuf restaurant *(p310)* have beautiful Belle Epoque interiors. The Musée d'Orsay *(pp144–7)* has many objects from this period.

The entrance to the metro at Porte Dauphine was the work of leading Art Nouveau designer Hector Guimard *(p226)*.

The doorway of No. 29 Avenue Rapp *(p191)*, in the Eiffel Tower quarter, is a fine example of Art Nouveau.

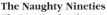

Captain Dreyfus was publicly humiliated for selling secrets to the Prussians. He was later found innocent.

1894–1906 Dreyfus affair

1907 Picasso paints *Les Demoiselles d'Avignon*

1913 Proust publishes first volume of *Remembrance of Things Past*

| 1895 | 1900 | 1905 | 1910 |

1898 Pierre and Marie Curie discover radium

1909 Blériot flies across the English Channel

1911 Diaghilev brings the Russian ballet to Paris

1895 Lumière brothers introduce cinematography

Avant-Garde Paris

From the 1920s to the 1940s, Paris became a mecca for artists, musicians, writers and film-makers. The city was alive with new movements such as Cubism and Surrealism represented by Cézanne, Picasso, Braque, Man Ray and Duchamp. Many new trends came from the USA, as writers and musicians including Ernest Hemingway, Gertrude Stein and Sidney Bechet took up residence in Paris. In architecture, the geometric shapes created by Le Corbusier changed the face of the modern building.

Office chair by Le Corbusier

EXTENT OF THE CITY

■ 1940   □ Today

Napoleon by Abel Gance
Paris has always been a city for film-makers. In 1927 Abel Gance made an innovative movie about Napoleon, using triple screens and wide-angle lenses.

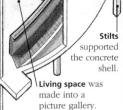

Occupied Paris
Paris was under occupation for most of World War II. The Eiffel Tower was a favourite spot for German soldiers.

Stilts supported the concrete shell.

Living space was made into a picture gallery.

Josephine Baker
Arriving in Paris in 1925, the outlandish dancer catapulted to fame in "La Revue Nègre" wearing nothing but feathers.

Sidney Bechet
In the 1930s and 1940s the jazz clubs of Paris resounded to the swing music of black musicians such as the saxophonist Sidney Bechet.

LA ROCHE VILLA BY LE CORBUSIER
Made from concrete and steel, with straight lines, horizontal windows and a flat roof, this house (1923) epitomized the new style.

TIMELINE

1919 Treaty of Versailles signed in the Hall of Mirrors

1924 Olympic Games held in Paris

1924 André Breton publishes Surrealist Manifesto

1925 Art Deco style first seen at the Exposition des Arts Décoratifs

PARIS-1925

| 1914 | 1916 | 1918 | 1920 | 1922 | 1924 | 1926 | 19 |

1914–18 World War I. Paris is under threat of German attack, saved by the Battle of the Marne. A shell hits St-Gervais-St-Protais.

World War I soldier in uniform

1920 Interment of the Unknown Soldier

An eternal flame for the Unknown Soldier burns under the Arc de Triomphe

Fashion in the 1940s
After World War II, the classic look for men and women was reminiscent of military uniforms.

The roof was designed as a garden terrace.

Airmail Poster
Airmail routes developed during the 1930s, especially to French North Africa.

The bedroom was above the dining room.

The kitchen was built at the back with a sloping glass roof.

The garage was built into the ground floor.

Windows were arranged in a horizontal strip.

The old Trocadéro was changed to the Palais de Chaillot *(see p200)* for the World Exhibition.

WHERE TO SEE AVANT-GARDE PARIS
La Roche Villa is now part of the Fondation Le Corbusier *(p254)* and can be visited in the Paris suburb of Auteuil. Hemingway's haunt, the barbrasserie La Closerie des Lilas in Montparnasse *(p179)*, has retained much of its period decor. For fashion don't miss the Musée Galliera *(p203)*.

Claudine in Paris by Colette
The Claudine series of novels, written by Colette Willy, known simply as "Colette", were extremely popular in the 1930s.

1931 Colonial Exhibition

A visitor to the exhibition in colonial dress

1937 Picasso paints Guernica in protest at the Spanish Civil War

1940 World War II: Paris bombed and occupied by Nazis

1930	1932	1934	1936	1938	1940	1942

1935 The talented Edith Piaf discovered dancing in the Paris streets

1934 Riots and strikes in response to the Depression

1937 Palais de Chaillot built

Symbol of Free French superimposed on the victory sign

Aug 1944 Liberation of Paris

The Modern City

In 1962 a programme of renovation began, with run-down districts like the Marais being restored. This work was continued by François Mitterrand's *Grands Travaux* (great works) scheme. Access was improved to historical monuments and art collections, such as the Grand Louvre *(see pp122–9)* and the Musée d'Orsay *(pp144–7)*. The scheme produced several monuments to the modern age, including the Opéra National de Paris Bastille *(p98)*, the Cité des Sciences *(pp236–9)* and the Bibliothèque Nationale at Quai de la Gare *(p246)*. With these, and the boldly modern Défense, Grande Arche, Stade de France and musée du quai Branly building, Paris prepared herself for the 21st century.

Late president, François Mitterrand

EXTENT OF THE CITY

■ 1959   □ Today

La Grande Arche
is taller and wider than Notre-Dame and runs in an axis linking the Arc de Triomphe and the Louvre Pyramid.

Christo's Pont Neuf
To create a work of art, the Bulgarian-born artist Christo wrapped Paris's oldest bridge, the Pont Neuf, in fabric in 1985.

Simone de Beauvoir
Influential philosopher and life-long companion of J-P Sartre, de Beauvoir fought for the liberation of women in the 1950s.

Shopping centre

Citroën Goddess (1956)
With its ultra-modern lines, this became Paris's most prestigious car.

TIMELINE

1950 Construction of UNESCO, and the Musée de Radio-France		**1962** André Malraux, Minister of Culture, begins renovation programme of run-down districts and monuments	*Ducting at the Pompidou Centre*		**1977** Pompidou Centre opens. Jacques Chirac is installed as first elected Mayor of Paris since 1871		**1980** Thousands greet Pope John-Paul on his official visit
1945	1950	1955	1960	1965	1970	1975	1980
		1958 Establishment of Fifth Republic with de Gaulle as President	**1964** Reorganization of the Ile de France	**1968** Student riots and workers strikes in the Latin Quarter	**1969** Les Halles market transfers to Rungis	**1973** Construction of Montparnasse Tower and the Périphérique (ring road)	

President de Gaulle

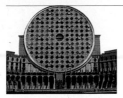

Chanel Designs
Paris is the centre of the fashion world with important shows each year.

Marne La Vallée
Like a gigantic loud speaker, this residential complex is in one of Paris's dormitory towns near Disneyland Resort Paris.

The Pompidou Centre
The nation's collection of modern art is housed here in this popular building (see pp110–13).

The Fiat Tower is one of Europe's tallest buildings.

Opéra National de Paris Bastille (1989)
It marks the bicentenary of the fall of the Bastille.

STUDENTS AT THE BARRICADES

In May 1968 Paris saw a revolution of a kind. The Latin Quarter was taken over by students and workers. What began as a protest against the war in Vietnam spread to other issues and became an expression of discontent with the Government. President de Gaulle rode out the storm but his prestige was severely damaged.

Rioting students clash with police

The Défense Palace, housing the centre for industry, is the oldest tower.

LA DÉFENSE

This huge business centre was started on the edge of Paris in 1958. Over 150,000 people work here with further expansion due by 2015.

Victorious French football team holding aloft the World Cup trophy in Paris

2002 The Euro replaces the Franc as exclusive legal tender

2007 The Vélib', a public rental bike scheme is launched

1985	1990	1995	2000	2005	2010	2015	2020

1985 Christo wraps Pont Neuf

1989 Bicentenary celebrations to mark the French Revolution

1994 Eurostar inaugurated: Paris to London in 3 hrs

1999 December hurricanes hit Paris: Versailles loses 10,000 trees

2007 Centre-right Nicolas Sarkozy elected president

1998 France hosts – and wins – the 1998 football World Cup tournament

PARIS AT A GLANCE

There are nearly 300 places of interest described in the *Area by Area* section of this book. A broad range of sights is covered: from the ancient Conciergerie and its grisly associations with the guillotine *(see p81)*, to the modern Opéra National de Paris Bastille *(see p98)*; from the oldest house in Paris, No. 51 Rue de Montmorency *(see p114)* to the exotic musée du quai Branly *(see pp192–3)*. To help make the most of your stay, the following 20 pages are a time-saving guide to the best Paris has to offer. Museums and galleries, historic churches, spacious parks, gardens and squares all have a section. There are also guides to Paris's famous personalities. Each sight has a cross reference to its own full entry. Below are the top tourist attractions to start you off.

PARIS'S TOP TOURIST ATTRACTIONS

Sacré-Coeur
See pp226–7.

Sainte-Chapelle
See pp88–9.

Palace of Versailles
See pp248–53.

Pompidou Centre
See pp110–13.

Jardin du Luxembourg
See p172.

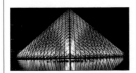

Musée du Louvre
See pp122–9.

Musée d'Orsay
See pp144–7.

Eiffel Tower
See pp194–5.

Bois de Boulogne
See pp254–5.

Notre-Dame
See pp82–5.

Arc de Triomphe
See pp210–11.

◁ The Dôme Church, adjoining the Hôtel des Invalides

Remarkable Parisians

By virtue of its strategic position on the Seine, Paris has always been the economic, political and artistic hub of France. Over the centuries, many prominent and influential figures from other parts of the country and abroad have come to the city to absorb her unique spirit. In return they have left their mark: artists have brought new movements, politicians new schools of thought, musicians and film-makers new trends, and architects a new environment.

Actress Catherine Deneuve

ARTISTS

Sacré-Coeur by Utrillo (1934)

In the early 18th-century, Jean-Antoine Watteau (1684–1721) took the inspiration for his paintings from the Paris theatre. Half a century later, Jean-Honoré Fragonard (1732–1806), popular painter of the Rococo, lived and died here, financially ruined by the Revolution. Later, Paris became the cradle of Impressionism. Its founders Claude Monet (1840–1926), Pierre-Auguste Renoir (1841–1919) and Alfred Sisley (1839–99) met in a Paris studio. In 1907, Pablo Picasso (1881–1973) painted the seminal work *Les Demoiselles d'Avignon* at the Bateau-Lavoir, *(see p228)* where Georges Braque (1882–1963), Amedeo Modigliani (1884–1920) and Marc Chagall (1887–1985) also lived. Henri de Toulouse-Lautrec (1864–1901) drank and painted in Montmartre. So did Salvador Dalí (1904–89) who frequented the Café Cyrano, centre of the Surrealists. The Paris School eventually moved to Montparnasse, home to sculptors Auguste Rodin (1840–1917), Constantin Brancusi (1876–1957) and Ossip Zadkine (1890–1967).

POLITICAL LEADERS

Hugh Capet, Count of Paris, became King of France in 987. His palace was on the Ile de la Cité. Louis XIV, XV and XVI lived at Versailles *(see pp248–53)* but Napoleon *(see pp32–3)* preferred the Tuileries. Cardinal Richelieu (1585–1642), the power behind Louis XIII, created the Académie Française and the Palais-Royal *(see p120)*. Today the President lives in the Palais de l'Elysée *(p209)*.

Portrait of Cardinal Richelieu by Philippe de Champaigne (about 1635)

FILMS AND FILM-MAKERS

Paris has always been at the heart of French cinema. The prewar and immediate post-war classics were usually made on the sets of the Boulogne and Joinville studios, where whole areas of the city were reconstructed, such as the Canal St-Martin for Marcel Carné's *Hôtel du Nord*. Jean-Luc Godard and other New Wave directors preferred to shoot outdoors. Godard's *A Bout de Souffle* (1960) with Jean-Paul Belmondo and Jean Seberg was filmed in and around the Champs-Elysées.

Simone Signoret (1921– 1985) and Yves Montand (1921–1991), the most celebrated couple of French cinema, were long associated with the Ile de la Cité. Actresses, such as Catherine Deneuve (b.1943) and Isabelle Adjani (b.1955), live in the city to be near their couturiers.

MUSICIANS

Jean-Philippe Rameau (1683–1764), organist and pioneer of harmony, is associated with St-Eustache *(see p114)*. Hector Berlioz (1803–69) had his *Te Deum* first performed there in 1855, and Franz Liszt (1811–86) his *Messe Solennelle* in 1866. A great dynasty of organists, the Couperins, gave recitals in St-Gervais–St-Protais *(see p99)*.

The stage of the Opéra *(see p217)* has seen many talents, but audiences have not always been appreciative. Richard Wagner (1813–83) had his *Tannhäuser* hooted down. George Bizet's *Carmen*

(1838–75) was booed, as was *Peléas et Mélisande* by Claude Debussy (1862–1918).

Soprano Maria Callas (1923–77) gave triumphal performances here. The composer and conductor Pierre Boulez (b.1925) has devoted his talent to experimental music at IRCAM near the Pompidou Centre *(see p346)*, which he helped to found.

The diminutive *chanteuse* Edith Piaf (1915–63), known for her nostalgic love-songs, began singing in the streets of Paris and then went on to tour the world. The acclaimed film about her life, *La Vie en Rose*, was released in 2007.

The Grand Trianon at Versailles, built by Louis Le Vau in 1668

Renée Jeanmaire as Carmen (1948)

ARCHITECTS

Gothic, Classical, Baroque and Modernist – all co-exist in Paris. The most brilliant medieval architect was Pierre de Montreuil, who built Notre-Dame and Sainte-Chapelle. Louis Le Vau (1612–70) and Jules Hardouin-Mansart (1646–1708) designed Versailles *(see pp248–53)*. Jacques-Ange Gabriel (1698–1782) built the Petit Trianon *(see p249)* and Place de la Concorde *(see p131)*. Haussmann (1809–91) gave the city its boulevards *(see pp34–5)*. Gustave Eiffel (1832–1923) built his tower in 1889. A century later, I M Pei added the Louvre's glass pyramid *(see p129)*, Jean Nouvel created the Institut du Monde Arabe *(see p164)* and the Musée du Quai Branly *(see pp192–3)*, while Dominique Perrault was behind the Bibliothèque Nationale de France *(see p246)*.

WRITERS

French has been dubbed "the language of Molière", after playwright Jean-Baptiste Poquelin, alias Molière, (1622–73), who helped create the Comédie-Française, now situated near his home in Rue Richelieu. On the Left Bank, the Odéon Théâtre de l'Europe was home to playwright Jean Racine (1639–99). It is near the statue of Denis Diderot (1713–84), who published his *L'Encyclopédie* between 1751 and 1776. Marcel Proust (1871–1922), author of the 13-volume *Remembrance of Things Past*, lived on the Boulevard Haussmann. To the existentialists, the district of St-Germain was the only place to be *(see pp142–3)*. Here Sylvia Beach welcomed James Joyce (1882–1941) to her bookshop on the Rue de l'Odéon. Ernest Hemingway (1899–1961) and F Scott Fitzgerald (1896–1940) wrote novels in Montparnasse.

Proust by J-E Blanche (about 1910)

SCIENTISTS

Paris has a Quartier Pasteur, a Boulevard Pasteur, a Pasteur metro and the world-famous Institut Pasteur *(see p247)*, all in honour of Louis Pasteur (1822–95), the great French chemist and biologist. His apartment and laboratory are faithfully preserved. The Institut Pasteur is today home to Professor Luc Montagnier, who first isolated the AIDS virus in 1983. Discoverers of radium, Pierre (1859–1906) and Marie Curie (1867–1934), also worked in Paris. The Curies have been the subject of a long-running play in Paris, *Les Palmes de M. Schutz*.

EXILED IN PARIS

The Duke and Duchess of Windsor married in France after his abdication in 1936 as King Edward VIII. The city granted them a rent-free mansion in the Bois de Boulogne. Other famous exiles have included Chou En-Lai (1898–1976), Ho Chi Minh (1890–1969), Vladimir Ilyich Lenin (1870–1924), Oscar Wilde (1854–1900) and ballet dancer Rudolf Nureyev (1938–93).

The Duke and Duchess of Windsor

Paris's Best: Churches

The Catholic Church has been the bastion of Parisian society through time. Many of the city's churches are worth visiting. Architectural styles vary and the interiors are often spectacular. Most churches are open during the day and many have services at regular intervals. Paris's tradition of church music is still alive. You can spend an evening enjoying the interiors while listening to an organ recital or classical concert *(see p346)*. A more detailed overview of Paris churches is on pages 48–9.

Early crucifix in St-Gervais-St-Protais

La Madeleine
Built in the style of a Greco-Roman temple, this church is known for its fine sculptures.

Chaillot Quarter

Champs-Elysées

Tuileries Qua

R I V E R   S E I N E

Invalides and Eiffel Tower Quarter

St-Germe des-Pré

Dôme Church
This memorial to the military engineer Vauban lies in the Dôme Church, where Napoleon's remains were buried in 1840.

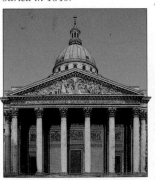

Montparnasse

Sainte-Chapelle
With its fine stained glass, this chapel is a medieval jewel.

Panthéon
The Neo-Classical Sainte-Geneviève, now the Panthéon, was inspired by Wren's St Paul's Cathedral in London.

0 kilometres

0 miles   0.5

Sacré-Coeur
Above the altar in this massive basilica, the chancel vault is decorated with a vast mosaic of Christ by Luc-Olivier Merson.

Montmartre

St-Eustache
With its mixture of Gothic and Renaissance styles, this is one of the finest churches in Paris.

St-Paul–St-Louis
This Christ figure is one of the many rich furnishings in this Jesuit church, built in 1641 for Cardinal Richelieu.

Beaubourg and
Les Halles

The Marais

Ile de la Cité

Ile St-Louis

Latin Quarter

Notre-Dame
The great cathedral was left to rot after the Revolution, until Victor Hugo led a restoration campaign.

Luxembourg
Quarter

Jardin des Plantes
Quarter

St-Séverin
The west door leads to one of the finest medieval churches in the city.

Mosquée de Paris
The minaret of this 1920s mosque is 33 m (100 ft) tall.

Exploring Paris's Churches

Some of Paris's finest architecture is reflected in the churches. The great era of church building was the medieval period but examples survive from all ages. During the Revolution *(see pp30–31)* churches were used as grain or weapons stores but were later restored to their former glory. Many churches have superb interiors with fine paintings and sculptures.

MEDIEVAL

Tower of St-Germain-des-Prés

Both the pointed arch and the rose window were born in a suburb north of Paris at the Basilique-Cathédrale de St-Denis, where most of the French kings and queens are buried. This was the first Gothic building, and it was from here that the Gothic style spread. The finest Gothic church in Paris is the city cathedral, **Notre-Dame**, tallest and most impressive of the early French cathedrals. Begun in 1163 by Bishop Maurice de Sully, it was completed over the next century by architects Jean de Chelles and Pierre de

Montreuil, who added the transepts with their fine translucent rose windows. Montreuil's masterpiece is Louis IX's medieval palace chapel, **Sainte-Chapelle**, with its two-tier structure. It was built to house Christ's Crown of Thorns. Other surviving churches in Paris are **St-Germain-des-Prés**, the oldest surviving abbey church in Paris (1050); the tiny, rustic Romanesque **St-Julien-le-Pauvre**; and the Flamboyant Gothic **St-Séverin**, **St-Germain l'Auxerrois** and **St-Merry**.

RENAISSANCE

The effect of the Italian Renaissance swept through Paris in the 16th century. It led to a unique architectural style in which fine Classical detail and immense Gothic proportions resulted in an impure, but attractive, cocktail known as "French Renaissance". The best example in Paris is **St-Etienne-du-Mont**, whose interior has the feel of a wide and light basilica. Another is **St-Eustache**, the massive market church in Les Halles, and the nave of **St-Gervais–St-Protais** with its stained glass and carved choir stalls.

Facade of Chapelle de la Sorbonne

BAROQUE AND CLASSICAL

Churches and convents flourished in Paris during the 17th century, as the city expanded under Louis XIII and his son Louis XIV. The Italian Baroque style was first seen on the majestic front of **St-Gervais–St-Protais**, built by Salomon de Brosse in 1616. The style was toned down to suit French tastes and the rational temperament of the Age of Enlightenment *(see pp28–9)*. The result was a harmonious and monumental Classicism in the form of columns and domes. One example is the **Chapelle de la Sorbonne**, completed by Jacques Lemercier in 1642 for Cardinal Richelieu. Grander and more richly decorated, with a painted dome, is the church built by François Mansart to honour the birth of the Sun King at the **Val-de-Grâce** convent. The true gem of the period is Jules Hardouin-Mansart's **Dôme Church**, with its enormous gilded

St-Gervais–St-Protais

TOWERS, DOMES AND SPIRES

Paris's many churches have dominated her skyline since early Christian times. The Gothic Tour St-Jacques, the only element still extant from a long-gone church, reflects the medieval love of the defensive tower. St-Etienne-du-Mont, with its pointed gable and rounded pediment, shows the transition from Gothic to Renaissance. The dome, a much-used feature of the French Baroque, was used to perfection in the Val-de-Grâce, while St-Sulpice with its severe arrangement of towers and portico is typically Neo-Classical. With its ornate spires, Ste-Clotilde is a Gothic Revival church. Modern landmarks include the mosque, with its minaret.

Tour St-Jacques

St-Etienne-du-Mont

Gothic

Renaissance

dome. Jesuit extravagance can be seen in **St-Paul–St-Louis** built in the style of Il Gesù in Rome. In contrast are Libéral Bruand's chapels, the **Salpêtrière** and **St-Louis-des-Invalides** with their severe geometry and unadorned simplicity. Other fine Classical churches are **St-Joseph-des-Carmes** and the 18th-century bankers' church, **St-Roch**, with its Baroque Marian chapel.

NEO-CLASSICAL

Interior of the Panthéon

An obsession with all things Greek and Roman swept France in the mid-18th century and well into the 19th century. The excavations at Pompeii (1738) and the influence of the Italian architect Andrea Palladio produced a generation of architects fascinated by the column, geometry and engineering. The best example of such churches is Jacques-Germain Soufflot's Sainte-Geneviève, now the **Panthéon**. Begun in 1773, its colonnaded dome was also inspired by Christopher Wren's St Paul's in London. The dome is supported by four pillars, built by Guillaume Rondelet, linking four great arches. The first colonnaded facade was Giovanni Niccolo Servandoni's **St-Sulpice**. Construction of this church began in 1733 and consisted of a two-storey portico, topped by a triangular pediment. **La Madeleine**, Napoleon's grand temple to his victorious army, was constructed on the ground plan of a Greco-Roman temple.

SECOND EMPIRE AND MODERN

Franz Christian Gau's **Sainte-Clotilde** of the 1840s is the first and best example in Paris of the Gothic Revival or *style religieux*. Showy churches were built in the new districts created by Haussmann in the Second Empire *(pp34–5)*. One of the most lovely is Victor Baltard's St-Augustin, at the intersection of the Boulevard Malesherbes and the Boulevard de la Madeleine. Here historic detail combines with modern iron columns and girders in a soaring interior space. The great basilica of the late 19th century, **Sacré-Coeur**, was built as a gesture of religious defiance. **St-Jean l'Evangéliste** by Anatole de Baudot is an interesting modern church combining the Art Nouveau style with Islamic arches. The modern gem of Islamic architecture, the **Mosquée de Paris**, is an attractive 1920s building in the Hispanic-Moorish style. It has a grand patio, inspired by the Alhambra, woodwork in cedar and eucalyptus, and a fountain.

The arches of St-Jean L'Evangéliste, reminiscent of Islamic architecture

FINDING THE CHURCHES

Baroque and Classical

Val-de-Grâce

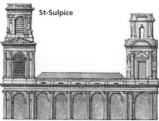

Neo-Classical

St-Sulpice

Second Empire

Sainte-Clotilde

Modern

Mosquée de Paris

Paris's Best: Gardens, Parks and Squares

Few cities can boast the infinite variety of styles found in Parisian gardens, parks and squares today. They date from many different periods and have been central to Parisian life for the past 300 years. The Bois de Boulogne and the Bois de Vincennes enclose the city with their lush, green open spaces, while elegant squares and landscaped gardens, such as the Jardin du Luxembourg, brighten the inner city and provide a retreat for those craving a few moments peace from the bustling city.

Parc Monceau
This English-style park features many follies, grottoes, magnificent trees and rare plants.

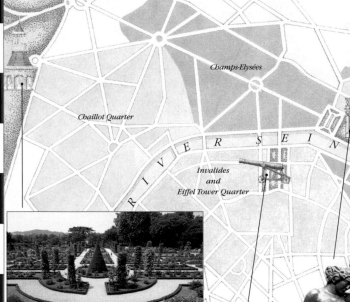

Champs-Elysées

Opéra Quar

Chaillot Quarter

Tuiler Quart

R I V E R   S E I N E

Invalides and Eiffel Tower Quarter

St-Germain-des-Prés

Luxembot Quarter

Bois de Boulogne
The Bagatelle gardens, set in this wooded park, have an amazing array of flowers including the spectacular rose garden.

Montparnasse

Esplanade des Invalides
From this huge square, lined with lime trees, are some brilliant views over the quays.

Jardin des Tuileries
These gardens are renowned for ornamental ponds, terraces and the collection of bronze figures by Aristide Maillol.

Parc des Buttes-Chaumont
Once a scraggy hilltop, this park was transformed to provide open spaces for the growing city. It is now beautifully landscaped with huge cliffs revealing caves.

0 kilometres 1

0 miles 0.5

Square du Vert-Galant
The square, named after Henri IV's nickname, forms the west point of the Ile de la Cité.

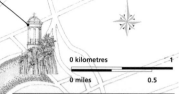

Place des Vosges
Considered one of the most beautiful squares in the world, it was finished in 1612 and is the oldest square in Paris.

Beaubourg
and
Les Halles

The Marais

Ile de la
Cité

Ile St-Louis

Jardin des Plantes
The botanical garden has a vast collection of plants and flowers from around the world.

Latin Quarter

Jardin des Plantes
Quarter

Jardin du Luxembourg
This park is a favourite with Parisians wanting to escape the bustle of the Latin Quarter.

Bois de Vincennes
The flower garden in this charming park is the perfect place to relax.

Exploring Gardens, Parks and Squares

Paris is dotted with many areas of parkland, intimate gardens and attractive tree-lined squares. Each is a reminder of the French capital's illustrious past. Many squares were formed during Napoleon III's transformation of the city, creating a pleasant environment for Parisians to live in (see pp34–5). This aim has been preserved right up to the present day. Paris's parks and gardens have their own character: some are ideal for a stroll, others for romance, while some provide space for sporting activities such as a game of boules.

Engraving of the Jardin du Palais Royal (1645)

HISTORIC GARDENS

The oldest public gardens in Paris were made for queens of France – the **Jardin des Tuileries** for Catherine de Médicis in the 16th century, and the **Jardin du Luxembourg** for Marie de Médicis in the 17th century. The Tuileries form the beginning of the axis running from the Arc de Triomphe du Carrousel through the Arc de Triomphe (pp210–11) to La Défense (p255). These gardens retain the formality devised by landscape architect André Le Nôtre, originally for the **Palace of Versailles**. Many of the Jardin des Tuileries's original sculptures survive, as well as modern pieces, notably the bronze nudes by Aristide Maillol (1861–1944).

The Jardin du Luxembourg also has the traditional formal plan – straight paths, clipped lawns, Classical sculpture and a superb 17th-century fountain. It is shadier and more intimate than the Tuileries, with lots of seats, pony rides and puppet shows to amuse the children.

The **Jardins des Champs-Elysées**, also by Le Nôtre, were reshaped in the English style during the 19th century. The gardens have Belle Epoque pavilions, three theatres (L'Espace Pierre Cardin, Théâtre Marigny and the Théâtre du Rond Point), smart restaurants – and the ghost of the novelist Marcel Proust, who once played here as a child.

A haven of peace in a busy district is the **Jardin du Palais**

Royal built by Cardinal Richelieu in the 17th century. An elegant arcade encloses the garden. The 19th-century **Parc Monceau**, in the English picturesque style, has follies and grottoes. The flat **Jardins des Invalides** and the landscaped **Champ-de-Mars** were the grounds of the Hôtel des Invalides and the Ecole Militaire. They were the site of the Paris Universal Exhibition, whose reminder is the Eiffel Tower (pp194–5).

An attractive public garden is attached to the lovely Hôtel Biron, home of the **Musée Rodin**. The 17th-century botanical garden **Jardin des Plantes** is famous for its ancient trees, flowers, alpine garden, hothouses and small zoo.

19TH-CENTURY PARKS AND SQUARES

Aquatic Garden, Bois de Vincennes

The great 19th-century parks and squares owe much to Napoleon III's long exile in London before he came to power. The unregimented planting and rolling lawns of Hyde Park and the leafy squares of Mayfair inspired him to bring trees, fresh air

Relaxing in Jardin du Luxembourg

FOLLIES AND ROTUNDAS

Dramatic features of Paris's parks and gardens are the many follies and rotundas. Every age of garden design has produced these ornaments. The huge Gloriette de Buffon in the Jardin des Plantes was erected as a memorial to the great naturalist (p166). It is the oldest metal structure in Paris. The pyramid in the Parc Monceau, the oriental temple in the Bois de Boulogne, and the 19th-century temple of love in the Bois de Vincennes reflect a more sentimental age. In contrast are the stark, painted-concrete follies that grace the Parc de la Villette.

Egyptian pyramid

Parc Monceau

and park benches to what was then Europe's most congested and dirty capital. Under his direction, landscape gardener Adolphe Alphand turned two woods at opposite ends of the city, the **Bois de Boulogne** (known as the "Bois") and the **Bois de Vincennes**, into English-style parks with duck ponds, lakes and flower gardens. He also added a racecourse to the "Bois". Its most attractive feature is the Bagatelle rose garden and the Jardin d'Acclimatation, a small theme park for families. The "Bois" is best avoided at night.

The two smaller Alphand parks are also pleasant, **Parc Montsouris** in the south and the **Parc des Buttes-Chaumont** in the northeast. The "Buttes" (hills), a favourite with the Surrealists, was a quarry transformed into two craggy mini-mountains with overhanging vegetation, suspended bridge, temple of love and a lake.

Part of the town-planning schemes for the old city included squares and avenues with fountains, sculptures, benches and greenery. One of the best is Ile de la Cité's **Square du Vert-Galant**. The Avenue de l'Observatoire in the **Jardin du Luxembourg** is rich in sculptures made by Jean-Baptiste Carpeaux

Fountains and sculpture in the Jardins du Trocadéro

Parc Montsouris

MODERN PARKS AND GARDENS

The shady **Jardins du Trocadéro** sloping down to the river from the Palais de Chaillot were planted after the 1937 Universal Exhibition. Here is the largest fountain in Paris and fine views of the river and the Eiffel Tower.

More recent Paris gardens eschew formality in favour of wilder planting, multiple levels, maze-like paths, children's gardens and modern sculpture. Typical are the **Parc André-Citroën**, the **Parc de la Villette** and the Jardins Atlantique, next to the Gare Montparnasse.

Pleasant strolls may be taken in Paris's waterside gardens: in the modern sculpture park behind Notre-Dame, at the Bassin de l'Arsenal at the Bastille, and along the quays of the Seine between the Louvre and the Place de la Concorde, or on the elegantly residential Ile St-Louis. The planted walkway above the **Viaduc des Arts** is a peaceful way to observe eastern Paris.

FINDING THE GARDENS, PARKS AND SQUARES

Jardin des Plantes · Gloriette de Buffon

Bois de Boulogne · Oriental temple

Bois de Vincennes · Temple of love

Parc de la Villette · Modern folly

Paris's Best: Museums and Galleries

Some of the oldest, the newest, and certainly some of the finest museums and galleries are to be found in Paris – many are superb works of art in their own right. They house some of the greatest and strangest collections in the world. Some of the buildings complement their themes, such as the Roman baths and Gothic mansion which form the Musée National du Moyen Age, or the Pompidou Centre, a modern masterpiece. Elsewhere there is pleasing contrast, such as the Picassos in their gracious 17th-century museum, and the Musée d'Orsay housed in its grand old railway station. Together they make an unrivalled feast for visitors.

Musée des Arts Décoratifs
Decorative and ornamental art like this Paris bathroom by Jeanne Lanvin is displayed here.

Chaillot Quarter

Champs-Elysées

S E I N E

R I V E R

Invalides and Eiffel Tower Quarter

Montparnasse

Petit Palais
A collection of works by the 19th-century sculptor Jean-Baptiste Carpeaux is housed here, including The Fisherman and Shell.

musée du quai Branly
This wooden sculpture from Papua New Guinea is one of 3,500 artifacts housed in this striking anthropological museum.

Musée Rodin
The museum brings together works bequeathed to the nation by sculptor Auguste Rodin, like the magnificent Gates of Hell *doors.*

Musée d'Orsay
Carpeaux's Four Quarters of the World *(1867–72) can be found among this collection of 19th-century art.*

Musée du Louvre
The museum boasts one of the world's great collections of paintings and sculpture, from the ancient civilizations to the 19th century. This Babylonian monument, the Code of Hammurabi, *is the oldest set of laws in existence.*

Pompidou Centre
Paris's modern art collection from 1905 to the present day is housed here. The centre also has art libraries and an industrial design centre.

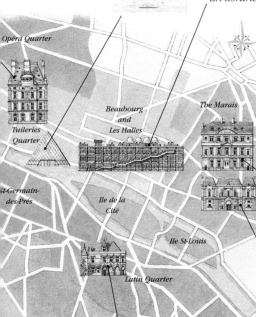

Opéra Quarter

St-Germain-des-Prés

Beaubourg and Les Halles

The Marais

Tuileries Quarter

Ile de la Cité

Ile St-Louis

Latin Quarter

Luxembourg Quarter

Jardin des Plantes Quarter

Musée Picasso
Sculptor and Model (1931) is one of many paintings on display in Picasso's private collection, "inherited" in lieu of tax by the French government after his death in 1973.

Musée Carnavalet
The museum is devoted to the history of Paris. Its historic buildings surround attractive garden courtyards.

Musée National du Moyen Age
The remains of the Gallo-Roman baths are part of this museum of ancient and medieval art.

0 kilometres	1
0 miles	0.5

Exploring Paris's Museums and Galleries

Paris holds great treasures in its museums and art galleries. The major national art collection is to be found at the **Musée du Louvre**, which began collecting 400 years ago and is still growing. Other important museums, such as the **Musée d'Orsay**, the **musée du quai Branly** and the **Pompidou Centre**, have their own treasures, but there are scores of smaller, specialized museums, each with its own interest.

Dante and Virgil in the Underworld (1822) by Delacroix, Musée du Louvre

GREEK, ROMAN AND MEDIEVAL ART

Altar, Musée National du Moyen Age

The **Musée du Louvre** has a fine collection of sculptures from Greek and Roman times, along with medieval sculptures and vestiges of the medieval Louvre under the Sully wing. The **Musée National du Moyen Age**, a superb 15th-century mansion, houses a major medieval collection. Highlights are the Unicorn Tapestries, the Kings' Heads from Notre-Dame and Basel Cathedral's golden altar. Third-century Roman baths adjoin the museum. Remains of houses from Roman and medieval Paris can be seen in the **Crypte Archéologique** near Notre-Dame cathedral.

OLD MASTERS

The *Mona Lisa* was one of the **Musée du Louvre's** first paintings, acquired 400 years ago. It also has other fine Leonardos. They are to be found along with superb

Titians, Raphaels and other Italian masters. Other works include Rembrandt's *Pilgrims at Emmäus*, Watteau's *Gilles* and Fragonard's *The Bathers*. The **Musée Cognacq-Jay** has a small, but exquisite, collection of paintings and drawings by 18th-century French painters. The **Musée Jacquemart-André** has works by such masters as Mantegna, Uccello, Canaletto, Rembrandt and Chardin.

IMPRESSIONIST AND POST-IMPRESSIONIST ART

Installed in a converted 19th-century railway station, the **Musée d'Orsay** boasts the world's largest collection of art from the period 1848–1904. Admired for its fine Impressionist and Post-Impressionist collections, it also devotes a lot of space to the earlier Realists and the formerly reviled 19th-century academic and "Salon" masters. There are superb selections of Degas, Manet, Courbet, including his controversial *L'Origine du Monde*, Monet, Renoir, Millet, Cézanne, Bonnard and Vuillard, and some fine Gauguins, Van Goghs and Seurats.

A great ensemble of late Monets is to be found at the **Musée Marmottan-Monet** and another at the **Musée de**

l'Orangerie, including Monet's last great waterlily murals (1920–25). Here also is a good collection of Cézannes and late Renoirs.

Three artists' studios and homes are now museums of their life and work. The **Musée Rodin**, in an attractive 18th-century mansion and garden, offers a complete survey of the master's sculptures, drawings and paintings. The **Musée Delacroix**, set in a garden near St-Germain-des-Prés, has sketches, prints and oils by the Romantic artist. The **Musée Gustave Moreau**, in an atmospheric 19th-century town house, has an extraordinary collection of intricately painted canvases of legendary *femmes fatales* and dying youths. The **Petit Palais** has an interesting collection of 19th-century paintings with four major Courbets, including *The Sleep*.

Dead Poet in Musée Gustave Moreau

MODERN AND CONTEMPORARY ART

As the international centre of the avant-garde from 1900 to 1940, Paris has a great concentration of modern painting and sculpture. The Pompidou Centre houses the **Musée National d'Art Moderne**, covering 1905 to the present. It has a good selection of Fauvist and Cubist works, particularly by Matisse, Rouault, Braque, Delaunay, and Leger, as well as works by the 1960s' *Nouveaux Réalistes*.

The **Musée d'Art Moderne de la Ville de Paris**, in the elegant 1930s Palais de Tokyo also has an excellent collection, including Delaunays, Bonnards and Fauvist paintings. The highlight is Matisse's 1932 mural, *The Dance*. In the opposite wing of the same building, the **Palais de Tokyo**, showcases some of today's most avant-garde artists.

Penelope by Bourdelle

The **Musée Picasso** in a lovely 17th-century mansion, has the world's largest Picasso collection, including paintings, drawings and sculptures. Picasso, Matisse, Modigliani, Utrillo and late Derains make up the collection on display at the **Musée de l'Orangerie**. For modern sculpture, the small **Musée Zadkine** has Cubist work by a minor school whose leading light was Ossip Zadkine. The **Musée Antoine Bourdelle** and the **Musée Maillol** house work by these two sculptors.

FURNITURE, DECORATIVE ARTS AND OBJETS D'ART

Pride of place after painting must go to furniture and the decorative arts, contained in a plethora of museums. Fine ensembles of French furnishings and decoration are in the **Louvre** (medieval to Napoleonic) and at the **Palace** of **Versailles** (17th–18th century). Furniture and *objets d'art* from the Middle Ages to the present century are arranged in period rooms at the **Musée des Arts Décoratifs**. The **Musée d'Orsay** has a large collection of 19th-century furniture, notably Art Nouveau. Louis XV (1715–74) and Louis XVI (1774–93) furniture and decoration can be found in the **Musée Nissim de Camondo**, a mansion from 1912 facing the Parc Monceau. Other notable collections are the **Musée Cognacq-Jay**; the **Musée Carnavalet** (18th-century); the **Musée Jacquemart-André** (French furniture and earthenware); the **Musée Marmottan-Monet** (Empire) and **Musée d'Art Moderne de la Ville de Paris** (Art Deco).

Jeweller's shop in the Carnavalet

SPECIALIST MUSEUMS

Devotees of antique sporting guns, muskets and hounds of the chase should make for the attractive Marais **Hôtel Guénégaud** (Musée de la Chasse et de la Nature). This museum also has some fine 18th-century animal paintings by Jean-Baptiste Oudry and Alexandre-François Desportes, as well as others by Rubens and Brueghel. **The Musée de la Contrefaçon** gives a fascinating insight into the world of counterfeit with examples from every luxury trade, including perfume, wines and spirits, and clothing. Numismatists will find an extensive coin and medallion collection housed in luxurious surroundings at the 18th-century Paris Mint at the **Musée de la Monnaie**. French coins are no longer minted here, but the old Mint still makes medals which are on sale. Stamps are on show at the **Musée de la Poste**. The history of postal services is also covered, as are all aspects of philately old and new, with temporary shows on current philatelic design. Visitors can discover how radio programmes are made at the **Musée de Radio-France**, which charts the history of communications from 1793 (when the first Chappe telegraph was sent) to the present day and Internet broadcasting. The collection of radio and television equipment includes some 2,000 objects.

Cabinet from Musée des Arts Décoratifs

FASHION AND COSTUME

The two rival fashion museums in Paris are the **Musée Galliera** at the Palais Galliera and the **Musée de la Mode** within the **Musée des Arts Décoratifs**. Neither has a permanent collection, but both hold regular shows devoted to the great Paris couturiers, such as Saint Laurent and Givenchy. They sometimes display fashion accessories as well and, more rarely but always fascinatingly, historical costumes.

PALAIS GALLIERA
10, avenue Pierre-1er-de-Serbie, Paris XVI
du 24 octobre 1991 au 15 mars 1992

Poster for the Musée Galliera

ASIAN, AFRICAN AND OCEANIAN ART

The major collection of Asian art in France is housed at the **Musée National des Arts Asiatiques Guimet**, covering China, Tibet, Japan, Korea, Indochina, Indonesia, India and Central Asia. It includes Chinese bronzes and lacquerware and some of the best Khmer art outside Cambodia. The **Musée Cernuschi** has a smaller but well-chosen Chinese collection, noted for its ancient bronzes and reliefs. France's premier showcase for African, Asian, American tribal and Oceanian arts and cultures is the **musée du quai Branly**, which displays more than 3,500 objects in truly breathtaking surroundings. The **Musée Dapper** also houses African art and is part of an important ethnographic research centre, housed in an elegant 1901 *hôtel particulier* with an "African" garden. Its collection of tribal masks is particularly dazzling.

Sri Lankan theatrical mask

HISTORY AND SOCIAL HISTORY

Café in Musée de Montmartre

Covering the entire history of the city of Paris, the **Musée Carnavalet** is housed in two historic Marais *hôtels*. It has period interiors, paintings of the city and old shop signs, a fascinating section covering events and artefacts from the French Revolution, and even Marcel Proust's bedroom. Also in the Marais, the **Musée d'Art et d'Histoire du Judaisme** explores the culture of French Jewry. The **Musée de l'Armée**, in the Hôtel des Invalides, recounts French military history, and the Musée de l'Histoire de France, in the Rococo **Hôtel de Soubise**, has historical documents from the national archives on display. Famous *tableaux vivants* and characters, both current and historical, await the visitor at the **Grévin** wax museum. The intriguing

Musée de Montmartre, overlooking Paris's last surviving vineyard, holds exhibitions on the history of Montmartre.

ARCHITECTURE AND DESIGN

The **Cité de l'Architecture et du Patrimoine** *(see p200)* charts the history of French architecture with scale models of its most iconic buildings. Superb scale models of fortresses built for Louis XIV and later are on display at the **Musée des Plans-Reliefs**. The work of the celebrated Franco-Swiss architect forms the basis of the **Fondation Le Corbusier**. The showpiece is his 1920s villa for his friend, art collector Raoul La Roche. Some of his furniture is also on display.

THE FRENCH IMPRESSIONISTS

Impression: Sunrise by Monet

Impressionism, the great art revolution of the 19th century, began in Paris in the 1860s, when young painters, influenced in part by the new art of photography, started to break with the academic values of the past. They aimed to capture the "impression" of what the eye sees at a given moment and used brushwork designed to capture the fleeting effects of light falling on a scene. Their favourite subjects were landscapes and scenes from contemporary urban life.

The movement had no founder, though Edouard Manet (1832–83) and the radical Realist painter Gustave Courbet (1819–77) both inspired many of the

Monet's sketchbooks

younger artists. Paintings of scenes of everyday life by Manet and Courbet often offended the academicians who legislated artistic taste. In 1863 Manet's *Le Déjeuner sur l'Herbe (see p144)* was exhibited at the Salon des Refusés, an exhibition set up for paintings rejected by the official Paris Salon of that year. The first time the term "Impressionist" was used to describe this new artistic movement was at another unofficial exhibition, in 1874. The name came from a painting by Claude Monet, *Impression: Sunrise*, a view of Le Havre in the mist from 1872. Monet was almost exclusively a landscape artist, influenced by the works of the English

Harvesting (1876) by Pissarro

The living room of La Roche Villa by Le Corbusier (1923)

SCIENCE AND TECHNOLOGY

In the Jardin des Plantes the **Muséum National d'Histoire Naturelle** has sections on palaeontology, minerology, entomology, anatomy and botany, plus a zoo and a botanical garden. In the Palais de Chaillot, the **Musée de l'Homme** is a museum of anthropology and prehistory.

It is due to reopen in 2012. Next door, the **Musée de la Marine** covers French naval history from the 17th century onwards, with interesting 18th-century models of ships and sculpted figure-heads. The **Musée des Arts et Métiers** displays the world of science and industry, invention and manufacturing. The **Palais de la Découverte** covers the history of science and has a good planetarium, somewhat overshadowed by the spectacular one at the **Cité des Sciences** in the Parc de la Villette. This museum is on several levels, with an IMAX 3D movie screen, the Géode.

Gabrielle (1910) by Renoir

artists, Constable and Turner. He always liked to paint out of doors and encouraged others to follow his example.

At the 1874 exhibition, a critic wrote that one should stand well back to see these "impressions" – the further back the better – and that members of the establishment should retreat altogether. Other exhibitors at the show were Pierre-Auguste Renoir, Edgar Degas, Camille Pissarro, Alfred Sisley and Paul Cézanne.

There were seven more Impressionist shows up to 1886. By then the power of the Salon had waned and the whole direction of art had changed. From then on, new movements were defined in terms of their relation to Impressionism. The leading Neo-Impressionist was Georges Seurat, who used thousands of minute dots of colour to build up his paintings. It took later generations to fully appreciate the work of the Impressionists. Cézanne was rejected all his life, Degas sold only one painting to a museum, and Sisley died unknown. Of the great artists whose genius is now universally recognized, only Renoir and Monet were ever acclaimed in their lifetimes.

Profile of a Model (1887) by Seurat

Artists in Paris

Monet's palette

The city first attracted artists during the reign of Louis XIV (1643–1715), and Paris became the most sophisticated artistic centre in Europe; the magnetism has persisted. During the 18th century, all major French artists lived and worked in Paris. In the latter half of the 19th century and early part of the 20th century, Paris was the European centre of modern and progressive art, and movements such as Impressionism and Post-Impressionism were founded and blossomed in the city.

BAROQUE ARTISTS

Champaigne, Philippe de (1602–74)
Coysevox, Antoine (1640–1720)
Girardon, François (1628–1715)
Le Brun, Charles (1619–90)
Le Sueur, Eustache (1616–55)
Poussin, Nicolas (1594–1665)
Rigaud, Hyacinthe (1659–1743)
Vignon, Claude (1593–1670)
Vouet, Simon (1590–1649)

ROCOCO ARTISTS

Boucher, François (1703–70)
Chardin, Jean-Baptiste-Siméon (1699–1779)
Falconet, Etienne-Maurice (1716–91)
Fragonard, Jean-Honoré (1732–1806)
Greuze, Jean-Baptiste (1725–1805)
Houdon, Jean-Antoine (1741–1828)
Oudry, Jean-Baptiste (1686–1755)
Pigalle, Jean-Baptiste (1714–85)
Watteau, Jean-Antoine (1684–1721)

Boucher's Diana Bathing *(1742), typical of the Rococo style (Louvre)*

1600	1650	1700	1750
BAROQUE		ROCOCO	NEO-CLASSICISM
1600	1650	1700	1750

1627 Vouet returns from Italy and is made court painter by Louis XIII. Vouet revived a dismal period in the fortunes of French painting

1667 First Salon, France's official art exhibition; originally held annually, later every two years

1793 Louvre opens as first national public gallery

Vouet's The Presentation in the Temple *(1641) with typically Baroque contrasts of light and shade (Louvre)*

Philippe de Champaigne's Last Supper *(about 1652). His style slowly became more Classical in his later years (Louvre)*

1648 Foundation of the Académie Royale de Peinture et de Sculpture, which had a virtual monopoly on art teaching

NEO-CLASSICAL ARTISTS

David, Jacques-Louis (1748–1825)
Gros, Antoine Jean (1771–1835)
Ingres, Jean-Auguste-Dominique (1780–1867)
Vigée-Lebrun, Elizabeth (1755–1842)

David's The Oath of the Horatii *(1784), in the Neo-Classical style (Louvre)*

ROMANTIC AND REALIST ARTISTS

Courbet, Gustave (1819–77)
Daumier, Honoré (1808–79)
Delacroix, Eugène (1798–1863)
Géricault, Théodore (1791–1824)
Rude, Francois (1784–1855)

Courbet's The Burial at Ornans
(1850) which showed Courbet to
be the foremost exponent of
Realism (Musée d'Orsay)

Rude's Departure of
the Volunteers in
1792 (1836), a
tribute to the French
Revolution (see p211)

MODERN ARTISTS

Arp, Jean (1887–1966)
Balthus (1908–2001)
Brancusi, Constantin (1876–1957)
Braque, Georges (1882–1963)
Buffet, Bernard (1928–1999)
Chagall, Marc (1887–1985)
Delaunay, Robert (1885–1941)
Derain, André (1880–1954)
Dubuffet, Jean (1901–85)
Duchamp, Marcel (1887–1968)
Epstein, Jacob (1880–1959)
Ernst, Max (1891–1976)
Giacometti, Alberto (1901–66)
Gris, Juan (1887–1927)
Léger, Fernand (1881–1955)
Matisse, Henri (1869–1954)
Miró, Joan (1893–1983)
Modigliani, Amedeo (1884–1920)
Mondrian, Piet (1872–1944)
Picasso, Pablo (1881–1973)
Rouault, Georges (1871–1958)
Saint Phalle, Niki de (1930–2002)
Soutine, Chaim (1893–1943)
Stael, Nicolas de (1914–55)
Tinguely, Jean (1925–91)
Utrillo, Maurice (1883–1955)
Zadkine, Ossip (1890–1967)

Giacometti's Standing
Woman II (1959), one of
his many tall, thin bronze
figures (see p112)

1904 Picasso
settles in Paris

1886 Van
Gogh moves
to Paris

1874 First
Impressionist
exhibition

1905 Birth of Fauvism, the first
of the "isms" in modern art

0	1850	1900	1950
MANTICISM/REALISM	IMPRESSIONISM	MODERNISM	
0	1850	1900	1950

1863 Manet's Le
Déjeuner sur l'Herbe
causes a scandalous
sensation at the Salon
des Refusés, both for
"poor moral taste",
and for its broad
brushstrokes. The
artist's Olympia was
thought just as
outrageous, but it was
not exhibited until
1865 (see p144)

1938
International
Surrealist
exhibition in
Paris

1977
Pompidou
Centre opens

Monet's Impression: Sunrise (1872),
which led to the name Impressionism

Delacroix's Liberty Leading the
People (1830) romantically
celebrates victory in war (Louvre)

1819 Géricault paints The Raft of the
Medusa, one of the greatest works of
French Romanticism (see p124)

IMPRESSIONIST AND POST-IMPRESSIONIST ARTISTS

Bonnard, Pierre (1867–1947)
Carpeaux, Jean-Baptiste (1827–75)
Cézanne, Paul (1839–1906)
Degas, Edgar (1834–1917)
Gauguin, Paul (1848–1903)
Manet, Edouard (1832–83)
Monet, Claude (1840–1926)
Pissarro, Camille (1830–1903)
Renoir, Pierre-Auguste (1841–1919)
Rodin, Auguste (1840–1917)
Rousseau, Henri (1844–1910)
Seurat, Georges (1859–91)
Sisley, Alfred (1839–99)
Toulouse-Lautrec, Henri de (1864–1901)
Van Gogh, Vincent (1853–90)
Vuillard, Edouard (1868–1940)
Whistler, James Abbott McNeill (1834–1903)

Tinguely and Saint Phalle's
Fontaine Igor Stravinsky (1980),
a modern kinetic sculpture
(Pompidou Centre)

PARIS THROUGH THE YEAR

Paris's pulling power is strongest in spring – the season for chestnuts in blossom and tables under trees. From June Paris is slowly turned over to tourists; the city almost comes to a standstill for the French Tennis Open, and the major race tracks stage the big summer races. Next comes the 14 July Bastille Day parade down the Champs-Elysées; towards the end of the month the Tour de France usually ends here.

The end of July also sees the end of Paris' three-month Jazz Festival, after which most Parisians abandon the city to visitors until *la rentrée*, the return to school and work in September. Dates of events listed on the following pages may vary. For details consult the listings magazines, or contact Paris Infos Mairie *(see p359)*. The Office du Tourisme *(see p367)* also produces an annual calendar of events.

SPRING

A good many of the city's annual 20 million visitors arrive in the spring. It is the season for fairs and concerts, when the marathon street race is held and the outdoor temperature is pleasant. Spring is also the time when hoteliers offer weekend packages, often with tickets for jazz concerts and with museum passes included.

MARCH

Spring flower shows
at Parc Floral (Bois de Vincennes, *p235*) and Bagatelle Gardens (Bois de Boulogne, *pp254–5*).
Banlieues Bleues Festival
(mid-Mar–early Apr), Paris suburbs. Jazz, blues, soul and funk.
Salon International d'Agriculture *(1st week)*, Paris-Expo, Porte de Versailles. Vast farming fair.
Printemps du Cinema *(3 days late Mar)*. Films can be seen for a very reasonable price

French Tennis Open, Stade Roland Garros

at cinemas across Paris and throughout France.
Foire du Trône *(late Mar–May)*, Bois de Vincennes *(p235)*. Large funfair.

APRIL

Chemin de la Croix *(Good Friday)*. Beautiful Stations of the Cross procession, from Montmartre to Sacré Coeur.
Blue Note Records Festival *(late Mar–early Apr)*, sees the big names of jazz, funk and soul perform across the city.
Paris International Marathon *(April)*, from Place de la Concorde to Avenue Foch.
Foire de Paris *(end Apr–1st week May)*, Paris Expo, Porte de Versailles. Food, wine, homes and gardens and tourism show.

MAY

Shakespeare Garden Festival *(until Oct)*, Bois de Boulogne *(pp254–5)*. Classic plays performed outdoors.
Carré Rive Gauche *(one week, mid-month)*. Exhibits at

antiques dealers in and around St-Germain-des-Prés *(p135)*.
Grandes Concerts de Versailles *(Apr–Jul: days vary)*, Versailles *(p248)*. Open-air concerts and pyrotechnical displays on Versailles lake.

Spring colour, Jardin du Luxembourg

French Tennis Open *(last week May–1st week Jun)*, Stade Roland Garros *(p358)*. Parisian society meets sport!
Le Printemps des Rues *(3rd w/end)*. Concerts and free street theatre in Bastille/ République area.

Paris International Marathon

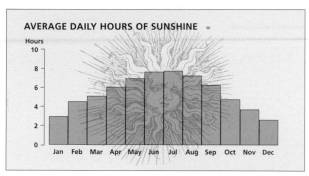

AVERAGE DAILY HOURS OF SUNSHINE

Hours

Sunshine Hours
*The northerly
position of Paris
gives it long and
light summer
evenings, but in
winter the daylight
recedes with few
truly bright days.*

SUMMER

Summer begins with the
French Tennis Open, and
there are many events and
festivities until July. Thereafter
the French begin thinking of
their own annual holiday, but
there are big celebrations on
Bastille Day (14 July) with
military displays for the
president and his guests.

Final lap of the Champs-Elysées during the Tour de France

Jardin du Luxembourg in summer

JUNE

Festival St-Denis, Basilique-
Cathédrale de St-Denis.
Concerts emphasise large-
scale choral works *(p346)*.
Fête du Cinéma, films shown
all over Paris for a nominal
entry fee *(p354)*.

Fête de la Musique
(21 Jun), all over Paris.
Nightlong summer solstice
musical celebrations.
Flower show, Bois de
Boulogne *(pp254–5)*.
Rose season in the
Bagatelle Gardens.
Gay Pride *(end Jun)*. Lively
parade around the Bastille.
Paris Jazz Festival *(May–Jul)*,
Parc Floral de Paris. Jazz
musicians come to play in
Paris *(pp349–50)*.
Prix de Diane-Hermès
(2nd Sun), Chantilly. French
equivalent of the British
Ascot high society horse-
racing event.
Les Grandes Eaux Nocturnes
(mid-Jun–mid-Aug),
Versailles. Son et lumiere in

the gardens with music,
dance and theatre *(p249)*.

JULY

**Paris Air and Space
Technology Show** *(Jul, alternate years)*, Le Bourget Airport.
**Festival du cinéma en plein
air** *(mid-Jul–Aug)*, Parc de
la Villette *(pp236–7)*.
Paris Quartier d'Eté *(mid-
Jul–mid-Aug)*. Dance, music,
theatre, ballet.
Tour de France *(late Jul)*.
The last stage of the world's
greatest cycle race comes to a
climax in the Champs-Elysées.
Paris-Plage *(mid-Jul–mid-
Aug)*. Sand and palm trees
deposited on the Right Bank
of the Seine create a beach.

March past of troops on Bastille Day (14 July)

AVERAGE MONTHLY TEMPERATURE

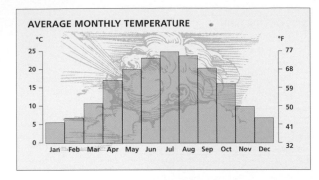

°C		°F
25		77
20		68
15		59
10		50
5		41
0	Jan Feb Mar Apr May Jun Jul Aug Sep Oct Nov Dec	32

Temperature
The chart shows the average temperatures for each month. It is hottest in July and August and coolest between December and February, though Paris is rarely freezing cold. Temperatures are pleasant in the spring when the number of visitors peaks, and also in autumn.

AUTUMN

September sees the start of the social season, with gala performances of new films, and parties in big houses on the Ile St-Louis. Paris is the world's largest congress centre and there is a rush of shows in September, ranging from gifts to leisure and music. The pace barely slackens in October and November when Parisians begin to indulge their great love for the cinema. French and Hollywood stars often make appearances at premieres staged on the Champs-Elysées.

The Prix de l'Arc de Triomphe (October)

SEPTEMBER

Festival d'Automne à Paris *(mid-Sep–end Dec)*, throughout Paris. Music, dance, theatre *(pp346–7)*.
La Villette Jazz Festival *(mid-Sep)*. Jazz artists come and blow their horns with gusto throughout the Cité de la Musique *(p236)*.
Journées du Patrimoine *(2nd or 3rd week Sep)*. Historic buildings, monuments and museums are open free to the public for two days, following an all-night party to kick off proceedings.

OCTOBER

Nuit Blanche *(one Sat in Oct)*. Museums stay open all night and there are art installations around the city.
Prix de l'Arc de Triomphe *(1st week)*, Longchamp. An international field competes for the richest prize in European horse-racing.
Salon de l'Automobile *(1st fortnight, alternate years)*, Paris-Expo, Porte de Versailles. Commercial motor show, alternated annually with a motorcycle show.
Foire Internationale d'Art Contemporain (FIAC) *(last week)*, Paris-Expo, Porte de Versailles. Paris's biggest international modern and contemporary art fair.

Jazz fusion guitarist Al di Meola playing in Paris

NOVEMBER

BNP Paribas Masters *(usually Nov)*, Palais Omnisports de Paris-Bercy *(pp358–9)*. Prestigious indoor men's tennis tournament.
Mois de la Photo *(Oct–Nov, every two years, next in 2012)*. Numerous photography shows, film screenings and public discussions.
Beaujolais Nouveau *(3rd Thursday Nov)*. Bars and cafés are crowded on this day, in a race to taste the new vintage.

Autumn in the Bois de Vincennes

AVERAGE MONTHLY RAINFALL

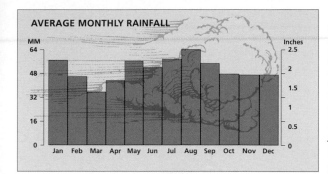

Rainfall
August is the wettest month in Paris as well as the hottest. In August and September you risk getting caught in storms. Sudden showers, sometimes with hail, can occur between January and April – notoriously in March. There is occasional snow in winter.

WINTER

Paris rarely sees snow; winter days tend to be invigorating rather than chilly. There are jazz and dance festivals, candlelit Christmas church services and much celebrating in the streets over the New Year. After New Year, the streets seem to become slightly less congested and on bright days the riverside quays are used as the rendezvous point of strollers and lovers.

DECEMBER

Christmas illuminations *(until Jan)* in the Grands Boulevards, Opéra, Ave Montaigne, Champs-Elysées and the Rue du Faubourg St-Honoré.
Crèche *(early Dec–early Jan)*, under a canopy in Place de l'Hôtel de Ville, Marais *(p102)*. Lifesize Christmas crib from a different country each year.

January fashion show

Snow in the Tuileries, a rare occurrence

Horse & Pony Show *(1st fortnight)*, Paris-Expo, Porte de Versailles.
Paris International Boat Show *(1st fortnight)*, Paris-Expo, Porte de Versailles.

JANUARY

Fête des Rois (Epiphany). *(6 Jan)*. The *boulangeries* are full of *galettes des rois*.
Prix d'Amérique *(mid-Jan)*. Europe's most famous trotting race, Hippodrome de Vincennes.
Fashion shows, summer collections. *(See* Haute Couture *p324.)*

FEBRUARY

Carnaval *(weekend before Mardi Gras)*, Quartier de St-Fargeau. **Floraisons** *(all month)*, Parc Floral de Paris, Bois de Vincennes *(p235)* and Parc de Bagatelle, Bois de Boulogne *(pp254–5)*. Say farewell to winter with these colourful displays of crocuses and snowdrops.

PUBLIC HOLIDAYS
New Year's Day
(1 Jan)
Easter Monday varies
Labour Day (1 May)
VE Day (8 May)
Ascension Day (6th Thu after Easter)
Bastille Day (14 Jul)
Assumption (15 Aug)
All Saints' Day
(1 Nov)
Remembrance Day
(11 Nov)
Christmas (25 Dec)

Eiffel Tower Christmas decorations

A RIVER VIEW
OF PARIS

Sculpture on the Pont Alexandre III

The remarkable French music-hall star Mistinguett described the Seine as a "pretty blonde with laughing eyes". The river most certainly has a beguiling quality, but the relationship that exists between it and the city of Paris is far more than one of flirtation.

No other European city defines itself by its river in the same way as Paris. The Seine is the essential point of reference to the city: distances are measured from it, street numbers determined by it, and it divides the capital into two distinct areas, with the Right Bank on the north side of the river and the Left Bank on the south side. These are as well defined as any of the supposedly official boundaries. The city is also divided historically, with the east more closely linked to the city's ancient roots and the west more closely linked to the 19th and 20th centuries.

Practically every building of note in Paris is either along the river or within a stone's throw. The quays are lined by fine bourgeois apartments, magnificent town houses, great museums and striking monuments.

Above all, the river is very much alive. For centuries fleets of small boats used it, but motorized land traffic stifled this once-bustling scene. Today, the river is busy with commercial barges and massive *bateaux mouches* pleasure boats cruising sightseers up and down the river.

The octagonal lake, in the Jardin de Luxembourg, is a favourite spot for children to sail their toy boats. The Seine is host to larger craft, including many pleasure cruisers.

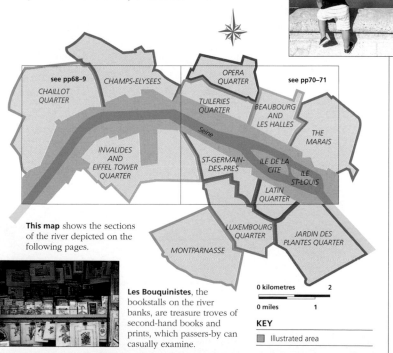

see pp68–9

CHAILLOT QUARTER

CHAMPS-ELYSEES

OPERA QUARTER

see pp70–71

TUILERIES QUARTER

BEAUBOURG AND LES HALLES

THE MARAIS

Seine

INVALIDES AND EIFFEL TOWER QUARTER

ST-GERMAIN-DES-PRES

ILE DE LA CITE

ILE ST-LOUIS

LATIN QUARTER

This map shows the sections of the river depicted on the following pages.

LUXEMBOURG QUARTER

JARDIN DES PLANTES QUARTER

MONTPARNASSE

Les Bouquinistes, the bookstalls on the river banks, are treasure troves of second-hand books and prints, which passers-by can casually examine.

0 kilometres   2

0 miles   1

KEY

☐ Illustrated area

◁ **Pont Alexandre III, encrusted with exuberant statuary**

From Pont de Grenelle to Pont de la Concorde

The soaring monuments and grand exhibition halls along this stretch of the river are remnants of the Napoleonic era and the Industrial Revolution with its great exhibitions. The exhilarating self-confidence of the Eiffel Tower, the Petit Palais and the Grand Palais is matched by more recent buildings, such as the Palais de Chaillot, the Maison de Radio-France and the skyscrapers of the Left Bank.

Palais de Chaillot
The curved wings and arching fountains make this a spectacular setting for three museums and a theatre (p200).

Palais de Tokyo
Figures by Bourdelle adorn this museum (p203).

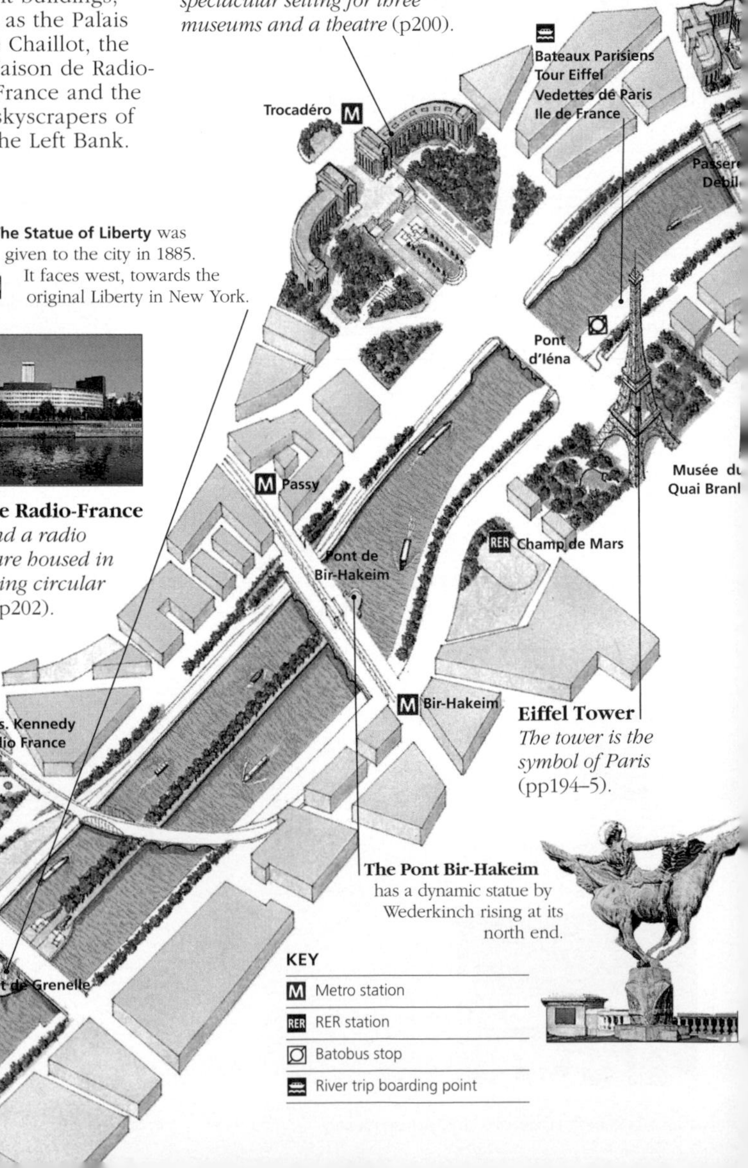

Bateaux Parisiens
Tour Eiffel
Vedettes de Paris
Ile de France

Trocadéro Ⓜ

Passer
Debi

The Statue of Liberty was given to the city in 1885. It faces west, towards the original Liberty in New York.

Pont d'Iéna

Ⓜ Passy

Musée du
Quai Branl

Maison de Radio-France
Studios and a radio museum are housed in this imposing circular building (p202).

RER Champ de Mars

Pont de
Bir-Hakeim

RER Prés. Kennedy
Radio France

Ⓜ Bir-Hakeim

Eiffel Tower
The tower is the symbol of Paris (pp194–5).

The Pont Bir-Hakeim has a dynamic statue by Wederkinch rising at its north end.

Pont de Grenelle

KEY

Ⓜ	Metro station
RER	RER station
Ⓞ	Batobus stop
⛴	River trip boarding point

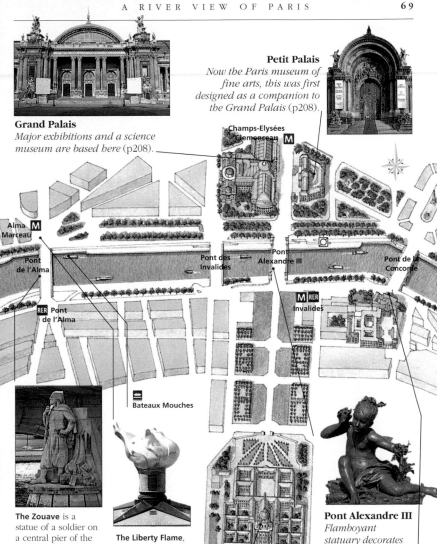

Grand Palais
Major exhibitions and a science museum are based here (p208).

Petit Palais
Now the Paris museum of fine arts, this was first designed as a companion to the Grand Palais (p208).

Champs-Elysées Clemenceau [M]

Alma Marceau [M]

Pont de l'Alma

RER Pont de l'Alma

Pont des Invalides

Pont Alexandre III

Pont de la Concorde

[M] RER Invalides

Bateaux Mouches

The Zouave is a statue of a soldier on a central pier of the bridge. It is used to measure the level of the Seine when it is in flood.

The Liberty Flame, commemorating French Resistance fighters, is also an unofficial memorial to Diana, Princess of Wales.

Pont Alexandre III
Flamboyant statuary decorates Paris's most ornate bridge (p208).

Dôme Church
The majestic gilded dome (pp188–9) is here seen from Pont Alexandre III.

Assemblée Nationale Palais-Bourbon
Louis XIV's daughter once owned this palace, which is now used by the Chambre des Députés as the national forum for political debate (p190).

From Pont de la Concorde to Pont de Sully

The historic heart of Paris lies on the banks and islands of the east river. At its centre is the Ile de la Cité, a natural stepping stone across the Seine and the cultural core of medieval Paris. Today it is still vital to Parisian life.

Jardin des Tuileries
These are in the formal style (p130).

Musée du Louvre
Before becoming the world's greatest museum and home to the Mona Lisa, this was Europe's largest royal palace (pp122–9).

Pont de la Concorde

Assemblée Nationale Ⓜ

Passerelle Solférino

Quai d'Orsay RER

Pont Royal

Pont du Carrousel

Passerelle des Arts

Musée de l'Orangerie
An important collection of 19th-century paintings is on display here (p131).

The Passerelle des Arts
is a steel reconstruction of Paris's first cast-iron bridge (1804), and was inaugurated in 1984.

Bâteaux Vedettes du Pont Neuf

Musée d'Orsay
Paris's most important collection of Impressionist art is housed in this converted railway station (pp144–7).

Hôtel des Monnaies
Built in 1771–75, this former Mint has a fine coin collection in its old milling halls (p141).

Ile de la Cité

The medieval identity of this small island was almost completely erased in the 19th century by Baron Haussmann's grand scheme. Sainte-Chapelle and parts of the Conciergerie are the only buildings of the period that remain today (pp76–89).

Conciergerie

During the Revolution this building, with its distinctive towers, became notorious as a prison (p81).

The Tour de l'Horloge, a 14th-century clock tower, features the first public clock in Paris. Germain Pilon's fine carvings continue to adorn the clock face.

Ile St-Louis

This has been a desirable address since the 17th century (p87).

St-Gervais–St-Protais

The oldest organ in Paris, dating from the early 17th century, is in this church (p99).

Pont Neuf Ⓜ

t Neuf

Ⓜ **Châtelet**

Hôtel de Ville Ⓜ

Pont au Change

Pont Notre-Dame

Cité Ⓜ

Pont d'Arcole

RER Ⓜ **St-Michel**

Petit Pont

Pont au Double

Pont St-Louis

Pont Louis Philippe

Ⓜ **Pont Marie**

Pont Marie

Pont de l'Archevêché

Pont de la Tournelle

Sully Morland Ⓜ

Pont de Sully

Notre-Dame

This towering cathedral surveys the river (pp82–5).

Bâteaux Parisiens

How to Take a River or Canal Trip

River Seine cruises on a variety of pleasure boats operate along the main sightseeing reaches of the river, taking in many of the city's famous monuments. The Batobus river service operates as a shuttle or bus service, allowing you to get on and off anywhere along the route. The main city canal trips operate along the old industrial St-Martin canal in the east of the city.

Pleasure-cruise boat passing by the Eiffel Tower

Types of Boats

Bateaux mouches, *the largest of the pleasure-cruise boats, are a spectacular sight with their passenger areas enclosed in glass for excellent all round viewing. At night floodlights are used to pick out river bank buildings. A more luxurious version of these is used on the Bateaux Parisien cruises. The* vedettes *are smaller and more intimate boats, with viewing through glass walls. The Canauxrama canal boats are flat-bottomed.*

SEINE CRUISES AND SHUTTLE SERVICES

The Seine cruises and shuttle services information below includes the location of boarding points, the nearest metro and RER stations, and the nearest bus routes. Lunch and dinner cruises must be booked in advance, and passengers must board them 30 minutes before departure.

vedettes de paris

Vedettes de Paris Seine Cruise

Passengers are carried in comfort and style on a cruise encompassing all the major sights along the river. Tickets can be bought that include a snack or champagne. The boarding point is:

Port de Suffren
Map 10 D3. **Tel** 01 44 18 19 50. Ⓜ *Bir Hakeim.* ᴿᴱᴿ *Champs de Mars.* 🚌 *22, 30, 32, 44, 63, 69, 72, 82, 87.*

Departures
10.30am–11pm (11am–7pm Oct–Feb) daily (every 30 min).
Duration *1 hr.*
www.vedettesdeparis.com

Croisière Dégustation Champagne

Enjoy a selection of champagnes while you cruise along the river. A *sommelier* provides tasting notes. The boarding point is:

Port de Suffren
Map 10 D3.
Tel 01 44 18 19 50.
Ⓜ *Bir Hakeim.*
Departures 6pm Thu–Sat. **Duration** 1 hr.
www.vedettesdeparis.com

Bateaux Parisiens Tour Eiffel Cruise

This company offers sightseeing and meal cruises with a commentary in 13 languages. The boarding point is:

Port de la Bourdonnais
Map 10 D2. **Tel** 08 25 01 01 01. Ⓜ *Trocadéro, Bir Hakeim.* ᴿᴱᴿ *Champs de Mars.* 🚌 *42, 82.*
Departures every 30 mins 10am–10.30pm daily (hourly Oct–Mar).
Duration 1 hr.
Lunch cruise 12.30pm.
Duration 2 hr. **Dinner cruise** 6.30pm, 8.30pm, 9pm. **Duration** up to 3 hr. Formal dress required.
www.bateauxparisiens.com

Bateaux Parisiens Notre-Dame Cruise

Same route as the Tour Eiffel Cruise, but in the opposite direction. The boarding point is:

Quai de Montebello
Map 13 B4. **Tel** 08 25 01 01 01. Ⓜ *Maubert-Mutualite, St-Michel.* ᴿᴱᴿ *St-Michel.* 🚌 *24, 27, 47.*
Departures 28 Mar–28 Aug: 11am–11pm; 29 Aug–26 Sep: 11am–10.30pm; 27 Sep–3 Nov: 1.30–6pm. Times may vary so call ahead to check.
Duration 1 hr.

Boarding Points

The boarding points for the river cruises and the Batobus services are easy to find

along the river. Here you can buy tickets, and there are amenities such as snack-bars. Major cruise companies also have foreign exchange booths. There is limited parking around the points, but none near the Pont Neuf.

River boarding point

BATOBUS CRUISES

Shuttle service. 1-, 2- and 5-day passes available. **Tel** 08 25 05 01 01. **Departures** daily. Early Feb–mid-Mar, mid-Nov–20 Dec: 10.30am–4.30pm; mid-Mar–May, early Sep–11 Nov: 10am–7pm; Jun–early Sep: 10am–9.30pm. Board at: **Eiffel Tower: Map** 10 D3. M Bir Hakeim. **Champs-Elysées: Map** 11 B1. M Champs-Elysées-Clemenceau. **Musée d'Orsay. Map** 12 D2. M Assemblée Nationale. **Louvre: Map** 12 E2. M Louvre. **St-Germain-des-Prés: Map** 12 E3. M St-Germain-des-Prés. **Notre-Dame: Map** 13 B4. M Saint-Michel. **Hôtel de Ville: Map** 13 B4. M Hôtel de Ville. www.batobus.com

Bateaux Mouches Cruise

One of Paris's best known pleasure boat companies, with a fleet of 14 boats. The boarding point is:

Pont de l'Alma
Map 10 F1. **Tel** 01 42 25 96 10. M Alma-Marceau. RER Pont de l'Alma. 28, 42, 49, 63, 72, 80, 83, 92.
Departures Apr–Sep: 10.15am–11pm daily (every 30 min, every 20 min 7–11pm); Oct–Mar: 11am–9pm (from 10.15am Sat & Sun; every 1 hr; 50 passengers min).
Duration 1 hr 15 min.
Lunch cruise 1pm Sat, Sun and bank hols (embark from 12.15pm).
Duration 1 hr 45 min.
Under-12s half price.
Dinner cruise 8.30pm daily (embark from 7.30pm).
Duration 2 hr 15 min.
Jacket and tie required.
www.bateaux-mouches.fr

Bateaux Vedettes Pont Neuf Cruise

This company runs a fleet of six small boats. The boats are of an older style, for a quainter cruise. Price reductions can be obtained when booking tickets online. The boarding point is:

Square du Vert-Galant
(Pont Neuf). **Map** 12 F3. **Tel** 01 46 33 98 38. M Pont Neuf. RER Châtelet. 27, 58, 67, 70, 72, 74, 75. **Departures** mid-Mar–Oct: 10.30am, 11.15am, noon; 1.30–10.30pm daily (every 30 min); Nov–mid-Mar: 10.30am, 11.15am, noon, 2–6.30pm (every 45 min), 8pm, 10pm Mon–Thu; 10.30am, 11.15am, noon, 2–6.30pm, 8pm, 9–10pm (every 45 min) Fri–Sun (24 & 31 Dec: last departure 5.45pm).
Duration 1 hr. www.vedettesdupontneuf.com

CANAL TRIPS

The Canauxrama company operates boat cruises along the city's Canal St-Martin and along the banks of the river Marne. The St-Martin journey passes along the tree-lined canal, which has nine locks, two swing bridges and eight romantic footbridges. The Bords de Marne cruise travels well into the suburbs, as far as Bry-sur-Marne. The **Paris Canal Company** (01 42 40 96 97; www. pariscanal.com) also has a St-Martin canal trip, from Parc de la Villette and extending beyond the canal, passing into the River Seine and as far as the Musée d'Orsay.

CANAUXRAMA

Canal St-Martin

The Canauxrama company offers many different trips along this canal, but it has two 125-passenger boats that operate regularly between the Bassin de la Villette and the Port de l'Arsenal. The boarding points are:
Bassin de la Villette. Map 8 E1. M Jaurès.
Port de l'Arsenal. Map 14 E4. M Bastille.
Tel 01 42 39 15 00. **Departures** Apr–Nov, times may vary so phone to check and to make a reservation: Bassin de la Villette 9.45am and 2.45pm; Port de l'Arsenal 9.45am and 2.30pm daily. On weekday mornings there are concessions for students, pensioners and children under 12. Children under six travel free. Concert cruises are available on chartered trips on the Canal St-Martin and the Seine.
Duration 2 hr 30 min. www.canauxrama.fr

Bords de Marne Croisière

This all-day cruise extends westwards out of Paris down the Marne. The trip includes a commentary, stories and dancing. Bring a picnic or eat lunch in a guinguette (open-air café). The boarding point is: **Port de l'Arsenal. Map** 14 E4. M Bastille. **Tel** 01 42 39 15 00. **Departures** Apr–Oct: 9am Thu–Sun (arrive 20 min before). Reservations necessary. **Duration** 8 hr.

Canal-cruise boat in the Bassin de la Villette

PARIS AREA
BY AREA

ILE DE LA CITE AND ILE ST-LOUIS

The history of the Ile de la Cité is the history of Paris. This island on the Seine was no more than a primitive village when the conquering Julius Caesar arrived in 52 BC. Ancient kings later made it the centre of political power and in medieval times it became the home of church and law. It no longer has such power, except to draw armies of tourists to the imposing Palais de Justice and to its Gothic masterpiece, Notre-Dame.

The medieval huddles of tiny houses and narrow streets that so characterized the island at one time

The motto of the city of Paris

were swept away by the spacious thoroughfares built in the 19th century. But there are still small areas of charm and relief, among them the colourful bird and flower market, the romantic Square du Vert-Galant and the ancient Place Dauphine.

At the island's eastern end the St-Louis bridge connects it to the smaller Ile St-Louis. This former swampy pastureland was transformed into an elegant 17th-century residential area, with picturesque, tree-lined quays. More recently, rich artists, doctors, actresses and heiresses have lived here.

SIGHTS AT A GLANCE

Historic Buildings and Streets
Ancien Cloître Quartier ❷
Hôtel Dieu ❻
Conciergerie ❽
Palais de Justice ❿
Hôtel de Lauzun ⓰

Churches and Cathedrals
Notre-Dame pp82–5 ❶
Sainte-Chapelle pp88–9 ❾
St-Louis-en-l'Ile ⓯

Monuments
Paris Mémorial
de la Déportation ❹

Markets
Marché aux Fleurs and Marché aux Oiseaux ❼

Squares and Gardens
Square Jean XXIII ❸
Place Dauphine ⓫
Square du Vert-Galant ⓭

Museums and Galleries
Crypte Archéologique ❺
Société Historique et Littéraire Polonaise ⓮

Bridges
Pont Neuf ⓬

GETTING THERE
This area is served by the metro stations at Cité and St-Michel on the Left Bank. The bus routes 38, 47, 58, 85 and 96 cross the Ile de la Cité, and 67, 86 and 87 cross the Ile St-Louis.

SEE ALSO

• *Street Finder,* map 12–13

• *St-Louis Walk* pp262–3

• *Where to Stay* p284

• *Restaurants* p300

0 metres   400
0 yards   400

KEY

◼ Street-by-Street map

Ⓜ Metro station

◁ View of the Conciergerie and the Pont au Change, previous page St-Sulpice church and rooftops

Street-by-Street: Ile de la Cité

The origins of Paris are here on the Ile de la Cité, the boat-shaped island on the Seine first inhabited over 2,000 years ago by Celtic tribes. One tribe, the Parisii, eventually gave its name to the city. The island offered a convenient river crossing on the route between northern and southern Gaul and was easily defended. In later centuries the settlement was expanded by the Romans, the Franks and the Capetian kings to form the nucleus of today's city.

There is no older place in Paris, and remains of the first buildings can still be seen today in the archaeological crypt under the square in front of Notre-Dame, the great medieval cathedral and place of pilgrimage for millions of visitors each year. At the other end of the island is another Gothic masterpiece, Sainte-Chapelle – a miracle of light.

★ Conciergerie
A grisly ante-chamber to the guillotine, this prison was much used in the Revolution ❽

The Cour du Mai is the impressive main courtyard of the Palais de Justice.

Metro Cité

★ Sainte-Chapelle
A jewel of Gothic architecture and one of the most magical sights in Paris, Sainte-Chapelle is noted for the magnificence of its stained glass ❾

To Pont Neuf

The Quai des Orfèvres owes its name to the goldsmiths *(orfèvres)* who frequented the area from medieval times onwards.

Palais de Justice
With its ancient towers lining the quays, the old royal palace is today a massive complex of law courts. Its history extends back over 16 centuries ❿

| 0 metres | 100 |
| 0 yards | 100 |

The Préfecture de Police is the headquarters of the police and was the scene of intense battles during World War II.

The Statue of Charlemagne commemorates the King of the Franks, who was crowned emperor in 800. He united all the Christian peoples of the West.

★ **Marché aux Fleurs et Oiseaux**
The flower market is a colourful, lively sight and is one of Paris's few remaining flower markets. Birds are sold at the Sunday market ⑦

LOCATOR MAP
See Central Paris Map pp14–15

Hôtel Dieu
Once an orphanage, this is now a city hospital ⑥

★ **Crypte Archéologique**
Deep under the square, lie the remains of houses from 2,000 years ago ⑤

STAR SIGHTS

- ★ Notre-Dame
- ★ Sainte-Chapelle
- ★ Conciergerie
- ★ Marché aux Fleurs et Oiseaux
- ★ Crypte Archéologique

KEY

– – – Suggested route

The Rue Chanoinesse has had many famous residents, such as the 17th-century playwright Racine.

Ancien Cloître Quartier
These quaint streets were once home to medieval clergymen and students ②

Point Zéro
is the point from which all distances are measured in France.

The Square Jean XXIII
is a peaceful square close to the river ③

★ **Notre-Dame**
This cathedral is a superb example of French medieval architecture ①

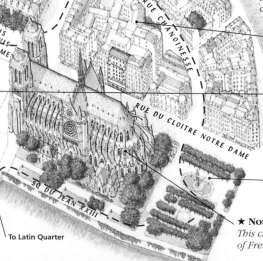

To Latin Quarter

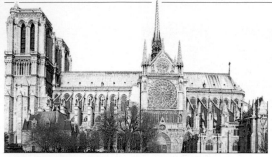

Notre-Dame from the Left Bank

Notre-Dame ❶

See pp82–5.

Ancien Cloître Quartier ❷

Rue du Cloître-Notre-Dame north to Quai des Fleurs 75004. **Map** 13 B4. Ⓜ *Cité*. 🚇 *St-Michel*.

On the northern side of Notre-Dame cathedral lies a warren of little-explored streets known as the "Old Cloister" quarter. They are all that remains of a once-bustling medieval hub frequented by cathedral seminary students. Today, the narrow streets with well-preserved medieval mansions make for an interesting stroll. The mansions in Rue des Chantres and Rue des Ursins in particular have pretty gardens and cobbled courtyards.

Square Jean XXIII ❸

Rue du Cloître-Notre-Dame 75004. **Map** 13 B4. Ⓜ *Cité*.

Notre-Dame's St Stephen's door (porte St-Etienne) opens on to this pleasant garden square, dedicated to Pope John XXIII. The garden runs alongside the river and is an excellent place for enjoying the sculptures, rose windows and flying buttresses of the east end of the cathedral.

From the 17th century, the square was occupied by the archbishop's palace, which was ransacked by rioters in 1831 and later demolished. A square was conceived to replace the Prefect of Paris, Rambuteau. The Gothic-style fountain of the Virgin in the square has been there since 1845.

Paris Mémorial de la Déportation ❹

Sq de l'Ile de France 75004. **Map** 13 B4. **Tel** *01 42 77 44 72*. Ⓜ *Cité*. 🚇 *St-Michel*. ☐ *10am–6pm Tue–Sun.*

The simple, modern memorial to the 200,000 French men, women and children deported to Nazi concentration camps in World War II (often via Drancy, just a few miles to the north of Paris) is covered with a roll-call of names of the camps to which they were deported. Earth from these camps has been used to form small tombs and the interior walls are decorated with poetry. At the far end is the tomb dedicated to the Unknown Deportee.

Inside the Paris Mémorial de la Déportation

The Square Jean XXIII behind Notre-Dame

Gallo-Roman ruins in the Crypte Archéologique

Crypte Archéologique ❺

Pl Jean Paul II, Parvis de Notre-Dame 75004. **Map** 13 A4. **Tel** 01 55 42 50 10. M Cité. ◯ 10am–6pm Tue–Sun (last adm: 30 min before closing). ◖ 1 Jan, 1 May, 8 May, 1 & 11 Nov, 25 Dec. ◳ free for children under 13. ▯ www.carnavalet.paris.fr

Situated on the main square (the *parvis*) in front of Notre-Dame and stretching 120 m (393 ft) underground, this crypt exhibits the remains of foundations and walls that pre-date the cathedral by several hundred years. There are traces of a sophisticated underground heating system in a house from Lutèce, the settlement of the Parisii, the Celtic tribe who inhabited the island 2,000 years ago, giving their name to the present city.

Hôtel Dieu ❻

1 Pl du Parvis Notre-Dame 75004. **Map** 13 A4. ◖ to the public for visits. M Cité.

On the north side of the place du Parvis Notre-Dame is the Hôtel Dieu, the hospital serving central Paris. It was built on the site of an

Hôtel Dieu, central Paris's hospital

orphanage between 1866 and 1878. The original Hôtel Dieu, built in the 12th century and stretching across the island to both banks of the river, was demolished in the 19th century to make way for one of Baron Haussmann's urban-planning schemes.

It was here in 1944 that the Paris police courageously resisted the Germans; the battle is commemorated by a monument in Cour de 19-Août.

Paris's main flower market

Marché aux Fleurs ❼

Pl Louis-Lépine 75004. **Map** 13 A3. M Cité. ◯ 8am–7.30pm daily.

The year-round flower market adds colour and scent to an area otherwise dominated by administrative buildings. It is the most famous and unfortunately one of the last remaining flower markets in the city of Paris, offering a wide range of specialist varieties such as orchids. Each Sunday it makes way for the cacophony of an animal market, which is best avoided by sensitive animal lovers.

Conciergerie ❽

2 Bd du Palais 75001. **Map** 13 A3. ▯ 01 53 40 60 80. M Cité. ◯ 9.30am–6pm daily (9am–5pm Nov–end Feb) (last adm: 30 min before closing). ◖ 1 Jan, 1 May, 25 Dec. ◳ (combined ticket with Ste-Chapelle, pp88–9, available.) ▱ phone to check. ▯

Occupying the north part of the old Capetian palace, the Conciergerie was under the administration of the palace "concierge", the keeper of the King's mansion. When the King moved to the Marais (in 1417), the palace remained the seat of royal administration and law; and the Conciergerie became a prison, with the "concierge" as its chief gaoler. Henry IV's assassin, Ravaillac, was imprisoned and tortured here.

During the Revolution it housed over 4,000 prisoners, including Marie-Antoinette, who was held in a tiny cell and Charlotte Corday, who stabbed Revolutionary leader Marat as he lay in his bath. Ironically, the Revolutionary judges Danton and Robespierre also became "tenants" before being sent to the guillotine.

The Conciergerie has a superb four-aisled Gothic Salle des Gens d'Armes (Hall of the Men-at-Arms), the dining hall for the castle's 2,000 members of staff. The building, renovated in the 19th century, retains the 11th-century torture chamber, the Bonbec Tower and the 14th-century public clock tower on the Tour de l'Horloge (Palais de Justice). It is the city's oldest and is still operating.

A portrait of Marie-Antoinette in the Conciergerie, awaiting her execution at the guillotine

Notre-Dame ❶

No other building is more associated with the history of Paris than Notre-Dame. It stands majestically on the Ile de la Cité, cradle of the city. Pope Alexander III laid the first stone in 1163, marking the start of 170 years of toil by armies of Gothic architects and medieval craftsmen. Ever since, a procession of the famous has passed through the three main doors below the massive towers.

The cathedral is a Gothic masterpiece, standing on the site of a Roman temple. At the time it was finished, in about 1330, it was 130 m (430 ft) long and featured flying buttresses, a large transept, a deep choir and 69-m (228-ft) high towers.

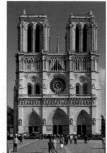

★ West Front
Three main doors with superb statuary, a central rose window and an openwork gallery are important details.

The south tower houses the cathedral's famous Emmanuel bell.

★ Galerie des Chimères
The cathedral's legendary gargoyles (chimères) hide behind a large upper gallery between the towers.

★ West Rose Window
This window depicts the Virgin in a medallion of rich reds and blues.

The Kings' Gallery features 28 Kings of Judah gazing down on the crowds.

Portal of the Virgin
The Virgin surrounded by saints and kings is a fine composition of 13th-century statues.

STAR FEATURES

★ West Front and Portals

★ Flying Buttresses

★ Rose Windows

★ Galerie des Chimères

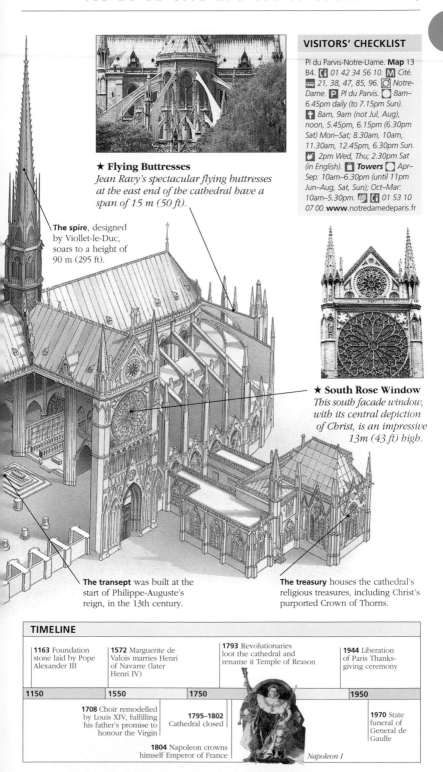

★ **Flying Buttresses**
Jean Ravy's spectacular flying buttresses at the east end of the cathedral have a span of 15 m (50 ft).

The spire, designed by Viollet-le-Duc, soars to a height of 90 m (295 ft).

VISITORS' CHECKLIST

Pl du Parvis-Notre-Dame. **Map** 13 B4. 01 42 34 56 10. *Cité.* 21, 38, 47, 85, 96. *Notre-Dame.* **P** *Pl du Parvis.* 8am–6.45pm daily (to 7.15pm Sun). 8am, 9am (not Jul, Aug), noon, 5.45pm, 6.15pm (6.30pm Sat) Mon–Sat; 8.30am, 10am, 11.30am, 12.45pm, 6.30pm Sun. 2pm Wed, Thu; 2.30pm Sat (in English). **Towers** Apr–Sep: 10am–6.30pm (until 11pm Jun–Aug, Sat, Sun); Oct–Mar: 10am–5.30pm. 01 53 10 07 00. **www**.notredamedeparis.fr

★ **South Rose Window**
This south facade window, with its central depiction of Christ, is an impressive 13m (43 ft) high.

The transept was built at the start of Philippe-Auguste's reign, in the 13th century.

The treasury houses the cathedral's religious treasures, including Christ's purported Crown of Thorns.

TIMELINE

1163 Foundation stone laid by Pope Alexander III	**1572** Marguerite de Valois marries Henri of Navarre (later Henri IV)	**1793** Revolutionaries loot the cathedral and rename it Temple of Reason	**1944** Liberation of Paris Thanks-giving ceremony
1150	**1550**	**1750**	**1950**
1708 Choir remodelled by Louis XIV, fulfilling his father's promise to honour the Virgin	**1795–1802** Cathedral closed		**1970** State funeral of General de Gaulle
	1804 Napoleon crowns himself Emperor of France	*Napoleon I*	

A Guided Tour of Notre-Dame

Notre-Dame's interior grandeur is instantly apparent on seeing the high-vaulted central nave. This is bisected by a huge transept, at either end of which are medieval rose windows, 13 m (43 ft) in diameter. Works by major sculptors adorn the cathedral. Among them are Jean Ravy's old choir screen carvings, Nicolas Coustou's *Pietà* and Antoine Coysevox's Louis XIV statue. In this majestic setting kings and emperors were crowned and royal Crusaders were blessed. But Notre-Dame was also the scene of turmoil. Revolutionaries ransacked it, banished religion, changed it into a temple to the Cult of Reason, and then used it as a wine store. Napoleon restored religion in 1804 and architect Viollet-le-Duc later restored the buildings, replacing missing statues, as well as raising the spire and fixing the gargoyles.

A jewelled chalice of Notre-Dame

⑨ **North Rose Window**
This 13th-century stained-glass window depicts the Virgin encircled by figures from the Old Testament.

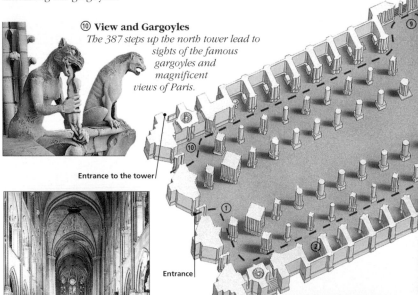

⑩ **View and Gargoyles**
The 387 steps up the north tower lead to sights of the famous gargoyles and magnificent views of Paris.

Entrance to the tower

Entrance

① **View of Interior**
From the main entrance, the view takes in the high-vaulted central nave looking down towards the huge transept, the choir and the high altar.

KEY

— — — Suggested route

② **Le Brun's "May" Paintings**
These religious paintings by Charles Le Brun hang in the side chapels. In the 17th and 18th centuries, the Paris guilds presented a painting to the cathedral on May Day each year.

⑧ **Carved Choir Stalls**
*Noted for their early
18th-century carved
woodwork, the choir
stalls were commis-
sioned by Louis XIII,
whose statue stands
behind the high altar.
Among the details
carved in bas-relief on
the back of the high
stalls are scenes from
the life of the Virgin.*

⑦ **Louis XIII Statue**
*After many years of childless marriage,
Louis XIII pledged to erect a high altar
and to redecorate the east chancel to
honour the Virgin if an heir was born
to him. The future Louis XIV was born
in 1638, but it took 60 years before
the promises were made good. One
of the surviving features from that
time is the carved choir stalls.*

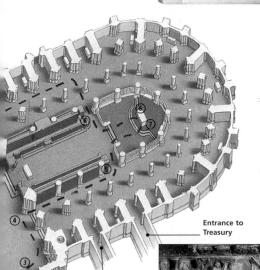

Entrance to
Treasury

Entrance to
Sacristy

⑥ **Pietà**
*Behind the high altar is Nicolas
Coustou's Pietà, standing on a
gilded base sculptured by
François Girardon.*

⑤ **Chancel Screen**
*A 14th-century high stone screen enclosed
the chancel and provided canons at prayer
with peace and solitude from noisy
congregations. Some of it has survived to
screen the first three north and south bays.*

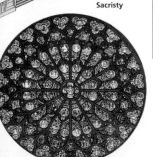

③ **South Rose Window**
*Located at the south end
of the transept, this window
retains some of its original
13th-century stained glass.
The window depicts Christ in
the centre, surrounded by
virgins, saints and the
12 Apostles.*

④ **Statue of the Virgin and Child**
*Against the southeast pillar of the
transept stands the 14th-century statue
of the Virgin and Child. It was brought
to the cathedral from the chapel of St
Aignan, and is known as Notre-Dame
de Paris (Our Lady of Paris).*

The Pont Neuf, extending to the north and south of the Ile de la Cité

Sainte-Chapelle ⑨

See pp88–9.

A Sainte-Chapelle decoration of angels with the Crown of Thorns

Palais de Justice ⑩

6 Blvd du Palais (entrance by the Cour de Mai) 75001. **Map** 13 A3. **Tel** *01 44 32 52 52.* Ⓜ *Cité.* ◯ *8.30am–6pm Mon–Fri.* ⌀

This huge block of buildings making up the law courts stretches the entire width of the Ile de la Cité. It is a splendid sight with its old towers lining the quays. The site has been occupied since Roman times and was the seat of royal power until Charles V moved the court to the Hôtel St-Paul in the Marais during the 14th century. In April 1793 the Revolutionary Tribunal began dispensing justice from the Première Chambre (gilded chamber). Today the site embodies Napoleon's great legacy – the French judicial system.

Place Dauphine ⑪

75001 (enter by Rue Henri-Robert). **Map** 12 F3. Ⓜ *Pont Neuf, Cité.*

East of Pont Neuf is this ancient square, laid out in 1607 by Henri IV and named after the Dauphin, the future Louis XIII. No. 14 is one of the few buildings to have avoided any subsequent restoration. This haven of 17th-century charm is popular with *pétanque* (boules) players and employees of the adjoining Palais de Justice.

Pont Neuf ⑫

75001. **Map** 12 F3. Ⓜ *Pont Neuf, Cité.*

Despite its name (New Bridge), this bridge is the oldest in Paris and has been immortalized by major literary and artistic figures since it was built. The first stone was laid by Henri III in 1578, but it was Henri IV who inaugurated it and gave it its name in 1607. The bridge has 12 arches and spans 275 m (912 ft). The first stone bridge to be built without houses, it heralded a new era in the relationship between the Cité and the river and has been popular ever since. Fittingly, Henri IV's statue stands in the central section.

A sculptured relief on the Palais de Justice

was founded in 1903 by his son. Part of the famous Polish library is at 74 rue Lauriston, but the archives remain here. They form the finest Polish collection outside Poland: paintings, books, maps and Frédéric Chopin memorabilia.

St-Louis-en-l'Ile

19 bis Rue St-Louis-en-l'Ile 75004. **Map** 13 C4. *Tel* 01 46 34 11 60. M Pont Marie. ◯ 9am–noon, 3pm–7pm Tue–Sat, 9am–6.30pm Sun. ◉ public hols. **Concerts** *Tel* 01 44 62 00 55.

The construction of this church was begun in 1664 from plans by the royal architect Louis Le Vau, who lived on the island. It was completed and consecrated in 1726. Among its outstanding exterior features are the 1741 iron clock at the entrance and the pierced iron spire.

The interior, in the Baroque style, is richly decorated with gilding and marble. There is a statue of St Louis holding a crusader's sword. A plaque in the north aisle, given in 1926, bears the inscription "in grateful memory of St Louis in whose honour the City of St Louis, Missouri, USA is named". The church is also twinned with Carthage cathedral in Tunisia, where St Louis is buried.

The interior of St-Louis-en-l'Ile

Henri IV in Square du Vert-Galant

Square du Vert-Galant ⑬

75001. **Map** 12 F3. M Pont Neuf, Cité.

One of the magical spots of Paris, this square bears the nickname of Henri IV. This amorous and colourful monarch did much to beautify Paris in the early 17th century, and his popularity has lasted to this day. From here there are splendid views of the Louvre and the Right Bank of the river, where Henri was assassinated in 1610. This is also the point from which the Vedettes du Pont Neuf pleasure boats depart *(see pp72–3)*.

Société Historique et Littéraire Polonaise ⑭

6 Quai d'Orléans 75004. **Map** 13 C4. *Tel* 01 55 42 83 83. M Pont Marie. ◯ 10am–1pm, 2–6pm Tue, 2–6pm Thu & Fri, 10am–1pm Sat. 3pm Wed, 11am, 3pm Sat; call to book. **www**.bibliotheque-polonaise-paris-shlp.fr

The Polish Romantic poet Adam Mickiewicz, who lived in Paris in the 19th century, was a major force in Polish cultural and political life, devoting his writing to helping his countrymen who were oppressed at home and abroad. His life is the focal point of the museum, which

A bust of Adam Mickiewicz

Hôtel de Lauzun ⑯

17 Quai d'Anjou 75004. **Map** 13 C4. *Tel* 01 44 54 19 30. M Pont Marie. ◯ for guided visits only. **www**.monuments-nationaux.fr

This splendid mansion was built by Louis Le Vau in the mid-1650s for Charles Gruyn des Bordes, an arms dealer. It was sold in 1682 to the French military commander Duc de Lauzun, who was a favourite of Louis XIV. It later became a focus for Paris's Bohemian literary and artistic life. It now belongs to the city of Paris and, for those lucky enough to see inside, offers an unsurpassed insight into wealthy lifestyles in the 17th century. Charles Le Brun worked on the decoration of its magnificent panelling and painted ceilings before moving on to Versailles.

The poet Charles Baudelaire (1821–67) lived on the third floor and wrote the major part of his controversial masterpiece *Les Fleurs du Mal* here in a room packed with antiques and bric-a-brac. The celebrated French Romantic poet, traveller and critic, Théophile Gautier (1811–72), had apartments here in 1848. Meetings of the Club des Haschischines (the Hashish-Eaters' Club) took place on the premises.

Other famous residents were the Austrian poet Rainer Maria Rilke, the English artist Walter Sickert and the German composer Richard Wagner. Nowadays it is used for public receptions by the mayor of Paris.

Sainte-Chapelle 9

Ethereal and magical, Sainte-Chapelle has been hailed as one of the greatest architectural master-pieces of the Western world. In the Middle Ages the devout likened this church to "a gateway to heaven". Today no visitor can fail to be transported by the blaze of light created by the 15 magnificent stained-glass windows, separated by the narrowest of columns that soar 15 m (50 ft) to the star-studded, vaulted roof. The windows portray over 1,000 religious scenes in a kaleidoscope of red, gold, green, blue and mauve. The chapel was built in 1248 by Louis IX to house Christ's purported Crown of Thorns (now housed in the Notre-Dame treasury).

The spire rises 75 m (245 ft) into the air. It was erected in 1853 after four previous spires burned down.

The Crown of Thorns decorates the pinnacle as a symbol of the first relic bought by Louis IX.

★ Rose Window
Best seen at sunset, the religious story of the Apocalypse is told in 86 panels of stained glass. The window was a gift from Charles VIII in 1485.

STAR FEATURES

- ★ Rose Window
- ★ Window of Christ's Passion
- ★ Apostle Statues
- ★ Window of the Relics

Main Portal
The two-tier structure of the portal, the lower half of which is shown here, echoes that of the chapel.

ST LOUIS' RELICS

Louis IX was extremely devout, and was canonized in 1297, not long after his death. In 1239 he acquired the Crown of Thorns from the Emperor of Constantinople and, in 1241, a fragment of Christ's Cross. He built this chapel as a shrine to house them. Louis paid nearly three times more for the relics than for the construction of Sainte-Chapelle. The Crown of Thorns is now kept at Notre-Dame.

LOUIS IX.

VISITORS' CHECKLIST

4 Blvd du Palais. **Map** 13 A3. ☎ 01 53 40 60 80. Ⓜ Cité. ▦ 21, 27, 38, 85, 96 to Ile de la Cité. Ⓡⓔⓡ St-Michel. ◎ Notre-Dame. Ⓟ Palais de Justice. ◯ daily. Mar–Oct: 9.30am–6pm; Nov–Feb: 9am–5pm. Last adm 30 mins before closing. ● 1 Jan, 1 May, 25 Dec. ▨ (combined ticket with Conciergerie, p81, is available.) ◎ ☒ ▯

The angel
once revolved so that its cross could be seen from anywhere in Paris.

Upper Chapel
The windows are a pictorial Bible, showing scenes from the Old and New Testaments.

UPPER CHAPEL WINDOWS

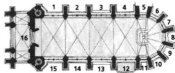

1	Genesis	
2	Exodus	
3	Numbers	
4	Deuteronomy: Joshua	
5	Judges	
6	*left* Isaiah *right* Rod of Jesse	
7	*left* St John the Evangelist *right* Childhood of Christ	
8	Christ's Passion	
9	*left* St John the Baptist *right* Story of Daniel	
10	Ezekiel	
11	*left* Jeremiah *right* Tobiah	
12	Judith and Job	
13	Esther	
14	Book of Kings	
15	Story of the Relics	
16	Rose Window: The Apocalypse	

★ **Window of Christ's Passion**
The Last Supper is shown here in one of the most beautiful windows in the upper chapel.

★ **Apostle Statues**
These magnificent examples of medieval stone carving adorn the 12 pillars of the upper chapel.

Lower Chapel
Servants and commoners worshipped here, while the chapel above was reserved for the use of the king and the royal family.

★ **Window of the Relics**
This shows the journey of the True Cross and the nails of the Crucifixion to Sainte-Chapelle.

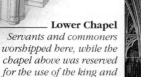

THE MARAIS

A place of royal residence in the 17th century, the Marais was all but abandoned during the Revolution, later descending into an architectural wasteland. Sensitive restoration brought the area to life again; some of Paris's most popular museums are now housed in its elegant mansions, while the main streets and narrow passageways bustle with smart boutiques, galleries and restaurants. Many traders have been driven out by high prices, but enough artisans, bakers and small cafés survive, as does the ethnic mix of Jews, former Algerian settlers, Asians and others. Today, the Marais is also the centre of the Parisian gay scene.

SIGHTS AT A GLANCE

Historic Buildings and Streets
Hôtel de Lamoignon ❷
Rue des Francs-Bourgeois ❸
Rue des Rosiers ❽
Hôtel de Ville ⓳
Hôtel de Rohan ㉒

Churches
St-Paul–St-Louis ⓯
St-Gervais–St-Protais ⓲
Cloître des Billettes ⓴
Notre-Dame-des-Blancs-Manteaux ㉑

Museums and Galleries
Musée Carnavalet pp96–7 ❶
Musée Cognacq-Jay ❹
Maison de Victor Hugo ❻
Hôtel de Sully ❼
Hôtel de Coulanges ❾
Musée Picasso pp100–1 ❿
Pavillon de l'Arsenal ⓫
Hôtel de Sens ⓰
Hôtel de Soubise ㉓
Hôtel Guénégaud (Musée de la Chasse et de la Nature) ㉔
Musée des Arts et Métiers ㉕
Musée d'Art et d'Histoire du Judaïsme ㉗

Monuments and Statues
Colonne de Juillet ⓭
Mémorial de la Shoah ⓱

Opera Houses
Opéra National de Paris Bastille ⓬

Squares
Place des Vosges ❺
Place de la Bastille ⓮
Square du Temple ㉖

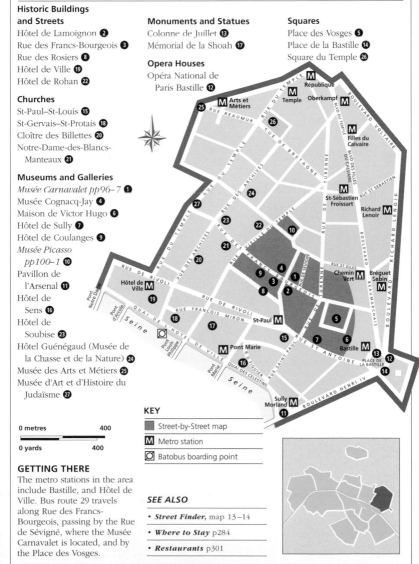

KEY

▨	Street-by-Street map
Ⓜ	Metro station
▣	Batobus boarding point

0 metres | 400
0 yards | 400

GETTING THERE

The metro stations in the area include Bastille, and Hôtel de Ville. Bus route 29 travels along Rue des Francs-Bourgeois, passing by the Rue de Sévigné, where the Musée Carnavalet is located, and by the Place des Vosges.

SEE ALSO

• *Street Finder,* map 13–14

• *Where to Stay* p284

• *Restaurants* p301

◁ Lunchtime at a Marais park café

Street by Street: The Marais

Once an area of marshland as its name suggests (*marais* means swamp), the Marais grew steadily in importance from the 14th century, by virtue of its proximity to the Louvre, the preferred residence of Charles V. Its heyday was in the 17th century, when it became the fashionable area for the monied classes. They built many grand and sumptuous mansions (*hôtels*) that still dot the Marais today. Many of these *hôtels* have been restored and turned into museums. Once again fashionable with the monied classes, designer boutiques, trendy restaurants, art galleries and cafés now line the streets.

To the Pompidou Centre

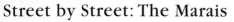

RUE BARBETTE

RUE ELZEVIR

RUE PAYENNE

RUE DES HOSPITALIERES ST GERVAIS

RUE DES ROSIERS

RUE MALHER

RUE PAVEE

Rue des Francs-Bourgeois
This ancient street is lined with intriguing buildings and trendy shops ❸

0 metres		100
0 yards		100

KEY
━ ━ ━ Suggested route

Rue des Rosiers
The smell of hot pastrami and borscht wafts from restaurants and shops in the heart of the Jewish area ❽

Musée Cognacq-Jay
An exquisite collection of 18th-century paintings and furniture is shown in perfect period setting ❹

STAR SIGHTS

★ Musée Picasso

★ Musée Carnavalet

★ Place des Vosges

Hôtel de Lamoignon
Behind the ornate doorway of this fine mansion is Paris's historical library ❷

★ **Musée Picasso**
The palatial home of a 17th-century salt-tax collector is the setting for the largest collection of Picassos in the world, the result of a family bequest to the state ⑪

LOCATOR MAP
See Central Paris Map pp14–15

The Hôtel le Peletier de St-Fargeau adjoins the Hôtel Carnavalet to form a museum of Paris history.

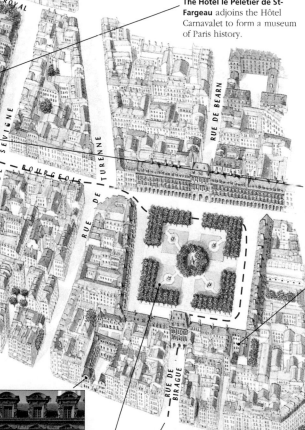

★ **Musée Carnavalet**
The statue of Louis XIV in Roman dress by Coysevox is in the courtyard of the Hôtel Carnavalet ①

Maison de Victor Hugo
Author of Les Misérables, *Victor Hugo lived at No. 6 Place des Vosges, where his house is now a museum of his life and work* ⑥

To Metro Sully Morland

★ **Place des Vosges**
Once the site of jousting and tournaments, the historic Place des Vosges, in the very heart of the Marais, is a square of perfect symmetry ⑤

Hôtel de Sully
This Renaissance hôtel *was built for a notorious gambler* ⑦

Musée Carnavalet ❶

See pp96–7.

Hôtel de Lamoignon ❷

24 Rue Pavée 75004. **Map** 14 D3.
***Tel** 01 44 59 29 40.* Ⓜ *St-Paul.*
◯ *1–6pm Mon–Sat.* ◯ *public hols*
& 1–15 Aug. ▢ *www.paris.fr*

The imposing Hôtel de Lamoignon is home to the historical library of the city of Paris. This mansion was built in 1585 for Diane de France, also known as the Duchesse d'Angoulême, daughter of Henri II. The building is noted for six high Corinthian pilasters topped by a triangular pediment and flourishes of dogs' heads, bows, arrows and quivers – recalling Diane's passion for hunting. The collection includes documents from the French Revolution and 80,000 prints covering the history of Paris.

Rue des Francs-Bourgeois ❸

75003, 75004. **Map** 14 D3.
Ⓜ *Rambuteau, Chemin-Vert.*

This street is an important thoroughfare in the heart of the Marais, linking the Rue des Archives and the Place

Courtyard of the Musée Carnavalet

des Vosges, with the imposing Hôtel de Soubise at one end and the Musée Carnavalet at the other. The street got its name from the *francs* (free from taxes) – almshouses built for the poor in 1334 at Nos. 34 and 36. These were later closed because of illegal financial activities, although the state kept its pawnshop nearby, still there today.

Musée Cognacq-Jay ❹

Hôtel Donon, 8 Rue Elzévir 75003.
Map 14 D3. ***Tel** 01 40 27 07 21.*
Ⓜ *St-Paul.* ◯ *10am–6pm Tue–Sun.*
◯ *public hols.* ▨ *pre-book.* ▢
www.cognacq-jay.paris.fr

This fine small collection of French 18th-century works of art and furniture was formed

by Ernest Cognacq and his wife, Louise Jay, founder of the Art Deco La Samaritaine, which was once Paris's largest department store *(see p115)*. The private collection was bequeathed to the city and is now housed in the heart of the Marais at the Hôtel Donon – an elegant building dating from 1575 with an 18th-century facade.

Place des Vosges ❺

75003, 75004. **Map** 14 D3.
Ⓜ *Bastille, St-Paul.*

This square is considered among the most beautiful in the world by Parisians and visitors alike *(see pp24–5)*. Its impressive symmetry – 36 houses, 9 on each side, of brick and stone, with deep slate roofs and dormer windows over arcades – is still intact after 400 years. It has been the scene of many historic events over the centuries. A three-day tournament was held here to celebrate the marriage of Louis XIII to Anne of Austria in 1615. The famous literary hostess, Madame de Sévigné, was born here in 1626; Cardinal Richelieu, pillar of the monarchy, stayed here in 1615; and Victor Hugo, the writer, lived here for 16 years.

A 19th-century engraving of the Place des Vosges

Maison de Victor Hugo ⑥

6 Pl des Vosges 75004. **Map** 14 D3.
Tel 01 42 72 10 16. **M** Bastille.
⬜ 10am–6pm Tue–Sun. ⬤ public
hols. 🖼 exhibitions only. 📷
Library.www.musee-hugo.paris.fr

The French poet, dramatist and
novelist lived on the second
floor of the former Hôtel
Rohan-Guéménée from 1832 to
1848. It was here that he wrote
most of *Les Misérables* and
completed many other famous
works. On display are some
reconstructions of the rooms in
which he lived, pen-
and-ink drawings,
books and
mementos from
the crucially
important
periods in his
life, from his
childhood to
his exile between
1852 and 1870.
Temporary exhibi-
tions on Hugo
take place
regularly.

**Marble bust of Victor Hugo by
Auguste Rodin**

Hôtel de Sully ⑦

62 Rue St-Antoine 75004. **Map** 14
D4. **Tel** 01 42 74 47 75. **M** St-Paul.
⬜ noon–7pm Tue–Fri; 10am–7pm Sat
& Sun. ⬤ 1 Jan, 1 May, 1 & 11 Nov,
25 Dec. 🖼 📷 www.jeudepaume.org

This fine 17th-century
mansion on one of Paris's
oldest streets has been
extensively restored, using
old engravings and drawings
as reference. It was built in
1624 for a notorious gambler,
Petit Thomas, who lost his
whole fortune in one night.
The Duc de Sully, Henri IV's
chief minister, purchased the
house in 1634 and added
some of the interior decoration
as well as the Petit Sully
orangery in the gardens. The
Hôtel de Sully has now joined
forces with the Tuileries' Jeu
de Paume museum (see p131),
showcasing contemporary
works on photography,
film and the moving arts.

Late-Renaissance facade of the Hôtel de Sully

Rue des Rosiers ⑧

75004. **Map** 13 C3. **M** St-Paul.

The Jewish quarter in and
around this street is one of the
most colourful areas of Paris.
The street's name refers to the
rosebushes within the old city
wall. Jews first settled here in
the 13th century, with a
second significant wave of
immigration occurring in the
19th century from Russia,
Poland and central Europe.
Sephardic Jews arrived from
Algeria, Tunisia, Morocco and
Egypt in the 1950s and 1960s.
Some 165 students were
rounded up and deported
from the old Jewish Boys'
school nearby at 10 rue de
Hospitalières-St-Gervais.
N'Oubliez pas (Lest we forget)
is engraved on the wall. Today
this area contains synagogues,
bakeries and kosher
restaurants (see p333).

Hôtel de Coulanges ⑨

35 rue des Francs Bourgeois, 75004.
Map 13 C3. **Tel** 01 44 61 85 95.
M St-Paul. ⬜ 1.30pm–7pm
Mon–Fri. ⬤ public hols.
www.paris-europe.eu

This hôtel is a magnificent
example of the architecture
of the early 18th century. The
right wing of the building,
separating the courtyard from
the garden, dates from the
early 17th century. The hôtel
was given in 1640 to Philippe
II de Coulanges, the King's
counsellor. Renamed the "Petit
hôtel Le Tellier" in 1662 by its
new owner Le Tellier, this is
where the children of Louis
XIV and Madame de Montespan
were raised in secrecy. It is
home to the Maison de
l'Europe, with exhibitions on
themes relating to Europe.

**Orthodox Jews in
the Marais**

Musée Carnavalet ●

Carnavalet entrance

Devoted to the history of Paris, this vast museum occupies two adjoining mansions, with entire decorated rooms with panelling, furniture and *objets d'art;* many works of art such as paintings and sculptures of prominent personalities; and engravings showing Paris being built. The main building is the Hôtel Carnavalet, built as a town house in 1548 and transformed in the mid-17th century by François Mansart. The neighbouring 17th-century mansion, Hôtel Le Peletier, features superb early 20th-century interiors, and the restored Orangery is devoted to Prehistory and Gallo-Roman Paris.

Marie Antoinette in Mourning *(1793) Alexandre Kucharski painted her at the Temple prison after the execution of Louis XVI.*

Memorabilia in this room is dedicated to 18th-century philosophers, in particular Jean-Jacques Rousseau and Voltaire.

★ **Charles Le Brun Ceiling**
Magnificent works by the 17th-century artist decorate the former study and great hall from the Hôtel de la Rivière.

★ **Mme de Sévigné's Gallery**
The gallery includes this portrait of Mme de Sévigné, the celebrated letter-writer, whose beloved home this was for the 20 years up to her death.

STAR EXHIBITS

- ★ Charles Le Brun Ceiling
- ★ Mme de Sévigné's Gallery
- ★ Hôtel d'Uzès Reception Room
- ★ Ballroom of the Hôtel de Wendel

★ **Hotel d'Uzès Reception Room**
The room was created in 1761 by Claude Nicolas Ledoux. The gold-and-white panelling is from a Rue Montmartre mansion.

Entran the mus

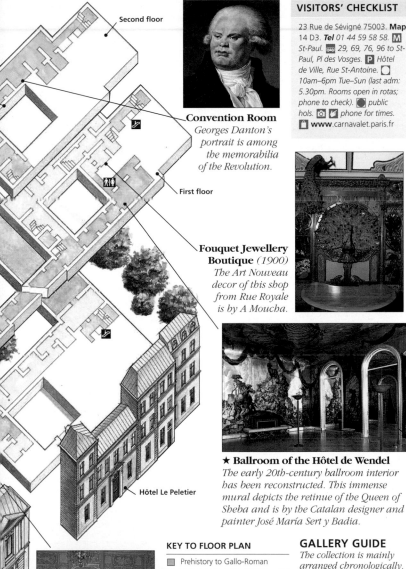

Second floor

First floor

Hôtel Le Peletier

Convention Room
*Georges Danton's
portrait is among
the memorabilia
of the Revolution.*

VISITORS' CHECKLIST

23 Rue de Sévigné 75003. **Map**
14 D3. *Tel* 01 44 59 58 58. Ⓜ
St-Paul. 🚌 *29, 69, 76, 96 to St-
Paul, Pl des Vosges.* Ⓟ *Hôtel
de Ville, Rue St-Antoine.* ⬭
*10am–6pm Tue–Sun (last adm:
5.30pm. Rooms open in rotas;
phone to check).* ⬤ *public
hols.* ⬜ 🎞 *phone for times.*
🔲 www.*carnavalet.paris.fr*

**Fouquet Jewellery
Boutique** *(1900)*
*The Art Nouveau
decor of this shop
from Rue Royale
is by A Moucha.*

★ **Ballroom of the Hôtel de Wendel**
*The early 20th-century ballroom interior
has been reconstructed. This immense
mural depicts the retinue of the Queen of
Sheba and is by the Catalan designer and
painter José María Sert y Badia.*

Louis XV Room
*This delightful room
contains art from the
Bouvier collection and
panelling from the
Hôtel de Broglie.*

KEY TO FLOOR PLAN

⬜	Prehistory to Gallo-Roman
⬜	Medieval Paris
⬜	Renaissance Paris
⬜	17th-century Paris
⬜	Louis XV's Paris
⬜	Louis XVI's Paris
⬜	Revolutionary Paris
⬜	19th Century
⬜	20th Century
⬜	Temporary exhibitions
⬜	Non-exhibition space

GALLERY GUIDE

*The collection is mainly
arranged chronologically.
It covers the history of Paris
up to 1789. The Renaissance
is on the ground floor, and
the exhibits covering the
17th century to the Revolution
are on the first floor. In the
Hôtel le Peletier the ground
floor covers the First–Second
Empires, with the Pre-history–
Gallo-Roman departments in
the Orangery; from the
Second Empire to the present
day is on the first floor, and
the second floor is devoted to
the Revolution.*

Musée Picasso ⑩

See pp100–1.

Pavillon de l'Arsenal ⑪

21 Bd Morland 75004. **Map** 14 D4.
Tel *01 42 76 33 97.* Ⓜ *Sully Morland,
Bastille.* ◯ *10.30am–6.30pm Tue–Sat,
11am–7pm Sun.* ◯ *1 Jan.* ▢ ▢ ▢
by appointment only. **www**.pavillon-
arsenal.com

The Pavillon de l'Arsenal
houses a small but fascinating
exhibition on the architectural
evolution of Paris. Using
films, models and panoramic
images, this permanent
exhibition explores how Paris
was built over the centuries,
as well as looking at future
plans for the city. Up to three
temporary exhibitions are also
programmed each year.

Opéra National de Paris Bastille ⑫

120 Rue de Lyon 75012.
Map 4 E4. 🎫 *08 92 89 90 90.*
Ⓜ *Bastille.* ◯ *phone for details.*
◯ *certain public hols.*
▨ ♿ ▢ *compulsory.*
See **Entertainment** *pp332–5.*
www.operadeparis.fr

The controversial "people's
opera" was officially opened
on 14 July 1989 to coincide
with the bicentennial
celebrations of the fall

**The "genius of liberty" on top of
the Colonne de Juillet**

of the Bastille. Carlos Ott's
imposing building is a notable
break with 19th-century
opera-house design,
epitomized by Garnier's
opulent Opéra in the heart
of the city *(see pp216–17).*
It is a massive, modern,
curved, glass building. The
main auditorium seats an
audience of 2,700; its design
is functional and modern
with black upholstered seats
contrasting with the granite
of the walls and the
impressive glass ceiling.
With its five moveable
stages, this opera house is
certainly a masterpiece of
technological wizardry.

Colonne de Juillet ⑬

Pl de la Bastille 75004. **Map** 14 E4.
Ⓜ *Bastille.* ◯ *to the public.*

Topped by the statue of the
"genius of liberty", this
column of hollow bronze
reaches 51.5 m (170 ft) into
the sky. It is a memorial to
those who died in the street
battles of July 1830 that led
to the overthrow of the
monarch *(see pp32–3).* The
crypt contains the remains of
504 victims of the violent
fighting and others who died
in the 1848 revolution.

Place de la Bastille ⑭

75004. **Map** 14 E4. Ⓜ *Bastille.*

Nothing is now left of the
prison stormed by the
revolutionary mob on 14 July
1789 *(see pp30–31)* – an event
celebrated annually by the
French at home and abroad –
although the stones were used
for the Pont de la Concorde. A
line of paving stones from Nos.
5 to 49 Blvd Henri IV traces the
former towers and fortifications.
Until recently, the large, traffic-
clogged square which marks
the site, was the border
between central Paris and the
eastern working-class areas
(faubourgs). Gentrification,
however, is well underway,
with a marina, the Port de
Plaisance de l'Arsenal, and
attractive cafés and shops.

**The glass facade of the Bastille
Opéra**

St-Paul–St-Louis 🄑

99 Rue St-Antoine 75004. **Map** 14
D4. **Tel** 01 42 72 30 32. Ⓜ St-Paul.
◻ 8am–8pm Mon–Fri, 8am–7.30pm
Sat, 9am–8pm Sun. **Concerts**

A Jesuit church, St-Paul–St-Louis was an important symbol of the influence which the Jesuits held from 1627, when Louis XIII laid the first stone, to 1762 when they were expelled from France. The Gesù church in Rome served as the model for the nave, while the 60-m high (180-ft) dome was the forerunner of those of the Invalides and the Sorbonne. Most of the church's treasures were removed during periods of turmoil, but Delacroix's masterpiece, *Christ in the Garden of Olives*, can still be seen. The church stands on one of the main streets of the Marais, but can also be approached by the ancient Passage St-Paul.

***Christ in the Garden of Olives* by Delacroix in St-Paul–St-Louis**

him to die of rage in 1594 on hearing that the Protestant Henri IV had entered Paris. Marguerite de Valois, lodged here by her ex-husband, Henri IV, led a life of breathtaking debauchery and scandal. This culminated in the beheading of an ex-lover, who had dared to assassinate her current favourite.

The memorial to the unknown Jewish martyr, dedicated in 1956

Hôtel de Sens 🄖

1 Rue du Figuier 75004. **Map** 13
C4. **Tel** 01 42 78 14 60. Ⓜ Pont-
Marie. ◻ 1pm–7.30pm Tue, Fri, Sat;
10am–7.30pm Wed, Thu. ◒ public
hols. 🈳 for exhibitions. 🎫
🈳 by appointment only.

This is one of the few medieval buildings left in Paris. It now houses the Forney fine arts library. In the 16th century, at the time of the Catholic League, it was turned into a fortified mansion and occupied by the Bourbons, the Guises and Cardinal de Pellevé, whose religious fervour led

Mémorial de la Shoah 🄗

17 Rue Geoffroy-l'Asnier 75004.
Map 13 C4. **Tel** 01 42 77 44 72.
Ⓜ Pont-Marie. ◻ 10am–6pm Sun–
Fri (10am–10pm Thu). 🈳 exhibitions.
🅰 🈳 www.memorialdelashoah.org

The eternal flame burning in the crypt here is the simple memorial to the unknown Jewish martyr of the Holocaust. Its striking feature is a large cylinder that bears the names of the concentration camps where Jewish victims of the Holocaust died. In 2005 a stone wall, engraved with the names of 76,000 Jews – 11,000 of them children – who were deported from France to the Nazi death camps, was also erected here.

St-Gervais– St-Protais 🄘

Pl St-Gervais 75004. **Map** 13 B3.
Tel 01 48 87 32 02. Ⓜ Hôtel de
Ville. ◻ 7am–10pm daily.

Named after Gervase and Protase, two Roman soldiers who were martyred by Nero, this remarkable church dates from the 6th century. It has the oldest Classical façade in Paris, which is formed of a three-tiered arrangement of columns: Doric, Ionic and Corinthian. Behind its facade lies a beautiful Gothic church renowned for its association with religious music. It was for the church's fine organ that François Couperin (1668–1733) composed his two masses. The church currently has a Roman Catholic monastic community whose liturgy attracts people from all over the world.

The Hôtel de Sens, now home to a fine arts library

The facade of St-Gervais–St-Protais with its Classical columns

Musée Picasso ⑩

On the death of the Spanish-born artist Pablo Picasso (1881–1973), who lived most of his life in France, the French State inherited many of his works in lieu of death duties. It used them to establish the Musée Picasso, which opened in 1985. The museum is housed in a large 17th-century mansion, the Hôtel Salé, in the Marais. The original character of the Hôtel, which was built in 1656 for Aubert de Fontenay, a salt-tax collector (*salé* means "salty"), has been preserved. The breadth of the collection reflects Picasso's development, including his Blue, Pink and Cubist periods. The museum closed in 2009 for major renovation work, which should be finished by spring 2013.

★ Self-Portrait
Poverty, loneliness and the onset of winter all made the end of 1901, when this picture was painted, a particularly difficult time for Picasso.

Violin and Sheet Music
This collage (1912) is from the artist's Synthetic Cubist period.

★ The Two Brothers
During the summer of 1906 Picasso returned to Catalonia in Spain, where he painted this picture.

★ The Kiss *(1969)*
Picasso married Jacqueline Roque in 1961, and at around the same time he returned to the familiar themes of the couple and of the artist and model.

GALLERY GUIDE
The collection is mainly presented in chronological order, starting on the first floor with the Blue and Pink periods, Cubist and Neo-Classical works. Exhibitions change regularly – not all paintings are on show at any one time. On the ground floor there is a sculpture garden and works from the late 1920s to late 1930s, and from the mid-1950s to 1973.

Basement ——————

KEY TO FLOORPLAN

☐	Paintings
☐	Illustrations
☐	Sculpture garden
☐	Ceramics
☐	Non-exhibition space

Woman with a Mantilla *(1949)*
Picasso extended his range when he began working in ceramics in 1948.

Painter with Palette and Easel (1928)
This Post-Cubist portrait in oils was painted at a time when Picasso's work was verging on Surrealism.

First floor

★ **Two Women Running on the Beach** (1922)
In 1924 this was used for the stage curtain design for Diaghilev's ballet The Blue Train. It proved to be his last major design work for any theatre.

Ground floor

Woman Reading (1932)
Purples and yellows were often used by Picasso when painting his model Marie-Thérèse Walter.

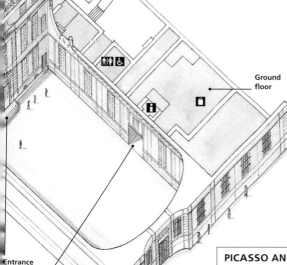

Entrance

Entrance

STAR PAINTINGS

★ Self-Portrait

★ The Two Brothers

★ Two Women Running on the Beach

★ The Kiss

PICASSO AND SPAIN

After 1934, Picasso never returned to his homeland due to his rejection of Franco's regime. However, throughout his life in France he used Spanish themes in his art, such as the bull (often in the form of a minotaur) and the guitar, which he associated with his Andalusian childhood.

The town hall (Hôtel de Ville), overlooking a delightful square

Hôtel de Ville ⑲

Pl de l'Hôtel de Ville 75004. **Map** 13
B3. *Tel 01 42 76 40 40.* Ⓜ *Hôtel-de-
Ville.* ◯ *10am–7pm Mon–Sat for
temporary exhibitions; groups: by
arrangement.* ● *public hols, official
functions.* ♿ ✉

Home of the city council,
the town hall is a 19th-
century reconstruction of the
17th-century town hall that
was burned down in 1871.
It is highly ornate, with
elaborate stonework, turrets
and statues overlooking a
pedestrianized square which
is a delight to stroll in,
especially at night when the
fountains are illuminated.

The square was once the
main site for hangings, burn-
ings and other executions. It
was here that Ravaillac, Henri
IV's assassin, was quartered
alive, his body ripped to
pieces by four strong horses.

Inside the Hôtel de Ville,
a notable feature is the long
Salle des Fêtes (ballroom), with
adjoining salons devoted to
science, literature and the arts.
The impressive staircase, the
decorated ceilings with their
chandeliers and the statues and
caryatids all add to the air of
ceremony and pomp. Whilst
these parts are mostly closed
to the public (except during
some of the Journées du
Patrimoine (*see p64*) and group
visits, certain annexes are used
for temporary exhibitions on
themes related to France (see
www.paris.fr for more info).

Cloître des Billettes ⑳

24 Rue des Archives 75004.
Map 13 B3. *Tel 01 42 72 37 08.*
Ⓜ *Hôtel-de-Ville.* ◯ **Cloister**
11am–7pm daily; **church** *6.30–8pm
Thu, 9.30am–4pm Sun.*

This is the only remaining
medieval cloister in Paris.
It was built in 1427 for the
Brothers of Charity, or
Billettes, and three of its four
original galleries are still
standing. The adjoining
church is a simple Classical
building which replaced the
monastic original in 1756.

The oldest cloister in Paris

Notre-Dame-des-Blancs-Manteaux ㉑

12 Rue des Blancs-Manteaux 75004.
Map 13 C3. *Tel 01 42 72 09 37.*
Ⓜ *Rambuteau.* ◯ *10am–noon,
3pm–7pm daily.* **Concerts.**

This church, built in 1685,
takes its name from the white
habits worn by the Augus-
tinian friars who founded a
convent on the site in 1258. It
has a splendid 18th-century
Rococo Flemish pulpit, and
its famous organ is best
appreciated at one of its
concerts of religious music.

Hôtel de Rohan ㉒

87 Rue Vieille-du-Temple 75003.
Map 13 C2. *Tel 01 40 27 60 00.*
Ⓜ *Rambuteau.* ◯ *for temporary
exhibitions only Sun pm.*

Although not resembling it
in appearance, the Hôtel de
Rohan forms a pair with the
Hôtel de Soubise. It was built
by the same architect,
Delamair, for Armand de
Rohan-Soubise, a cardinal
and Bishop of Strasbourg.
The hôtel has been home to
a part of the national archives
(one of the largest in the
world) since 1927. In the
courtyard over the doorway
of the stables is the 18th-
century sculpture *Horses of
Apollo* by Robert Le Lorrain.

Horses of Apollo by Le Lorrain

Hôtel de Soubise ㉓

60 Rue des Francs-Bourgeois 75003.
Map 13 C2. **Tel** 01 40 27 60 96. Ⓜ
Rambuteau. **Musée de l'Histoire de
France** ◻ *10am–12.30pm, 2–5.30pm
Wed–Fri, 2–5.30pm Sat & Sun.* ▨

The Hôtel de Soubise

This imposing mansion, built
from 1705 to 1709 for the
Princesse de Rohan, is one of
two main buildings housing
the national archives. (The
other is the Hôtel de Rohan).
The Hôtel de Soubise displays
a majestic courtyard and a
magnificent interior decoration dating from 1735 to 1740
by some of the most gifted
painters and craftsmen of the
day: Carl Van Loo, Jean
Restout, Charles Natoire and
François Boucher.
Natoire's *rocaille* work on
the Princess's bedroom, the
Oval Salon, forms part of the
Musée de l'Histoire de France.
Other exhibits include
Napoleon's will, in which he
asks for his remains to be
returned to France, and letters
by Joan of Arc and Voltaire.

Hôtel Guénégaud ㉔

60 Rue des Archives 75003.
Map 13 C2. **Tel** 01 53 01 92 40.
Ⓜ *Hôtel de Ville.* ◻ *11am–6pm
Tue–Sun.* ◐ *public hols.* ▨ ◻ ◻
www.chassenature.org

The celebrated architect
François Mansart built this
superb mansion in the mid-
17th century for Henri de
Guénégaud des Brosses, who
was Secretary of State and
Keeper of the Seals. One wing

now contains the Musée
de la Chasse et de la Nature
(Hunting Museum) inaugur-
ated by André Malraux in
1967. The exhibits include a
fine collection of hunting
weapons from the 16th to the
19th centuries, many from
Germany and Central Europe.
There are also drawings and
paintings by Oudry, Rubens
(including *Diane and her
Nymphs Preparing to Hunt*)
and Rembrandt.

Musée des Arts et Métiers ㉕

60 Rue Réaumur 75003. **Map** 13 B1-
C1. **Tel** 01 53 01 82 00. Ⓜ *Arts et
Métiers.* ◻ *10am–6pm Tue–Sun (to
9.30pm Thu).* ◐ *public hols.* ▨ ◻
♿ ◻ ◻ www.arts-et-metiers.net

Housed within the old
Abbey of Saint-Martin-des-
Champs, the Arts and Crafts
museum was founded in
1794 and closed down two
centuries later for interior
restructuring and renovation.
It reopened in 2000 as a high-
quality museum of science
and industry displaying 5,000
items (it has 75,000 other items
in store available to academics
and researchers). The theme
is man's ingenuity and the
world of invention and
manufacturing, covering such
topics as textiles, photography
and machines. Among the most
entertaining displays are ones
of musical clocks, mechanical
music instruments and
automata (mechanical figures),
one of which, the "Joueuse
de Tympanon", is said to
represent Marie-Antoinette.

Square du Temple ㉖

75003. **Map** 13 C1. Ⓜ *Temple.*

A quiet and pleasant square
today, this was once a
fortified centre of the medieval
Knights Templar. A state within a state, the area contained
a palace, a church and shops
behind high walls and a draw-
bridge, making it a haven for
those who were seeking to
escape from royal jurisdiction.
Louis XVI and Marie-Antoinette
were held here after their
arrest in 1792 *(see pp30–31).*
The king left from here for his
execution on the guillotine.

Musée d'Art et d'Histoire du Judaïsme ㉗

Hôtel de St-Aignan, 71 rue du Temple
75003. **Map** 13 B2. **Tel** 01 53 01 86
60. Ⓜ *Rambuteau.* ◻ *11am–6pm
Mon–Fri, 10am–6pm Sun (last
admission at 5.15pm).* ◐ *Jewish hols.*
▨ ♿ ◻ ◻ ◻ www.mahj.org

Housed in an elegant Marais
mansion, the museum unites
collections formerly scattered
around the city, and commemorates the culture of French
Jewry from medieval times to
the present. There has been a
sizeable Jewish community in
France since Roman times, and
some of the world's greatest
Jewish scholars were French.
Much exquisite craftsmanship
is displayed, with elaborate
silverware and Torah covers.
There are also historical
documents, photographs,
paintings and cartoons.

"Being a Jew in Paris in 1939", a display in the Jewish Museum

BEAUBOURG AND LES HALLES

This Right Bank area is dominated by the modernistic Forum des Halles and the Pompidou Centre. These two spectacular undertakings are thriving public areas of contact for shoppers, art lovers, students and tourists. Literally millions flow between the two squares. The Halles is for street fashion, with most of the shops underground, and the clientele strolling under the concrete and glass bubbles is young. Above ground, there are gardens and mini-pavilions. The surrounding streets are coloured by popular cheap shops and bars, but there are still enough specialist food shops, butchers and small markets to recall what Les Halles must have been like in its prime as the city's thriving market. All roads round Les Halles lead to the Beaubourg area and the Pompidou Centre, an avant-garde assembly of vast pipes, ducts and cables, renovated in the 1990s to cope with its 20,000 daily visitors. The adjoining streets, such as Rue St-Martin and Rue Beaubourg, house small contemporary art galleries in crooked, gabled buildings.

Fountain in the Place Igor Stravinsky

SIGHTS AT A GLANCE

Historic Buildings and Streets
No. 51 Rue de Montmorency ❿
Tour Jean Sans Peur ⓫
Bourse du Commerce ⓭
La Samaritaine ⓯
Tour St-Jacques ⓰

Churches
St-Merry ❸
St-Eustache ⓬
St-Germain l'Auxerrois ⓮

Museums and Galleries
Pompidou Centre pp110–13 ❶
Galerie Marian Goodman ❺
Forum des Images ❼
Musée de la Poupée ❾

Modern Architecture
Place Igor Stravinsky ❷
Forum des Halles ❽

Cafés
Café Beaubourg ❻

Fountains
Fontaine des Innocents ❹

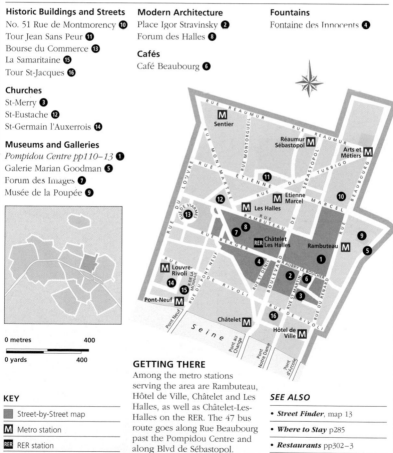

0 metres 400
0 yards 400

KEY
▢ Street-by-Street map
Ⓜ Metro station
RER RER station

GETTING THERE
Among the metro stations serving the area are Rambuteau, Hôtel de Ville, Châtelet and Les Halles, as well as Châtelet-Les-Halles on the RER. The 47 bus route goes along Rue Beaubourg past the Pompidou Centre and along Blvd de Sébastopol.

SEE ALSO
• *Street Finder*, map 13

• *Where to Stay* p285

• *Restaurants* pp302–3

◁ St-Eustache and sculptured head, *l'Ecoute*, by Henri de Miller

Street-by-Street: Beaubourg and Les Halles

When Emile Zola described Les Halles as the "belly of Paris" he was referring to the meat, vegetable and fruit market that had thrived here since 1183. Traffic congestion in the 1960s forced the market to move to the suburbs and Baltard's giant umbrella-like market pavilions were pulled down, despite howls of protest, and replaced by a shopping and leisure complex, the Forum. The conversion worked: today, Les Halles and the Pompidou Centre, which lies in the Beaubourg quarter and has been one of Paris's main tourist attractions ever since it opened in 1977, draw the most mixed crowds in Paris.

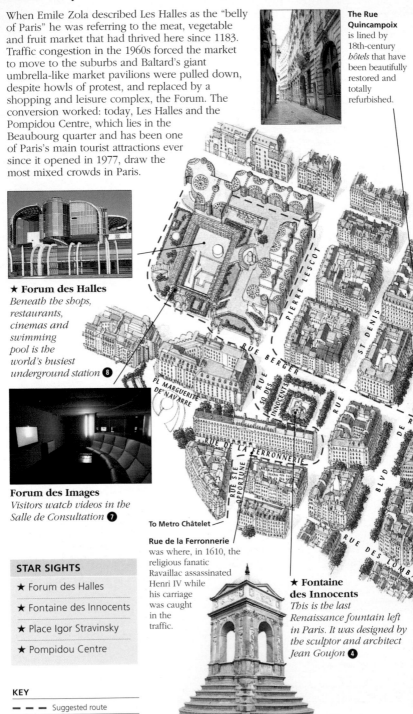

The Rue Quincampoix is lined by 18th-century *hôtels* that have been beautifully restored and totally refurbished.

★ **Forum des Halles**
Beneath the shops, restaurants, cinemas and swimming pool is the world's busiest underground station ⑧

Forum des Images
Visitors watch videos in the Salle de Consultation ⑦

To Metro Châtelet

Rue de la Ferronnerie was where, in 1610, the religious fanatic Ravaillac assassinated Henri IV while his carriage was caught in traffic.

★ **Fontaine des Innocents**
This is the last Renaissance fountain left in Paris. It was designed by the sculptor and architect Jean Goujon ④

STAR SIGHTS

★ Forum des Halles

★ Fontaine des Innocents

★ Place Igor Stravinsky

★ Pompidou Centre

KEY

— — — Suggested route

**Le Défenseur
du Temps**
This impressive brass-
and-steel mechanical
clock and sculpture was
designed by Jacques
Monastier in 1979. It
portrays a soldier
defending the passage
of time against savage
beasts which represent
the elements.

LOCATOR MAP
See Central Paris Map pp14–15

**Metro
Rambuteau**

0 metres   100

0 yards   100

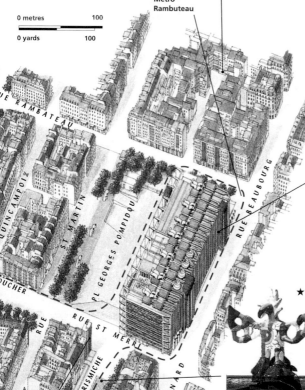

★ **Pompidou Centre**
*Paris's museum of modern
art is housed here, along
with extensive art libraries
and an industrial design
centre* ❶

★ **Place Igor Stravinsky**
*is dominated by the
first contemporary
Parisian fountain,
created by Niki de
Saint Phalle and Jean
Tinguely* ❷

St-Merry
*The pulpit of this beautiful
church was designed by the
Stodtz brothers in the mid-
18th century and is
supported by a pair of
carved palm trees, one on
either side* ❸

RCAM is a
research centre
dedicated to pioneering
new ways of making music.

Pompidou Centre ❶

See pp110–13.

Place Igor Stravinsky ❷

Map 13 B2. Ⓜ *Rambuteau.*

This lively square on the south side of the Pompidou Centre is filled with modern sculptures and street performers. Since 1983 it has contained the Stravinsky Fountain, which features 16 moving, water-spraying sculptures of skeletons, dragons and a large pair of red lips. The black iron and colourful polyester mechanical sculptures were created by husband-and-wife team Jean Tinguely and Niki de Saint Phalle and pay homage to Igor Stravinsky. Each sculpture represents one of his compositions, including *The Firebird* and *The Rite of Spring*.

Stravinsky's music paved the way for the pioneering work of IRCAM (Institut de la Researche et de la Coordination Acoustique/ Musique), which has an entrance on the west side of the square. Founded by the composer Pierre Boulez, it is a research centre dedicated to creating new technologies for contemporary music, as well as a venue for concerts. Much of the Institute is underground, with an overground extension by Renzo Piano, one of the Pompidou Centre's architects. IRCAM runs an annual festival, which usually takes place for up to two weeks in June.

St-Merry ❸

76 Rue de la Verrerie 75004. **Map** 13 B3. **Tel** 01 42 71 93 93. Ⓜ *Hôtel-de-Ville.* ◯ *3–7pm daily.* 🎵 *1st & 3rd Sun, pm.* **Concerts.**

The site of this church dates back to the 7th century. St Médéric, the abbot of St-Martin d'Autun, was buried here at the beginning of the 8th century. The saint's name, which was eventually

A Nativity scene from the stained-glass windows in St-Merry

corrupted to Merry, was given to a chapel built nearby. The building of the church – in the Flamboyant Gothic style – was not completed until 1552. The west front is particularly rich in decoration, and the northwest turret contains the oldest bell in Paris, dating from 1331. It was the wealthy parish church of the Lombard moneylenders, who gave their name to the nearby Rue des Lombards.

Fontaine des Innocents ❹

Sq des Innocents 75001. **Map** 13 A2. Ⓜ *Les Halles.* ⓇⒺⓇ *Châtelet-Les-Halles.*

This carefully-restored Renaissance fountain stands in the Square des Innocents, the area's main crossroads. Erected in 1549 on the Rue St-Denis, it was moved to its present location in the 18th century, when the square was constructed on the site of a former graveyard. Originally set into a wall, the fountain had only three sides so a fourth had to be constructed. The fountain is popular with the city's youth as a meeting place, and is one of the landmarks of Les Halles.

Galerie Marian Goodman ❺

79 rue du Temple 75003. **Map** 13 C2. **Tel** 01 48 04 70 52. Ⓜ *Rambuteau.* ⓇⒺⓇ *Châtelet-Les-Halles.* ◯ *11am–7pm Tue–Sat.* **www**.mariangoodman.com

One of many art spaces in the area, this cutting edge gallery is the sister of Marian Goodman Gallery, New York which has played an important role in presenting European artists to American audiences since the 1970s. Many important contemporary artists, from the continent and the US, have been exhibited in the Paris gallery, including Gerhard Richter, Jeff Wall, Chantal Akerman and Cristina Iglesias.

Housed in a beautiful 17th-century mansion, the contemporary works on display and the Manhattan-style interior contrast in an appealing, if strikingly anachronistic way with the period façade.

Café Beaubourg ❻

100 Rue St-Martin, 75004. **Map** 13 B2. **Tel** 01 48 87 63 96. Ⓜ *Les Halles.* ⓇⒺⓇ *Châtelet-Les-Halles.* ◯ *8am–1am Mon–Wed, Sun; 8am–2am Thu–Sat.*

Opened by Gilbert Costes in 1987, this stylish café was designed and decorated by one of France's star architects, Christian de Portzamparc,

Decoration on the Fontaine des Innocents

The terrace of the Café Beaubourg

who created the impressive Cité de la Musique in the Parc de la Villette (see p236). Its vast terrace is lined with comfortable wicker chairs. The spacious and coolly elegant interior is decorated with rows of books, which soften its severely Art Deco ambience. The café is a favourite meeting point for art dealers from the surrounding galleries and Pompidou Centre staff. It serves light meals and brunch. If the crush gets too much around Les Halles, the Café Beaubourg is the ideal place to soothe the nerves.

François Truffaut's *Baisers Volés*

Forum des Images ❼

2 Rue du Cinéma, Forum des Halles 75001. **Map** 13 A2. **Tel** *01 44 76 63 00.* Ⓜ *Les Halles.* RER *Châtelet-Les-Halles.* 🕐 *12.30–11.30pm Tue–Fri, 2–11.30pm Sat & Sun.* 🎫 ♿ 🖥 **www**.forumdesimages.fr

At the forum you can choose from thousands of cinema, television, and amateur films. Many feature the city of Paris. There is footage on the history of Paris since 1895 including a remarkable news-reel of General de Gaulle avoiding sniper fire during the Liberation of Paris in 1944. There are countless movies such as Truffaut's

Baisers Volés. On Friday evenings, the forum also hosts "Cours de Cinéma", when classic films are analysed. There are also regular film festivals, "midnight movies" screenings and short film evenings. Special screenings of films for parents with babies take place fortnightly on Tuesdays.

Forum des Halles ❽

75001. **Map** 13 A2. Ⓜ *Les Halles.* RER *Châtelet-Les-Halles.*

The present Forum des Halles, known simply as Les Halles, was built in 1979, amid much controversy, on the site of the famous old fruit and vegetable market. Emile Zola named the area *Le Ventre de Paris* (The Belly of Paris). The present

Pygmalion by Julio Silva in the Forum des Halles

complex occupies 7 ha (750,000 sq ft), above and below ground. The underground levels 2 and 3 are occupied by a varied array of shops, from chic boutiques to megastores, a multi-screen cinema, swimming pool as well as the fantastic Forum des Images film archive centre. Beneath this is a metro station and major urban railway (RER) hub. Above ground there are well-tended gardens, pergolas and mini-pavilions.

Sadly, the area can be rather seedy, and is not recommended at night. However, Les Halles is going to be revamped under the direction of architect David Mangin, and a major and much-needed remodelling project will hopefully transform the area as well as bring back a food market. The project is expected to take around six years, with the gardens due to be finished by the end of 2013, but a start date for the rest has yet to be decided. Remember to explore the surrounding streets, including the trendy rue Montorgueil to the north.

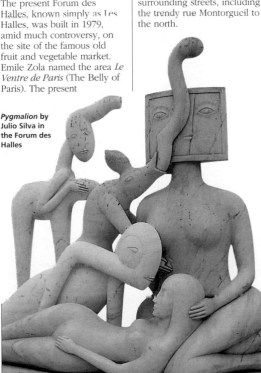

Pompidou Centre ●

The Pompidou is like a building turned inside out: escalators, lifts, air and water ducts and even the massive steel struts that are the building's skeleton have all been placed on the outside. This allowed the architects, Richard Rogers, Renzo Piano and Gianfranco Franchini, to create an uncluttered and flexible space within it for the Musée National d'Art Moderne and for the Pompidou's other activities. Among the schools represented in the museum are Fauvism, Cubism and Surrealism. Outside in the piazza, crowds gather to watch the street performers. The Pompidou also hosts temporary exhibitions that thrust it into the heart of the international art scene.

The escalator that rises step by step up the facade overlooking the piazza runs through a glass conduit. From the top there is a spectacular view over Paris that includes Montmartre, La Défense and the Eiffel Tower.

KEY

☐ Exhibition space

▨ Non-exhibition space

GALLERY GUIDE

The permanent collections are on Levels 5 & 4: works from 1905 to 1960 are on the former, with the latter reserved for contemporary art from 1960s onwards. Levels 1 & 6 are for major exhibitions, while Levels 1, 2 & 3 house an information library. The lower levels make up "The Forum", the focal public area, which include a performance centre for dance, theatre and music, a cinema and a children's workshop.

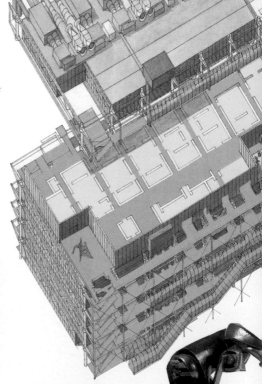

Portrait of the Journalist Sylvia von Harden *(1926)*
The surgical precision of Dix's style makes this a harsh caricature.

Le Cheval Majeur
This bronze horse (1914–16) by Duchamp-Villon is one of the finest examples of Cubist sculpture.

To Russia, the Asses and the Others (1911)
Throughout his life Chagall drew inspiration from the small Russian town of Vitebsk, where he was born.

VISITORS' CHECKLIST

Pl Georges Pompidou. **Map** 13
B2. *Tel* 01 44 78 12 33. Ⓜ
Rambuteau, Châtelet, Hôtel de
Ville. 🚌 21, 29, 38, 47, 58, 69,
70, 72, 74, 75, 76, 81, 85, 96. 🅡🅔🅡
Châtelet-Les-Halles. ◻ MNAM &
temp exhibs: 11am–9pm Wed–
Mon; Library: noon–10pm Wed–
Mon (from 11am Sat, Sun & pub
hols); Atelier Brancusi: 2–6pm
Wed–Mon. 🅟 ♿ 🖼 🎫 🚻 🍴
🔲 www.centrepompidou.fr

Basin and
Sculpture
Terrace

**The Breakfast
Table** (1915)
*Juan Gris'
fragmented
objects with
sharp-edges
represent the
synthetic Cubism
style of art.*

Le Duo (1937)
*Georges Braque, like
Picasso, developed the
Cubist technique of repre-
senting different views of a
subject in a single picture.*

Basin and
Sculpture
Terrace

COLOUR-CODING

The coloured pipes that are the most striking
feature at the back of the Pompidou, on the rue
du Renard, moved one critic to compare the
building to an oil refinery. Far from being merely
decorative, the colours serve to distinguish the
pipes' various functions: air-conditioning ducts
are blue, water pipes green and electricity lines
are painted yellow. The areas through which
people move vertically (such as escalators) are
red. The white funnels are ventilation shafts for
the underground areas, and structural beams are
clad in stainless steel. The architects' idea was to
help the public understand the way the
dynamics of a building function.

Exploring the Pompidou's Modern Art Collection

With over 60,000 works of art from over 5,000 artists, the Pompidou holds Europe's largest collection of modern and contemporary art. Classic disciplines – painting, sculpture, drawing and photography – are integrated with cinema, architecture, design, and audio-visual archives, to form a complete, chronological overview of modern and contemporary art. Works are often loaned out so some pieces may not be on show.

The Two Barges (1906) by André Derain

FROM 1905–60

The "historical" collections bring together the great artistic movements of the first half of the 20th century, from Fauvism to Abstract Expressionism to the changing currents of the 1950s. The rich collection of Cubist sculptures, of which the *Cheval Majeur* by Duchamp-Villon (1914–1916) is a fine example, is displayed, as well as examples of the great masters of the 20th century. Matisse, Picasso, Braque, Duchamp, Kandinsky, Léger, Miró, Giacometti and Dubuffet command large

With the Black Arc (1912) by Vassily Kandinsky

areas at the heart of the collection. Towards the end of his life, Matisse made several collages from cut-up large sheets of gouache-painted paper. Among others, the museum possesses *Jazz* (1943–7). With *Homme à la Guitare* (Man with a Guitar), Braque demonstrates his command of the Cubist technique which he pioneered along with Picasso. Considered as one of the first, if not the first, Abstract painter,

Kandinsky transformed works inspired by nature into constructions of colour and form. The museum has a large collection of the Russian painter's works, of which the Impressions *(Impressions V, Parc,* 1911) mark the end of his Expressionist period before his plunge into Abstract art with *Improvisations XIV* or *Avec l'Arc Noir* (With the Black Arc) both dating from 1912 compositions.

The collection also shows the groups and the movements on which the history of modern art is based, or by which it has been affected, including Dada, Abstract Art and Informal. A pioneer of Informal art, Jean Fautrier is represented in the collections with *Otages* (Hostages), a commemoration of the suffering of the resistance fighters.

At the heart of this chronological progression, various thematic displays are a revelation. One set shows non-figurative art from "Groupe Espace and the Magazine"; a collaboration between painters, sculptors, architects and engineers. Another room recreates the atmosphere of André Breton's workshop in which the works of his Surrealist friends are also shown. Silent pauses have also been allowed for: the room reserved for Miró has vast, moody canvasses such as *La Sieste* that give visitors reason to meditate on the explosion and revolutions of modern art.

BRANCUSI'S STUDIO

The Atelier Brancusi, on the rue Rambuteau side of the piazza, is a reconstruction of the workshop of the Romanian-born artist Constantin Brancusi (1876-1957), who lived and worked in Paris from 1904. He bequeathed his entire collection of works to the French state on condition that his workshop be rebuilt as it was on the day he died. The collection includes sculptures and plinths, photographs and a selection of his tools. Also featured are some of his more personal items such as documents, pieces of furniture and his book collection.

Miss Pogany (1919–20) by Constantin Brancusi

The Good-bye Door (1980) by Joan Mitchell

ART SINCE 1960

The contemporary art section occupies the fourth floor of the Pompidou Centre and consists of approximately 500 works. Jean-Michel Alberola's exceptional, boldly coloured mural, *Vous avez le bonjour de Marcel* (2002) welcomes visitors and sets the tone for the contemporary collection.

The collection starts with works by leading French artists of the second half of the twentieth century: artist and sculptor Louise Bourgeois whose work is strongly influenced by the surrealists, abstract expressionism and minimalism, Pierre Soulages, Jean-Pierre Raynaud, François Morellet and Bertrand Lavier.

Yayoï Kusama's restored masterpiece *My Flower Bed* (1965-6), made of painted mattress springs and stuffed gloves, is also on view.

The display is organized around a central aisle from which the rooms holding the museum's collections lead off. The central aisle is dotted with sculptures including works by Toni Grand, John Chamberlain and Xavier Veilhan. This hall is however dedicated principally to painting with works by Gerhard Richter, Brice Marden,

Mobile on Two Planes (1955) by Alexander Calder

Jean-Michel Basquiat, Philip Guston, Bernard Piffaretti and Katharina Grosse.

Room three is an homage to artist, philosopher and art critic Pontus Hulten, chosen by President Georges Pompidou to plan and run the national museum of modern art that was to be one of the four departments of the Pompidou Centre.

Homogenous Infiltration (1966) by Joseph Beuys

Pontus Hulten was director of the Musée National d'Art Moderne from 1973 to 1981, and was responsible for making it the open and cross-disciplinary museum that its founder had intended. Works by Jean Tinguely, Andy Warhol and Niki de Saint Phalle are to be found in this room.

Certain areas in the Pompidou Centre have been designated to bring together different disciplines around a theme such as minimalist painting or conceptual art rather than a school or movement. Other rooms, however, are artist specific with rooms dedicated to New Realist Martial Raysse, Robert Filliou, Christian Botanski, Sarkis, Joseph Beuys and Marcel Broodthaers. These rooms explore installation and photography as well as painting.

The fourth floor allows different aspects of the

museum's collections to be discovered, often reflecting a preference for the more ironic and conceptual forms. German artist Joseph Beuys's *Plight* (1985), for example, consists of a grand piano in a room where the walls are covered from floor to ceiling with about seven tonnes of thick felt arranged in rolls.

With regards to design and architecture, inflatable structures are explored in an unprecedented way with acidically coloured inflatable pieces on display.

A room is dedicated to French designer Philippe Starck's work with items from the sixties through to the present day on display.

Another room focuses on leading young international architects and designers of the moment, along with a space dedicated to Japanese artists, including Shigeru Ban, the architect behind the construction of the Pompidou Centre's sister gallery in Metz.

Lastly, there is a "global" room bringing together major contemporary pieces by African, Chinese, Japanese, and American artists. *Denkifuku* (1956), a dress made from light-bulbs, is a key work by Atsuko Tanaka of Japan.

The museum gallery allows temporary exhibitions to be mounted from works held in reserve. A graphic arts exhibition room and a video area complete the arrangement. A screening room gives access to the museum's entire collection of videos of a wide range of modern artists.

Le Rhinocéros (1999) by Xavier Veilhan

Musée de la Poupée ❾

Impasse Berthaud 75003.
Map 13 B2. **Tel** 01 42 72 73 11.
Ⓜ *Rambuteau.* ◯ *10am–6pm Tue–Sun.* 🎨 🎫 *for groups, by appt.*
www.museedelapoupeeparis.com

An impressive collection of hand-made dolls, from the mid-19th century to the present day, are on show in this charming museum. Thirty-six of the displays contain French dolls with porcelain heads ranging from 1850 to 1950. Another 24 display windows are devoted to themed exhibitions of dolls from around the world.

Father and son, Guido and Samy Odin, who own the museum, are at your service if your doll needs medical care. The museum shop stocks everything you need to preserve and maintain these unique works of art. The Odins also offer comprehensive classes on doll-making for both adults and children.

A 19th-century French doll with porcelain head

No. 51 Rue de Montmorency ❿

75003. **Map** 13 B1. Ⓜ *Réaumur-Sébastopol.* ◯ *to the public.*

This house is considered to be the oldest in Paris. No. 51 was built in 1407 by Nicolas Flamel, a book-keeper and alchemist. His house was always open to the poor, from whom he asked nothing more than that they should pray for those who were dead. Today, the house is a French restaurant.

The interior of St-Eustache in the 1830s

Tour Jean Sans Peur ⓫

20 Rue Etienne-Marcel 75002.
Map 13 A1. **Tel** 01 40 26 20 28.
Ⓜ *Etienne-Marcel.* ◯ *early Nov–end Mar: 1.30–6pm Wed, Sat, Sun; Apr–early Nov: 1.30pm–6pm Wed–Sun.*
🎨 🎫 **www.**tourjeansanspeur.com

After the Duc d'Orléans was assassinated on his orders in 1408, the Duc de Bourgogne feared reprisals. To protect himself, he had this 27-m (88-ft) tower built on to his home, the Hôtel de Bourgogne, and moved his bedroom up to the fourth floor (reached by a flight of 140 steps).

No. 51 Rue de Montmorency, the oldest house in Paris

St-Eustache ⓬

Pl du Jour 75001. **Map** 13 A1. **Tel** 01 42 36 31 05. Ⓜ *Les Halles.* 🚇 *Châtelet-Les-Halles.* ◯ *9.30am–7pm Mon–Fri; 10am–7pm Sat & Sun.* 🅿 🕂 *12.30pm, 6pm Mon–Fri; 6pm Sat; 9.30am, 11am, 6pm Sun.*
Organ recitals 5.30pm Sun.

With its Gothic plan and Renaissance decoration, St-Eustache is one of the most beautiful churches in Paris. Its interior plan is modelled on Notre-Dame, with five naves and side and radial chapels. The 105 years (1532–1637) it took to complete the church saw the flowering of the Renaissance style, which is evident in the arches, pillars and columns. The stained-glass windows in the chancel are created from cartoons by Philippe de Champaigne.

The church has associations with many famous figures: Molière was buried here; the Marquise de Pompadour, official mistress of Louis XV, was baptized here, as was Cardinal Richelieu.

Entrance to the Bourse du Commerce, the old corn exchange

Bourse du Commerce 🔞

2 Rue de Viarmes 75001.
Map 12 F2. **Tel** 01 55 65 55 65.
Ⓜ Les Halles. RER Châtelet-Les-Halles. ⏱ 9am–5pm Mon–Fri.
🏛 groups by appt. ♿

Compared dismissively by Victor Hugo to a jockey's cap without a peak, the old grain exchange building was France's first iron structure. It was constructed in the 18th century and remodelled in 1889. Today its huge, domed hall is filled with the hustle and bustle of the Chambre de Commerce et d'Industrie de Paris. It is still worth entering to marvel at the architecture, in particular the beautifully restored cupola and its decor. Also worth a look are the murals depicting French trade and industry through the ages, which were painted in 1889 and restored in 1998.

St-Germain l'Auxerrois 🔞

2 Pl du Louvre 75001. **Map** 12 F2.
Tel 01 42 60 13 96. Ⓜ Louvre,
Pont-Neuf. ⏱ 8am–7pm Mon–Sat
(to 8.30pm Wed). 9am–8pm Sun.
Musical Hour 4–5pm Sun.

This church has been built in a combination of Renaissance and Gothic styles. The first church on the site was constructed in the 12th century, of which only the foundations of the bell tower

remain. The splendid rose stained-glass windows date from the Renaissance period.

After the Valois Court decamped to the Louvre from the Ile de la Cité in the 14th century, this became the favoured church of kings.

The church's many historical associations include the horrific St Bartholomew's Day Massacre on 24 August 1572, the eve of the royal wedding of Henri of Navarre and Marguerite de Valois. Thousands of Huguenots who had been lured to Paris for the wedding were murdered as the church bell tolled.

Later, after the Revolution, the church was used as a barn and as a police station. Despite many restorations, it is a jewel of Gothic architecture.

La Samaritaine 🔞

119 Rue de la Monnaie 75001.
Map 12 F2. Ⓜ Pont-Neuf.
⬤ to the public.

This former department store was founded in 1900 by Ernest Cognacq. Built in 1926 with a framework of iron and wide expanses of glass, La Samaritaine is an outstanding example of the Art Deco style.

Cognacq was also a collector of 18th-century art, and his collection is now on display in the Musée Cognacq-Jay in the Marais quarter (see p94).

The building is no longer open to the public and may be redeveloped to create luxury apartments.

The Tour St-Jacques with its ornate decoration

Tour St-Jacques 🔞

Square de la Tour St-Jacques
75004. **Map** 13 A3. Ⓜ Châtelet.
⬤ to the public.

This imposing late Gothic tower, dating from 1523, is all that remains of an ancient church that was a rendezvous for pilgrims setting out on long journeys. The church was destroyed after the Revolution. Earlier, Blaise Pascal, the 17th-century mathematician, physicist, philosopher and writer, used the tower for experiments. There is a memorial statue to him on the ground floor. Queen Victoria passed by on her state visit in 1854, giving her name to the nearby Avenue Victoria. Visitors are not allowed inside the building, but the gardens make for a pretty resting spot.

The St Bartholomew's Day Massacre (c. 1572–84) by François Dubois

TUILERIES QUARTER

The Tuileries area is bounded by the vast expanse of the Concorde square at one end and the Grand Louvre at the other. This was a place for kings and palaces. The Sun King (Louis XIV) lives on in the Place des Victoires, which was designed solely to show off his statue. In Place Vendôme, royal glitter has been replaced by the precious stones of Cartier, Boucheron and

Ornate lamppost on Place de la Concorde

Chaumet, and the fine cut of Arab, German and Japanese bankers, not to mention the chic ladies visiting the luxurious Ritz. The area is crossed by two of Paris's most magnificent shopping streets – the long Rue de Rivoli, with its arcades, expensive boutiques, bookshops and luxury hotels, and the Rue St-Honoré, another extensive street, bringing together the richest and humblest in people and commerce.

SIGHTS AT A GLANCE

Historic Buildings
Palais Royal ❸
Banque de France ⓲

Museums and Galleries
Musée du Louvre pp122–9 ❶
Musée des Arts Décoratifs ❾
Galerie Nationale du
Jeu de Paume ⓭
Musée de
l'Orangerie ⓮
Village Royal ⓰

Monuments and Fountains
Fontaine Molière ❻
Arc de Triomphe du Carrousel ❿

Squares, Parks and Gardens
Jardin du Palais Royal ❺
Place des Pyramides ❽
Jardin des Tuileries ⓬
Place de la Concorde ⓯
Place Vendôme ⓱
Place des Victoires ⓳

Theatres
Comédie Française ❹

Shops
Louvre des Antiquaires ❷
Rue de Rivoli ⓫

Churches
St-Roch ❼

GETTING THERE
This area is well served by the metro system, with stations at Tuileries, Pyramides, Palais Royal and Louvre. Many buses pass through the area. Routes 24, 27, 72 and 95 travel along the quayside passing the Jardin des Tuileries and the Musée du Louvre.

KEY

- Street-by-Street map
- M Metro station
- Batobus boarding point
- Tourist information

SEE ALSO

- *Street Finder*, map 6, 11–12
- *Where to Stay* pp285–6
- *Restaurants* pp303–04

◁ View of the Place de la Concorde and the Obelisk

Street by Street: Tuileries Quarter

Elegant squares, formal gardens, street arcades and courtyards give this part of Paris its special character. Monuments to monarchy and the arts coexist with contemporary luxury: sumptuous hotels, world-famous restaurants, fashion emporiums and jewellers of international renown. Sandblasting and washing have given a refreshing glow to the facades of the Louvre and the Palais Royal square, where Cardinal Richelieu's creation, the royal palace, is now occupied by government offices. From here the Ministry of Culture surveys the cleaning and restoration of the city's great buildings. The other former royal palace, the Louvre, is now one of the great museums of the world.

St-Roch
The papal statue stands in this remarkably long 17th-century church, unusually set on a north-south axis. St-Roch is a treasure house of religious art **7**

Metro Pyramides

The Paris Convention and Visitors' Bureau

M

The Normandy is an elegant hotel in the Belle Epoque style, a form of graceful living that prevailed in Paris at the turn of the 20th century.

★ Jardin des Tuileries
Pony rides are a popular attraction in these formal gardens, which were designed by the royal gardener André Le Nôtre in the 17th century **14**

Place des Pyramides
Frémiet's gilded statue of Joan of Arc is the focus of pilgrimage for royalists **8**

To the Quai du Louvre

Musée des Arts Décoratifs
A highlight of the museum's displays of art and design is the Art Nouveau collection **11**

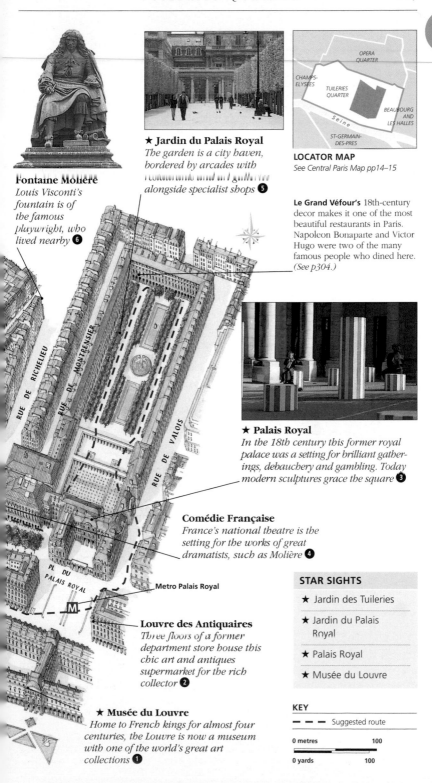

★ Jardin du Palais Royal
The garden is a city haven, bordered by arcades with columns and an I garden view alongside specialist shops ⑤

Fontaine Molière
Louis Visconti's fountain is of the famous playwright, who lived nearby ⑥

LOCATOR MAP
See Central Paris Map pp14–15

Le Grand Véfour's 18th-century decor makes it one of the most beautiful restaurants in Paris. Napoleon Bonaparte and Victor Hugo were two of the many famous people who dined here. (See p304.)

★ Palais Royal
In the 18th century this former royal palace was a setting for brilliant gatherings, debauchery and gambling. Today modern sculptures grace the square ③

Comédie Française
France's national theatre is the setting for the works of great dramatists, such as Molière ④

Metro Palais Royal

Louvre des Antiquaires
Three floors of a former department store house this chic art and antiques supermarket for the rich collector ②

★ Musée du Louvre
Home to French kings for almost four centuries, the Louvre is now a museum with one of the world's great art collections ①

STAR SIGHTS

★ Jardin des Tuileries

★ Jardin du Palais Royal

★ Palais Royal

★ Musée du Louvre

KEY

– – – Suggested route

0 metres	100
0 yards	100

The five-arched Pont Royal linking the Louvre with the Left Bank

Musée du Louvre ❶

See pp122–9.

Louvre des Antiquaires ❷

2 Pl du Palais Royal 75001. **Map** 12 E2. *Tel* 01 42 97 27 27. ☐ 11am–7pm *Tue–Sun (Jul & Aug: Tue–Sat).* ● 1 Jan, 25 Dec. 🍴 🖵 *See* **Shopping** *pp336–7.* **www.**louvre-antiquaires.com

One of the shops in the Louvre des Antiquaires market

A large department store – the Grands Magasins du Louvre – was converted at the end of the 1970s into this three-floor collection of art galleries and antique shops. Few bargains are found here, but the 250 shops of this chic market provide clues about what *nouveaux riches* collectors are seeking.

Palais Royal ❸

Pl du Palais Royal 75001. **Map** 12 E1. Ⓜ *Palais Royal.* **Buildings not open** *to public.*

This former royal palace has had a turbulent history. Starting out in the early 17th century as Richelieu's Palais Cardinale, it passed to the Crown on his death and became the childhood home of Louis XIV. Under the control of the 18th-century royal dukes of Orléans it was the scene of brilliant gatherings, interspersed with periods of debauchery and gambling. The cardinal's theatre, where Molière had performed, burned down in 1763, but was replaced by the Comédie Française. After the Revolution, the palace became a gambling house. It was reclaimed in 1815 by the future King Louis-Philippe, one of whose librarians was Alexandre Dumas. The building narrowly escaped the flames of the 1871 uprising.

After being restored again, between 1872 and 1876, the palace reverted to the state, and it now houses both the Council of State, the supreme legal body for administrative matters, and its more recent "partner", the Constitutional Council. Another wing of the palace is occupied by the Ministry of Culture.

Comédie Française ❹

1 Place Colette 75001. **Map** 12 E1. 🎟 0825 101 680. Ⓜ *Palais Royal.* ☐ *for performances.* 🎭 11am Sun. 📷 🚫 *See* **Entertainment** *pp342–4.*

A stone plaque to Pierre Corneille

Overlooking two charming, if traffic-choked, squares named after the writers Colette and André Malraux, sits France's national theatre. The company has its roots partly in Molière's 17th-century players. In the foyer is the armchair in which Molière collapsed, dying, on stage in 1673 (ironically while he was performing *Le Malade Imaginaire – The Hypochondriac*). Since the company's founding in 1680 by Louis XIV, the theatre has enjoyed state patronage as a centre of national culture, and it has been based in the present building since 1799. The repertoire includes works of Corneille, Racine, Molière and Shakespeare, as well as those of modern playwrights.

Daniel Buren's stone columns (1980s) in the Palais Royal courtyard

Statue in the Jardin du Palais Royal

Jardin du Palais Royal ❺

Pl du Palais Royal 75001. **Map** 12 F1.
Ⓜ *Palais Royal.*

The present garden is about a
third smaller than the original
one, laid out by the royal
gardener for Cardinal
Richelieu in the 1630s. This is
due to the construction,
between 1781 and 1784, of 60
uniform houses bordering
three sides of the square.
Today restaurants, art galleries
and specialist shops line the
square, which maintains a
strong literary history – Jean
Cocteau, Colette and Jean
Marais are among its famous
former residents.
  The courtyard contains the
controversial black-and-white
striped stone columns that
form conceptual artist Daniel
Buren's *Les Deux Plateaux.*
The columns were installed in
the pedestrianized Palais
Royal courtyard in 1986, in
the face of strong opposition.
These columns are now
beloved of children and
skateboarders alike.

Fontaine Molière ❻

Rue de Richelieu 75001. **Map** 12 F1.
Ⓜ *Palais Royal.*

France's most famous play-
wright lived near here, in a
house on the site of No. 40
Rue de Richelieu. The 19th-
century fountain is by Louis
Visconti, who also designed
Napoleon's tomb at Les
Invalides *(see pp188–9).*

Vien's *St Denis Preaching to the Gauls* (1767) in St-Roch

St-Roch ❼

296 Rue St-Honoré 75001. **Map** 12
E1. **Tel** *01 42 44 13 20.* Ⓜ *Tuileries.*
◯ *8am–7pm daily.* ● *non-religious
public hols.* ✝ *Daily, times vary.*
Concerts. ◙

This huge church was designed
by Lemercier, architect of the
Louvre, and its foundation
stone was laid by Louis XIV
in 1653. Jules Hardouin-

Seated statue of Molière

Mansart added the large Lady
Chapel with its richly
decorated dome and ceiling
in the 18th century and two
further chapels extended the
church to 126 m (413 ft), just
short of Notre-Dame. It is a
treasure house of religious
art, much of it from now-
vanished churches and
monasteries. It also contains
the tombs of the playwright
Pierre Corneille, the royal
gardener André Le Nôtre and
the philosopher Denis
Diderot. The facades reveal
marks of Napoleon's attack,
in 1795, on royalist troops
who were defending the
church steps.

Place des Pyramides ❽

75001. **Map** 12 E1. Ⓜ *Tuileries,
Pyramides.*

Joan of Arc, wounded nearby
fighting the English in 1429,
is commemorated by a 19th-
century equestrian statue by
the sculptor Emmanuel Frémiet.
The statue is a rallying point
for royalists.

Musée du Louvre ❶

The Musée du Louvre, containing one of the most important art collections in the world, has a history extending back to medieval times. First constructed as a fortress in 1190 by King Philippe-Auguste to protect Paris against Viking raids, it lost its imposing keep in the reign of François I, who replaced it with a Renaissance-style building. Thereafter, four centuries of French kings and emperors improved and enlarged it. A glass pyramid designed by I M Pei was added to the main courtyard in 1989. All the galleries can be reached from here.

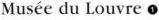

The east facade, facing St-Germain l'Auxerrois

The Jardin du Carrousel, now part of the Jardin des Tuileries, was once the grand approach to the Tuileries Palace which was burned down in 1871 by the Communards.

Pavillon des Sessions

BUILDING THE LOUVRE

Over many centuries the Louvre was enlarged by a succession of French rulers, shown below with their dates.

MAJOR ALTERATIONS

- ☐ Reign of François I (1515–47)
- ☐ Catherine de' Médici (about 1560)
- ■ Reign of Henri IV (1589–1610)
- ■ Reign of Louis XIII (1610–43)
- ■ Reign of Louis XIV (1643–1715)
- ■ Reign of Napoleon I (1804–15)
- ■ Reign of Napoleon III (1852–70)
- ■ I M Pei (1989) (architect)

The Carrousel du Louvre underground visitors' complex, with galleries, cloakrooms, shops, lavatories, parking and an information desk, lies beneath the Arc de Triomphe du Carrousel.

Denon Wing

The inverted glass pyramid brings light to the subterranean complex, echoing the museum's main entrance in the Cour Napoléon.

★ Arc de Triomphe du Carrousel
This triumphal arch was built to celebrate Napoleon's victories in 1805.

STAR FEATURES

- ★ Arc de Triomphe du Carrousel
- ★ Medieval Moats
- ★ Perrault Colonnade
- ★ Pyramid Entrance

Pavillon Richelieu
This imposing 19th-century pavilion is part of the Richelieu Wing, once home to the Ministry of Finance but now converted into magnificent galleries.

VISITORS' CHECKLIST

Map 12 F2. Automatic ticket booths are located in the Carrousel du Louvre (99 Rue de Rivoli). 01 40 20 50 50. Palais Royal, Musée du Louvre. 21, 24, 27, 39, 48, 68, 69, 72, 81, 95. RER Châtelet-Les-Halles. Louvre. Carrousel du Louvre (entrance via Ave du General Lemonnier), IV du Louvre, Rue St-Honoré. 9am–6pm Wed–Mon (to 10pm Wed, Fri). 1 Jan, 1 May, 25 Dec. (free 1st Sun of each month), tickets can be bought online. partial (01 40 20 59 90). phone 01 40 20 52 09. **Lectures, films, concerts** (01 40 20 55 55). www.louvre.fr

Cour Marly is the glass-roofed courtyard that now houses the Marly Horses *(see p125)*.

Richelieu Wing

★ **Pyramid Entrance**
The main entrance, designed by the architect I M Pei, was opened in 1989.

Cour Puget

Cour Khorsabad

Sully Wing

Cour Carrée

★**Perrault's Colonnade**
The east facade with its majestic rows of columns was built by Claude Perrault, who worked on the Louvre with Louis Le Vau in the mid-17th century.

Cour Napoléon

The Salle des Caryatides
takes its name from the statues of women created by Jean Goujon in 1550 to support the upper gallery.

The Louvre of Charles V
In about 1360, Charles V transformed Philippe-Auguste's robust old fortress into a royal residence.

★ **Medieval Moats**
The base of the twin towers and the drawbridge support of Philippe-Auguste's fortress can be seen in the excavated area.

The Louvre's Collection

The Louvre's treasures can be traced back to the collection of François I (1515–47), who purchased many Italian paintings including the *Mona Lisa (La Gioconda)*. In Louis XIV's reign (1643–1715) there were a mere 200 works, but donations and purchases augmented the collection. The Louvre was first opened to the public in 1793 after the Revolution, and has been continually enriched ever since.

The Lacemaker
In this exquisite picture from about 1665, Jan Vermeer gives us a glimpse into everyday domestic life in Holland. The painting came to the Louvre in 1870.

The Raft of the Medusa *(1819)*
Théodore Géricault derived his inspiration for this gigantic and moving work from the shipwreck of a French frigate in 1816. The painting shows the moment when the few survivors sight a sail on the horizon.

Cour Marly

Richelieu Wing

Main entrance

Underground visitors' complex

GALLERY GUIDE
The main entrance is beneath the glass pyramid. The works are displayed on four floors: the painting and sculpture collections are arranged by country of origin. There are eight departments: Near Eastern antiquities; Egyptian antiquities; Greek, Etruscan and Roman antiquities; Islamic art; sculptures; decorative arts; paintings; and prints and drawings.

Pavillon des Sessions

Denon Wing

KEY TO FLOORPLAN

☐	Painting
☐	Objets d'art
☐	Sculpture
☐	Antiquities
☐	Non-exhibition space

★ Venus de Milo
Found in 1820 on the island of Milos in Greece, this ideal of feminine beauty was made in the Hellenistic Age at the end of the 2nd century BC.

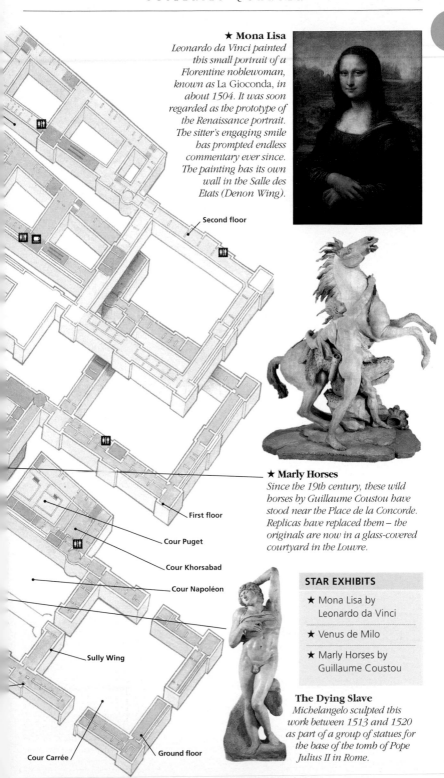

★ **Mona Lisa**
Leonardo da Vinci painted this small portrait of a Florentine noblewoman, known as La Gioconda, *in about 1504. It was soon regarded as the prototype of the Renaissance portrait. The sitter's engaging smile has prompted endless commentary ever since. The painting has its own wall in the Salle des Etats (Denon Wing).*

Second floor

★ **Marly Horses**
Since the 19th century, these wild horses by Guillaume Coustou have stood near the Place de la Concorde. Replicas have replaced them – the originals are now in a glass-covered courtyard in the Louvre.

First floor

Cour Puget

Cour Khorsabad

Cour Napoléon

Sully Wing

Cour Carrée

Ground floor

STAR EXHIBITS

★ Mona Lisa by
Leonardo da Vinci

★ Venus de Milo

★ Marly Horses by
Guillaume Coustou

The Dying Slave
Michelangelo sculpted this work between 1513 and 1520 as part of a group of statues for the base of the tomb of Pope Julius II in Rome.

Exploring the Louvre's Collections

It is important not to underestimate the size of these vast collections and useful to set a few viewing priorities before starting. The collection of European paintings (1400–1850) is comprehensive and 40 per cent of the works are by French artists, while the selection of sculptures is less complete. The museum's antiquities – Oriental, Egyptian, Greek, Etruscan and Roman – are of world renown and offer the visitor an unrivalled range of objects. The *objets d'art* on display are very varied and include furniture and jewellery.

The Fortune Teller (about 1594) by Caravaggio

EUROPEAN PAINTING: 1200 TO 1850

Painting from northern Europe is well covered. One of the earliest Flemish works is Jan van Eyck's *Madonna of Chancellor Rolin* (about 1435) which shows the Chancellor of Burgundy kneeling in prayer before the Virgin and Child. Hieronymus Bosch's *Ship of Fools* (1500) is a fine,

Portrait of Erasmus (1523)
by Hans Holbein

satirical account of the futility of human existence. In the Dutch collection, Van Dyck's portrait *King Charles out Hunting* (1635) shows Charles I of England in all his refined elegance. Jacob Jordaens, best known for scenes of gluttony and lust, reveals unusual sensitivity in his *Four Evangelists*. The saucy smile of the *Gipsy Girl* (1628) displays Frans Hals' effortless virtuosity, in sharp contrast to Vermeer's highly-finished *Lacemaker*. Rembrandt's *Self-portraits, Disciples at Emmaus* (1648) and *Bathsheba* (1654) are fine examples of his genius.

There is relatively little German painting, but the three major German painters of the 15th and 16th centuries are represented by important works. There is a *Self-portrait* by Albrecht Dürer as a young artist of 22 (1493), a *Venus* by Lucas Cranach (1529) and a portrait of the great humanist scholar Erasmus by Hans Holbein. Works by English artists include Thomas Gainsborough's *Conversation*

in a Park (around 1746), Sir Joshua Reynolds' *Master Hare* (1788) and France's only painting by J M W Turner, *Landscape with a River and a Distant Bay* (around 1840).

Many of the master works in the Spanish collection depict the tragic side of life: El Greco's *Christ on the Cross Adored by Donors* (1576) and Francisco de Zurbarán's *Lying-in-State of St Bonaventura* (about 1629) with its dark-faced corpse are two of the Louvre's prize pieces. The subject of José de Ribera's *Club-Footed Boy* (1642) is a poor mute, who carries a scrap of paper requesting alms. Portraits by Goya from the late 18th and early 19th century are in a lighter vein.

The museum's large collection of Italian paintings covers the period 1200 to 1800. The father figures of the early Renaissance, Cimabue and Giotto, are here, as is Fra Angelico, with his *Coronation of the Virgin* (around 1430–1432), and Raphael, with his stately *Portrait of Baldassare Castiglione* (around 1514). There is also a fine portrait in profile of Sigismondo Malatesta by Piero della Francesca (around 1450) and an action-packed battle scene by Paolo Uccello. Several paintings by Leonardo da Vinci, for instance the *Virgin with the Infant Jesus and St Anne*, are as enchanting as his *Mona Lisa*.

The collection of French painting ranges from the 14th century to 1848. Paintings after this date are housed in the Musée d'Orsay *(see*

Gilles or Pierrot (about 1717)
by Jean-Antoine Watteau

LEONARDO DA VINCI IN FRANCE

Leonardo, artist, engineer and scientist, was born in 1452 and became a leading figure in the Italian Renaissance. François I met Leonardo in 1515 and invited him to live and work in France. The painter brought the *Mona Lisa* with him. Already in poor health, he died three years later in the arms of the king.

Self-portrait (early 16th century)

pp144–7). Outstanding early works are Jean Fouquet's *Portrait of Charles VIII* (around 1450) and *Gabrielle d'Estrée*, mistress of Henri IV, in her bathtub with her sister (1594). From the 16th and 17th centuries there are several splendid works by Georges de la Tour.

That great 18th-century painter of melancholy, Jean Watteau, is represented, as is J H Fragonard, master of the Rococo. His delightfully frivolous subjects are evident in *The Bathers* from 1770. In stark contrast is the Classicism of Nicolas Poussin and the history painting of J L David. Most of J D Ingres' work is in the Musée d'Orsay, but the Louvre kept the erotic *Turkish Bath* of 1862.

EUROPEAN SCULPTURE: 1100 TO 1850

Early Flemish and German sculpture in the collection has many masterpieces such as Tilman Riemenschneider's *Virgin of the Annunciation* from the end of the 15th century and an unusual life-size, nude figure of the penitent Mary Magdalen by Gregor Erhart (early 16th century). An ornate gilded-wood altarpiece of the same period exemplifies Flemish church art. Another important work of Flemish sculpture is Adrian de Vries's long-limbed *Mercury and Psyche* from 1593, which was originally made for the court of Rudolph II in Prague.

The French section opens with early Romanesque works, such as the figure of Christ by a 12th-century Burgundian sculptor and a head of St Peter. With its eight black-hooded mourners, the tomb of Philippe Pot (a high-ranking official in Burgundy) is one of the more unusual pieces. Diane de Poitiers, mistress of Henri II, had a large figure of her namesake Diana, goddess of the hunt, installed in the courtyard of her castle west of Paris. It is now in the Louvre. The works of Pierre Puget (1620–94), the great sculptor from Marseilles, have been assembled inside a glass-covered courtyard, Cour Puget. They include a figure of Milo of Crotona, the Greek athlete who got his hands caught in the cleft of a tree stump and was eaten by a lion. The wild horses of Marly now stand in the glass-roofed Cour Marly, surrounded by other masterpieces of French sculpture, including Houdon's early 19th-century busts of Diderot and Voltaire, and two equestrian pieces by Coysevox.

The Italian sculpture collection includes pre-Renaissance work by Duccio and Donatello, and later masterpieces such as Michelangelo's *Slaves* and Cellini's Fontainebleau *Nymph*.

Tomb of Philippe Pot (late 15th century) by Antoine le Moiturier

NEAR EASTERN, EGYPTIAN, GREEK, ETRUSCAN AND ROMAN ANTIQUITIES

The range of antiquities in the Louvre is impressive. There are objects from the Neolithic period (about 6000 BC) to the fall of the Roman Empire. Important works of Mesopotamian art include the seated figure of Ebih-il, from 2400 BC, and several portraits of Gudea, Prince of Lagash, from about 2255 BC. A black basalt block bearing the code of the Babylonian King Hammurabi, from about 1700 BC, is one of the world's oldest legal documents.

The warlike Assyrians are represented by delicate carvings and a spectacular reconstruction of part of Sargon II's (722–705 BC) palace with its huge, winged bulls. A fine example of Persian art is the enamelled brickwork depicting the king of Persia's personal guard of archers (5th century BC). It decorated his palace at Susa.

Most Egyptian art was made for the dead, who were provided with the things that they needed for the after-life. It often included vivid images of daily life in ancient Egypt. One example is the tiny funeral chapel built for a high official in about 2500 BC. It is covered with exquisite carvings: men in sailing ships, catching fish, tending cattle and fowl.

It is also possible to gain insights into family life in ancient Egypt through a number of life-like funeral portraits, like the squatting scribe, and several sculptures of married couples. The

earliest sculpture dates from 2500 BC, the latest from 1400 BC.

From the New Kingdom (1555–1080 BC) a special crypt dedicated to the god Osiris contains some colossal sarcophagi, and a large number of mummified animals.

Some smaller objects of considerable charm include a 29-cm (11-inch) headless body of a woman, sensually outlined by the transparent veil of her dress and thought to be Queen Nefertiti (about 1365–1349 BC).

The department of Greek, Roman and Etruscan antiquities contains a vast array of fragments, among them some exceptional pieces. There is a large, geometric head from the Cyclades (2700 BC) and an elegant, swan-necked bowl, quite modern in its unadorned simplicity. It is hammered out of a single gold sheet and dates from about 2500 BC.

The Archaic Greek period, from the 7th to the 5th century BC, is represented by the *Auxerre Goddess*, one of the earliest-known pieces of Greek sculpture, and the *Hera of Samos* from the Ionian Islands. From the height of the Classical Greek period (about the 5th century BC)

Winged Victory of Samothrace (Greece, late 3rd–early 2nd century BC)

Winged Bull with Human Head from 8th century BC, found in Khorsabad, Assyria

there are several fine male torsos and heads such as the *Laborde Head*. This head has been identified as part of the sculpture that once decorated the west pediment of the Parthenon in Athens.

The two most famous Greek statues in the Louvre, the *Winged Victory of Samothrace* and the *Venus de Milo (see p 124)*, belong to the Hellenistic period (late 3rd to 2nd century BC) when more natural-looking human forms were beginning to be produced.

The undisputed star of the Etruscan collection is the terracotta *Sarcophagus of the Cenestian Couple*, who appear

Etruscan sarcophagus (6th century BC)

as though they are attending an eternal banquet.

The sculptures in the Roman section demonstrate the great debt owed to the art of ancient Greece. There are many fine pieces: a bust of Agrippa, a basalt head of Livia, the wife of Augustus, and a splendid, powerful bronze head of Emperor Hadrian from the 2nd century AD. This has the look of a true portrait, unlike so many Imperial heads which are uninspired and impersonal.

Squatting Scribe (Egyptian, about 2500 BC)

DECORATIVE ARTS

The term *objets d'art* (art objects) covers a vast range of "decorative art" objects: from jewellery, silver and glassware, to French and Italian bronzes, porcelain, snuffboxes and armour. The Louvre has well over 8,000 items, from many ages and regions.

Many of these precious objects were in the Abbey of St-Denis, where the kings of France were crowned. Long before the Revolution, a regular flow of visitors had made it something of a museum. After the Revolution all the objects were removed and presented to the nation. Much was lost or stolen during the move but what remains is still outstanding.

The treasures include a serpentine stone plate from the 1st century AD with a 9th-century border of gold and precious stones. (The plate itself is inlaid with eight golden dolphins.) There is also a porphyry vase which Suger, Abbot of St-Denis, had mounted in gold in the shape of an eagle, and the golden sceptre made for King Charles V in about 1380.

The French crown jewels include the coronation crowns of Louis XV and Napoleon, sceptres, swords and other accessories of the coronation ceremonies. On view is also the Regent, one of the purest diamonds in the world. It was bought in 1717 and worn by Louis XV at his coronation in 1722.

One whole room is taken up with a series of tapestries called the *Hunts of Maximilian*, which were originally executed for Emperor Charles V in 1530 after drawings by Bernard Van Orley.

The large collection of French furniture ranges from the 16th to the 19th centuries and is assembled by period,

The Eagle of Suger (mid-12th century)

or in rooms devoted to donations by distinguished collectors such as Isaac de Camondo. On display are important pieces by exceptionally prominent furniture-makers such as André-Charles Boulle, cabinet-maker to Louis XIV, who worked at the Louvre in the late 17th to mid-18th centuries. He is noted for his technique of inlaying copper and tortoiseshell. From a later date, the curious inlaid steel and bronze writing desk, created by Adam Weisweiler for Queen Marie-Antoinette in 1784, is one of the more unusual pieces in the museum's collection.

In 2012 the Islamic Art Department will open in the Cour Visconti I with around 2,000 objects on display covering 3,000 years of history from three continents.

THE GLASS PYRAMID

Plans for the modernization and expansion of the Louvre were first conceived in 1981. They included the transfer of the Ministry of Finance from the Richelieu wing of the Louvre to offices elsewhere, and a new main entrance to the museum. A Chinese-American architect, I M Pei, was chosen to design the changes. He designed the pyramid as both the focal point and entrance to the Louvre. Made out of glass, it enables the visitor to see the historic buildings that surround it while allowing light down into the underground visitors' reception area.

Musée des Arts Décoratifs **⑨**

Palais du Louvre, 107 Rue de Rivoli 75001. **Map** 12 E2. **Tel** 01 44 55 57 50. Ⓜ *Palais Royal, Tuileries.* ◯ *11am–6pm Tue–Fri (until 9pm Thu); 10am–6pm Sat & Sun (last adm 30 mins before closing).* **Library** ◯ *pub hols.* 🖼 & **www.lesartsdecoratifs.fr**

With five floors and over 100 rooms, this museum offers an eclectic display of decorative and ornamental art and design from the Middle Ages to the present. Among the highlights are the Art Nouveau and Art Deco rooms, jewellery and Gallé glass. The doll collection is remarkable.

The Galerie des Bijoux is particularly interesting, with a huge collection of more than 1,300 pieces, from medieval brooches to Cartier designs.

The chic restaurant offers breathtaking views over the Tuileries Gardens.

Also open for temporary exhibitions are the adjoining Musée de la Mode and the Musée de la Publicité. Musée de la Mode frequently shows parts of its vast *haute couture* collections. Past exhibitions have included a tribute to Christian Lacroix with a retrospective of his designs.

With a catalogue of over 40,000 historic posters dating from the 18th century to 1949, the Musée de la Publicité brings together thousands of objects linked to advertising as well as films. The entry fee includes access to all three museums. Dual tickets can also be purchased that allow access to the Musée Nissim de Camondo too *(see p232)*.

Lemot's Restoration group of statues with the gilded figure of Victory

Arc de Triomphe du Carrousel **⑩**

Pl du Carrousel 75001. **Map** 12 E2. Ⓜ *Palais Royal.*

Built by Napoleon in 1806–8 as an entrance to the former Palais des Tuileries, this vast arch's marble columns are topped by Grande Armée soldiers. They replaced the Horses of St Mark's which were returned to Venice in 1815.

Arcades along the Rue de Rivoli

Rue de Rivoli **⑪**

75001. **Map** 11 C1 & 13 A2. Ⓜ *Louvre, Palais Royal, Tuileries, Concorde.*

The long arcades with their shops, topped by Neo-Classical apartments, date back to the early 18th century,

though they were only finished in the 1850s. Commissioned by Napoleon after his victory at Rivoli, in 1797, the street completed the link between the Louvre and the Champs-Elysées, and became an important artery as well as an elegant centre for commerce. The Tuileries walls were replaced by railings and the whole area opened up.

Today along the Rue de Rivoli there are makers of expensive men's shirts and bookshops towards the Place de la Concorde, and popular department stores near the Châtelet and Hôtel de Ville. Angélina's, at No. 226, is said to serve the best hot chocolate in Paris *(see p318).*

Jardin des Tuileries **⑫**

75001. **Map** 12 D1. **Tel** 01 40 20 90 43. Ⓜ *Tuileries, Concorde.* ◯ *7.30am–7pm (or sunset).*

These formal gardens were once the gardens of the old Palais des Tuileries. They are an integral part of the landscaped area running parallel to the Seine from the Louvre to the Champs-Elysées and the Arc de Triomphe.

The gardens were laid out in the 17th century by André Le Nôtre, royal gardener to Louis XIV. Restoration created an additional garden as well as filling the entire gardens with striking modern and contemporary sculpture.

A 17th-century engraving of the Jardin des Tuileries by G Perelle

Galerie Nationale du Jeu de Paume ⑬

Jardin des Tuileries, Pl de la Concorde 75008. **Map** 11 C1.
Tel 01 47 03 12 50. Ⓜ Concorde.
⬤ noon–7pm Tue–Sun (to 9pm Tue, from 10am Sat, Sun). ⬤ 1 Jan, 1 May, 25 Dec. 🖼 📸 👥 ✏ ▢ 📷
📷 www.jeudepaume.org

The Jeu de Paume – or *réal* tennis court – was built by Napoleon III in 1851. When *réal* (royal) tennis was replaced in popularity by lawn tennis, the court was used to exhibit art. Eventually an Impressionist museum was founded here. In 1986, the collection moved to the Musée d'Orsay *(see pp144–7)*. The Jeu de Paume now houses the Centre National de la Photographie, and shows exhibitions of contemporary art. Its sister site is the Hôtel de Sully *(see p95)*.

Monet's water lilies, on display in the Musée de l'Orangerie

Entrance to the Jeu de Paume

Musée de l'Orangerie ⑭

Jardin des Tuileries, Pl de la Concorde 75008. **Map** 11 C1. **Tel** 01 44 77 80 07. Ⓜ Concorde. ⬤ 9am–6pm Wed–Mon. ⬤ 1 May, 25 Dec. 🖼 📷 👥 ✏ by appt. 📷 www. musee-orangerie.fr

Claude Monet's crowning work, the water lily series, or *Nymphéas*, can be found here. The series was painted in his garden at Giverny, near Paris, and presented to the public in 1927. This superb work is complemented well by the outstanding Walter-Guillaume collection of artists of the Ecole de Paris, from the late Impressionist era to the interwar period. This is a remarkable concentration of

masterpieces, including a room of dramatic works by Soutine and some 14 works by Cézanne – still lifes, portraits *(Madame Cézanne)* and landscapes, such as *Dans le Parc du Château Noir*.

Renoir is represented by 27 canvases, including *Les Fillettes au Piano (Young Girls at the Piano)*. There are early Picassos, works by Henri Rousseau – notably *La Carriole du Père Junier (Old Junier's Cart)* – Matisse and a portrait of Paul Guillaume by Modigliani. All are bathed in the natural light which flows through the window. Temporary exhibitions are shown on the lower ground floor.

Place de la Concorde ⑮

75008. **Map** 11 C1. Ⓜ Concorde.

This is one of Europe's most magnificent and historic squares, covering more than 8 ha (20 acres) in the middle of Paris. Starting out as Place Louis XV, for displaying a statue of the king, it was built in the mid-18th century by architect Jacques-Ange Gabriel, who chose to make it an open octagon with only the north side containing

The 3,200-year-old obelisk from Luxor

mansions. In the square's next incarnation, as the Place de la Révolution, the statue was replaced by the guillotine. The death toll in the square in two and a half years was 1,119, including Louis XVI, Marie-Antoinette (who died in view of the small, secret apartment she kept at No. 2 Rue Royale) and the revolutionary leaders Danton and Robespierre.

Renamed Concorde (originally by chastened Revolutionaries) in a spirit of reconciliation, the grandeur of the square was enhanced in the 19th century by the 3,200-year-old Luxor obelisk, two fountains and eight statues personifying French cities. It has become the culminating point of triumphal parades down the Champs-Elysées each 14 July, most notably on the memorable Bastille Day of 1989 when the Revolution's bicentenary was celebrated by a million people, and many world leaders.

Colonnaded entrance to the Village Royale

Village Royal ⑯

75008. **Map** 5 C5. M *Madeleine.* *Galerie Royale* ◯ *10am–7pm Tue–Sat.* ◉ *public hols.*

This delightful enclave of 18th-century town houses sits discreetly between the Rue Royale and the Rue Boissy d'Anglas. The Galerie Royale is the former home of the Duchess d'Abrantès. It was converted in 1994 by architect Laurent Bourgois who has combined both classical and modern elements in superb style. The village was formerly the home of glassworkers and silversmiths, and for a while examples of

antique glass and silverware were on display. Nowadays, chic shoppers flock in droves to the designer boutiques that are here, such as Chanel, Dior and Eric Bompard Cashmere, or they stop by for a coffee break in the up-market café, Le Village.

Place Vendôme ⑰

75001. **Map** 6 D5 M *Tuileries.*

Perhaps the best example of 18th-century elegance in the city, the architect Jules Hardouin-Mansart's royal square was begun in 1698. The original plan was to house academies and embassies behind the arcaded facades. However, bankers moved in and created opulent homes. Miraculously the square has remained virtually intact, and is home to jewellers and bankers. Among the famous, Frédéric Chopin died here in 1848 at No. 12 and César Ritz established his famous hotel at the turn of the 20th century at No. 15.

Banque de France ⑱

39 Rue Croix des Petits Champs 75001. **Map** 12 F1. M *Palais Royal.* ◯ *for details phone 01 44 54 19 30.*

Founded by Napoleon in 1800, France's central bank is housed in a building intended for quite different purposes. The 17th-century architect François Mansart designed this mansion for Louis XIII's wealthy Secretary of State,

Napoleon's statue in Place Vendôme

FORMAL GARDENS IN PARIS

The South Parterre at Versailles (see pp248–9)

For the past 300 years the main formal gardens in Paris have been open to the public and are a firm fixture in the city's life. The Jardin des Tuileries *(see p130)* is gradually being renovated, with ongoing replanting; the Jardin du Luxembourg *(see p172)*, the private garden of the French Senate, is still beloved of Left Bankers; and the Jardin du Palais Royal *(see p121)* is enjoyed by those who seek peace and privacy.

French landscaping was raised to an art form in the 17th century, thanks to Louis XIV's talented landscaper André Le Nôtre, who created the gardens of Versailles *(see pp248–9)*. He achieved a brilliant marriage between the traditional Italian Renaissance garden and the French love of rational design.

The role of the French garden architect was not to tend nature but to transform it, pruning and planting to

The long Galerie Dorée in the Banque de France

Louis de la Vrillière, with the sumptuous 50-m (164-ft) long Galerie Dorée specially created for hanging his great collection of historical paintings. The house was later sold to the Comte de Toulouse, son of Louis XIV and Madame de Montespan. The building was extensively reconstructed in the 19th century after the ravages of the Revolution. The bank's most famous modern alumnus is Jacques Delors, president of the European Commission 1985–1994.

Place des Victoires ⑲

75002. **Map** 12 F1. Ⓜ *Palais Royal.*

This circle of elegant mansions was built in 1685 solely to offset the statue of Louis XIV by Desjardins, which was placed in the middle, with torches burning day and night. The proportions of the buildings and even the arrangement of the surrounding streets were all designed by the architect and courtier Jules Hardouin-Mansart to display the statue to its best advantage.

Unfortunately, the 1792 mobs were less sycophantic and tore down the statue. A replacement, of a different style, was erected in 1822, to the detriment of the whole system of proportions of buildings to statue. Yet the square retains much of the original design, and today it is the address of major names in the fashion business, most notably Thierry Mugler and Kenzo.

Louis XIV on Place des Victoires

A Bagatelle garden with floral colour *(see p255)*

In the 17th century, as now, French formal gardens served two purposes: as a setting or backdrop for a château or palace, and for enjoyment. The best view of a formal garden was from the first floor of the château, from which the combination of boxwood hedges, flowers and gravel came together in an intricate, abstract pattern, a blossoming tapestry which complemented the château's interior. Paths of trees drew the eye into infinity, reminding the onlooker of how much land belonged to his host, and therefore establishing his undoubted wealth. So, early on the formal garden became a status symbol, and it still is. This is obvious in both private gardens and in grand public projects. Napoleon Bonaparte completed his vista from the Jardin des Tuileries with a triumphal arch. The late President Mitterrand applied the principle in building his Grand Arche de la Défense (*see pp40–41, 255*) along the same axis as the Tuileries and Arc de Triomphe.

But formal gardens were also made to be enjoyed. People in the 17th century believed that walking in the fresh air kept them in good health. What more perfect spot than a formal garden bedecked with statues and fountains for additional entertainment. The old and infirm could be pushed around in sedan chairs and people could meet one another around a boxwood hedge or on a stone bench under the marbly gaze of the goddess Diana.

create leafy sculptures out of trees, bushes and hedges. Complicated geometrical designs that were created in beds and paths were interspersed with pebbles and carefully thought-out splashes of floral colour. Symmetry and harmony were the landscaper's passwords, a sense of grandeur and magnificence his ultimate goal.

ST-GERMAIN-DES-PRES

This Left Bank area is fuller and livelier, its streets and cafés more crowded than when it was at the forefront of the city's intellectual life in the 1950s. The leading figures of the time have now gone, and the rebellious disciples have retreated to their bourgeois backgrounds. But the new philosophers are there, the radical young thinkers who emerged from the 1960s upheavals, and the area still has its major publishing houses, whose executives entertain treasured writers and agents at the celebrated cafés. But they now share the area with the smart set, those who patronize Yves St-Laurent's opulent premises and the elegant Rue Jacob's smart interior designers. On the south side of Boulevard St-Germain the streets are quiet and quaint, with lots of good restaurants, and at the Odéon end there are brassy cafés and a profusion of cinemas.

Musée d'Orsay clock

SIGHTS AT A GLANCE

Historic Buildings and Streets
Palais Abbatial ❷
Boulevard St-Germain ❼
Rue du Dragon ❽
Rue de l'Odéon ❿
Cour de Rohan ⓬
Cour du Commerce St-André ⓭
Institut de France ⓯
Ecole Nationale Supérieure des Beaux-Arts ⓰
Ecole Nationale d'Administration ⓱
Quai Voltaire ⓲

Churches
St-Germain-des-Prés ❶

Museums and Galleries
Musée Eugène Delacroix ❸
Musée de la Monnaie ⓮
Musée d'Orsay pp144–7 ⓳
Musée Nationale de la Légion d'Honneur ⓴

Theatres
Odéon Théâtre de L'Europe ⓫

Cafés and Restaurants
Les Deux Magots ❹
Café de Flore ❺
Brasserie Lipp ❻
Le Procope ❾

GETTING THERE

Metro stations St-Germain-des-Prés and Odéon and the RER station at Musée d'Orsay serve the area. Bus route 63 travels down Boulevard St-Germain and route 95 goes along Rue Bonaparte. Route 70 passes along Rue Mazarine.

| 0 metres | 400 |
| 0 yards | 400 |

KEY

◼ Street-by-Street map
Ⓜ Metro station
◻ Batobus boarding point
RER RER station

SEE ALSO

• **Street Finder**, map 11–12
• **Where to Stay** pp286–7
• **Restaurants** pp304–06

◁ **Les Deux Magots café beside the church of St-Germain-des-Prés**

Street-by-Street: St-Germain-des-Prés

After World War II, St-Germain-des-Prés became synonymous with intellectual life centred around bars and cafés. Philosophers, writers, actors and musicians mingled in the cellar nightspots and brasseries, where existentialist philosophy co-existed with American jazz. The area is now smarter than in the heyday of Jean-Paul Sartre and Simone de Beauvoir, the haunting singer Juliette Greco and the New Wave film-makers. The writers are still around, enjoying the pleasures of sitting in Les Deux Magots, Café de Flore and other haunts. The 17th-century buildings have survived, but signs of change are evident in the plethora of affluent shops dealing in antiques, books and fashion.

Organ grinder in St-Germain

Les Deux Magots
The café is famous for the patronage of celebrities such as Hemingway ❹

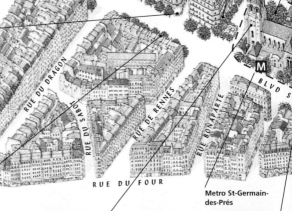

Café de Flore
In the 1950s, French intellectuals wrestled with new philosophical ideas in the Art Deco interior of the café ❺

RUE DU DRAGON

RUE DU SABOT

RUE DE RENNES

RUE BONAPARTE

RUE DU FOUR

M BLVD ST

RUE BONAPARTE

Metro St-Germain-des-Prés

Brasserie Lipp
Colourful ceramics decorate this famous brasserie once frequented by politicians ❻

★ **St-Germain-des-Prés**
Descartes and the king of Poland are among the notables buried here in Paris's oldest church ❶

★ **Boulevard St-Germain**
Café terraces, boutiques, cinemas, restaurants and bookshops characterize the central section of the Left Bank's main street ❼

Picasso's sculpture Homage to Apollinaire *is a tribute to the artist's friend, the poet Guillaume Apollinaire. It was erected in 1959, near the Café de Flore, where the poet held court.*

LOCATOR MAP
See Central Paris Map pp14–15

★ **Musée Delacroix**
Here, Delacroix created the splendid mural, Jacob Wrestling, *for St-Sulpice (see p172)* ❸

Rue de Fürstenberg is a tiny square with old-fashioned street lamps and shady trees. It is often used as a film setting.

STAR SIGHTS

★ St-Germain-des-Prés

★ Boulevard St-Germain

★ Musée Delacroix

KEY

– – – Suggested route

0 metres   100

0 yards   100

Rue de Buci was for centuries an important Left Bank street and the site of some Réal Tennis courts. It now holds a lively market every day.

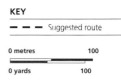

RUE MAZARINE

RUE DE BUCI

GERMAIN

M

RUE DE MONTFAUCON

RUE DE SEINE

RUE DE L'ANCIENNE COMEDIE

Palais Abbatial
This was the residence of abbots from 1586 till the 1789 Revolution ❷

Metro Odéon

M

RUE MABILLON

RUE FÉLIBIEN

CARREFOUR DE L'ODÉON

Metro Mabillon

Marché St-Germain is an old covered food market which was opened in 1818, taking over the site of a former fairground. *(See p334.)*

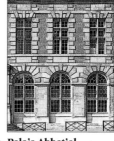

Danton's statue *(1889), by Auguste Paris, is a tribute to the Revolutionary leader.*

St-Germain-des-Prés ❶

3 Pl St-Germain-des-Prés 75006.
Map 12 E4. **Tel** 01 55 42 81 33. Ⓜ
St-Germain-des-Prés. ⬭ 8am–7pm
daily. **Concerts** 8pm Tue, Thu. ✝
12.15pm, 7pm Mon–Fri; 12.15pm
Sat; 9am, 11am, 7pm Sun. 🎦 🏠

This is the oldest church in
Paris, originating in 542 when
King Childebert built a basilica
to house holy relics. This
became an immensely
powerful Benedictine abbey,
which was suppressed during
the Revolution, when most of
the buildings were destroyed
by a fire in 1794. One of the
Revolution's most horrific
episodes took place in a
nearby monastery
when 318 priests
were hacked to
death by the mob
on 3 September
1792. The present
church dates from
about the 11th
century and was
heavily restored
in the 19th
century. One of
the three original
towers survives,
housing one of
the oldest belfries
in France. The
interior is an
interesting mix of
architectural styles,
with some 6th-
century marble
columns, Gothic
vaulting and Romanesque
arches. Famous tombs include
those of René Descartes, the
poet Nicolas Boileau and John
Casimir, king of Poland, who
later became abbot of St-
Germain-des-Prés in 1669.

**Our Lady of
Consolation statue
in St-Germain-
des-Prés**

Palais Abbatial ❷

1–5 Rue de l'Abbaye 75006.
Map 12 E4. Ⓜ St-Germain-des-Prés.
Not open to the public.

This brick and stone palace
was built in 1586 for Charles
of Bourbon who was
cardinal-abbot of St-Germain
and, very briefly, king of
France. Ten more abbots
lived here until the Revolution, when the building was

**An ironwork detail from the
facade of the Palais Abbatial**

sold. James Pradier, the 19th-
century sculptor who was
famous for his female figures,
established a studio here. The
palace is now noted for its
mixture of building materials
and its vertical windows.

Musée Eugène Delacroix ❸

6 Rue de Fürstenberg 75006.
Map 12 E4. **Tel** 01 44 41 86 50.
Ⓜ St-Germain-des-Prés. ⬭ 9.30am–
5pm Wed–Mon (last adm: 4.30pm).
🎦 🏠 www.musee-delacroix.fr

Eugène Delacroix

The leading non-conformist
Romantic painter, Eugène
Delacroix, known for his
passionate and highly-
coloured canvases, lived and
worked here from 1857 to his
death in 1863. Here he
painted *The Entombment
of Christ* and *The Way to
Calvary* (which now hang in
the museum). He also created
superb murals for the Chapel
of the Holy Angels in the
nearby St-Sulpice church,
which is part of the reason
why he moved to this area.

The first-floor apartment and
garden studio now form a
national museum, where
regular exhibitions of
Delacroix's work are held.
The apartment has a portrait
of George Sand, self-portraits,
studies for future works and
artistic memorabilia.

The charm of Delacroix's
garden is reflected in the tiny
Fürstenberg square. With its
pair of rare catalpa trees and
old-fashioned street lamps,
the square is one of Paris's
most romantic corners.

Les Deux Magots ❹

6 Pl St-Germain-des-Prés 75006.
Map 12 E4. **Tel** 01 45 48 55 25.
Ⓜ St-Germain-des-Prés.
⬭ 7.30am–1am daily.
● for one week in Jan.
www.lesdeuxmagots.com

The café still trades on its
reputation as the meeting place
of the city's literary and
intellectual elite. This derives
from the patronage of
Surrealist artists and writers
including Ernest Hemingway
in the 1920s and 1930s, and
existentialist philosophers and
writers in the 1950s.

The present clientele is
more likely to be publishers
or people-watchers than the
new Hemingway. The café's
name comes from the two
wooden statues of Chinese
commercial agents *(magots)*
that adorn one of the pillars.
This is a good place for
enjoying an old-fashioned hot
chocolate and watching the
world go by.

The interior of Les Deux Magots

Facade of the Café de Flore, former meeting-place of existentialists

Café de Flore ❺

26 Rue St-Benoît 75006.
Map 12 E3. **Tel** 01 45 48 55 26.
Ⓜ St-Germain-des-Prés. ◯ 7.30am–
1.30am daily. ♿ restricted.
www.cafedeflore.fr

The classic Art Deco interior of this café, all-red seating, mahogany and mirrors, has changed little since the war. Like its rival Les Deux Magots, Café de Flore has hosted most of the French intellectuals during the post-war years. Jean-Paul Sartre and Simone de Beauvoir developed their philosophy of existentialism here.

A waiter at the Brasserie Lipp

Brasserie Lipp ❻

151 Blvd St-Germain 75006.
Map 12 E4. **Tel** 01 45 48 53 91.
Ⓜ St-Germain-des-Prés
◯ 9am–1am daily.
www.brasserie-lipp.fr

Third of the famous cafés around St-Germain-des-Prés, Brasserie Lipp combines Alsatian beer, sauerkraut and sausages (it was founded by a refugee from Alsace) with excellent coffee to produce a Left Bank fixture once

popular with French politicians and fashion gurus, and now with visitors. Originally opened in the late 19th century, it is regarded by many as the quintessential Parisian brasserie, although the experience is more atmospheric than culinary these days. The interior is bright with ceramic tiles of parrots and cranes.

Boulevard St-Germain ❼

75006, 75007. **Map** 11 C2 &
13 C5. Ⓜ Solférino, Rue du Bac, St-
Germain-des-Prés, Mabillon, Odéon.

The left bank's most celebrated thoroughfare, over 3 km (2 miles) long, curves across three districts from the Ile St-Louis to the Pont de la Concorde. The architecture is homogeneous because the boulevard was another of Baron Haussmann's bold strokes of 19th-century urban planning, but it encompasses a wide range of different lifestyles as well as a number of religious and cultural institutions. From the east (the low street numbers) the

boulevard passes the late François Mitterrand's private town residence in the Rue de Bièvre, as well as the Maubert-Mutualité market square, the Musée de Cluny and the Sorbonne university, before crossing the lively Boulevard St-Michel.

It continues past the Ecole de Médecine and the Place de l'Odéon to St-Germain-des-Prés, with its historic church and café terraces. Fashion boutiques, cinemas, restaurants and bookshops give this central portion its distinctive character. It is also here that one is most likely to see a celebrity. The area is active from midday to the early morning hours.

Continuing further, beyond this section the boulevard becomes more exclusively residential and then distinctly political with the Ministry of Defence and the National Assembly buildings.

Rue du Dragon ❽

75006. **Map** 12 D4.
Ⓜ St-Germain-des-Prés.

This short street, between the Boulevard St-Germain and the Carrefour de la Croix Rouge, dates back to the Middle Ages and still has houses from the 17th and 18th centuries. Notice their large doors, tall windows and ironwork balconies. A group of Flemish painters lived at No. 37 before the Revolution. The novelist Victor Hugo rented a garret at No. 30 when he was a 19-year-old bachelor.

A plaque at No. 30 Rue du Dragon commemorating Victor Hugo's house

Le Procope ❾

13 Rue de l'Ancienne-Comédie
75006. **Map** 12 F4. **Tel** 01 40 46 79
00. Ⓜ Odéon. ◯ noon–1am daily.
See **The History of Paris** pp26–7.
www.procope.com

Founded in 1686 by the
Sicilian Francesco Procopio
dei Coltelli, this claims to be
the world's first coffee house.
It quickly became popular
with the city's political and
cultural elite.

The rear facade of Le Procope restaurant

Its patrons have included
the philosopher Voltaire – who
supposedly drank 40 cups of
his favourite mixture of coffee
and chocolate every day – and
the young Napoleon, who
would leave his hat as security
while he went searching for
the money to pay the bill.
Le Procope is now an 18th-
century style restaurant run by
the famous Frères Blanc group.

**Odéon Théâtre de l'Europe, former
home of the Comédie-Française**

Rue de l'Odéon ❿

75006. **Map** 12 F5. Ⓜ Odéon.

Sylvia Beach's bookshop
Shakespeare & Company
(see pp331–2) stood at No. 12
from 1921 to 1940. She
befriended many struggling
American and British writers,
such as Ezra Pound, T S Eliot,
Scott Fitzgerald and Ernest
Hemingway. It was largely
due to her support – as
secretary, editor, agent and
banker – that James Joyce's
Ulysses was first published in
English. Adrianne Monnier's
French equivalent at No. 7
opposite, Les Amis des Livres,
was frequented by André
Gide and Paul Valéry.
    Opened in 1779 to improve
access to the Odéon theatre,
this was the first street in
Paris to have pavements with
gutters and it still has many
attractive houses and shops,
most of them dating from the
18th century.

Odéon Théâtre de l'Europe ⓫

1 Pl Paul-Claudel 75006. **Map** 12 F5.
Tel 01 44 85 40 40. Ⓜ Odéon,
Luxembourg. ◯ for performances
only. See **Entertainment** pp342–4.
www.theatre-odeon.fr

This Neo-Classical theatre was
built in 1779 in the grounds
of the former Hôtel de Condé.
The site had been purchased
by the king and given to the
city to house the Comédie
Française. The premiere of The
Marriage of Figaro, by Beaumarchais, took place here in
1784. With the arrival of a new
company in 1797 the name of
the theatre was changed to
Odéon. In 1807 the theatre was
consumed by fire. It was rebuilt
later the same year by the
architect Jean-François Chalgrin.
    Following World War II, the
theatre specialized in modern
drama and was the best attended in Paris. Today, plays are
often performed in foreign
languages, including English.
The auditorium is very impressive, not least for its ceiling,
painted by André Masson
in 1965.

A young Hemingway in the 1920s

Cour de Rohan ⓬

75006. **Map** 12 F4. Ⓜ Odéon.
Access from the Rue du Jardinet
until 8pm; 8pm–8am access from
the Blvd St-Germain.

**The unusual middle courtyard in
the Cour de Rohan**

This picturesque series
of three courtyards was
originally part of the 15th-
century pied-à-terre of the
archbishops of Rouen
(corrupted to "Rohan"). The
middle courtyard is the most
unusual. Its three-legged
wrought-iron mounting block,
known as a pas-de-mule, was
used at one time by elderly
women and overweight
prelates to mount their mules.
It is probably the last
mounting block left in Paris.
Overlooking the yard is the
facade of a fine Renaissance
building, dating from the
beginning of the 17th century.
One of its important former
residents was Henri II's
mistress, Diane de Poitiers.
    The third courtyard opens
on to the tiny Rue du
Jardinet, where the composer
Saint-Saëns was born in 1835.

Cour du Commerce St-André ⑬

75006. **Map** 12 F4. Ⓜ *Odéon.*

No. 9 has a particularly grisly past, because it was here that Dr Guillotin is supposed to have perfected his "philanthropic decapitating machine". In fact, although the idea was Guillotin's, it was Dr Louis, a Parisian surgeon, who was responsible for putting the humane plan into action. When the guillotine was first used for execution in 1792 it was known as a *Louisette*.

A print of a Revolutionary mob at a guillotine execution

Musée de la Monnaie ⑭

11 Quai de Conti 75006. **Map** 12 F3. *Tel* 01 40 46 56 66. Ⓜ *Pont-Neuf, Odéon.* ⏱ *11am–5.30pm Tue–Fri, noon–5.30pm Sat & Sun.* 🎬 📷 ✉ *Films.* **www**.monnaiedeparis.fr

When Louis XV decided to rehouse the Mint in the late 18th century, he hit upon the idea of launching a design competition for the new building. The present Hôtel des Monnaies is the result of this competition. It was completed in 1777, and the architect, Jacques Antoine, lived here until his death.

Coins were minted in the mansion until 1973, when the process was moved to Pessac in the Gironde. The minting and milling halls now contain the coin and medallion museum. The extensive collection is displayed in vertical glass stands so that both sides of the coins are visible, and everything is presented in the context of the history of the day. The permanent exhibitions are closed until late 2013 while renovations are carried out, but visitors can still enjoy some temporary exhibits.

Instead of minting coins, the building's workshops are now devoted to the creation of medallions, a selection of which are on sale in the museum shop.

Institut de France ⑮

23 Quai de Conti 75006. **Map** 12 E3. *Tel* 01 44 41 44 41. Ⓜ *Pont-Neuf, St-Germain-des-Prés.* ⏱ *Sat & Sun by appointment only.* 📷 ✉ **www**.institut-de-france.fr

Now home to the illustrious Académie Française, this Baroque building was built as a school in 1688 and was given over to the Institut de France in 1805. Its distinctive cupola was designed by the palace's architect, Louis Le Vau, to harmonize with the Palais du Louvre.

The Académie Française is the most famous of the five academies within the institute. It was founded in 1635 by

A sign to the former Mint, which is now a museum

Cardinal Richelieu and charged with the compilation of an official dictionary of the French language. From the beginning, membership has been limited to 40, who are entrusted with working on the dictionary.

Ecole Nationale Supérieure des Beaux-Arts ⑯

13 Quai Malaquais 75006. **Map** 12 E3. *Tel* 01 47 03 50 00. Ⓜ *St-Germain-des-Prés.* ⏱ *daily to groups by appt only (phone 01 42 46 92 02 to arrange).* 📖 **Library**. **www**.ensba.fr

The main French school of fine arts occupies an enviable position at the corner of the Rue Bonaparte and the river-side Quai Malaquais. The school is housed in several buildings, the most imposing being the 19th-century Palais des Etudes.

A host of budding French and foreign painters and architects have crossed the large courtyard to study in the ateliers of the school. Young American architects, in particular, have studied there over the past century.

The facade of the Ecole Nationale Supérieure des Beaux-Arts

THE CELEBRATED CAFES OF PARIS

One of the most enduring images of Paris is the café scene. For the visitor it is the romantic vision of great artists, writers or eminent intellectuals consorting in one of the Left Bank's celebrated cafés. For the Parisian the café is one of life's constants, an everyday experience, providing people with a place to tryst, drink and meet friends, or to conclude business deals, or to simply watch the world go by.

The first café anywhere can be traced back to 1686, when the café Le Procope *(see p140)* was opened. In the following century cafés became a vital part of Paris's social life. And with the widening of the city's streets, particularly during the 19th century and the building of Haussmann's Grands Boulevards, the cafés spread out on to the pavements, evoking Emile Zola's comment as to the "great silent crowds watching the street live".

The nature of a café was sometimes determined by the interests of its patrons. Some were the gathering places for those interested in playing chess, dominoes or billiards. Literary gents gathered in Le Procope during Molière's time in the 17th century. In the 19th century, First Empire Imperial guards officers were drawn to the Café d'Orsay and Second Empire financiers gathered in the cafés along the Rue de la Chaussée d'Antin. The smart set patronized the Café de Paris and Café Tortini, and theatre-goers met at the cafés around the Opéra, including the Café de la Paix *(see p215)*.

Newspaper reading is still a typical café pastime

Ecole Nationale d'Administration ⓱

13 Rue de l'Université 75007.
Map 12 D3. **Tel** 01 49 26 45 45.
Ⓜ *Rue du Bac.* ◑ *to the public.*

This fine 18th-century mansion was originally built as two houses in 1643 by Briçonnet. In 1713 they were replaced by a *hôtel*, built by Thomas Gobert for the widow of Denis Feydeau de Brou. It was passed on to her son, Paul-Espirit Feydeau de Brou, until his death in 1767. The *hôtel* then became the residence of the Venetian ambassador. It was occupied by Belzunce in 1787 and became a munitions depot during the Revolution until the restoration of the monarchy in 1815.

It once housed the Ecole Nationale d'Administration (now in Strasbourg), where many of the elite in politics, economics and science were once students. Today the building is used by France's famous Science Po University.

Plaque marking the house in Quai Voltaire where Voltaire died

Quai Voltaire ⓲

75006 and 75007. **Map** 12 D3.
Ⓜ *Rue du Bac.*

Formerly part of the Quai Malaquais, then later known as the Quai des Théatins, the Quai Voltaire is now home to some of the most important antiques dealers in Paris. It is also noted for its attractive 18th-century houses and for the famous people who lived in many of them, making it an especially interesting and pleasant street to walk along.

The 18th-century Swedish ambassador Count Tessin lived at No. 1, as did the sculptor James Pradier, famed for his statues and for his wife, who swam naked across the Seine. Louise de Kéroualle, spy for Louis XIV and created Duchess of Portsmouth by the infatuated Charles II of England, lived at Nos. 3–5.

Famous past residents of No. 19 included the composers Richard Wagner and Jean Sibelius, the novelist Charles Baudelaire and the exiled Irish writer and wit Oscar Wilde.

The French philosopher Voltaire died at No. 27, the Hôtel de la Villette. St-Sulpice, the local church, refused to accept his corpse (on the grounds of his atheism) and his body was rushed into the country to avoid a pauper's grave.

Entertainment in the Claude Alain café in the Rue de Seine during the 1950s

problems of Russia and the world over a *petit café*. Cultural life flourished in the 1920s, when Surrealists, like Salvador Dalí and Jean Cocteau, dominated café life, and later when American writers led by Ernest Hemingway and Scott Fitzgerald talked, drank and worked in various cafés, among them La Coupole *(see p178)*, Le Sélect

his intellectual peers and followers, among them the writers Simone de Beauvoir and Albert Camus, the poet Boris Vian and the enigmatic singer Juliette Greco, gathered to work and discuss their ideas in Les Deux Magots *(see p138)* and the nearby rival Café de Flore *(see p139)*. The traditional habitué of these cafés is still to be seen, albeit mixing with the international jet-set and with self-publicizing intellectuals hunched over their notebooks.

The most famous cafés are on the Left Bank, in St-Germain and Montparnasse, where the literati of old used to gather and where the glitterati of today love to be seen. Before World War I, Montparnasse was haunted by hordes of Russian revolutionaries, most eminently Lenin and Trotsky, who whiled away their days in the cafés, grappling with the

and La Closerie des Lilas *(see p179)*.

After the end of World War II, the cultural scene shifted northwards to St-Germain. Existentialism had become the dominant creed and Jean-Paul Sartre its tiny charismatic leader. Sartre and

Works by one of St-Germain's elite, Albert Camus (1913–60)

Musée d'Orsay ⑲

See pp144–7.

Musée Nationale de la Légion d'Honneur ⑳

2 Rue de la Légion d'Honneur (Parvis du Musée d'Orsay) 75007. **Map** 11 C2. **Tel** 01 40 62 84 25. M Solférino. RER Musée d'Orsay. 1–6pm Wed–Sun. public hols. **www**.musee-legiondhonneur.fr

Next to the Musée d'Orsay is the truly massive Hôtel de Salm. It was one of the last

Napoleon III's Great Cross of the Legion of Honour

The Musée d'Orsay, converted from a railway station into a museum

great mansions to be built in the area (1702). The first owner was a German count, Prince de Salm-Kyrbourg, who was guillotined in 1794.

Today the building contains a museum where one can learn all about the Legion of Honour, a decoration launched by Napoleon I. Those awarded the honour

wear a small red rosette in their buttonhole. The impressive displays of medals and insignia are complemented by paintings. In one of the rooms, Napoleon's Legion of Honour is on display with his sword and breastplate.

The museum also covers decorations from most parts of the world, among them the British Victoria Cross and the American Purple Heart.

Musée d'Orsay ⑲

In 1986, 47 years after it had closed as a mainline railway station, Victor Laloux's superb late 19th-century building was reopened as the Musée d'Orsay. Commissioned by the Orléans railway company to be its Paris terminus, it avoided demolition in the 1970s. During the conversion much of the original architecture was retained. The museum, which has undergone extensive renovation, was set up to present each of the arts of the period from 1848 to 1914 in the context of its contemporary society and all other forms of creative activity happening at the time. Renovations to the upper levels have expanded exhibition spaces to improve the display of works.

The Museum, from the Right Bank
Victor Laloux designed the building for the Universal Exhibition in 1900.

Chair by Charles Rennie Mackintosh
The style developed by Mackintosh was an attempt to express ideas in a framework of vertical and horizontal forms, as in this tearoom chair (1900).

★ **The Gates of Hell** *(1880–1917)*
Rodin included figures that he had already created, such as The Thinker *and* The Kiss, *in this famous gateway.*

★ **Le Déjeuner sur l'Herbe** *(1863)*
Manet's painting, first exhibited in Napoleon III's Salon des Refusés, *is presently on display in the first area of the upper level.*

KEY TO FLOORPLAN

- ☐ Architecture & Decorative Arts
- ☐ Sculpture
- ☐ Painting before 1870
- ☐ Impressionism
- ☐ Neo-Impressionism
- ☐ Naturalism and Symbolism
- ☐ Art Nouveau
- ☐ Temporary exhibitions
- ☐ Non-exhibition space

GALLERY GUIDE

The collection occupies three levels. On the ground floor there are works from the mid to late 19th century. The middle level features Art Nouveau decorative art and a range of paintings and sculptures from the second half of the 19th century to the early 20th century. The upper level has an outstanding collection of Impressionist and Neo-Impressionist art.

The Dance *(1867–8)*
Carpeaux's sculpture caused a scandal when first exhibited.

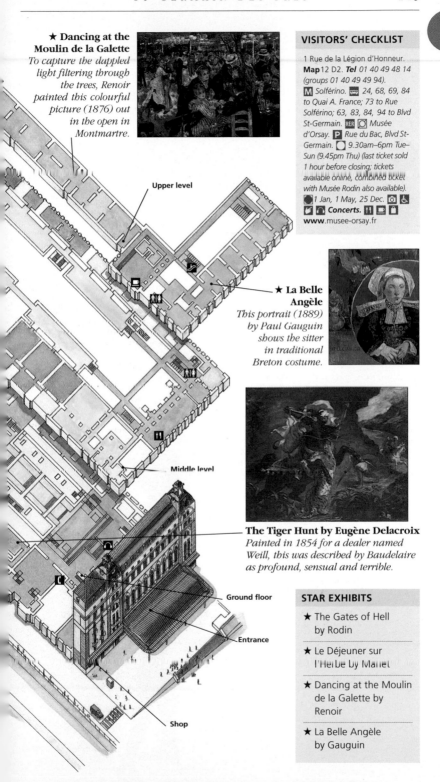

★ **Dancing at the Moulin de la Galette**
To capture the dappled light filtering through the trees, Renoir painted this colourful picture (1876) out in the open in Montmartre.

Upper level

VISITORS' CHECKLIST

1 Rue de la Légion d'Honneur.
Map 12 D2. **Tel** *01 40 49 48 14 (groups 01 40 49 49 94).*
M *Solférino.* 🚌 *24, 68, 69, 84 to Quai A. France; 73 to Rue Solférino; 63, 83, 84, 94 to Blvd St-Germain.* **RER** 🅾 *Musée d'Orsay.* **P** *Rue du Bac, Blvd St-Germain.* 🕘 *9.30am–6pm Tue–Sun (9.45pm Thu) (last ticket sold 1 hour before closing; tickets available online, combined ticket with Musée Rodin also available).*
🅾 *1 Jan, 1 May, 25 Dec.* 📷 ♿
🎫 🎪 **Concerts.** 🍴 🛗 💻
www.musee-orsay.fr

★ **La Belle Angèle**
This portrait (1889) by Paul Gauguin shows the sitter in traditional Breton costume.

Middle level

The Tiger Hunt by Eugène Delacroix
Painted in 1854 for a dealer named Weill, this was described by Baudelaire as profound, sensual and terrible.

Ground floor

Entrance

Shop

STAR EXHIBITS

★ The Gates of Hell by Rodin

★ Le Déjeuner sur l'Herbe by Manet

★ Dancing at the Moulin de la Galette by Renoir

★ La Belle Angèle by Gauguin

Exploring the Musée d'Orsay

The Musée d'Orsay picks up where the Louvre ends, showing works from 1848 to 1914. Its star attraction is a superb collection of Impressionist art, but it also holds world-class temporary exhibitions and excellent lunchtime and evening concerts. In addition to the main exhibition, there are displays that explain the social, political and technological context in which the art was created, including exhibits on the history of cinematography.

Ceiling design (1911) by the artist and designer Maurice Denis

ART NOUVEAU

The Belgian architect and designer Victor Horta was among the first to give free rein to the sinuous line that gave Art Nouveau its French sobriquet of *Style Nouille* (noodle style). Taking its name from a gallery of modern design that opened in Paris in 1895, Art Nouveau flourished throughout Europe until World War I.

In Vienna, Otto Wagner, Koloman Moser and Josef Hoffmann combined high craft with the new design, while the School of Glasgow, under the impetus of Charles Rennie Mackintosh, developed a more rectilinear approach which anticipated the work of Frank Lloyd Wright in the United States.

René Lalique introduced the aesthetics of Art Nouveau into jewellery and glassware, while Hector Guimard, inspired by Horta, is most famous today for his once-ubiquitous Art Nouveau entrances to the Paris metro.

One exhibit not to be missed is the carved wooden bookcase by Rupert Carabin (1890), with its proliferation of allegorical seated female nudes, bronze palm fronds and severed bearded heads.

SCULPTURE

The museum's central aisle overflows with an oddly-assorted selection of sculptures. These illustrate the eclectic mood around the middle of the 19th century when the Classicism of Eugène Guillaume's *Cenotaph of the Gracchi* (1848–53) co-existed with the Romanticism of François Rude. Rude created the relief on the Arc de Triomphe (1836), often referred to as *La Marseillaise (see p211)*.

There is a wonderful series of 36 busts of members of parliament (1832) – bloated, ugly, unscrupulous and self-important – by the satirist Honoré Daumier, and work by the vital but short-lived genius Jean-Baptiste Carpeaux, whose first major bronze, *Count Ugolino* (1862), was a character from Dante. In 1868 he produced his Dionysian delight, *The Dance*, which caused a storm of protest: it was "an insult to public morals". This contrasts with the derivative and mannered work of such sculptors as Alexandre Falguière and Hyppolyte Moulin.

Edgar Degas' famous *Young Dancer of Fourteen* (1881) was displayed during his lifetime, but the many bronzes on show were made from wax sculptures found in his

studio after his death. In contrast, the sculpture of Auguste Rodin was very much in the public eye, and his sensuous and forceful work makes him pre-eminent among 19th-century sculptors. The museum contains many of his works, including the original plaster of *Balzac* (1897). Rodin's talented companion, Camille Claudel, who spent much of her life in an asylum, is represented by a grim allegory of mortality, *Maturity* (1899–1903).

The turn of the 20th century is marked by the work of Emile-Antoine Bourdelle and Aristide Maillol.

PAINTING BEFORE 1870

The surprising diversity of styles in 19th-century painting is emphasized by the close juxtaposition on the ground floor of all paintings prior to 1870 – the crucial year in which Impressionism first made a name for itself. The raging colour and almost Expressionistic vigour of Eugène Delacroix's *Lion Hunt* (1854) stands next to Jean-Dominique Ingres' cool Classical *The Spring* (1820–56). As a reminder of the academic manner that dominated the century up to that point, the uninspired waxwork style of Thomas Couture's monumental *The Romans in the Age of Decadence* (1847) dominates the central aisle. In a class of their own are Edouard Manet's provocative *Olympia* and *Le Déjeuner sur l'Herbe* (1863), while works painted around the same time by his friends, Claude Monet, Pierre-Auguste Renoir, Frédéric Bazille and Alfred Sisley, give a glimpse of the Impressionists before the Impressionist movement began.

Young Dancer of Fourteen **(1881) by Edgar Degas**

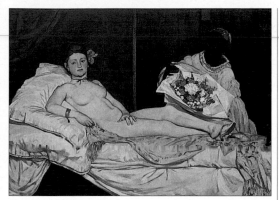

Olympia (1863) by Edouard Manet

IMPRESSIONISM

Rouen Cathedral caught at various moments of the day (1892–3) is one of the many works on show by Claude Monet, the leading figure of the Impressionist movement. Pierre-Auguste Renoir's plump nudes and his young people *Dancing at the Moulin de la Galette* (1876) were painted at the high point of his Impressionist period. Other artists on display include Camille Pissarro, Alfred Sisley and Mary Cassatt.

Edgar Degas, Paul Cézanne and Vincent Van Gogh are included here although their techniques differed from those of the Impressionists. Degas often favoured crisp Realism, though he was quite capable of using the sketchy manner of the Impressionists, as, for instance, in *L'Absinthe* (1876). Cézanne was more concerned with substance than light, as can be seen in his *Apples and Oranges* (1895–1900). Van Gogh was momentarily influenced by the movement but then went his own way, illustrated here by works from the collection of Dr Gachet.

Breton Peasant Women (1894) by Paul Gauguin

NEO-IMPRESSIONISM

Although labelled Neo-Impressionism, the work of Georges Seurat (which includes *The Circus* from 1891) was quite unrelated to the older movement. He, along with Maximilien Luce and Paul Signac, painted by applying small dots of colour that blended together when viewed from a distance. *Jane Avril Dancing* (1892) is just one of many pictures by Henri de Toulouse-Lautrec on display. The work Paul Gauguin did at Pont-Aven in Brittany is shown next to that of younger artists who knew him at the time, such as Emile Bernard and the Nabis group. There are also a number of paintings from his Tahitian period.

The Nabis (which included Pierre Bonnard) tended to treat the canvas as a flat surface out of which a sense of depth emerged as the viewer gazed upon it.

The dream like visions of Odilon Redon are in the Symbolist vein, while the naïve art of Henri (Douanier) Rousseau is represented by *War* (1894) and *The Snake Charmer* (1907).

NATURALISM AND SYMBOLISM

Three large rooms are devoted to paintings that filled the Salons from 1880 to 1900. The work of the Naturalists was sanctioned by the Third Republic and widely reproduced at the time. Fernand Cormon's figure of *Cain* was highly acclaimed when it first appeared in the 1880 Salon. Jules Bastien-Lepage's interest lay in illustrating peasant life, and in 1877 he painted *Haymaking*, which established him as one of the leading Naturalists. His fairly free handling of paint was influenced by what he had learned from Manet and his friends. More sombrely (and effectively) naturalistic is Lionel Walden's view of *The Docks of Cardiff* (1894).

Symbolism developed as a reaction against Realism and Impressionism and tended to be dominated by images of dreams and thoughts. This resulted in a wide variety of subjects and modes of expression. There is the over-sweet vision of levitating harpists, *Serenity* by Henri Martin (1899), Edward Burne-Jones' monumental work *Wheel of Fortune* (1883) and Jean Delville's *School of Plato* (1898). One of the most evocative paintings in this section is Winslow Homer's lyrical *Summer Night* (1890).

Blue Waterlilies (1919) by Claude Monet

LATIN QUARTER

15th-century stained glass in Musée de Cluny

Student bookshops, cafés, cinemas and jazz clubs fill this ancient riverside quarter between the Seine and the Luxembourg Gardens. Famous institutes of learning abound, among them the two most prestigious *lycées*, Henri IV and Louis le Grand, through which passes a large percentage of the future French elite.

As the leaders of the 1968 revolt *(see pp40–41)* disappeared into the mainstream of French life, so the Boulevard St-Michel, the area's spine, turned increasingly to commerce, not demonstrations. Today, there are cheap shops and fast-food outlets, and the maze of narrow, cobbled streets off the boulevard are full of inexpensive ethnic shops, quirky

boutiques and avant-garde theatres and cinemas. But the area's 800 years of history are difficult to efface. The Sorbonne retains much of its old character and the eastern half of the area has streets dating back to the 13th century. And the Rue St-Jacques still remains the long Roman road stretching out of the city, and the forerunner of all the city's streets.

A young musician playing music under the Pont St-Michel is part of the Latin Quarter's long tradition as a focus for the young from all walks of life.

SIGHTS AT A GLANCE

Historic Buildings and Streets
Boulevard St-Michel **2**
La Sorbonne **7**
Collège de France **8**

Museums and Galleries
Musée National du Moyen Age pp154–7 **1**
Musée de la Préfecture de Police **6**

GETTING THERE
Metro stations in the area include those at St-Michel and Cluny La Sorbonne. The Balabus and routes 24 and 87 travel along Blvd St-Germain, and 38 travels along Blvd St-Michel, passing the Sorbonne and the Musée National du Moyen Age.

Churches and Temples
St-Séverin **3**
St-Julien-le-Pauvre **4**

Squares
Place Maubert **5**

Chapelle de la Sorbonne **9**
St-Etienne-du-Mont **10**
Panthéon pp158–9 **11**

KEY

	Street-by-Street map
M	Metro station
	Batobus boarding point
RER	RER station

SEE ALSO

◁ **A peaceful spot along a Latin Quarter quay**

Street-by-Street: Latin Quarter

Since the Middle Ages this riverside quarter has been dominated by the Sorbonne, and acquired its name from the early Latin-speaking students. It dates back to the Roman town across from the Ile de la Cité; at that time the Rue St-Jacques was one of the main roads out of Paris. The area is generally associated with artists, intellectuals and the bohemian way of life; it also has a history of political unrest. In 1871, the Place St-Michel became the centre of the Paris Commune, and in May 1968 it was the site of the student uprisings. Today the eastern half has become sufficiently chic, however, to contain the homes of some of the Establishment.

Place St-Michel
contains a fountain
by Davioud. The
bronze statue by
Duret shows St
Michael killing
the dragon.

Metro St-Michel

Little Athens is a lively place in the evening, especially at the weekend, when the Greek restaurants situated in the touristy streets around St-Séverin are at their busiest.

**Metro Cluny
La Sorbonne**

★ Boulevard St-Michel
The northern end of the Boul'Mich, as it is affectionately known, is a lively mélange of cafés, book and clothes shops, with bars and experimental cinemas nearby **❷**

★ Musée National du Moyen Age
One of the finest collections of medieval art in the world is kept here in a superb late 15th-century building **❶**

No. 22 Rue St-Séverin is the narrowest house in Paris and used to be the residence of Abbé Prévost, author of *Manon Lescaut*.

★ St-Séverin
*Begun in the 13th century,
this beautiful church took
three centuries to build and
is a fine example of the
flamboyant Gothic style* ❸

Rue du Chat qui Pêche (meaning
"street of the fishing cat") is the
narrowest street in Paris at just
1.8 m (6 ft) wide.

LOCATOR MAP
See Central Paris Map pp14–15

Shakespeare & Co *(see
pp331–2)* at No.37 Rue
de la Bûcherie is a
delightful, if chaotic,
bookshop. Any books
purchased here are
stamped with
*Shakespeare & Co
Kilomètre Zéro Paris.*

★ St-Julien-le-Pauvre
*Rebuilt in the 17th
century, this church was
used to store animal feed
during the Revolution* ❹

Rue du Fouarre
used to host
lectures in the
Middle Ages. The
students sat on straw
(fouarre) in the street.

Ⓜ
**Metro
Maubert
Mutualité**

STAR SIGHTS

★ Boulevard St-Michel

★ Musée National du
Moyen Age

★ St-Séverin

★ St-Julien-le-Pauvre

KEY

 Suggested route

| 0 metres | 100 |
| 0 yards | 100 |

Rue Galande was home
to the rich and chic
in the 17th century,
but subsequently
became notorious for
its taverns.

Musée National du Moyen Age ❶

See pp154–7.

Boulevard St-Michel ❷

75005 & 75006. **Map** 12 F5 & 16 F2.
Ⓜ *St-Michel, Cluny-La Sorbonne.*
ℝℇℝ *Luxembourg.*

Cut through the area in 1869, the boulevard initially gained fame from its many literary cafés, but nowadays many have been replaced by clothes shops. Nos. 60–64 house the Ecole Nationale Supérieure des Mines, one of France's leading engineering schools *(see p173).* In the Place St-Michel, marble plaques commemorate the many students who died here in 1944 fighting the Nazis.

Gargoyles adorning St-Séverin

St-Séverin ❸

1 Rue-des-Prêtres-St-Séverin 75005.
Map 13 A4. **Tel** 01 42 34 93 50.
Ⓜ *St-Michel.* ◯ *11am–7.30pm Mon–Sat, 9am–8.30pm Sun.* 📷
Concerts. www.saint-severin.com

One of the most beautiful churches in Paris, St-Séverin is a perfect example of the Flamboyant Gothic style. It is named after a 6th-century hermit who lived in the area and persuaded the future St Cloud, grandson of King Clovis, to take holy orders. Construction finished in the early 16th century and included a remarkable double ambulatory circling the

Inside St-Julien-le-Pauvre

chancel. In 1684 the Grande Mademoiselle, cousin to Louis XIV, adopted St-Séverin after breaking with St-Sulpice and had the chancel modernized.

The burial ground here, which is now a garden, was the site of the first operation for gall stones in 1474. An archer who had been condemned to death was offered his freedom by Louis XI if he consented to the operation and lived. (It was a success, and the archer went free.) In the garden stands the church's medieval gable-roofed charnel house.

St-Julien-le-Pauvre ❹

1 Rue St-Julien-le-Pauvre 75005.
Map 13 A4. **Tel** 01 43 54 52 16.
Ⓜ *St-Michel.* ◯ *9.30am–1.30pm, 3pm–6pm daily.* **Concerts.**
See **Entertainment** *p336.*

At least three saints can claim to be patron of this church, but the most likely is St Julian the Hospitaller. The church, together with St-Germain-des-Prés, is one of the oldest in Paris, dating from between 1165 and 1220. The university held its official meetings in the church until 1524, when a student protest created so much damage that university meetings were barred from the church by parliament. Since 1889 it has belonged to the Melchite sect of the Greek Orthodox Church, and it is now the setting for chamber and religious music concerts.

Place Maubert ❺

75005. **Map** 13 A5.
Ⓜ *Maubert-Mutualité.*

From the 12th to the middle of the 13th century, "La Maub" was one of Paris's scholastic centres, with lectures given in the open air. After the scholars moved to the new colleges of the Montagne St-Geneviève, the square became a place of torture and execution, including that of the philosopher Etienne Dolet, who was burnt at the stake in 1546.

So many Protestants were burnt here in the 16th century that it became a place of pilgrimage for the followers of the new faith. Its dark reputation has been replaced by respectability and a notable street market.

Musée de la Préfecture de Police ❻

4 Rue de la Montagne Ste-Geneviève 75005. **Map** 13 A5.
Tel 01 44 41 52 50. Ⓜ *Maubert-Mutualité.* ◯ *9am–5pm Mon–Fri; 10am–5pm Sat (last adm: 4.30pm).*
◉ *public hols.*

Weapons in the police museum

A darker side to Paris's history is illustrated in this small, rather old-fashioned museum. Created in 1909, the collection traces the development of the police in Paris from the Middle Ages to the 20th century. Curiosities on show include arrest warrants for figures such as the famous revolutionary Danton, and a rather sobering display of weapons and tools used by famous criminals. There is also a section on the part the police played in the Resistance and subsequent liberation of Paris.

La Sorbonne **7**

47 Rue des Ecoles 75005.
Map 13 A5. **Tel** 01 40 46 22 11.
Ⓜ *Cluny-La Sorbonne, Maubert-Mutualité.* ⬜ *by appointment only.*
🖼 *by appointment only: write to Service des Visites.*

The Sorbonne, seat of the University of Paris, was established in 1253 by Robert de Sorbon, confessor to Louis IX, for 16 poor students to study theology. From these modest beginnings the college soon became the centre of scholastic theology. In 1469 the rector had three printing machines brought over from Mainz, thereby founding the first printing house in France. The college's opposition to liberal 18th-century philosophy led to its suppression during the Revolution. It was re-established by Napoleon in 1806. The buildings built by Richelieu in the early 17th century were replaced by the ones seen today, with the exception of the chapel.

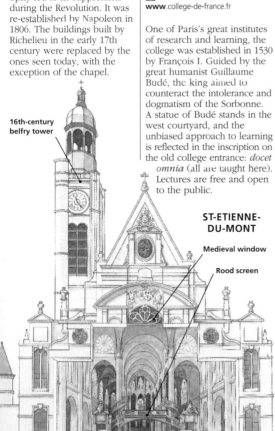

16th-century belfry tower

ST-ETIENNE-DU-MONT

Medieval window

Rood screen

Statues outside the college

Collège de France **8**

11 Pl Marcelin-Berthelot 75005.
Map 13 A5. **Tel** 01 44 27 12 11.
Ⓜ *Maubert-Mutualité.*
⬜ *Oct–Jun: 9am–6pm Mon–Fri.*
www.college-de-france.fr

One of Paris's great institutes of research and learning, the college was established in 1530 by François I. Guided by the great humanist Guillaume Budé, the king aimed to counteract the intolerance and dogmatism of the Sorbonne. A statue of Budé stands in the west courtyard, and the unbiased approach to learning is reflected in the inscription on the old college entrance: *docet omnia* (all are taught here). Lectures are free and open to the public.

Chapelle de la Sorbonne **9**

Pl de la Sorbonne 75005.
Map 13 A5. **Tel** 01 40 46 22 11.
Ⓜ *Cluny-La Sorbonne, Maubert-Mutualité.* 🚇 *Luxembourg.*
⬜ *for temporary exhibitions only.* 🖼

Designed by Lemercier and built between 1635 and 1642, this chapel is, in effect, a monument to Richelieu, with his coat of arms on the dome supports and his white marble tomb, carved by Girardon in 1694, in the chancel. The chapel's attractive lateral facade looks on to the main courtyard of the Sorbonne.

Chapelle de la Sorbonne clock

St-Etienne-du-Mont **10**

Pl Ste-Geneviève 75005. **Map** 17 A1.
Tel 01 43 54 11 79. Ⓜ *Cardinal Lemoine.* ⬜ *8.45am–7.30pm Tue–Fri, 8.45am–12pm, 2.30–7.45pm Sat & Sun.* 📷 ⬜

This remarkable church houses not only the shrine of Sainte Geneviève, patron saint of Paris, but also the remains of the great literary figures Racine and Pascal. Some parts are in the Gothic style and others date from the Renaissance, including a magnificent rood screen which crosses the nave like a bridge. The stained glass windows are also of note.

Panthéon **11**

See pp158–9.

Musée National du Moyen Age ●

Head of St John the Baptist

Previously known as the Musée de Cluny, the museum is housed in the former townhouse of the Abbots of Cluny. Surrounded by imaginatively recreated medieval gardens, the museum is a unique combination of Gallo-Roman ruins, incorporated into a medieval mansion, and one of the world's finest collections of medieval art.

Medieval Mansion
The museum building, completed in 1500, was erected by Jacques d'Amboise, Abbot of Cluny.

Medieval chapel

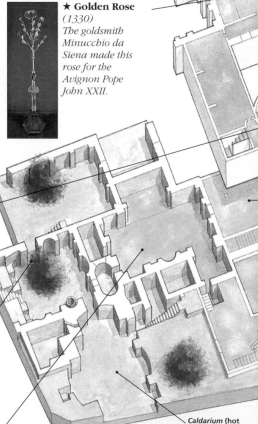

★ **Golden Rose**
(1330)
The goldsmith Minuccio da Siena made this rose for the Avignon Pope John XXII.

★ **Lady with the Unicorn**
This outstanding series of six tapestries is a fine example of the millefleurs style, which was developed in the 15th and early 16th centuries. The style is noted for its graceful depiction of plants, animals and people.

Gallo-Roman Baths
Built in AD 200, the baths lasted for about 100 years before being sacked by the barbarians.

Caldarium (hot bath room)

STAR EXHIBITS

★ Lady with the Unicorn

★ Golden Rose

★ Gallery of the Kings

Gallo-Roman Frigidarium
The arches of this cold bath room, dating from the 1st and 2nd centuries, were once decorated with pairs of carved ship prows, the symbol of the association of Paris boatmen (nautes).

Books of Hours

The museum possesses two Books of Hours from the first half of the 15th century. The illuminated pages include scenes showing the Labours of the Months, accompanied by the relevant sign of the zodiac.

VISITORS' CHECKLIST

6 Pl Paul-Painlevé. **Map** 13 A5.
[F] 01 53 73 78 16/00. [M]
Cluny-La-Sorbonne, St-Michel,
Odéon. [bus] 63, 86, 87, 21, 27,
38 to Rue Soufflot, Rue des Ecoles.
[RER] St-Michel, Cluny-La Sorbonne.
[P] Blvd St-Germain, Pl Edmond
Rostand. [ ] 9.15am–5.45pm
Wed–Mon. [ ] 1 Jan, 1 May, 25
Dec. [icons] **Concerts.**
Workshops. www.musee-
moyenage.fr

★ Gallery of the Kings

In 1977, 21 of the 28 stone heads of the Kings of Judah (carved around 1220 during the reign of Philippe Auguste) were unearthed during excavations in the Rue de la Chaussée-d'Antin behind the Opéra.

GALLERY GUIDE

The collection is spread throughout the two floors of the building. It is mainly medieval and covers a wide range of items, including illuminated manuscripts, tapestries, textiles, precious metals, alabaster, ceramics, sculpture and church furnishings. A number of Gallo-Roman artifacts are displayed around the sides of the frigidarium, and the small circular room nearby contains some capitals.

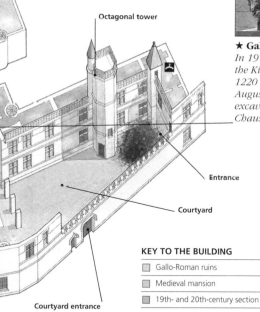

Octagonal tower

Entrance

Courtyard

Courtyard entrance

KEY TO THE BUILDING

- ◻ Gallo-Roman ruins
- ◻ Medieval mansion
- ◼ 19th- and 20th-century section

TIMELINE

200	1450	1750	1800	1850
c. 300 Public baths built	**1747** Octagonal tower used as observatory	**1789** Seized in the Revolution and sold by the State	**1833** Acquired by Alexandre du Sommerard, collector of medieval artefacts
1500 Building of mansion by Jacques d'Amboise completed			**1844** Opened as a museum

c. 300 Baths sacked and burned by barbarians

1600 Hôtel becomes residence of papal nuncios

1819 Baths excavated on the orders of Louis XVIII

Louis XVIII at his desk

1842 House and collection bought by State

Exploring the Moyen Age's Collection

Alexandre du Sommerard took over the Hôtel de Cluny in 1833 and installed his art collection with great sensitivity to the surroundings and a strong sense of the dramatic. After his death the Hôtel and its contents were sold to the State and turned into a museum.

The Grape **Harvest tapestry**

TAPESTRIES

The museum's tapestries are remarkable for their quality, age and state of preservation. The images present a surprising mixture of the naïve with more complex notions. One of the earliest, *The Offering of the Heart* (early 15th century), shows a man who is literally proffering his heart to a seated medieval beauty. More everyday scenes are shown in the magnificent series *The Noble Life* (about 1500). Upstairs is the mysterious *Lady with the Unicorn* series.

CARVINGS

The diverse techniques of medieval European woodcarvers are well represented. From the Nottingham workshops in England, there are wood as well as alabaster works which were widely used as altarpieces all over Europe. Among the smaller works of this genre are *The School*, which is touchingly realistic and dates from the early 16th century.

Upstairs there are some fine Flemish and south German woodcarvings. The multi-coloured figure of St John is typical. Two notable altarpieces on display are the intricately carved and painted *Lamentation of Christ* (about 1485) from the Duchy of Clèves, and the Averbode altarpiece, which was made in 1523 in Antwerp, and depicts three scenes including the Last Supper. Not to be missed is a beautiful full-length figure of Mary Magdalene.

STAINED GLASS

Most of the Cluny's glass from the 12th and 13th centuries is French. The oldest examples were originally installed in the Basilique-Cathédrale de St-Denis in 1144. There are also three fragments from the Troyes Cathedral, destroyed by fire, two of which illustrate the life of St Nicholas while the third depicts that of Christ.

Numerous panels came to the Cluny from Sainte-Chapelle (*see pp88–9*), during its mid-19th-century restoration, and were never returned, including five scenes from the story of Samson dating from 1248.

The technique of contrasting coloured glass with surrounding grisaille (grey-and-white panels) developed in the latter half of the 13th century. Four panels from the royal château at Rouen illustrate this.

Stained-glass scenes from Brittany (1400)

The School **woodcarving (English, early 16th century)**

Head of a queen from St-Denis from before 1120

SCULPTURE

The highlight here is the Gallery of the Kings, a display of heads and decapitated figures from Notre-Dame. There is also an very graceful statue of Adam, sculpted in the 1260s.

In the vaulted room opposite are displays of fine Romanesque sculpture retrieved from French churches. Among the earliest are the 12 capitals from the nave of St-Germain-des-Prés, from the early 11th century. Retrieved from the portal of St-Denis is a boldly sculpted head of a queen (c.1140) which, though badly mutilated, is still compelling.

Other Romanesque and early Gothic capitals include six finely sculpted works from Catalonia and four of the museum's most famous statues, early 13th-century apostles made for Sainte-Chapelle.

EVERYDAY OBJECTS

Household goods show another side to medieval life, and this large collection is grouped in a sensitive way to illustrate their use – from wallhangings and caskets to kitchenware and clothing. Children's toys bring a very human aspect to the display, while travel cases and religious emblems evoke journies of exploration and pilgrimage.

PRECIOUS METALWORK

The museum has a fine collection of jewellery, coins, metal and enamelwork from Gallic times to the Middle Ages. The showcase of Gallic jewellery includes gold torques, bracelets and rings, all of a simple design. In between these is one of the Cluny's most precious exhibits, the Golden Rose, a delicately wrought piece commissioned by Pope John XXII in 1330 and the oldest known of its kind.

The earliest enamelwork on display is the late Roman and Byzantine *cloisonné* pieces, culminating in the remarkable Limoges enamels, which flourished in the late 12th century. There are also two exceptional altarpieces, the Golden Altar of Basel and the Stavelot altarpiece.

Cross from Italy (late 15th century)

LADY WITH THE UNICORN TAPESTRIES

This series of six tapestries was woven in the late 15th century in the southern Netherlands. It is valued for its fresh harmonious colours and the poetic elegance of the central figure. Allegories of the senses are illustrated in the first five: sight (gazing into a mirror), hearing (playing a portable organ), taste (sampling sweets), smell (sniffing carnations) and touch (the lady holding the unicorn's horn).

The Pillar of the Nautes

GALLO-ROMAN RUINS

One of the main reasons for visiting the Musée National du Moyen Age is to see the scale and layout of its earliest function, the Gallo-Roman baths. The vaulted *frigidarium* (cold bath room) was the largest of its kind in France. Here there is another of the museum's highlights, the restored Pillar of the Nautes (boatmen), unearthed during excavations beneath Notre-Dame in 1711. Composed of five carved stone blocks representing Gallic and Roman divinities, its crowning element is presumed to depict the Seine's boatmen. There are also the ruins of the *caldarium* and *tepidarium* (hot and tepid baths), and visitors can tour the underground vaults.

Unicorn on the sixth tapestry

The enigmatic sixth tapestry (showing jewels being placed in a box) includes the words "to my only desire" and is now thought to represent the principle of free choice.

Panthéon ⑪

When Louis XV recovered from desperate illness in 1744, he was so grateful to be alive that he conceived a magnificent church to honour Sainte Geneviève. The design was entrusted to the French architect Jacques-Germain Soufflot, who planned the church in Neo-Classical style. Work began in 1764 and was completed in 1790, ten years after Soufflot's death, under the control of Guillaume Rondelet. But with the Revolution underway the church was soon turned into a pantheon – a location for the tombs of France's good and great. Napoleon returned it to the Church in 1806, but it was secularized and then desecularized once more before finally being made a civic building in 1885.

The Facade
Inspired by the Rome Pantheon, the temple portico has 22 Corinthian columns.

The arches of the dome show a renewed interest in the lightness of Gothic architecture and were designed by Rondelet. They link four pillars supporting the dome, which weighs 10,000 tonnes and is 83 m (272 ft) high.

Pediment Relief
David d'Angers' pediment bas-relief depicts the mother country (France) granting laurels to her great men.

The Panthéon Interior
The interior has four aisles arranged in the shape of a Greek cross, from the centre of which the great dome rises.

Entrance

STAR FEATURES

* ★ Iron-Framed Dome

* ★ Frescoes of Sainte Geneviève

* ★ Crypt

★ Frescoes of Sainte Geneviève
Murals along the south wall of the nave depict the life of Sainte Geneviève. They are by Pierre Puvis de Chavannes, the 19th-century fresco painter.

The dome lantern
allows only a little light
to filter into the church's
centre. Intense light was
thought inappropriate
for the place where
France's heroes rested.

VISITORS' CHECKLIST

Pl du Panthéon. **Map** 17 A1.
Tel 01 44 32 18 00. Ⓜ Jussieu,
Cardinal-Lemoine. 🚌 84 to
Panthéon; 21, 27, 38, 82, 84, 85,
89 to Gare du Luxembourg.
🚆 Luxembourg. 🅿 Pl E Rostand.
⏲ Apr–Sep: 10am–6.30pm
daily; Oct–Mar: 10am–6pm daily
(last adm 45 mins before). ⬤
1 Jan, 1 May, 25 Dec. 🎫 📷 ✏

★ Iron-Framed Dome
*The tall dome, with its stone
cupolas and three layers of
shells, was inspired by St
Paul's in London and the
Dôme Church (see pp188–9).*

The dome galleries afford a
magnificent panoramic view
of France's capital.

Colonnade
*The colonnade encircling the
dome is both decorative
and part of an
ingenious supporting
system.*

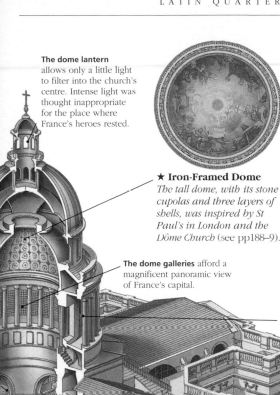

Monument to Diderot
*This is Alphonse Terroir's
statue (1925) to the political
writer Denis Diderot.*

★ Crypt
*Covering the entire area under
the building, the crypt divides
into galleries flanked by Doric
columns. Many French notables
rest here.*

THE PANTHEON'S ENSHRINED

The first of France's great men to be
entombed was the popular orator
Honoré Mirabeau. (Later, under the
revolutionary leadership of Maximilien
Robespierre, he fell from grace and his
body was removed.) Voltaire followed.
A statue of Voltaire by Jean Antoine
Houdon stands in front of his tomb. In
the 1970s the remains of the wartime
Resistance leader Jean Moulin were
reburied here. Pierre and Marie Curie's
remains were transferred here in 1995,
followed by Alexandre Dumas in 2002.
Others here include Jean-Jacques
Rousseau, Victor Hugo and Emile Zola.

JARDIN DES PLANTES QUARTER

This area, traditionally, has been one of the most tranquil corners of Paris. It takes its character from the 17th-century botanical gardens where the kings of the *ancien régime* grew medicinal herbs and where the National Natural History Institute stands today. The many hospitals in the area, notably Paris's largest, Pitié-Salpêtrière, add to the atmosphere. A market takes over the lower part of Rue Mouffetard every day, and the streets off Mouffetard are redolent of life in medieval times.

SIGHTS AT A GLANCE

Museums and Galleries
Musée de la Sculpture en Plein Air ❷
Collection des Minéraux de l'Université ❹
Muséum National d'Histoire Naturelle ❿
La Manufacture des Gobelins ⓭

Modern Architecture
Institut du Monde Arabe ❶

Churches and Temples
St-Médard ❽
Mosquée de Paris ❾

Squares, Parks and Gardens
Ménagerie ❸
Place de la Contrescarpe ❻
Jardin des Plantes ⓫

Historic Buildings and Streets
Arènes de Lutèce ❺
Rue Mouffetard ❼
Groupe Hospitalier Pitié-Salpêtrière ⓬

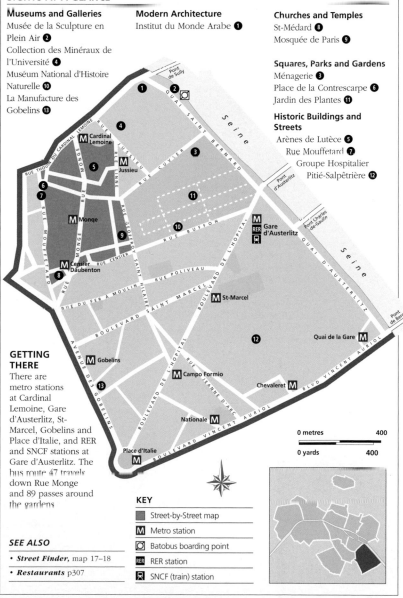

GETTING THERE
There are metro stations at Cardinal Lemoine, Gare d'Austerlitz, St-Marcel, Gobelins and Place d'Italie, and RER and SNCF stations at Gare d'Austerlitz. The bus route 47 travels down Rue Monge and 89 passes around the gardens

SEE ALSO

KEY
▇ Street-by-Street map
Ⓜ Metro station
Ⓞ Batobus boarding point
RER RER station
🚉 SNCF (train) station

◁ **Picturesque Rue Mouffetard, one of Paris's oldest neighbourhoods**

Street-by-Street: Jardin des Plantes Quarter

Two physicians to Louis XIII, Jean Hérouard and Guy de la Brosse, obtained permission to establish the royal medicinal herb garden in the sparsely populated St-Victor suburb in 1626. The herb garden and gardens of various religious houses gave the region a rural character. In the 19th century the population and thus the area expanded and it became more built up, until it gradually assumed the character it has today: a well-to-do residential patchwork of 19th- and early 20th-century buildings interspersed with much older and some more recent buildings.

Metro Cardinal Lemoine

Place de la Contrescarpe
This village-like square filled with restaurants and cafés buzzes with student life after dusk **6**

★ Rue Mouffetard
Locals flock to the daily open-air market here which is one of the oldest Paris street markets. A hoard of louis d'or *gold coins from the 18th century was found at No. 53 during its demolition in 1938* **7**

Pot de Fer fountain is one of 14 that Marie de Médicis had built on the Left Bank in 1624 as a source of water for her palace in the Jardin du Luxembourg. The fountain was rebuilt in 1671.

Metro Monge

Passage des Postes is an ancient alley which was opened in 1830. Its entrance is in the Rue Mouffetard.

St-Médard
This church was started in the mid-15th century and completed by 1655. In 1784 the choir was made Classical in style, and the nave's 16th-century windows were replaced with contemporary stained glass **8**

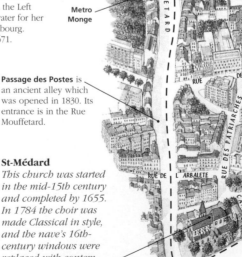

★ **Arènes de Lutèce**
The Roman amphitheatre of Lutetia was used for burials in the 4th century ❺

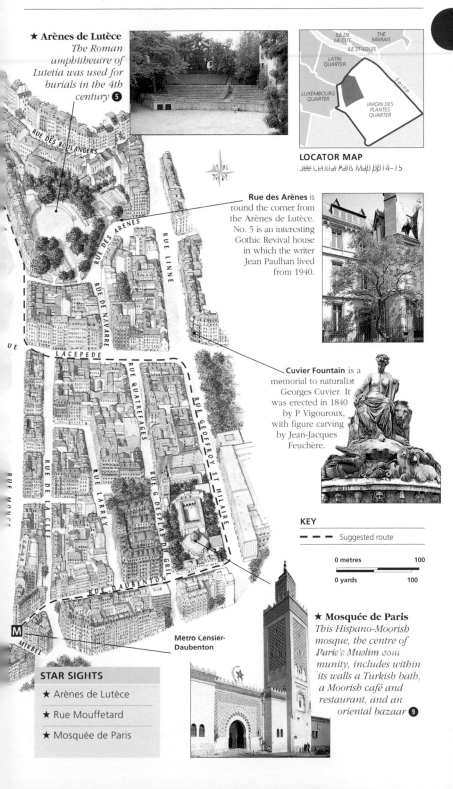

LOCATOR MAP
See Central Paris Map pp14–15

Rue des Arènes is round the corner from the Arènes de Lutèce. No. 5 is an interesting Gothic Revival house in which the writer Jean Paulhan lived from 1940.

Cuvier Fountain is a memorial to naturalist Georges Cuvier. It was erected in 1840 by P Vigouroux, with figure carving by Jean-Jacques Feuchère.

KEY

— — — Suggested route

0 metres	100
0 yards	100

Metro Censier-Daubenton

★ **Mosquée de Paris**
This Hispano-Moorish mosque, the centre of Paris's Muslim community, includes within its walls a Turkish bath, a Moorish café and restaurant, and an oriental bazaar ❾

STAR SIGHTS

★ Arènes de Lutèce

★ Rue Mouffetard

★ Mosquée de Paris

Institut du Monde Arabe ❶

1 Rue des Fossées St-Bernard 75005.
Map 13 C5. **Tel** 01 40 51 38 38.
Ⓜ Jussieu, Cardinal-Lemoine. ◯
Museum & temp exhibs: 10am–
6pm Tue–Sun. **Library:** 1–8pm
Tue–Sat. ◯ public hols. 🏷 ♿ 🎫
Lectures. 🍴 🖥 www.imarabe.org

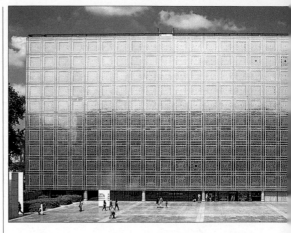

This cultural institute was founded in 1980 by France and 20 Arab countries with the intention of fostering cultural links between the Islamic world and the West. It is housed in a magnificent modern building designed by the French architect Jean Nouvel (also responsible for the musée du quai Branly, *see p192–3*), that combines modern materials with the spirit of traditional Arab architecture. The white marble book tower, which can be seen through the glass of the west wall, spirals upwards bringing to mind the minaret of a mosque. The emphasis that is traditionally placed on interior space in Arab architecture has been used here to create an enclosed courtyard reached by a narrow gap splitting the building in two.

From floors four to seven, there is a fascinating display of Islamic works of art from the 9th to the 19th centuries, including glassware, ceramics, sculpture, carpets and astrolabes. There is also a library and media archive.

Musée de la Sculpture en Plein Air ❷

75004/75005. **Map** 13 C5. Ⓜ
Gare d'Austerlitz, Sully-Morland.

Butting up to the left hand corner of the Institut du Monde Arabe, the Pont de Sully links the Ile St Louis with both banks of the Seine. Opened in 1877 and built of cast iron, the Pont de Sully is not an especially beautiful structure. Despite this, it is well worth pausing for a moment on the bridge for a fabulous view of Notre-Dame rising dramatically behind the wonderfully graceful Pont de la Tournelle.

Running along the river from the Pont de Sully as far as the Pont d'Austerlitz is the peaceful Quai St-Bernard. Not always so sedate, Quai St-Bernard was famous during the 17th century as a spot for nude bathing, until scandalized public opinion made it illegal. The grassy slopes adjoining the quai make a perfect spot to enjoy a picnic. Opened in 1975, they are known as the Jardin Tino Rossi in honour of the celebrated Corsican singer. The garden has a display of open-air sculpture known as the Musée de la Sculpture en Plein Air. Vandalism and other problems have unfortunately necessitated the removal of some of the exhibits.

Ménagerie ❸

57 Rue Cuvier 75005. **Map** 17 C1.
Tel 01 40 79 37 94. Ⓜ Jussieu,
Austerlitz. ◯ 9am–5.30pm daily (last
adm 30 mins before). 🏷 🍴 🖥
www.mnhn.fr

France's oldest public zoo is situated in the lovely surroundings of the Jardin des Plantes. It was set up during the Revolution to house survivors from the Royal menagerie at Versailles – all four of them. The state then rounded up animals from circuses and exotic creatures were sent from abroad. Unfortunately, during the Prussian siege of Paris (1870–71), most of them were slaughtered to feed the hungry citizens (*see p226*). Today the zoo specializes in small mammals, insects, birds, primates and reptiles.

It is a great favourite with children as it allows them to get quite close to the animals, either in the petting enclosure, or during feeding times. The lion house contains panthers from China and other attractions include a large monkey house, a waterfowl aviary, and wild sheep and goats.

The displays in the vivarium (enclosures of live animals in natural habitat) are changed at regular intervals and there is a permanent exhibition of micro-arthropods (also known as creepy-crawlies!).

Child playing at the zoo

Light Screens

The south elevation is made up of 1,600 high-tech metal screens which filter the light entering the building. Their design is based on moucharabiyahs (*carved wooden screens found on the outsides of buildings from Morocco to Southeast Asia*).

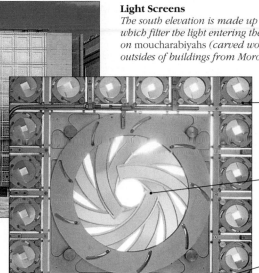

Each screen contains 21 irises which are controlled electronically, opening and closing in response to the amount of sunlight falling on photosensitive screens.

The central iris is made up of interlocking metal blades which move to adjust the size of the central opening.

The peripheral irises are linked to one another and to the central iris. They open and close in unison forming a delicate pattern of light and shade inside the institute.

Collection des Minéraux de l'Université **4**

Paris VI-Jussieu, 4 Pl Jussieu 75005. **Map** 17 B1. **Tel** 01 44 27 52 88.
Ⓜ Jussieu. ◯ 1pm–6pm Wed–Mon. ● 1 Jan, Easter, 1 May, 14 Jul, 1 Nov, 25 Dec. ⍁ 🔌 📷 🎧 groups Tue pm. ⅙

This fascinating small museum is housed in the main university building, named after the distinguished scientists. The collection comprises cut and uncut gemstones and rock crystal from all over the world, shown to maximum advantage through the clever use of specialized lighting.

Topaz

Arènes de Lutèce **5**

Rue de Navarre 75005. **Map** 17 B1.
Ⓜ Jussieu. See p21.

The remains of this vast Roman arena (Lutetia was the Roman name for Paris) date from the late 1st century. Its destruction began towards the end of the 3rd century at the hands of the Barbarians, and later, parts of it were used to build the walls of the Ile de la Cité. The arena was then gradually buried and its exact location preserved only in old documents and the local name Clos des Arènes. It was rediscovered in 1869 during the construction of the Rue Monge and the allocation of building plots nearby.

Action towards its restoration began with the campaigning of Victor Hugo (among others) in the 19th century but work did not get really underway until 1918.

With a seating capacity of 15,000, arranged in 35 tiers, the original arena was used both for theatrical performances and as an amphitheatre for the more gruesome spectacle of gladiator fights. This type of combined use was peculiar to Gaul (France), and the arena is similar to the other French ones in Nîmes and Arles.

The public park at the Arènes de Lutèce

BUFFON AND THE JARDIN DES PLANTES

At the age of 32 Georges Louis Leclerc, Comte de Buffon (1707–88), became the curator of the Jardin des Plantes at a time when the study of natural history was at the forefront of contemporary thought – Charles Darwin's *The Origin of Species* was to be published 120 years later. Buffon masterminded the reorganization of the Jardin, propelling it to a pre-eminent position within the scientific world. He was elected to the Académie Française in 1752 following the publication of his two main works, *Natural History* and *The Epoques of Nature*. He died in his house in the Jardin.

Illustration of a primate from Buffon's *Natural History*

Place de la Contrescarpe ⑥

75005. **Map** 17 A1. Ⓜ *Place Monge.*

At one time this site lay outside the city walls. It gets its name from the backfilling of the moat that ran along Philippe-Auguste's wall. The present square was laid out in 1852. At No. 1 there is a memorial plaque to the old "pine-cone club" immortalized in the writings of Rabelais; here a group of writers known as *La Pléiade* (named after the constellation of The Pleiades) used to meet in the 16th century.

The area has always been used for meetings and festivals. Today it is extremely lively at weekends, and on Bastille Day *(see p65)* a delightful ball is held here.

Part of the medieval city wall

Rue Mouffetard ⑦

75005. **Map** 17 B2. Ⓜ *Censier-Daubenton, Place Monge.* ⃝ **Market** *Place Maubert: 7am–2.30pm Tue, Thu, Sat (to 3pm Sat); Place Monge: 7am–2.30pm Wed, Fri, Sun (to 3pm Sun).* See **Shops and Markets** *p339.*

A major thoroughfare since Roman times, when it linked Lutetia (Paris) and Rome, this street is one of the oldest in the city. In the 17th and 18th centuries it was known as the Grande Rue du Faubourg St-Marcel, and many of its buildings date from that time. Some of the small shops still have ancient painted signs, and some houses have mansard roofs. No. 125 has an attractive, restored Louis XIII facade, and the entire front of No. 134 has beautiful decoration of wild beasts, flowers and plants. At No. 60, the *Fontaine de Pot-de-Fer* is a small fountain dating from Roman times. Later on it was connected to an aqueduct used by Marie de Médicis to take water to the Palais du Luxembourg and its gardens.

The area is known for its open-air markets, especially those in Place Maubert, Place Monge, and Rue Daubenton, a side street where a lively African market takes place.

At night, the street bustles with people enjoying Greek, Italian, Argentinian and other cuisines on offer at the many small restaurants.

St-Médard ⑧

141 Rue Mouffetard 75005. **Map** 17 B2. **Tel** 01 44 08 87 00. Ⓜ *Censier-Daubenton.* ⃝ *8am–12.30pm, 2.30–7.30pm Tue–Sat; 8.30am–12.30pm, 4–8pm Sun.* 📷 ♿

The origins of this charming church go back to the 9th century. St Médard, counsellor to the Merovingian kings, was known for giving a wreath of white roses to young girls noted for their virtue. The churchyard became notorious in the 18th century as the centre of the cult of the Convulsionnaires, whose hysterical fits were brought on by the contemplation of miracle cures. The interior has many fine paintings, including the 17th-century *St Joseph Walking with the Christ Child* by Francisco de Zurbarán.

Decoration inside the mosque

Mosquée de Paris ⑨

2 bis Pl du Puits de l'Ermite 75005. **Map** 17 C2. **Tel** 01 45 35 97 33; 01 43 31 38 20 (tearoom, Turkish baths). Ⓜ *Place Monge.* ⃝ *9am–noon, 2pm–6pm Sat–Thu.* 📷 *Muslim hols.* 📷 🔟 📖 📷 **Library.** www.mosquee-de-paris.org. **Café & baths** www.la-mosquee.com

Built in the 1920s in the Hispano-Moorish style, this group of buildings is the spiritual centre for Paris's Muslim community and the home of the Grand Imam. The complex comprises religious, educational and commercial sections; at its heart is a mosque. Each of the mosque's domes is decorated differently, and the minaret stands nearly 33 m (100 ft) high. Inside is a grand patio with mosaics on the walls and tracery on the arches.

Once used only by scholars, the mosque's place in Parisian life has grown over the years. The Turkish baths can be enjoyed by both men and women, but on different days. A tearoom and restaurant serve Moorish specialities.

Muséum National d'Histoire Naturelle ⑩

2 Rue Buffon 75005. **Map** 17 C2. **Tel** 01 40 79 54 79. Ⓜ *Jussieu, Austerlitz.* ◯ *10am–6pm Wed–Mon.* ◉ *1 May.* ◩ ⑤ *restricted.* ▣ 🅸 **Library.** www.mnhn.fr

Skull of the reptile dimetrodon

The highlight of the museum is the Grande Galerie de l'Evolution. There are also four other departments: palaeontology, featuring skeletons, casts of various animals and an exhibition showing the evolution of the vertebrate skeleton; palaeo-botany, devoted to plant fossils; mineralogy, including gemstones; and entomology, with some of the oldest fossilized insects on earth. The bookshop is in the house that was occupied by the naturalist Buffon, from 1772 until his death in 1788.

Jardin des Plantes ⑪

57 Rue Cuvier 75005. **Map** 17 C1. **Tel** 01 40 79 56 01. Ⓜ *Jussieu, Austerlitz.* ◯ *8am–6.45pm (to 5.30pm winter) daily.*

The botanical gardens were established in 1626, when Jean Hérouard and Guy de la Brosse, Louis XIII's physicians,

obtained permission to found a royal medicinal herb garden here and then a school of botany, natural history and pharmacy. The garden was opened to the public in 1640 and flourished under Buffon's direction. Now one of Paris's great parks, it includes a natural history museum, botanical school and zoo.

As well as beautiful vistas and walkways flanked by ancient trees and punctuated with statues, the park has a remarkable alpine garden with plants from Corsica, Morocco, the Alps and the Himalayas and an unrivalled display of herbaceous and wild plants. It also has the first Cedar of Lebanon to be planted in France, originally from Britain's Kew Gardens.

Groupe Hospitalier Pitié-Salpêtrière ⑫

47 Blvd de l'Hôpital 75013. **Map** 18 D3. Ⓜ *St-Marcel, Austerlitz.* Ⓡ *Gare d'Austerlitz.* ◯ **Chapel** *8.30am– 6.30pm daily.* ✝ *3.30pm daily.* ◉ ⑤

The vast Salpêtrière Hospital stands on the site of an old gunpowder factory and derives its name from the saltpetre used in the making of explosives. It was founded by Louis XIV in 1656 to help sick or socially-disadvantaged women and children and later became renowned for its pioneering humane treatment of the insane. It was here that Princess Diana died in 1997, following an automobile accident in a Paris underpass.

The Cedar of Lebanon in the Jardin

Outside the Hôpital Salpêtrière

La Manufacture des Gobelins ⑬

42 Ave des Gobelins 75013. **Map** 17 B3. **Tel** 01 44 08 53 49. Ⓜ *Gobelins.* ◯ *11am–6pm Tue– Sun. Groups by appt.* ◩ ◉ *1 Jan, 1 May, 25 Dec.* **www. mobiliernational.culture.gouv.fr**

Versailles tapestry by Le Brun

Originally a dyeing workshop set up in about 1440 by the Gobelin brothers, the building became a tapestry factory early in the 17th century. Louis XIV took it over in 1662 and gathered together the greatest craftsmen of the day – carpet weavers, cabinet makers and silversmiths – to furnish his new palace at Versailles (*see pp248–53*). Working under the direction of court painter Charles Le Brun, 250 Flemish weavers laid the foundations for the factory's international reputation. Today weavers continue to work in the traditional way but with modern designs, including those of Picasso and Matisse.

LUXEMBOURG QUARTER

Many a Parisian dreams of living in the vicinity of the Luxembourg Gardens, a quieter, greener and somehow more reflective place than its neighbouring areas. Luxembourg is one of the most captivating places in the capital. Its charm is in its old gateways and streets, its bookshops, and in the sumptuous yet intimate gardens. Though spirits of the eminence of Paul Verlaine and André Gide no longer stroll in its groves, the paths, lawns and avenues are still full of charm, drawing to them the numerous students from the nearby *grandes écoles* and *lycées*. And on

warm days old men meet under the chestnut trees to play chess or the traditional game of *boules*.

To the west the buildings are public and official, and on the east the houses are shaded by the tall chestnut trees of the Boulevard St-Michel.

Sailing boats are hired by children and adults to sail in the *grand bassin* (ornamental pond) in the Luxembourg Gardens.

SIGHTS AT A GLANCE

Museums
Musée du Luxembourg **8**
Ecole Nationale Supérieure des Mines **11**

Historic Buildings
Palais du Luxembourg **3**
Institut Catholique de Paris **6**

Churches
St-Sulpice **2**
St-Joseph-des-Carmes **7**
Val-de-Grâce **10**

Squares and Gardens
Place St-Sulpice **1**
Jardin du Luxembourg **5**

Fountains
Fontaine Médicis **4**
Fontaine de l'Observatoire **9**

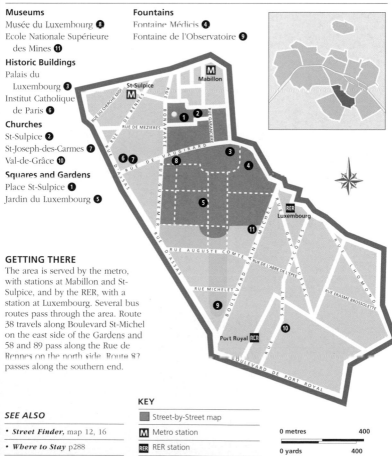

GETTING THERE

The area is served by the metro, with stations at Mabillon and St-Sulpice, and by the RER, with a station at Luxembourg. Several bus routes pass through the area. Route 38 travels along Boulevard St-Michel on the east side of the Gardens and 58 and 89 pass along the Rue de Rennes on the north side. Route 82 passes along the southern end.

SEE ALSO

• **Street Finder,** map 12, 16

• **Where to Stay** p288

KEY

▦	Street-by-Street map
M	Metro station
RER	RER station

0 metres 400
0 yards   400

◁ Playing chess in the Jardin du Luxembourg

Street-by-Street: Luxembourg Quarter

Situated only a few steps
from the bustle of St-
Germain-des-Prés, this
graceful and historic area
offers a peaceful haven in
the heart of a modern city.
The Jardin du Luxembourg
and Palais du Luxembourg
dominate the vicinity. The
gardens became fully open
to the public in the 19th
century under the ownership of the
Comte de Provence (later Louis XVIII),
when for a small fee visitors could come
in and feast on fruit from the orchard.
Today the gardens, palace and old
houses on the streets to the north remain
unspoilt and attract many visitors.

★ St-Sulpice
*This Classical church was built
over 134 years to Daniel Gittard's
plans. It has a facade by the Italian
architect Giovanni Servandoni* ❷

To St-Germain-des-Prés

Place St-Sulpice
*The Fontaine des
Quatre Points
Cardinaux depicts
four church leaders
at the cardinal points
of the compass.* Point
*also means "never":
the leaders were
never made
cardinals* ❶

The Monument to Delacroix
(1890) by Jules Dalou is
situated near the private
gardens of the French
Senate. Beneath
the bust of the
leading Romantic
painter Eugène
Delacroix are the
allegorical figures of
Art, Time and Glory.

STAR SIGHTS

★ St-Sulpice

★ Jardin du
  Luxembourg

★ Palais du
  Luxembourg

★ Fontaine de
  Médicis

★ Jardin du Luxembourg
*Many fine statues were erected
in the Luxembourg gardens in
the 19th century during the reign
of Louis-Philippe* ❺

The Rue de Tournon is full of elegant architecture, boutiques and old bookshops. At No. 12 is the Grand Hôtel d'Entragues, reconstructed by Neveu in the 18th century during Louis XVI's reign.

LOCATOR MAP
See Central Paris Map pp14–15

KEY

– – – Suggested route

0 metres   100
0 yards   100

★ **Palais du Luxembourg**
In 1794, during the Revolution, the painter Jacques-Louis David was imprisoned here and made sketches for the Intervention of the Sabine Women ❸

★ **Fontaine Médicis**
The 17th-century fountain is in the style of an Italian grotto and is thought to have been designed by Salomon de Brosse ❹

Sainte Geneviève, the patron saint of Paris, was a wealthy 5th-century Gallo-Roman land-owner. When Paris was invaded by the Huns in AD 451, she prayed with women friends that the city would be spared – their prayers were answered. This statue by Michel-Louis Victor (1845) pays homage to her.

The Octagonal Lake (Grand Bassin), attributed to Jean-François Chalgrin, is surrounded by formal terraces where visitors to the gardens often sunbathe.

Place St-Sulpice

75006. **Map** 12 E4. **M** *St-Sulpice.*

This large square, which is dominated on the east side by the enormous church from which it takes its name, was built in the last half of the 18th century.

Two main features of the square are the Fountain of the Four Bishops by Joachim Visconti (1844) and the pink-flowering chestnut trees. There is also the Café de la Mairie, a rendezvous of writers and students, which is often featured in French films.

Stained-glass window of St-Sulpice

St-Sulpice

Pl St-Sulpice 75006. **Map** 12 E5. *Tel 01 42 34 59 98.* **M** *St-Sulpice.* ☐ *7.30am–7.30pm daily.* ☐ *daily.* ☐

It took more than a century, from 1646, for this huge and imposing church to be built. The result is a simple two-storey west front with two tiers of elegant columns. The overall harmony of the building is marred only by the towers, one at each end, which do not match.

Large arched windows fill the vast interior with light. By the front door are two huge shells given to François I by the Venetian Republic – they rest on rock-like bases sculpted by Jean-Baptiste Pigalle.

In the side chapel to the right of the main door are three magnificent murals by Eugène Delacroix: *Jacob Wrestling with the Angel (see p137), Heliodorus Driven from the Temple* and *St-Michael Killing the Dragon*. If you are lucky you can catch an organ recital.

Palais du Luxembourg

15 Rue de Vaugirard 75006. **Map** 12 E5. *Tel 01 42 34 20 60 (groups); 01 44 54 19 49 (individuals).* **M** *Odéon.* **RER** *Luxembourg.* ☐ *one Sat each mth.* ☑ www.senat.fr

Now the home of the French Senate, this palace was designed by Salomon de Brosse in the style of Florence's Pitti Palace to remind Marie de Médicis, widow of Henri IV, of her native town. By the time it was finished (1631), Marie had been banished, but it remained a royal palace until the Revolution, when it temporarily served as a prison. In World War II it was the headquarters of the Luftwaffe, with air-raid shelters built under its gardens. The Musée du Luxembourg, in the east gallery, hosts renowned art exhibitions *(see p173)*.

Figures on the Fontaine Médicis

Fontaine Médicis

15 Rue de Vaugirard 75006. **Map** 12 F5. **RER** *Luxembourg.*

Built in 1624 for Marie de Médicis by an unknown architect, this vigorous Baroque fountain stands at the end of a long pond filled with goldfish and shaded by trees. The mythological figures were added much later by Auguste Ottin (1866).

Jardin du Luxembourg

Blvd St-Michel 75006. **Map** 12 E5. *Tel 01 42 34 23 89.* **RER** *Luxembourg.* ☐ *dawn–dusk daily.* ☐

A green oasis covering 25 ha (60 acres) in the heart of the Left Bank, this is the most popular park in the whole of Paris. The layout of the gardens is centred around the Luxembourg Palace and is dominated by a splendid octagonal pool – usually full of toy sailing boats.

Apart from the aesthetic attraction of its formal terraces and broad avenues, statues of various queens of France are also dotted throughout the park, as well as an impressive figure of Saint Genevieve, the patron of Paris, and, by way of contrast, a Cyclops.

The park also includes an open-air café, a puppet theatre, a large children's play area, numerous tennis courts, a bandstand and a bee-keeping school.

Sculptures on Palais du Luxembourg

Institut Catholique de Paris ⑥

21 Rue d'Assas 75006. **Map** 12 D5.
Tel 01 44 39 52 00. Ⓜ St-Placide,
Rennes. **Musée Bible et Terre
Sainte** ⬜ 4–6pm Sat during term
time or by appt. ⬤ Jul–Sep.
Tel 01 45 44 09 55. **www**.icp.fr

Founded in 1875, this is one of
the most distinguished teaching
institutions in France with
some 23,000 students. It
also houses a small
museum: the Musée
Bible et Terre Sainte
which displays objects
excavated in the
Holy Land. They
give an interesting
insight into daily
life in Palestine
throughout
the ages.

**Courtyard statue at
the Institut Catholique**

St-Joseph-des-Carmes ⑦

70 Rue de Vaugirard 75006.
Map 12 D5. **Tel** 01 45 44 89 77.
Ⓜ St-Placide. ⬜ 7am–7pm Mon–
Sat; 9am–7pm Sun. ⬤ Easter Mon,
Pentecost. ♿ restricted. 🎧 3pm Sat.
www.sjdc.fr

Completed in 1620, this
church was built as the
chapel for a Carmelite convent but was used as a prison
during the Revolution. In
1792 more than a hundred
priests met a grisly end in the
church's courtyard as part of
the September Massacres
(see pp30–31). Their remains
are now in the crypt.

Facade of St-Joseph-des-Carmes

Carpeaux's fountain sculpture

Musée du Luxembourg ⑧

19 Rue de Vaugirard 75006.
Map 12 E5. **Tel** 01 40 13 62 00.
Ⓜ St-Sulpice. 🚉 Luxembourg.
⬜ 10am–8pm daily (until 10pm Fri &
Sat). ♿ 🎧 📷 📷
www.museeduluxembourg.fr

In 1615, under the orders of
Marie de Médicis, architect
Salomon de Brosse built the
Palais du Luxembourg. The
two adjoining galleries were
designed to hang the Queen's
collection of paintings by
Rubens. In 1750, the east
wing became France's first
public gallery, housing works
by artists such as Leonardo da
Vinci, Rembrandt and Van
Dyck. Today it hosts impressive temporary exhibitions as
directed by the French Ministry
of Culture and the Senate.

Fontaine de l'Observatoire ⑨

Pl Ernest Denis, Ave de l'Observatoire.
Map 16 E2. 🚉 Port Royal.

Situated at the southern tip of
the Jardin du Luxembourg,
this is one of the liveliest
fountains in Paris. Made of
bronze, it has four women
holding aloft a globe

representing four continents –
the fifth, Oceania, was left out
for reasons of symmetry.
There are some subsidiary
figures, including dolphins,
horses and a turtle. The
sculpture was erected in 1873
by Jean-Baptiste Carpeaux.

Val-de-Grâce ⑩

1 Pl Alphonse-Laveran 75005.
Map 16 F2. **Tel** 01 40 51 51 92.
Ⓜ Gobelins. 🚉 Port Royal.
⬜ noon–6pm Tue, Wed, Sat & Sun.
🎧 (except for nave). ♿ frequent,
pm. 🎧 by appt. **Museum** ⬜ as
church. **www**.valdegrace.org

One of the most beautiful
churches in France, Val-de-
Grâce was built for Anne of
Austria (wife of Louis XIII) in
thanks for the birth of her son.
Young Louis XIV laid the first
stone in 1645. François Mansart
is the great architect behind it.
    The church is noted for its
beautiful imposing lead-and-
gilt dome, which stands at an
impressive 41 m (135 ft). In the
cupola is Pierre Mignard's
enormous fresco, with over
200 triple-life-size figures.
    The six huge marble columns
that frame the altar are similar
to those at St Peter's in Rome.
    Henrietta of France (wife of
Charles I) is buried at this
site, along with 26 members
of the French royal family.
    Today the church is part of
a military hospital complex,
which also houses a museum
of military medicine.

Ecole Nationale Supérieure des Mines ⑪

60 Blvd St-Michel. **Map** 16 F1.
Tel 01 40 51 91 39. 🚉 Luxembourg.
⬜ 1.30–6pm Tue–Fri; 10am–
12.30pm, 2–5pm Sat. 🎧 📷 🎧

Louis XIV set up the School
of Mines in 1783 to train
mining engineers. Today, it is
one of the most prestigious
grandes écoles – schools that
provide the élite for the civil
service and professions. It
also houses the national
collection of minerals – the
Musée de Minéralogie.

MONTPARNASSE

In the first three decades of the 20th century, Montparnasse was a thriving artistic and literary centre. Many modern painters and sculptors, new novelists and poets, the great and the young were drawn to this area. Its ateliers, conviviality and renowned Bohemian lifestyle made it a magnet for genius, some of it French, much of it foreign. The great epoch ended with World War II, and change continued with the destruction of many ateliers and the construction of the soaring Tour Montparnasse, Paris's tallest office tower, which heralded the more modern *quartier*. But the area has not lost its appeal. The great cafés remain and attract a lively international crowd. Small café-theatres have opened and the area springs to life at the weekends with cinema crowds.

Monument to Charles Augustin Ste-Beauve in the Cimetière du Montparnasse

SIGHTS AT A GLANCE

Historic Buildings and Streets
Rue Campagne-Première ❸
Catacombes ❿
Observatoire de Paris ⓫

Cafés and Restaurants
La Coupole ❶
La Closerie des Lilas ⓬

Museums and Galleries
Musée Zadkine ❷
Musée Antoine Bourdelle ❻
Musée de la Poste ❼

Musée du Montparnasse ❽
Fondation Cartier ❾

Modern Architecture
Tour Montparnasse ❺

Cemeteries
Cimetière du Montparnasse pp180–81 ❹

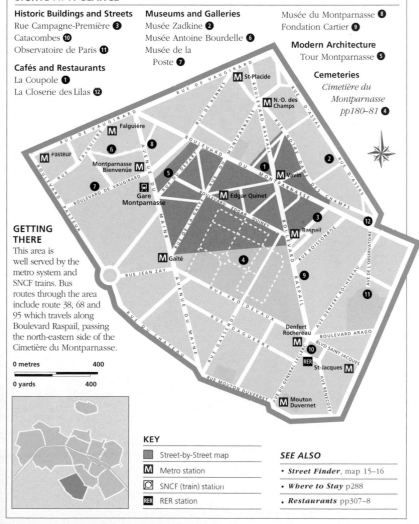

GETTING THERE
This area is well served by the metro system and SNCF trains. Bus routes through the area include route 38, 68 and 95 which travels along Boulevard Raspail, passing the north-eastern side of the Cimetière du Montparnasse.

| 0 metres | 400 |
| 0 yards | 400 |

KEY

▨	Street-by-Street map
Ⓜ	Metro station
▣	SNCF (train) station
RER	RER station

SEE ALSO

• *Street Finder*, map 15–16
• *Where to Stay* p288
• *Restaurants* pp307–8

◁ **View of Tour Montparnasse from the Cimetière du Montparnasse**

Street-by-Street: Montparnasse

Renowned for its mix of art and high
living, Montparnasse continues to live up
to its name: Mount Parnassus was the
mountain dedicated by the ancient
Greeks to Apollo, god of poetry, music
and beauty. That mix was especially
potent in the 1920s and 1930s, when
such artists and writers as Picasso,
Hemingway, Cocteau, Giacometti,
Matisse and Modigliani were to be seen
in the local bars, cafés and cabarets.

★ La Coupole
*This traditional
brasserie-style café,
with its large
enclosed terrace,
opened in 1927 and
became a famous
meeting place for
artists and
writers* ❶

**★ Cimetière du
Montparnasse**
This fine sculpture, The
Separation of a Couple
*by de Max, stands in
the smallest of the city's
major cemeteries* ❹

The Théâtre Montparnasse at
No. 31, with its fully-restored
original 1880s decor.

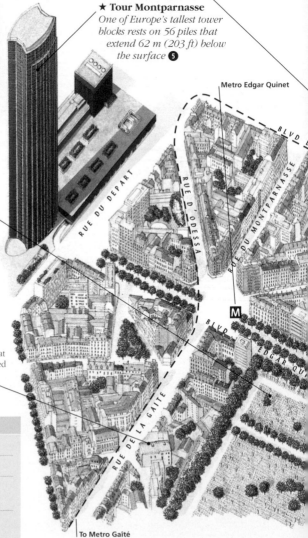

★ Tour Montparnasse
*One of Europe's tallest tower
blocks rests on 56 piles that
extend 62 m (203 ft) below
the surface* ❺

Metro Edgar Quinet

BLVD E

RUE DU DEPART

RUE D'ODESSA

RUE DU MONTPARNASSE

M

BLVD

EDGAR QUI

RUE DE LA GAÎTE

To Metro Gaîté

STAR SIGHTS

★ La Coupole

★ Tour Montparnasse

★ Rue Campagne-
Première

★ Cimetière du
Montparnasse

Académie de la Grande-Chaumière at no. 14 offers tuition in painting and sculpture. Former students of note include Alberto Giacometti and Amedeo Modigliani.

Rue Bréa has a variety of shops, restaurants and hotels, all within 90 m (300 ft).

The statue of Balzac by Auguste Rodin was erected in 1939, and stands 3 m (10 ft) tall.

Metro Vavin

LOCATOR MAP
See Central Paris Map pp14–15

★ **Rue Campagne-Première**
The block of artists' studios at No. 31 was built in 1911, and the facade was decorated by the ceramicist Paul Bigot

3

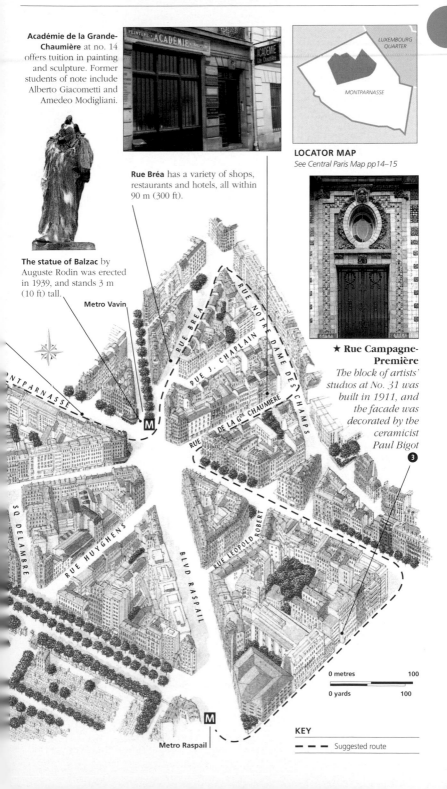

Metro Raspail

0 metres	100
0 yards	100

KEY

– – – Suggested route

The interior of La Coupole

La Coupole ❶

102 Blvd du Montparnasse 75014.
Map 16 D2. **Tel** 01 43 20 14 20. Ⓜ
Vavin, Montparnasse. ⏰ 8.30am–
1am Mon–Thu, 8.30am–1.30am Fri–
Sun. See **Restaurants and Cafés**
p307. **www**.flobrasseries.com

Established in 1927, this historic
café-restaurant and dance hall
underwent a face-lift in the
1980s. Its red velvet seats and
famous columns, decorated by
various artists, have survived.
Among its clientele have been
Jean-Paul Sartre, Josephine
Baker and Roman Polanski.

The museum's **Les Trois Belles**
(1950) by Ossip Zadkine

Musée Zadkine ❷

100 bis Rue d'Assas 75116.
Map 16 E1. **Tel** 01 55 42 77 20.
Ⓜ Notre-Dame-des-Champs.
⏰ 10am–6pm Tue–Sun. ⚫ public
hols. 🅿 ⓞ 🗐 by appt. ♿ limited.
www.zadkine.paris.fr

The Russian-born sculptor
Ossip Zadkine lived here

from 1928 until his death in
1967. The small house, studio
and daffodil-filled garden
contain his works. Here he
produced his great commemorative sculpture, *Ville Détruite*,
commissioned by Rotter-
dam after World War II,
and two monuments to
Vincent Van Gogh, one for
Holland and one for Auvers-
sur-Oise, where Van Gogh
died. The museum's works
span the development of
Zadkine's style, from his Cubist
beginnings to Expressionism
and Abstractionism.

Rue Campagne-Première ❸

75014. **Map** 16 E2. Ⓜ Raspail.

This street has some
interesting Art Deco buildings
and a long artistic tradition.
Modigliani, ravaged by opium
and tuberculosis, lived at No. 3
during his last years. Between
the wars many artists resided
here, including Picasso, Joan
Miró and Kandinsky.

Cimetière du Montparnasse ❹

See pp180–81.

Tour Montparnasse ❺

Pl Raoul Dautry 75014. **Map** 15 C2.
Ⓜ Montparnasse-Bienvenüe. **Tel** 01
45 38 52 56. ⏰ Apr–Sep: 9.30am–
11.30pm daily (last lift 11pm); Oct–
Mar: 9.30am–10.30pm daily (to
11pm Fri & Sat). 🅿 🍴 🗐 🗐
www.tourmontparnasse56.com

This was Europe's largest office
block when it was built
in 1973 as the focal
point of a new
business sector. At
210 m (690 ft) high, it
totally dominates the
area's skyline. The
views from the 59th
floor are spectacular
(up to 40 km on a
clear day). The tower
also boasts Europe's
fastest lift (56 floors in
38 seconds) and a
panoramic restaurant.

The Archer (1909) by Antoine
Bourdelle

Musée Antoine Bourdelle ❻

18 Rue Antoine Bourdelle 75015.
Map 15 B1. **Tel** 01 49 54 73 73.
Ⓜ Montparnasse-Bienvenüe.
⏰ 10am–6pm Tue–Sun.
⚫ public hols. 🅿 ♿ limited.
www.bourdelle.paris.fr

The prolific sculptor, Antoine
Bourdelle, lived and worked
in the studio here from 1884
until his death in 1929. The
house, studio and garden are
now a museum devoted to
his life and work. Among the
900 sculptures on display are
the original plaster casts of
his monumental works
planned for wide public
squares. They are housed in
the Great Hall in an extension
and include the group of
sculptures for the relief
decoration of the Théâtre
des Champs-Elysées.

Musée de la Poste ❼

34 Blvd de Vaugirard 75015.
Map 15 B2. 📧 01 42 79 24 24.
Ⓜ Montparnasse-Bienvenüe. ⏰
10am–6pm Mon–Sat.
⚫ public hols. 🅿 🗐
♿ **Library**. **www**.
museedelaposte.fr

A view of the tower

Every conceivable
aspect of the history
of the French postal
service and methods
of transportation is
covered in this well
laid out collection.
There is even a
room devoted to

mail delivery in times of war – carrier pigeons were used during the Franco-Prussian War with postmarks stamped on their wings. Postage stamp art is displayed in the gallery.

A Miró-designed postage stamp

Musée du Montparnasse ⑧

21 Ave du Maine 75015. **Map** 15 C1. **Tel** 01 42 22 91 96. Ⓜ *Montparnasse-Bienvenüe, Falguière.* ⓄⒼ *12.30–7pm Tue–Sun.* ✉ www. museedumontparnasse.net

During World War I, this was a canteen for needy artists which, by its status as a private club, was not subject to curfew, and so the likes of Picasso, Braque, Modigliani and Léger could eat for 65 centimes and then party until late at night. This symbolic place is now dedicated to temporary art exhibitions, usually of an African theme, and also hosts evenings of music and poetry recitals.

Fondation Cartier ⑨

261 Blvd Raspail 75014. **Map** 16 E3. **Tel** 01 42 18 56 50. Ⓜ *Raspail.* Ⓞ *11am–8pm Tue–Sun (until 10pm Tue).* ● *1 Jan, 25 Dec.* ✉ 🅴 🅲 http://fondation.cartier.com

This foundation for contemporary art is housed in a building designed by architect Jean Nouvel. He has created an air of transparency and light, as well as incorporating a cedar of Lebanon planted in 1823 by François-René de Chateaubriand. The structure complements the nature of the exhibitions of progressive art, which showcase personal, group or thematic displays, often including works by young unknowns.

Catacombes ⑩

1 Ave du Colonel Henri Rol-Tanguy 75014. **Map** 16 E3. **Tel** 01 43 22 47 63. Ⓜ *Denfert-Rochereau.* Ⓞ *10am–5pm Tue–Sun (last adm: 4pm).* ● *public hols.* 🅰 🅾 🅲 www.carnavalet.paris.fr

In 1786 a monumental project began here: the removal of the millions of skulls and bones from the unsanitary city cemetery in Les Halles to the ancient quarries formed by excavations at the base of the three "mountains": Montparnasse, Montrouge and Montsouris. It took 15 months to transport the bones and rotting corpses across the city in huge carts to their new resting place; the transportation was carried out at night.

Just before the Revolution, the Comte d'Artois (later Charles X) threw wild parties in the catacombs, and during World War II the French Resistance set up its headquarters here. Above the door outside are the words "Stop! This is the empire of death."

Observatoire de Paris ⑪

61 Ave de l'Observatoire 75014. **Map** 16 E3. **Tel** 01 45 07 74 78 (2–4pm Mon–Fri) Ⓜ *Denfert-Rochereau.* **Visits** (2 hrs) Tue or Thu 2pm; apply by email: paris@obspm.fr or call 01 40 51 23 97; groups by appt. ● *Aug.* 🅰 🅲 www.obspm.fr

In 1667 Louis XIV was persuaded by his scientists and astronomers that France needed a royal observatory.

Building began on 21 June, the day of summer solstice, and took five years to complete.

Astronomical research undertaken here included the calculation of the exact dimensions of the solar system in 1672, calculations of the dimensions of longitude, the mapping of the moon in 1679 and the discovery of the planet Neptune in 1846.

The facade of the Observatoire

La Closerie des Lilas ⑫

171 Blvd du Montparnasse 75014. **Map** 16 E2. **Tel** 01 40 51 34 50. Ⓜ *Vavin.* 🆁 *Port Royal.* Ⓞ *Bar: 11–2am, brasserie: noon–1am daily.* www.closeriedeslilas.fr

Lenin, Trotsky, Hemingway and Scott Fitzgerald all frequented the Montparnasse bars, but the Closerie was their favourite. Much of Hemingway's novel *The Sun Also Rises* takes place here which he wrote on the terrace in just six weeks. Today the terrace is ringed with trees and the area more elegant, but much of the original decor remains (see pp38–9).

Skulls and bones stored in the catacombs

Cimetière du Montparnasse ❹

The Montparnasse Cemetery was planned by Napoleon outside the city walls to replace the numerous, congested small cemeteries within the old city, viewed as a health hazard at the turn of the 19th century. It was opened in 1824 and became the resting place of many illustrious Parisians, particularly Left Bank personalities. Like all French cemeteries it is divided into rigidly aligned paths forming blocks or divisions. The Rue Emile Richard cuts it into two parts, the Grand Cimetière and the Petit Cimetière.

★ Charles Baudelaire Cenotaph
This is a monument to the great poet and critic (1821–67), author of The Flowers of Evil.

Samuel Beckett, the great Irish playwright renowned for *Waiting for Godot*, spent most of his life in Paris. He died in 1989.

The Pétain tomb contains the family of the marshal who collaborated with the Germans during World War II. Pétain himself is buried on Ile d'Yeu, where he was imprisoned.

Guy de Maupassant was a 19th-century novelist.

Alfred Dreyfus was a Jewish army officer whose unjust trial for treason in 1894 provoked a political and social scandal.

Frédéric Auguste Bartholdi was the sculptor of the Statue of Liberty (1886) in New York.

André Citroën, an engineer and industrialist who died in 1935, founded the famous French car firm.

AVE DU MIDI

AVE THIERRY

RUE EMILE RICHARD

AVE DE L'EST

★ Charles Pigeon Family Tomb
This wonderfully pompous Belle Epoque tomb depicts the French industrialist and inventor in bed with his wife.

Charles-Augustin Sainte-Beuve was a critic of the French Romantic generation, and is generally described as the "father of modern criticism".

STAR FEATURES

- ★ Charles Baudelaire Cenotaph
- ★ Charles Pigeon Family Tomb
- ★ Jean-Paul Sartre and Simone de Beauvoir
- ★ Serge Gainsbourg

The Kiss by Brancusi
This is the famous Primitivo-Cubist sculpture (a response to Rodin's Kiss) by the great Romanian artist, who died in 1957 and is buried just off the Rue Emile Richard.

Camille Saint-Saëns, the pianist, organist and composer who died in 1921, was one of France's great post-Romantic musicians.

★ **Serge Gainsbourg**
The French singer, composer and pop icon of the 1970s and 1980s is best known for his wistful and irreverent songs. He was married to the actress Jane Birkin.

VISITORS' CHECKLIST

3 Blvd Edgar Quinet. **Map** 16 D3. **Tel** 01 44 10 86 50. M Edgar Quinet. ▦ 38, 83, 91 to Port Royal. RER Port Royal. P Rue Campagne-Première, Blvd St-Jacques. ◯ Mid-Mar–early Nov: 8am–6pm daily; early Nov–mid-Mar closes 5.30pm. **Adm free.** 📷 ♿

The Tower is all that remains of a 17th-century windmill. It was part of the old property of the Brothers of Charity on which the cemetery was built.

Génie du Sommeil Eternel
Horace Daillion's wistful bronze angel of Eternal Sleep (1902) is the cemetery's centrepiece.

Tristen Tzara, the Romanian writer, was leader of the literary and artistic Dada movement in Paris in the 1920s.

Henri Laurens
The French sculptor (1885–1954) was a leading figure in the Cubist movement.

Man Ray was an American photographer who immortalized the Montparnasse artistic and café scene in the 1920s and 1930s.

Charles Baudelaire, the 19th-century poet, is buried here in his detested stepfather's family tomb, along with his beloved mother.

Chaïm Soutine, a poor Jewish Lithuanian, was a Montparnasse Bohemian painter of the 1920s. He was a friend of the Italian artist Modigliani.

Jean Seberg
The Hollywood actress, chosen by Jean-Luc Godard as the star for his film A bout de souffle, *was the epitome of American blonde beauty, youth and candour.*

★ **Jean-Paul Sartre and Simone de Beauvoir**
The famous existentialist couple, undisputed leaders of the post-war literary scene, lie here close to their Left Bank haunts.

INVALIDES AND EIFFEL TOWER QUARTER

Musée de l'Armée cannon

Everything in the area of Invalides is on a monumental scale. Starting from the sprawling 18th-century buildings of the Ecole Militaire on the corner of the Avenue de la Motte Picquet, the Parc du Champ de Mars stretches down to the Eiffel Tower and the Seine. The avenues around the Tower are lined with luxurious buildings, some in the Art Nouveau style, and numerous embassies. The area was already highly prized between the World Wars when the noted actor Sacha Guitry lived there. Even earlier, in the 18th century, wealthy residents of the Marais moved to this part of the city, building the aristocratic town houses that line the Rue de Varenne and Rue de Grenelle.

SIGHTS AT A GLANCE

Historic Buildings and Streets
Hôtel des Invalides ❻
Hôtel Matignon ❽
Assemblée Nationale
  Palais-Bourbon ⓫
Rue Cler ⓬
Les Egouts ⓭
Champ-de-Mars ⓯
No. 29 Avenue Rapp ⓱
Ecole Militaire ⓳

Museums and Galleries
Musée de l'Ordre de la
  Libération ❸
Musée de l'Armée ❹
Musées des Plans-Reliefs ❺

Musée Rodin ❼
Musée Maillol ❾
musée du quai Branly ⓮

Churches and Temples
Dôme Church pp188–9 ❶
St-Louis-des-Invalides ❷
Sainte-Clotilde ❿

Monuments and Fountains
Eiffel Tower pp194–5 ⓰

Modern Architecture
Village Suisse ⓲
UNESCO ⓴

GETTING THERE
The metro system serves this area well, with stations at Invalides, Solférino, Sèvres Babylone, Varenne, Latour Maubourg and Ecole Militaire. There are also several bus routes through the area. Route 69 passes along Rue St-Dominique heading east and along Rue de Grenelle on the way back. Route 82 travels along the Avenue de Suffren and 28 past L'Ecole Militaire.

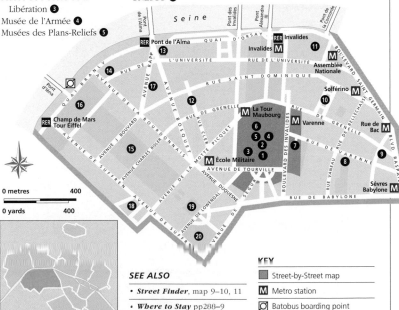

SEE ALSO
- **Street Finder**, map 9–10, 11
- **Where to Stay** pp288–9
- **Restaurants** pp308–09

KEY
▨	Street-by-Street map
Ⓜ	Metro station
▣	Batobus boarding point
RER	RER station

◁ **View of the Eiffel Tower**

Street-by-Street: Invalides

The imposing Hôtel des Invalides, from which the area takes its name, was built from 1671 to 1676 by Louis XIV for his wounded and homeless veterans and as a monument to his own glory. At its centre lies the glittering golden roof of the Sun King's Dôme Church, which marks the final resting place of Napoleon Bonaparte. The emperor's body was brought here from St Helena in 1840, 19 years after he died, and placed inside the majestic red sarcophagus, designed by Joachim Visconti, that lies at the centre of the Dôme's circular glass-topped crypt. Just to the east of the Hôtel on the corner of the Boulevard des Invalides, the superb Musée Rodin offers artistic relief from the pomp and circumstance of the surrounding area.

Mounted military policeman

Metro La Tour Maubourg

PL DE

AVE DE LA MOTTE PICQUET

The façade of the Hôtel is 196 m (645 ft) long and is topped by dormer windows, each decorated in the shape of a different trophy. A head of Hercules sits above the central entrance.

★ Musée de l'Armée
This vast museum covers military history from the Stone Age to World War II. It contains the third-largest collection of armoury in the world **4**

AVE DE TOURVILLE

Musée de l'Ordre de la Libération
The Order was set up to honour feats of heroism during World War II **3**

AVE DE SEGOR

STAR SIGHTS

- ★ Dôme Church and Napoleon's Tomb

- ★ St-Louis-des-Invalides

- ★ Musée de l'Armée

- ★ Musée Rodin

Musées des Plans-Reliefs
This museum contains military models of forts and towns, as well as a display on model-making **5**

KEY

– – – Suggested route

General de Gaulle's Liberation Order and compass

0 metres	100
0 yards	100

Hôtel des Invalides
After the two World Wars, Louis XIV's Hôtel was returned to its original use as a hospital for veterans **6**

LOCATOR MAP
See Central Paris Map pp14–15

The Invalides gardens were designed by de Cotte in 1704 and are lined by bronze cannons from the 17th and 18th centuries.

Metro Varenne

The Cour d'Honneur is still used for military parades. Seurre's statue of Napoleon, known as the Little Corporal, stands above the south side.

★ St-Louis-des-Invalides
From St-Louis, the soldier's chapel, it is possible to see into the Dôme, which was built as Louis XIV's private chapel **2**

★ Musée Rodin
By the time he died in 1917, Auguste Rodin had revolutionized the art of sculpture. All his key works, including The Thinker *(about 1880), are on display* **7**

★ Dôme Church and Napoleon's Tomb
The Dôme took 27 years to build. In the crypt lies Napoleon, whose final wish was to have his ashes "rest on the banks of the Seine" **1**

Dôme Church ❶

See pp188–9.

St-Louis-des-Invalides ❷

Hôtel des Invalides 75007. **Map** 11 A3. Ⓜ *Varenne, La Tour-Maubourg.* **Tel** *01 44 42 37 65.* ◻ *Apr–Sep: 10am–5.30pm daily; Oct–Mar: 10am–4.30pm daily.*

Also known as the "soldiers' church", this is the chapel of the Hôtel des Invalides. It was built from 1679 to 1708 by Jules Hardouin-Mansart from the original designs by Libéral Bruand, architect of the Hôtel des Invalides. The imposing, but stark, interior is decorated with banners seized in battle.

The fine 17th-century organ was built by Alexandre Thierry. The first performance of Berlioz's *Requiem* was given on it in 1837, with an orchestra accompanied by a battery of outside artillery.

Musée de l'Ordre de la Libération ❸

51 bis Blvd de La Tour-Maubourg 75007. **Map** 11 A4. **Tel** *01 47 05 04 10.* Ⓜ *La Tour-Maubourg.* ◻ *Apr–Sep: 10am–6pm daily (6.30pm Sun); Oct–Mar: 10am–5pm daily (5.30pm Sun).* ◻ *1st Mon of mth, some pub hols.* 📷◻📷

This museum is devoted to the wartime Free French and their

The altar of St-Louis-des-Invalides

The facade of the Musée de l'Ordre de la Libération

leader, General Charles de Gaulle. The Order of Liberation was created by de Gaulle in 1940. It is France's highest honour and was eventually bestowed on those who made an outstanding contribution to the final victory in World War II. Those who received the honour were French civilians and members of the armed forces, plus some overseas leaders, including King George VI, Winston Churchill and General Dwight Eisenhower.

Cannons at the Musée de l'Armée

Musée de l'Armée ❹

Hôtel des Invalides 75007. **Map** 11 A3. **Tel** *08 10 11 33 99.* Ⓜ *La Tour-Maubourg, Varenne.* Ⓡ *Invalides.* ◻ *10am–6pm (Oct–Mar: 5pm; Apr–Sep: 9pm Tue) daily (last adm: 45 mins before closing time).* ◻ *1st Mon of month (unless a bank hol), 1 Jan, 1 May, 1 Nov, 25 Dec.* 📷 *(ticket includes entry to the Musée de l'Ordre de la Libération and the Musée des Plans-Reliefs.)* 📷 ♿ *ground floor only.* 📷◻📷 **Film.** **www.**invalides.org

This is one of the most comprehensive museums of military history in the world, with exhibits ranging from the Stone Age to the final days of World War II. The third-largest collection of armoury in the world is housed here.

Situated in the northeast refectory, the Ancient Armoury department is worth visiting for the collection on display as much as for the extensively restored 17th-century murals by Joseph

Parrocel adorning the walls. These celebrate Louis XIV's military conquests.

The life of Charles de Gaulle and his role in World War II are documented in the *Historial de Gaulle*, a film and multimedia attraction (closed on Mondays).

The Département Moderne is in two parts: the first (1648–1792) covers the reign of Louis XIV, while the second (1792–1871) displays a collection of Napoleon's mementoes. Items include his famous frock coat and felt hats, as well as his stuffed dog.

Musées des Plans-Reliefs ❺

Hôtel des Invalides 75007. **Map** 11 B3. **Tel** *01 45 51 95 05.* Ⓜ *La Tour-Maubourg, Varenne.* ◻ *10am–6pm (5pm Oct–Mar) daily.* ◻ *1st Mon of mth, 1 Jan, 1 May, 1 & 11 Nov, 25 Dec.* 📷📷📷 **www.**museedesplansreliefs.culture.fr

A map of Alessandria, Italy (1813)

The detailed models of French forts and fortified towns, some dating back to Louis XIV's reign, were considered top secret until the 1950s, when they were put on public display. The oldest model is that of Perpignan, dating to 1686. It shows the fortifications drawn up by the legendary 17th-century military architect Vauban, who built the defences around several French towns, including Briançon.

Hôtel des Invalides

75007. **Map** 11 A3. **Tel** 01 44 42 38 77. M *La Tour-Maubourg, Varenne.* ⏰ *10am–6pm daily (5pm winter).* ● *1 Jan, 1 May, 1 Nov, 25 Dec.* ✔ www. invalides.org

The Invalides main entrance

Founded by Louis XIV, this was the first military hospital and home for French war veterans and disabled soldiers who had hitherto been reduced to begging. The decree for building this vast complex was signed in 1670, and construction, following the designs of Libéral Bruand, was finished five years later.

Today the harmonious Classical facade is one of the most impressive sights in Paris, with its four storeys, cannon in the forecourt, garden and tree-lined esplanade stretching to the Seine. The south side leads to St-Louis-des-Invalides, the soldiers' church, which backs on to the magnificent Dôme church of Jules Hardouin-Mansart. The dome was regilded in 1989 and now glitters anew.

Musée Rodin 7

79 Rue de Varenne 75007. **Map** 11 B3. **Tel** 01 44 18 61 10. M *Varenne.* ⏰ *Apr–Sep: 10am–5.45pm Tue–Sun; Oct–Mar: 10am–4.45pm Tue–Sun (to 0.45pm Wed). Garden closes at 6pm.* ● *1 Jan, 1 May, 25 Dec.* 📷 & *restricted.* 🖥️ 🏠 ✔ *occas.* www.musee-rodin.fr

Auguste Rodin, widely regarded as the greatest 19th-century French sculptor, lived and worked in the elegant Hôtel Biron from 1908 until his death in 1917. In return for a state-owned flat and studio, Rodin left his work to the nation, and it is now exhibited here. Some of his most celebrated sculptures are on display in the garden: *The Burghers of Calais, The Thinker, The Gates of Hell* and *Balzac*.

Inside, exhibits arranged in chronological order span the whole of Rodin's career, with highlights such as *The Kiss* and *Eve*. There are also works by his pupil and mistress, Camille Claudel.

Hôtel Matignon 8

57 Rue de Varenne 75007. **Map** 11 C4. M *Solférino, Rue du Bac.* ● *to the public.*

One of the most beautiful mansions in the Faubourg area, this was built by Jean Courtonne in 1721 and has been substantially remodelled since. Former owners include Talleyrand, the statesman and diplomat who held legendary parties and receptions here, and several members of the nobility. It has been the official residence of the French Prime Minister since 1958 and has the largest private garden in Paris.

Rodin's *The Kiss* (1886) at the Musée Rodin

Musée Maillol 9

61 Rue de Grenelle 75007. **Map** 11 C4. **Tel** 01 42 22 59 58. M *Sèvres-Babylone, Rue du Bac.* ⏰ *10.30am–7pm Wed–Mon (to 9.30pm Fri; last adm 45 mins before).* ● *pub hols.* & 🖥️ 🏠 www.museemaillol.com

Once the home of novelist Alfred de Musset, this museum was created by Dina Vierny, former model of Aristide Maillol. All aspects of the artist's work are here: drawings, engravings, paintings, sculpture and decorative objects. Also displayed is Vierny's private collection, including works by Matisse, Picasso and Rodin.

Large allegorical figures of the city of Paris and the four seasons decorate Bouchardon's fountain in front of the house.

Sculptured figures at Ste-Clotilde

Sainte-Clotilde 10

12 Rue de Martignac 75007. **Map** 11 B3. 🖼️ 01 44 18 62 60. M *Solférino, Varenne, Invalides.* ⏰ *9am–7.30pm Mon–Fri, 10am–8pm Sat & Sun.* ● *non-religious public hols.* 🏠 🏛️ www.sainte-clothilde.com

Designed by the German-born architect François-Christian Gau and the first of its kind to be built in Paris, this Neo-Gothic church was inspired by the mid-19th-century enthusiasm for the Middle Ages, made fashionable by such writers as Victor Hugo. The church is noted for its imposing twin towers, visible from across the Seine. The interior decoration includes sculpted stations of the cross by James Pradier and stained-glass windows. The composer César Franck was the church organist here for 32 years.

Dôme Church ❶

Jules Hardouin-Mansart was asked in 1676 by the Sun King, Louis XIV, to build the Dôme Church among the existing buildings of the Invalides military refuge. A soldiers' church had already been built, but the Dôme was to be reserved for the exclusive use of the Sun King and for the location of royal tombs. The resulting masterpiece complements the surrounding buildings and is one of the greatest examples of 17th-century French architecture.

After Louis XIV's death, plans to bury the royal family in the church were abandoned, and it became a monument to Bourbon glory. In 1840 Louis-Philippe decided to install Napoleon's remains in the crypt, and the addition of the tombs of Vauban, Marshal Foch and other figures of military prominence have since turned this church into a French military memorial.

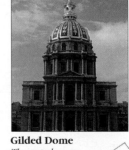

Gilded Dome
The cupola was first gilded in 1706.

① **Tomb of Joseph Bonaparte**
The sarcophagus of Napoleon's older brother, the King of Naples and later of Spain, is in the side chapel to the right as visitors enter.

Main entrance

② **Memorial to Vauban**
Commissioned by Napoleon I in 1808, this contains an urn with Sébastien le Prestre de Vauban's heart. He was Louis XIV's great military architect and engineer who died in 1707. His long military career culminated in his appointment as Marshal of France in 1703. He revolutionized siege warfare when he introduced his ricochet-batteries. His reclining figure by Antoine Etex lies on top of the memorial, mourned by Science and War.

⑥ Glass Gallery
Access to the glass-topped crypt containing Napoleon's tomb is by the curved stairs in front of the altar. The glass partition behind the altar separates the Dôme from the older Invalides chapel beyond.

VISITORS' CHECKLIST

Hôtel National des Invalides, 129 Rue de Grenelle. **Map** 11 A3. **Tel** 08 10 11 33 99. Ⓜ *La Tour-Maubourg, Varenne.* 🚌 *28, 63, 69, 80, 82, 83, 87, 92, 93 to Les Invalides.* ⓇⒺⓇ *Invalides.* 🅾️ *Tour Eiffel.* 🅿️ *Rue de Constantine.* 🕙 *10am–5pm daily (Apr–Jun: to 6pm; Jul, Aug: to 7pm).* ⬤ *1st Mon of mth, 1 Jan, 1 May, 1 Nov, 25 Dec.* 🎫 📷 ♿ *restricted (01 47 05 36 47).* 📷 *groups.* ⬜ ⬜ ⬜

KEY

▬ ▬ ▬ Tour route

⑤ St Jérôme's Chapel
Passing across the centre of the church, the side chapel to the right of the main entrance contains the tomb of Napoleon's younger brother, Jérôme, King of Westphalia.

Stairs to crypt

④ Dôme Ceiling
Looking upwards, Charles de la Fosse's circular painting (1692) on the ceiling shows the Glory of Paradise, *with Saint Louis presenting his sword to Christ.*

③ Tomb of Marshal Foch
Ferdinand Foch's imposing bronze tomb was built by Paul Landowski in 1937.

NAPOLEON'S RETURN

King Louis-Philippe decided to bring the Emperor Napoleon's body back from St Helena *(see pp32–3)* as a gesture of reconciliation to the Republican and Bonapartist parties contesting his regime. The Dôme Church, with its historical and military associations, was an obvious choice for Napoleon's final resting place. His body was encased in six coffins and finally placed in the crypt in 1861, in the culmination of a grand ceremony which was attended by Napoleon III.

Neo-Classical facade of the Assemblée Nationale Palais-Bourbon

Assemblée Nationale Palais-Bourbon ⓫

126 Rue de l'Université 75007.
Map 11 B2. **Tel** 01 40 63 60 00.
Ⓜ Assemblée-Nationale. RER
Invalides. ◯ to group visits only. Call
the above number for more
information. 🛗 📷
www.assemblee-nationale.fr

Built in 1722 for the Duchesse de Bourbon, daughter of Louis XIV, the Palais-Bourbon was confiscated during the Revolution. It has been home to the lower house of the French Parliament since 1830.

During World War II, the palace became the Nazi administration's seat of government. The public can enter to watch parliament in action. The grand Neo-Classical facade with its fine columns was added in 1806, partly to mirror the facade of La Madeleine church facing it across the Seine. The adjacent Hôtel de Lassay, built by the Prince de Condé, is now the residence of the president of the National Assembly.

Rue Cler ⓬

75007. **Map** 10 F3. Ⓜ Ecole-Militaire,
La Tour-Maubourg. **Market** ◯ Tue–
Sat. See **Shops and Markets** p338.

This is the street market of the seventh arrondissement, the richest in Paris, for here live the bulk of senior civil servants, captains of industry and many diplomats. The market area occupies a pedestrian precinct stretching south from the Rue de Grenelle.

It is colourful, but very much an exclusive market, with the best-dressed shoppers in town. As one would expect, the produce is excellent, the pâtisserie and cheese shops in particular.

Les Egouts ⓭

Opposite 93 Quai d'Orsay 75007.
Map 10 F2. 🛗 01 53 68 27 81. Ⓜ
Alma-Marceau. RER Pont de l'Alma.
◯ 11am–5pm (4pm in winter) Sat–
Wed. ● 2 wks Jan. 🐾 📷 📹

One of Baron Haussmann's finest achievements, the majority of Paris's sewers (*égouts*) date from the Second Empire (*see pp32–3*). If laid end to end the 2,100 km (1,300 miles) of sewers would stretch from Paris to Istanbul. In the 20th century the sewers became a popular attraction. All tours are limited to a small area around the Quai d'Orsay entrance and are on foot (the sewers may close after heavy rain). Be aware that the smell can be very pungent, especially during summer. Visitors can discover the mysteries of underground Paris at the Sewer Museum.

musée du quai Branly ⓮

See pp192–3.

The fruit and vegetable market in the Rue Cler

Doorway at No. 29 Avenue Rapp

Champ-de-Mars **⑮**

75007. **Map** 10 E3. **M** Ecole-Militaire.
RER Champ-de-Mars–Tour-Eiffel.

The gardens stretching from the Eiffel Tower to the Ecole Militaire were originally a parade ground for the officer cadets of the Ecole Militaire. The area has since been used for horse-racing, balloon ascents and the mass celebrations for 14 July, the anniversary of the Revolution.

 *(balloon illustration, mid-column)*

An illustration of a balloon

The first ceremony was held in 1790 in the presence of a glum, captive Louis XVI. Vast exhibitions were held here in the late 19th century, including the 1889 World Fair for which the Eiffel Tower was erected. *Le Mur de la Paix*, Jean-Michel Wilmotte's monument to world peace, stands at one end.

Eiffel Tower **⑯**

See pp194–5.

No. 29 Avenue Rapp **⑰**

75007. **Map** 10 E2. **M** Pont-de-l'Alma.

A prime example of Art Nouveau architecture is No. 29 and it won its designer, Jules Lavirotte, first prize at the Concours des Facades de la Ville de Paris in 1901. Its ceramics and brickwork are decorated with animal and flower motifs intermingling with female figures. These are superimposed on a multi-coloured sandstone base to produce a facade that is deliberately erotic, and was certainly subversive in its day. Also worth visiting is Lavirotte's building, complete with watchtower, which can be found in the Square Rapp.

Village Suisse **⑱**

38-78 Ave de Suffren 75015.
Map 10 E4. **M** Dupleix.
☐ 10.30am–7pm Thu–Mon.

The Swiss government built a mock-Alpine village for the 1900 Universal Exhibition held in the Champ-de-Mars nearby. It was later used as a centre for dealing in secondhand goods. In the 1950s and 1960s antique dealers moved in, and everything became more fashionable and expensive. The village was renovated in the late 1960s.

Ecole Militaire **⑲**

1 Pl Joffre 75007. **Map** 10 F4.
M Ecole-Militaire. **Visits** by special permission only – contact the Commandant in writing. 📷

The Royal Military Academy of Louis XV was founded in 1751 to educate 500 sons of impoverished officers. It was designed by architect Jacques-Ange Gabriel, and one of the features is the central pavilion. This is a magnificent example of the French Classical style, with eight Corinthian pillars and a quadrangular dome. The interior is decorated in Louis XVI style; of main interest are the chapel and a superb Gabriel-designed wrought-iron banister on the main staircase.

An early cadet at the academy was Napoleon, whose passing-out report stated that "he could go far if the circumstances are right".

A 1751 engraving showing the planning of the Ecole Militaire

UNESCO **⑳**

7 Pl de Fontenoy 75007. **Map** 10 F5.
Tel 01 45 68 10 00. 📞 01 45 68 10 60 (in English). **M** Ségur, Cambronne.
☐ guided visits 3pm Mon (Eng) & 3pm Wed (Fre); by appt only, apply 3 months ahead: 01 45 68 03 59.
● public hols. 🖼 ♿ 📷 🎫 📷
Exhibitions, **films**. www.unesco.org

This is the headquarters of the United Nations Educational, Scientific and Cultural Organization (UNESCO). The organization's stated aim is to contribute to international peace and security through education, science and culture.

UNESCO is a trove of modern art, notably a huge mural by Picasso, ceramics by Joan Miró and sculptures by Henry Moore.

Moore's *Reclining Figure* at UNESCO (erected 1958)

musée du quai Branly ⑭

Widely regarded as former President Jacques Chirac's legacy to Paris's cultural scene, quai Branly has proved a major tourist pull since it opened in 2006. The stylish Jean Nouvel building displays 3,500 exhibits from the French state's vast non-western art collection, one of the world's most prolific. Outside, the grounds offer visitors breathing space and in summer, the museum's 500-seat auditorium opens onto an outdoor theatre for music and dance. The rooftop restaurant boasts breathtaking views.

Interior
Subdued natural light creates intimacy, while an undulating open-plan design reflects the diversity and convergence of different cultures.

Brass pendant (India, 19–20th century)
Topped by three heads, this pendant is associated with headhunting, a tradition once practised by Naga warriors.

Musical instrument tower

Collection of slit drums (Vanuatu, mid-20th century)
Used for dance and transmitting messages, these vertical drums produce different sounds depending on the thickness of the slit cut into them.

Ramp to main collection

Ticket desks and entrance

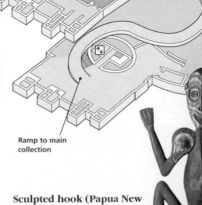

Sculpted hook (Papua New Guinea, early 20th century)
Tribal men would hang ritual offerings on the hook protruding from this sculpted female figure.

STAR EXHIBITS

★ Androgynous statue

★ Museum architecture

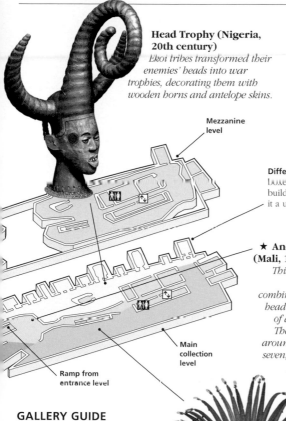

Head Trophy (Nigeria, 20th century)
Ekoi tribes transformed their enemies' heads into war trophies, decorating them with wooden horns and antelope skins.

Mezzanine level

VISITORS' CHECKLIST

37 Quai Branly. **Map** 10 E2.
Tel 01 56 61 70 00. Ⓜ️ *Alma-Marceau, Bir-Hakeim, Iéna.* 🚌 42, 63, 72, 80, 82, 92. RER *Pont de l'Alma.* 🅾️ *Tour Eiffel.* 🅿️ *on site.* ⬜ *11am–7pm Tue, Wed, Sun, (to 9pm Thu–Sat).* ♿ 📷 ✏️ 🍴 🖥️ 🎭 **Exhibitions, film, library, theatre.** www.quaibranly.fr

Different-sized display boxes jut out of the building facade, lending it a unique shape.

★ Androgynous statue (Mali, 10–11th century)
This 1.91 m (6.3 ft) wooden statue combines a regal male head with the breasts of a fertile woman. The bracelets worn around the wrist total seven, the number of perfect union.

Main collection level

Ramp from entrance level

GALLERY GUIDE
Tickets are bought outside the main building. Once inside, visitors take a 180-metre (590-ft) ramp that spirals up around a large glass tower displaying the museum's reserve of musical instruments. This leads to the main collection level, where a suggested route passes through four colour-coded zones of Oceania, Asia, Africa and the Americas. There are stairs from the main collection level to the three mezzanine galleries, one of which is for multimedia resources.

Giant headdress (Bolivia)
Worn for the Macheteros warrior dance, this colourful headdress weighs almost 10 kg (22 lb).

KEY

☐	Asia
☐	Africa
☐	The Americas
☐	Oceania
☐	Temporary exhibition space
☐	Multimedia gallery
☐	Musical instrument tower
☐	Non-exhibition space

★ Museum architecture
Set on pillars above the verdant museum gardens, architect Jean Nouvel's elegant building resembles the elongated shadow of the nearby Eiffel Tower. An exterior glass wall and thickets of trees help shield the museum from the outside world.

Eiffel Tower ⑯

Eiffel Tower from the Trocadéro

Originally built to impress visitors to the 1889 Universal Exhibition, the Eiffel Tower (Tour Eiffel) was meant to be a temporary addition to the Paris skyline. Designed by the engineer Gustave Eiffel, it was fiercely decried by 19th-century aesthetes. The author Guy de Maupassant lunched there to avoid seeing it. The world's tallest building until 1931, when New York's Empire State Building was completed, the tower is now the symbol of Paris. Freshly painted every 7 years, with a light show that plays every night on the hour, the Tour Eiffel has never looked better.

Ironwork Pattern
According to Eiffel, the complex pattern of pig-iron girders came from the need to stabilize the tower in strong winds. But Eiffel's design quickly won admirers for its pleasing symmetry.

Lift Engine Room
Eiffel emphasized safety over speed when choosing the lifts for the tower.

STAR FEATURES

★ Cineiffel

★ Hydraulic Lift Mechanism

★ Viewing Gallery

★ Eiffel Bust

★ Cineiffel
This small museum tells the history of the tower through a short film. It includes footage of famous personalities who have visited the tower, including Charlie Chaplin, Josephine Baker and Adolf Hitler.

THE DARING AND THE DELUDED

The tower has inspired many crazy stunts. It has been climbed by mountaineers, cycled down by a journalist, and used by trapeze artists and as a launch pad by parachutists. In 1912 an Austrian tailor, Franz Reichelt, attempted to fly from the parapet with only a modified cape for wings. He plunged to his death in front of a large crowd. According to the autopsy, he died of a heart attack before even touching the ground.

Birdman Reichelt

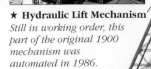
★ Hydraulic Lift Mechanism
Still in working order, this part of the original 1900 mechanism was automated in 1986.

The third level, 276 m (905 ft) above the ground, can hold 400 people at a time.

★ **Viewing Gallery**
On a clear day it is possible to see for 72 km (45 miles), including a distant view of Chartres Cathedral.

Double-Decker Lifts
During the tourist season, the limited capacity of the lifts means that it can take up to a couple of hours to reach the top. Queuing for the lifts requires patience and a good head for heights.

The second level is at 115 m (376 ft), separated from the first level by 359 steps, or a few minutes in the lift.

Le Jules Verne Restaurant is one of the best restaurants in Paris, offering superb food and panoramic views *(see p309)*.

The first level, at 57 m (187 ft) high, can be reached by lift or by 345 steps. The restaurant 58 Tour Eiffel is here.

VISITORS' CHECKLIST

Champ de Mars. Map 10 D3. **Tel** 08 92 70 12 39. **M** Bir Hakeim. **41** 42, 69, 72, 82, 87 to Champ de Mars. **RER** Champ de Mars. **O** Tour Eiffel. **P** on site. **O** Sep–mid-Jun: 9.30am–11.45pm daily (6.30pm for stairs); mid-Jun–Aug: 9am–0.45am (last adm 45 mins before, last lift to top 1 hr 15 mins before). **I O I** limited. **I I** **I** Films. www.tour-eiffel.fr

THE TOWER IN FIGURES

• the top (including the antennae) is 324 m (1,063 ft) high
• the top can move in a curve of 18 cm (7 in) under the effect of heat
• 1,665 steps to the third level
• 2.5 million rivets hold the tower together
• never sways more than 7 cm (2.5 in)
• 10,100 tonnes in weight
• 60 tonnes of paint are used every seven years

A workman building the tower

★ **Eiffel Bust**
Eiffel's (1832–1923) achievement was crowned with the Légion d'Honneur in 1889. Another honour was the bust by Antoine Bourdelle, placed beneath the tower in 1929.

Gilded bronze
statues by a number
of sculptors
decorating the
central square of the
Palais de Chaillot

Porte Dauphine M
Avenue Foch RER 11

BLVD FLANDRIN
RUE DE LA FAISANDERIE
RUE
DE
AVE VICT
Avenue
Henri Martin
RER
AVE HENRI MARTIN
RUE
DE
RUE
DE

M La Muet
RUE DE PA
RER
Boulainvilliers-
La Muette
RUE DES VIGN
RUE DE BOULAINVILLIERS
RUE

CHAILLOT QUARTER

The village of Chaillot was absorbed into Paris in the 19th century and transformed into an area rich in grand Second Empire avenues *(see pp34–5)* and opulent mansions. Some of the avenues converge on the Place du Trocadéro, once renowned for its elegant cafés, which leads to the Avenue du Président Wilson, with

Sculptures at the base of the Chaillot pool

a greater concentration of museums than any other street in Paris. Many of the area's private mansions are occupied by embassies, including the imposing Vatican embassy, and by major company headquarters. To the west is the territory of the *haute bourgeoisie*, one of Paris's most exclusive, if staid, residential neighbourhoods.

SIGHTS AT A GLANCE

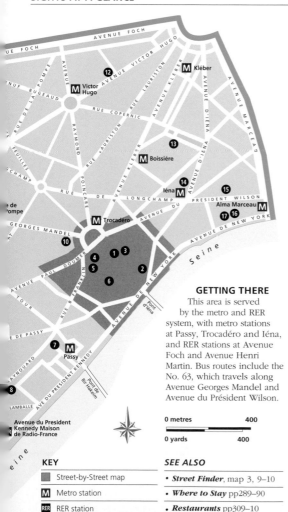

Museums and Galleries
Cité de l'Architecture et du Patrimoine ❸
Musée de l'Homme ❹
Musée de la Marine ❺
Musée du Vin ❼
Maison de Balzac ❽
Maison de Radio-France ❾
Musée de la Contrefaçon ⓫
Musée Dapper ⓬
Galerie-Musée Baccarat ⓭
Musée National des Arts Asiatiques Guimet ⓮
Musée Galliera ⓯
Musée d'Art Moderne de la Ville de Paris ⓰
Palais de Tokyo ⓱

Gardens
Jardins du Trocadéro ❻

Aquariums
Cinéaqua ❷

Modern Architecture
Palais de Chaillot ❶

Cemeteries
Cimetière de Passy ❿

GETTING THERE
This area is served by the metro and RER system, with metro stations at Passy, Trocadéro and Iéna, and RER stations at Avenue Foch and Avenue Henri Martin. Bus routes include the No. 63, which travels along Avenue Georges Mandel and Avenue du Président Wilson.

| 0 metres | 400 |
| 0 yards | 400 |

KEY
▉ Street-by-Street map
Ⓜ Metro station
RER RER station

SEE ALSO
- *Street Finder*, map 3, 9–10
- *Where to Stay* pp289–90
- *Restaurants* pp309–10

Street-by-Street: Chaillot

The Chaillot hill, with its superb position overlooking the Seine, was the site chosen by Napoleon for "the biggest and most extraordinary" palace that was to be built for his son – but by the time of his downfall only a few ramparts had been completed. Today, the monumental Palais de Chaillot, with its two massive curved wings, stands on the site. From the terrace in front of the Palais there is a magnificent view over the Trocadéro gardens and the Seine to the Eiffel Tower.

The statue of Marshal Ferdinand Foch, who led the Allies to victory in 1918, was unveiled on 11 November 1951. The monument was built by Robert Wlérick and Raymond Martin to commemorate the centenary of Foch's birth and the 33rd anniversary of the 1918 Armistice.

Metro Trocadéro

The Place du Trocadéro was created for the Universal Exhibition of 1878. Initially it was known as the Place du Roi-de-Rome, in honour of Napoleon's son.

★ **Musée de la Marine**
With a focus on France's maritime history, this museum includes exhibits of navigational instruments ❺

★ **Palais de Chaillot**
This Neo-Classical building was created for the World Fair of 1937. It replaced the Palais du Trocadéro, which was originally built in 1878 ❶

Musée de l'Homme
The main collection is due to reopen in 2012. Until then enjoy the interesting temporary exhibitions held here ❹

The Théâtre National de Chaillot, beneath the terrace, includes a multi-purpose cultural centre and a modern 1,200-seat theatre. *(See pp342–4.)*

Jardins du Trocadéro
The present layout of the gardens was created by R Lardat after the World Fair of 1937 ❻

LOCATOR MAP
See Central Paris Map pp14–15

Cinéaqua
Built to blend in with the Chaillot hillside, this aquarium also has a cinema complex ❷

Cité de l'Architecture et du Patrimoine
This vast complex houses an architecture museum, a school, library and archive, and various heritage organizations ❸

The Trocadéro fountains are operated in sequence, culminating in the massive water cannons in the centre firing towards the Eiffel Tower. They are illuminated at night.

The Pont d'Iéna was built by Napoleon to celebrate his victory in 1806 over the Prussians at Jena (Iéna) in Prussia. It was widened in 1937 to complement the building of the Palais de Chaillot.

KEY

— — — Suggested route

0 metres   100

0 yards   100

STAR SIGHTS

★ Palais de Chaillot

★ Musée de la Marine

Trocadéro fountains in front of the Palais de Chaillot

Palais de Chaillot ●

17 Pl du Trocadéro 75016.
Map 9 C2. Ⓜ *Trocadéro.*
🍴 🖥 🛗

The Palais, with its huge, curved colonnaded wings each culminating in an immense pavilion, was designed in Neo-Classical style for the 1937 Paris Exhibition by Léon Azéma, Louis-Hippolyte Boileau and Jacques Carlu. It is adorned with sculptures and bas-reliefs. On the walls of the pavilions there are gold inscriptions by the poet and essayist Paul Valéry.

The *parvis* or square, situated between the two pavilions is decorated with large bronze sculptures and ornamental pools. On the terrace in front of the *parvis* stand two bronzes, *Apollo* by Henri Bouchard and *Hercules* by Albert Pommier. Stairways

lead from the terrace to the Théâtre National de Chaillot *(see pp342–3)*, which, since World War II, has enjoyed huge fame for its avant-garde productions.

Cinéaqua ●

5 Ave Albert de Mun 75016. **Map** 9 C2. **Tel** 01 40 69 23 23. Ⓜ *Trocadéro.* ◯ *10am–7pm daily; last adm 1 hour before closing.* 🏷 ♿ **www**.cineaqua.com

Originally built in 1878 for the Universal Exhibition, this is now a state-of-the-art aquarium which is home to over 500 species of sea creatures, including seahorses, clownfish, stonefish and some spectacular sharks and rays.

The building is located in a former quarry and has been designed to blend in entirely with the Chaillot hillside.

Cinema screens showing cartoons and animal documentaries are interspersed with the aquariums. There is also a restaurant with a wall that is part of the aquarium.

Church model from Bagneux, Cité de l'Architecture et du Patrimoine

Cité de l'Architecture et du Patrimoine ●

Palais de Chaillot, Pl du Trocadéro 75016. **Map** 9 C2. **Tel** 01 58 51 52 00. Ⓜ *Trocadéro.* ◯ *11am–7pm Wed–Mon (to 9pm Thu).* 🏷 📷 🍴 **www**.citechaillot.fr

In the east wing of the Palais de Chaillot, this museum charts the development of French architecture through the ages. Among the unmissable displays is the Galerie des Moulages, which covers the period from the Middle Ages to the Renaissance. Here you will find three-dimensional models of great French cathedrals, such as Chartres. Also worth a look is the Galerie Moderne et Contemporaine, with a reconstruction of a Le Corbusier-designed apartment.

Shark basin, one of the 43 tanks at the Cinéaqua aquarium

Musée de l'Homme ❹

Palais de Chaillot, 17 Pl du Trocadéro 75016. **Map** 9 C2. *Tel* 01 44 05 72 72. Ⓜ Trocadéro. ◯ 10am–5pm Mon, Wed–Fri; 10am–6pm Sat, Sun. ⬤ public hols. 🎫 **Exhibitions, films.** 🍴 🖥 📷 www.mnhn.fr

Situated in the west wing of the Chaillot palace, this museum traces the process of human evolution, from prehistoric times to the present, through a series of anthropological exhibits from around the world.

The museum is currently undergoing extensive renovations that will lead to its housing one of the most comprehensive prehistoric collections in the world. Until the possible end date in 2012, visitors can enjoy a series of temporary exhibitions.

Gabon mask at Musée de l'Homme

Musée de la Marine ❺

Palais de Chaillot, 17 Pl du Trocadéro 75016. **Map** 9 C2. *Tel* 01 53 65 69 69. Ⓜ Trocadéro. ◯ 10am–6pm Wed–Mon (last adm 45 min before). ⬤ 1 Jan, 1 May, 25 Dec. 🎫 📷 📷 **Films, videos.** www.musee-marine.fr

French maritime history from the days of the royal wooden warships to today's aircraft carriers and nuclear submarines is told through wonderfully exact scale models (most of them two centuries old), mementos of naval heroes, paintings and navigational instruments. The museum was set up by Charles X in

Relief outside the Musée de la Marine

1827, and was then moved to the Chaillot palace in 1943. Exhibits include Napoleon's barge, models of the fleet he assembled at Boulogne-sur-Mer in 1805 for his planned invasion of Britain, and displays on underwater exploration and fishing vessels.

Jardins du Trocadéro ❻

75016. **Map** 10 D2. Ⓜ Trocadéro.

These lovely gardens cover 10 ha (25 acres). Their centrepiece is a long rectangular ornamental pool, bordered by stone and bronze-gilt statues, which look spectacular at night when the fountains are illuminated. The statues include *Man* by P Traverse and *Woman* by G Braque, *Bull* by P Jouve and *Horse* by G Guyot. On either side of the pool, the slopes of the Chaillot hill lead down to the Seine and the Pont d'Iéna. There is a freshwater aquarium in the northeast corner of the gardens, which are richly laid out with trees, walkways, small streams and bridges

Bridge in the Trocadéro gardens

Musée du Vin ❼

Rue des Eaux, 5 Sq Charles Dickens 75016. **Map** 9 C3. *Tel* 01 45 25 63 26. Ⓜ Passy. ◯ 10am–6pm Tue– 🍴 📷 groups only. 🍴 lunchtime only Tue–Sat. www.museeduvinparis.com

Waxwork figures and cardboard cut-outs graphically illustrate the history of wine-making in these atmospheric vaulted medieval cellars,

which were once used by the monks of Passy. The exhibits include a collection of old wine bottles, glasses and corkscrews, as well as an array of scientific instruments that were used in the wine-making and bottling processes. There is also an atmospheric restaurant, wine for sale and tours which include a wine-tasting session.

Balzac's modest house

Maison de Balzac ❽

47 Rue Raynouard 75016. **Map** 9 B3. *Tel* 01 55 74 41 80. Ⓜ Passy, La Muette. ◯ 10am–6pm Tue–Sun (last adm: 5.30pm). ⬤ public hols. 🎫 📷 📷 📷 www.balzac.paris.fr

The novelist Honoré de Balzac lived here from 1840 to 1847 under a false name, Monsieur de Brugnol, to avoid his numerous creditors. During this time he wrote many of his most famous novels, among them *La Cousine Bette* (1846).

The house now contains a reference library, with first editions and manuscripts, and a museum with memorabilia from his life. Many of the rooms have drawings and paintings portraying Balzac's family and close friends. The Madame Hanska room is devoted to the memory of the Russian woman who corresponded with Balzac for 18 years and was his wife for the five months before his death in 1850.

The house has a back entrance leading into Rue Berton, which was used to evade unwelcome callers. Rue Berton, with its ivy-covered walls, has retained much of its old, rustic charm.

Debussy's grave in the Cimetière de Passy, in the shadow of the Eiffel Tower

Maison de Radio-France **9**

116 Ave du Président-Kennedy 75016. **Map** 9 B4. **Tel** 01 56 40 15 16. Ⓜ Ranelagh. 🕐 for concerts only, check website for details. ♿ www.radiofrance.fr

Maison de Radio-France is an impressive building designed by Henri Bernard in 1963 as the headquarters of France's public radio network. The largest single structure in France, it is made up of three concentric circular buildings with a rectangular tower and covers 2 ha (5 acres).

The 70-odd studios and main public auditorium are the home of French national public radio. Radio France sponsors more than 100 concerts each year, including performances by the Orchestre National de France – several of these concerts are held at the Maison de Radio-France.

Cimetière de Passy **10**

2 Rue du Commandant-Shloesing 75016. **Map** 9 C2. Ⓜ Trocadéro. 🕐 8.30am–5.30pm Mon–Sat, 9am–5.30pm Sun (to 6pm 16 Mar–5 Nov).

Located in the elegant 16th arrondissement, this small cemetery, which opened in 1820, is packed with the graves of eminent Parisians, including the composers Claude Debussy and Gabriel Fauré and painter Edouard Manet, as well as many

politicians and aristocrats, such as Ghislaine Dommanget, Princess of Monaco.

Musée de la Contrefaçon **11**

16 Rue de la Faisanderie 75016. **Map** 3 A5. **Tel** 01 56 26 14 00. Ⓜ Porte Dauphine. 🕐 2–5.30pm Tue–Sun. ● public hols, Aug, 2 Nov. 🖼 🎫

French cognac and perfume producers, and the luxury trade in general, have been plagued for years by counterfeiters operating around the world. This museum was set up by the manufacturers' union and illustrates the history of this type of fraud, which has been going on since Roman times. Among the impressive display of forgeries are copies of Louis Vuitton luggage, Cartier watches and fake wine.

Musée Dapper **12**

35 bis Rue Paul-Valéry, 75116. **Map** 3 C4. **Tel** 01 45 00 91 75. Ⓜ Victor-Hugo. 🕐 11am–7pm Wed–Mon. 🖼 🛒 www.dapper.com.fr

Not just a museum, but a world-class ethnographic research centre called the Dapper Foundation, this lively centre showcases African art and culture. Located in an attractive building with an "African" garden, it is a treasure house of vibrant colour and powerful, evocative work from sub-Saharan Africa. The emphasis

is on pre-colonial folk arts, with sculpture, carvings, and tribal work, but there is later art too. The highlight is the collection of tribal masks, with a dazzling array of richly carved religious, ritual and funerary masks, as well as theatrical masks used for comic, magical or symbolic performances, some dating back to the 12th century.

Galerie-Musée Baccarat **13**

11 Place des Etats-Unis 75016. **Tel** 01 40 22 11 00. Ⓜ Boissière, Iéna. 🕐 10am–6.30pm Mon, Wed–Sat. ● public hols. 🖼 📷 🎫 www.baccarat.fr

The Galerie-Musée Baccarat shows off some 1,200 articles made by the Baccarat crystal glass company, which was founded in 1764 in Lorraine. These include services created for the royal and imperial courts of Europe and one-off pieces created in the workshops.

Khmer art in the Musée National des Arts Asiatiques Guimet

Musée National des Arts Asiatiques Guimet **14**

6 Pl d'Iéna 75116. **Map** 10 D1. **Tel** 01 56 52 53 00. Ⓜ Iéna. 🕐 10am–6pm Wed–Mon (last adm: 5.15pm). 🖼 🛒 ♿ 🎫 🚻 📷 📱 Panthéon Bouddhique (additional galleries) at 19 Ave d'Iéna **Tel** 01 40 73 88 00. www.guimet.fr

The Musée Guimet has the finest collection of Khmer (Cambodian) art in the West.

It was originally set up in Lyon in 1879 by the industrialist and orientalist Emile Guimet.

Moved to Paris in 1884, it meticulously represents every artistic tradition from Afghanistan to India, China, Japan and the rest of south-east Asia. With over 45,000 artworks, the museum is acclaimed for some especially unusual collections, including the Cambodian Angkor Wat sculptures and 1600 artworks from the Himalayas. Other highlights include Chinese bronzes and lacquerware, and many statues of Buddha. Seasonal tea ceremonies are held in the Panthéon Bouddhique. Call for details.

times, have been donated by such fashionable women as Baronne Hélène de Roths-child and Princess Grace of Monaco. The various garments are displayed in rotation twice per year.

Gabriel Forestier's sculpted doors, Musée d'Art Moderne

Musée Galliera 🅖

10 Ave Pierre 1er de Serbie 75116. **Map** 10 E1. **Tel** 01 56 52 86 00.
Ⓜ Iéna, Alma Marceau. **Library & documentation centre** ◯ 10am–1pm, 2–5.30pm Tue, 10am–1pm Wed–Fri. **Museum** ◯ for renovation until spring 2012. 🅖 **Children's room**. www.galliera.paris.fr

Devoted to the evolution of fashion, this museum is housed in the Renaissance-style palace built for the Duchesse Maria de Ferrari Galliera in 1892. The collection comprises more than 100,000 outfits, from the 18th century to the present day. Some, from more recent

Musée d'Art Moderne de la Ville de Paris 🅟

Palais de Tokyo, 11 Ave du Président-Wilson 75116. **Map** 10 E1. **Tel** 01 53 67 40 00. Ⓜ Iéna, Alma Marceau. ◯ 10am–6pm Tue–Sun (to 10pm Thu). 🅖 temporary exhibitions. ♿ 🅖🅖🅖 **Films**. www.mam.paris.fr

This large lively museum houses the city of Paris's own renowned collection of modern art, covering all major 20th-century movements and artists (the 21st century will be included). Established in 1961, the museum occupies the vast east wing of the

Palais de Tokyo, which was built for the 1937 World Fair.

One of the museum's highlights is Raoul Dufy's gigantic mural *La Fée Electricité (The Spirit of Electricity)*, which traces the history of electricity through the ages. One of the largest paintings in the world, measuring 600 sq metres (6,500 sq ft), this curved mural takes up a whole room at the museum. Also notable are the Cubists, Amadeo Modigliani, Georges Rouault and the Fauves. This group of avant-garde artists was dominated by Henri Matisse, whose celebrated mural, *La Danse*, is on display here in both versions.

Sculpture in the forecourt of the Palais de Tokyo

Palais de Tokyo 🅠

Palais de Tokyo, 13 Ave du Président-Wilson 75116. **Map** 10 E1. **Tel** 01 47 23 54 01. Ⓜ Iéna, Alma Marceau. ◯ noon–midnight Tue–Sun. ● 1 Jan, 1 May, 25 Dec. ♿ 🅖🅖 🅖 www.palaisdetokyo.com

This open-space modern art museum is located in an adjacent wing to the Musée d'Art Moderne de la Ville de Paris, within the imposing 1937 Palais de Tokyo building. It presents an innovative, ever-changing programme of contemporary art exhibitions, fashion shows and avant-garde performances. Quirky installations, by artists such as Pierre Joseph, Wang Du and Frank Scurti have earned the Palais de Tokyo a reputation as one of the most cutting-edge art houses in Europe.

Garden and rear facade of the Musée Galliera

CHAMPS-ELYSEES

Two great streets dominate this area – the Avenue des Champs-Elysées and the Rue St-Honoré. The former is the capital's most famous thoroughfare. Its breadth is spectacular. The pavements are wide and their cafés, cinemas and shops attract throngs of people, who come to eat and shop, but also to see and to be seen. Rond Point des Champs-Elysées is the pretty end, with shady chestnut trees and pavements colourfully bordered by flower beds. Luxury and political power are nearby. Five-star hotels, fine restaurants and upmarket shops line the nearby streets and avenues. And along Rue St-Honoré are the heavily guarded presidential Palais de l'Elysée, the sumptuous town mansions of business chiefs, and the many embassies and consulates.

Ornate lamp-post on
Pont Alexandre III

SIGHTS AT A GLANCE

Historic Buildings and Streets
Palais de l'Elysée **5**
Avenue Montaigne **6**
Avenue des Champs-Elysées **8**
Place Charles de Gaulle
(l'Etoile) **9**

Monuments
Arc de Triomphe pp210–11 **10**

Bridges
Pont Alexandre III **1**

Museums and Galleries
Grand Palais **2**
Palais de la Découverte **3**
Petit Palais **4**
Musée Jacquemart-
André **7**

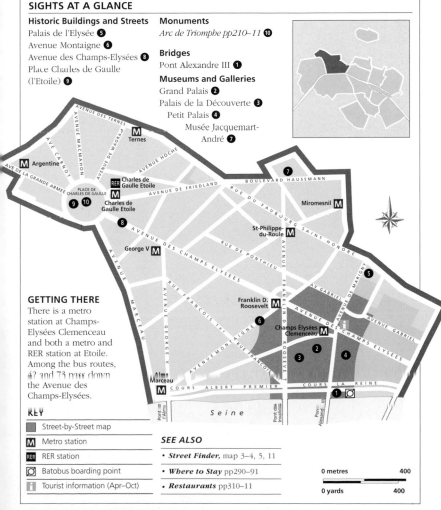

GETTING THERE

There is a metro station at Champs-Elysées Clemenceau and both a metro and RER station at Etoile. Among the bus routes, 42 and 73 pass down the Avenue des Champs-Elysées.

KEY

▢	Street-by-Street map
M	Metro station
RER	RER station
▢	Batobus boarding point
ℹ	Tourist information (Apr–Oct)

SEE ALSO

- **Street Finder,** map 3–4, 5, 11
- **Where to Stay** pp290–91
- **Restaurants** pp310–11

0 metres   400

0 yards   400

◁ **View of the Arc de Triomphe at night**

Street-by-Street: Champs-Elysées

The formal gardens that line the Champs-Elysées from the Place de la Concorde to the Rond-Point have changed little since they were laid out by the architect Jacques Hittorff in 1838. They were used as the setting for the World Fair of 1855, which included the Palais de l'Industrie, Paris's answer to London's Crystal Palace. The Palais was later replaced by the Grand Palais and Petit Palais, which were created as a showpiece of the Third Republic for the Universal Exhibition of 1900. They sit on either side of an impressive vista that stretches from Place Clémenceau across the elegant curve of the Pont Alexandre III to the Invalides.

The Théâtre du Rond-Point was the home of the Renaud-Barrault Company. There are plaques on the back door of the theatre representing Napoleon's campaigns.

Metro Franklin D Roosevelt
Ⓜ

Avenue Montaigne
Christian Dior and other haute couture *houses are based in this chic avenue* ❻

★ **Grand Palais**
Designed by Charles Girault, this grand 19th-century building is still used for major exhibitions ❷

The Lasserre restaurant is decorated in the style of a luxurious ocean liner from the 1930s.

RUE JEAN GOUJON

RUE FRANÇOIS PREMIER

AVE FRANKLIN D ROOSEVELT

AVE G. EISENHOWER

PL DU CANADA

COURS LA REIN

PONT DES INVALIDES

STAR SIGHTS

★ Avenue des Champs-Elysées

★ Grand Palais

★ Petit Palais

★ Pont Alexandre III

Palais de la Découverte
Outside this museum of scientific discoveries is a pair of equestrian statues ❸

KEY

‒ ‒ ‒ Suggested route

0 metres   100

0 yards   100

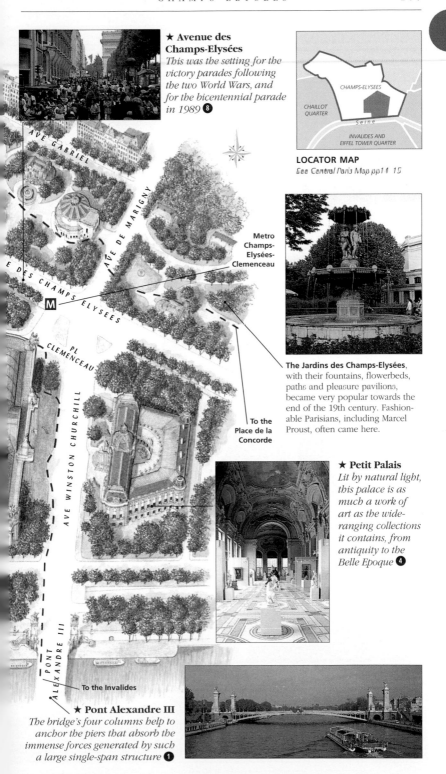

★ **Avenue des Champs-Elysées**
This was the setting for the victory parades following the two World Wars, and for the bicentennial parade in 1989 **8**

LOCATOR MAP
See Central Paris Map pp14-15

The Jardins des Champs-Elysées, with their fountains, flowerbeds, paths and pleasure pavilions, became very popular towards the end of the 19th century. Fashionable Parisians, including Marcel Proust, often came here.

Metro Champs-Elysées-Clemenceau

To the Place de la Concorde

★ **Petit Palais**
Lit by natural light, this palace is as much a work of art as the wide-ranging collections it contains, from antiquity to the Belle Epoque **4**

To the Invalides

★ **Pont Alexandre III**
The bridge's four columns help to anchor the piers that absorb the immense forces generated by such a large single-span structure **1**

Pont Alexandre III ❶

75008. **Map** 11 A1. Ⓜ *Champs-Elysées-Clemenceau.*

This is Paris's prettiest bridge with its exuberant Art Nouveau decoration of lamps, cherubs, nymphs and winged horses at either end. It was built between 1896 and 1900, in time for the Universal Exhibition, and it was named after Tsar Alexander III, whose son Nicholas II laid the foundation stone in October 1896.

The style of the bridge reflects that of the Grand Palais, to which it leads on the Right Bank. The construction of the bridge is a marvel of 19th-century engineering, consisting of a 6-m (18-ft) high single-span steel arch across the Seine. The design was subject to strict controls that prevented the bridge from obscuring the view of the Champs-Elysées or the Invalides. So today you can still enjoy magnificent views from here.

Pont Alexandre III

Grand Palais ❷

Porte A, Ave Général Eisenhower 75008. **Map** 11 A1. 🎫 *01 44 13 17 17.* Ⓜ *Champs-Elysées-Clemenceau.* ◯ *for temporary exhibitions (usually 10am–8pm Thu–Mon,10am–10pm Wed, but call to check).* ◑ *1 May, 25 Dec.* 🖼 🗷 ♿ 🗓 *usually 3pm Mon, Fri, Sat, 7pm Wed but call to check.* 🔊 🖥 📷 www.grandpalais.fr

Built at the same time as the Petit Palais and the Pont Alexandre III, the exterior of this massive palace combines an imposing Classical stone

facade with a riot of Art Nouveau ironwork. The enormous glass roof (15,000 sq metres/160,000 sq ft) has Récipon's colossal bronze statues of flying horses and chariots at its four corners. The metal structure supporting the glass weighs 8,500 tonnes, some 500 tonnes more than the Eiffel Tower. Today, the restored Grand Palais hosts contemporary art exhibitions and other events; major temporary and touring exhibitions are held at the Galeries Nationales in the same building.

Palais de la Découverte

Palais de la Découverte ❸

Ave Franklin D Roosevelt 75008. **Map** 11 A1. 🎫 *01 56 43 20 21.* Ⓜ *Franklin D Roosevelt.* ◯ *9.30am–6pm Tue–Sat, 10am–7pm Sun & public hols.* ◑ *1 Jan, 1 May, 14 Jul, 15 Aug, 25 Dec.* 🖼 📷 *by permission.* 🔊 🖥 www.palais-decouverte.fr

Opened in a wing of the Grand Palais for the World Fair of 1937, this science museum is a much-loved Paris institution. Demonstrations and displays, including a planetarium, cover many subjects and explain such phenomena as electromagnetism.

Entrance to the Petit Palais

Petit Palais ❹

Ave Winston Churchill 75008. **Map** 11 B1. **Tel** *01 53 43 40 00.* Ⓜ *Champs-Elysées-Clemenceau.* ◯ *10am–6pm Tue–Sun.* ◑ *public hols.* 🖼 📷 📷 *for exhibitions.* 🖥 www.petitpalais-paris.fr

Built for the Universal Exhibition in 1900, to stage a major display of French art, this jewel of a building now houses the Musée des Beaux-Arts de la Ville de Paris. Arranged around a pretty semi-circular courtyard and garden, the palace is similar in style to the Grand Palais, and has Ionic columns, a grand porch and a dome, which echoes that of the Invalides (*see p187*).

The Cours de la Reine wing, nearest the river, is used for temporary exhibitions, while the Champs-Elysées side of the palace houses the permanent collections. These are divided into sections: Greek and Roman; medieval and Renaissance ivories and sculptures; Renaissance clocks and jewellery; and 17th-, 18th-and 19th-century art and furniture. There are also many works by the Impressionists.

Exhibition space   **Iron supports**

GRAND PALAIS

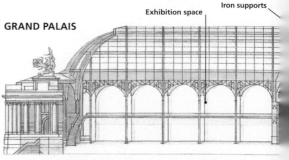

Palais de l'Elysée ❺

55 Rue du Faubourg-St-Honoré
75008. **Map** 5 B5. M *St-Philippe-du-Roule.* **Not open** to the public.

Backing onto splendid English-style gardens, the Elysée Palace was built in 1718 for the Comte d'Evreux and has been the official residence of the President of the Republic since 1873. From 1805 to 1808 it was occupied by Napoleon's sister, Caroline, and her husband, Murat. Two charming rooms have been preserved from this period: the Salon Murat and the Salon d'Argent. General de Gaulle used to give press conferences in the Hall of Mirrors. Today, the President's modernized apartments can be found on the first floor opposite the Rue de l'Elysée.

Elysée guard

Avenue Montaigne ❻

75008. **Map** 10 F1. M *Franklin D Roosevelt.*

In the 19th century this avenue was famous for its dance halls and its Winter Garden, where Parisians went to hear Adolphe Sax play his newly-invented saxophone. Today it is still one of Paris's most fashionable streets, bustling with restaurants, cafés, hotels and designer boutiques.

Glass cupola

Inside the Musée Jacquemart-André

Musée Jacquemart-André ❼

158 Blvd Haussmann 75008. **Map** 5 A4. **Tel** 01 45 62 11 59. M *Miromesnil, St-Philippe-du-Roule.* ◯ *10am–6pm daily.* 🖼 ⌀ 🏠 🔊 🖥 **www**.musee-jacquemart-andre.com

This museum is known for its fine collection of Italian Renaissance and French 18th-century works of art, as well as its beautiful frescoes by Tiepolo. Highlights include works by Mantegna, Uccello's masterpiece *St George and the Dragon* (circa 1435), paintings by Boucher and Fragonard and 18th-century tapestries and furniture.

Avenue des Champs-Elysées ❽

75008. **Map** 5 A5. M *Franklin D Roosevelt, George V.*

Paris's most famous and popular thoroughfare had its beginnings in about 1667, when the landscape garden designer, André Le Nôtre, extended the royal view from the Tuileries by creating a tree-lined avenue which eventually became known as the Champs-Elysées (Elysian Fields). It has been France's national "triumphal way" ever since the home-coming of Napoleon's body from St Helena in 1840. With the addition of cafés and restaurants in the second half of the 19th century, the Champs-Elysées became the place in which to be seen.

Place Charles de Gaulle (l'Etoile) ❾

75008. **Map** 4 D4. M *Charles de Gaulle-Etoile.*

Known as the Place de l'Etoile until the death of Charles de Gaulle in 1969, the area is still referred to simply as l'Etoile, the star. The present *place* was laid out in accordance with Baron Haussmann's plans of 1854 (*see pp34–5*). For motorists, it is the ultimate challenge.

Arc de Triomphe from the west

Arc de Triomphe ❿

See pp210–11.

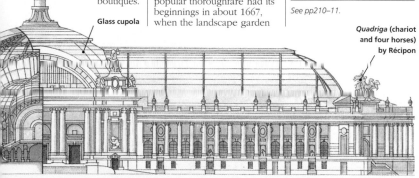

Quadriga (chariot and four horses) by Récipon

Arc de Triomphe ⑩

The east facade of the Arc de Triomphe

After his greatest victory, the Battle of Austerlitz in 1805, Napoleon promised his men, "You shall go home beneath triumphal arches." The first stone of what was to become the world's most famous triumphal arch was laid the following year. But disruptions to architect Jean Chalgrin's plans and the demise of Napoleonic power delayed the completion of this monumental building until 1836. Standing 50 m (164 ft) high, the Arc is now the customary starting point for victory celebrations and parades.

Thirty shields just below the Arc's roof each bear the name of a victorious Napoleonic battle fought in either Europe or Africa.

East facade

The frieze was executed by Rude, Brun, Jacquet, Laitié, Caillouette and Seurre the Elder. This east facade shows the departure of the French armies for new campaigns. The west side shows their return.

The Battle of Aboukir, a bas-relief by Seurre the Elder, depicts a scene of Napoleon's victory over the Turkish army in 1799.

Triumph of Napoleon
J P Cortot's high-relief celebrates the Treaty of Vienna peace agreement of 1810.

STAR FEATURES

★ Departure of the Volunteers in 1792

★ Tomb of the Unknown Soldier

★ **Tomb of the Unknown Soldier**
An unknown French soldier from World War I is buried here.

TIMELINE

1806 Napoleon commissions Chalgrin to build triumphal Arc

1836 Louis-Philippe completes the Arc

1885 Victor Hugo's body lies in state under the Arc

1944 Liberation of Paris. De Gaulle leads the crowd from the Arc

1800	1850	1900	1950

1815 Downfall of Napoleon. Work on Arc ceases

1840 Napoleon's cortège passes under the Arc

1919 Victory parade of Allied armies through the Arc

NAPOLEON'S NUPTIAL PARADE

Napoleon divorced Josephine in 1809 because she was unable to bear him children. A diplomatic marriage was arranged in 1810 with Marie-Louise, daughter of the Austrian emperor. Napoleon was determined to impress his bride by going through the Arc on their way to the wedding at the Louvre, but work had barely been started. So Chalgrin built a full-scale mock-up of the arch on the site for the couple to pass beneath.

VISITORS' CHECKLIST

Pl Charles de Gaulle. **Map** 4 D4.
Tel 01 55 37 73 77. Ⓜ 🆁🅴🆁 Charles
de Gaulle–Étoile. 🚌 22, 30, 31,
52, 73, 92 to Pl C de Gaulle. 🅿 off
Pl C de Gaulle. **Museum** ◯ Apr–
Sep: 10am–11pm daily; Oct–Mar:
10am–10.30pm daily (last adm:
30 mins earlier). ◯ am only 1 Jan,
1 May, 8 May, 14 Jul & 11 Nov;
all day 25 Dec. 🖼 🗖 🗖 🗖 🖾

The viewing platform affords one of the best views in Paris, overlooking the Champs-Elysées on one side, and the Grande Arche de la Défense on the other.

General Marceau's Funeral
Marceau defeated the Austrians in 1795, only to be killed the following year, still fighting them.

The Battle of Austerlitz by Gechter shows Napoleon's army breaking up the ice on the Satschan lake in order to drown thousands of enemy troops

Officers of the Imperial Army are listed on the walls of the smaller arches.

Entrance to museum

★ **Departure of the Volunteers in 1792**
François Rude's work shows citizens leaving to defend the nation.

Place Charles de Gaulle
Twelve avenues radiate from the Arc at the centre. Some bear the names of important French military leaders, such as Avenues Marceau and Foch.
(See pp34–5.)

OPERA QUARTER

The Opéra quarter bustles with bankers and stockbrokers, newspapermen and shoppers, theatre-goers and sightseers. Much of its 19th-century grandeur survives in the Grands Boulevards of Baron Haussmann's urban design. These are still a favourite with thousands of Parisian and foreign promenaders, drawn by the profusion of shops and department stores, which range from the exclusively expensive to the popular.

Much more of the area's older character is found in the many *passages*, delightful narrow shopping arcades with steel and glass roofs. Fashion's bad boy, Jean-Paul Gaultier, has a shop adjoining one of

**Les Coulisses de l'Opéra
(1889) by J Beraud**

the smartest, Galerie Vivienne. But more authentically old-style Parisian are the Passage des Panoramas and the Passage Jouffroy, the Passage Verdeau, with its old cameras and comics, and the tiny Passage des Princes. Two of Paris's finest food shops are in the area. Fauchon and Hédiard are noted for mouthwatering mustards, jams, pâtés and sauces. The area still has a reputation as a press centre, although *Le Monde* has moved out, and a history of cinema and theatre – the Lumière brothers held the world's first public film show here in 1895. The Opéra National de Paris Garnier is famous for its dazzling Belle Epoque interior.

SIGHTS AT A GLANCE

Historic Buildings and Streets
Place de la Madeleine ❷
Les Grands Boulevards ❸
Palais de la Bourse ❿
Avenue de l'Opéra ⓬

Churches
La Madeleine ❶

Opera Houses
Opéra National de Paris
   Garnier ❹

Museums and Galleries
Bibliothèque-Musée de l'Opéra ❺
Paris Story ❻
Grévin ❽
Bibliothèque Nationale
   Richelieu ⓫

Shops
Drouot (Hôtel des Ventes) ❼
Les Passages ❾

GETTING THERE
This area is served by the metro and RER systems. Metro lines 3, 7 and 8 serve the station at the Opéra, line 14 stops at Madeleine and the RER Line A stops at Auber. Among the bus routes passing through the area, 42 and 52 travel along Boulevard Madeleine, and 21, 27, 29 and 95 along Avenue de l'Opéra.

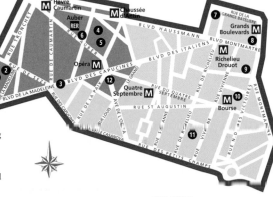

0 metres   400

0 yards   400

KEY

▦ Street-by-Street map

Ⓜ Metro station

ᴿᴱᴿ RER station

SEE ALSO

• *Street Finder*, map 5–6
• *Where to Stay* p291
• *Restaurants* pp311–12

◁ Jean-Baptiste Carpeaux's *La Danse* outside the Opéra National de Paris Garnier

Street-by-Street: Opéra Quarter

It has been said that if you sit for long enough at the Café de la Paix (opposite the Opéra National de Paris Garnier) the whole world will pass by. During the day, the area is a mixture of commerce – France's top three banks are based here – and tourism. A profusion of shops, ranging from the chic, exclusive and expensive to the popular department stores, draw the crowds. In the evening, the theatres and cinemas attract a totally different crowd, and the cafés along the Boulevard des Capucines throb with life.

Statue by Gumery on the Opéra

Place de la Madeleine
On the north side of the square, the windows of the Fauchon shop are filled with exquisite delicacies **2**

KEY

- – – Suggested route

0 metres   100
0 yards   100

RUE AUBE

RUE TRONCHET

RUE VIGNON

RUE GODOT DE MAUROY

RUE CAUMARTIN

PL DE LA MADELEINE

BLVD D

BLVD DE LA MADELEINE

M — Metro Madeleine

STAR SIGHTS

★ La Madeleine

★ Boulevard des Capucines

★ Opéra National de Paris Garnier

★ **La Madeleine**
The final design of this church, which is dedicated to Mary Magdalene, differs from this original model, now in the Musée Carnavalet (see pp96–7) **1**

★ **Opéra National de Paris Garnier**
with a mixture of styles ranging from Classical to Baroque, this building from 1875 has come to symbolize the opulence of the Second Empire ❹

LOCATOR MAP
See Central Paris Map pp14–15

PL DIACHILEV

Metro Chaussée d'Antin 🄼

RUE GLUCK

RUE HALEVY

PL J ROUCHE

RUE SCRIBE

RUE

PL CH GARNIER

Bibliothèque-Musée de l'Opéra
The world of opera is celebrated here ❺

The Place de l'Opéra
was designed by Baron Haussmann and is one of Paris's busiest intersections.

PL DE L'OPERA

Metro Opéra 🄼

PUCINES

RUE DAUNOU

AVE DE L'OPERA

The Café de la Paix maintains its old-fashioned ways and still has its 19th-century decor, designed by Charles Garnier. Vanilla slices are legendary. (See p319.)

Harry's Bar was named after Harry MacElhone, a bartender who bought the bar in 1913. Past regulars have included F Scott Fitzgerald and Ernest Hemingway.

★ **Boulevard des Capucines**
At No. 14 a plaque tells of the world's first public screening of a movie, by the Lumière brothers in 1895; it took place in the Salon Indien, a room in the Grand Café ❸

Charles Marochetti's *Mary Magdalene Ascending to Heaven* (1837) behind the high altar of La Madeleine

La Madeleine ❶

Pl de la Madeleine 75008.
Map 5 C5. **Tel** 01 44 51 69 00.
Ⓜ Madeleine. ⬚ 9.30am–7pm
daily. ✦ frequent. **Concerts.** ⬚
⬚ See **Entertainment** pp346–7.

This church, which is
dedicated to Mary
Magdalene, is one of
the best-known build-
ings in Paris because
of its prominent
location and great
size. It stands facing
south to Place de la
Concorde and is the
architectural counter-
point of the Palais-
Bourbon (home of the
Assemblée Nationale,
the French parliament)
across the river. It was
started in 1764 but not
consecrated until 1845. There
were proposals to convert it
into a parliament, a stock
exchange or the city's first
train station.

Napoleon decided to build
a temple dedicated to military
glory and he commissioned
Pierre Vignon to design it,
after the battle of Jena (Iéna)
in 1806. A colonnade of 20 m
high (64 ft) Corinthian
columns encircles the
building and supports a
sculptured frieze. The bas-
reliefs on the bronze doors
are by Henri de Triqueti and
show the Ten Commandments.

The inside is decorated with
marble and gilt, and has some
fine sculpture, notably François
Rude's *Baptism of Christ.*

Place de la Madeleine ❷

75008. **Map** 5 C5. Ⓜ
Madeleine. **Flower market**
⬚ 8am–7.30pm Tue–Sun.

The place de la
Madeleine was
created at the same
time as the Madeleine
church. It is a food
lover's paradise, with
many shops special-
izing in luxuries such
as truffles, champagne,
caviar and handmade

Fauchon tin

chocolates. Fauchon, the
millionaires' supermarket, is
situated at No. 26 and stocks
more than 20,000 items *(see
pp333–5)*. The large house at
No. 9 is where Marcel Proust
spent his childhood. To the
east of La Madeleine is a small
flower market *(see p338)* and
some excellently preserved
19th-century public toilets.

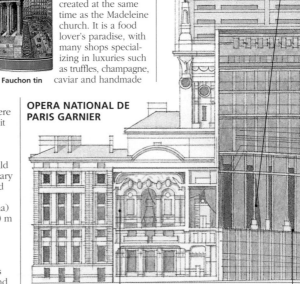

Scenery backdrop
operated by pulley

**OPERA NATIONAL DE
PARIS GARNIER**

Backstage area   Stage

Les Grands Boulevards ❸

75002 & 75009. **Map** 6 D5–7C5.
Ⓜ *Madeleine, Opéra, Richelieu-Drouot, Grands Boulevards.*

A broad thoroughfare divided into eight boulevards – Madeleine, Capucines, Italiens, Montmartre, Poissonnière, Bonne Nouvelle, St-Denis and St-Martin – runs from La Madeleine to the Place de la République. The route was constructed in the 17th century to turn obsolete city fortifications into fashionable promenades – *boulevard* came from the Middle Dutch *bulwerc*, which means bulwark or rampart. The boulevards became so famous in the 19th century that the name *boulevardier* was coined for one who cuts a figure on the boulevards.

Around the Madeleine church and the Opéra it is still possible to gain an impression of what the Grands Boulevards looked like in their heyday, lined with cafés and chic shops. Elsewhere, most of the cafés and restaurants have long since gone, and the old facades are now hidden by neon advertising. However, the Grands Boulevards and the nearby department stores on the Boulevard Haussmann still attract large crowds.

Boulevard des Italiens

Opéra National de Paris Garnier ❹

Pl de l'Opéra 75009. **Map** 6 E4. 🛈
08 92 89 90 90. Ⓜ *Opéra.* ⏰ 10am–5pm daily (1pm on show days). ⬤ public hols. 🎫 📷 See **Entertainment** *pp345–7.* **www.operadeparis.fr**

Sometimes compared to a giant wedding cake, this sumptuous building was designed by Charles Garnier for Napoleon III; construction started in 1862. Its unique appearance is due to a mixture of materials (including stone, marble and bronze) and styles, ranging from Classical to Baroque, with a multitude of columns, friezes and sculptures on the exterior. The building was not completed until 1875; work was interrupted by the Prussian War and 1871 uprising.

In 1858 Count Orsini had attempted to assassinate the emperor outside the old opera house. This prompted Garnier to include a pavilion on the east side of the new building, with a curved ramp leading up to it so that the sovereign could safely step out of his carriage into the suite of rooms adjoining the royal box.

The functions performed by each part of the building are reflected in the structure. Behind the flat-topped foyer, the cupola sits above the auditorium, while the triangular pediment that rises up behind the cupola marks the front of the stage. Underneath the building is a small lake, which provided inspiration for the phantom's hiding place in Paul Leroux's *Phantom of the Opera*, and is used by firemen for water rescue safety training.

Don't miss the magnificent Grand Staircase, made of white marble with a balustrade of red and green marble, and the Grand Foyer, with its domed ceiling covered with mosaics. The five-tiered auditorium is a riot of red velvet, plaster cherubs and gold leaf, which contrast with the false ceiling painted by Marc Chagall in 1964.

Most operas are performed at the Opéra Nationale de Paris Bastille (*see p98*), but the ballet remains here.

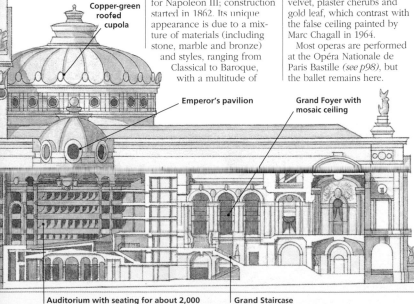

Statue by Millet

Copper-green roofed cupola

Emperor's pavilion

Grand Foyer with mosaic ceiling

Auditorium with seating for about 2,000

Grand Staircase

Sign outside the Grévin waxwork museum

Bibliothèque-
Musée de l'Opéra **⑤**

Pl de l'Opéra 75009. **Map** 6 E5.
Tel 01 47 42 07 02. Ⓜ Opéra.
◯ 10am–5pm daily. ● 1 Jan,
1 May. 🈺 🈲 🈳

The way in to this small, charming museum was once the emperor's private entrance to the Opéra. The museum tells the history of opera and ballet through a large collection of scores, manuscripts, photographs and artists' memorabilia, such as the Russian dancer Vaslav Nijinsky's ballet slippers and tarot cards. Other exhibits include models of stage sets and busts of major composers. The museum also houses a superb library, containing books and manuscripts on theatre, dance and music.

Paris Story **⑥**

11 bis Rue Scribe 75009. **Map** 6 D4.
Tel 01 42 66 62 06. Ⓜ Opéra.
◯ 10am–6pm daily. 🈺 🈳
www.paris-story.com

Especially useful for the first-time visitor, this small museum covers everything you need to know about the history and architecture of Paris in an hour-long film and interactive display. The film covers 2,000 years of history from Lutèce (the Roman name for Paris) to the Paris of today. The show is narrated by a holographic figure of Victor Hugo and visitors can listen to it in English via headphones. A 3D model of the city allows you to pin-point and learn about various monuments with a description of the 156 most important and interesting sites. The Explore Paris gallery consists of five plasma screens showing 3D films on Paris.

Drouot (Hôtel des
Ventes) **⑦**

9 Rue Drouot 75009. **Map** 6 F4.
Tel 01 48 00 20 20. Ⓜ Richelieu
Drouot. ◯ 11am–6pm Mon–Sat,
sales 2pm. 🈲 🈺 🈳 See **Shops
and Markets** pp336–7. **www**.
drouot.com

This is the leading French auction house (Hôtel des Ventes) and it takes its name from the Comte de Drouot who was Napoleon's aide-de-camp. There has been an auction house on the site since 1858, and in 1860 Napoleon III visited the Hôtel and

purchased a couple of earthenware pots. It has been known as the Nouveau Drouot ever since the 1970s, when the existing building was demolished and replaced with today's rather dull structure.

Although overshadowed internationally by Christie's and Sotheby's, auctions at the Nouveau Drouot nevertheless provide a lively spectacle and involve a fascinating range of rare objects. Its presence in the area has attracted many antique and stamp shops.

Grévin **⑧**

10 Blvd Montmartre 75009. **Map** 6
F4. **Tel** 01 47 70 85 05. Ⓜ Grands
Boulevards. ◯ 10am–6:30pm Mon–
Fri, 10am–7pm Sat & Sun (last
admission 1 hour before closing).
🈺 🈳 **www**.grevin.com

This waxwork museum was founded in 1882 and is now a Paris landmark, on a par with Madame Tussauds in London. It contains tableaux of vivid historical scenes (such as Louis XIV at Versailles and the arrest of Louis XVI), the Palais des Mirages – a giant walk-in kaleidoscope, and the Cabinet Fantastique, which includes regular conjuring shows given by a live magician. Famous figures from the worlds of art, sport and politics are also on show, with new celebrities replacing faded and forgotten stars.

Les Passages **⑨**

75002. **Map** 6 F5. Ⓜ Bourse.

The early 19th-century Parisian shopping arcades (known as *passages* or *galeries*) are located between the Boulevard Montmartre and the Rue St-Marc (the extensive Passage des Panoramas). Other arcades are found between the Rue du Quatre Septembre and the Rue des Petits Champs. At the time of their construction, the Passages represented a new traffic-free area for commerce, workshops and apartments. They fell into disuse, but were

Model of a set for *Les Huguenots* (1875) in the Musée de l'Opéra

The colonnaded Neo-Classical facade of the Palais de la Bourse

dramatically revamped in the 1970s and now house an eclectic mixture of small shops selling anything from designer jewellery to rare books. They have high, vaulted roofs of iron and glass. Many have seen better days but one of the most charming is the Galerie Vivienne (off the Rue Vivienne or the Rue des Petits Champs) with its mosaic floor and excellent tearoom.

Galerie Vivienne

Palais de la Bourse ⑩

(Bourse des Valeurs) 4 Pl de la Bourse 75002. **Map** 6 F5.
Tel 01 49 27 14 70. Ⓜ *Bourse.*
⬤ *to the public.*

This Neo-Classical temple of commerce was commissioned by Napoleon and was home to the French Stock Exchange from 1826 to 1987. Today the French stock market is located at 29 Rue Cambon (not open to visits). The hectic floor trading of the Palais de la Bourse has been considerably reduced and is limited to the Matif (the futures market) and the Monep (the traded options market).

Bibliothèque Nationale Richelieu ⑪

58 Rue de Richelieu 75002. **Map** 6 F5. *Tel* 01 53 79 59 59. Ⓜ *Bourse.*
◯ *10am–7pm Tue–Sat, noon–7pm Sun.* ⬤ *public hols.* **www**.bnf.fr

The Bibliothèque Nationale (National Library) originated with the manuscript collections of medieval kings, to which, by law, a copy of every French book printed since 1537 has been added. The collection, which includes two Gutenberg bibles, is partially housed in this complex, created in the 17th century by Cardinal Mazarin. Despite the removal of the printed books, periodicals and CD-Roms to the Bibliothèque Nationale François Mitterand *(see p246)* at Tolbiac, the rue Richelieu buildings still contain a huge variety of items, including original manuscripts by Victor Hugo and Marcel Proust. The library also has the richest collection of engravings and photographs in the world, and departments for maps and plans, theatrical arts, and musical scores. Sadly, the 19th-century reading room is not open to the public.

Bibliothèque Nationale

Avenue de l'Opéra ⑫

75001 & 75002. **Map** 6 E5.
Ⓜ *Opéra, Pyramides.*

This broad avenue is a notable example of Baron Haussmann's dramatic modernization of Paris in the 1860s and 1870s *(see pp34–5)*, and is the city's only tree-less avenue. Much of the medieval city (including a mound from which Joan of Arc began her crusade against the English) was cleared to make way for the wide thoroughfares. The Avenue de l'Opéra, running from the Palais Royal to the Opéra National de Paris Garnier, was completed in 1876. The uniformity of the five-storey buildings that line it contrast with those found in nearby streets, which date from the 17th and 18th centuries. Nearby, in Place Gaillon, is the bar and restaurant Drouant where the Goncourt Prize for literature is decided. The avenue is dominated by travel and luxury shops. The Institut d'Etudes Supérieures des Arts is at No. 5.

Avenue de l'Opéra

MONTMARTRE

Montmartre and art are inseparable. By the end of the 19th century the area was a mecca for artists, writers, poets and their disciples, who gathered to sample the bordellos, cabarets, revues and other exotica which made Montmartre's reputation as a place of depravity in the eyes of the city's more sober, up-standing citizens. Many of the artists and writers have long since left the area and the lively night life no longer has the same charm.

But the hill of Montmartre (the Butte) still has its physical charms

Street theatre in Montmartre

and the village atmosphere remains remarkably intact. Mobs of eager tourists ascend the hill, mostly congregating on the old village square, the Place du Tertre, which is packed with easel painters, and also in front of the Sacré-Coeur church. Elsewhere there are tiny, exquisite squares, winding streets, small terraces, long stairways, plus the Butte's famous vineyard where the few grapes are harvested in early autumn. And there are spectacular views of the city from various points, most especially from the monumental Sacré-Coeur.

SIGHTS AT A GLANCE

Historic Buildings and Streets
Bateau-Lavoir ⑪
Moulin de la Galette ⑭
Avenue Junot ⑮

Churches
Sacré-Coeur pp224–5 ❶
St-Pierre de Montmartre ❷
Chapelle du Martyre ❽
St-Jean l'Evangéliste de Montmartre ❿

Museums and Galleries
Espace Dalí Montmartre ❹
Musée de Montmartre ❺
La Halle Saint Pierre ❼

Squares
Place du Tertre ❸
Place des Abbesses ❾

Cemeteries
Cimetière de Montmartre ⑬

Theatres and Nightclubs
Au Lapin Agile ❻
Moulin Rouge ⑫

GETTING THERE
Abbesses and Pigalle are the nearest metro stations. The Montmartobus leaves Pigalle for the village area. Route 30 runs from the Arc de Triomphe to the foot of the Sacré-Coeur hill and the 85 from the Louvre to Clignancourt.

KEY

▨	Street-by-Street map
M	Metro station
ℹ	Tourist information

0 metres   400
0 yards   400

SEE ALSO

◁ **The narrow Rue St-Rustique winding up the hill to Sacré-Coeur**

Street-by-Street: Montmartre

The steep *butte* (hill) of Montmartre has been associated with artists for 200 years. Théodore Géricault and Camille Corot came here at the start of the 19th century, and in the 20th century Maurice Utrillo immortalized the streets in his works. Today street painters thrive on a lively tourist trade as travellers flock to this picturesque district which in places still preserves the atmosphere of prewar Paris. The name of the area is ascribed to local martyrs tortured in Paris around AD 250, hence *mons martyrium*.

Streetside painter

Montmartre vineyard is one of the last surviving vineyards in Paris. The grape harvest is celebrated on the first Saturday in October.

Metro Lamarck Caulaincourt

★ Au Lapin Agile
This rustic café was a popular meeting point for artists including Picasso ❻

A La Mère Catherine was a favourite eating place of Russian Cossacks in 1814. They would bang on the table and shout *"Bistro!"* (Russian for "quick") – hence the Paris bistro was born.

Espace Dalí Montmartre
This is France's only permanent collection of the Surrealist master's sculptures, paintings and graphic works ❹

KEY

– – – Suggested route

0 metres   100
0 yards   100

STAR SIGHTS

★ Au Lapin Agile

★ Place du Tertre

★ Musée de Montmartre

★ Sacré-Coeur

★ Place du Tertre
The bustling square is the tourist centre of Montmartre and is full of portraitists and other easel artists. Cafés and bars surround the square ❸

★ Musée de Montmartre
The museum features the work of artists who lived in the area: this Portrait of a Woman *(1918) is by the Italian painter and sculptor Amedeo Modigliani* ❺

LOCATOR MAP
See Central Paris Map pp14–15

★ Sacré-Coeur
This Romano-Byzantine church, started in the 1870s and completed in 1914, has many treasures, such as this figure of Christ by Eugène Benet (1911) ❶

RUE DU MONT CENIS
RUE DU CHEVALIER
RUE DU CARDINAL GUIBERT
RUE LAMARCK
RUE PAUL ALBERT
PL DU PARVAIS DU SACRE COEUR
RUE AZAIS
RUE ST ELEUTHERE
RUE DU CARDINAL DUBOIS
SQ WILLETTE
RUE CH NODIER
RUE CHAPPE
PL ST-PIERRE
RUE TARDIEU
RUE STEINKERQUE
— To metro Anvers

St-Pierre de Montmartre
This church became the Temple of Reason during the Revolution ❷

The funiculaire, or cable railway, at the end of the Rue Foyatier takes you to the foot of the basilica of the Sacré-Coeur. Metro tickets are valid on it.

Square Willette lies below the *parvis* (forecourt) of the Sacré-Coeur. It is laid out on the side of the hill in a series of descending terraces with lawns, shrubs, trees and flowerbeds.

La Halle Saint Pierre
The museum hosts exhibitions of Art Brut and Naïve Art. This oil painting, L'Opéra de Paris *(1986), is by L Milinkov* ❼

Montmartre streetside paintings

Sacré-Coeur ❶

See pp226–7.

St-Pierre de Montmartre ❷

2 Rue du Mont-Cenis 75018.
Map 6 F1. *Tel* 01 46 06 57 63.
Ⓜ *Abbesses.* ◻ 8.45am–7pm daily.
✝ 6pm Sat, 9am, 11am Sun. ◙ ♿
Concerts. **www.**sacre-coeur-montmartre.com

Situated in the shadow of
Sacré-Coeur, St-Pierre de
Montmartre is one of the
oldest churches in Paris. It is
all that remains of the great
Benedictine Abbey of
Montmartre, founded in 1133
by Louis VI and his wife,
Adelaide of Savoy, who, as its
first abbess, is buried here.
    Inside are four marble
columns supposedly from a
Roman temple which once
stood on the site. The vaulted
choir dates from the 12th
century, the nave
was remodelled in
the 15th century
and the west front
in the 18th. During
the Revolution the
abbess was
guillotined, and
the church fell into
disuse. It was
reconsecrated in
1908. Gothic-style
stained glass
windows replace
those destroyed by
a bomb in World
War II. The tiny
cemetery opens to the public
only on 1 November.

Doors to St-Pierre church

Place du Tertre ❸

75018. **Map** 6 F1. Ⓜ *Abbesses.*

Tertre means "hillock", or
mound, and this picturesque
square is the highest point in
Paris at some 130 m (430 ft).
It was once the site of the
abbey gallows but is associated with artists, who began
exhibiting paintings here in
the 19th century. It is lined
with colourful restaurants –
La Mère Catherine dates back
to 1793. The house at No. 21
was formerly the home of the
irreverent "Free Commune",
founded in 1920 to perpetuate
the Bohemian spirit of the
area. The Old Montmartre
information office is now here.

Surrealist artist Salvador Dalí

Espace Dalí Montmartre ❹

11 Rue Poulbot 75018.
Map 6 F1. *Tel* 01 42
64 40 10. Ⓜ *Abbesses.*
◻ 10am–6pm daily.
🖼 🎟 groups by appt.
✝ www.*daliparis.com*

A permanent
exhibition of 330
works by the
prolific painter and
sculptor Salvador
Dalí is displayed
here at the heart of
Montmartre. Inside,
the vast, dark
setting reflects the
dramatic character of this
20th-century genius as

moving lights grace first one,
then another, of his Surrealist
works to a soundtrack of Dalí's
recorded voice. This fascinating museum also houses a
commercial art gallery, a
library and a shop selling
books, prints and postcards.

Musée de Montmartre ❺

12 Rue Cortot 75018. **Map** 2 F5.
Tel 01 49 25 89 37. Ⓜ *Abbesses,
Anvers, Blanche, Lamarck-
Caulaincourt.* ◻ 11am–6pm Tue–
Sun. ◙ 1 Jan, 25 Dec. 🖼 ⌀ 🛡
www.*museedemontmartre.fr*

During the 17th century this
charming home belonged to
the actor Roze de Rosimond
(Claude de la Rose), a member
of Molière's theatre company
who, like his mentor Molière,
died during a performance of
Molière's play *Le Malade
Imaginaire*. From 1875 the
big white house, undoubtedly
the finest in Montmartre,
provided living and studio
space for numerous artists,
including Maurice Utrillo and
his mother, Suzanne Valadon,
a former acrobat and model
who became a talented
painter, as well as Raoul Dufy
and Pierre-Auguste Renoir.
    The museum recounts the
history of Montmartre from
the days of the abbesses to
the present, through artefacts,
drawings and photographs. It
is particularly rich in memorabilia of Bohemian life, and
has a reconstruction of the
Café de l'Abreuvoir, Utrillo's
favourite watering hole.

Café de l'Abreuvoir reconstructed

The deceptively rustic exterior of Au Lapin Agile, in the heart of Montmartre

Au Lapin Agile ⑥

22 Rue des Saules 75018. **Map**
2 F5. *Tel* 01 46 06 85 87. Ⓜ
Lamarck-Caulaincourt. ◯ *9pm–*
2am Tue–Sun. See Entertainment
pp342–3. www.au-lapin-agile.com

The former Cabaret des
Assassins derived its current
name from a sign painted by
the humorist André Gill. His
picture of a rabbit escaping
from a cooking pot *(Le Lapin
à Gill)* is a pun on his own
name. The club enjoyed
popularity with intellectuals
and artists at the start of the
20th century. Here in 1911
the novelist Roland Dorgelès
and a group of other regulars
staged one of the modern art
world's most celebrated
hoaxes, with the help of the
café owner's donkey, Lolo. A
paintbrush was tied to Lolo's
tail, and the resulting daub
was shown to critical acclaim
at the Salon des Indépendants,
under the enlightening title
Sunset over the Adriatic,
before the joke was revealed.
  In 1903 the premises were
bought by the cabaret
entrepreneur Aristide Bruand
(painted in a series of posters
by Toulouse-Lautrec). The
venue was depicted by Pablo
Picasso in an oil painting
which was sold for $20 by
the cabaret's owner in 1912.

In 1989, the painting was sold
at auction for $67.5 million.
  Today the cabaret venue
manages to retain much of its
original atmosphere.

Halle Saint Pierre ⑦

Halle St-Pierre, 2 Rue Ronsard
75018. **Map** 7 A1. *Tel* 01 42 58 72
89. Ⓜ *Anvers.* ◯ *10am–6pm daily,*
(Aug: noon–6pm, Mon–Fri). ◯ *some*
public hols. 🎨 🚫 ♿ 🖥 🎬
www.hallesaintpierre.org

In 1945 the French painter
Jean Dubuffet developed the
concept of *Art Brut* (Outsider
or Marginal Art) to describe
works created outside the
boundaries of "official" culture,
often by insane asylum
inmates or the mentally handi-
capped. The Halle Saint Pierre,
at the foot of the Butte, is a

Art Brut at Halle Saint Pierre

museum and gallery devoted
to these "raw" art forms. It
also hosts avant-garde theatre
and musical productions,
holds regular literary evenings
and debates and runs
children's workshops. The
permanent collection includes
more than 500 works of Naïve
art collected by the publisher
Max Fourny in the 1970s.
There is also a specialised
bookshop and café.

Chapelle du Martyre ⑧

9 Rue Yvonne-Le-Tac 75018.
Map 6 F1. Ⓜ *Pigalle.*
◯ *10am–noon, 3pm–5pm Fri–Wed.*

This 19th-century chapel
stands on the site of a
medieval convent chapel,
which was said to mark the
place where the early Christian
martyr and first bishop of
Paris, Saint Denis, was
beheaded by the Romans in
AD 250. It remained a major
pilgrimage site throughout the
Middle Ages. In 1534, in the
crypt of the original chapel,
Ignatius de Loyola, founder of
the Society of Jesus (the mighty
Jesuit order designed to save
the Catholic Church from the
onslaught of the Protestant
Reformation), took his Jesuit
vows with six companions.

Sacré-Coeur ❶

South-east rose window (1960)

At the outbreak of the Franco Prussian War in 1870, two Catholic businessmen made a private religious vow to build a church dedicated to the Sacred Heart of Christ, should France be spared the impending Prussian onslaught. The two men, Alexandre Legentil and Hubert Rohault de Fleury, lived to see Paris saved from invasion despite the war and a lengthy siege – and the start of work on the Sacré-Coeur basilica. The project was taken up by Archbishop Guibert of Paris. Work began in 1875 to Paul Abadie's designs. They were inspired by the Romano-Byzantine church of St-Front in Périgueux. The basilica was completed in 1914, but its consecration was forestalled by the Great War until 1919, when France was victorious.

The Principal Facade
The best view of the domed and turreted Sacré-Coeur is from the gardens below.

The belltower (1895) is 83 m (252 ft) high and contains one of the heaviest bells in the world. The bell itself weighs 18.5 tonnes and the clapper 850 kg (1,900 lb).

★ **Great Mosaic of Christ**
The colossal mosaic (1912–22) dominating the chancel vault was designed by Luc Olivier Merson and Marcel Magne.

Virgin Mary and Child *(1896)*
This Renaissance-style silver statue is one of two in the ambulatory by P Brunet.

★ **Crypt Vaults**
A chapel in the basilica's crypt contains Legentil's heart in a stone urn.

THE SIEGE OF PARIS

Prussia invaded France in 1870. During the four-month siege of Paris, instigated by the Prusso-German statesman Otto von Bismarck, hungry Parisians were forced to eat the city's horses and other animals.

STAR FEATURES

★ Great Mosaic of Christ

★ Bronze Doors

★ Ovoid Dome

★ Crypt Vaults

VISITORS' CHECKLIST

Place du Parvis de Notre Dame 75018. **Map** 6 F1.
Tel 01 53 41 89 00.
Ⓜ Abbesses (then take the funiculaire to the steps of the Sacré-Coeur), Anvers, Barbès-Rochechouart, Lamarck-Caulaincourt. 🚍 30, 31, 54, 80, 85. Ⓟ Blvd de Clichy, Rue Custine. **Basilica** ◯ 6am–10.30pm daily. **Dome and crypt** ◯ 9am–5.45pm daily.
🎫 for crypt and dome.
✝ 7am, 11.15am, 6.30pm, 10pm Mon–Fri (processional at 3pm Fri); 7am, 11.15am, 10pm Sat; 7am, 11am Sun. 🚭 ♿ restricted. 🖥 www.sacre-coeur-montmartre.com

★ Ovoid Dome
This is the second-highest point in Paris, after the Eiffel Tower.

Spiral staircase

The inner structure supporting the dome is made from stone.

The stained-glass gallery affords a view of the whole of the interior.

Statue of Christ
The basilica's most important statue is symbolically placed above the two bronze saints.

Equestrian Statues
The statue of Joan of Arc is one of a pair by H Lefèbvre. The other is of Saint Louis.

★ Bronze Doors
Relief sculptures on the doors in the portico entrance illustrate scenes from the life of Christ, such as the Last Supper.

Main entrance

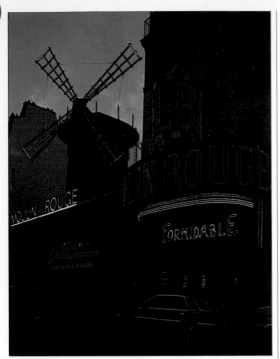

The famous silhouette of the Moulin Rouge nightclub

Place des Abbesses **9**

75018. **Map** 6 F1. M *Abbesses.*

This is one of Paris's most picturesque squares. It is sandwiched between the rather dubious attractions of Place Pigalle with its strip clubs and the Place du Tertre which is mobbed by hundreds of tourists. Be sure not to miss the Abbesses metro station with its unusual green wrought-iron arches

Entrance to the Abbesses metro

and amber lights. Designed by the architect Hector Guimard, it is one of the few original Art Nouveau stations.

St-Jean l'Evangéliste de Montmartre **10**

19 Rue des Abbesses 75018. **Map** 6 F1. *Tel* 01 46 06 43 96. M *Abbesses.* ◯ *9am–7pm Mon– Sat; noon–7pm Sun.* ✝ *frequent.* ◉ ✂ *Fourth Sun each month at 4pm.*

Designed by Anatole de Baudot and completed in 1904, this church was the first to be built from reinforced concrete. The flower motifs on the interior are typical of Art Nouveau, while its interlocking arches suggest Islamic architecture. The red-brick facing has earned it the nickname St-Jean-des-Briques.

Detail of St-Jean l'Evangéliste facade

Bateau-Lavoir **11**

13 Pl Emile-Goudeau 75018. **Map** 6 F1. M *Abbesses.* ◉ *to public.*

This ramshackle tenement building took its name from its resemblance to the laundry boats that used to operate along the River Seine. Between 1890 and 1920 it was home to some of the most talented artists and poets of the day. They lived in squalid conditions with only one tap and took it in turns to sleep in the beds. Picasso, Raoul Dufy, Van Dongen, Marie Laurencin, Juan Gris, Modigliani and Jean Cocteau were just a few of the residents. It was here that Picasso painted *Les Demoiselles d'Avignon* in 1907, usually regarded as the painting that inspired Cubism. The original building burned down in 1970, but a concrete replica has been built – with studio space for up-and-coming artists.

Moulin Rouge **12**

82 Blvd de Clichy 75018. **Map** 6 E1. *Tel* 01 53 09 82 82. M *Blanche.* ◯ *Dinner: 7pm; shows: 9pm and 11pm daily.* 🎟 *See Entertainment pp343–4.* www.moulinrouge.fr

Built in 1885, the Moulin Rouge was turned into a dance hall as early as 1900. The cancan originated in Montparnasse, in the polka gardens of the Rue de la Grande-Chaumière, but it will always be associated with the Moulin Rouge where the wild and colourful dance shows were immortalized in the posters and drawings of Henri de Toulouse-Lautrec. The high-kicking routines of famous "Dorriss girls" such as Yvette Guilbert and Jane Avril continue today in a glittering, Las Vegas-style revue that includes sophisticated light shows and displays of magic.

place, conveying some of the heated energy and artistic creativity of Montmartre a century ago.

Nearby, close to Square Roland Dorgelès, there is another, smaller, often overlooked Montmartre cemetery – **Cimetière St-Vincent.** Here lie more of the great artistic names of the district, including the Swiss composer Arthur Honegger and the writer Marcel Aymé. Most notable of all at St-Vincent is the grave of the great French painter Maurice Utrillo, the quintessential Montmartre artist, many of whose works are now some of the most enduring images of the area.

Vaslav Nijinsky lies in Montmartre

Cimetière de Montmartre ⓭

20 Ave Rachel 75018. **Map** 2 D5.
Tel 01 53 42 36 30. Ⓜ Place de Clichy, Blanche. ◯ 8am–5.30pm daily (opens 8.30am Sat, 9am Sun; closes 6pm daily in summer). ♿

This has been the resting place for many artistic luminaries since the beginning of the 19th century. The composers Hector Berlioz and Jacques Offenbach (who wrote the famous cancan tune) are buried here, alongside many other celebrities such as La Goulue (stage name of Louise Weber, the high-kicking *danseuse* who was the cancan's first star performer and Toulouse-Lautrec's model), the painter Edgar Degas, writer Alexandre Dumas *fils*, German poet Heinrich Heine, Russian dancer Vaslav Nijinsky, and film director François Truffaut. It's an evocative, atmospheric

Moulin de la Galette ⓮

T-junction at Rue Tholozé and Rue Lepic 75018. **Map** 2 E5.
Ⓜ Lamarck-Caulaincourt, Abbesses.

Once some 14 windmills dotted the Montmartre skyline and were used for grinding wheat and pressing grapes. Today only two remain: the Radet, now a restaurant confusingly named Moulin de la Galette which stands further along the Rue Lepic, and the rebuilt Moulin de la Galette, originally built in 1622 and formerly known as the Blute-fin. One of its mill owners, Debray, was supposedly crucified on the windmill's sails during the 1814 Siege of Paris. He had been trying to repulse the invading Cossacks. At the end

of the 19th century both mills became famous dance halls providing inspiration for many artists, notably Pierre-Auguste Renoir and Vincent Van Gogh.

The steep Rue Lepic is a busy shopping area. The Impressionist painter Armand Guillaumin once lived on the first floor of No. 34. Van Gogh inhabited its third floor, and painted the view from there.

Moulin de la Galette

Avenue Junot ⓯

75018. **Map** 2 E5. Ⓜ Lamarck-Caulaincourt.

Opened in 1910, this broad, peaceful street includes many painters' studios and beautiful Art Deco houses. No. 13 has mosaics designed by its former resident, illustrator Francisque Poulbot, who was famous for his drawings of children and street urchins. At No. 15 is Maison Tristan Tzara, named after its previous owner, the Romanian Dadaist poet. Its eccentric design by the Austrian architect Adolf Loos aimed to complement the poet's character. No. 23 is Villa Léandre, with its quaint Anglo-Norman style houses. Just off the Avenue Junot up the steps of the Allée des Brouillards is an 18th-century architectural folly, the Château des Brouillards. In the 19th century it was the home of the French Symbolist writer Gérard de Nerval, who took his pet lobster for walks in the Palais Royal gardens.

Sacré-Coeur, Montmartre, by Maurice Utrillo

FURTHER AFIELD

Many of the châteaux outside Paris originally built as country retreats for the aristocracy and post-revolutionary bourgeoisie are now preserved as museums. Versailles is without doubt the finest, but if your tastes are Modernist, there's also Le Corbusier architecture to see. Disneyland Resort Paris and Parc de la Villette offer plenty to amuse adults and children alike, and there are delightful parks to relax in when the bustle of the city gets too much.

SIGHTS AT A GLANCE

Museums and Galleries
Musée Nissim de Camondo **3**
Musée Cernuschi **4**
Musée Gustave Moreau **5**
Musée du Fumeur **12**
Cité Nationale de l'Histoire de l'Immigration **16**
Musée Marmottan-Monet **29**
Musée des Années 30 **31**

Churches
St-Alexandre-Nevsky Cathedral **1**
Basilique-Cathédrale de Saint-Denis **7**
Notre-Dame du Travail **23**

Famous Buildings and Streets
Bercy **18**
Bibliothèque Nationale de France **19**
13th Arrondissement **20**
Cité Universitaire **22**
Institut Pasteur **24**
Versailles pp248–53 **26**
Rue de la Fontaine **27**
Fondation Le Corbusier **28**
La Défense **32**
Château de Malmaison **33**

Markets
Marché aux Puces de St-Ouen **6**
Portes St-Denis et St-Martin **8**
Marché d'Aligre **15**

Parks, Gardens and Canals
Parc Monceau **2**
Canal St-Martin **9**
Parc des Buttes-Chaumont **10**
Château et Bois de Vincennes **17**
Parc Montsouris **21**
Parc André Citroën **25**
Bois de Boulogne **30**

Cemeteries
Cimetière du Père Lachaise pp240–41 **13**

Leisure Parks
Parc de la Villette pp236–9 **11**
Disneyland Resort Paris pp242–5 **14**

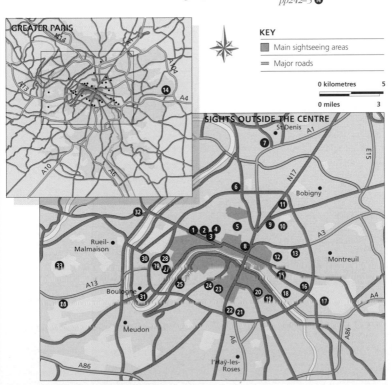

KEY

▮ Main sightseeing areas

▬ Major roads

0 kilometres   5

0 miles   3

North of the City

St-Alexandre-Nevsky Cathedral

St-Alexandre-Nevsky Cathedral ❶

12 Rue Daru 75008. **Map** 4 F3.
Tel 01 42 27 37 34. **M** Courcelles.
⏰ 3pm–5pm Tue, Fri, Sun.
✝ 6pm Sat, 10.30am Sun. ⊘ ♿

This imposing Russian Orthodox cathedral with its five golden-copper domes signals the presence of a large Russian community in Paris. Designed by members of the St Petersburg Fine Arts Academy and financed jointly by Tzar Alexander II and the local Russian community, the cathedral was completed in 1861. Inside, a wall of icons divides the church in two. The Greek-cross plan and the rich interior mosaics and frescoes are Neo-Byzantine

in style, while the exterior and gilt domes are traditional Russian Orthodox.

The Russian population in the city increased dramatically following the Bolshevik Revolution of 1917, when thousands of Russians fled to Paris for safety. The Rue Daru, in which the cathedral stands, and the surrounding area form "Little Russia", with its Russian schools and the many dance academies, and delightful tea shops and bookshops where visitors can browse.

Parc Monceau ❷

Blvd de Courcelles 75017. **Map** 5 A3.
Tel 01 42 27 39 56. **M** Monceau.
⏰ 7am–8pm daily (to 9.30pm summer). See **Eight Guided Walks** pp258–9.

This green haven dates back to 1778 when the Duc de Chartres (later Duc d'Orléans) commissioned the painter-writer and amateur landscape designer Louis Carmontelle to create a magnificent garden. Also a theatre designer, Carmontelle created a "garden of dreams", an exotic landscape full of architectural follies in imitation of English and German fashion of the time. In 1783 the Scottish landscape gardener Thomas Blaikie laid out an area of the garden in English style. The park was the scene of the first recorded parachute landing, made by

André-Jacques Garnerin on 22 October 1797. Over the years the park changed hands and in 1852 it was acquired by the state and half the land sold off for property development. The remaining 9 ha (22 acres) were made into public gardens. These were restored and new buildings erected by Adolphe Alphand, architect of the Bois de Boulogne and the Bois de Vincennes.

Today the park remains one of the most chic in the capital but has lost many of its early features. A *naumachia* basin flanked by Corinthian columns remains. This is an ornamental version of a Roman pool used for simulating naval battles. There are also a Renaissance arcade, pyramids, a river and the Pavillon de Chartres, a charming rotunda designed by Nicolas Ledoux which was once used as a tollhouse. Just south of here is a huge red pagoda, which now houses a gallery devoted to Asian art.

Musée Nissim de Camondo ❸

63 Rue de Monceau 75008.
Map 5 A3. ☎ 01 53 89 06 40, 01 53 89 06 50. **M** Monceau, Villiers.
⏰ 10am–5.30pm Wed–Sun (last adm: 4.30pm). ● public hols. 📷 📷
www.lesartsdecoratifs.fr

Comte Moïse de Camondo, a leading Jewish financier during the Belle Epoque, commissioned this mansion in 1914. It was built in the style of the Petit Trianon, at Versailles *(see pp248–9)*, to house a rare collection of 18th-century furniture, tapestries, paintings and other precious objects. The museum has been faithfully and lovingly restored to recreate an aristocratic town house of the Louis XV and XVI eras. In the museum there are Savonnerie carpets, Beauvais tapestries and the Buffon service

Colonnade beside the *naumachia* basin in Parc Monceau

233

(Sèvres porcelain). The very latest gadgets, for the period, are now displayed in the restored kitchen and service quarters, equipped with the utmost efficiency, taste and forethought by their owner.

Musée Nissim de Camondo

Musée Cernuschi ❹

7 Ave Vélasquez 75008. **Map** 5 A3. **Tel** 01 53 96 21 50. Ⓜ Villiers, Monceau. ◯ 10am–6pm Tue–Sun. ⬤ public hols. 🚫 🎥 📷 🛗 www.cernuschi.paris.fr

This mansion near Parc Monceau contains an intriguing private collection of late East Asian art which was amassed by the Milanese-born politician and banker Enrico Cernuschi (1821–96). The original bequest of 5,000 lacquered, ceramic, bronze and ivory items has been augmented by donations and acquisitions over the years. The wide-ranging collection, now about ten thousand items, includes a 5th-century seated Bodhisattva (Buddhist divine being) from Yunkang; *La Tigresse* (a 12th-century BC bronze vase); and *Horses and Grooms*, an 8th-century T'ang painting on silk attributed to the era's greatest horse painter, court artist Han Kan.

Bodhisattva in the Musée Cernuschi

Musée Gustave Moreau ❺

14 Rue de la Rochefoucauld 75009. **Map** 6 E3. **Tel** 01 48 74 38 50. Ⓜ Trinité. ◯ 10am–12.45pm, 2–5.15pm Wed–Mon. ⬤ 1 Jan, 1 May, 25 Dec. 🎥 📷 🛗 www.musee-moreau.fr

The Symbolist painter Gustave Moreau (1825–98), known for his vivid, imaginative works depicting biblical and mythological fantasies, left to the French state a vast collection of more than 1,000 oils, watercolours and some 7,000 drawings in his town house. One of Moreau's best-known and most outstanding works, *Jupiter and Semele*, can be seen here. There is also a superb collection of his unfinished sketches.

Angel Traveller by Gustave Moreau, in the Musée Gustave Moreau

Marché aux Puces de St-Ouen ❻

Rue des Rosiers, St-Ouen 75018. **Map** 2 F2. Ⓜ Porte-de-Clignancourt. ◯ 9.30am–6pm Sat–Mon. 🎥 call 01 40 11 77 36. See **Markets** p339. www.les-puces.com

This is the oldest, most expensive and largest of the Paris flea markets, covering 6 ha (15 acres). In the 19th century, rag merchants and tramps would gather outside the city limits and offer their wares for sale.

Marché aux Puces du St-Ouen, an antiques and bric-a-brac market

By the 1920s there was a proper market here, where masterpieces could sometimes be purchased cheaply from the often uninformed sellers. Today it is divided into specialist markets. Known especially for its profusion of furniture and ornaments from the Second Empire (1852–70), few bargains are to be found these days, yet some 150,000 bargain-hunters, tourists and dealers still flock here to browse among more than 2,000 stalls *(see p339)*.

Basilique-Cathédrale de Saint-Denis ❼

1 Rue de la Légion D'Honneur, 93200 St-Denis. **Tel** 01 48 09 83 54. Ⓜ St-Denis-Basilique. ᴿᴱᴿ St-Denis. ◯ Apr–Sep: 10am–6.15pm Mon–Sat, noon–6.15pm Sun; Oct–Mar: 10am–5.15pm Mon–Sat, noon–5.15pm Sun (last adm: 30 mins before closing). 🕭 8.30am, 10am Sun. 🎥 📷 🎥 🛗

Constructed between 1137 and 1281, the cathedral is on the site of the tomb of St Denis, the first bishop of Paris, who was beheaded in AD 250. The building was the original influence for Gothic art. From Merovingian times it was a burial place for rulers of France. During the Revolution many tombs were desecrated and scattered, but the best were stored, and now represent a collection of funerary art. Memorials include those of Dagobert (died 638), Henri II (died 1559) and Catherine de' Medici (died 1589), and Louis XVI and Marie-Antoinette (died 1793).

Portes St-Denis et St-Martin ^⑧

Blvds St-Denis & St-Martin 75010.
Map 7 B5. Ⓜ *Strasbourg-St-Denis.*

These gates give access to the two ancient and important north–south thoroughfares whose names they bear. They once marked the entrance to the city. The Porte St-Denis is 23 m (76 ft) high and was built in 1672 by François Blondel. It is decorated with figures by Louis XIV's sculptor, François Girardon. They commemorate victories of the king's armies in Flanders and the Rhine that year. Porte St-Martin is 17 m (56 ft) tall and was built in 1674 by Pierre Bullet. It celebrates Besançon's capture and the defeat of the Triple Alliance of Spain, Holland and Germany.

Western arch of the Porte St-Denis, once the entrance to the city

Boats berthed at Port de l'Arsenal

East of the City

Canal St-Martin ^⑨

Map 8 E2. Ⓜ *Jaurès, J Bonsergent, Goncourt. See pp260–61.*

The 5-kilometre (3-mile) canal, opened in 1825, provides a short-cut for river traffic between loops of the Seine. It has long been loved by novelists, film directors and tourists alike. It is dotted with barges and pleasure boats that leave from the Port de l'Arsenal. At the north end of the canal is the Bassin de la Villette waterway and the elegant Neo-Classical Rotonde de la Villette, spectacularly floodlit at night.

Parc des Buttes-Chaumont ^⑩

Rue Manin 75019 (main access from Rue Armand Carrel). Ⓜ *Botzaris, Buttes-Chaumont.* ⃝ *7am–8.15pm daily (1 Jun–15 Aug: to 10.15pm; May, 16 Aug–30 Sep: to 9.15pm).* ⑪ *See pp268–9.*

For many this is the most pleasant and unexpected park in Paris. The panoramic hilly site was converted in the 1860s by Baron Haussmann from a rubbish dump and quarry with a gallows below. Haussmann worked with the landscape architect/designer Adolphe Alphand, who organized a vast programme to furnish the new pavement-lined avenues with benches and lampposts. Others involved in the creation of this park were the engineer Darcel and the landscape gardener Barillet-Deschamps. They created a lake, made an island with real and artificial rocks, gave it a Roman-style temple and added a waterfall, streams, foot-bridges leading to the island and beaches. Today visitors will also find boating facilities and donkey rides.

Parc de la Villette ^⑪

See pp236–9.

Musée du Fumeur ^⑫

7 Rue Pache 75011. *Tel 01 46 59 05 51.* Ⓜ *Voltaire.* ⃝ *12.30–7pm Tue–Sat.* ⬤ *1–8 Jan, 1 May, 1–22 Aug, 25 Dec.* ▧ ▯

As France's public spaces are now refreshingly tobacco free, this quaint museum nostalgically documents the history of tobacco and smoking through the ages. Objects used by smokers across the world, including 17th-century clay pipes, rare snuff boxes, and period engravings, sit alongside

Parc des Buttes-Chaumont

modern works of art dedicated to smoking. Aficionados can consult the library which offers essays and articles from tobacco magazines, plus regular film-showings covering subjects such as how tobacco is cultivated and how to roll a cigar.

Cimetière du Père Lachaise ⑬

See pp240–41.

Disneyland Paris ⑭

See pp242–5.

Marché d'Aligre ⑮

Place d'Aligre 75012. **Map** 14 F5.
Ⓜ Ledru-Rollin. ⏰ 9am–1pm,
4–7.30pm Tue–Fri; 9am–1pm,
3.30–7.30pm Sat; 9am–1.30pm Sun.

On Sunday mornings this lively market offers one of the most colourful sights in Paris. French, Arab and African traders hawk fruit, vegetables, flowers and clothing on the streets, while the adjoining covered market, the Beauveau St-Antoine, offers meats, cheeses, pâtés and many intriguing international delicacies.

Aligre is where old and new Paris meet. Here the established community of this old artisan quarter coexists with a more recently established group of hip urban professionals, who have been lured here by the transformation of the nearby Bastille area (see p98).

Cité Nationale de l'Histoire de l'Immigration ⑯

293 Ave Daumesnil 75012.
Tel 01 53 59 58 60. Ⓜ Porte Dorée.
⏰ 10am–5.30pm Tue–Fri, 10am–
7pm Sat, Sun. 🅿 ♿ restricted. 📷
www.histoire-immigration.fr

This museum and aquarium is housed in a beautiful Art Deco building that was designed especially for the

The imposing Château de Vincennes

1931 Colonial Exhibition. The impressive facade has a vast frieze by A Janniot, depicting the contributions of France's overseas territories.

Formerly the home of the Musée National des Arts d'Afrique et d'Océanie (whose collection was moved to the musée du quai Branly in 2003, see pp192–3), the Palais de la Porte Dorée now houses the Cité Nationale de l'Histoire de l'Immigration. This acts as both a museum and a cultural centre, with regular live performances and films on the subject of the history of immigration in France.

The magnificent 1930s Hall d'Honneur and the Salle des Fêtes (ballroom) are also open to the public. In the basement there is a magnificent tropical aquarium filled with colourful fish, as well as terrariums containing tortoises and crocodiles.

Exterior relief on the Cité Nationale de l'Histoire de l'Immigration

Château et Bois de Vincennes ⑰

Ⓜ Château de Vincennes. RER
Vincennes. Château Ave de Paris
94300 Vincennes. **Tel** 01 48 08 31
20. ⏰ 10am–5pm daily (to 6pm
Apr–Sep; various options are available
for guided visits. Call for details).
● public hols. 📷 📷 📷 📷 **Bois
de Vincennes** ⏰ dawn to dusk daily.
www.chateau-vincennes.fr

The Château de Vincennes, enclosed by a defensive wall and a moat, was once a royal residence. It was here that Henry V of England died painfully of dysentery in 1422. His body was boiled in the Château's kitchen to prepare it for shipping back to England. Abandoned when Versailles was completed, the château was converted into an arsenal by Napoleon.

The 14th-century *donjon*, or keep, is the tallest in Europe and is a fine example of medieval military architecture. It houses the Château's museum. Building work on the Gothic chapel started in 1380, but was not finished until around 1550. The chapel has beautiful stone rose windows and a magnificent single aisle. Two 17th-century pavilions house a museum of army insignia.

Once a royal hunting ground, the forest of Vincennes was given to the City of Paris by Napoleon III in 1860. Baron Haussman's landscape architect added ornamental lakes and cascades. Among its main attractions is the largest funfair in France (from Palm Sunday to end of May).

Parc de la Villette ⓫

The old slaughterhouses and livestock market of Paris have been transformed into this Bernard Tschumi-designed urban park. Its vast facilities stretch across 55 ha (136 acres) of a previously run-down part of the city. The plan is to revive the tradition of parks for meetings and activities and to stimulate interest in the arts and sciences. Work began in 1984, and the park has grown to include a science museum, a concert hall, an exhibition pavilion, a spherical cinema, a circus and a music centre. Linking them all is the park itself, with its *folies*, walkways, gardens and playgrounds. In the summer the park holds an open-air film festival.

The *Folies*
These red cubes punctuate the park and provide a variety of services, such as a café and a children's workshop.

Children's Playground
The maze-like setting, complete with sand pits and colourful play equipment makes this playground a paradise for young children.

★ Grande Halle
The old cattle hall has been transformed into a flexible exhibition space with mobile floors and auditorium.

Entrance

STAR BUILDINGS

- ★ Cité des Sciences et de l'Industrie
- ★ Grande Halle
- ★ Cité de la Musique
- ★ Zénith Theatre

★ Cité de la Musique
This quirky but elegant all-white complex holds the music conservatory, a concert hall, library, studios and a museum.

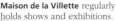

Maison de la Villette regularly holds shows and exhibitions.

Entrance

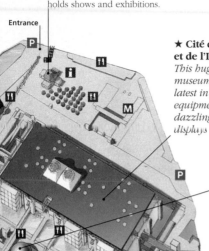

★ **Cité des Sciences et de l'Industrie**
This huge science museum boasts the latest in futurist equipment and has dazzling hands-on displays (see pp236–9).

La Géode
The cinema's gigantic 180° movie screen combines visual and sound effects to create fantastic experiences, such as the sense of travelling in space.

★ **Zénith Theatre**
This vast polyester tent was built as a venue for pop concerts with a capacity to seat more than 6,000 spectators.

Musicians from Guadeloupe performing outside the Museum

LE MUSEE DE LA MUSIQUE

This museum brings together a collection of over 4,500 instruments, objects, tools and works of art covering the history of music since the Renaissance. The permanent collection of over 900 items is displayed chronologically and can be traced using infrared audio headphones.

L'Argonaute
The exhibit consists of a 1950s submarine and a nearby navigation museum.

Cité des Sciences et de l'Industrie

This hugely popular science and technology museum occupies the largest of the old Villette slaughterhouses, which now form part of a massive urban park. Architect Adrien Fainsilber has created an imaginative interplay of light, vegetation and water in the high-tech, five-storey building, which soars 40 m (133 ft) high, stretching over 3 ha (7 acres). At the museum's heart is the Explora exhibit, a fascinating guide to the worlds of science and technology. Visitors can take part in computerized games on space, the earth and ocean, computers and sound. On other levels there are a children's science city, cinemas, a science newsroom, a library and shops.

A young visitor at La Villette

Planetarium
In this 260-seat auditorium you can watch eclipses and fly over Martian landscapes, thanks to their "Allsky" video system.

Le Nautile
This full-scale model of the Nautile, France's technologically advanced exploration submarine, represents one of the most sophisticated machines in the world.

★ The Story of the Universe
An exploration of the birth of the universe, this exhibit takes you back 13.7 billion years to the creation of the first atom.

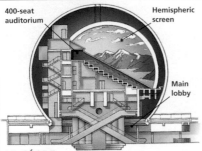

400-seat auditorium

Hemispheric screen

Main lobby

LA GÉODE
This vast sphere houses a hemispherical cinema screen, 1,000 sq m (11,000 sq ft), showing IMAX and 3D films. The Géode is prohibited for women more than six-months pregnant.

The moat was designed by Fainsilber so that natural light could penetrate into the lower levels of the building.

The main hall is vast, with a soaring network of shafts, bridges, escalators and balconies, and has a cathedral-like atmosphere.

STAR EXHIBITS

★ Children's City

★ Story of the Universe

★ La Géode

VISITORS' CHECKLIST

30 av Corentin-Cariou 75019.
📞 01 40 05 80 00. Ⓜ Porte
de la Villette. 🚌 75, 139, 150,
152, 375, PC2. 🅿 Quai de la
Charente. ☐ 10am–6pm Tue–
Sat (7pm Sun). 📷 ♿ 🍴 📖 📷
📷 Shows, films, videos,
library, conference centre.
www.cite-sciences.fr

Cupolas
*The two glazed domes,
17 m (56 ft) in diameter,
filter the flow of natural
light into the main hall.*

The greenhouse is a
square hothouse, 32 m
(105 ft) high and wide,
linking the park to the
building.

To La Géode

Mirage Aircraft
*A full-size model of the
French-built jet fighter is one
of the exhibits illustrating
advances in technology.*

Walkways
*The walkways cross the
encircling moat to link the
various floors of the museum
to the Géode and the park.*

★ Children's City
*In this lively, extensive
area children can
experiment and play
with machines that
show how scientific
principles work.*

Cimetière du Père Lachaise ⑬

Paris's most prestigious cemetery is set on a wooded hill overlooking the city. The land was once owned by Père de la Chaise, Louis XIV's confessor, but it was bought by order of Napoleon in 1803 to create a new cemetery. The cemetery became so popular with the Paris bourgeoisie that it was expanded six times during the century. Here were buried celebrities such as the writer Honoré de Balzac and the composer Frédéric Chopin, and more recently, the singer Jim Morrison and the actor Yves Montand. Famous graves and striking funerary sculpture make this a pleasant place for a leisurely, nostalgic stroll.

The Columbarium was built at the end of the 19th century. The American dancer Isadora Duncan is one of the many celebrities whose ashes are housed here.

Marcel Proust
Proust brilliantly chronicled the Belle Epoque in his novel Remembrance of Things Past.

★ Simone Signoret and Yves Montand
France's most famous post-war cinema couple were renowned for their left-wing views and long turbulent relationship.

Allan Kardec was the founder of a 19th-century spiritual cult, which still has a strong following. His tomb is forever covered in pilgrims' flowers.

Sarah Bernhardt
The great French tragedienne, who died in 1923 aged 78, was famous for her portrayal of Racine heroines.

Monument aux Morts
by Paul Albert Bartholomé is one of the best monumental sculptures in the cemetery. It dominates the central avenue.

Entrance

Frédéric Chopin, the great Polish composer, belonged to the French Romantic generation.

Théodore Géricault
The French Romantic painter's masterpiece, The Raft of the Medusa *(see p124), is depicted on his tomb.*

STAR FEATURES

★ Oscar Wilde
★ Jim Morrison
★ Edith Piaf
★ Simone Signoret and Yves Montand

★ Oscar Wilde
The Irish dramatist, aesthete and great wit was cast away from virtuous Britain to die of drink and dissipation in Paris in 1900. Jacob Epstein sculpted the monument.

The remains of Molière, the great 17th-century actor and dramatist, were transferred here in 1817 to add historic glamour to the new cemetery.

VISITORS' CHECKLIST

16 Rue du Repos. *Tel 01 55 25 82 10.* **M** *Père Lachaise, Alexandre Dumas.* 🚌 *60, 69, 26 to Pl Gambetta.* **P** *Pl Gambetta.* ⬤ *8am–5.30pm daily (from 8.30am Sat, 9am Sun; mid-Mar–early Nov: to 6pm).* 📷 ✔ 🚻 ℹ

Mur des Fédérés is the wall against which the last Communard rebels were shot by government forces in 1871. It is now a place of pilgrimage for left-wing sympathizers.

★ Edith Piaf
Known as "the little sparrow" because of her size, Piaf was the 20th century's greatest French popular singer. In her tragic voice she sang of the sorrows and love woes of the Paris working class.

Victor Noir
The life-size statue of this 19th-century journalist shot by Pierre Bonaparte, a cousin of Napoleon III, is said to have fertility powers.

George Rodenbach, the 19th-century poet, is depicted as rising out of his tomb with a rose in the hand of his outstretched arm.

Elizabeth Demidoff, a Russian princess who died in 1818, is honoured by a three-storey Classical temple by Quaglia.

★ Jim Morrison
The death of The Doors' *lead singer in Paris in 1971 is still a mystery.*

François Raspail
The tomb of this much-imprisoned partisan of the 1830 and 1840 revolutions is in the form of a prison.

Disneyland Resort Paris ⓮

Disneyland Resort Paris is built on a massive scale – the 2,000-ha (5,000-acre) site encompasses two theme parks; seven hotels (several with swimming pools); a shopping, dining and entertainment village; a seasonal ice skating rink; lakes; two convention centres; and a golf course. One stop down the line from their very own train station lies Val d'Europe, a huge shopping mall with more than 180 shopping outlets, including 60 discount stores, and a Sea World centre.

Unbeatable for complete escapism, combined with vibrant excitement and sheer energy, the Parks offer extreme rides and gentle experiences, all accompanied by phenomenal visual effects.

The Queen of Hearts' Castle, in Alice's Curious Labyrinth

THE PARKS

Disneyland Resort Paris consists of Disneyland Park and Walt Disney Studios Park. Disneyland Park is based on the Magic Kingdom of California and has more than 40 rides or attractions. The newest is Walt Disney Studios Park, where interactive exhibits and live shows bring alive the wizardry of the movie and television industry. Find out more at: www.disneylandparis.com or call 08 705 03 03 03 (UK), 0825 30 60 30 (France).

GETTING THERE

By Car
Disneyland Resort Paris lies 32 km (20 miles) east of Paris, and has its own link (exit 14) from the A4 east-bound from Paris and west-bound A4, from Strasbourg. Follow the signs to Marne la Vallée (Val d'Europe) until you see the Disneyland signs. (The Davy Crockett Ranch is exit 13.)

By Air
Both Orly and Charles de Gaulle Airports have a shuttle bus (VEA) which runs every 30 minutes (45 in low season). No booking is necessary. The fare is about €13–17 per person.

By Train
The Paris RER A runs directly to the parks at Marne la Vallée, as does the TGV with connections throughout Europe, including with the Eurostar.

PARKING

There is space for over 12,000 vehicles, and an efficient moving sidewalk conveys you to the exit. Parking costs €8 per day for cars, and €13 for campers and coaches. Parking at Disneyland Resort Paris hotels is free to guests, and the Disneyland and New York hotels offer valet parking.

OPENING HOURS

The Parks tend to open at 9am in high season and 10am otherwise. Disneyland Park closes at 11pm in high season and 8pm in low season. The Walt Disney Studios Park closes at 8pm in high season and 6pm in low season. Special events, such as Hallowe'en, can mean extended hours.

WHEN TO VISIT

The busiest times are Christmas and New Year, mid-February to early April and July to early September, and mid-October. Busiest days are Saturday–Monday; Tuesday and Wednesday are quietest.

LENGTH OF VISIT

To experience everything Disneyland Resort Paris has to offer you really need to spend three or four days at the resort. Although it is possible to tour the Parks in one day each, to enjoy them at less than breakneck pace you need at least two days for Disneyland Park alone, and if you want to include Buffalo Bill's Wild West show or visit some of the

EATING AND DRINKING

There's no need to leave the park to eat during the day. **Au Chalet de la Marionnette** (Fantasyland) is excellent for kids (and almost deserted at 3pm) as is the **Cowboy Cookout Barbecue** (Frontierland), which tends to be rather more crowded. **Colonel Hathi's Pizza Outpost** (Adventureland) is worth a visit just to see the authentic colonial gear, whilst **Café Hyperion – Videopolis** (Discoveryland) offers good food plus excellent entertainment, but service is very slow.

You pay a premium for full-service restaurants but the experience of eating in **Blue Lagoon Restaurant** (Adventureland) is one you will remember. You dine on the "shore" of a Caribbean Pirate hideaway while the boats from Pirates of the Caribbean glide past. **Walt's**, on Main Street, USA, is also a good but pricey restaurant offering American fare. If you're lucky, they'll seat you so that you can watch the afternoon Main Street parade in comfort from an upstairs window.

In Disney Village **Annette's Diner** is staffed by roller-skating waitresses against a background of '50s records. **Planet Hollywood** is another good option, and the **Rainforest Café** provides an interestingly animated meal. Bavarian specialities are on the menu in **King Ludwig's Castle**, while a giant **McDonald's** serves the usual fare. The hotel restaurants are more expensive the nearer they are located to the park.

nightclubs in Disney Village, then you'll be pushed to manage it all in under four days. Locals turn up on a daily basis from Paris, which is only 35 minutes away on the RER, but most guests from further afield will stay in hotels. Disney offer several packages for those who wish to stay on site. These include passes for the Parks, and accommodation with continental breakfast included. All-inclusive packages can also be booked.

TICKETS

Tickets can be bought online, as part of a package or from any Disney Store before you leave home, or at the Park upon arrival – though this means queuing. One-, two- or three-day tickets are available. Hopper tickets allow same day entry to both Parks. The Paris transport system RATP also sells tickets combining RER travel and entry to the Parks. Once inside, you can use your ticket to get a fast pass for certain rides with a specific time slot to enable entry without queuing.

GETTING AROUND

Disney provides an efficient transport system between the Parks and the hotels (excluding Davy Crockett Ranch) with buses on the half hour. In summer, a fleet of little open-top buses drives slowly around Lake Disney, ferrying guests between the three lakeside hotels and Disney Village. If you're staying at any of the on-site hotels it's only a short walk (20 minutes at most) to the Park gates.

Sleeping Beauty Castle, the centrepiece of the Park

WHICH HOTEL?

There are six hotels on site, and one in woodland 2 km (3 miles) away. The best hotels are the closest to the Parks.

Hotel Santa Fe: basic, small and reasonably inexpensive. The only hotel offering parking immediately outside your room.
Hotel Cheyenne: a Wild West theme hotel, about 17 minutes' walk from the park. Small rooms (with bunks for the kids), a Native American village play area. Inexpensive and a great experience. Kids love this hotel.
Sequoia Lodge: a lakeside "hunter's lodge", moderately priced with more than 1,000 rooms. Ask for a room in the main building. Rooms at the front have great views.
Newport Bay Club: a huge, nautically-themed, hotel on the lakeside. Moderately priced, this massive hotel has a huge convention centre, magnificent swimming pool and three floors offering extra services for a supplement.
Hotel New York: expensive and business-oriented with a large convention centre. An ice-skating rink is available Oct–Mar.
Disneyland Hotel: the jewel in the crown. Expensive, but right at the entrance to the Disneyland Park. Full of delightful touches, such as grandfather clocks and ever-present Disney characters. The Castle Club is a 50-room hotel-within-a-hotel. If you can afford it, a week of decadent fawning and unrestrained hedonism can be yours!
Davy Crockett Ranch: log cabins sleeping 4–6 are grouped around a woodland trail, as well as traditional camping facilities. The best choice for family activities with some excellent facilities: the pool ranks as one of the best in Disneyland Resort Paris.

MONEY

Credit cards are accepted everywhere within the resort. ATMs and commission-free foreign exchange are available immediately inside the Park entrances and at reception in all the hotels.

DISABLED TRAVELLERS

City Hall (immediately within Disneyland Park) has a brochure outlining the facilities for the disabled, and a Disabled Guest Guide can be pre-ordered (free) from the website. The complex is designed very much with the disabled in mind and wheelchairs can be hired, but note that cast members are not allowed to assist with lifting people or moving wheelchairs.

STAYING IN A DISNEY HOTEL

The on-site hotels offer rooms at a wide range of prices; generally, those closest to the Parks are the most expensive. Advantages include virtually no travelling to reach the

The runaway mine-train track of Big Thunder Mountain

Parks, fast passes (ask at reception about restrictions) and "early bird" entry to the parks on selected dates (usually at peak times).

If you stay at a Disney hotel you will be given a hotel ID card which is very important. As well as being used to charge anything you buy back to your hotel room (and have it delivered there), it also allows you entry to the Disneyland hotel grounds early in the morning while they're still shut to day trippers (the grounds also act as an entrance to the Park).

For children (of any age), one of the most exciting bonuses of staying in an on-site hotel is the chance to dine with Disney characters.

Exploring Disneyland Resort Paris

The resort consists of two large entertainment areas, Disneyland Park and the Walt Disney Studios Park. The former celebrates Hollywood folklore and fantasies, both past and future, while the latter highlights the ingenuity of the production processes involved in cinema, animation and television. The resort offers a plethora of attractions and themed parades chosen from the "Wonderful World Of Disney".

DISNEYLAND PARK

MAIN STREET, USA

Main Street represents a fantasy small-town America, right down to the traffic, which includes horse-drawn rail cars, a paddy wagon and other vintage transport in a system that runs between Town Square and Central Plaza. The Victorian facades offer a wealth of detail, and front several interesting stores. The Emporium is the place for gifts. Further along, you can snack at Casey's Corner or succumb to the aromas from Cookie Kitchen or the Cable Car Bake Shop. Either side of the shops are the Discovery and Liberty Arcades, offering a covered route to the Central Plaza and hosting displays and cute small stalls.

At night, thousands of lights set Main Street's paving aglow. Disney's Fantillusion, a fantasy of music, live action and illuminated floats, begins at Town Square. From Main Street you can ride a 19th-century "steam" engine. Do note that boarding elsewhere than Main Street is not always possible before noon.

FRONTIERLAND

This homage to America's Wild West hosts some of the Park's most popular attractions. Big Thunder Mountain, a rollercoaster ride, is circled by the Thunder Mesa river boat that takes a musical cruise around America's finest natural monuments. Phantom Manor is an excellent ghost ride with realistic special effects. Pocahontas Indian Village

and Legends of the Wild West are both popular with younger children.

ADVENTURELAND

Enjoy the wild rides and Audio-Animatronics™ of Adventureland. Indiana Jones™ and the Temple of Peril hurtles you through a derelict mine. The ride has torches, steep drops and tight 360° loops.

Pirates of the Caribbean is a great boat ride through underground prisons and past fighting galleons. La Cabane des Robinson, based on Jonathan Wyss's *Swiss Family Robinson*, starts with a shaky climb up a 27-m (88-ft) Banyan Tree. From here you explore the rest of the island, including the caves of Ben Gunn from *Treasure Island* and the awe-inspiring suspension bridge near Spy-glass Hill. The children's playground, Pirates' Beach, and Aladdin's Enchanted Passage are also well worth a visit.

FANTASYLAND

The buildings here are mod–elled on those in animated movies. Many attractions are for younger children, such as Snow White and the Seven Dwarfs, and Pinocchio's Fantastic Journey. The very young will love Dumbo the Flying Elephant. Peter Pan's Flight is a triumph of imag–ination and technology, flying you high over the streets of London. A popular diversion is Alice's Curious Labyrinth.

Hourly, there's a musical parade of clockwork figures at "It's a small world". Aboard a boat, you meander through lands of animated models to the strains of the eponymous

song. Le Pays des Contes des Fées (Storybook Land) is another boat ride. Next, hop aboard Casey Jr for a train ride circling the boats.

DISCOVERYLAND

Science fiction and the future are the themes here. The multi-loop ride Space Mountain draws crowds from the outset, but at the end of the day you can often walk straight on. Les Mystères du Nautilus takes you right into the submarine from *20,000 Leagues Under the Sea*. Autopia, where you can drive a real, petrol-engined car, is a magnet for youngsters. Orbitron features spaceships whilst Star Tours takes you on a breathtaking journey in a star shuttle. Buzz Lightyear Laser Blast takes you into the world of toys where you have to shoot Emperor Zurg's electronic army.

The best shows are in Videopolis. Honey, I Shrunk the Audience is a masterpiece of total sensory stimulation.

WALT DISNEY STUDIOS PARK

FRONT LOT

Inside the giant studio gates, you can't miss Mickey Mouse as he appears in *The Sorceror's Apprentice*. Also hard to miss is the "Earful Tower", a massive studio icon based on the water tower at the Disney Studios in California. Disney Studio 1 houses a film set boulevard, complete with stylised street facades and venues such as the 1930's-style Club Swankedero, the Liki Tiki tropical bar and the ultra cool rat-packesque Hep Cat Club. Also behind the facades is the Legends of Hollywood store.

TOON STUDIO

A huge *Sorcerer's Apprentice* hat marks the entrance to the Art of Disney Animation, an interactive attraction tracing the history of moving imagery.

Animagique brings together some of the greatest moments from the Disney corpus. In Flying Carpets over Agrabah, the genie from *Aladdin* invites spectators to take part in an astonishing magic carpet ride. Crushes Coaster takes you into the underwater animated world of Nemo where you face sharks. Toy Story Playland, which opened in summer 2010, takes visitors to "Andy's Back Yard" for exhilarating fun, including a simulated parachute dive.

PRODUCTION COURTYARD

At the Walt Disney Television Studios you can see behind the scenes of television production, while Ciné–Magique is a must for film buffs, as it covers the history of both American and European cinema. Must dos are the Studio Tram Tour and a go on the latest rides Stitch and Twilight Zone of Terror where you are plunged thirteen floors down inside a haunted hotel.

BACKLOT

This area focuses on special effects, film music recording and crazy dare-devil stunts. Armageddon Special Effects presents a tour of film trickery, while Rock 'n' Roller Coaster is a high-speed attraction (in fact, it is the fastest ride in any Disney theme park) that combines a once-in-a-lifetime ride with neon lights and pulsating Aerosmith music.

RIDES AND ATTRACTIONS

This chart is designed to help you make the best use of your time at Disneyland.

	Queues	Height / Age Restriction	Best Time to Ride or Visit	Fastpass	Scary Rating	May Cause Motion Sickness	Rating Overall
Phantom Manor	◗		Any		❷		★
Rivers of the Far West	○		Any		❶		▼
Big Thunder Mountain	●	1.2m	FT	✔	❷		★
Pocahontas Indian Village	○		Any		❶		▼
Indiana Jones & the Temple of Peril	●	1.4m	LT	✔	❸	✔	★
Adventure Isle	○		Any		❶		▼
La Cabane des Robinson	○		Any		❶		▼
Pirates of the Caribbean	○		Any		❶		★
Peter Pan's Flight	●		FT	✔	❶		◆
Snow White & the Seven Dwarfs	●		►11		❶		◆
Pinocchio's Fantastic Journey	●		►11		❶		▼
Dumbo the Flying Elephant	●		FT		❶		▼
Mad Hatter's Teacups	◗		►12		❶		▼
Alice's Curious Labyrinth	○		Any		❶		▼
"It's a Small World"	○		Any		❶		◆
Casey Jr – Le Petit Train du Cirque	○		►11		❶		◆
Le Pays des Contes des Fees	○		Any		❶		◆
Buzz Lightyear Laser Blast	◗		Any	✔	❶	✔	◆
Star Tours	○	1.32m	Any	✔	❶		★
Space Mountain	●	1.32m	LT	✔	❸	✔	★
Honey, I Shrunk the Audience	○		Any		❶		★
Autopia	●		FT		❶		▼
Orbitron	●	1.2m	FT		❶		▼
Disney Studio 1	◗		Any		❶		◆
Art of Disney Animation	◗		Any		❶		▼
Animagique	●		Any		❶		◆
Crushes Coaster	○	1.07m	Any		❶	✔	★
Flying Carpets Over Agrabah	●	1.2m	FT		❶	✔	◆
Walt Disney Television Studios	●		Any		❶		◆
CinéMagique	◗		Any		❶		◆
Stitch Live	◗		FT		❶		◆
Studio Tram Tour	●		FT		❶		★
Twilight Zone Tower of Terror	●	1.02m	Any	✔	❸	✔	★
Armageddon Special Effects	●		Any		❶		▼
Rock 'n' Roller Coaster	●	1.2m	Any	✔	❸	✔	★

Short - ○ Medium - ◗ Long - ● Anytime - Any Before 11 - ►11 First thing - FT Last thing - LT
Not Scary - ❶ Slightly - ❷ Very - ❸ Quite good - ▼ Very good - ◆ Outstanding - ★

Bercy ⑱

75012. **Map** 18 F3. Ⓜ *Bercy, Cour St-Emilion.*

This former wine-trading quarter east of the city centre, with its once-grim warehouses, pavilions and slum housing, has been transformed into a modern district. An automatic metro line (Line 14) links it to the heart of the city.

The centrepiece of Bercy is the Palais Omnisports de Paris-Bercy, now the city centre's principal venue. The vast pyramidal structure has become a contemporary landmark. Many sports events are held here, as well as classical operas and rock concerts (*see pp345 and 349*).

Other architecturally adventurous buildings dominate Bercy, notably Chemetov's building for the Ministry of Finance, and Frank Gehry's American Center. This houses the Cinemathèque Française, a wonderful cinema museum that hosts frequent retrospectives on famous directors.

At the foot of these structures, the imaginatively designed 70-ha (173-acre) Parc de Bercy provides a welcome green space for this part of the city. The park's attractions for children include a traditional carousel.

Former wine stores and cellars along Cours St Emilion have been restored as bars, restaurants and shops, and one of the warehouses now contains the Musée des Arts Forains (Fairground Museum),

Bibliothèque Nationale de France

which is open only for private tours. There is also a multiscreen cinema and numerous hotels.

Bibliothèque Nationale de France ⑲

Quai François-Mauriac 75013. **Map** 18 F4. Ⓕ *01 53 79 59 59.* Ⓜ *Bibliothèque F Mitterrand, Quai de la Gare.* ◯ *9am–7pm daily (from 2pm Mon, from 1pm Sun).* ◯ *pub hols & 2 wks mid-Sep.* 📶 ♿ 🅿 🛒 www.bnf.fr

Dominique Perrault's 1996 landmark national library is the most striking of all the *Grands Projets* with which President Mitterand revitalized this area. Four towers house 12,000,000 volumes, with reference and research libraries in the central podium. Resources include 50,000 digitized illustrations, sound archives and CD-ROMs. Exhibitions on its hidden collections are often held.

South of the City

13th Arrondissement ⑳

Zac Paris Rive Gauche, 75013. Ⓜ *Bibliotheque F Mitterrand.* **Map** 18 F5.

Following a ten-year redevelopment project, the Zac Paris Rive Gauche, Paris's 13th arrondissement has become an area of startling urban regeneration. The once-disused area of land between Gare d'Austerlitz and Ivry-sur-Seine has now been revived to house a university with some 30,000 students. The area also boasts the MK2 Bibliothèque, a vast cinema complex with 14 screens, cafés and exhibition areas.

Connected to Bercy by a bridge, the area also offers new housing, schools and business opportunities.

Parc Montsouris ㉑

Blvd Jourdan 75014. Ⓜ *Porte d'Orléans.* ⒭ *Cité Universitaire.* ◯ *8am–5.30pm Mon–Fri; 9am–dusk weekends. Times may vary.* ▢

This English-style park was laid out by the landscape architect Adophe Alphand between 1865 and 1878. It has a restaurant, lawns, slopes and a lake that is home to many species of birds. Children will enjoy the playgrounds, pony rides and puppet theatre. The park is the second largest in central Paris and is also home to a weather station.

Bercy's striking American Center, designed by Frank Gehry

Cité Universitaire 22

17–21 Blvd Jourdan 75014.
Tel 01 44 16 64 00. RER Cité
Universitaire. **www**.ciup.fr

This is an international city in
miniature for more than 5,000
foreign students attending
university in Paris. Created in
the 1920s, it now contains 37
houses and, fascinatingly,
each is in an architectural
style linked to different
countries. The Swiss House
and the Franco-Brazilian
House were designed by the
Modernist architect Le
Corbusier. The International
House, donated by John D
Rockefeller in 1936, has a
library, restaurant, swimming
pool and theatre. The student
community makes this a lively
and stimulating area of the
city to visit.

Japan House at Cité Universitaire

Notre-Dame du Travail 23

59 Rue Vercingétorix 75014. **Map** 15
B3. **Tel** 01 44 10 72 92. M Pernety.
🕐 7.30am–7.45pm Mon–Fri, 9am–
7.30pm Sat, 8.30am–7pm Sun. 🕀
9am, 12.15pm, 7pm Mon–Fri, 6.30pm
Sat, 9am, 10.45am, 7pm Sun.

This church dates from 1901
and is made of an unusual
mix of materials: stone, rubble
and bricks over a riveted steel
and iron framework. It was
the creation of Father
Soulange-Boudin, a priest
who organized cooperatives
and sought to reconcile
labour and capitalism. Local

**The Sebastopol Bell in Notre-
Dame du Travail**

parishioners raised the money
for its construction, but lack
of funds meant that many
features, such as the bell
towers, were never built. On
the façade hangs the
Sebastopol Bell, a trophy
from the Crimean War given
to the people of the Plaisance
district by Napoleon III. The
Art Nouveau interior has been
completely restored, and
features paintings of saints.

Institut Pasteur 24

25–28 Rue du Docteur Roux 75015.
Map 15 A2. **Tel** 01 45 68 00 00.
M Pasteur. 🕐 2pm–5.30pm Mon–
Fri (last adm: 4.45pm). 🔴 Aug,
public hols. 📷 🚫 **Films, videos**.
📷 compulsory. 🖥 **www**.pasteur.fr

The Institut Pasteur is France's
leading medical research
centre and was founded by
the world-renowned
scientist
Louis Pasteur in
1888–9. He
discovered the
process of milk
pasteurization as
well as vaccines
against rabies and
anthrax. The centre
houses a museum
which includes a
reconstruction of
Pasteur's apartment
and laboratory. It was
designed by his grand-
children (also scientists) and
is faithful to the original down
to the last detail. Pasteur's tomb
is in a basement crypt built in
the style of a small Byzantine
chapel. The tomb of Dr Emile
Roux, the inventor of the

Louis Pasteur

treatment of diphtheria by
serum injection, lies in the
garden. The institute has
laboratories for pure and
applied research, lecture
theatres, a reference section,
and a hospital founded to
apply Pasteur's theories.
There is also a library – the
institute's original building
from 1888 – where research
into AIDS is carried out, led
by pioneering Professor Luc
Montagnier who discovered
the HIV virus in 1983.

Garden in the Parc André Citroën

Parc André Citroën 25

Rue Balard 75015. **Tel** 01 56 56 11
56. M Javel, Balard. 🕐 8am–dusk
Mon–Fri (9am Sat, Sun & public hols).

Opened in 1992, this park
offers the city's third large
scale vista on the Seine, along
with Les Invalides and the
Champ-de-Mars. Designed
by both landscapers and
architects, it is a fascinating
blend of styles, ranging
from a wildflower
meadow in the north
to the sophisticated
monochrome
mineral and sculpture
gardens of the southern
section. Modern water
sculptures dot the park,
and huge glasshouses
nurture a range of
environments. During
the summer, there is a
tethered hot-air balloon
from which groups of
visitors can enjoy great views
of the city.

Versailles 26

See pp248–53.

The Palace and Gardens of Versailles ㉖

Visitors passing through the rich interior of this colossal palace, or strolling in its vast gardens, will understand why it was the glory of the Sun King's reign. Starting in 1668 with his father's modest hunting lodge, Louis XIV built the largest palace in Europe, housing 20,000 people at a time. Architects Louis Le Vau and Jules Hardouin-Mansart designed the buildings, Charles Le Brun did the interiors, and André Le Nôtre, the great landscaper, redesigned the gardens. The gardens are formally styled into regular patterns of paths and groves, hedges and flowerbeds, pools of water and fountains.

Garden statue of a flautist

★ Formal Gardens
Geometric paths and shrubberies are features of the formal gardens.

The Orangery was built beneath the Parterre du Midi to house exotic plants in winter.

The South Parterre's shrubbery and ornate flowerbeds overlook the Swiss pond.

★ The Château
Louis XIV made the château into the centre of political power in France (see pp250–53).

The Water Parterre's vast pools of water are decorated with superb bronze statues.

Fountain of Latona
Marble basins rise to Balthazar Marsy's statue of the goddess Latona.

Dragon Fountain
The fountain's centrepiece is a winged monster.

The King's Garden with Mirror Pool are a 19th-century English garden and pool created by Louis XVIII.

Colonnade
Mansart designed this circle of marble arches in 1685.

VISITORS' CHECKLIST

Versailles. 📞 *01 30 83 78 00*, 🚌 *171 from Pont de Sèvres to Versailles.* **Château** 🕐 *9am–6.30pm Tue–Sun (last adm 5pm Nov–Mar, 6pm Apr–Oct).* ♿

Grand Trianon & Petit Trianon
🕐 Apr–Oct: noon–7pm daily; Nov–Mar: noon–5.30 daily. ♿ ♿
📷 📁 🛍 🍴 🎵 *Les Grandes Concerts de Versailles (Apr–Sep); Le Parcours du Roi (Jun–Aug: Sat); Les Grandes Eaux Nocturnes (Jun–Aug: Sat).* www.chateauversailles.fr

The Grand Canal was the setting for Louis XIV's many boating parties.

Petit Trianon
Built in 1762 as a retreat for Louis XV, this small château became a favourite of Marie-Antoinette.

Fountain of Neptune
Groups of sculptures spray spectacular jets of water in Le Nôtre and Mansart's 17th-century fountain.

★ Grand Trianon
Louis XIV built this small palace of stone and pink marble in 1687 to escape the rigours of court life, and to enjoy the company of his mistress, Madame de Maintenon.

STAR SIGHTS

★ The Château

★ Formal Gardens

★ Grand Trianon

The Main Palace Buildings of Versailles

Gold crest from the Petit Trianon

The present palace grew as a series of envelopes enfolding the original hunting lodge, whose low brick front is still visible in the centre. In the 1660s, Louis Le Vau built the first envelope, a series of wings which expanded into an enlarged courtyard. It was decorated with marble busts, antique trophies and gilded roofs. On the garden side, columns were added to the west facade and a great terrace was created on the first floor. Mansart took over in 1678 and added the two immense north and south wings and filled Le Vau's terrace to form the Hall of Mirrors. He designed the chapel, which was finished in 1710. The Opera House (*L'Opéra*) was added by Louis XV in 1770.

South Wing
The wing's original apartments for great nobles were replaced by Louis-Philippe's museum of French history.

The Royal Courtyard
was separated from the Ministers' Courtyard by elaborate grillwork during Louis XIV's reign. It was accessible only to royal carriages.

Louis XIV's statue, erected by Louis Philippe in 1837, stands where a gilded gateway once marked the beginning of the Royal Courtyard.

STAR SIGHTS

★ Marble Courtyard

★ L'Opéra

★ Chapelle Royale

Ministers' Courtyard

Main Gate
Mansart's original gateway grille, surmounted by the royal arms, is the entrance to the Ministers' Courtyard.

TIMELINE

Louis XV

1667 Grand Canal begun

1668 Construction of new château by Le Vau

1722 12-year-old Louis XV occupies Versailles

1793 Louis XVI and Marie-Antoinette executed

1833 Louis-Philippe turns the château into a museum

1650	1700	1750	1800	1850

1671 Interior decoration by Le Brun begun

1715 Death of Louis XIV. Versailles abandoned by court

1789 King and queen forced to leave Versailles for Paris

1661 Louis XIV enlarges château

1682 Louis XIV and Marie-Thérèse move to Versailles

1774 Louis XVI and Marie-Antoinette live at Versailles

1919 Treaty of Versailles signed on 28 June

The Clock
Hercules and Mars flank the clock overlooking the Marble Courtyard.

★ Marble Courtyard
The courtyard is decorated with marble paving, urns, busts and a gilded balcony.

North Wing
The chapel, Opéra and picture galleries occupy this wing, which originally housed royal apartments.

★ L'Opéra
Built for the 1770 marriage of the future Louis XVI and Marie-Antoinette, the Opéra is now used as a theatre.

★ Chapelle Royale
Mansart's last great work, this two-storey Baroque chapel, was Louis XIV's last addition to Versailles.

Inside the Château of Versailles

The sumptuous main apartments are on the first floor of the vast château complex. Around the Marble Courtyard are the private apartments of the king and the queen. On the garden side are the state apartments where official court life took place. These were richly decorated by Charles Le Brun with coloured marbles, stone and wood carvings, murals, velvet, silver and gilded furniture. Beginning with the Salon d'Hercule, each state room is dedicated to an Olympian deity. The climax is the Hall of Mirrors, where 17 great mirrors face tall arched windows.

STAR SIGHTS

★ Chapelle Royale

★ Salon de Vénus

★ Hall of Mirrors

★ Queen's Bedroom

KEY

☐	South wing
☐	Coronation room
☐	Madame de Maintenon's apartments
☐	Queen's apartments and private suite
☐	State apartments
☐	King's apartments and private suite
☐	North wing
☐	Non-exhibition space

★ Queen's Bedroom
In this room the queens of France gave birth to the royal children in full public view.

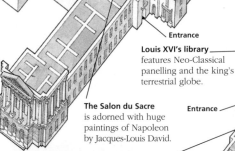

Entrance

Louis XVI's library features Neo-Classical panelling and the king's terrestrial globe.

The Salon du Sacre is adorned with huge paintings of Napoleon by Jacques-Louis David.

Entrance

★ Salon de Vénus
A Louis XIV statue stands amidst the rich marble decor of this room.

★ Chapelle Royale
The chapel's first floor was reserved for the royal family and the ground floor for the court. The interior is richly decorated in white marble, gilding and Baroque murals.

★ Hall of Mirrors
Great state occasions were held in this multi-mirrored room stretching 70 m (233 ft) along the west façade. The Treaty of Versailles was ratified here in 1919, ending World War I.

Oeil-de-Boeuf

The King's Bedroom
is where Louis XIV died in 1715, aged 77.

Salon de la Guerre
The room's theme of war is dramatically reinforced by Antoine Coysevox's stuccoed relief of Louis XIV riding to victory.

The Cabinet du Conseil is where the king received his ministers and his family.

Salon d'Apollon
Designed by Le Brun and dedicated to the god Apollo, this was Louis XIV's throne room. A copy of Hyacinthe Rigaud's famous portrait of the king (1701) hangs here.

Salon d'Hercule

Stairs to ground floor reception area

PURSUIT OF THE QUEEN

On 6 October 1789, a Parisian mob invaded the palace seeking the despised Marie-Antoinette. The queen, roused in alarm from her bed, fled towards the king's rooms through the anteroom known as the Oeil-de-Boeuf. As the mob tried to break into the room, the queen beat on the door of the king's bedroom. Once admitted she was safe, at least until morning, when she and the king were removed to Paris by the cheering and triumphant mob.

West of the City

An Art Nouveau window in the Rue la Fontaine

Rue la Fontaine ㉗

75016. **Map** 9 A4. Ⓜ *Jasmin, Michel-Ange Auteuil.*

The Rue la Fontaine and surrounding streets act as a showcase for some of the most exciting architecture of the early 20th century. At No. 14 stands the Castel Béranger, a stunning apartment block made from cheap building materials to keep costs low, yet featuring stained glass, convoluted ironwork, balconies and mosaics. It established the reputation of Art Nouveau architect Hector Guimard, who went on to design the entrances for the Paris metro. Several more examples of his work can be seen further along the street, such as the Hôtel Mezzara at No. 60.

Fondation Le Corbusier ㉘

8–10 Square du Docteur Blanche 75016. **Tel** *01 42 88 41 53.* Ⓜ *Jasmin.* ◯ *1.30–6pm Mon; 10am– 12.30pm, 1.30–6pm Tue–Fri (to 5pm Fri); 10am–5pm Sat (Villa La Roche only).* ⬤ *public hols, Aug, 24 Dec– 2 Jan.* 🎥 ⊙ *Films, videos.* 📷 *See History of Paris pp38–9.* **www**.fondationlecorbusier.asso.fr

In a quiet corner of Auteuil are the villas La Roche *(see p265)* and Jeanneret, the first two Parisian houses built by the 20th-century architect Charles-Edouard Jeanneret, known as Le Corbusier. Built in the 1920s, they show his revolutionary use of white concrete in Cubist forms. Rooms flow into each other allowing maximum light, and the houses stand on stilts with windows along their entire length.
Villa La Roche was owned by the art patron Raoul La Roche. Today both villas serve as a fascinating documentation centre on Le Corbusier.

Musée Marmottan-Monet ㉙

2 Rue Louis Boilly 75016. 🛈 *01 40 50 65 84.* Ⓜ *Muette.* ◯ *11am–6pm Tue–Sun (to 9pm Tue).* ⬤ *1 Jan, 1 May, 25 Dec.* 🎥 🚻 📷 **www**.marmottan.com

The museum was created in the 19th-century mansion of the art historian Paul Marmottan in 1932, when he

bequeathed his house and his Renaissance, Consular and First Empire collections of paintings and furniture to the Institut de France. The focus of the museum changed after the bequest by Michel Monet of 65 paintings by his father, the Impressionist Claude Monet. Some of his most famous paintings are here, including *Impression – Sunrise*, a beautiful canvas from the Rouen Cathedral series, and several *Water Lilies*.
Part of Monet's personal art collection also passed to the museum, including paintings by Camille Pissarro and the Impressionists Pierre Auguste Renoir and Alfred Sisley. The museum also displays medieval illuminated manuscripts.

La Barque (1887) by Claude Monet, in the Musée Marmottan

Bois de Boulogne ㉚

75016. Ⓜ *Porte Maillot, Porte Dauphine, Porte d'Auteuil, Sablons.* ◯ *24 hrs daily.* 🎥 *to specialist gardens and museum.* 🚻
Shakespeare garden ◯ *9.30am– dusk daily.* 🎥
Open-air theatre ◯ *May–Sep.*
Bagatelle & Rose gardens ◯ *9.30am. Closing times vary from 4.30pm to 8pm according to season.*
Jardin d'Acclimatation Tel *01 40 67 90 82.* ◯ *10am–7pm daily (Oct–May: 6pm).* 🔲 🎡
www.jardindacclimatation.fr
Musée en Herbe Tel *01 40 67 97 66.* ◯ *10am–6pm daily.* 🎥 🚻
www.musee-en-herbe.com

Between the western edges of Paris and the River Seine this 865-ha (2,137-acre) park offers greenery for strolling, boating, picnicking or spending a day at the races. The Bois de Boulogne is all

Villa La Roche, home of the Fondation Le Corbusier

Kiosque de l'Empereur, on an island in the Grand Lac, Bois de Boulogne

that remains of the vast Forêt du Rouvre. In the mid-19th century Napoleon III had it redesigned and landscaped by Haussmann along the lines of London's Hyde Park.

There are many beautiful areas within the Bois. The Pré Catelan is a self-contained park with the widest beech tree in Paris, and the charming Bagatelle gardens feature architectural follies and an 18th-century villa famous for its rose garden, where an international rose competition is held in June. The villa was built in 64 days as a bet between the Comte d'Artois and Marie-Antoinette. The Bois de Boulogne has a reputation as a seedy area after dark so is best avoided at night.

Musée des Années 30 ❸

28 Ave André Morizet, Boulogne-Billancourt 92100. *Tel* 01 55 18 53 00. Ⓜ *Marcel Sembat.* ◯ 11am–6pm Tue–Sun. ◉ 1–15 Aug. ⬤ ⬤
⬤ ⬤ www.annees30.com

La Grande Arche in La Défense

Inaugurated in 1998, this museum of the 1930s forms part of an arts complex, the Espace Landowski, named after Paul Landowski, a sculptor who lived in Boulogne-Billancourt from 1905 until his death in 1961, and his musician brother, Marcel. Several of Paul's works are on show here among the collection of some 800 sculptures, 2,000 paintings, furniture and ceramics.

The museum gives a vivid impression of the aesthetic mood of the era and its decorative arts through the work of artists such as Juan Gris and Robert Mallet-Stevens, classics of industrial design, and film-makers such as Renoir and Pagnol. The museum organizes temporary exhibitions, as well as themed tours of the architectural and industrial heritage of Boulogne-Billancourt.

La Défense ❸

1 Parvis de la Défense. *Tel* 01 49 07 27 27. Ⓜ ⭐ *La Défense.* ◯ 10am–7pm daily (Apr–Sep: to 8pm). ⬤ ⬤
ℹ See **History of Paris** pp38–9. www.grandearche.com

This skyscraper business district on the western edge of Paris is one of Europe's largest modern office developments and covers 80 ha (198 acres). It was launched in the

1960s to create a new home for leading French and multi-national companies. Since then, a major artistic scheme has transformed many of the squares into fascinating open-air museums.

In 1989 La Grande Arche was added to the complex, an enormous hollow cube large enough to contain Notre-Dame cathedral. This was designed by Danish architect Otto von Spreckelsen as part of major construction works, or *Grands Travaux*, which were initiated by (and are now a memorial to) the late President François Mitterrand.

The arch now houses an exhibition gallery and a conference centre, and commands a superb view over the city of Paris.

Château de Malmaison ❸

Ave du Château 92500 Rueil-Malmaison. *Tel* 01 41 29 05 55. ⭐ *La Défense then bus 258.* ◯ Apr–Sep: 10am 12.30pm, 1.30 5.15pm Wed–Sun (6.15pm Sat, Sun); Oct–Mar: 10am–12.30pm, 1.30–5.15pm Wed–Sun (5.45pm Sat, Sun). ⬤ ⬤ See **History of Paris** pp32–3. www.chateau-malmaison.fr

The Empress Josephine's bed in the Château de Malmaison

This 17th-century château was bought in 1799 by Josephine de Beauharnais, wife of Napoleon I. A magnificent veranda, Classical statues and a small theatre were added. After his campaigns, Napoleon and his entourage would come here to relax. The Château became Josephine's main residence after their divorce. Today, it is an important Napoleonic museum, together with the nearby Château de Bois-Préau. Furniture, portraits, artifacts and mementos of the imperial family are displayed in rooms reconstructed in the style of the First Empire.

Part of the original grounds still exists, including Josephine's famous rose garden.

EIGHT GUIDED WALKS

Paris is a city for walking. It is more compact and easier to get around than many other great capitals. Most of its great sights are within walking distance of one another and they are close to the heart of the city, the Ile de la Cité.

There are 14 classic tourist areas described in the *Area by Area* section of this book, each with a short walk marked on its *Street-by-Street* map, taking you past many of the most interesting sights. Yet Paris offers a wealth of lesser-known but equally remarkable areas, whose special history, architecture and local customs reveal other facets of the city.

The eight walks around the following neighbourhoods take in the main sights and also introduce visitors to their subtle details, such as street markets, quirky churches, canals, gardens, old village streets and bridges. And the literary, artistic and historical associations allow the past and present to blend into the changing and vibrant life of the modern city.

Auteuil is renowned for its luxury modern residential architecture, Monceau for its sumptuous Second Empire mansions and Ile St-Louis for its *ancien régime* town houses and narrow streets. The old-fashioned charm of the iron footbridges survives along Canal St-Martin, and steep village streets that were once home to famous artists still enrich Montmartre. A tranquil village atmosphere also pervades two lesser-known hilltop districts – Buttes Chaumont, with one of Paris's loveliest parks, and Butte-aux-Cailles, whose quaint, cobbled alleyways belie its association with the ill-fated Paris Commune of 1871, while the once working-class area of Faubourg St-Antoine has been given a new lease of life as an artisans' quarter with a pleasure-boat harbour.

All the walk areas are readily accessible by public transport and the nearest metro stations and bus routes are listed in the *Tips for Walkers* boxes. For each walk there are suggestions on convenient resting points, such as cafés and squares, along the route.

Parc Monceau statue

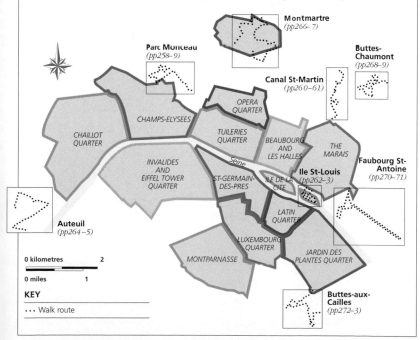

Montmartre
(pp266–7)

Parc Monceau
(pp258–9)

Buttes-Chaumont
(pp268–9)

Canal St-Martin
(pp260–61)

OPERA QUARTER

CHAMPS-ELYSEES

CHAILLOT QUARTER

TUILERIES QUARTER

BEAUBOURG AND LES HALLES

THE MARAIS

Faubourg St-Antoine
(pp270–71)

INVALIDES AND EIFFEL TOWER QUARTER

Seine

ST-GERMAIN-DES-PRES

ILE DE LA CITE

Ile St-Louis
(pp262–3)

Auteuil
(pp264–5)

LATIN QUARTER

LUXEMBOURG QUARTER

JARDIN DES PLANTES QUARTER

MONTPARNASSE

0 kilometres 2

0 miles 1

KEY

••• Walk route

Buttes-aux-Cailles
(pp272–3)

◁ **Bridge over the Canal St-Martin**

A 90-Minute Walk around Parc Monceau

This leisurely walk passes through the exquisite late-18th-century Parc Monceau, the centrepiece of a smart Second Empire district. It then follows a route along surrounding streets, where groups of opulent mansions stunningly convey the magnificence in which some Parisians live, before ending at Place St-Augustin. For details on Monceau sights, see pages 232–3.

Ruysdaël gate

Parc Monceau to Avenue Velasquez

The walk starts at the Monceau metro station ① on the Boulevard de Courcelles. Enter the park where Nicolas Ledoux's 18th-century tollhouse ② stands. On

Parc Monceau's tollhouse ②

either side are sumptuously gilded 19th-century wrought-iron gates which support ornate lampposts.

Take the second path on the left past the monument to Guy de Maupassant ③ (1897). This is only one of a series of six Belle Epoque monuments of prominent French writers and musicians which are picturesquely scattered throughout the park. Most of them feature a solemn bust of a great man who is accompanied by a swooning muse.

Straight ahead is the most important remaining folly, a moss-covered Corinthian colonnade ④ running around the edge of a charming tiny lake with the requisite island in the centre. Walk around the colonnade and under a 16th-century arch ⑤ transplanted from the old Paris Hôtel de Ville (see p102), which burned down in 1871.

Turn left on the Allée de la Comtesse de Ségur and go into Avenue Velasquez, a

wide tree-lined street with 19th-century Neo-Classical mansions. At No. 7 is the splendid Cernuschi museum ⑥, which houses a collection of Far Eastern art.

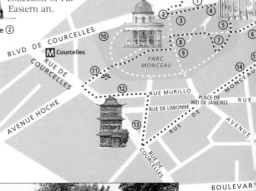

Colonnade in Parc Monceau ④

Ambroise Thomas statue ⑧

Avenue Velasquez to Avenue Van Dyck

Re-enter the park and turn left into the second small winding path, which is bordered by an 18th-century mossy pyramid ⑦, antique tombs, a stone arcade, an obelisk and a small Chinese stone pagoda. The romantically melancholy tone of these false ruins suits the spirit of the late 18th century.

Turn right on the first path past the pyramid and walk back to the central avenue. Straight ahead a Renaissance bridge fords the little stream running from the lake. Turn left and walk past the

monument (1902) to the musician Ambroise Thomas ⑧. Immediately behind there is a lovely artificial mountain with cascade. Turn left on the next avenue and walk to the monument (1897) to the composer Charles Gounod ⑨ on the left. From here follow the first winding path to the right towards the Avenue Van Dyck exit. Ahead to the right, in the corner of the park, is the Chopin monument ⑩ (1906), and looking along the Allée de la Comtesse de Ségur, the monument to the 19th-century French poet Alfred de Musset.

Avenue Van Dyck to Rue de Monceau

Leave the park and pass into Avenue Van Dyck. No. 5 on the right is an impressive Parc Monceau mansion ⑪, a Neo-Baroque structure built by chocolate manufacturer Emile Menier; No. 6 is in the French Renaissance style that came back into favour in the 1860s. Straight ahead, beyond the ornate grille, there is a fine view of Avenue Hoche and in the distance the Arc de Triomphe. Walk past the gate

The mountain cascade ⑧

and turn left into Rue de Courcelles and left again into Rue Murillo, bordered by more elaborate town houses in 18th-century and French Renaissance styles ⑫. At the crossing of Rue Rembrandt, on the left, is another gate into the park and on the right a massive apartment building from 1900 (No. 7) and an elegant French Renaissance house with an elaborately carved wooden front door (No. 1). At the corner of the Rue Rembrandt and the Rue de Courcelles is the oddest of all the neighbourhood buildings, a striking five-storey red Chinese pagoda ⑬. It is an exclusive emporium of Chinese art.

Turn left on to the Rue de Monceau, walk past Avenue Ruysdaël and continue to the Musée Nissim de Camondo at No. 63 Rue de Monceau ⑭. Some nearby buildings worth having a look at are Nos. 52, 60 and 61 ⑮.

Boulevard Malesherbes

At the junction of Rue de Monceau and Boulevard Malesherbes turn right. This long boulevard with dignified six-storey apartment buildings is typical of the great avenues cut through Paris by Baron Haussmann, Prefect of the Seine during the Second Empire (see pp34–5). They

greatly pleased the Industrial Age bourgeoisie, but horrified sensitive souls and writers who compared them with the buildings of New York.

No. 75 is the posh marble front of Benneton, the most fashionable Paris card and stationery engraver ⑯. On the left, approaching the Boulevard Haussmann, looms the greatest 19th-century Paris church, St-Augustin ⑰, built by Victor-Louis Baltard. Enter the church through the back door on Rue de la Bien-faisance. Walk through the church and leave by the main door. On the left is the massive stone building of the French Officers' club, the Cercle Militaire ⑱. Straight ahead is a bronze statue of Joan of Arc ⑲. Continue on to Place St-Augustin to St-Augustin metro station.

Joan of Arc statue ⑲

KEY

••• Walk route

☼ Good viewing point

Ⓜ Metro station

| 0 metres | 250 |
| 0 yards | 250 |

Five-storey Chinese pagoda ⑬

TIPS FOR WALKERS

Starting point: Blvd de Courcelles.
Length: 3 km (2 miles).
Getting there: The nearest metro is Monceau, reached by bus No. 30; No. 84 goes to metro Courcelles and No. 94 stops between Monceau & Villiers metros.
St Augustin church: Open 8.30am–7pm Mon–Fri, 8.30am–noon, 2.30–7.30pm Sat, 8.30am–12.30pm, 4–7.30pm Sun.
Stopping-off points: Near the Renaissance bridge in the Parc Monceau a kiosk serves coffee and sandwiches (summer only). There is a brasserie at Place de Rio de Janeiro and several cafés around Place St-Augustin. The Square M Pagnol off Ave C Claire is a pleasant place to take in the beauty of the park.

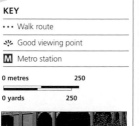

A 90-Minute Walk along the Canal St-Martin

The walk along the quays on either side of the Canal St-Martin is an experience of Paris very different from that of smarter districts. Here, the older surviving landmarks of the neighbourhood – the factories, warehouses, dwellings, taverns and cafés – hint at life in a thriving 19th-century industrial, working-class world. But there are also the gentler charms of the old iron footbridges, the tree-lined quays, the inevitable fishermen, the river barges, and the still waters of the broad canal basins. A walk along the canal, which connects the Bassin de la Villette with the Seine, will evoke images of the Pernod-drinking, working-class Paris of Jean Gabin and Edith Piaf.

The 18th-century
Rotonde de la Villette ②

Bassin de la Villette looking north ③

Place de Stalingrad to Avenue Jean-Jaurès

From the Stalingrad metro station ①, follow Boulevard de la Villette to the square in front of the Rotonde de la Villette ②. This is one of the few remaining 18th-century tollhouses in Paris, designed by the celebrated Neo-Classical architect

Nicolas Ledoux in the 1780s. The fountains, square and terraces were designed in the 1980s to provide an attractive setting and fine views of the Bassin de la Villette ③ to the north.

Walk towards Avenue Jean-Jaurès. On the left is the first lock ④ leading down to the canal, as well as the art-house cinema chain MK2's landmark complexes, which are linked together by a boat.

TIPS FOR WALKERS

Starting point: Place de Stalingrad.
Length: 3.5 km (2 miles).
Getting there: The nearest metro is Stalingrad: bus No.54 stops there, and No.26 at metro Jaurès.
Hôpital St-Louis: Chapel open 2–5pm Fri–Sun; the courtyard is open daily.
Stopping-off points: Ethnic food shops and restaurants abound in the lively Rue du Faubourg du Temple and nearby streets. The Quai de Valmy and Rue Beaupaire offer plenty of modish restaurants and bars (Le Point Ephémère, The Hôtel Du Nord ⑰, Chez Prune). There is a shady public garden on Boulevard Jules Ferry.

View from Rue E Varlin bridge ⑦

KEY

••• Walk route

☆ Good viewing point

Ⓜ Metro station

0 metres   500

0 yards   500

Courtyard garden of Hôpital St-Louis ⑭

Iron footbridges over the canal ⑤

Quai de Valmy to Rue Bichat

Cross over to the Quai de Jemmapes, which runs the length of the east side of the canal and down to the first bridge on Rue Louis Blanc ⑤. Cross the bridge to the Quai de Valmy. From the corner there is a glimpse of the oblique granite and glass front of the Paris Industrial Tribunal ⑥ on the Rue Louis Blanc.

Continue along Quai de Valmy. At Rue E Varlin cross the bridge ⑦, from where there is an attractive view of the second canal lock, lock-keeper's house, public gardens and old lampposts. At the other side of the bridge and slightly to the left, go along the pedestrianized Rue Haendel, which provides a

good view of the towering buildings of a social housing estate ⑧. Nearby is the French Communist Party headquarters ⑨ on Place du Colonel Fabien, with its curving glazed tower.

Return to the Quai de Jemmapes, where at No. 134 ⑩ stands one of the few surviving brick-and-iron industrial buildings that used to line the canal in the 19th century. At No. 126 ⑪ is another notable modern building, a residence for the aged, with monumental concrete arches and glazed bay windows. Further along, at No. 112 ⑫, is an Art Deco apartment building with bay windows, decorative iron balconies and tiles. On the ground floor is a modernized former 1930s proletarian café. Here the canal curves gracefully into the third lock, spanned by a charming transparent iron footbridge ⑬.

Hôpital St-Louis to Rue Léon-Jouhaux

Turn left into Rue Bichat, which leads to the remarkable 17th-century Hôpital St-Louis ⑭. Enter through the hospital's old main gate with its high-pitched roof and massive stone arch. Pass into the courtyard. The hospital was founded in 1607 by Henri IV, the first Bourbon king, to care for the victims of the plague. Leave the courtyard from the central gate on the wing on your left. Here you pass by the 17th-century hospital chapel ⑮ and out into the Rue de la Grange aux Belles.

Turn left and walk back to the canal. At the junction of Rue de la Grange Batelière and the Quai de Jemmapes stood, until 1627, the notorious Montfaucon gallows ⑯, one of the chief public execution spots of medieval Paris. Turn into the Quai de Jemmapes. At No. 101 ⑰ is the original front of the Hôtel du Nord, made famous in the eponymous 1930s film. It features an iron footbridge and a draw-bridge ⑱ for traffic, providing a charming setting with views of the canal on either side. Cross over and continue down the Quai de Valmy until the last footbridge ⑲ at the corner of the Rue Léon-Jouhaux. From here the canal can be seen disappearing under the surface of Paris, to continue its journey through a great stone arch.

Entrance to Hôpital St-Louis ⑭

Square Frédéric Lemaître to Place de la République

Walk along Square Frédéric Lemaître ⑳ to the start of Boulevard Jules Ferry, which has a public garden stretching down its centre. The garden was built over the canal in the 1860s. At its head stands a charmingly nostalgic statue of a flower girl of the 1830s, *La Grisette* ㉑. This is the cross-roads of a busy working-class street, Rue du Faubourg du Temple ㉒, with flourishing ethnic shops and restaurants. Follow the street to the right and on to the metro station in the Place de la République.

Shop, Rue du Faubourg du Temple ㉒

A 90-Minute Walk around the Ile St-Louis

The walk around this charming tiny island passes along the enchanting, picturesque tree-lined quays from Pont Louis-Philippe to Quai d'Anjou, taking in the sumptuous 17th-century *hôtels* that infuse the area with such a powerful sense of period. It then penetrates into the heart of the island along the main street, Rue St-Louis-en-l'Ile, enlivened by chic restaurants, cafés, art galleries and boutiques, before returning to the north side of the island and back to Pont Marie. For more information on the main sights, see pages 77 and 87.

Left Bank view of the Ile St-Louis

Fishing on a St-Louis quayside

Metro Pont Marie to Rue Jean-du-Bellay

From the Pont Marie metro station ① walk down Quai des Celestins and Quai de l'Hôtel de Ville, lined with bookstands, with views of Ile St-Louis. Turn left at Pont Louis-Philippe ② and, having crossed it, take the steps down to the lower quay immediately to the right. Walk around the tree-shaded west point of the island ③, then up the other side to the Pont St-Louis ④.

Opposite the bridge, on the corner of Rue Jean-du-Bellay, is Le Flore en l'Ile ⑤, the smartest café-cum-tea salon on the island.

Quai d'Orléans

From the corner of the Quai d'Orléans and the Rue Jean-du-Bellay there are fine views of the Panthéon's dome and Notre-Dame. Along the quay, Nos. 18–20, the Hôtel Rolland, has unusual Hispano-Moorish windows. No. 12 ⑥ is one of several stately 17th-century houses with handsme wrought-iron balconies. At No. 6 the former Polish library, founded

KEY

••• Walk route

🌣 Good viewing point

Ⓜ Metro station

0 metres	250
0 yards	250

in 1838, now houses the Société Historique et Littéraire Polonaise *(see p87)*, focusing on the life of Polish poet Adam Mickiewicz ⑦; it also contains some Chopin scores and autographs by George Sand and Victor Hugo. On the right, the Pont de la Tournelle ⑧ links the island to the Left Bank.

Seine barge passing a St-Louis quay

Quai de Béthune to Pont Marie

Continue beyond the bridge and into Quai de Béthune, where the Nobel-laureate Marie Curie lived at No. 36 ⑨, and where beautiful wrought-iron balconies gracefully decorate Nos. 34 and 30. The Hôtel Richelieu ⑩ at No. 18 is one of the island's most beautiful houses.

St-Louis church door ⑰

It features a fine garden where it has retained its original Classical blind arcades.

If you turn left down Rue Bretonvilliers there is an imposing 17th-century house ⑪, with a high-pitched roof resting on a great Classical arch spanning the street. Back on the Quai de Béthune, proceed to the Pont de Sully ⑫, a late 19th-century bridge joining the river banks. Ahead is the charming 19th-century Square Barye ⑬, a shady public garden at the east point of the island, from where there are fine river views. From here travel towards the Quai d'Anjou as far as the corner of Rue St-Louis-en-l'Ile to see the most famous house on

small, chic, bistro-style restaurants with pleasantly old-fashioned decors. No. 31 is the original Berthillon ice cream shop ⑱, No. 60 an art gallery ⑲ with an original 19th-century window front, and at No. 51 is one of the few 18th-century *hotels* on the island, Hôtel Chernizot ⑳, with a superb Rococo balcony resting on leering gargoyles.

Gargoyle at No. 51 Rue St-Louis-en-l'Ile ⑳

Turn right into Rue Jean-du-Bellay and along to Pont Louis-Philippe. Turn right again into the Quai de Bourbon, lined by one of the island's finest rows of *hôtels*, the most notable being Hôtel Jassaud at No. 19 ㉑. Continue to the 17th-century Pont Marie ㉒ and cross it to the Pont Marie metro on the other side.

The 17th-century Pont Marie ㉒

the island, the Hôtel Lambert ⑭ (*see pp26–7*). Continue into the Quai d'Anjou where Hôtel de Lauzun ⑮ at No. 17 has a severe Classical front and a beautiful gilded balcony. Now turn left into Rue Poulletier and note the convent of the Daughters of Charity ⑯ at No. 1105. Further on, at the corner of Rue Poulletier and Rue St-Louis-en-l'Ile, is the island church, St-Louis ⑰ (*see p87*), with its unusual tower, projecting clock and carved main door.

Proceed along Rue St-Louis-en-l'Ile, which abounds in

Windows of the Hôtel Rolland

TIPS FOR WALKERS

Starting point: Pont Marie metro.
Length: 2.6 km (1.6 miles).
Getting there: The walk starts from the Pont Marie metro. However, bus route 67 takes you to Rue du Pont Louis-Philippe and also crosses the island along Rue des Deux Ponts and Blvd Pont de Sully; routes 86 and 87 also cross the island along Blvd Pont de Sully.
Stopping-off points: There are cafés, such as Flore en l'Ile and the Berthillon shops for ice cream (see p317). Restaurants on the Rue St-Louis-en-l'Ile include Auberge de la Reine Blanche (No. 30) and Le Fin Gourmet (No. 42), as well as a pâtisserie and a cheese shop. Good resting-points are the tree-shaded quays and Square Barye at the eastern end of the island.

A 90-Minute Walk in Auteuil

Part of the fascination of the walk around this bastion of bourgeois life in westernmost Paris lies in the contrasting nature of the area's streets. The old village provincialism of Rue d'Auteuil, where the walk begins, leads on to the masterpieces of luxurious modern architecture along Rue La Fontaine and Rue du Docteur Blanche. The walk ends at the Jasmin metro station. For more on the sights of Auteuil, see page 254.

Rue d'Auteuil

The walk begins at Place d'Auteuil ①, a leafy village square with a striking Guimard-designed metro station entrance, an 18th-century funerary obelisk, and the 19th-century Neo-Romanesque Notre Dame d'Auteuil. Walk down Rue d'Auteuil, the main street of the old village, and take in the sense of a past provincial world. The Auberge du Mouton Blanc brasserie at No. 40 ② now occupies the premises of the area's oldest tavern, favoured by Molière and his actors in the 1600s. The house at Nos. 45–47 ③ was the residence of American presidents John Adams and his son John Quincy Adams. Move on to the pleasantly shaded Place Jean Lorrain ④, the site of the local market. Here there is a Wallace drinking fountain,

Wallace fountain ④

donated by the English millionaire, Richard Wallace in the 19th century. On the right, down Rue Donizetti, is the Villa Montmorency ⑤, a private enclave of luxury villas, built on the former country estate of the Comtesse de Boufflers.

Rue La Fontaine

Continue the walk along Rue La Fontaine, renowned for its many Hector Guimard buildings. Marcel Proust was born at No.96. Henri Sauvage's ensemble of artists' studios at No. 65 ⑥ is one of the most original Art Deco buildings in Paris. No. 60 is a Guimard Art Nouveau house ⑦ with elegant cast-iron balconies. Further along there is a small Neo-Gothic chapel at No. 40 ⑧ and Art Nouveau apartment buildings at Nos. 19 and 21 ⑨. No. 14 is Guimard's most spectacular building, the Castel Béranger ⑩, with a superb iron gate.

TIPS FOR WALKERS

Starting point: Place d'Auteuil.
Length: 3 km (2 miles).
Getting there: The nearest metro station to the starting point is Eglise d'Auteuil, and buses that take you there are Nos. 22, 52 and 62.
Stopping-off points: At No. 40 Rue d'Auteuil is the inexpensive trendy brasserie, L'Auberge du Mouton Blanc, with 1930s décor. At No. 35bis Rue La Fontaine is Acajou, serving innovative cuisine and owned by a young chef. Place Jean Lorrain is a pleasantly shaded square where walkers can rest, and on Rue La Fontaine there is a small park in front of the Neo-Gothic chapel at No. 40. Further on at Place Rodin there is a pleasant public garden.

Obelisk, Place d'Auteuil ①

Doorway of No. 28 Rue d'Auteuil.

KEY

••• Walk route

☆ Good viewing point

Ⓜ Metro station

| 0 metres | 250 |
| 0 yards | 250 |

Rue de l'Assomption to Rue Mallet-Stevens

At the corner of Rue de l'Assomption there is a view of the massive Maison de Radio-France ⑪ built in 1963 to house French radio and television *(see p202)*. It was one of the first modern postwar buildings in the city. Turn left into Rue de l'Assomption and walk to the fine 1920s apartment building at No. 18 ⑫. Turn left into Rue du Général Dubail and follow the street to Place Rodin, where the great sculptor's bronze

Shuttered bay window at No. 3 Square Jasmin

nude, *The Age of Bronze* (1877) ⑬, occupies the centre of the roundabout.

Take the Avenue Théodore Rousseau back to Rue de l'Assomption and turn left

towards Avenue Mozart. Cut through in the 1880s, this is the principal artery of the 16th arrondissement, linking north and south and lined with typical bourgeois apartment buildings of the late 19th century. Cross the avenue and continue to the Avenue des Chalets where there is a typical collection of weekend villas ⑭ recalling the quieter suburban Auteuil of the mid-19th century. Further along Rue de l'Assomption, Notre-Dame de l'Assomption ⑮ is a Neo-Renaissance 19th-century church. Turn left into Rue du Docteur Blanche. At No. 9 and down the adjoining Rue Mallet-Stevens ⑯ there is a row of celebrated modern houses in the International Modern style by the architect Robert Mallet-Stevens. In this expensive, once avant-garde enclave lived architects, designers, artists and their modern-minded clients. The original proportions, however,

were altered dramatically by the addition of an extra three storeys in the 1960s.

Continue on Rue du Docteur Blanche until coming to Villa du Docteur Blanche on the left. At the end of this small cul de sac is the most celebrated modern house in Auteuil, Le Corbusier's Villa Roche ⑰. Together with the adjoining Villa Jeanneret, it is now part of the Corbusier Foundation *(see pp254–5)*. Built for an art collector in 1924 using the new technique of reinforced concrete, the house, with its geometric forms and lack of ornamentation, is a model of early Modernism.

No. 18 Rue de l'Assomption, detail ⑫

Rue du Docteur Blanche to Rue Jasmin

Walk back to Rue du Docteur Blanche and turn right into Rue Henri Heine. No. 18 bis ⑱ is a very elegant Neo-Classical 1920s apartment building offering a good contrast to one of Guimard's last creations from 1926 next door – an Art Nouveau facade much tamer than that at Castel Béranger but still employing brick, and with projecting bay windows and a terraced roof. Turn left on Rue Jasmin. In the second cul de sac on the left there is another Guimard house at No. 3 Square Jasmin ⑲. Towards the end of Rue Jasmin is the metro station.

Courtyard of No. 14 Rue La Fontaine

The Age of Bronze ⑬

A 90-Minute Walk in Montmartre

The walk begins at the base of the sandstone *butte* (hill), where old theatres and dance halls, once frequented and depicted by painters from Renoir to Picasso, have now been taken over by rock clubs. It continues steeply uphill to the original village, along streets which still retain the atmosphere caught by artists like Van Gogh, before winding downhill to end at Place Blanche. For more on the main sights of Montmartre and the Sacré-Coeur, see pages 220–29.

Montmartre seen from a distance

Place Pigalle to Rue Ravignan

The walk starts at the lively Place Pigalle ① and follows Rue Frochot to the Rue Victor Massé. At the corner is the ornate entrance to an exclusive private street bordered by late 19th-century chalets ②. Opposite, at No. 27 Rue Victor Massé, is an ornate mid-19th-century apartment building, and No. 25 is where Vincent Van Gogh and his brother Theo lived in 1886 ③. The famous Chat Noir ④, Montmartre's most renowned artistic cabaret in the 1890s, flourished at No. 12. At the end of the street begins the wide tree-lined Avenue Trudaine. Take Rue Lallier on the left to Boulevard de Rochechouart. Continue east. No. 84 is the first address of the Chat Noir and No. 80 was the Grand Trianon ⑤, Paris's oldest-surviving cinema, from the early 1890s. It is now

Entrance gate to Avenue Frochot

TIPS FOR WALKERS

Starting point: Place Pigalle.
Length: 2.3 km (1.4 miles). The walk goes up some very steep streets to the top; if you do not feel like the climb, consider taking the Montmartrobus, which covers most of the walk and starts at Place Pigalle.
Getting there: The nearest metro is Pigalle; buses that take you there are Nos. 30, 54 and 67.
Stopping-off points: There are many cafés and shops in Rue Lepic and the Rue des Abbesses. Le Saint Jean (16 Pl des Abbesses) remains a locals' haunt and serves well-priced brasserie food. For shade and a rest, Place Jean-Baptiste Clément and Square S Buisson at Avenue Junot are charming public squares.

a theatre. Further along, No. 72 is the original front of Montmartre's first great cancan dance hall, the Elysée-Montmartre ⑥. Today it is a nightclub and concert hall.

Turn left on to Rue du Steinkerque, which leads to Sacré-Coeur gardens, and then left into Rue d'Orsel, which leads to the leafy square, Place Charles Dullin, where the small early 19th-century Théâtre de l'Atelier ⑦ stands. Continue up the hill on Rue des Trois Frères and turn left on Rue Yvonne le Tac, which leads to Place des Abbesses ⑧. This is one of the most pleasant and liveliest squares in the area. It has conserved its entire canopied Art Nouveau metro entrance by Hector Guimard. Opposite is St-Jean l'Evangéliste ⑨, an

Rue André Antoine ⑩

unusual brick and mosaic Art
Nouveau church. To the right
of the church a flight of steep
steps leads to the tiny Rue
André Antoine, where the
Pointillist painter Georges
Seurat lived at No. 39 ⑩.
Continue along Rue des
Abbesses and turn right at
Rue Ravignan.

Rue Ravignan
From here there is a sweeping
view of Paris. Climb the steps
straight ahead to the deeply
shaded Place Emile Goudeau
⑪. To the left, at No. 13, is the
original entrance to the Bateau-
Lavoir, the most important
cluster of artists'

KEY

••• Walk route

☀ Good viewing point

Ⓜ Metro station

0 metres   250

0 yards   250

St-Jean l'Evangéliste, detail ⑨

studios in Montmartre. Here
Picasso lived and worked in
the early 1900s. Further up, at
the corner of Rue Orchampt
and Rue Ravignan, there is a
row of picturesque 19th-
century artists' studios ⑫.

Rue Ravignan to Rue Lepic
Continue up the hill along the
small public garden, Place
Jean-Baptiste Clément ⑬.
At the top, cross Rue Norvins.
Opposite is an old Monmar-
tois restaurant, Auberge de
la Bonne Franquette ⑭,
which used to be a favourite
gathering place for 19th-
century artists. Continue
along the narrow Rue St-
Rustique, from where Sacré-
Coeur can be seen. At the
end and to the right is Place
du Tertre ⑮, the main village
square. From here go north
on Rue du Mont Cenis and
turn left to Rue Cortot. Erik
Satie, the eccentric composer,
lived in No. 6 ⑯, and at No. 12
is the Musée de Montmartre ⑰.
Turn right on Rue des Saules
and walk past the very pretty
Montmartre vineyard ⑱ to the
Au Lapin Agile ⑲ at the corner

of Rue St-Vincent. Go back
down Rue des Saules and right
on Rue de l'Abreuvoir, an
attractive street of late 19th-
century villas and gardens.
Continue into l'Allée des
Brouillards, a leafy pedestrian
alley. No. 6 ⑳ was Renoir's last
house in Montmartre. Take the
steps down into the Rue Simon
Dereure and immediately turn
left into a small park, which
can be crossed to reach
Avenue Junot. Here, No. 13
㉑ was the house of Dadaist
Tristan Tzara in the early 1920s.
Continue up Avenue Junot,
turn right on Rue Girardon and
right again on Rue Lepic.

Au Lapin Agile cabaret ⑲

Rue Lepic to Place Blanche
At the corner is one of the
area's few surviving windmills,
the Moulin du Radet ㉒, now a
restaurant confusingly called
Moulin de la Galette. Continue
along Rue Lepic: to the right at
the top of a slope is another
windmill, the original Moulin
de la Galette ㉓, now a private
home. Turn left on Rue de
l'Armée d'Orient, with its quaint
artists' studios ㉔, and left again
into Rue Lepic. Van Gogh lived
at No. 54 ㉕ in June 1886.
Continue to Place Blanche, and
on Boulevard de Clichy to the
right is the Moulin Rouge ㉖.

Moulin Rouge cabaret near the Place Blanche ㉖

A 90-Minute Walk in Buttes-Chaumont

This area in the east of the city is little known to many visitors, yet it contains one of Paris's biggest and most beautiful parks and some fascinating architecture. The walk is quite strenuous with many steps, and takes in a charming micro-village, the Butte Bergeyre, which is perched high above the city and has rare houses in contrasting styles. After descending from the village, the walk continues in Buttes-Chaumont park, a vast hill complete with a lake with a huge island and folly, rocky outcrops and a wonderful variety of trees and plants.

a small garden ⑩. This is owned by the city but tended by local residents who can often be found working here.

Head back down the Rue Georges Lardennois to the Rue Michel Tagrine and take the ivy-draped steps back down to the main road ⑪. Continue straight and then turn right onto the Avenue Mathurin-Moreau, noting the fine Art Deco building ⑫ at 42 with its glittering gold-coloured tile detail. At the end of the road, cross the Rue Manin to the entrance to the park.

View across city towards Sacré-Coeur ⑧

The Butte Bergeyre

From the metro Buttes-Chaumont ① take the Rue Botzaris, turning right onto the Avenue Simon Bolivar until you reach the stairs at 54 ②, which lead up into the Butte Bergeyre. At the top of the stairs pause to absorb the enchanting atmosphere of this micro-village of five little streets. Construction started in the 1920s but there are also some modern buildings. Carry on into the Rue Barrelet de Ricou ③ to admire the ivy-covered house at 13 ④, then continue to the end of the road to take a left into the Rue Philippe Hecht ⑤ where the chalet-style house at 7 ⑥ is an interesting contrast to the creeper-covered Art Deco gem at 13 ⑦. At the end of the street take a left up to the corner of the Rue Georges Lardennois and the Rue Rémy-de-Gourmont for a wonderful view across the city ⑧ of Montmartre with its wedding-cake Sacré-Coeur on top. Be sure to admire the tiny patch of grapevines ⑨ in the residents' garden below. Close to this mini-vineyard is

Some of the lovely mature trees in the park

The suspension bridge, for the best view of the park ⑱

PARC DES BUTTES CHAUMONT

climb them to the top. Go on along a tree-lined path to join the Avenue du General Puebla Liniers and follow this until reaching the Carrefour de la Colonne ⑭ where there is a red brick mansion house. With your back to this go ahead to a little bridge lined with terracotta tiles. Cross the bridge ⑮. Take the right branch of steps and head up to the top of the cliff. Cross a tiny bridge ⑯ and turn left up some steps to the folly ⑰, a copy of the Temple of Sibyl near Rome. This is the highest point in the park, providing views across the city all the way to the Sacré-Coeur. Now take the path on the right back to the first bridge. Then branch right down the steps within man-made rock to an impressive 63-m (206-ft) long bridge ⑱. Towering over the lake, this provides wonderful views of the park. The bridge may be closed for repairs, so in that instance use the terracotta-tiled bridge as before. Cross the bridge and follow the path down to the lake. The lake ⑲ is encircled by weeping willows and benches for breaks to admire

the 50-m (164-ft) high man-made island ⑳. Follow the lake round until you hear rushing water. One of the park's most impressive features is the 32-m (105-ft) high waterfall ㉑ hidden inside a grotto. Walk right up to the waterfall looking up to see a patch of sky and some glorious man-made stalactites. Take a stepping-stone to the other side of the cave and then exit and rejoin the path round the lake, heading left. Ascend the few steps, then veer to the left and up the hill ㉒. Follow the path around to the Carrefour de la Colonne and continue along the Avenue de la Cascade to the exit ㉓. From here you can take the metro from Botzaris.

Clifftop folly, the park's summit ⑰

The Buttes-Chaumont Park

Commissioned by Napoleon III and Baron Haussmann in 1864, the park covers 25 ha (61 acres) and took four years to complete. It was built by the engineer Adolphe Alphand and the architect Gabriel Davioud. It is packed with mature trees including planes, poplars, ash, maples, chestnuts, sequoias and beautiful magnolias. At the entrance to the park there is a man-made rock structure ⑬ with steps carved out of the facade;

KEY

••• Walk route

⚜ Good viewing point

Ⓜ Metro station

0 metres	200
0 yards	200

Man-made waterfall, inside the grotto ㉑

A 90-Minute Walk in Faubourg St-Antoine

In the east of the city a few steps away from the bustle of the Bastille lies the Faubourg St-Antoine district, traditionally a working-class neighbourhood full of furniture designers, carpenters and artisans and this legacy can still be seen today. From the Place de la Bastille, the walk takes in Paris's pleasure-boat port, the artisan area around the Viaduc des Arts – a former viaduct with arts and crafts studios nestling in the arches – and onto the Promenade Plantée for a fascinating tree-filled stroll.

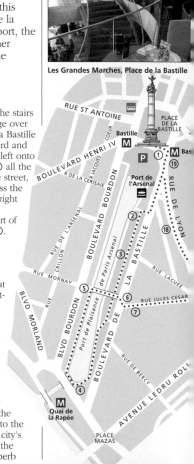

Les Grandes Marches, Place de la Bastille

The Port de Plaisance, with many pleasure boats ④

Port de Plaisance

Tucked away near the traffic of Place de La Bastille ① lies an area of tranquillity that's of interest to boat-lovers and landlubbers alike. The Port de Plaisance and Paris-Arsenal garden ② was inaugurated in 1983 to provide a harbour for pleasure craft. Linking the Seine to the Canal St-Martin, the harbour was previously where commercial barges loaded and unloaded cargo. Today, it's a pretty spot full of yachts, dinghies and Parisians out for a stroll. The cobbled stones on the quayside and old-fashioned lamp-posts add to the port's atmosphere. The lawns are perfect for a picnic and the children's play areas, while small, are well stocked with rocking chairs, slides and climbing apparatus ③. Continue to the end of the marina to the lock ④. Cross over the lock bridge, observing the pedestrian crossing sign, and head down on the other quayside turning back towards the Place de La Bastille. Just before the grey

steel bridge ⑤, take the stairs up and then the bridge over to the Boulevard de la Bastille ⑥. Cross the Boulevard and take a right and then left onto the Rue Jules César ⑦ all the way to the end of the street, turn left and then cross the Rue de Lyon turning right onto the Avenue Daumesnil and the start of the Viaduc des Arts ⑧.

Viaduc des Arts

In 1859 the Paris Viaduct was built to take a railway line that linked the Faubourg St-Antoine district with the suburbs. In 1994 the restored and revamped Viaduc des Arts opened with 50 shops and studios nestling in the bridge's rose stone archways.

In keeping with the tradition of the area, the ateliers are all linked to the arts, and some of the city's master craftsmen call the arches home. The superb

Place de la Bastille with the impressive Opéra de Paris Bastille ①

window displays at the first studio "Maison Guillet" ⑨ give a hint of the quality of craftsmanship to come. Guillet specializes in providing silk flowers for Paris's top theatre and fashion houses. The "Ateliers du Temps Passé" ⑩ at 5 is a restorer of paintings, while Lorenove at 11 restores period glass. Number 13 is the base for hot interior designer Cherif, and the whimsical "Le Bonheur des Dames" ⑪ at 17 provides all sorts of materials for embroidery fans. For refreshment, stop at the Viaduc Café at 43 ⑫, which dishes up simple meals and hearty salads to the area's hip creatives. Vertical at 63 ⑬

One of the arts and crafts shop fronts under the Viaduc des Arts ⑧

mixes art and nature with twisting "botanical sculptures". Moving on past the metal furnituremaker Baguès at 73, the antique lace restorers Marie Lavande at 83, the Atelier Le Tallec 93/95, which specializes in hand-painted porcelain, it is clear that the spirit of the old artisans' area is alive and well. For those of a musical bent, Allain Cadinot repairs and sells Boehm flutes at 99, while Roger Lanne is a violin- and cello-maker at 103 ⑭. With the coppersmith at 111, the terracotta tile specialist at 113 and the frame-maker at 117, you are close to the end of the viaduct, where the last atelier Jean-

Vincennes woods. For a longer walk, turn right along the Promenade and follow it to the city's edge. Or turn left and head back towards the Bastille. This narrow walkway offers wonderful views of the rooftops, and you can see into some apartments. With roses, lavender and maples, the walkway is a delight. At the end ⑰, take the steps down to the Rue de Lyon ⑱ leading to the Bastille metro, pausing only to ponder the modern architecture of the Opéra de Paris Bastille ⑲ (see p98).

Promenade Plantée, a lovely rooftop walkway ⑯

Charles Brosseau ⑮ perhaps sums up the street's diversity specializing in making hats, scent and cutlery.

Promenade Plantée

Turn left, follow the signs and take the steps up to the Promenade Plantée ⑯, a walkway on top of the viaduct. It is 4.5km (2.8 miles) long and goes all the way to the

TIPS FOR WALKERS

Starting point: Bastille Metro
Length: 2.6 km (1.6 miles).
Getting there: Bastille Metro is served by lines 1, 8 and 5. Bus Nos. 29, 65, 69, 76, 86, 87, 91 and more. Get off at "Place de la Bastille" stop.
Stopping off points: The area is full of great cafés, bars and restaurants. Les Grandes Marches (Place de la Bastille) is a chic place for lunch, dinner or just coffee before you start or afterwards. Nearby Rue de Charonne is lined with some fun bars. During the walk, take a break at the Viaduc Café (43 Viaduc des Arts).

KEY

••• Walk route

••• Detour route

☆ Good viewing point

Ⓜ Metro station

Montgallet Ⓜ
300 metres / 330 yards

Bois de Vincennes
3 km / 2 miles

Dugommier Ⓜ
450 metres / 500 yards

0 metres 200
0 yards 200

A 90-Minute Walk in Butte-aux-Cailles

This walk takes place in and around the Butte-aux-Cailles, a lovely "village" set on a hill that is all quiet streets, leafy squares and buzzy local bistros. The area made history in 1783 when the first manned balloon flight touched down here. In the 1800s it was home to many workers from the small factories in the area and was one of the first areas to fight during the Paris Commune. However, it only really developed after 1910 and the architecture reflects the social ideals of the day – that individual houses and green spaces aid health.

to the Place de la Commune de Paris ⑫, which today looks unremarkable yet was the site of a major street battle in May 1871. Continue up the Rue de la Butte-aux-Cailles. Les Abeilles at 21 ⑬ is a curious store dedicated to bee-keeping and a delight for honey lovers. Pancakes in the old-fashioned crêperie Des Crêpes et des Cailles at 13 may satisfy if you are just peckish, but further down at 18 is the area's best-known restaurant Le Temps de Cerises ⑭. Fittingly, as it's only a few minutes' walk from the Place de la Commune, it's run as a co-operative

Quiet, cobbled streets typify the Butte-aux-Cailles ⑪

Corvisart Ⓜ

RUE DE TOLBIAC

Buttes-aux-Cailles

Take the "Auguste Blanqui" exit out of the Place d'Italie metro station ①, noting the Guimard decoration. Follow the bustling Rue Bobillot until you reach the Rue Paulin-Méry ② and take your first steps into the peace of the Butte-aux-Cailles. The contrast is surprising as you walk the quiet, narrow, cobbled streets with their old-fashioned street lamps. Note the painted shutters on 5 ③ and the trees in the small garden in front of the house opposite. Continue straight ahead, cross over the Rue du Moulin-des-Prés and turn left into the Rue Gérard past the red brick terraces and plant decked villas ④. Keep on into the Rue Samson and then turn right onto the Rue Jonas and left onto the Rue des Cinq Diamants ⑤. At 43 ⑥ there is a hip Franco-Thai restaurant, Le 43. Those interested in history may appreciate the Association des Amis de la Commune de Paris at 46 ⑦, which sells T-shirts, books

and pamphlets on that bloody episode in Parisian history. Turn right into the Passage Barrault, a cobbled alleyway with ivy-covered walls and a countryside feel ⑧. At the end of the passage, turn left onto the Rue Barrault and continue up the street until the right turn into the Rue Daviel. At 10 Rue Daviel the row of cottages known as "Little Alsace" ⑨ because of their chalet style are, in fact, one of the first public housing schemes in Paris. The public can visit their intimate courtyards during the day. Opposite, walk down the Villa Daviel ⑩, a tiny street of terraces with small front gardens overflowing with greenery. Retrace your steps back up to the Rue Barrault, turn left and then right onto the artery of the area, the Rue de la Butte-aux-Cailles ⑪. Head up the street

Road sign in the Butte-aux-Cailles area

RUE DE LA BUTTE AUX CAILLES

13e Arrt

Les Abeilles, for honey enthusiasts ⑬

Le Temps des Cerises, full of bohemian atmosphere ⑭

KEY

••• Walk route

Ⓜ Metro station

0 metres   200

0 yards   200

and is also the unofficial neighbourhood HQ. At the end of the road is the Place Paul Verlaine ⑮. On the other side of the square is the red brick Art Nouveau swimming pool ⑯. Built in 1924, it houses one indoor pool and two lovely outdoor swimming areas. Take the steps in front of the building to find the modern fountain on the Place ⑰. This is supplied by le puits artésian, a local well 580 m (1,902 ft) deep, dating from 1863. You may see locals queuing to fill plastic bottles here. Exit the square, take a right and then another right past the chic restaurant Chez Nathalie with its flowery terrace, which is always packed in summer, into the Rue Vandrezanne, continuing down this pedestrianized street into the passage Vandrezanne, a steep cobbled alleyway with antiquated lampposts ⑱. Cross over the Rue Moulinet and take the Rue Moulin des Prés until you come to the Rue Tolbiac. Cross this busy road then take a right stepping back into another time at the Square des Peupliers ⑲. Built in 1926, each house is different, reflecting the ideals of the time. All have pretty little gardens, most have lovely Art Nouveau porches and the ornate gilded lamp posts are very special. Leave the Square des Peupliers and

Crêpes from Des Crêpes et des Cailles

take a right back onto the Rue du Moulin-des-Prés. Head down the street, noting the interesting rough stone houses ⑳, straight past an unusual purple Art Nouveau-style house at 104 ㉑. Take a right onto the Rue Damesme, turn right into the Rue du Docteur Leray and then right again onto Rue Dieulafoy ㉒. Here are several unique, colourful cottages with flower-filled front gardens behind railings. At the end of the row, take a right onto the Rue Henri Pape, a left onto the Rue Damesme, walk up to the Rue Tolbiac and back out into modern, busy, Paris. Turn right and walk up to the metro Tolbiac ㉓.

Square des Peupliers, with its unique houses ⑲

TRAVELLERS'
NEEDS

WHERE TO STAY

Paris has more guest rooms than almost any other city in Europe. Its hotels vary from magnificent luxury operations like the Ritz (the French call them *palaces*) and the exclusive L'Hôtel, where Oscar Wilde died beyond his means, to much simpler hotels in charming older parts of Paris. It is worth noting that *hôtel* does not always mean "hotel". It can also mean a town hall *(hôtel de ville)*, hospital *(Hôtel-Dieu)* or mansion.

We have inspected hotels in all price brackets and have selected a broad range, all of which offer good value for money. The listings on pp284–91 are organized by area, as in the sightseeing section of the guide, and according to hotel price. Other types of accommodation such as bed and breakfast rooms, self-catering apartments and hostels *(see pp278–9)* are also well worth considering, especially for visitors who are on a tight budget.

WHERE TO LOOK

Hotels in Paris tend to cluster by type in particular areas. As a very broad generalisation, luxury and big-business hotels tend to be on the Right Bank and *hôtels de charme* on the Left Bank.

In the fashionable districts near the Champs-Elysées and the Opéra Garnier lie many of the city's grandest hotels, including the Royal Monceau, Raffles Paris, the Bristol, the Four Seasons George V, the Meurice and the Plaza Athénée. Several less well known but elegant hotels can be found in the residential and ambassadorial quarter near the Palais de Chaillot.

To the east, still on the Right Bank, in the regenerated Marais, a number of the old mansions have been converted into exceptionally attractive small hotels at reasonable prices. The nearby areas around Les Halles and the

Rue St-Denis, however, attract prostitutes and drug addicts. Just south of the Marais across the Seine, the Ile St-Louis and Ile de la Cité have several charming hotels.

The Left Bank covers some of the most popular tourist areas and has an excellent range of small hotels of great character. The atmosphere subtly changes from the much upgraded Latin Quarter and the chic and arty areas north and south of Boulevard St-Germain, to the rather tatty Boulevard itself and the staid institutional area towards Les Invalides and the Eiffel Tower. The hotels tend to reflect this.

Further from the centre, Montparnasse has several large business hotels in high-rise blocks, and the Porte de Versailles area to the south is usually packed with trade fair participants. The station areas around Gare du Nord and Gare de Lyon offer a number of basic hotels (choose

Hôtel de Crillon *(see pp282, 285)*

carefully). Montmartre has one or two pleasant hotels if you don't mind the hilly location, but beware of hotels allegedly in Montmartre but actually in the red-light, sex-show district of Pigalle. If you are looking for a hotel in person, the best times for inspecting are late morning or mid-afternoon. If the hotels are fully booked, try again after 6pm, when unclaimed provisional bookings become free. Don't rely on the impression of a hotel given by reception: ask to see the room offered. (For airport hotels *see p377*.)

HOTEL PRICES

Hotel prices aren't always cheaper in low season (mid-November to March or July and August) because fashion shows and other major events throughout the year can pack rooms, raising prices. However, in the older hotels

The Hôtel du Louvre *(see p285)*, between the Louvre and the Palais Royal

◁ River view of Notre-Dame

differences in the size and position of rooms can have a marked effect on cost.

Twin rooms are slightly more expensive than doubles; single occupancy rates are as high or nearly as high as for two people sharing (tariffs are almost always quoted per room, not per person). Rooms without a bath tend to be about 20 per cent cheaper than those with. You might find a half-board arrangement unnecessary when the city has such a wide choice of good restaurants to suit all budgets.

It is always worth asking for a discount: you may get an Internet rate, for instance. In some hotels special deals are offered for students, families or senior citizens. Discounts are often available when booking online or when booking a package trip.

HIDDEN EXTRAS

By law, tax and service must be included in the price quoted or displayed at the reception desk or in the rooms. Tips are unnecessary other than for exceptional service – if the concierge books you a show, for instance, or if the maid does some washing for you. However, before you make a reservation you should always establish whether breakfast is included in the price or not. Beware of extras such as drinks or snacks from a mini-bar, which will probably be pricy, as will

The Plaza Athénée (see p291) in Champs-Elysées

laundry services, garage parking and telephone calls from your room – especially telephone calls made through the switchboard.

Exchange rates in hotels invariably tend to be lower than in a bank, so make sure you have enough cash to pay your bill unless you are paying by credit card or using travellers' cheques.

HOTEL GRADINGS

French hotels are classified by the tourist authorities into five broad categories: one to four stars, plus a five-star rating which was introduced in 2009. Some very simple places are unclassified. Star ratings serve to provide an indication of the level of facilities you can expect (for example, any hotel with more than three stars should have a lift). Increasingly, the French rating system also tries to take account of such factors as friendliness, cleanliness and decor.

FACILITIES

Few Parisian hotels below a four star rating have a restaurant, although there is nearly always a breakfast room. Many hotel restaurants close in August. Older hotels may also lack a public lounge area. More modern or expensive hotels have correspondingly better facilities and usually some kind of bar. Inexpensive hotels may not have a lift – significant when you are dragging suitcases upstairs. Usually only the more expensive hotels have parking facilities. For exceptions to this rule, see the listings on pages 284–91. If you are driving you may prefer to stay in one of the peripheral motel-style chains (see pp279–80). All but the very simplest of city hotels will have a telephone in the bedroom, many also have television. Business facilities (fax and Internet) are available in grander hotels, and WiFi is now commonplace. Two people sharing can ask for a double (grand lit) or twin beds (lits jumeaux).

Four Seasons George V (see p290)

Statue in the Hôtel Relais Christine (see pp283, 287)

The Meurice *(see p285)* in the Tuileries Quarter

WHAT TO EXPECT

Some hotel beds still use the time-honoured French bolster, a sausage-shaped headrest that can be uncomfortable if you are unused to it. If you prefer pillows, first check in the wardrobe as they may be kept there or ask for *oreillers*. Most hotels offer en suite bathrooms, but be sure to check if you want a bath *(baignoire)* rather than a shower *(douche)*. Simpler places may offer shared facilities on the landing *(au palier)*. A duplex room is a suite on two floors.

In Paris, the traditional French hotel breakfast of fresh coffee, croissants, jam and orange juice is gradually changing into an elaborate buffet breakfast with cold meats and cheeses. Some of the luxury hotels are now such popular venues for breakfast that it is worth reserving a place in the breakfast area if you don't want to eat in your room. A pleasant alternative is to head for the nearest café, where French workers enjoy breakfast over a newspaper.

Check-out time is usually noon and if you stay longer you may pay for an extra day.

SPECIAL BREAKS

Because Paris is such a popular destination with leisure as well as business travellers, weekend packages are often available via travel agents or the Internet. Providing there are no major events taking place, you can reduce costs by visiting in low season and negotiating a discount, or by seeking out an all-inclusive package.

TRAVELLING WITH CHILDREN

Families with young children will often find they can share a room at no or very little extra cost, and some operators offer packages with this in mind. Few hotels refuse to accept children, though facilities specifically for children are not universal. Some hotels will arrange babysitting.

TRAVELLERS WITH SPECIAL NEEDS

Our information about wheelchair access to hotels was gathered by questionnaire and therefore relies on the hotels' own assessment of their suitability. Not many are well geared for use by disabled visitors. **J'Accede** and the **Groupement pour l'Insertion des Personnes Handicapées Physiques (GIHP)** have pertinent information. *(For addresses see p369.)*

SELF-CATERING

Self-catering accommodation is a popular alternative for visitors staying in Paris. The **Citadines Apart'hotel** chain offers fully furnished studios and apartments with kitchens in several central Paris locations (as well as in many other major European cities). These are a good self-catering option for either a short break or an extended stay. Some hotel-type facilities are available, including laundry services, babysitting and grocery delivery, but you pay extra for them.

The **Office du Tourisme et des Congrès de Paris** provides a full list of self-catering accommodation agencies. The better known ones include **Allo Logement Temporaire, At Home In Paris, Haven in Paris, Paris Appartements Services** and **Holidays France Rentals**. **Good Morning Paris** and **France-Lodge** also arrange self-catering apartments, as well as being B&B agencies

The quiet and comfortable Hôtel des Grands Hommes *(see p287)*

The courtyard of the Relais Christine (see p287)

(see Directory *p280).* All offer furnished apartments for stays from one week to six months, sometimes in the apartment of a Parisian who is abroad. Prices are comparable to other apartment accommodation, sometimes slightly cheaper for the larger apartments.

The stylish reception area of the Atala (see p290)

STAYING IN PRIVATE HOMES

Bed and breakfast, that typically-British phenomenon, is known as *chambre d'hôte* or *café-couette* ("coffee and a quilt"). B&B accommodation is available at moderate prices, between €45 and €80 for a double room per night. **Alcôve & Agapes** offers rooms in some enviable districts of Paris, all within walking distance of a metro station. It is worth enquiring about suites and rooms with a private lounge, kitchen or terrace. All homes are routinely inspected.

France-Lodge is a good-value agency specialising in long-stay room rentals and apartments. A registration fee of €15 a year is payable but rentals are generally cheaper than with other agencies.

Good Morning Paris provides guest rooms and tourist information. A two-night minimum stay is required when booking *(for details see* Directory *p280).*

CHAIN HOTELS

A mushroom crop of motel-style establishments on the outskirts of Paris now take large numbers of both business and leisure visitors. The very cheapest chains such as Formule 1, Première Class and Fast Hotel really have nothing except price to recommend them. Further up the ladder are **Campanile, Ibis** and **Choice Hotels**. These places are practical, relatively inexpensive and useful if you have a car, but lack any real Parisian atmosphere or character. Many are in charmless locations on busy roads and may suffer from traffic noise. The newer motels of these chains are better equipped and more smartly decorated than the older ones. Several chains (**Sofitel, Novotel** and **Mercure**) are geared to business travellers, providing better facilities at higher prices; indeed some of the more central ones are positively luxurious. Reductions can make these hotels good value at weekends. Many of the hotels have restaurants

attached. Most of the chains produce their own brochures, often with useful maps detailing the motel's precise location *(see* Directory *p280).*

HOSTELS AND DORMITORY ACCOMMODATION

There are several hostel networks in Paris. **Maisons Internationales de la Jeunesse et des Etudiants (MIJE)** provides dormitory rooms for the 18–30s in 3 splendid mansions in the Marais. There is no advance booking (except for groups) – call at the central offices on the day.

The **Bureau Voyage Jeunesse (BVJ)** has two 'hotels' with double rooms and dormitory accommodation (€30–€42 and €28 respectively), with breakfast and nearly private bathrooms. Bookings cannot be made more than a fortnight in advance.

La Maison de l'UCRIF (Union des Centres de Rencontres Internationales de France) has six centres in and around Paris with individual, shared and dormitory rooms.

Fédération Unie des Auberges de Jeunesse (FUAJ) is a member of the International Youth Hostels Federation. There is no age limit at their three Paris area hostels.

St Christopher's Paris, on the Canal St Martin, provides excellent facilities and offers tours of Paris.

The Four Seasons George V Hotel (see p290)

DIRECTORY

OFFICE DU TOURISME

25 Rue des Pyramides 75001.
Tel 01 49 52 42 03.
See also p367.
www.parisinfo.com

AGENCIES

Ely 12 12
182 Rue du Faubourg
St-Honoré 75008.
Tel 01 43 59 12 12.
www.ely1212.com

SELF-CATERING

Allo Logement Temporaire
64 Rue du Temple 75003.
Tel 01 42 72 00 06.
www.allo-logement-temporaire.asso.fr

At Home in Paris
15 Ave de Friedland
75008.
Tel 01 42 12 40 40.
Fax 01 42 12 40 48.
www.athomeinparis.fr

Citadines Apart'hotel
Tel 01 41 05 79 05.
www.citadines.com

Haven In Paris
37 Somerset Rd,
Lexington, MA 02420-3519, USA.
Tel 1 61 7395 4243.
www.haveninparis.com

Holiday France Rentals
Tel 01 55 37 97 36.
www.holiday-france-rentals.com

Paris Appartements Services
20 Rue Bachaumont
75002. *Tel 01 40 28 01 28.* www.paris-apts.com

RESIDENCES DE TOURISME

Pierre et Vacances
Tel 0892 70 21 80.
www.pierre-vacances.fr

Résidence du Roy
8 Rue François-1er 75008.
Tel 01 42 89 59 59.
www.residence-du-roy.com

BED & BREAKFAST

Alcôve & Agapes
Tel 01 44 85 06 05.
Fax 01 44 85 06 14.
www.bed-and-breakfast-in-paris.com

France-Lodge
2 Rue Meissonier 75017.
Tel 01 56 33 85 85.
Fax 01 56 33 85 89.
www.apartments-in-paris.com

Good Morning Paris
43 Rue Lacépède, 75005.
Tel 01 47 07 28 29.
Fax 01 47 07 44 45.
www.goodmorning paris.fr

CHAIN HOTELS

Campanile
Tel 0825 003 003
(central reservations).
www.campanile.fr

Choice Hotels
Tel 08 00 12 12 12
(central reservations).
www.choicehotels.com

Hilton
57 Rue de Courcelles
75008.
Tel 01 58 36 67 00.
www.hilton.com

Holiday Inn République
10 Pl de la République
75011.
Tel 0800 905 649.
www.holidayinn.com

Holiday Inn St-Germain-des-Prés
92 Rue de Vaugirard.
Tel 0800 905 649.
www.holidayinn.com

Hôtel All Seasons Paris Bercy
77 Rue de Bercy 75012.
Tel 01 53 46 50 50.
www.accorhotels.com

Ibis
Tel 0892 686 686.
www.ibishotel.com

Mercure Paris Austerlitz
6 Blvd Vincent Auriol
75013.
Tel 01 45 82 48 00.
www.accorhotels.com

Mercure Paris Montparnasse
20 Rue de la Gaîté 75014.
Tel 01 43 35 28 28.
www.accorhotels.com

Mercure Paris Porte de Versailles
69 Blvd Victor 75015.
Tel 01 44 19 03 03.
www.accorhotels.com

Mercure Paris Tour-Eiffel
64 Blvd de Grenelle
75015.
Tel 01 45 78 90 90.
www.accorhotels.com

Méridien Montparnasse
19 Rue du Commandant
René Mouchotte 75014.
Tel 01 44 36 44 36.
www.lemeridien-montparnasse.com

Novotel Paris Bercy
85 Rue de Bercy 75012.
Tel 01 43 42 30 00.
www.novotel.com

Novotel Paris Les Halles
8 Pl Marguerite de
Navarre 75001.
Tel 01 42 21 31 31.
www.novotel.com

Novotel Tour Eiffel
61 Quai de Grenelle
75015. *Tel 01 40 58 20 00.* www.novotel.com

Paris Rive Gauche Hotel and Conference Centre
17 Blvd St-Jacques 75014.
Tel 01 40 78 79 80.
www.marriott.com

Royal Garden St-Honoré
218 Rue du Faubourg
St-Honoré 75008.
Tel 01 49 53 40 04.
www.royal gardenparis.com

Sofitel Le Faubourg
15 Rue Boissy d'Anglas
75008. *Tel 01 44 94 14 14.* www.sofitel.com

Sofitel Paris La Défense
33 Voie des Sculpteurs
92800. *Tel 01 47 76 44 43.* www.sofitel.com

Sofitel Scribe
1 Rue Scribe 75009.
Tel 01 44 71 24 24.
www.sofitel.com

Warwick Champs-Elysées
5 Rue de Berri 75008.
Tel 01 45 63 14 11.

HOSTELS

BVJ
20 Rue Jean-Jacques
Rousseau 75001.
Tel 01 53 00 90 90.
www.bvj-hotel.com

FUAJ – Le d'Artagnan
80 Rue Vitruve 75020.
Tel 01 40 32 34 56.
www.fuaj.org

La Maison de l'UCRIF
27 Rue de Turbigo 75002.
Tel 01 40 26 57 64.
www.ethic-etapes.fr

MIJE
11 Rue du Fauconnier
75004. *Tel 01 42 74 23 45.* www.mije.com

St Christopher's Paris
64–72 Quai de Seine
75019. *Tel 01 40 34 34 40.*
www.st-christophers.co.uk

CAMPING

Camping du Bois de Boulogne
2 Allée du Bord de l'Eau
75016. *Tel 01 45 24 30 00.* www.campingparis.fr

Camping International de Jablines
Jablines-Annet 77450. *Tel 01 60 26 09 37.* www.camping-jablines.com

Camping International Maisons-Laffitte
1 Rue Johnson 78600.
Tel 01 39 12 21 91.
www.campint.com

FFCC
78 Rue de Rivoli 75004.
Tel 01 42 72 84 08.
www.ffcc.fr

CAMPING

The only campsite in Paris itself is the **Camping du Bois de Boulogne/Ile de France** (around €15–€40 per night). This well-equipped site next to the Seine is open all year round but is usually fully booked during the summer. Pitches for tents, caravans as well as rental of mobile homes are available. There are many other campsites in the surrounding region, some close to an RER line. The **Camping International de Jablines** (around €25 per night) is conveniently located just 9km (5.5 miles) from Disneyland Paris and a 25-minute RER train ride from central Paris. **Camping International Maisons-Laffitte** (around €25 per night) is located in a pleasant suburb on the River Seine and is open from April to October. The local RER station is a 10-minute walk away. Trains from here take 20 minutes to the city centre and 50 minutes to Disneyland Paris. Versailles is 20 minutes from the campsite by car. Details of other sites can be obtained from the Paris tourist office or from a booklet produced by the **Fédération Française de Camping-Caravaning (FFCC)** *(see* Directory *p280).*

HOW TO BOOK

Paris is busiest at Christmas and New Year, and during France's school breaks around Easter and October. Tourists pour in from May to September, but Parisians pour out *en masse* in August, when many shops and restaurants close. Disneyland Resort Paris has further increased the pressure to find accommodation, as many visitors choose to stay in the capital and commute to the park on the RER.

If you have decided on a hotel, it is vital to book ahead by at least a month as Paris is a popular destination. The hotels in the listings are among the best in their category and will fill particularly quickly. Make a reservation six weeks in advance between May and

Tourist information desk, Charles de Gaulle airport

October. The best way is to book directly with the hotel. If you make your initial inquiry by telephone, ring during the day if possible – you are more likely to find staff authorized to take bookings. You should send confirmation of your reservation (websites or email addresses are provided where available); credit card details are often required to guarantee your booking.

It is usually possible to make a reservation through your hotel's website. It can be worth doing this as some hotels offer special deals for visitors who book online.

If you prefer to use an agency, **Ely 12 12** can book hotels and other kinds of accommodation, as well as excursions such as boat trips along the Seine.

If you aren't too fussy about where you stay, or if all the hotels are reportedly full, you can book via the **Office du Tourisme et des Congrès de Paris**, which offers an on-the-spot booking service for a reasonable fee.

DEPOSITS

If you make a reservation by telephone you will be asked for either your credit card number (from which any cancellation fee may be deducted) or a deposit (*arrhes*). These *arrhes* can be as much as the price of a night's stay, but usually will cost only about 15 per cent of this. Pay your deposit by credit card or by sending an international money order. You can sometimes send an

ordinary cheque for an amount equivalent to the deposit as evidence of your intention to keep the booking. Usually the hotel will simply keep your foreign cheque as security until you arrive, then return it to you and give you one total bill when you leave. But do check with the hotel before sending an ordinary cheque. It's also quite acceptable in France to specify your choice of room when you book.

Try to arrive at your hotel by 6pm on the day you have booked, or at least telephone to say you will be late, otherwise you may well lose the room. A hotel that breaks a confirmed, prepaid booking is breaking a contract, and the client is entitled to compensation of at least twice any deposit paid. Alternatively, the hotel must offer you equivalent or better accommodation elsewhere. If you have any problems, consult the Office du Tourisme.

TOURIST INFORMATION DESKS

You can book hotels at all airport information desks but only in person and for the same day. The Gare de Lyon, Gare du Nord and Pyramides information desks provide a similar booking arrangement for all forms of accommodation. Many Paris information desks also keep a complete list of city hotels and some book entertainment and excursions *(see* Practical Information *p367).*

Caravans at Camping International Maisons-Laffitte

Paris's Best: Hotels

Paris is famous for its hotels. It excels in all categories from the glittering opulent *palaces* (the top luxury hotels) to the *hôtels de charme*, full of character and romantic appeal, to the simpler good-value family hotels in quiet back streets. As a centre of culture and fashion, the city has long been a mecca for the rich and famous, great and good from all walks of life. Not surprisingly, therefore, it can boast some of the most magnificent hotels in the world and has more than a thousand hotels in the inner city alone. Whatever the price level, however, the hotels in our listings *(see pp284–91)* all show that inimitable style and taste that Parisians bring to everything they do. These are a selection of the very best.

Bristol
In the chic heart of Paris, this epitomizes luxury. (See p290.)

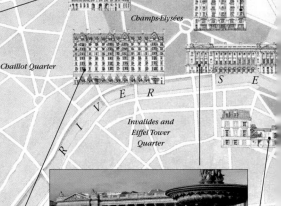

Champs-Elysées

Chaillot Quarter

Invalides and Eiffel Tower Quarter

RIVER

S E

Balzac
Small but stylish, this hotel exudes period charm. The restaurant, Pierre Gagnaire, is highly rated. (See p290.)

Hôtel de Crillon
One of the great palace hotels, this was built for Louis XV. (See p285.)

Plaza Athénée
In the heart of haute couture *Paris, this is the favourite haunt of the fashion world. Magnificent decor and a superb restaurant are the main attractions.* (See p291.)

Duc de St-Simon
Bedrooms overlook a leafy garden in this comfortable and peaceful hôtel de charme *situated in an 18th-century mansion south of the Seine.* (See p289.)

Le Grand Hôtel Intercontinental
Built for Napoleon III in 1862, this historic hotel has been patronized by the rich and famous from Mata Hari to Winston Churchill. (See p291.)

L'Hôtel
Best known as the last home of Oscar Wilde, this stylish hotel boasts rooms both impressive and slightly bizarre. One room was furnished and occupied by the music hall star Mistinguett. (See p286.)

Relais Christine
An oasis of calm in the hub of the city, this charming hotel offers traditional comforts such as a welcoming open fire in the drawing room. (See p287.)

Opéra Quarter

Tuileries Quarter

Beaubourg and Les Halles

E

St-Germain-des-Prés

The Marais

Ile de la Cité

Ile St-Louis

Luxembourg Quarter

Latin Quarter

Jardin des Plantes Quarter

Hôtel du Jeu de Paume
This cleverly converted hotel was once a court for playing real tennis – jeu de paume. (See p284.)

0 kilometres 1

0 miles 0.5

Lutétia
This was decorated by top designer Sonia Rykiel. (See p286.)

Hôtel de l'Abbaye
A pleasant garden and courtyard and attractive rooms are features of this small secluded hotel near the Jardins du Luxembourg. (See p286.)

Choosing a Hotel

The hotels listed in the following pages have been
selected for their facilities, good value and location. The
list covers all the areas and price categories. Check the
websites for special deals. Most hotels provide cots, can
reserve babysitters and have Internet access or Wi-Fi.
Hotels within the same category are listed alphabetically.

PRICE CATEGORIES
For a standard double room per night
including breakfast and necessary
charges:
€ under €100
€€ €100–€150
€€€ €150–€190
€€€€ €190–€280
€€€€€ over €280

ILE DE LA CITÉ AND ILE ST-LOUIS

Hôtel des Deux-Iles   €€€€
59 Rue St-Louis-en-l'Ile, 75004 **Tel** *01 43 26 13 35* **Fax** *01 43 29 60 25* **Rooms** *17*   **Map** *13 C4*

It's a privilege to be able to stay on the Ile St-Louis, and this converted 17th-century mansion offers an affordable
way to do so. Here the atmosphere is peaceful, the small bedrooms are attractive and breakfast is served in the
medieval vaults. **www.deuxiles-paris-hotel.com**

Hôtel du Jeu de Paume   €€€€€
54 Rue St-Louis-en-l'Ile, 75004 **Tel** *01 43 26 14 18* **Fax** *01 40 46 02 76* **Rooms** *30*   **Map** *13 C4*

Standing on the site of a former real tennis court, the hotel has been skilfully converted into a warm, elegant place
to stay. Features include a glass-walled lift, wooden beams, old terracotta paving, a sauna, a gym and several
charming duplex rooms. **www.hoteljeudepaume.com**

Paris Yacht   €€€€€
11 Quai St-Bernard, 75005 **Tel** *06 88 70 26 36* **Rooms** *2*   **Map** *13 C5*

This cosy houseboat docked opposite Ile St-Louis makes a unique and tranquil place to stay. It sleeps four people and
has a fully equipped kitchen, Internet access and a TV. Feel the river ripple as the Bateaux Mouches sail by, and enjoy
the views from the upstairs deck. Minumum three-night booking. **www.paris-yacht.com**

THE MARAIS

Hôtel de la Bretonnerie   €€
22 Rue Ste-Croix de la Bretonnerie, 75004 **Tel** *01 48 87 77 63* **Fax** *01 42 77 26 78* **Rooms** *29*   **Map** *13 C3*

Carved stone walls and an arched dining room in the basement are some of the charming features of Hôtel de la
Bretonnerie, housed in a 17th-century mansion. One of the most comfortable hotels in the area, it has spacious
bedrooms with wooden beams and antique furniture. Service is warm and friendly. **www.bretonnerie.com**

St-Merry   €€€
78 Rue de la Verrerie, 75004 **Tel** *01 42 78 14 15* **Fax** *01 40 29 06 82* **Rooms** *12*   **Map** *13 B3*

A historic hotel which was the presbytery of the adjoining church in the 17th century and later became a bordello, is
today a simply lovely place to stay. Furnished in Gothic style, note the flying buttresses crossing room 9.
www.hotel-paris-saintmerry-marais.com

Hôtel du Bourg Tibourg   €€€€
19 Rue du Bourg Tibourg, 75004 **Tel** *01 42 78 47 39* **Fax** *01 40 29 07 00* **Rooms** *30*   **Map** *13C*

This stylish spot was decorated by top interior designer Jacques Garcia and is extremely popular with fashionable
visitors to Paris. Rooms are opulent and all bathrooms are fully clad in black marble. The beautiful interior courtyard is
a pleasant surprise. **www.bourgtibourg.com**

Hôtel Duo   €€€€
11 Rue du Temple, 75004 **Tel** *01 42 72 72 22* **Fax** *01 42 72 03 53* **Rooms** *58*   **Map** *13 B3*

A family-run hotel for three generations, the former Axial Beaubourg is still in the same hands, but has had a trendy
makeover. The stylish, contemporary decor features teal and brown and there is a bijou bar and Japanese garden.
All just steps from the Pompidou Centre. **www.duo-paris.com**

St-Paul-le-Marais   €€€€
8 Rue de Sévigné, 75004 **Tel** *01 48 04 97 27* **Fax** *01 48 87 37 04* **Rooms** *28*   **Map** *14 D3*

Close to the historic Place des Vosges, this hotel has wooden beams and old stone, although the furnishings are
bright and modern. Some rooms abound in busy, but tasteful, patterned wallpaper and drapes. Ask for bedrooms
facing the courtyard to avoid the noise of traffic coming from the Rue de Sévigné. **www.hotel-paris-marais.com**

Key to Symbols *see back cover flap*

Pavillon de la Reine

🖥 P 🖵 ▤   €€€€€

28 Pl des Vosges, 75003 **Tel** *01 40 29 19 19* **Fax** *01 40 29 19 20* **Rooms** *54*   **Map** *14 D3*

Set back from the marvellous Place des Vosges, the Pavillon de la Reine is the best hotel in the Marais. Incredibly romantic, the courtyard is a haven of peace and the bedrooms are sumptuous and furnished with excellent reproduction antiques. Facilities include a gym, steam room and spa. **www.pavillon-de-la-reine.com**

BEAUBOURG AND LES HALLES

Hôtel Britannique

🖥 ⛷ ▤   €€€

20 Avenue Victoria, 75001 **Tel** *01 42 33 74 59* **Fax** *01 42 33 83 65* **Rooms** *39*   **Map** *13 A3*

The Britannique has many repeat visitors, who return for the central location beside Châtelet, as well as the Grand Tour atmosphere and helpful staff. A small hôtel de charme, with beautiful, characterful rooms and an abundance of old-fashioned charm. **www.hotel-britannique.fr**

TUILERIES QUARTER

Hôtel Louvre Sainte Anne

🖥 ⛷ ▤   €€€

32 Rue Sainte Anne 75001 **Tel** *01 40 20 02 35* **Fax** *01 40 15 91 13* **Rooms** *20*   **Map** *12 E1*

This small, pleasant hotel is close to the Louvre and the Opéra and has clean rooms and helpful staff. The rooms have been renovated and the reception area is rather splendid, with a trompe l'oeil painting. The hotel is popular with Japanese guests as this road is filled with sushi restaurants. **www.paris-hotel-louvre.com**

Brighton

🖥 ▤   €€€€

218 Rue de Rivoli, 75001 **Tel** *01 47 03 61 61* **Fax** *01 42 60 41 78* **Rooms** *61*   **Map** *12 D1*

A real insiders' location, the Brighton provides a much-sought after Rivoli address without the sky-high prices. The bedrooms have beautiful, high ceilings and large windows that look out either on to the Jardin des Tuileries or on to the courtyard. **www.paris-hotel-brighton.com**

Hôtel Costes

🖥 P 🍽 ♨ 🖵 ▤   €€€€€

239 Rue St Honoré, 75001 **Tel** *01 42 44 50 00* **Fax** *01 42 44 50 01* **Rooms** *82*   **Map** *12 D1*

One of the most fashionable places to stay in Paris, the Costes is a favourite with models and film stars. A sumptuous affair, it is designed to resemble a Second Empire palace. The balcony rooms are the most in demand. In summer, eat in the Italianate courtyard. **www.hotelcostes.com**

Hôtel de Crillon

🖥 P 🍽 🖵 ▤   €€€€€

10 Pl de la Concorde, 75008 **Tel** *01 44 71 15 00* **Fax** *01 44 71 15 02* **Rooms** *147*   **Map** *11 C1*

With its magnificent location on the glittering Place de la Concorde, the Crillon offers unsurpassed elegance. The hotel has a fine Royal Suite and terrace, one of the most beautiful dining rooms in Paris, Les Ambassadeurs, and a fabulous winter garden. **www.crillon.com**

Hôtel du Louvre

🖥 P 🍽 🖵 ▤   €€€€€

Pl André Malraux, 75001 **Tel** *01 44 58 38 38* **Fax** *01 44 58 38 01* **Rooms** *177*   **Map** *12 E1*

The first luxury hotel in France was built in 1855 by order of Napoleon III. The lavish rooms have spectacular views: the Pissarro Suite is where the artist painted his view of Place du Théâtre Français, while if you book room 551 you can admire the opera house from your bath! **www.hoteldulouvre.com**

Meurice

🖥 P 🍽 🖵 ▤   €€€€€

228 Rue de Rivoli, 75001 **Tel** *01 44 58 10 10* **Fax** *01 44 58 10 15* **Rooms** *160*   **Map** *12 D1*

The Meurice is a perfect example of successful restoration, with excellent replicas of the original plasterwork and furnishings. The staff here are unstintingly helpful and the hotel offers personalised shopping and art buying tours. The hotel also has France's only Valmont spa. **www.meuricehotel.fr**

Ritz Paris

🖥 P 🍽 ♨ 🖵 ▤   €€€€€

15 Pl Vendôme, 75001 **Tel** *01 43 16 30 30* **Fax** *01 43 16 31 78* **Rooms** *162*   **Map** *6 D5*

A legendary address, the Ritz still lives up to its reputation, combining elegance and decadence. The Louis XVI furniture and chandeliers are all originals, and the floral arrangements are works of art. The Hemingway Bar is home to the glitterati and an ideal spot for a cocktail. **www.ritzparis.com**

Saint James Albany Hotel and Spa

🖥 P 🍽 ♨ 🖵 ▤   €€€€€

202 Rue de Rivoli, 75001 **Tel** *01 44 58 43 21* **Fax** *01 44 58 43 11* **Rooms** *200*   **Map** *12 E1*

This quiet and tidy hotel in a 17th-century building offers luxurious rooms with modern facilities. It is perfectly situated in the heart of Paris, opposite the Tuileries gardens, and boasts a charming courtyard, spa and swimming pool area. **www.clarionsaintjames.com**

The Westin Paris

3 Rue de Castiglione, 75001 **Tel** *01 44 77 11 11* **Fax** *01 44 77 14 60* **Rooms** *438*

Map *12 D1*

This elegant late 19th-century hotel is situated between the Jardin des Tuileries and the Place Vendôme. It was designed by Charles Garnier, architect of the Paris Opéra. Bedrooms are quiet – the best overlook one of the courtyards. The Jacques Garcia-decorated restaurant is excellent. **www.westin.com**

ST-GERMAIN-DES-PRES

Grand Hôtel des Balcons

3 Rue Casimir Delavigne, 75006 **Tel** *01 46 34 78 50* **Fax** *01 46 34 06 27* **Rooms** *50*

Map *12 F5*

Embellished with Art Nouveau features, this hotel has a beautiful hall with stained-glass windows and striking 19th-century-style lamps and wood panelling. Most guestrooms, which are quiet and well-decorated, enjoy a balcony. High-speed Internet access with Wi-Fi available. **www.hotelgrandsbalcons.com**

Hôtel du Quai Voltaire

19 Quai Voltaire, 75007 **Tel** *01 42 61 50 91* **Fax** *01 42 61 62 26* **Rooms** *33*

Map *12 D2*

Overlooking the river, this hotel was once the favourite of Blondin, Baudelaire and Pissarro, and has featured in several films. Bedrooms on the quay are better avoided, as they suffer from traffic noise. Higher floors are quieter, though, and the views are superb. **www.quaivoltaire.fr**

Hôtel des Marronniers

21 Rue Jacob, 75006 **Tel** *01 43 25 30 60* **Fax** *01 40 46 83 56* **Rooms** *37*

Map *12 E3*

Situated between a courtyard and a garden, this hotel provides perfect peace. The decor is homely, with bold patterns and textured fabrics, and bedrooms on the fourth floor, garden side, provide very special views over the Parisian rooftops and the St-Germain-des-Prés church steeple. **www.hotel-marronniers.com**

Hôtel des Sts-Pères

65 Rue des Sts-Pères, 75006 **Tel** *01 45 44 50 00* **Fax** *01 45 44 90 83* **Rooms** *39*

Map *12 E3*

The hotel occupies one of the old aristocratic mansions of St-Germain-des-Prés, the former home of Louis XIV's architect. The lounge bar is very popular with authors from the publishing houses nearby. The bedrooms are quiet and roomy – the best has an outstanding ceiling fresco. **www.paris-hotel-saints-peres.com**

Hôtel Lenox

9 Rue de l'Université, 75007 **Tel** *01 42 96 10 95* **Fax** *01 42 61 52 83* **Rooms** *34*

Map *12 D3*

The charm of the Lenox lies in its simplicity and literary history – T.S. Eliot, Ezra Pound and James Joyce all lived here. The hotel has an Art Deco interior, the staff are extremely friendly and the cocktail bar is lovely. It enjoys a great location in the heart of St-Germain-des-Prés. **www.hotelparislenoxsaintgermain.com**

Hôtel de Fleurie

32/34 Rue Grégoire de Tours, 75006 **Tel** *01 53 73 70 00* **Fax** *01 53 73 70 20* **Rooms** *29*

Map *12 F4*

The statue-filled facade is enough to make one want to stay in this welcoming, family-run hotel. Inside, the woodwork and white stone create the same light feel, as do the bedrooms, all of which are beautifully decorated, with well-equipped bathrooms. Keep a lookout for the excellent Internet deals. **www.hoteldefleurieparis.com**

Hôtel de l'Abbaye St-Germain

10 Rue Cassette, 75006 **Tel** *01 45 44 38 11* **Fax** *01 45 48 07 86* **Rooms** *44*

Map *12 D5*

A 17th-century abbey, just steps from the Jardin du Luxembourg, this charming hotel has been a preferred hideout for artists and writers. Its finely furnished guestrooms and apartments have been tastefully done up and provided with modern facilities. The four duplex apartments make for an extra special stay. **www.hotelabbayeparis.com**

Le Bellechasse

8 Rue de Bellechasse, 75007 **Tel** *01 45 50 22 31* **Fax** *01 45 51 52 36* **Rooms** *34*

Map *11 C2*

Situated just one minute from the Musée d'Orsay, this boutique hotel has been designed by Christian Lacroix with characteristic flair and imagination. Huge butterflies, fish and painted ladies create a magical, Italianate setting. Rooms around the small courtyard have a more rustic feel. Wi-Fi is free. **www.lebellechasse.com**

Lutétia

45 Blvd Raspail, 75006 **Tel** *01 49 54 46 46* **Fax** *01 49 54 46 00* **Rooms** *230*

Map *12 D4*

The Lutétia is a mainstay of glamour on the south side of the river. The building is partly Art Nouveau and partly Art Deco, and has been restored throughout. Publishers and chic shoppers are regular customers in the restaurant. Convenient location. **www.lutetia-paris.com**

L'Hôtel

13 Rue des Beaux-Arts, 75006 **Tel** *01 44 41 99 00* **Fax** *01 43 25 64 81* **Rooms** *20*

Map *12 E3*

A riot of exuberance and opulence, this Jacques Garcia-designed hotel is gloriously decadent. Each room is different; the hotel's most famous one is the Oscar Wilde suite, named after the author who died in the hotel in 1900, which boasts period furnishings. There's also a beautiful spa and a one-star Michelin restaurant. **www.l-hotel.com**

Key to Price Guide *see p284* **Key to Symbols** *see back cover flap*

Montalembert

⬚ 🍴 ▤ €€€€€

3 Rue de Montalembert, 75007 **Tel** *01 45 49 68 68* **Fax** *01 45 49 69 49* **Rooms** *56*   **Map** *12 D3*

Situated in the heart of the publishing district, this fashionable hotel combines modernity and timeless elegance. The bedrooms boast fine wood and designer fabrics with excellent quality linen sheets, towels and bathrobes. The eighth-floor suites have good views. **www.montalembert.com**

Relais Christine

⬚ 🅿 🍴 ▤ €€€€€

3 Rue Christine, 75006 **Tel** *01 40 51 60 80* **Fax** *01 40 51 60 81* **Rooms** *51*   **Map** *12 F4*

Always full, the Relais Christine is the epitome of the *hôtel de charme*. It is part of the cloister of a 16th-century abbey and is a romantic haven of peace. The bedrooms are bright and spacious, especially the duplex rooms. There are spa and sauna facilities available. **www.relais-christine.com**

Villa St-Germain

⬚ ▤ €€€€€

29 Rue Jacob, 75006 **Tel** *01 43 26 60 00* **Fax** *01 46 34 63 63* **Rooms** *31*   **Map** *12 F3*

A very chic, contemporary hotel decorated in wenge wood, velvets and faux crocodile leather, La Villa has all the style of the Montalembert *(see p287)* but without the hefty price tag. A gourmet breakfast is served either in your room or in the pleasant dining room. **www.villa-saintgermain.com**

LATIN QUARTER

Esmeralda

€

4 Rue St-Julien-le-Pauvre, 75005 **Tel** *01 43 54 19 20* **Fax** *01 40 51 00 68* **Rooms** *16*   **Map** *13 A4*

The much-loved bohemian Esmeralda lies in the heart of the Latin Quarter. With old stone walls, beamed ceilings and marvellously old-fashioned wallpaper, its charm has seduced the likes of Terence Stamp and Serge Gainsbourg. The best rooms overlook Notre-Dame. No breakfast provided. **www.hotel-esmeralda.fr**

Hôtel des Grandes Ecoles

⬚ 🅿 €€

75 Rue Cardinal Lemoine, 75005 **Tel** *01 43 26 79 23* **Fax** *01 43 25 28 15* **Rooms** *51*   **Map** *13 B5*

This hotel is a cluster of three small houses around a beautiful garden, where you can breakfast in good weather. The rooms are all comfortable and furnished with traditional 18th-century-style floral wallpaper, some open onto the courtyard. **www.hotel-grandes-ecoles.com**

Hôtel des Grands Degrés de Notre Dame

🍴 €€

10 Rue des Grands Degrés, 75005 **Tel** *01 55 42 88 88* **Fax** *01 40 46 95 34* **Rooms** *10*   **Map** *13 B4*

An exceptionally friendly place to stay. The staff are genuinely welcoming and the wood-panelling and oak beams around the building make it even more special. Lovely, very clean bedrooms with Internet access available. The Bar Restaurant and Tea Room serves great food at a low price. **www.lesdegreshotel.com**

Hôtel des Grands Hommes

⬚ ▤ €€

17 Pl du Panthéon, 75005 **Tel** *01 46 34 19 60* **Fax** *01 43 26 67 32* **Rooms** *31*   **Map** *1/ A1*

This quiet family hotel close to the Jardin du Luxembourg boasts a great view of the Panthéon from the attic rooms on the upper floor. The bedrooms are comfortable and decorated in a daring Neo-Baroque and Empire style. Wi-Fi services available. **www.hoteldesgrandshommes.com**

Hôtel du Collège de France

⬚ 👥 ▤ €€

7 Rue Thénard, 75005 **Tel** *01 43 26 78 36* **Fax** *01 46 34 58 29* **Rooms** *29*   **Map** *13 A5*

One of the best-value small hotels in Paris, the Hôtel du Collège de France is conveniently situated in a quiet street near the Musée de Cluny (and opposite the excellent bistro Le Pré Verre). It offers a warm and charming decor, very helpful staff and free Wi-Fi in all the rooms. **www.hotel-collegedefrance.com**

Hôtel de Notre-Dame

⬚ ▤ €€€€

19 Rue Maître Albert, 75005 **Tel** *01 43 26 79 00* **Fax** *01 46 33 50 11* **Rooms** *34*   **Map** *13 B5*

The picturesque Hôtel de Notre-Dame overlooks Notre-Dame cathedral and the Seine on one side and the Panthéon on the other. The furnishings are functional, but some rooms have beams or an old stone wall. The main appeal here is the location. The hotel has its own sauna. **www.hotel-paris-notredame.com**

Hôtel Residence Henri IV

⬚ €€€€

50 Rue des Bernardins, 75005 **Tel** *01 44 41 31 81* **Fax** *01 46 33 93 22* **Rooms** *14*   **Map** *13 B5*

Overlooking a pretty park square and with window boxes full of geraniums in season, this hotel is a real jewel. Bedrooms are bright and airy and all have attached kitchens. There is also a flat for four people. The setting is very quiet for the area. **www.residencehenri4.com**

Hôtel Sorbonne

⬚ 👥 ▤ €€€€

6 Rue Victor Cousin, 75005 **Tel** *01 43 54 58 08* **Fax** *01 40 51 05 18* **Rooms** *38*   **Map** *12 F5*

Long a favourite with the parents of Sorbonne students, this hotel has been decorated in luscious turquoise, green and orange. The hotel's modern style is complemented by state-of-the art bathrooms, unlimited free Wi-Fi and iMacs in every room. It is situated near fashion boutiques and nightclubs. **www.hotelsorbonne.com**

LUXEMBOURG QUARTER

Aviatic   🛗 P 📧   €€€€
105 Rue de Vaugirard, 75006 **Tel** *01 53 63 25 50* **Fax** *01 53 63 25 55* **Rooms** *43*   **Map** *12 E5*

The much-loved Aviatic combines bohemian style with modern comforts. The rooms are individually decorated with charming pieces found at local flea markets and warm, bright textiles. Complimentary aperitifs are served in the evening. Staff are very friendly. Parking is available for €30 per day. **www.aviatic.fr**

Hôtel Louis II   🛗 🧍 📧   €€€€
2 Rue St-Sulpice, 75006 **Tel** *01 46 33 13 80* **Fax** *01 46 33 17 29* **Rooms** *22*   **Map** *12 E4*

A hotel for those who love the rustic charm of exposed beams and sloping walls, the Louis II is tastefully decorated and filled with light. Rooms overlook either Rue St-Sulpice or Rue de Condé, and the Jardin du Luxembourg is just a short walk away. The suites in the roof are particularly charming. **www.hotel-louis2.com**

MONTPARNASSE

Hôtel Apollon Montparnasse   🛗 P 📧   €€
91 Rue Ouest, 75014 **Tel** *01 43 95 62 00* **Fax** *01 43 95 62 10* **Rooms** *33*   **Map** *15 C3*

The Apollon offers clean, stylish, well-equipped rooms close to the Pernety metro station. The hotel also has good access by bus to the city centre. Breakfast is served at an extra cost, but there are plenty of pleasant cafés and restaurants nearby. The hotel provides free Wi-Fi and the staff are friendly and helpful. **www.paris-hotel-paris.net**

Hôtel Delambre   🛗 📧   €€
35 Rue Delambre, 75014 **Tel** *01 43 20 66 31* **Fax** *01 45 38 91 76* **Rooms** *30*   **Map** *16 D2*

Located a few steps away from Montparnasse cemetery, and close to the Jardin du Luxembourg and Latin Quarter, this hotel stylishly mixes modern and classical styles. Guestrooms are simply furnished in warm tones with all mod cons. **www.delambre-paris-hotel.com**

Hotel Danemark   🛗   €€€
21 Rue Vavin, 75006 **Tel** *01 43 26 93 78* **Fax** *01 46 34 66 06* **Rooms** *15*   **Map** *16 D1*

Ideally situated between the Jardin du Luxembourg and the bustling cafés of Montparnasse, this hotel combines excellent customer service with Parisian charm. The elegant rooms have stone walls and occasional beams, while bathrooms are artfully tiled. Free Wi-Fi access. **www.hoteldanemark.com**

Le Saint-Grégoire   🛗 P 📧   €€€€
43 Rue de l'Abbé Grégoire, 75006 **Tel** *01 45 48 23 23* **Fax** *01 45 48 33 95* **Rooms** *20*   **Map** *11 C5*

Le Saint-Grégoire is a fashionable townhouse hotel with immaculately-decorated bedrooms and 19th-century furnishings. At the centre of the drawing room is a charming fireplace with a real fire. Book a room with a delightful private terrace. Small pets are accepted. **www.hotellesaintgregoire.com**

Ste-Beuve   🛗 📧   €€€€
9 Rue Ste Beuve, 75006 **Tel** *01 45 48 20 07* **Fax** *01 45 48 67 52* **Rooms** *22*   **Map** *16 D1*

The Ste-Beuve is a small, carefully restored hotel for aesthetes and habitués of the Rive Gauche galleries. There is a fireplace in the hall, the rooms are pleasantly decorated in pastel shades and there are several classic, contemporary paintings. **www.hotel-sainte-beuve.fr**

Villa des Artistes   🛗 📧   €€€€
9 Rue de la Grande Chaumière, 75006 **Tel** *01 43 26 60 86* **Fax** *01 43 54 73 70* **Rooms** *ww*   **Map** *16 D2*

The Villa des Artistes aims to recreate Montparnasse's artistic heyday when Modigliani, Beckett and Fitzgerald were visitors here. The bedrooms are all individually decorated, with particularly eye-catching rooms inspired by Cubism, Fauvism and Surrealism. In summer the patio garden is a real draw at breakfast-time. **www.villa-artistes.com**

INVALIDES AND EIFFEL TOWER QUARTER

Grand Hôtel Levêque   🛗 📧   €€
29 Rue Cler, 75007 **Tel** *01 47 05 49 15* **Fax** *01 45 50 49 36* **Rooms** *50*   **Map** *10 F3*

On a street with a quaint fruit-and-vegetable market, the Levêque lies between the Eiffel Tower and the Invalides, near the Musée Rodin and the Louvre. The great location isn't the only attraction – guestrooms are well-kept and the hotel also provides Internet facilities. **www.hotel-leveque.com**

Key to Price Guide *see p284* **Key to Symbols** *see back cover flap*

Duquesne Eiffel
🖼️📧 €€€€

23 Ave Duquesne, 75007 **Tel** *01 44 42 09 09* **Fax** *01 44 42 09 08* **Rooms** *40* **Map** *11 A4*

Built in 1798 to accommodate students from the nearby Ecole Militaire, this hotel combines historic charm with elegantly renovated rooms, some of which have balconies with views of the Eiffel tower. The hotel is close to a metro stop, and the staff are friendly and helpful. **www.duquesneeiffel.com**

Hôtel Bourgogne et Montana
🖼️📧 €€€€

3 Rue de Bourgogne, 75007 **Tel** *01 45 51 20 22* **Fax** *01 45 56 11 98* **Rooms** *32* **Map** *11 B2*

Situated in front of the Assemblée Nationale, the hotel has an air of sobriety. Features include an old lift and an all-white circular hall with brightly coloured sofas. The bedrooms have been refurbished in a classical style. Extremely stylish. **www.bourgogne-montana.com**

Hôtel de Suède St-Germain
🖼️📧 €€€€

31 Rue Vaneau, 75007 **Tel** *01 47 05 00 08* **Fax** *01 47 05 69 27* **Rooms** *30* **Map** *11 B4*

Located near the Orsay and Rodin museums, the Hôtel de Suède St Germain offers elegant rooms, decorated in late 18th-century style, and the owners' welcome is exceptionally warm. Deluxe rooms offer a view over the park. A lovely little garden to breakfast in completes the picture. **www.hoteldesuede.com**

Hôtel de Varenne
🖼️📧 €€€€

44 Rue de Bourgogne, 75007 **Tel** *01 45 51 45 55* **Fax** *01 45 51 86 63* **Rooms** *25* **Map** *11 B2*

Beyond its severe facade, this hotel conceals a narrow courtyard garden where guests breakfast in the summer. The bedrooms, decorated in elegant Louis XVI or Empire inspired styles, are impeccable. The hotel is popular with French government officials. **www.varenne-hotel-paris.com**

Duc de St-Simon
🖼️📧 €€€€

14 Rue de St-Simon, 75007 **Tel** *01 44 39 20 20* **Fax** *01 45 48 68 25* **Rooms** *34* **Map** *11 C3*

The Hôtel Duc de St-Simon is justifiably one of the most sought-after hotels on the south side of the Seine. A charming 18th-century mansion furnished with antiques, it lives up to its aristocratic pretensions. **www.hotelducdesaintsimon.com**

CHAILLOT QUARTER

Hameau de Passy
🖼️ €€

48 Rue de Passy, 75016 **Tel** *01 42 88 47 55* **Fax** *01 42 30 83 72* **Rooms** *32* **Map** *9 B3*

In the heart of the residential quarter of Passy, a stone's throw from the Eiffel Tower and the Trocadero, Hameau de Passy lies in a private lane, which is an oasis of greenery. The basic but comfortable rooms overlook the garden. Breakfast can be served in your room upon request. **www.paris-hotel-hameaudepassy.com**

Hôtel du Bois
€€€€

11 Rue du Dôme, 75016 **Tel** *01 45 00 31 96* **Fax** *01 45 00 90 05* **Rooms** *41* **Map** *4 D5*

Two minutes from the Arc de Triomphe and the Champs Elysées, Hôtel du Bois is ideal for haute-couture boutique lovers. Behind a typically Parisian facade is an interior exuding modern style, decorated in chocolate, pistachio and fuchsia pink. You can even buy the art on the walls. **www.hoteldubois.com**

Concorde La Fayette
🖼️🅿️🍴📺📧 €€€€€

3 Pl du Général Koenig, 75017 **Tel** *01 40 68 50 68* **Fax** *01 40 68 50 43* **Rooms** *950* **Map** *3 C2*

The formulaic Concorde La Fayette with its fascinating egg-shaped tower is thoroughly high-tech. It has numerous facilities, including a fitness club, a bar on the 33rd floor, restaurants, a shopping gallery, and identical bedrooms with some absolutely splendid views. **www.concorde-lafayette.com**

Hôtel Elysées Regencia
🖼️🏃📧 €€€€€

41 Avenue Marceau, 75016 **Tel** *01 47 20 42 65* **Fax** *01 49 52 03 42* **Rooms** *43* **Map** *4 E4*

Colour is the central theme at this fashionably decorated hotel right in the heart of the designer shopping district. Choose your room from a palette of blue, fuchsia, aniseed (lime green) or lavender. The hotel also boasts a grand piano in the reception area, a panelled bar and a massage room. **www.regencia.com**

Hotel Square
🖼️🅿️🍴📺📧 €€€€€

3 Rue de Boulainvilliers, 75016 **Tel** *01 44 14 91 90* **Fax** *01 44 14 91 99* **Rooms** *22* **Map** *9 A4*

An exceptional hotel, the curvy granite facade hides 22 rooms and suites furnished with exotic fabrics and woods. The hotel boasts a fashionable restaurant and night club, a Nuxe spa and, most unusually, a small but well-stocked modern art gallery. **www.hotelsquare.com**

L'Hôtel K
🖼️🅿️🍴🛗📺📧 €€€€€

81 Ave Kléber, 75016 **Tel** *01 44 05 75 75* **Fax** *01 44 05 74 74* **Rooms** *83* **Map** *4 D5*

This hotel, situated steps from the Eiffel Tower, is a piece of modern art by Spanish architect Ricardo Bofill, who used sycamore, stucco, marble and stainless steel in the construction. Cool Asian interiors grace the guestrooms and there's a small heated swimming pool. **www.lhotelk.com**

St-James Paris

43 Ave Bugeaud, 75016 **Tel** *01 44 05 81 81* **Fax** *01 44 05 81 82* **Rooms** *48*

Map *3 B5*

The St-James occupies a mansion with a small park near the Avenue Foch and the Bois de Boulogne. Reminiscent of a gentleman's club, guests here become "temporary members" and a token fee is included in the room price. Aristocratic atmosphere. **www.saint-james-paris.com**

CHAMPS-ELYSÉES

Royal Magda Etoile

7 Rue Troyon, 75017 **Tel** *01 47 64 10 19* **Fax** *01 47 64 02 12* **Rooms** *37*

Map *4 D3*

Just minutes from the Etoile in a quiet cobbled street, the Royal Magda Etoile mixes contemporary chic with classic elegance. Rooms are on the small side, but the staff are exceptionally helpful and friendly, and will go out of their way to help guests, especially families. **www.paris-hotel-magda.com**

Atala

10 Rue Chateaubriand, 75008 **Tel** *01 45 62 01 62* **Fax** *01 42 25 66 38* **Rooms** *48*

Map *4 E4*

Situated in a quiet corner near the Champs-Elysées, this boutique hotel's rooms overlook a tranquil garden with tall trees. The bedrooms are comfortable and spacious. Book a room on the eighth floor with spectacular views of the Eiffel Tower. **www.hotelatala.com**

Balzac

6 Rue Balzac, 75008 **Tel** *01 44 35 18 00* **Fax** *01 44 35 18 05* **Rooms** *70*

Map *4 F4*

This calm and luxurious hotel is housed in a typically Parisian Belle Epoque building. Its trendy address is nothing compared to its top-floor suite, Paris's only "rooftop penthouse" with a view over "le tout Paris". The bar is a favourite destination for fashionable night owls. **www.hotelbalzac.com**

Bristol

112 Rue du Faubourg-St-Honoré, 75008 **Tel** *01 53 43 43 00* **Fax** *01 53 43 43 01* **Rooms** *188*

Map *5 A4*

One of Paris's finest hotels, the Bristol's large rooms are sumptuously decorated with antiques and magnificent marble bathrooms. The period dining room, with its Flemish tapestries and glittering crystal chandeliers, has been winning rave reviews. Wonderful swimming pool. **www.hotel-bristol.com**

Four Seasons George V

31 Ave George V, 75008 **Tel** *01 49 52 70 00* **Fax** *01 49 52 70 10* **Rooms** *246*

Map *4 E5*

This legendary hotel, dotted with salons, old furniture and art, lost a little of its charm when it was renovated. But it gained a stunning restaurant, Le Cinq, which boasts the world's top sommelier and an award-winning chef. Great spa. **www.fourseasons.com/paris**

Hotel Claridge Paris

37 Rue François 1er, 75008 **Tel** *01 47 23 54 42* **Fax** *01 47 23 08 84* **Rooms** *42*

Map *4 F5*

The Claridge has a truly traditional feel. It is quiet, sober and efficiently run, and is luxuriously furnished throughout with tapestries and antiques. The hotel is ideally located between the Champs-Elysées and the Seine, with easy access to the area's attractions. **www.hotelclaridgeparis.com**

Hôtel de Sers

41 Ave Pierre 1er de Serbie, 75008 **Tel** *01 53 23 75 75* **Fax** *01 53 23 75 76* **Rooms** *52*

Map *4 E5*

A luxury hotel in the Golden Triangle with a unique style that combines Old Master paintings with contemporary furniture and technology. There is a fabulous apartment on the top floor, but all the rooms are spacious and airy. The terrace restaurant is perfect for summer brunches. **www.hoteldesers.com**

Hôtel de la Trémoille

14 Rue de la Trémoille, 75008 **Tel** *01 56 52 14 00* **Fax** *01 40 70 01 08* **Rooms** *93*

Map *10 F1*

The Hôtel de la Trémoille is an impressive, yet relaxed, establishment. Rooms are decorated with comfortable antiques and the bathrooms are extremely luxurious. A fashionable restaurant, Louis II is now a hit with Paris's beautiful people. **www.hotel-tremoille.com**

Hôtel Fouquet's Barrière

46 Ave George V, 75008 **Tel** *01 40 69 60 00* **Rooms** *107*

Map *4 E5*

This beautiful palace-hotel is in a fine location on the Champs-Elysées. It is equipped with all the state-of-the-art technology you would expect in a modern, luxury establishment. The rooms are ultra stylish and are decorated in mahogany, silk and velvet. **www.fouquets-barriere.com**

Hôtel Vernet

25 Rue Vernet, 75008 **Tel** *01 44 31 98 00* **Fax** *01 44 31 85 69* **Rooms** *50*

Map *4 E4*

Gustave Eiffel, architect of the Eiffel Tower, created the dazzling glass roof of the dining room here. The hotel lobby is impressive with white and gold panelling, and sumptuous fabrics. The large, quiet bedrooms are pleasantly furnished, and offer flatscreen TVs and Wi-Fi. **www.hotelvernet.com**

Key to Price Guide *see p284* **Key to Symbols** *see back cover flap*

Plaza Athénée   🛏 🅿 🍴 🍽 📋   €€€€€

25 Ave Montaigne, 75008 **Tel** *01 53 67 66 65* **Fax** *01 53 67 66 66* **Rooms** *191*   **Map** *10 F1*

The legendary Plaza Athénée is popular with honeymooners, aristocracy and haute-couture shoppers. The restaurant by Alain Ducasse is wonderfully romantic, while Le Bar du Plaza is now the hottest address in Paris for cocktails. The last word in luxury. **www.plaza-athenee-paris.com**

San Régis   🛏 🍴 📋   €€€€€

12 Rue Jean Goujon, 75008 **Tel** *01 44 95 16 16* **Fax** *01 45 61 05 48* **Rooms** *44*   **Map** *11 A1*

Since it opened in 1923 the San Régis has been popular with the jet set, who enjoy its quiet but central location. This particularly welcoming, intimate luxury hotel is full of excellent antiques, overstuffed sofas and a distinctly opulent air. **www.hotel-sanregis.fr**

OPÉRA QUARTER

Hôtel Chopin   🛏 ♿ 🍴   €

46 Passage Jouffroy, 75009 **Tel** *01 47 70 58 10* **Fax** *01 42 47 00 70* **Rooms** *36*   **Map** *6 F4*

The well-loved Chopin gets booked up far in advance due to its low prices, friendly welcome and unusual location in a historic covered passage. There is no air conditioning, but it is so quiet that you can sleep with the windows open on summer nights. The top floor has a romantic rooftop view. **http://hotelbretonnerie.com**

Edouard VII Hotel   🛏 🍴 ♿ 📋   €€€€€

39 Ave de l'Opéra, 75002 **Tel** *01 42 61 56 90* **Fax** *01 42 61 47 73* **Rooms** *69*   **Map** *6 E5*

The only hotel on the impressive Avenue de l'Opéra, the Edouard VII is centrally located between the Louvre and the Opéra Garnier, which makes it perfect for sightseeing. Ask for a room at the front for a breathtaking view over the Opéra House. **www.edouard7hotel.com**

Le Grand Hôtel InterContinental   🛏 🅿 🍴 🍽 📋   €€€€€

2 Rue Scribe, 75009 **Tel** *01 40 07 31 77* **Fax** *01 40 07 32 02* **Rooms** *470*   **Map** *6 D5*

Directly next to the Opéra Garnier, the hotel is a sumptuous example of good taste. The bedrooms all have pictures with a musical theme reflecting the hotel's location. The renowned restaurant, the Café de La Paix, is an opulent affair in Opéra Quarter. **www.intercontinental.com**

MONTMARTRE

Regyn's Montmartre   €

18 Pl des Abbesses, 75018 **Tel** *01 42 54 45 21* **Fax** *01 42 23 76 69* **Rooms** *22*   **Map** *6 E1*

Near Sacré-Coeur, this is an impeccably kept hotel with retro-style decor. Top-floor guestrooms have views of the Eiffel Tower. Round the corner from here is Tabac des Deux Moulins on 15 Rue le Pic, where Amélie worked in the 2001 film *Amélie*. **www.paris-hotels-montmartre.com**

Relais Montmartre   🛏 ♿ 📋   €€€

6 Rue Constance, 75018 **Tel** *01 70 64 25 25* **Fax** *01 70 64 25 00* **Rooms** *26*   **Map** *6 E1*

In the heart of Montmartre's network of steep winding streets, this charming hotel is all femininity with delicate floral fabrics, antique furniture and painted beams. Quiet, intimate and romantic with the added bonus of being well situated for neighbourhood restaurants. **www.relaismontmartre.fr**

Hôtel Particulier Montmartre   📋   €€€€€

23 Ave Junot, 75018 **Tel** *01 53 41 81 40* **Rooms** *5*   **Map** *2 E5*

Hidden away behind a cluster of trees, this intimate three-storey mansion is Montmartre's best kept secret. With only five suites, each the size of a small apartment, comfort reigns. The individually designed rooms create a fabulous mix of avant-garde modern design. The garden is a haven of peace. **www.hotel-particulier-montmartre.com**

FURTHER AFIELD

Mama Shelter   🛏 🅿 🍴 ♿ 📋   €€

109 Rue Bagnolet, 75020 **Tel** *01 43 48 48 48* **Fax** *01 43 48 49 49* **Rooms** *170*

This concept hotel designed by Philippe Starck offers exceptionally low prices for non-refundable reservations; if you require flexibility the prices double. The contemporary rooms all have iMacs, satin-cotton sheets and microwaves. There is a trendy lounge bar and restaurant too. **www.mamashelter.com**

RESTAURANTS, CAFES AND BARS

The French national passion for good cuisine makes eating out one of the greatest pleasures of a visit to Paris. Everywhere in the city you see people eating – in restaurants, bistros, tea salons, cafés and wine bars.

Most restaurants serve French food but there is a range of Chinese, Vietnamese and North African eateries in many areas as well as Italian, Greek, Lebanese and Indian places. The restaurants in the listings *(see pp300–15)* have been selected from the best that Paris can offer across all price ranges. The listings are organized by area, as in the sightseeing section of the guide, and by price. Most places serve lunch from noon to about 2pm, and the menu often includes fixed-price meals. Parisians usually start to fill restaurants for dinner around 8.30pm and most places serve from around 7.30pm until 11pm. *(See also* Cafés, Tea Salons and Bars *pp316–19.)*

WHAT TO EAT

A tremendous range of food is available in Paris, from the rich meat dishes and perfect pâtisserie for which France is most famous to simpler French regional cuisines *(see pp296–7)*. The latter are available in brasseries and bistros – the type usually depends on the birthplace of the chef. At any time of day simple, tasty meals can be had in cafés, wine and beer bars, and brasseries, bistros and cake shops – or pâtisseries – abound.

The best ethnic food comes from France's former colonies: Vietnam and North Africa. North African places are known as *couscous* restaurants and serve filling, somewhat spicy, inexpensive food that varies in quality. Vietnamese restaurants are also good value and provide a light alternative to rich French food. Paris also has some good Japanese restaurants, notably around Rue Monsieur le Prince (6th arrondissement); Rue Ste-Anne (2nd) and Avenue de Choisy (13th) have others.

WHERE TO FIND GOOD RESTAURANTS AND CAFES

You can eat well in almost any part of Paris. Wherever you are, as a rule of thumb you will find that the most outstanding restaurants and cafés are those that cater predominantly to a French clientele.

The Left Bank probably has the greatest concentration of restaurants, especially in tourist areas like St-Germain-des-Prés and the Latin Quarter. The quality of food varies, but there are some commendable bistros, outdoor cafés and wine bars – see pages 316–19 for a selection of the best places to go in Paris for light meals and snacks. The Latin Quarter also has a high

Le Pré Verre restaurant *(see p306)*

concentration of Greek and Turkish restaurants centred chiefly around Rue de la Huchette.

In the Marais and Bastille areas, small bistros, tea salons and cafés are plentiful, some modern and fashionable. There are also many good, traditional long-established bistros and brasseries.

The Champs-Elysées and Madeleine area offer everything from smart, traditional cafés to fast-food outlets and a scattering of delectable tea rooms. There are some very good expensive restaurants here too.

Montparnasse still has some great cafés from the 1920s, including Le Sélect and La Rotonde, on the Boulevard du Montparnasse *(see p319)*. Sensitive renovation has recaptured much of their old splendour. This area is also well known for its many pancake restaurants. Rue de Montparnasse, for example,

The prim Mariage Frères shop and tea room *(see p318)*

is lined with *crêperies* serving *galettes*, sweet *crêpes* and Normandy cider.

There are many noteworthy restaurants, bistros and cafés in the Louvre-Rivoli area, competing with tourist-oriented, overpriced cafés. Just to the east, Les Halles is choc-a-bloc with fast food joints and mediocre restaurants but there are a few places of note.

Good Japanese food can be found near the Opera together with some fine brasseries, but otherwise the area around the Opéra and Grands Boulevards is not the best for restaurants. Near the Bourse are a number of reputable restaurants and bistros frequented by stockbrokers.

Montmartre has a predictable number of tourist restaurants, but it also has a few very pleasant small bistros. One traditional bistro, complete with a zinc bar, is Un Zèbre à Montmartre *(see p312)*, which serves delicious, inexpensive food.

Quiet neighbourhoods in the evening, the Invalides, Eiffel Tower and Palais de Chaillot tend to have less noisy, more serious restaurants than areas with lively nightlife. Prices can be high.

Two Chinatowns, one in the area south of the Place d'Italie, the other in the traditionally working-class, hill-top area of Belleville, have concentrations of ethnic food but few French restaurants of note. There are a number of Vietnamese eating places as well as large, inexpensive Chinese ones, and Belleville is also packed with small North African restaurants.

Le Grand Véfour in the Palais Royal *(see p304)*

TYPES OF RESTAURANTS AND CAFES

One of the most enjoyable aspects of eating in Paris is the diversity of places to eat. Bistros are small, often moderately priced restaurants with a limited selection of dishes. Those from the Belle Epoque era are particularly beautiful, with zinc bars, mirrors and attractive tiles. The food is generally, but not always, regional and traditional. Many chefs from the smartest restaurants have now also opened bistros and these can be very good value.

Brasseries are generally large bustling eateries, many with an Alsatian character serving carafes of Alsatian wine and platters of sauerkraut and sausage. They have immense menus, and most serve food throughout the day and are open late. Outside you may well see impressive pavement displays of shellfish, with apron-clad oyster shuckers working late into the night.

Cafés open early in the morning, and apart from the large tourist cafés, the majority close by around 10pm. They serve drinks and food all day long from a short menu of salads, sandwiches, omelettes and grills. At lunch most also offer a small choice of hot

A typical bistro menu

daily specials. Café prices vary from area to area, in direct proportion to the number of tourists. Smarter cafés, like Café de Flore and Les Deux Magots serve food until late at night. Those cafés specializing in beer almost always include onion tarts, French fries and hearty bowls of steamed mussels on the menu. Brunch is now served in many places at weekends, from around €17.

Wine bars are informal. They usually have a moderately priced, simple lunch menu and serve wine by the glass. Some serve snacks at any time of day – such as marvellous open sandwiches *(tartines)* made with sourdough Poilâne bread topped with cheese, sausage or pâté. A few stay open for dinner.

Tea salons open for breakfast or mid-morning until the early evening. Many offer lunch, as well as a selection of sweet pastries for afternoon tea. They are at their best in the middle of the afternoon and offer coffee and hot chocolate as well as fine teas. Some, like Le Loir dans la Théière, are casual with sofas and big tables, while Mariage Frères is more formal. Angélina on the Rue de Rivoli is famous for its hot chocolate, and Ladurée has excellent macaroons. *(For addresses see pp318–19.)*

Tour d'Argent decoration *(see p306)*

VEGETARIAN FOOD

Wholly vegetarian restaurants
in Paris are still relatively few,
and standard restaurant
menus typically offer only a
few vegetarian options. You
can often fare well by
ordering two courses from
the list of *entrées* (first
courses). North African
restaurants will serve
couscous with vegetables
only, but these may have
come out of the meat pot.

Never be timid about
asking for a change in a dish.
If you see a salad with ham,
bacon or *foie gras*, ask the
waiter for it without the meat.
If you are going to a smart
restaurant, telephone ahead
and ask the manager if it is
possible to prepare a special
meal for you. Most restaurants
will be happy to oblige.

Organic produce is
increasingly used in French
cuisine – look out for
biologique or *bio* on the
menu. Some places can also
provide gluten-free dishes.

HOW MUCH TO PAY

Prices for meals in Paris range
from extremely economic to
astronomical. You can still
enjoy a hearty restaurant or
café lunch for €18, but a
typical good bistro, brasserie
or restaurant meal in central
Paris will average €30–€40
with wine. (Remember that

Le Carré des Feuillants *(see p304)*

the better French wines will
increase the size of your
bill significantly.)

More expensive restaurants
begin at about €45 with wine
and go up to €200 for the top
places. Many places offer a
formule or *prix-fixe* (fixed
price) menu, especially at
lunch, and this will almost
always offer the best value.
Some restaurants feature two
course menus for under €15 –
a few at this price include
wine. Coffee usually carries
an extra charge.

All French restaurants are
obliged by law to display
their menu outside. The
posted rates include service
but a tip for particularly good
service will always be
appreciated (any amount
from one Euro to five per
cent of the total).

The most widely accepted
credit card is Visa.
Few restaurants
accept American
Express, and some
bistros do not
accept credit cards
at all, so it is wise
to enquire when
you book.
Travellers' cheques
are not accepted
either, and many
cafés require cash.

MAKING
RESERVATIONS

It is best to
reserve a table
in all restaurants,
brasseries and
bistros. Although
you can usually
get into a

The stunning Senderens restaurant *(see p312)*

brasserie without making a
reservation, you may have to
wait for a table.

DRESS CODE

Except for some chic restaurants which can be rather
formal, you can dress up or
down in Parisian restaurants –
within reason. Even when
dressed casually, the French
are generally well turned out.
The restaurant listings *(see
pp300–319)* indicate which
places require formal dress.

READING THE MENU
AND ORDERING

Menu boards in small
restaurants and bistros, and
even in big brasseries, are
often handwritten and can be
difficult to decipher, so ask
for help if necessary.

The waiter usually takes
your choice of *entrée* (first

The Angélina restaurant, also
known for its tea room *(see p318)*

course), then the *plat* (main
course). Dessert is ordered
after you have finished your
main course, apart from some
hot desserts that have to be
ordered at the start of the
meal. The waiter will tell you
this, or the dessert section of
the menu will be marked *à
commander avant le repas*.

The first course generally
includes a choice of seasonal
salads or vegetables, pâté and
small hot or cold vegetable
dishes or tarts. Small fish
dishes like smoked salmon,
grilled sardines, herring,
fish salads and tartares are
also offered. Brasseries have
shellfish such as oysters,
which can also be eaten as
a main course.

Le Train Bleu station restaurant in the Gare de Lyon *(see p315)*

Main dishes usually include a selection of meat, poultry and fish and upmarket restaurants offer game in autumn. Most restaurants also offer daily specials *(plats du jour)*. These dishes will incorporate fresh, seasonal produce and are usually good value.

Cheese is eaten either as a dessert or as a pre-dessert course. Some people have a green salad with their cheese. Coffee is served after, not with, dessert. You will need to ask specifically if you want it *au lait* (with milk). Decaffeinated coffee *(décaféiné)* and herbal teas *(tisanes)* are also popular after-dinner beverages.

In most restaurants you will be asked if you would like a drink before ordering food. A typical apéritif is *kir* (white wine with a drop of crème de cassis, a blackcurrant liqueur) or *kir royal* (champagne with crème de cassis). Beer, however, is rarely drunk before a meal in France *(see* What to Drink in Paris *pp298–9)*.

Bistros and brasseries usually include the wine list with the menu. The more expensive restaurants have separate wine lists, which are generally brought to the table by the wine waiter *(sommelier)* after you have seen the meal menu. The wine waiter will be able to advise on choosing the wine if you wish.

SERVICE

The lunchtime service in popular Paris eateries is generally very brisk, if sometimes a little brusque, due to the sheer pressure of numbers. Evening service can usually be enjoyed at a more leisurely pace.

CHILDREN

French children are introduced early to eating in restaurants and as a rule are well-behaved. Consequently, children are usually very welcome, but are expected to behave sensibly. However, there may be little room inside a busy restaurant to bring in push-chairs or prams, and few restaurants provide special facilities such as high-chairs or baby seats.

SMOKING

France has now joined several other countries in enforcing strict anti-tobacco laws. It is therefore against the law to smoke inside public places such as bars and restaurants. Smoking is permitted, however, on restaurant, café and pub terraces provided they are not enclosed.

WHEELCHAIR ACCESS

Parisian restaurants are generally accommodating, and a word when you book should ensure that you are given a more conveniently situated table when you arrive. It is always worth checking that toilets can also be used by wheelchair users, since access can be restricted.

PICNICS

Picnicking is the best way to enjoy the wonderful fresh produce, local bread, cheeses, *charcuterie* and pastries from the markets and enticing shops to be found all over the city. For more details see pages 333–5. It is also a good way of eating cheaply and enjoying the many parks that Paris has to offer.

An elegant Parisian restaurant

The Flavours of Paris

From the glittering temples of haute cuisine to the humblest neighbourhood bistro, Paris is a paradise for food lovers, whether you dine on foie gras and truffles or steak-frites, a seafood platter or a perfumed Moroccan couscous. France is immensely proud of its food, from classic haute cuisine to the most rustic of regional dishes. All are available in the capital and, though the French themselves will debate endlessly about the ideal sauce to complement meat or fish, or the right wine to accompany them, they will always be in total agreement that theirs is the best food in the world.

Girolles (chanterelles) on a stall in rue Mouffetard market

the season. Even if you are not shopping for food to cook, the markets are worth browsing and, after an hour or so in the crowded, narrow streets of the rue de Buci or rue Mouffetard you will be more than ready for lunch.

The food of the French provinces, once despised for its rusticity, is now celebrated and almost every region is represented in the capital,

from the rich, bourgeois cuisines of Burgundy and Lyon to the celebrated healthy Mediterranean diet of Provence. Paris itself is surrounded by top quality market gardens which supply young peas, carrots and potatoes. Salmon, asparagus, and wild mushrooms come from the Loire; Normandy brings salt-marsh lamb, apples and Camembert.

What all French chefs agree on is the importance of using the finest quality ingredients, and there is no better place to appreciate the quality of French produce than in the markets of Paris. Here, top chefs may be spied early in the morning, alongside local shoppers, seeking inspiration and the prize ingredients of

Comté

Brie

Tomme de chevre

Ami du Chambertin

Roquefort

Selection of fine French cheeses in perfect condition

CLASSIC FRENCH CUISINE

What is usually thought of as classic French cuisine was developed in royal palaces and noble châteaux, with the emphasis on luxury and display, not frugality or health. Dishes are often bathed in rich sauces of butter or cream, enhanced with luxurious ingredients like truffles, foie gras, rare mushrooms and alcohol. Meat is treated with reverence, and you will usually be asked how you want your beef, lamb or duck cooked; the French tend to like their beef rare (*bleu* or *saignant*) and their lamb and duck pink (*rose*). For well-cooked meat, ask for "*bien cuit*" but still expect at least a tinge of pinkness. The most famous country classics include slowly cooked casseroles like *coq au vin* and *boeuf bourguignonne*, as well as the bean, sausage and baked duck dish *cassoulet*, from the southwest.

Escargots à la Bourguignonne *are plump Burgundy snails served in their shells with garlic, butter and parsley.*

Salers beef and lentils come from the Auvergne; beef and Bresse chickens from Burgundy; not forgetting Basque ham, Collioure anchovies, lamb from the Pyrenees, or fragrant Provençal melons.

THE NEW STYLE

In recent years, innovative chefs have developed new styles of cooking, reacting against the richness of traditional cookery, and using fresh ingredients, lightly cooked to retain their flavour.

Mouthwatering display in a Parisian patisserie

Sealed jars of whole duck-liver foie gras, a luxury item

Sauces are made of light reductions to enhance, not obscure, the main ingredient of a dish. A wave of invention and originality has resulted in a plethora of unusual ingredients, fresh twists on the classics, and sometimes wonderful new combinations and flavours, such as sea bass with bean purée and red wine sauce, or with fermented grape juice; sole with quince juice and tarragon; tempura of langoustines with cinnamon beurre blanc; rabbit with Indian spices and tomato polenta; and rosemary ice cream or lavender sorbet.

FOREIGN FOOD

Paris can also offer diners an amazing selection of world flavours, especially those of France's former colonies – for example, Moroccan tajines and Cambodian fish with coconut milk. Most fascinating of all is to observe how these cuisines are developing, as young chefs adapt and combine traditional ingredients and culinary styles with those of France.

ON THE MENU

Andouillettes Sausages made from pork intestines

Blanquette de veau Veal stew with a creamy sauce

Crottin chaud en salade Goat's cheese on toast with salad

Cuisses de grenouille Frogs' legs in garlic butter

Iles flottantes Meringues floating in a custard sauce

Plateau de fruits de mer Platter of raw and cooked seafood

Ris de veau Veal sweetbreads

Rognons à la moutarde Kidneys in mustard sauce

Salade frisée aux lardons Endive salad with fried bacon

Sole meunière Fried sole with melted butter

Moules marinière *are mussels steamed in a fragrant sauce of white wine, garlic, parsley and sometimes cream.*

Coq au vin *is a male chicken braised with red wine, herbs, garlic, baby onions and button mushrooms.*

Tarte tatin *is a caramelized upside-down buttery apple tart, created at the hotel Tatin in the Loire Valley.*

What to Drink in Paris

Paris is the best place in France to sample a wide range of the country's many different wines. It's cheapest to order wine by the carafe, normally referred to by size: 25cl (*quart*), 33cl (*fillette*), 50cl (*demi*) or 75cl (*pichet*, equivalent to a bottle*). Cafés and wine bars usually offer wine by the glass – *un petit blanc* is a small glass of white, a larger glass of red, *un ballon de rouge*. House wine is nearly always reliable.

Paris's last vineyard, near Sacré-Coeur *(see p222)*

RED WINE

Some of the world's finest red wines come from the Bordeaux and Burgundy regions, but for everyday drinking choose from the vast range of basic southern French or Côtes du Rhône wines. Or try one of the Beaujolais *crus*, such as Morgon or Fleurie from southern Burgundy, or lighter reds from the Loire, such as Chinon or Saumur-Champigny.

Distinctive bottle shapes for Bordeaux and Burgundy

Bordeaux châteaux include Margaux, which makes some of the world's most elegant red wines.

Burgundy includes some big, strong red wines from the village of Gevrey-Chambertin in the Côte de Nuits.

Beaujolais Nouveau, the fruity first taste of the year's new wine, is released on the third Thursday of November.

The Loire has very good red wines from the area around Chinon. They are usually quite light and very dry.

Southern Rhône is famous for its dark, rich red wines from Châteauneuf-du-Pape, north of Avignon.

Northern Rhône has some dark, spicy red wines, best aged for at least 10 years, from Côte-Rôtie near Vienne.

FINE WINE VINTAGE CHART

	2009	2008	2007	2006	2005	2004	2003	2002	2001
BORDEAUX									
Margaux, St-Julien, Pauillac, St-Estèphe	10	8	7	8	9	7	8	6	7
Graves, Pessac-Léognan (red)	9	8	7	8	9	7	6	6	7
Graves, Pessac-Léognan (white)	7	8	7	8	9	8	7	6	7
St-Emilion, Pomerol	9	8	7	8	9	7	6	5	8
BURGUNDY									
Chablis	9	8	9	8	9	8	7	8	8
Côte de Nuits (red)	9	7	6	7	9	7	7	8	7
Côte de Beaune (white)	9	7	7	8	9	8	7	8	8
LOIRE									
Bourgueil, Chinon	9	8	8	7	9	7	7	8	7
Sancerre (white)	9	8	7	8	9	8	7	7	8
RHONE									
Hermitage (red)	9	7	10	7	9	7	7	4	7
Hermitage (white)	9	8	10	7	9	7	6	4	8
Côte-Rôtie	8	7	8	7	9	7	6	4	7
Châteauneuf-du-Pape	9	8	9	8	9	7	6	3	7

The quality scale from 1 to 10 represents an overall rating for the year and is only a guideline

Alsace Riesling and Burgundy

WHITE WINE

The finest white Bordeaux and Burgundies are best with food, but for everyday drinking try a light dry wine such as Entre-Deux-Mers from Bordeaux, or Anjou Blanc or Sauvignon de Touraine from the Loire. Alsace makes some reliable white wines. Sweet wines such as Sauternes, Barsac or Coteaux du Layon are delicious with *foie gras*.

Alsace wines are usually labelled by grape variety. Gewürztraminer is one of the most distinctive.

Loire wines include Pouilly-Fumé, from the east of the region. It is very dry, often with a slightly smoky perfume.

Burgundy wines include Chablis, a fresh, full-flavoured dry wine from the northernmost vineyards.

The Loire has the perfect partner to seafood dishes in Muscadet, a dry white wine from the Atlantic Coast.

SPARKLING WINE

In France champagne is the first choice for a celebration drink, and styles range from non-vintage to deluxe. Many other wine regions make sparkling wines by the champagne method which tend to be a lot cheaper. Look out for Crémant de Loire, Crémant de Bourgogne, Vouvray Mousseux, Saumur Mousseux and Blanquette de Limoux.

Champagne

Champagne vineyards east of Paris produce the famous sparkling wine. Billecart-Salmon is a light, pink Champagne.

Sweet Bordeaux are luscious, golden-coloured dessert wines, the most famous being Barsac and Sauternes.

APERITIFS AND DIGESTIFS

Kir, white wine mixed with a small amount of blackcurrant liqueur or *crème de cassis*, is the ubiquitous apéritif. Also common is aniseed-flavoured *pastis* which is served with ice and a pitcher of water and can be very refreshing. Vermouths, especially Noilly-Prat, are also common apéritifs. *Digestifs*, or after-dinner drinks, are often ordered with coffee and include *eaux-de-vie*, the strong colourless spirits infused with fruit, and brandies such as Cognac, Armagnac and Calvados.

Kir: white wine with cassis

BEERS

Beer in France is sold either by the bottle or, more cheaply, on tap by the glass – *un demi*. The cheapest is lager-type *bière à pression*, but the best brands are Meteor and Mutzig, followed by "33", "1664" and Kronenbourg. Pelforth makes very good dark beer and lager. Some bars and cafés specialize in foreign beers, especially from Belgium, and these are very malty and strong – Leffe, for example, comes as *brune* (dark, fully flavoured) or as a lighter *blonde* (lager). There are bars that brew their own beer. (For beer bars see p317.)

OTHER DRINKS

The brightly-coloured drinks consumed in cafés all over Paris are mixtures of flavoured syrups and mineral waters, called *sirops à l'eau*. The emerald-green drinks use mint syrup, the red ones grenadine. Fruit juices and tomato juice are sold in bottles unless you specify *citron pressé* or *orange pressée* (freshly-squeezed lemon or orange), which is served with a pitcher of water and with sugar or sugar syrup for you to dilute and sweeten to taste. If you ask for water, you will be served mineral water, sparkling *(gazeuse)* or still *(naturelle)*; if you don't want to be charged, ask for tap water *(eau de robinet)*.

Fresh lemon juice is served with water and sugar

Choosing a Restaurant

The restaurants listed on the following pages have been
selected for their good value or exceptional food. The
chart below lists restaurants in Paris by area, and the
entries are alphabetical within each price category.
Details on snack and sandwich bars are in Light Meals
and Snacks on pages 316–19.

PRICE CATEGORIES
For a three-course meal per person,
with a half-bottle of house wine,
including tax and service.
€ under €25
€€ €26–€35
€€€ €36–€50
€€€€ €51–€75
€€€€€ over €75

ILE DE LA CITÉ AND ÎLE SAINT-LOUIS

La Charlotte de l'Isle   €

24 Rue St-Louis en l'Ile, 75004 **Tel** *01 43 54 25 83*   **Map** *13 C4*

This little tea room founded in 1972 serves the most potent hot chocolate in town, with a little pot of milk to thin its
near-solid consistency. The rustic cakes are also delicious, though these are probably best enjoyed with one
of the flavoured teas. Puppet shows are held on Wednesdays.

Kitchen Galerie Bis   €€€€

25 Rue des Grands Augustins, 75006 **Tel** *01 46 33 00 85*   **Map** *13 A4*

Ideally situated, this sleek, minimalist restaurant and art gallery attracts a trendy crowd. The innovative menu serves
contemporary French cuisine with an Asian twist. The selection of tapas style *zors-d'œuvre* starters is particularly
recommmended. The gallery displays changing exhibitions of modern art.

Isami   €€€

4 Quai Orléans, 75004 **Tel** *01 40 46 06 97*   **Map** *13 C4*

As you walk through the door of this little Seine-side restaurant the hostess will warn you that they "serve only raw
fish here", which is why this restaurant is so popular with Japanese expats and locals who come here for sushi of a
quality rarely found in Paris. Japanese crockery lines the shelves and a peaceful atmosphere prevails.

Nos Ancêtres les Gaulois   €€€

39 Rue St-Louis en l'Ile, 75004 **Tel** *01 46 33 66 07*   **Map** *13 C4*

This restaurant has a jolly atmosphere and caters to big appetites. Only one set menu, which includes assorted
salads, a buffet of cooked meats, one grilled meat, cheeseboard, fruit, dessert and plenty of wine. Satisfying and
entertaining. Children's menu available for €10.

Mon Vieil Ami   €€€€

69 Rue St-Louis en l'Ile, 75004 **Tel** *01 40 46 01 35*   **Map** *13 C4*

This fabulous, minimalist dining room is not vegetarian, but vegetables take pride of place on the inventive menu.
Tuck into dishes such as slow-braised shoulder of roebuck with celery, quince and prunes or an Alsatian casserole
served with garlicky white beans and tomatoes topped with squid. Closed Mon, Tue, three weeks in Jan and Aug.

THE MARAIS

Chez Hannah   €

54 Rue des Rosiers, 75004 **Tel** *01 42 74 74 99*   **Map** *13 C3*

L'As du Fallafel down the street is better known, but Chez Hannah serves falafel sandwiches to rival any in this street
filled with Jewish delis. They come packed with crunchy chickpea balls, tahini sauce, melting aubergine and chilli, to
be eaten in the lively dining room or standing in the street. A locals' favourite.

Caves St-Gilles   €€

4 Rue St-Gilles, 75003 **Tel** *01 48 87 22 62*   **Map** *14 D3*

Soak up St-Gille's lively atmosphere with locals waiting at the bar for a table and friendly waiters shouting *"chaud
devant!"* (it's hot, move out of the way) as they bring out copious dishes of Spanish tapas, including Iberian ham,
mussels, lamb and chicken *brochettes*, and stuffed peppers and courgettes. Paella is served at the weekend.

Chez Cham   €€

3 Rue du Roi Doré, 75003 **Tel** *01 42 74 31 22*   **Map** *14 D2*

Off the beaten tourist track, Chez Cham wins all round: an intimate dining room in a medieval building that serves
fine contemporary French cuisine like *magret* of duck in honey and coriander sauce and a dreamy salted caramel
panna cotta. All ingredients are organic. Caters for vegetarians and those on gluten-free diets. Excellent wine list.

Key to Symbols *see back cover flap*

Chez Jenny
39 Blvd du Temple, 75003 **Tel** *01 44 54 39 00*
Map *14 D1*

This huge brasserie on the Place de la République has been a bastion of Alsatian cooking since it was founded over 60 years ago. Service by women in Alsatian dress adds to the atmosphere. The *choucroute* (sauerkraut) *spéciale Jenny* makes a hearty meal with a fruit tart or sorbet, served with a fruit liqueur for dessert.

Le Colimaçon
44 Rue Vieille du Temple, 75004 **Tel** *01 48 87 12 01*
Map *13 C3*

Le Colimaçon (snail) refers to the restaurant's centrepiece: a corkscrew staircase. A listed building dating to 1732, it has period wooden beams in the ceiling. Snails are also on the menu along with frogs' legs in parsley and tomato sauce and *gigot de sept heures* (seven-hour lamb). Open for dinner only.

Le Petit Marché
9 Rue de Béarn, 75003 **Tel** *01 42 72 06 67*
Map *14 D3*

Around the corner from the Place des Vosges, this is one of the few bistros in Paris to open every day of the week, all year round. There is a pavement terrace and a cosy Moroccan-style lounge downstairs for cold days. Service can be rushed, but the modern bistro fare, such as sesame-crusted tuna, is reliable. Gluten-free dishes are available.

Les Philosophes
28 Rue Vieille du Temple, 75003 **Tel** *01 48 87 49 64*
Map *13 C3*

Among the many cafés run by Xavier Denamour in this street, Les Philosophes is the most popular at meal times for its above-average bistro fare: the steak-*frites* are just as they should be and tomato *tarte tatin* is a speciality. The terrace is perfect for people-watching and service is jovial if rushed. Finish with the creamy vanilla *crème brûlée*.

Le Potager du Marais
22 Rue Rambuteau, 75003 **Tel** *01 42 72 17 79*
Map *13 C3*

Organic vegetarian food gets pride of place in this popular restaurant. The food is delicious, imaginative and comes in generous portions. Specialities include aubergine curry, leek gratin and chocolate mousse. Their wines are organic as well. Gluten-free dishes are available. Even meat eaters aren't disappointed. Advance booking is recommended.

Bistrot de L'Oulette
38 Rue des Tournelles, 75004 **Tel** *01 42 71 43 33*
Map *14 E3*

A tiny restaurant with good quality food at reasonable prices. The fixed-price menu is particularly good value. The Southwestern cuisine includes a delicious homemade cassoulet and braised oxtail. For dessert, delights include caramelized pears with spiced bread or chocolate and raspberry fondant.

Brasserie Bofinger
3 Rue de la Bastille, 75004 **Tel** *01 42 72 87 82*
Map *14 E4*

Established in 1864, Bofinger claims to be the oldest brasserie in Paris. It is certainly one of the prettiest, with stained glass, leather banquettes, brass decorations and murals by the Alsatian artist Hansi. It serves good shellfish, as well as respectable *choucroute*, and grilled meats.

Le Gaigne
12 Rue Pecquay, 75004 **Tel** *01 44 59 86 72*
Map *13 C2*

Young chef Mickaël Gaignon had years of haute cuisine training under his belt before opening this intimate ivory-and-plum dining room with food paintings on the walls. His inventive cooking focuses on the quality of the ingredients, such as scallop tartare flavoured with citron and served with red chicory.

Le Repaire de Cartouche
8 Blvd des Filles du Calvaire, 75011 **Tel** *01 47 00 25 86*
Map *14 D2*

Like its sister establishment, Le Villaret, this restaurant is run by former employees of Astier, to the same excellent standards. It too has a changing seasonal menu, which includes roast pigeon with leeks in a vinegar sauce and rabbit terrine with chocolate. Its decor is reassuringly traditional.

La Guirlande de Julie
25 Pl des Vosges, 75003 **Tel** *01 48 87 94 07*
Map *14 D3*

Consummate restaurant professional Claude Terrail of the Tour d'Argent (*see p306*) has employed a good chef here, and the decor is fresh and appealing. For the best views, ask for a table near the window in the first dining room. In good weather meals are served under the cool vaulted stone arcades.

Le Dôme du Marais
53bis Rue des Francs Bourgeois, 75004 **Tel** *01 42 74 54 17*
Map *14 D3*

Come here for serious French cuisine: sweetbreads, wild boar and *tête de veau* are all regulars on the menu. Other, more delicate, features include fillet of sea bream with a spiced crust, and cod cooked in champagne. Decent service and the remarkable domed building contribute to a truly memorable dining experience. Book ahead.

L'Ambroisie
9 Pl des Vosges, 75004 **Tel** *01 42 78 51 45*
Map *14 D3*

Housed in a former jewellery shop restored by Chef Monsieur Pacaud, this is one of only twelve Michelin three-star restaurants in Paris. The cuisine includes a mousse of sweet red peppers, *truffle feuilleté* (layered pastry) and langoustines. Reservations are accepted one month in advance.

BASTILLE

Bistrot du Peintre
€€
116 Ave Ledru Rollin, 75011 **Tel** *01 47 00 34 39*   **Map** *14 F5*

This laid-back bistro with Art Deco mouldings is popular with local artists and media types who are drawn here by the decent prices and busy terrace. Simple but good quality food is served such as steak as well as some excellent fish dishes, all accompanied with *frites* and vegetables.

L'Encrier
€€
55 Rue Traversière, 75012 **Tel** *01 44 68 08 16*   **Map** *14 F5*

The speciality at this local's haunt is pear served with Roquefort and a glass of sweet Jurançon wine. Other dishes include traditional recipes of lamb roasted in herbs, and salmon with poached eggs and warm lentils. This place is very popular so make sure you book and expect to get to know your neighbours on the tightly squeezed tables.

Le Souk
€€
1 Rue Keller, 75011 **Tel** *01 49 29 05 08*   **Map** *14 F4*

There are many North African restaurants to choose from in Paris, but few have the atmosphere of this buzzy Moroccan den with its mosaic tables, ochre walls and cushioned banquettes. The food is not that cheap but very good: try the lamb tagine with almonds and prunes or the mixed couscous. Friendly service.

Le Bistrot Paul Bert
€€€
18 Rue Paul Bert, 75011 **Tel** *01 43 72 24 01*

This bistro's popularity is not surprising, given its combination of vintage decor – complete with zinc bar – and classic bistro cooking. Staff are welcoming, the steak-*frites* are some of the best in town, and the dining room is always buzzing with a mix of Parisians and international gourmets. The wine list is exceptional too.

BEAUBOURG AND LES HALLES

Café Beaubourg
€€
100 Rue St-Martin, 75004 **Tel** *01 48 87 63 96*   **Map** *13 B2*

With views of the animated piazza of the Beaubourg museum, Café Beaubourg has an elegant and contemporary decor. Simple and reliable, if slightly overpriced, fare is guaranteed – a variety of salads, omelettes, tartares, grilled meats and fish. The Beaubourg is popular for Sunday brunch.

La Fresque
€€
100 Rue Rambuteau, 75001 **Tel** *01 42 33 17 56*   **Map** *13 A2*

Possibly the best value lunch menu in Les Halles (€14 for two courses and coffee) and wine is just €2. Tables are packed in like sardines and the jovial staff run around with their arms laden with plates full of French fare like salmon tartare and lamb with *ratatouille* and potatoes. The evening menu is more expensive but still good value.

Le Hangar
€€
12 Impasse Berthaud, 75003 **Tel** *01 42 74 55 44*   **Map** *13 B2*

Anyone who has found this locals' favourite in its quiet spot next door to the doll museum is sure to go back for the simple yet seductive cooking: two trademark dishes are the pan-fried *foie gras* on olive oil mash and the runny chocolate cake. There isn't much in the way of decor, but the food more than makes up for it.

Le Tambour
€€
41 Rue Montmartre, 75002 **Tel** *01 42 33 06 90*   **Map** *13 A1*

This Halles institution, decorated with wacky Parisian memorabilia, serves food until 3.30am (until 1am Sun and Mon), making it a prized destination for Paris's nighthawks. Its late night hours don't reduce the quality of the hearty bistro fare which includes such staples as steak-*frites*.

Le Tir Bouchon
€€
22 Rue Tiquetonne, 75002 **Tel** *01 42 21 95 51*   **Map** *13 A1*

The chef elaborates on various regional classics adding a gourmet touch – try *millefeuille* of potatoes, *foie gras* and mushroom sauce or swordfish with raspberry vinaigrette. One of the popular dishes served at the restaurant is the honey-roasted *Magret de canard au miel*.

Les Fines Gueules
€€
43 Rue Croix-des-Petits-Champs 75001 **Tel** *01 42 61 35 41*   **Map** *12 F1*

This bright corner bistro has become the place in Paris to eat hand-chopped steak tartare. Made with beef from master-butcher Hugo Desnoyers, the dish is served with roasted mini-potatoes and salad dressed with truffle oil. The "natural" wines come from small producers. Frequent live jazz.

Key to Price Guide *see p300* **Key to Symbols** *see back cover flap*

Au Pied de Cochon

6 Rue Coquillière, 75001 **Tel** *01 40 13 77 00*   **Map** 12 F1

This colourful brasserie was once popular with high society, who came to observe the workers in the old market and to relish the onion soup. Although touristy, this gigantic place is fun, and has a menu with something for everyone (including excellent shellfish). Still one of the best places after a night out. Open 24/7.

Deda

8–10 Rue Coquillière, 75001 **Tel** *01 53 40 82 40*   **Map** 12 F1

Georgian cuisine was almost unknown in Paris until this restaurant, wine cellar and *epicerie* with its own traditional bread oven opened in 2008. Perhaps the best way to discover the east-meets-west cuisine is with the Supra, a set menu of multiple dishes to be shared with everyone at the table. The Georgian wines are worth trying too.

Le 404

69 Rue Gravilliers, 75003 **Tel** *01 42 74 57 81*   **Map** 13 D1

Magnifil early for a tan to the finoru a faur mae auni for a serious a Letroa Henri IV's mistress in the 16th century. Le 404 is impeccably run by debonair actor Smaïn, who also owns London's Momo restaurant. The food is deeply rooted in his native Morocco: genuine-tasting *couscous*, tajine and vegetarian delicacies. Cheaper lunches.

Le Grizzli

7 Rue St-Martin, 75004 **Tel** *01 48 87 77 56*   **Map** 13 B3

A change of ownership has breathed new life into the Grizzli, founded in 1903 when it was one of the last Parisian places to have dancing bears! The owner orders much produce from his native Southwest including local ham, lamb chops cooked on a sizzling slate, cheeses and wines made by his family.

Le Pharamond

24 Rue de la Grande-Truanderie, 75001 **Tel** *01 40 28 45 18*   **Map** 13 A1

Founded in 1870, this bistro is a charming remnant of its age, with tiles and mosaics, handsome woodwork and mirrors. Specialities include *tripes à la mode de Caen* (tripe cooked with onions, leeks, cider and Calvados) and grilled *andouillette* (homemade sausage). The Normandy cider is strongly recommended.

Chez la Vieille

1 Rue de Bailleul, 75001 **Tel** *01 42 60 15 78*   **Map** 12 F2

Portions are getting smaller in Paris restaurants, but not in this old-fashioned bistro where diners are encouraged to help themselves to pâtés, salads and desserts such as chocolate mousse and home-made tarts. Main dishes are equally hearty; think tripe stew or *blanquette de veau* (veal in white sauce).

Benoît

20 Rue St-Martin, 75004 **Tel** *01 42 72 25 76*   **Map** 13 B2

A gem of a Parisian bistro, super-chef Alain Ducasse has retained the faux-marble, polished-brass and lace-curtain decor created in 1912. The menu includes house *foie gras, ris de veau* (calves' sweetbreads) and *cassoulet* (white bean and meat stew). The wine list is outstanding.

Georges

19 Rue Beaubourg, 75004 **Tel** *01 44 78 47 99*   **Map** 13 B2

On the top floor of the Pompidou Centre, the Georges offers stunning views. Light and inspired cuisine, such as cherry tomato and goat's cheese cake, *sole meunière*, lamb with chutney and macaroons. Roasted scallops with lemon butter is a hit. Terrace seating too. Decor is minimalist, with lots of steel and aluminium. Reservations required.

TUILERIES QUARTER

Salon de Thé Angélina

226 Rue de Rivoli, 75001 **Tel** *01 42 60 82 00*   **Map** 11 C1

The speciality of this smart tearoom is the *Mont Blanc*: a soft, chewy meringue topped with whipped cream and chestnut cream. The hot chocolate is also one of the best in town, and the Belle Epoque setting is the ideal background for a quick lunch or a sticky treat.

La Muscade

36 Rue Montpensier, 75001 **Tel** *01 42 97 51 36*   **Map** 12 E1

The epitome of French classicism: a Regency-style dining room nestled at the heart of the Palais Royal gardens. Mediterranean-inspired food such as the orange, glazed tomatoes and veal tagine. Tearoom in the afternoon, with pastries such as fig pastilla (in filo).

Le Fumoir

6 Rue de l'Amiral Coligny, 75001 **Tel** *01 42 92 00 24*   **Map** 12 F2

A café by day and a rather sultry restaurant-bar at night, Le Fumoir serves remarkably good food with a Scandinavian touch that often appears in condiments such as cranberries or horseradish. Cocktails are good and there is an intimate library at the back with big leather armchairs.

Le Grand Louvre

🏃 ♿ €€€

Le Louvre, 75001 **Tel** *01 40 20 53 41*

Map *12 F2*

It's rare to find such a good restaurant situated under the Louvre's glass pyramid entrance. The menu draws inspiration from Southwest France – stuffed goose neck, *foie gras, entrecôte* steak, prune ice cream with Armagnac – and was originally developed by André Daguin, one of the region's gastronomic stars.

1 Place Vendôme

🏃 🍴 €€€€

1 Place Vendôme, 75001 **Tel** *01 55 04 55 00*

Map *12 D1*

In the middle of the world's most expensive square, 1 Place Vendôme is a haven of fine dining. The talented chef Nicolas Rucheton prepares dishes like Erquy scallops with saffron risotto and suckling lamb with amadine truffle potatoes and mushrooms. Finish off with a chestnut soufflé. The bar has the biggest collection of whiskies in Paris.

Café Marly

🏃 🔲 🍴 €€€€

93 Rue de Rivoli, 75001 **Tel** *01 49 26 06 60*

Map *12 E2*

Wonderful views of the Louvre and inventive French cuisine: *carpaccio*, caramel and coconut duck, salmon with spinach cream and raspberry macaroons. Beef with Roquefort cream sauce is one of the main draws, while for the raw-fish lovers, there's spiced avocado and tuna *tartare*.

Goumard

🅿 🏃 ♿ 🍴 €€€€

9 Rue Duphot, 75001 **Tel** *01 42 60 36 07*

Map *5 C5*

Opened in 1872 and still possessing many original features such as glass chandeliers and inlaid wood panelling. There is quality seafood on the menu including *bouillabaisse* and sea bass with oyster sauce as well as plenty of Champagne (over 150 vintages).

Restaurant du Palais Royal

🏃 ♿ 🔲 €€€€

110 Galerie de Valois, 75001 **Tel** *01 40 20 00 27*

Map *12 F1*

This contemporary bistro has an enviable setting inside the Palais Royal gardens: the terrace tables are hotly sought-after in summer, though the jewel-toned dining room is just as pleasant in cooler weather. Classics on the menu include steak with *pommes Pont Neuf* (thick chips), seasonal variations on risotto and rum baba.

Le Grand Véfour

🅿 🏃 ♿ 🍴 €€€€€

17 Rue de Beaujolais, 75001 **Tel** *01 42 96 56 27*

Map *12 F1*

This 18th-century restaurant is considered by many to be Paris's most attractive. The chef Guy Martin effortlessly maintains his Michelin stars with dishes such as scallops with potatoes, tofu and caviar, *foie gras* ravioli with a truffle cream and endive *galette* (pancake).

Le Meurice

🏃 ♿ 🍴 🍴 €€€€€

228 Rue de Rivoli, 75001 **Tel** *01 44 58 10 55*

Map *12 D1*

Yannick Alleno has established himself as one of the finest chefs in Paris, and a meal here is as carefully orchestrated as a ballet. Alleno has a subtle yet elegant style, as illustrated in his signature dish: crabmeat in citrus dressing with herb cream and caviar. *Millefeuilles* assembled before your eyes are a delicious speciality.

SAINT-GERMAIN-DES-PRÈS

Coco & Co

€

11 Rue Bernard Palissy, 75006 **Tel** *01 45 44 02 52*

Map *12 E4*

Paris's one and only egg-themed restaurant is perfect for a homely snack. Nothing but eggs are served with over 22 varieties of omelette, oeuf-en-cocotte (baked eggs in cream or wine), boiled, scrambled or fried eggs and much more. To match the menu, the minimalist décor is also egg-themed.

La Crèmerie

🏃 🍴 €

9 Rue Quatre Vents, 75006 **Tel** *01 43 54 99 30*

Map *12 F4*

A former dairy store dating from 1880, this little shop with a painted glass ceiling has been a wine bar since the 1950s. The current owners, a pair of former architects, focus on "natural" wines served with bread and butter from Brittany, hams from Spain, sausage from the Ardèche and burrata cheese from Puglia in Italy.

Le Petit Saint-Benoît

🏃 ♿ 🔲 €

4 Rue St-Benoît, 75006 **Tel** *01 42 60 27 92*

Map *12 E3*

This is the place for anyone who wants to mix with the locals; the waitresses speak their mind and you might be seated at a table with others. Not much has been done to the decor, but the good-value food is simple and homely. Its *cuisine du marché* offers six *plats du jour*, different every day.

Aux Charpentiers

🏃 🔲 €€

10 Rue Mabillon, 75006 **Tel** *01 43 26 30 05*

Map *12 E4*

There are no surprises at this old-established bistro, popular with St-Germain-des-Prés locals. The menu changes daily but you can count on bistro stand-bys such as *cuisse de canard* (duck leg), *boeuf à la mode* and homely pastries, served at reasonable prices. Extra charges for dinner.

Key to Price Guide *see p300* **Key to Symbols** *see back cover flap*

L'Epigramme 🚶 🗻 €€

9 Rue de l'Eperon, 75006 **Tel** *01 44 41 00 09* **Map** *12 F4*

With terracotta tiles, wood beams and windows looking onto a leafy courtyard, L'Epigramme has plenty of Left Bank charm. The glassed-in kitchen turns out impeccable modern bistro food such as Basque farmer's pork on a bed of turnip *choucroute*; also look for game in season. Service is equally polished.

Le Timbre 🚶 🍴 €€

3 Rue Ste-Beuve, 75006 **Tel** *01 45 49 10 40* **Map** *16 D1*

Brit Chris Wright runs this wonderful "stamp-sized" (*timbre*) restaurant on a quiet street near the Luxembourg Gardens. Only the finest regional products go into his cuisine – *andouillette* with Puy lentils, pan-fried girolle mushrooms and scallops with parsnip purée. The wine list is consistently excellent too.

Polidor 🚶 ♿ €€

41 Rue Monsieur le Prince, 75006 **Tel** *01 43 26 95 34* **Map** *12 F5*

Once frequented by Verlaine and Rimbaud, this is bohemian Paris incarnate. The place has kept its reputation by sticking to traditional cuisine at affordable prices. Grilled steak, *daube de boeuf* and *blanquette de veau*. Various tarts such as chocolate, lemon or apple.

Alcazar 🚶 ♿ €€€

62 Rue Mazarine, 75006 **Tel** *01 53 10 19 99* **Map** *12 F4*

A fashionable club in the 1970s, Alcazar was bought by Sir Terence Conran in 1999. He converted it into a brasserie-bar, and the result is this huge, elegant and thoroughly modern establishment which serves simple but well-made cuisine. Cheaper lunches.

Bouillon Racine 🅿 🚶 ♿ €€€

3 Rue Racine, 75006 **Tel** *01 44 32 15 60* **Map** *12 F5*

Stuffed roast suckling pig, liquorice-flavoured lamb and seafood risotto are all served at Bouillon Racine. This was where the *bouillons*, the popular meat-flavoured soups, first made an appearance. Its listed building, dating to 1906, is an Art Nouveau masterpiece.

J'Go 🚶 🗻 🍴 €€€

Rue Clément, 75006 **Tel** *01 43 26 19 02* **Map** *12 E4*

This lively Toulousian wine bar doubles as a *rotisserie* serving juicy spit-roasted lamb from Quercy, whole-roasted chicken and black pig from Bigorre. The set menu is excellent value, offering pâté, a giant salad and delicious lamb with creamy white beans. Tapas are also served and the wine (by the bottle or the glass) is consistently excellent.

Joséphine Chez Dumonet 🗻 🍴 €€€€

117 Rue du Cherche-Midi, 75006 **Tel** *01 45 48 52 40* **Map** *11 C5*

Pre-World War II bistros with old-fashioned menus have become a rarity in Paris, which explains the popularity of Joséphine. Start with the help-yourself marinated herrings before superb steak tartare or perhaps a rib-sticking cassoulet; desserts are equally gargantuan. The wine list is lengthy and expensive.

Procope €€€€

13 Rue de l'Ancienne Comédie, 75006 **Tel** *01 40 46 79 00* **Map** *12 F4*

Opened in 1686, Paris's oldest café welcomed literary and political figures such as Voltaire and Diderot. Nowadays, it's still a hub for the intelligentsia, who sit alongside those curious about this historical monument. *Coq au vin* is the speciality. Shellfish platters, too.

Rôtisserie d'en Face 🅿 🚶 €€€€

2 Rue Christine, 75006 **Tel** *01 43 26 40 98* **Map** *12 F4*

Jacques Cagna's rôtisserie is located opposite his eponymous gastronomic restaurant. Perfectly mastered traditional recipes on the menu: veal chop with morel sauce and mashed potato and pan-fried red mullet with capers, lemon and caramelized chicory (endive).

Tan Dinh 🍽 🚶 ♿ €€€€

60 Rue de Verneuil, 75007 **Tel** *01 45 44 04 84* **Map** *12 D3*

The relatively high prices in this Franco-Vietnamese restaurant run by the discreet Vifian family are due to a combination of the good quality cuisine and an outstanding wine list with one of the biggest collections of Pomerols in the city. There are no Oriental lanterns here – the interior decor is sober.

Jacques Cagna 🅿 🚶 ♿ 🍴 €€€€€

14 Rue des Grands Augustins, 75006 **Tel** *01 43 26 49 39* **Map** *12 F4*

This elegant 17th-century townhouse showcases chef-owner Jacques Cagna's trinkets and excellent classic-cum-modern cuisine. Try the red mullet salad with *foie gras*, pigeon *confit* with turnips, and a classic Paris-Brest (choux pastry filled with praline-flavoured cream). The wine list is admirable.

Lapérouse 🅿 ♿ 🍴 €€€€€

51 Quai des Grands Augustins, 75006 **Tel** *01 43 26 68 04* **Map** *12 F4*

This famous establishment from the 19th century was once one of the glories of Paris. Under the impeccable management of owner-chef Alain Hacquard, this is still the case. The series of salons have kept their 1850s decor. The best tables are by the window. Valet parking available.

LATIN QUARTER

Breakfast In America   €
17 Rue des Ecoles, 75005 **Tel** *01 43 54 50 28*   **Map** *13 A5*

For all-day breakfasts of crispy bacon, sausages, eggs, hotdogs, burgers, steaks, pancakes, maple syrup and crispy fries, head to this wonderful American diner. It is so popular with Parisian families that queueing is inevitable – but it's worth it once you're inside. There's a second address in the Marais on Rue Malher.

Le Grenier de Notre Dame   P 🚶 ♿ 🔳   €
18 Rue de la Bûcherie, 75005 **Tel** *01 43 29 98 29*   **Map** *13 A4*

Le Grenier de Notre Dame opened in the 1970s and still exudes its original hippie atmosphere. Mostly organic ingredients are used to make the filling meals such as seitan *brochettes* (tofu skewers), vegetarian casserole or vegetarian escalope in breadcrumbs. The wine list offers a good choice of reasonably priced labels.

Itinéraires   🚶 ♿   €€
5 Rue de Pontoise, 75005 **Tel** *01 46 33 60 11*   **Map** *13 B5*

Chef Sylvain Sendra had a hard act to follow when he opened this modern bistro in 2008: his own success with his first restaurant Le Temps au Temps near the Bastille. Despite the occasional ill-judged dish, Itinéraires has quickly become one of the best places to eat in the area. Solo diners can sit at the bar or the long shared table.

Le Pré Verre   🚶 🍴   €€
19 Rue du Sommerard, 75005 **Tel** *01 43 54 59 47*   **Map** *13 A5*

The brothers Marc and Philippe Delacourcelle run this plum-walled bistro whose cooking draws liberally on Asian ingredients with dishes such as celery and salmon marinated with ginger, or beef with wasabi and chickpea purée. Wines come from small producers and the dining room is always lively.

Loubnane   🚶 🔳   €€
29 Rue Galande, 75005 **Tel** *01 43 26 70 60 or 01 43 54 21 27*   **Map** *13 A4*

A Lebanese restaurant where specialities include delicious and generous *mezzes*, served under the watchful eye of a patron whose main aim in life actually seems to be the happiness of his customers. Live Lebanese music is often performed in the basement.

Perraudin   🚶   €€
157 Rue St-Jacques, 75005 **Tel** *01 46 33 15 75*   **Map** *16 F1*

From the red-and-white tablecloths to the zinc-topped bar and the cuisine, everything at Perraudin looks and feels like a genuine 1900s bistro. On the menu are staples like *carré* of lamb and *frites*, *carpaccio* of beef with parmesan, and creamy *riz au lait* (rice pudding). Reservations for 7–8pm only – or wait at the bar (tables turn over quickly).

Christophe   €€€
8 Rue de Descartes, 75005 **Tel** *01 43 26 72 49*   **Map** *13 A4*

You must not be put off by the somewhat lacklustre decor, because it is what they present on the plates that makes Christophe's a restaurant not to be missed. The menu includes a wide range of imaginative dishes, such as sautéed langoustines in filo pastry and wonderful 66 per cent chocolate *moelleux* that oozes onto the plate.

Le Petit Pontoise   🚶 🔳   €€€
9 Rue Pontoise, 75005 **Tel** *01 46 29 25 20*   **Map** *13 B5*

Popular neighbourhood venue. Inventive use of herbs and spices: pan-fried quail with honey, dried fruits and nuts and prawns Provençal. A perfect menu will probably be composed of roasted camembert drizzled with honey followed by a duck *parmentier* and stir-fried *foie gras* and, finally, a hot vanilla *soufflé*. Reservations recommended.

Rôtisserie du Beaujolais   ♿   €€€
19 Quai de la Tournelle, 75005 **Tel** *01 43 54 17 47*   **Map** *13 B5*

Facing the Seine and owned by Claude Terrail of the Tour d'Argent next door, the restaurant has a large rôtisserie for roasting poultry and meats. Many of the meats and cheeses are ordered specially from the best suppliers in Lyon. A Beaujolais is, of course, the wine you should order here.

Brasserie Le Balzar   €€€€
49 Rue des Ecoles, 75005 **Tel** *01 43 54 13 67*   **Map** *13 A5*

Located in the heart of the Latin Quarter is this bistro with dark wooden panelling, vast mirrors and banquette seating. In a dining room that bustles with a mix of locals from the nearby Sorbonne and tourists, friendly waiters serve classic dishes such as onion soup, pepper steak, *sauerkraut* with sausages and for dessert, *tarte tatin*.

La Tour d'Argent   P 🚶 ♿ 🍴   €€€€€
15–17 Quai de la Tournelle, 75005 **Tel** *01 43 54 23 31* **Map** *13 B5*

Established in 1582, the Tour appears to be eternal. Owner André Terrail has hired young chefs who have rejuvenated the classic menu. The ground-floor bar is also a gastronomic museum; from here take a lift to the panoramic restaurant. One of the finest wine cellars. Lunch is much cheaper than dinner.

Key to Price Guide *see p300* **Key to Symbols** *see back cover flap*

JARDIN DES PLANTES QUARTER

La Mosquée de Paris
€€
39 Rue Geoffroy Saint Hilaire, 75005 **Tel** *01 43 31 38 20*
Map *17 B2*

On a sunny day there are few more agreeable places to sip mint tea in Paris than under the fig tree of the Paris Mosque café. Inside, you can choose your sticky pastry at the counter or have a more substantial meal in the warren of warmly decorated dining rooms.

Marty Restaurant
€€€
20 Ave des Gobelins, 75005 **Tel** *01 43 31 39 51*
Map *17 D3*

Authentic Art Deco interior but the cuisine steals the show. Serves a hearty fare, such as roast duck or rabbit casserole. Insist on seasonal dishes such as gazpacho. Excellent crème brûlée. The Marty was established by E Marty in 1913 and is still family-run.

Mavrommatis
€€€€
42 Rue Daubenton, 75005 **Tel** *01 43 31 17 17*
Map *17 B2*

With an elegant decor, this restaurant is manned by the Mavrommatis brothers, one in the kitchen, the other welcomes guests. Its Greek specialities include roast lamb and *moussaka*. The Hellenic excursion continues with Greek yogurt and *baklava* for dessert.

MONTPARNASSE

La Cantine du Troquet
€€
101 Rue de l'Ouest, 75014 **Tel** *01 45 40 04 98*
Map *15 B4*

This is the third restaurant of Christian Etchebest, best known for his bistro Le Troquet in the 15th arrondissement *(see p308)*. Here, long shared tables and a menu of simple bistro classics creates a canteen-like atmosphere, but Etchebest's expert chef's touch still shines through. No reservations so get there early or expect to queue.

La Cerisaie
€€
70 Blvd Edgar Quinet, 75014 **Tel** *01 43 20 98 98*
Map *16 D2*

Somewhat overshadowed by the Montparnasse tower, this bistro serves generous portions of traditional dishes such as mackerel with creamy potato purée and pork with asparagus. The excellent wine list includes a number of small but talented producers.

La Cagouille
€€€
10–12 Pl Constantin Brancusi, 75014 **Tel** *01 43 22 09 01*
Map *15 C3*

This large venue, on the stark Place Brancusi in the rebuilt Montparnasse district, is one of Paris's best fish restaurants. Big fish are served simply with few fancy sauces or adornments. You might also find unusual seasonal delicacies like black bay scallops and *vendangeurs* (tiny red mullet). There's a cognac cellar too.

La Coupole
€€€
102 Blvd du Montparnasse, 75014 **Tel** *01 43 20 14 20*
Map *16 D2*

This famous brasserie has been popular with the fashionistas, artists and thinkers since its creation in 1927. Under the same ownership as Brasserie Flo, it has a similar menu: shellfish, smoked salmon and good desserts. Lamb curry is a speciality. Open from breakfast to 2am.

Restaurant l'Assiette
€€€
181 Rue du Château, 75014 **Tel** *01 43 22 64 86*
Map *15 C4*

Long run by cigar-smoking chef Lulu and frequented by socialist politicians, this insider's bistro was taken over by the Alain Ducasse-trained David Rathgeber in 2008. His menu of bistro classics such as marinated herrings with warm potato salad and crème caramel "revisited" is attracting a younger set of celebrities.

Le Jeu de Quilles
€€€
45 Rue Boulard, 75014 **Tel** *01 53 90 76 22*
Map *16 D4*

This restaurant with an *épicerie* at the front is the perfect illustration of a trend in Paris: top-notch ingredients, simply prepared and served in simple surroundings. Meat from star-butcher Hugo Desnoyer finds its way into dishes such as veal with fresh porcini mushrooms and golden *frites*. Open Wednesday to Saturday.

Le Parc aux Cerfs
€€€
50 Rue Vavin, 75006 **Tel** *01 43 54 87 83*
Map *16 D1*

Parc aux Cerfs means "deer park". Although the area surrounding this bistro is quite built up, the inner courtyard, perfect for an alfresco dining experience, adds a touch of the outdoors. The menu is good value and the food inventive, with creative twists on traditional French dishes.

Wadja
10 Rue de la Grande-Chaumière, 75006 **Tel** *01 46 33 02 02*   **Map** *16 D2*

This is a favourite hangout for local families and arty types on a budget, thanks to its excellent-value *menu du jour*. Game, meat and fish are permanent fixtures, the wine list is suitably eclectic, and the waiters are always ready to advise on the right wine to go with the dishes you have chosen.

INVALIDES AND EIFFEL TOWER QUARTER

Sip Babylone
46 Bd Raspail, 75007 **Tel** *01 45 48 87 17*   **Map** *12 D4*

Close to Le Bon Marché and great for a tasty shopping break, this is more a snack bar than a restaurant. Tea and pastries are served all day long in the elaborate dining room. For lunch, try the cheese platters, bacon and Parmesan salad or a plate of smoked salmon, *taramasalata* and aubergine (eggplant).

La Billebaude
29 Rue de l'Exposition, 75007 **Tel** *01 45 55 20 96*   **Map** *10 F3*

This friendly restaurant offers good home-cooking, using the freshest ingredients at reasonable prices. Specialities from Burgundy include excellent home-made foie gras, scallops and rabbit, as well as a perfect pot-roasted calves' liver served with a confiture d'oignons.

Les Cocottes de Christian Constant
135 Rue St-Dominique, 75007 **Tel** *01 45 50 10 31*   **Map** *10 F3*

If you love bistro food but don't have two hours to spare, Les Cocottes has the answer. Here, star-chef Christian Constant has cooked up a series of *cocottes* (dishes served in cast-iron casseroles), soups and salads for the diner in a hurry. It is all served at a long counter to keep turnover high. No reservations.

Au Bon Accueil
14 Rue Monttessuy, 75007 **Tel** *01 47 05 46 11*   **Map** *10 E2*

Au Bon Accueil looks like a bistro from the outside with its terrace looking onto the Eiffel Tower but, once inside, the quality of the food and chic contemporary decor make it feel like a mini *haute cuisine* restaurant. If you are on a budget try the amazing-value *prix fixe* menus at lunch and dinner, which don't skimp on ingredients.

L'Ami Jean
27 Rue Malar, 75007 **Tel** *01 47 05 86 89*   **Map** *10 F2*

This Basque-style restaurant with a tavern-like interior is one of the most popular bistros in Paris: try to reserve a table about 10 days in advance. The man behind its success is Stéphane Jego, who puts an innovative spin on southwestern French cooking with dishes such as lamb sweetbreads with paper-thin chorizo "leaves".

La Villa Corse
164 Bd de Grenelle, 75015 **Tel** *01 53 86 70 81*   **Map** *10 E5*

In a pleasant neighbourhood, La Villa Corse is regarded as one of the city's best, serving fresh and strongly flavoured Corsican-Mediterranean cuisine. The menu features wild boar stew, olive veal, Brocciu cheese and chestnut bread, a speciality from the city of Bonifacio. Good choice of Corsican wines.

Le Troquet
21 Rue François Bonvin, 75015 **Tel** *01 45 66 89 00*   **Map** *10 F5*

This is a jewel in an unlikely, quiet residential street with a view of the Eiffel Tower. Locals soak up the friendly atmosphere and devour Basque chef Christian Etchebest's fabulous cooking. Expect unusual dishes such as smoked eel tart with avocado purée and apples.

Thoumieux
79 Rue St-Dominique, 75007 **Tel** *01 47 05 49 75*   **Map** *11 A2*

This bustling traditional French bistro with Art Deco mirrors, crystal chandeliers and velvet banquette seating is run by the Costes group. The menu is both inventive (think a gourmet, inflated pizza) and refined – the *Chateaubriand* melts in the mouth. One of the best tables in town.

L'Arpège
84 Rue de Varenne, 75007 **Tel** *01 45 51 47 33*   **Map** *11 B3*

Alain Passard's three-star restaurant near the Musée Rodin is one of the most highly regarded in Paris. It has striking pale-wood decor and sprightly young service as well as good food. Passard's menu might include lobster with black truffles and *ris de veau* (sweetbreads) with horseradish. Don't miss the apple tart, smothered in pastry roses.

Le Jules Verne
2nd platform, Eiffel Tower, 75007 **Tel** *01 45 55 61 44*   **Map** *10 D3*

This is no tourist trap: the Jules Verne on the second platform of the Eiffel Tower is now one of the hardest dinner reservations to obtain in Paris. The sleek, all-black decor suits the monument perfectly and the pretty, flavourful cuisine is very good indeed. Reserve at least three months in advance.

Key to Price Guide *see p300* **Key to Symbols** *see back cover flap*

Vin sur Vin

20 Rue de Monttessuy, 75007 **Tel** *01 47 05 14 20*

Map 10 E2

Owner Patrice Vidal is justly proud of his eight-table restaurant. The menu is seasonal and original, the wine list fabulous with interesting wines at reasonable prices. Dishes might include *pot-au-feu de foie gras*, *salade folle* and *côte de veau de Cantal*.

CHAILLOT AND PORTE MAILLOT

6 New York

6 Ave de New York, 75116 **Tel** *01 40 70 03 30*

Map 10 E1

A trendy restaurant, with an impressive minimalist interior, 6 New York marries pale wood and soft tones of grey. Though known to be a fashionable venue, it serves a surprisingly traditional cuisine, featuring pig's trotters, Niçoise sole and vegetable risotto.

Chez Géraud

31 Rue Vital, 75016 **Tel** *01 45 20 33 00*

Map 9 B3

Géraud Rongier, the jovial owner, is a scrupulous observer of *cuisine du marché*, using what's best at the market that day to create dishes like shoulder of lamb cooked on a spit, *sabodet* sausage in red wine sauce, skate with mustard, roast pigeon with port sauce and bitter chocolate cake. The mural was specially created.

La Plage

Port de Javel 75015 **Tel** *01 40 59 41 00*

Map 9 B5

A spectacular site facing the Statue of Liberty on the Ile aux Cignes. Thankfully, the cuisine's as good as the view. The huge terrace is the place to be seen at lunchtime, as well as an idyllic spot for a candlelit dinner on a balmy summer's eve. The decor is an attractive mix of wood and pastel tones.

L'Huîtrier

16 Rue Saussier Leroy, 75017 **Tel** *01 40 54 83 44*

Map 4 E2

This freshly-decorated restaurant specializes in shellfish, especially oysters which you order by the half-dozen or dozen. It also serves several hot fish dishes and makes a good restorative stop before or after visiting the animated market in the nearby Rue Poncelet.

La Grande Armée

3 Ave de la Grande Armée, 75016 **Tel** *01 45 00 24 77*

Map 4 D4

A few steps from the Arc de Triomphe and opposite the Champs-Elysées, this brasserie run by the Costes brothers is a handy address to have up your sleeve. Napoleon's army is the theme of the slightly tongue-in-cheek decor, and the menu has something for everyone, from Caesar salad to Argentinian steak.

Le Relais du Parc

55–57 Ave Raymond Poincaré, 75016 **Tel** *01 44 05 66 10*

Map 9 C1

This historic townhouse was originally run by Alain Ducasse and Joel Robuchon, who joined forces to create a menu of "classic" dishes. Ducasse-trained Alexandre Nicolas took over in 2009 and has added a light, modern touch to the restaurant. In summer opt for one of the lovely terrace tables.

Le Timgad

21 Rue Brunel, 75017 **Tel** *01 45 74 23 70*

Map 3 C3

This has been Paris's best-known, most elegant Maghrebian restaurant for years, hence the need to reserve in good time. The menu has many different briks, tagines and couscous dishes as well as specialities like grilled pigeon, *pastilla* and *méchoui* (whole roast lamb), which needs to be ordered in advance.

Prunier

16 Ave Victor Hugo, 75116 **Tel** *01 44 17 35 85*

Map 4 D4

One of the prettiest seafood restaurants, Prunier was founded in 1925. Its dazzling Art-Deco interior features wooden panels in the upstairs dining room. Wonderful seafood including smoked salmon and a variety of caviars. The menu changes monthly. Hotel parking available.

Zebra Square

3 Pl Clément Ader, 75016 **Tel** *01 44 14 91 91*

Map 9 B4

Part of the Hotel Square complex, a modern building with minimalist decor spiced up by splashes of zebra prints. Equally modern fare: crab cakes, aubergine (eggplant) *carpaccio* and salmon tartare. Brunch on Sundays. Stylish rooms done up in rich, soothing colours. A hit with the fashion and media crowd.

Antoine

10 Ave de New York, 75116 **Tel** *01 40 70 19 28*

Map 10 E1

This chic seafood restaurant offers views across the Seine onto the Eiffel Tower. Gourmands will love the tempura langoustines in a mango dressing, red mullet with thyme risotto and *bouillabaisse* (fish soup) made with saffron from Quercy. Desserts are good too, especially the *rhum baba* with roasted pineapple.

L'Astrance
P   €€€€€

4 Rue de Beethoven, 75016 **Tel** *01 40 50 84 40*   **Map** *9 C3*

The inventive cuisine of L'Astrance's two chefs has made it so popular that you must book several months ahead. Dishes include sautéd pigeon with a caramelized hazelnut sauce and apple and celery minestrone with roasted spice ice cream. The Menu Surprise is as lovely as the mountain flower this restaurant is named after.

CHAMPS-ELYSÉES

Granterroirs
€

30 Rue Miromesnil, 75008 **Tel** *01 47 42 18 18*   **Map** *5 B4*

In the modish Champs-Elysées area it is a surprise to come across this *epicerie*-restaurant decorated like a country kitchen, with long, shared wooden tables. More than 800 products line the shelves, many of which can be tasted in salad and open sandwich plates; a different hot dish is served every day. Lunch only.

Ladurée
€

75 Ave des Champs-Elysées, 75008 **Tel** *01 40 75 08 75*   **Map** *4 F5*

Celebrated as one of the best tearooms in town since 1862, Ladurée hasn't lost any of its class. This elegant tearoom, famous for its Renaissance-style interior, still serves its renowned macaroons, which come in all sorts of inventive flavours: aniseed, caramel, chestnut, lime and basil.

Atelier Renault
€€

53 Ave des Champs-Elysées, 75008 **Tel** *08 11 88 28 11*   **Map** *4 F5*

This futuristic looking café, clad in glass and aluminium, awaits car lovers above the Renault showroom. It is ideal for a quick bite on the Champs Elysées with everything from sandwiches to pasta dishes and, for something more filling, three-course menus offering a French take on World food; think scallops served in a tagine with lemon zest.

Bistrot Napolitain
€€

18 Ave Franklin D Roosevelt, 75008 **Tel** *01 45 62 08 37*   **Map** *5 A5*

In a neighbourhood where looks often count more than substance it is a surprise to come across this restaurant with paper tablecloths and arguably the best pizza in town (try the rocket-topped version). The dining room is always crowded and noisy, and the waiters can seem brusque, but it is all part of the fun.

Flora Danica
€€€

142 Ave des Champs-Elysées, 75008 **Tel** *01 44 13 86 26*   **Map** *4 E4*

On the ground floor of the House of Denmark, this venue is more relaxed and less pricey than Copenhague upstairs. Original Scandinavian cuisine, with just a touch of France. Specialities include grilled salmon and strawberries with mulled wine. Interiors are prettily done in Danish style. Valet parking available.

Savy
€€€

23 Rue Bayard, 75008 **Tel** *01 47 23 46 98*   **Map** *10 F1*

Opened in 1923, this Art-Deco restaurant with cosy booths in the front room is dedicated to the hearty cooking of the Aveyron region in central France. Order a marbled steak or the lamb shoulder for two, served with crisp shoestring *frites*, with one of the excellent wines from the cellar, perhaps a Mercury from Burgundy.

La Fermette Marbeuf 1900
€€€€

5 Rue Marbeuf, 75008 **Tel** *01 53 23 08 00*   **Map** *4 F5*

Fabulous Belle Époque mosaics, tiles and ironwork were discovered beneath the formica walls of this Champs-Elysées bistro. La Fermette Marbeuf also serves good brasserie-style food including a commendable set menu with many *appellation contrôlée* wines – a measure of their quality.

L'Avenue
€€€€

41 Ave Montaigne, 75008 **Tel** *01 40 70 14 91*   **Map** *10 F1*

Located at the hub of *couture* fashion, L'Avenue attracts an elegant crowd. The unusual Neo-1950s decor is fresh and colourful. Service can get a bit hectic at peak lunch and dinner times, but then this is a brasserie. The cuisine is varied and supper is served until late.

Les Saveurs de Flora
€€€€

36 Avenue George V, 75008 **Tel** *01 40 70 10 49*   **Map** *4 E5*

At this restaurant with a romantic pink decor, chef Flora Mikula's menu reflects her Provençal cooking roots as well as her travels around the world, with combinations like grilled sea bass with North African-style aubergine. End with the excellent cheese board or a show-stopping dessert. The set menu is great value.

Guy Savoy
€€€€€

18 Rue Troyon, 75017 **Tel** *01 43 80 40 61*   **Map** *4 D3*

A handsome dining room and professional service further complement the remarkable cuisine of Guy Savoy himself. The three-starred Michelin menu includes iced, poached oysters, steam-baked Bresse chicken with lemongrass, stuffed pigeon breast studded with black radish and then an extraordinary dessert.

Key to Price Guide *see p300* **Key to Symbols** *see back cover flap*

La Maison Blanche
`P` `♿` `♿` `🍴` `T` €€€€€

15 Ave Montaigne, 75008 **Tel** *01 47 23 55 99* **Map** *10 F1*

The popular Maison Blanche restaurant affixed 15 Avenue Montaigne to its name when it moved here. Although the decor is modern, the restaurant is almost opulently vast. The cuisine, with its Provençale and Southwestern influences, is flavoursome and is the main attraction for its worldly clientele.

Lasserre
`T` €€€€€

17 Ave Franklin D. Roosevelt, 75008 **Tel** *01 43 59 02 13* **Map** *11 A1*

Built for the 1937 World Fair to imitate the interior of a luxury liner, this Michelin-starred restaurant, once favoured by Marc Chagall and Dali, combines opulent décor with deliciously refined cuisine by chef Christophe Moret. His dishes are inspired by 19th-century recipes such as macaroni with black truffles. Service is faultless.

Le Cinq
`P` `♿` `🍴` `T` `P` €€€€€

31 Ave George V, 75008 **Tel** *01 49 52 70 00* **Map** *4 E5*

For a rare splurge, it is hard to do better than this sumptuous restaurant in the George V. The technically stunning food is not stuck in a time warp; ingredients such as wasabi and harissa make their way into some dishes. The €85 lunch menu is something of a bargain, given the quality of the food.

Pavillon Ledoyen
`P` `♿` `T` €€€€€

1 Ave Dutuit, 75008 **Tel** *01 53 05 10 02* **Map** *11 B1*

The refined cuisine at Pavillon Ledoyen mainly features turbot breast and mashed potatoes with truffle *butte* (a sea fish recipe) and *mille-feuilles de Krampouz croustillante avec crème de citron*. Ask for a table in the dining room – a re-creation of a 1950s grill room – or on the terrace.

OPÉRA QUARTER

Chartier
`♿` `♿` €

7 Rue du Faubourg Montmartre, 75009 **Tel** *01 47 70 86 29* **Map** *6 F4*

Despite its impressive, listed 1900s decor, Chartier still caters to people on a budget, mostly students and tourists, though some of the old habitués still come for the basic cuisine (hard-boiled eggs with mayonnaise, house pâté, roast chicken and pepper steak). No frills, and expect to wait: the waiters are very busy.

Le Grand Colbert
€€€

2–4 Rue Vivienne, 75002 **Tel** *01 42 86 87 88* **Map** *6 F5*

Situated in the Galérie Colbert owned by the Bibliothèque Nationale, this must be one of the prettiest brasseries in Paris. The menu offers classic brasserie fare – herring fillets with potatoes or cream, snails, onion soup, classic whiting Colbert (in breadcrumbs) and grilled meats.

Le Vaudeville
`♿` `🍴` €€€

29 Rue Vivienne, 75002 **Tel** *01 40 20 04 62* **Map** *6 F5*

This is one of seven brasseries owned by Paris's reigning brasserie king, Jean-Paul Bucher. Good shellfish, Bucher's famous smoked salmon, many different fish dishes as well as classic brasserie standbys like pig's trotters and *andouillette*. A quick, friendly service and noisy ambience make it lots of fun.

Les Alchimistes
`♿` €€€

16 Rue Favart, 75002 **Tel** *01 42 96 69 86* **Map** *6 F5*

In the shadow of the Opéra Comique, this friendly restaurant offers dishes such as veal parmentier with oyster mushrooms, and warm chocolate tart with white-chocolate ice cream. The decor is a mix of old and new, with red walls and dark furniture.

Les Noces de Jeannette
`♿` `♿` €€€

14 Rue Favart, 75002 **Tel** *01 42 96 36 89* **Map** *6 F5*

A typical Parisian bistro, named for the one-act curtain-raising opera performed at the Opéra Comique across the street. An ornate interior belies the cosy atmosphere. The fixed-price menu offers a wide choice of classic dishes. Try the vichyssoise or terrine de crustacés à la crème d'Oseille. Menu changes regularly.

Willi's Wine Bar
`♿` €€€

13 Rue des Petits-Champs, 75001 **Tel** *01 42 61 05 09* **Map** *12 F1*

Original wine posters cover the walls and over 250 vintages are in the cellar at Willi's Wine Bar. The menu includes onion tart with a salad topped with pine nuts, beef *fricassée* with braised chicory (endive) and rosemary sauce and bitter chocolate terrine.

La Fontaine Gaillon
`P` `♿` `🍴` €€€€€

1 Rue de la Michodière, 75002 **Tel** *01 47 42 63 22* **Map** *6 E5*

In a 17th-century mansion, Fontaine Gaillon is partly owned by legendary film actor, Gérard Depardieu. The menu showcases sautéed John Dory, Merlan Colbert with sorrel purée, *confit de canard* and lamb chops. Comfortable interiors and a good wine list.

Senderens

🔲🍴 €€€€€

9 Pl de la Madeleine, 75008 **Tel** *01 42 65 22 90*   **Map** *5 C5*

Super-chef Alain Senderens has just given up the Michelin stars of his Lucas Carton restaurant to open this more informal eatery, on the same spot as its famous predecessor. His legendary creations include *foie gras* with cabbage, spicy duck Apicius and a mango *mille-feuille vanille*. The Belle-Époque decor is stunning and the crowd glamorous.

MONTMARTRE

Musée de la Halle St-Pierre

📗🧍♿ €

2 Rue Ronsard, 75018 **Tel** *01 42 58 72 89*   **Map** *7 A1*

Formerly a covered market, this venue now hosts a library, an Art Brut museum and a café. This is a popular spot for afternoon tea and pastries. At lunch, the menu is more substantial with savoury bites such as quiche, pies and tarts. Children's activities provided.

Rose Bakery

🧍♿🖼 €

46 Rue des Martyrs, 75009 **Tel** *01 42 82 12 80*   **Map** *6 F3*

Who knew that Parisians would develop such a soft spot for British baking? Ever since Rose and Jean-Charles Carrarini opened this industrial-looking café in 2004, Paris locals have come from far and wide for the carrot cake and scones. Quiches, salads, risotto and soups are equally delicious. Brunch on weekends.

La Bourse ou la Vie

🧍🍴 €€

12 Rue Vivienne, 75002 **Tel** *01 42 60 08 83*   **Map** *6 F5*

You may well find the best steak-*frites* in Paris at this restaurant with a red-and-yellow, 1940s decor near the old stock exchange. The secret here is top-quality meat (order your steak doused in creamy cracked-peppercorn sauce) and the animal fat used for the *frites*. A soundtrack of French *chansons* adds to the atmosphere.

Le Miroir

🍴 €€

94 Rue des Martyrs, 75018 **Tel** *01 46 06 50 73*   **Map** *6 F3*

At this well kept secret near Montmartre, Ducasse-trained chef Sébastien Guénard prepares seasonal menus with modern flair. The reasonably priced lunch menu might include shellfish with courgette and tomato purée served with artichoke cream or Basque pork with cepe mushrooms. The wine list is equally impressive. Closed Sun dinner.

Un Zèbre à Montmartre

🖼 €€

38 Rue Lepic, 75018 **Tel** *01 42 23 97 80*   **Map** *6 E1*

This Lyonnais café, with its traditional zinc bar and bohemian clientele, is one of the best value eateries in Montmartre. For just €15 (lunch) and €17 (evening), you can enjoy a two course meal of dishes such as Lyonnais sausage, confit of duck and a scrumptious chocolate mousse. The cocktails are recommended.

Le Wepler

🅿🧍♿🖼 €€€

14 Pl de Clichy, 75018 **Tel** *01 45 22 53 24*   **Map** *6 D1*

Retro-style brasserie open until late into the night. Good for afternoon tea, early evening cocktails and pre- or post-show suppers. Large shellfish platters as well as sauerkraut, *andouillette* and *confit de canard*. An institution, established in 1892.

Une Journée à Peyrassol

🍴 €€€

13 Rue Vivienne, 75002 **Tel** *01 42 60 12 92*   **Map** *6 F5*

The Commanderie de Peyrassol, one of the best vineyards in Provence, runs this restaurant dedicated to truffles, wine and other products from the area. The two rustic-meets-modern dining rooms have a warm Provençal atmosphere, reinforced by the earthy aroma of dishes such as truffle-laced scrambled eggs.

Drouant

🍴 €€€€

16–18 Place Gaillon, 75002 **Tel** *01 42 65 15 16*   **Map** *6 E5*

This former Alsatian brasserie founded in 1880 is now a contemporary restaurant run by Antoine Westermann (who is also behind the bistro Mon Vieil Ami, see p300). Order *à la carte* to sample his generous hors d'oeuvres, which fill the table with little bowls and plates. Upstairs are several private salons for groups.

FURTHER AFIELD

Au Pied de Fouet

🧍♿ €

96 Rue Oberkampf, 75011 **Tel** *01 48 06 46 98*   **Map** *14 F1*

The latest addition to the eponymous bistro trio (with sister addresses on Rue de Babylone in the 7th, and Rue Saint-Benoît in the 6th), Au Pied de Fouet offers a traditional zinc bar, red-checkered tablecloths, hearty daily specials and a friendly welcome (complete with the house apéritif).

Key to Price Guide *see p300* **Key to Symbols** *see back cover flap*

Beyrouth
16 Rue de la Vacquerie, 75011 **Tel** *01 43 79 27 46*

In a residental street near the cemetery of Père Lachaise, this is a wonderful Lebanese restaurant frequented by a mixture of locals, media types (from the TV studio next door) and drama students. The food is as copious and delicious as it is well priced, and the service is friendly.

Chez Gladines
30 Rue des Cinq Diamantes, 75013 **Tel** *01 45 80 70 10*   **Map** *17 C4*

In the villagey Butte-aux-Cailles quarter, hidden behind the high-rises of Place d'Italie, this is a haven of decent, no-frills food. The place is so popular, it is always busy. Giant salads are among the favourite items on the menu: they are served in massive bowls and are often covered in sautéed potatoes.

Le Baron Rouge
1 Rue Théophile Roussel, 75012 **Tel** *01 43 43 14 32*   **Map** *14 F5*

Right next to the lively Marché d'Aligre (*see p338*), Parisians rush here at weekends to sample the divine oysters, brought straight from Cap Ferret on the Atlantic coast. These can be eaten out on the pavement, standing round large wine barrels. Also a good wine bar during the week.

Astier
44 Jean-Pierre Timbaud, 75011 **Tel** *01 43 57 16 35*   **Map** *14 E1*

Quality here is among the best for the price in Paris, and the dining rooms are always full in this hugely popular bistro. The food is very good, including mussel soup with saffron, rabbit in mustard sauce, duck breast with honey, and good cheeses and wines.

Chez Prune
36 Rue Beaurepaire, 75010 **Tel** *01 42 41 30 47*   **Map** *8 D4*

With wonderful views of Canal Saint-Martin, this is a top spot for brunch on Sundays, with a choice of smoked salmon or ham with croissants. Upmarket cuisine for lunch: saffron and lime fish and three-cheese ravioli. Platters of cold meats and cheeses in the evening. Daily food based on *cuisine du marché*.

Favela Chic
18 Rue Faubourg du Temple, 75011 **Tel** *01 40 21 38 14*   **Map** *8 D5*

Not much of Brazil is missing from this lively haven, where the food is accompanied by loud music and dancing. The *caipirinha* (fresh lime, cane-sugar alcohol and lots of crushed ice) has lost none of its buzz, and the *feijoada* tastes just as it does back in Salvador Bahia. The place gets noisy as the evening progresses, so come early.

La Marine
55 Quai Valmy, 75010 **Tel** *01 42 39 69 81*   **Map** *8 D5*

For several years now this establishment has been a popular mainstay of the Canal St-Martin district, and as such, is usually packed, so book ahead. The main courses are good and mainly fishy, such as red mullet in puff pastry, fish steak with a creamy nettle sauce, and fish stew.

La Maroquinerie
23 Rue Boyer, 75002 **Tel** *01 40 33 35 05*

This former workshop has been converted into an excellent restaurant with a shaded terrace. Modern French food includes hearty portions of pork *mignon* with vanilla, artichokes and mushrooms and a delicious Nutella *crème-brûlée*. The venue also houses a club, a café and a very popular concert space.

La Mère Lachaise
78 Bd de Ménilmontant, 75020 **Tel** *01 47 97 61 60*

This is a friendly bistro with a split personality. A great terrace and two dining rooms – one traditional and the other plastered in aluminium. Uncomplicated food includes asparagus and citrus fruit salad, beef with potato gratin, charcuterie and crumble with seasonal fruit.

Le 20ème Art
46 Rue des Vignoles, 75020 **Tel** *01 43 67 22 29*

Don't be put off by the surroundings of this excellent locals' restaurant; the area is being revamped and looks a little worse for wear. The square where the restaurant is located is, however, charming, as is the decor inside, with art by local artists on the stone walls. Both the meat and fish dishes are innovative, mixing unexpected flavours.

Le Baratin
3 Rue Jouye Rouve, 75020 **Tel** *01 43 49 39 70*

The haunt of top Paris chefs such as pastry maestro Pierre Hermé, this wine bar-bistro focusing on small producers is worth the hike to the top of Belleville. Argentinian-born Raquel Carena turns out dishes such as *pollack tartare* with sea urchin "tongues" and roast Basque lamb with baby potatoes and spinach.

Le Volant Basque
13 Rue Beatrix Dussane, 75015 **Tel** *01 45 75 27 67*   **Map** *10 D5*

The owner of Le Volant Basque (*volant* means steering wheel) is fanatical about motorcar racing. There's nothing racy, however, about the cooking: it is simple, traditional French cuisine at its best; *boeuf bourguignon*, mouth-watering homemade fruit tarts and the never-to-be-forgotten chocolate mousse.

Ma Pomme/Colimaçon   🚶 €€
107 Rue de Ménilmontant, 75020 **Tel** *01 40 33 10 40*

It is worth the 10-minute walk up steep Rue de Ménilmontant to get to this well-kept secret. Excellent food is served with a smile in a bright-yellow dining room with temporary art collections on the walls. Expect unusual dishes with ingredients such as ostrich and kangaroo.

Pause Café   🚶♿🔲 €€
41 Rue de Charonne, 75011 **Tel** *01 48 06 80 33*   **Map** *14 F4*

Since the shooting of the 1996 film *Chacun Cherche son Chat*, this has been a top spot to be seen. Luckily this has not ruined the friendly ambience nor the fine cuisine: light dishes such as steak tartare, tarts with salads and excellent homemade pastries. The stone and glass interior lends a rustic-elegant charm.

Brasserie Flo   🅿🚶♿🔲 €€€
7 Cour des Petites-Ecuries, 75010 **Tel** *01 47 70 13 59*   **Map** *7 B4*

This authentic Alsatian brasserie is situated in a passageway in a slightly unsavoury neighbourhood. But it is worth the effort to find it: the rich wood and stained-glass decor is unique and very pretty and the straightforward brasserie menu includes good shellfish and *choucroute* (sauerkraut).

Brasserie Julien   🅿🚶 €€€
16 Rue du Faubourg St-Denis, 75010 **Tel** *01 47 70 12 06*   **Map** *7 B5*

With its superb 1880s decor, Julien is upmarket but reasonable. Under the same ownership as Brasserie Flo, it has the same friendly service and wide dessert variety. The imaginative brasserie cuisine includes hot *foie gras* with lentils, breaded pig's trotter and Julien's version of *cassoulet*.

Le Bistro d'à Côté Flaubert   🚶🔲 €€€
10 Rue Gustave Flaubert, 75017 **Tel** *01 42 67 05 81*   **Map** *4 E2*

This was the first and remains the most appealing of star-chef Michel Rostang's boutique bistros. Many Lyonnais dishes are served including lentil salad, *cervelas* or *sabodet* sausage, *andouillette*, and macaroni gratin. Popular with executives at lunch and with the upper layers of the bourgeoisie at night.

Le Bistro des Deux Théâtres   🚶 €€€
18 Rue Blanche, 75009 **Tel** *01 45 26 41 43*   **Map** *6 D3*

If you are on a strict budget this formula restaurant in the theatre district is a real find. The reasonable set menu includes an apéritif, a choice of first and main courses, cheese or dessert and a half bottle of wine. The food is reliably good, including duck *foie gras*, smoked salmon, *magret de canard* (duck breast) and *profiteroles*.

Le Clocher Pereire   🚶♿ €€€
42 Blvd Pereire, 75017 **Tel** *01 44 40 04 15*

Two chefs with an impressive *haute cuisine* background run this restaurant on the edge of Paris. The slightly old-fashioned dining room is nearly always packed with locals who come for the great-value €32 menu. The best dishes include scallop carpaccio, *cochon au lait* (roast pork) with stuffed peppers and pineapple with lychee sorbet.

Le Paprika   🚶♿🔲 €€€
28 Ave Trudaine, 75009 **Tel** *01 44 63 02 91*   **Map** *6 F2*

Gourmet Hungarian cuisine and live gypsy music at weekends. A dish such as the *csáky bélszin* (beef with morels and *foie gras*) is familiar to the French palate, but desserts such as apple and cinnamon strudel offer a taste of Central Europe. Friendly staff give a warm welcome.

L'Epicuriste   🔲🍷 €€€
41 Blvd Pasteur, 75015 **Tel** *01 47 34 15 50*

The former owners of L'Epigramme continue their Parisian gastronomic legacy in the 15th arrondissement. Enjoy their changing market-based specialities such as scallops roasted in butter and parsley or beef cheeks with winter vegetables. The slightly cold, modern decor is quickly warmed up by the friendly staff.

Le Villaret   ♿ €€€
13 Rue Ternaux, 75011 **Tel** *01 43 57 89 76*   **Map** *14 E2*

Tucked away on the Oberkampf district's northern fringes, this restaurant is run by the former staff from Astier close by. Well-known for its *cuisine du marché* (using the freshest ingredients from the day's market), carefully chosen and prepared meat and big cheese selection. Packed at weekends.

Les Zygomates   €€€
7 Rue Capri, 75012 **Tel** *01 40 19 93 04*

This former butcher's shop is now a popular eatery – surprising, given its out-of-town-centre address. The ceiling is painted tin and the dining room is filled with other interesting touches. Food is plentiful and wonderfully innovative, with dishes such as turkey in a salted rosemary crust or snail and mushroom ravioli. Closed in August.

L'Ourcine   🚶♿ €€€
92 Rue Broca, 75013 **Tel** *01 47 07 13 65*   **Map** *17 A3*

The cream-and-red decor of this little bistro is unassuming but welcoming and you can see the young chef at work in his small kitchen at the back. Expect exemplary bistro dishes such as pork cheeks with lentils and *foie gras*, and lime cream with an orange *tuile* for dessert. Wines are a bit pricey.

Key to Price Guide *see p300* **Key to Symbols** *see back cover flap*

Villa Pereire

116 Blvd Pereire, 75017 **Tel** *01 43 80 88 68*

Map *4 E1*

The perfect place if you are looking to rub shoulders with the chic locals. The French fusion menu includes delights such as crayfish and vegetable spring rolls in sweet and sour sauce and *confit de canard* with truffle oil and mashed potatoes. It is also open for breakfast.

La Gazzetta

29 Rue de Cotte, 75012 **Tel** *01 43 47 47 05*

Map *14 F5*

The young chef at this delightful restaurant is Petter Nilsson and he creates a superb gastronomic harmony with contemporary French dishes, such as venison with polenta, dried figs and dandelion leaves. The food is served in a relaxing Neo-Art Deco setting.

Le Chalet des Îles

14 Chemin de Ceinture du Lac Inferieur du Bois de Boulogne, 75116 **Tel** *01 42 88 04 69*

Map *3 A4*

Idyllic setting, method on an island in the middle of a lake. The country-style interior suits the bucolic environment, but the cuisine showcases a modern approach: pan-fried sole with a Creole-style sauce, coconut and lemon chicken with red rice and chocolate cake with a red berry *coulis*.

Le Chardenoux

1 Rue Jules Vallès, 75011 **Tel** *01 43 71 49 52*

This classic bistro, run by star TV chef Cyril Lignac, is one of the prettiest in Paris. Both fish and meat feature on the traditional French menu, with dishes such as roasted cod, preserved duck and fricassée of kidney. The wine list covers all of France's wine regions. The menu changes depending on the market.

Le Pavillon Montsouris

20 Rue Gazan, 75014 **Tel** *01 43 13 29 00*

This restored building once counted Trotsky, Mata Hari and Lenin among its clientele. Today the attractive interior and terrace make fine surroundings for a good value set menu. Specialities include lobster *à la plancha*, wild boar with bacon and wine sauce, and *crème brulée à la vanille Bourbon*.

Le Train Bleu

Pl Louis Armand, 75012 **Tel** *01 43 43 09 06*

Map *18 E1*

Train station restaurants were once grand places for a meal. Today this is not usually so, but the Train Bleu (named after the fast train that once took the élite to the Riviera) in the Gare de Lyon is a pleasant exception. Upmarket brasserie cuisine such as hot Lyonnais sausage, with excellent pastries. The Belle Époque decor is a landmark.

L'Oulette

15 Pl Lachambeaudie, 75012 **Tel** *01 40 02 02 12*

L'Oulette's vast premises may lack intimacy, but Chef Marcel Baudis's cuisine, reflecting his native Quercy, remains excellent. Dishes include duck *foie gras* with chestnuts and glazed anchovies, lamb from the Pyrenées, and *pain d'épices* (a kind of spiced cake).

Augusta

98 Rue de Tocqueville, 75017 **Tel** *01 47 63 39 97*

Map *5 A1*

This reliable restaurant serves exclusively fish and seafood. The *salade augusta* is generously garnished with shellfish and the house speciality *bouillabaisse* with potatoes must be one of the best in Paris. An unusual dish is langoustines flavoured with tarragon and saffron.

Au Trou Gascon

40 Rue Taine, 75012 **Tel** *01 43 44 34 26*

This authentic 1900s bistro owned by star-chef Alain Dutournier (of Carré des Feuillants) is one of Paris's most popular places. The delicious Gascon food includes ham from the Chalosse region, great *foie gras*, lamb from the Pyrenees and local poultry. Dutournier's desserts are also worth finding room for.

Dessirier

9 Pl du Maréchal Juin, 75017 **Tel** *01 42 27 82 14*

Map *4 E1*

Dedicated to seafood since 1883, this is one of Paris's best-known fish restaurants. Oyster risotto, whole grilled sea bass and langoustine salad feature. A combination of fish brasserie and wet-fish market, it offers a variety of fish-based dishes, depending on the season. Affordable wine list available. Valet parking.

Le Pré Catelan

Route de Suresnes, Bois de Boulogne, 75016 **Tel** *01 44 14 41 14*

This elegant Belle Époque restaurant in the Bois is a delight, either in midsummer when you can dine on the terrace, or in midwinter when the lights inside are magical. The menu is luxurious, with huge langoustines, veal with truffles and sea urchin soufflé. Divine desserts. There is a cheaper menu at lunchtime.

Murano Urbano Hotel Restaurant

13 Bvd du Temple, 75003 **Tel** *01 42 71 20 00*

Map *14 D1*

Mediterranean cuisine is on the menu inside this trendy restaurant, whose funky decor complements that of the adjoined hotel. Opt for a table inside the almost all-white dining room, or, on a sunny day, relax and enjoy your meal in the outdoor courtyard instead.

Cafés, Tea Salons and Bars

Good food and drink is so much a part of everyday life in Paris that you can eat and drink well without ever going to a restaurant. Whether you want to enjoy a meal or casual drink at a café, wine bar or tearoom, buy a crêpe from a street stand or a quiche or crusty *baguette* sandwich from a bakery, or buy a market picnic of cheeses, breads, salads and *pâtés*, informal eating is one of the city's great gastronomic strengths.

Paris is also a wonderful city for drinking. Wine bars in every quarter offer various wines by the glass. Beer bars have astounding selections, and Irish pubs are much-loved spots which serve Guinness in a relaxed, sometimes rowdy atmosphere. Or choose from chic hotel bars or fun late-night bars. *(See also pp298–9.)*

CAFES

Paris is famous for its cafés, and rightly so. You can't walk far in this city without passing one. They range in size from tiny to huge, some with pinball machines, a tobacconist and betting stations, some with elegant Belle Epoque decorations and immaculately attired waiters. Every Parisian has their favourite local café and these establishments function as the heart of any neighbourhood. The life of a café changes throughout the day and it's always fascinating to check out the locals at leisure, sipping their morning espresso, tucking into a hearty lunch or drinking an *apéritif* after work. Most cafés will serve you light food and drink at any time of day.

Breakfast definitely is one of the busiest times and fresh croissants and *pains au chocolat* (chocolate-filled pastries) sell fast. The French often eat these dipped in a bowl or large cup of milky coffee or hot chocolate. Eating breakfast out at a café, or at least grabbing a quick caffeine fix in the morning is a fundamental part of the French lifestyle.

The café lunch usually includes *plats du jour* (daily specials) and, in the smaller cafés, these are great Parisian bargains, rarely costing more than €16 for two courses. The specials are often substantial meat dishes such as *sauté d'agneau* (sautéed lamb) or *blanquette de veau* (veal with a white sauce),

with fruit tarts for dessert. For a simpler lunch, salads, sandwiches and omelettes are usually available at any time of day. One of the best places for this kind of food is **Le Bourdonnec Pascal** in St-Germain-des-Prés. **Le Rostand** by the Luxembourg Gardens is also an excellent place to eat as is **Café Constant** *(see p319)* in the Invalides district.

Most museums have reliable cafés, but those at the Pompidou Centre *(see pp110–11)* and the Musée d'Orsay *(see pp144–5)* are especially good. When visiting the Louvre, it is worth waiting till you re-emerge from the galleries and stopping at the upmarket **Café Marly** in front of the glass pyramid under the arcades for an expensive, yet memorable drink or meal. Should you find yourself in the department store **Galeries Lafayette** *(see p321)*, it's worth going to the café for the fabulous views over Paris.

Cafés in the main tourist and nightlife areas (Boulevard St-Germain, Les Halles, Avenue des Champs-Elysées, Boulevard Montparnasse, the Opéra and Bastille) generally stay open late – some not closing their doors until 2am.

It is important to note that prices change depending on where in the café you choose to enjoy your drink. Standing at the bar is usually a little cheaper than sitting at one of the tables, and heading outside to the terrace will normally cost you more again.

TEA SALONS

Tearooms have become increasingly popular in Paris over the last few years and the selection of teas is normally impressive. Some tea salons also offer light lunches, as well as breakfast and afternoon tea, including **Angélina**, with its Belle Epoque decor. **Mariage Frères** in the Marais is well known for its exhaustive drink list and also sells loose tea and lovely teapots to take home. **Ladurée** on the Champs Elysées is a Parisian institution where well-heeled ladies sip tea and nibble the house speciality macaroons. For a more exotic atmosphere, visit the mosaic-tiled **Café de la Mosquée**, at Paris's mosque in the Jardin des Plantes area, for sticky pastries and excellent mint tea.

WINE BARS

Most Parisian wine bars are small, convivial neighbourhood places. They open early, many doubling as cafés for breakfast, and offer a small, good-quality lunch menu. It's best to get there early or after 1.30pm if you want to avoid the crowd. Most wine bars are usually closed by 9pm.

Wine bar owners tend to be passionate about wine, most of them buying directly from producers. Young Bordeaux wines and those from the Loire, Rhône and the Jura can be surprisingly good, and wine bar owners usually seek out interesting tipples. The **L'Ecluse** chain specializes in Bordeaux, but for the most part you will find delicious lesser-known wines at very reasonable prices. Serious oenophiles might like to visit wine bars attached to leading wine shops so that any interesting vintages tasted can be ordered by the caseload and enjoyed at home. There are several examples of this type of place in Paris – **Juvenile's**, **Lavinia** and **Legrand Filles et Fils** in the Opéra district are among the finest. Juveniles is a small shop with a zinc bar run by a Scotsman. The selection is very good, especially for wines from the New World, and great food is also served here. Lavinia is Europe's largest wine store, the choice is vast, there are regular tastings and the sleek bar serves many wines by the glass. Legrand is an old-fashioned vintner whose bar is extremely popular with Parisian wine buffs. Another fashionable wine bar of this type is **Wine and Bubbles** in the Beaubourg and Les Halles district. The delightful **Rouge Passion**, situated below Montmartre, is a great place to spend a whole evening. Wine-tasting classes with guest *sommeliers* are a regular feature in this bar.

BEER BARS AND PUBS

Paris has both pubs and beer bars. Whereas pubs are simply for drinking, beer bars also serve a particular style of food and are larger. *Moules-frites* (a generous bowl of steamed mussels served with French fries), *tarte aux poireaux* (leek tart) and *tarte aux oignons* (onion tart) are classic examples of the food they serve. The chief reason for going to a beer bar, however, is for the beer. The lists are often vast: some specialize in Belgian *gueuze* (heavy, malty, very alcoholic beer), others have beers from all around the world.

Some beer bars are open from noon, whereas pubs may open later in the afternoon. Pubs are usually open every day, often until 1 or 2am. The pubs in Paris have a good mix of expatriate and French clients. Some pubs are also micro-breweries serving beer brewed on the premises. The **Frog and Princess** and the **Frog and Rosbif** are good examples of this type of pub, serving several types of home-brewed beer. The bar staff are very friendly and will happily help you choose the beer that's right for you. Aside from traditionally English pubs such as **The Bombardier** in

the Latin Quarter, Paris has dozens of Irish pubs and a few Scottish pubs. The best Irish pubs include **Coolin** and **Corcoran's** in St-Germain-des-Prés, **Kitty O'Sheas** and **Carrs** in the Tuileries district and **O'Sullivans by the Mill** in Montmartre. A Highland fling and good whisky can be found in the **Highlander** in St-Germain-des-Prés and **The Auld Alliance** in the Marais.

BARS

Being such an elegant city, it's no surprise that Paris has more than its share of cocktail and late-night bars too. Some pretty Paris brasseries, such as **La Coupole**, **La Rotonde** and **La Closerie des Lilas**, have long wooden or zinc bars, accomplished bartenders, a glamorous ambience and a sense of distinguished times past. Hotel bars are some of the loveliest places for cock-tails in Paris. **The Hemingway Bar** at the Ritz *(see p285)* is the most famous hotel bar in Paris. It is full of nostalgia, small, intimate, lined with heavy wood and has been run since 1994 by one of the world's top barmen, Colin Peter Field. The cocktails here are wonderful and each drink for a lady comes complete with a fresh flower. Other hotel bars of note include the bar at the Four Seasons George V *(see p290)* where the bartenders will shake your martini at your table and present it in an individual silver shaker, the perennially popular bar in the hotel Balzac *(see p290)* and the fashionable bar at the hotel Plaza Athénée *(see p292)*.

La Mezzanine de l'Alcazar is one of Paris's most fashionable bars, while **Yono** is young and trendy. Other hip bars include **Le Fumoir** next to the Louvre with its long elegant bar and excellent cocktails, **Andy Wahloo** which is tiny with a Moroccan design, **De LaVille** café which is popular as a pre-club destination, **Le China**, which has a wonderful cocktail menu and **The Lizard Lounge**, which attracts a noisy, young crowd. The

Philippe Starck-designed bar and restaurant **Kong**, on top of the Kenzo store near the Pont Neuf, is currently Paris's trendiest place for drinks.

Bars which are less trendy but great for a relaxing drink include the tiny, stone-clad **Stolly's** in the Marais and legendary **Harry's Bar**, which claims to have invented the Bloody Mary.

TAKE-AWAY FOOD

Crêpes are the traditional Parisian street food. Although there are fewer good crêpe stands than there used to be, they still exist. Sandwich bars provide *baguettes* with a wide range of fillings; a Parisien – a type of *baguette* – is normally Emmental cheese with ham. Camembert-filled sandwiches tend to be delicious, but beware the misguidingly named *crudités* (salad) which may include non-vegetarian ingredients too. The best fast food in Paris is freshly-baked flat *fougasse* (foccacia) bread sprinkled with savoury flavourings. It is sold fresh from a wood-burning oven and filled with one or more fillings of your choice. You can buy it at **Cosi** in Rue de Seine. Busy tourist areas also have their share of kebab shops for a speedy snack.

Ice-cream stands open around noon, and stay open late in summer. It's worth queuing for the city's best ice cream at **Maison Berthillon**. Seasoned gourmets come from across the city to queue around the block for a scoop or two of their delicious concoctions. Chocoholics will be delighted with their intense cocoa ice cream, whilst fruit fans can expect sorbets packed with flavour. There are several branches of Berthillon in the city but the Ile St Louis store is recom-mended: nothing beats strolling along the Seine catching the drips from a divine ice-cream cone. Ice-cream obsessives might also like to head to **Amorino** which makes Italian-style *gelati*. Don't miss the *amaretto gelato* which comes sprinkled with crushed *amaretti* biscuits.

DIRECTORY

ILE DE LA CITÉ AND ILE ST-LOUIS

TEA SALONS

Le Flore en l'Ile
42 Quai d'Orléans 75004.
Map 13 B4.

ICE-CREAM PARLOURS

Amorino
47 Rue St-Louis-en-l'Ile
75004.
Map 13 C4.

Maison Berthillon
31 Rue St-Louis-en-l'Ile
75004.
Map 13 C4.

TUILERIES QUARTER

CAFÉS

Café Marly
93 Rue de Rivoli Cour
Napoleon du Louvre
75001.
Map 12 F1.

WINE BARS

La Cloche des Halles
28 Rue Coquillière 75001.
Map 12 E2.

Le Rubis
10 Rue du Marché St-Honoré 75001.
Map 12 D1.

Juvenile's
47 Rue de Richelieu
75001. **Map** 12 E1.

TEA SALONS

Angélina
226 Rue de Rivoli 75001.
Map 12 D1.

Ladurée
16 Rue Royale 75008.
Map 5 C5.

PUBS

Carr's
1 Rue Mont Thabor
75001. **Map** 12 D1.

Kitty O'Sheas
10 Rue des Capucines
75002. **Map** 6 D5.

BARS

Bars du Ritz
15 Pl Vendôme 75001.
Map 6 D5.

THE MARAIS

Harry's Bar
5 Rue Daunou 75002.
Map 6 E5.

CAFÉS

Au Petit Fer à Cheval
30 Rue Vieille du Temple
75004. **Map** 13 C3.

L'Etoile Manquante
34 Rue Vieille du Temple
75004. **Map** 13 C3.

Ma Bourgogne
19 Pl des Vosges 75004.
Map 14 D3.

Le Trésor
7 Rue du Trésor 75004.
Map 13 C3.

TEA SALONS

Le Loir dans la Théière
3 Rue des Rosiers
75004. **Map** 13 C3.

Mariage Frères
30–32 Rue du Bourg-Tibourg 75004.
Map 13 C3.

BEER BARS

Café des Musées
49 Rue de Turenne
75003. **Map** 14 D3.

WINE BARS

La Belle Hortense
31 Rue Vieille du Temple
75004. **Map** 13 C3.

La Trinquette
67 Rue des Gravilliers
75003.
Map 13 C1.

Le Coude Fou
12 Rue du Bourg-Tibourg 75004.
Map 13 C3.

PUBS

The Auld Alliance
80 Rue François Miron
75004. **Map** 13 C3.

Stolly's
16 Rue Cloche Perce
75004. **Map** 13 C3.

BARS

L'Apparement Café
18 Rue des Coutures
St-Gervais 75003.
Map 14 D2.

Les Philosophes
28 Rue Vieille du Temple
75004. **Map** 13 C3.

The Lizard Lounge
18 Rue du Bourg-Tibourg
75004. **Map** 13 C3.

Yono
37 Rue Vieille du
Temple 75004.
Map 13 C3.

BEAUBOURG AND LES HALLES

CAFÉS

Café Beaubourg
100 Rue St Martin 75004.
Map 13 B2. *(See p108).*

WINE BARS

La Garde Robe
41 Rue de l'Arbre Sec
75001.
Map 12 E2.

Wine and Bubbles
3 Rue Françoise 75001.
Map 13 A1.

PUBS

Frog and Rosbif
116 Rue Saint-Denis
75002. **Map** 13 B1.

Quigley's Point
5 Rue du Jour 75001.
Map 13 A2.

BARS

Andy Wahloo
69 Rue des Gravilliers
75003. **Map** 13 B1.

Kong
1 Rue du Pont Neuf
75001. **Map** 13 A2.

Le Comptoir
37 Rue Berger 75001.
Map 12 F2.

Le Fumoir
6 Rue de l'Amiral-de-Coligny 75001.
Map 12 F2.

ST-GERMAIN-DES-PRÉS

CAFÉS

Le Bourdonnec Pascal
75 Rue de Seine 75006.
Map 12 E4.

Café de Flore
(See p139).

Café de la Mairie
8 Place St-Sulpice 75006.
Map 12 E4.

Les Deux Magots
(See p138).

La Palette
43 Rue de Seine 75006.
Map 12 E4.

SANDWICH BARS

Cosi
54 Rue de Seine 75006.
Map 12 E4.

WINE BARS

Au Sauvignon
80 Rue des Sts-Pères
75007.
Map 12 D4.

Bistro des Augustins
39 Quai des Grands-Augustins 75006.
Map 12 F4.

PUBS

Coolin
15 Rue Clément 75006.
Map 12 E4.

Corcoran's
28 Rue Saint-André
des Arts 75006.
Map 12 F4.

Frog and Princess
9 Rue Princesse 75006.
Map 12 E4.

Highlander
8 Rue de Nevers 75006.
Map 12 F3.

The Moose
16 Rue des Quatre-Vents
75006. **Map** 12 F4.

BARS

Le Bar Dix
10 Rue de l'Odéon
75006.
Map 12 E4.

Birdland
8 Rue Guisarde
75006. **Map** 12 E4.

Café Mabillon
164 Blvd St-Germain
75006.
Map 12 E4.

Don Carlos
66 Rue Mazarine 75006.
Map 12 F4.

DIRECTORY

Fubar
5 Rue St Sulpice 75006.
Map 12 F4.

La Mezzanine de l'Alcazar
62 Rue Mazarine 75006.
Map 12 F4.

Zéro de Conduite
14 Rue Jacob 75006.
Map 12 E3.

LATIN QUARTER

CAFÉS

Panis
21 Quai Montebello
75005. **Map** 13 A4.

WINE BARS

Les Pipos
2 Rue de l'Ecole Polytechnique 75005. **Map** 13 A5.

Le Vin qui Danse
4 Rue des Fossés-St-Jacques 75005.
Map 17 A1.

BEER BARS

La Gueuze
19 Rue Soufflot 75005.
Map 12 F5.

PUBS

The Bombardier
2 Place du Panthéon
75005. **Map** 17 A1.

BARS

Le Caveau des Oubliettes
52 Rue Galande 75005.
Map 13 A4.

JARDIN DES PLANTES

CAFÉS

Café Littéraire de l'Institut du Monde Arabe
1 Rue des Fossés-St-Bernard 75005.
Map 13 C5.

TEA SALONS

Café de la Mosquée
39 Rue Geoffroy St-Hilaire
75005. **Map** 17 C2.

PUBS

Bière Academy
7 Rue des Ecoles 75005.
Map 13 B5.

ICE-CREAM PARLOURS

Häagen-Dazs
3 Pl de la Contrescarpe
75005. **Map** 17 A1.

LUXEMBOURG QUARTER

CAFÉS

Au Petit Suisse
16 Rue de Vaugirard
75006. **Map** 21 F5.

Le Rostand
6 Place Edmond
Rostand 75006.
Map 12 F5.

BEER BARS

L'Académie de la Bière
88 Blvd de Port-Royal
75005. **Map** 17 B3.

MONTPARNASSE

CAFÉS

Café de la Place
23 Rue d'Odessa 75014.
Map 15 C2.

La Rotonde
7 Pl 25 Août 1944 75014.
Map 16 D2.

Le Sélect Montparnasse
99 Blvd du Montparnasse
75006.
Map 16 D2.

WINE BARS

Le Rallye Peret
6 Rue Daguerre
75014.
Map 16 D4.

TEA SALONS

Justine
96 Rue Oberkampf
75011.
Map 14 E1.

BARS

La Closerie des Lilas
171 Blvd du
Montparnasse 75006.
Map 16 D2.

La Coupole (Café Bar)
102 Blvd du
Montparnasse 75014.
Map 16 D2.
(See p178).

Cubana Café
45 Rue Vavin 75006.
Map 12 F5.

Le Café Tournesol
9 Rue de la Gaîté 75014.
Map 2 E2.

INVALIDES AND EIFFEL TOWER QUARTER

CAFÉS

Café Constant
139 Rue St-Dominique
75007. **Map** 11 B2.

PUBS

O'Brien's
77 Rue Saint-Dominique
75007. **Map** 10 F3.

BARS

Comptoir du 7
39 Ave de la Motte-
Picquet 75007.
Map 10 F4.

CHAMPS-ELYSÉES

WINE BARS

L'Ecluse
64 Rue François Premier
75008. **Map** 4 F5.

Ma Bourgogne
133 Blvd Haussmann
75008. **Map** 5 B4.

TEA SALONS

Ladurée
75 Ave des Champs-
Elysées 75008. **Map** 4 F5.

BARS

Le Bar du Plaza at the Plaza Athénée
(See p291).

Le V at Four Seasons George V
(See p290).

OPÉRA QUARTER

CAFÉS

Café de la Paix
12 Blvd des Capucines
75009.
Map 6 E5. *(See p213).*

WINE BARS

Bistro du Sommelier
97 Blvd Haussmann
75008. **Map** 5 C4.

Lavinia
3-5 Blvd de la Madeleine
75001. **Map** 6 D5.

Legrand Filles et Fils
1 Rue de la Banque
75002. **Map** 12 F1.
Tel 01 42 60 07 12.

MONTMARTRE

CAFÉS

Le Saint Jean
16 Place des Abbesses
75018. **Map** 6 F1.

Le Sancerre
35 Rue des Abbesses
75018. **Map** 6 E1.

WINE BARS

Rouge Passion
14 Rue Jean Baptiste
Pigalle 75009.
Map 6 D2.

PUBS

O'Sullivans by the Mill
92 Blvd de Clichy 75018.
Map 6 E21.

FURTHER AFIELD

WINE BARS

Le Verre Volé
67 Rue de Lancry 75010.
Map 8 D1.

BARS

L'Autre Café
62 Rue Jean-Pierre
Timbaud 75011.
Map 8 F5.

Café Charbon
109 Rue Oberkampf
75011.
Map 14 E1.

Chez Prune
36 Rue Beaurepaire
75010. **Map** 8 D4.

Le China
50 Rue de Charenton
75012. **Map** 14 F5.

Pause Café
41 Rue de Charonne
75011. **Map** 14 F4.

GLUTEN FREE

Des Si et des Mets
63 Rue Lépic 75018.
Map 6 E1.

SHOPS AND MARKETS

Paris seems to be the very definition of luxury and good living. Beautifully dressed people sip wine by the banks of the Seine against a backdrop of splendid architecture, or hurry down gallery-lined streets carrying parcels from specialist shops. The least expensive way of joining the chic set is to create French style with accessories or costume jewellery.

Alternatively, splash out on the fashion, or the wonderful food and related items from kitchen gadgets to tableware. Remember too that Parisian shops and markets are the ideal place to indulge in the French custom of strolling through the streets, seeing and being seen. For high fashion there are the exquisite *couture* house window displays on Avenue Montaigne, or you can browse at the bookstalls along the Seine. A survey of some of the most famous places to shop follows.

OPENING HOURS

Shops are usually open from 10am to 7pm, Monday to Saturday, but hours can vary. Many department stores stay open late on Thursday, while boutiques may shut for an hour or two at midday. Markets and local neighbourhood shops close on Mondays. Some places shut for the summer, usually in August, but they may leave a note on the door suggesting an open equivalent nearby.

HOW TO PAY

Cash is readily available from the ATMs in most banks, which accept both credit and bank debit cards. Visa and MasterCard are the most widely accepted credit cards.

VAT EXEMPTION

A sales tax (TVA) of 5.5– 19.6 per cent is imposed on most goods and services in EU countries. Non-EU residents shopping in France are entitled to a refund of this if they spend a minimum of €175 in one shop in one day. You must have been resident in France for less than six months and either carry the goods with you out of the country within three months of purchase or get the shop to forward them to you. If shopping in a group, you can usually buy goods together in order to reach the minimum.

Larger shops will generally supply a form (*bordereau de détaxe* or *bordereau de vente*) and help you to fill it in. When you leave France or the EU you present the form to Customs, who either permit you to be reimbursed straight away, or forward your claim to the place where you bought the merchandise; the shop eventually sends you a refund. If you know someone in Paris it may be quicker if they can pick up the refund for you at the

Shopping in Avenue Montaigne

shop. Alternatively at large airports such as Orly and Roissy some banks may have the facilities to refund you on the spot. Though the process involves a lot of paperwork, it can be worth it. There is no refund on food, drink, tobacco, cars and motorbikes. Bicycles, however, can be reimbursed.

SALES

The best sales (*soldes*) are held in January and July, although you can sometimes find sale items before Christmas. If you see goods labelled *Stock*, it means that they are stock items. *Dégriffé* means designer labels marked down, frequently from the previous year's collections. *Fripes* indicates that the clothes are second-hand. The sales tend to occupy prime floor space for the first month and are then relegated to the back of the store.

Au Printemps, the *grande dame* of Parisian department stores

DEPARTMENT STORES

Much of the pleasure of shopping in Paris is derived from going to the small specialist shops. But if time is short, try the *grands magasins* (department stores). Some still operate a ticket system for selling goods. The shop assistant writes up a ticket for goods from that same boutique which you take to one of the cashiers. You then return with your validated ticket to pick up your purchase. This can be time-consuming, so go early in the morning and don't shop on Saturdays. The French don't pay much attention to queues, so be assertive! One peculiarity of a visit is that the security guards may ask to inspect your bags as you leave. These are random checks and should not be taken as an implication of theft.

Department stores vary in style and content, but all have places to eat. **Au Printemps** is noted for its exciting and innovative household goods section, and large menswear store. The clothes departments for women and children are well-stocked. The lovely domed restaurant in the cupola often hosts chic after-hours parties;

Kenzo designerwear in the Place des Victoires *(see pp324–5)*

Snails from the *charcuterie*

these are private, but do visit the restaurant during shopping hours.

BHV (Le Bazar de l'Hôtel de Ville) is a DIY enthusiast's paradise. It also sells a host of other items related to home decor. The Left Bank **Le Bon Marché** was Paris's first department store and today is its most chic. The designer clothing sections are well-sourced, the high-end accessories are excellent and the own-brand linen has a good quality to price ratio. The prepared food sections serve restaurant-quality fare to take away.

Galeries Lafayette is perhaps the best-known department store and has a wide range of clothes available at all price levels. Its first-floor trends section plays host to lots of innovative designers. Having taken over part of the old Marks & Spencer, Galeries Lafayette boasts a wonderful food hall, Lafayette Gourmet, which offers a vast array of mouthwatering goodies.

Virgin Megastore is open until late and has an excellent record selection and an impressive book section. **FNAC** sells records, books (foreign editions can be found at Les Halles) and electronic equipment. The branch on the Champs-Elysées specializes in music, videos and DVDs and concert tickets. **FNAC Digitale** sells a wide range of the latest technological equipment.

Apollonia Poilâne's bread bearing her trademark "P" *(see pp333–5)*

ADDRESSES

Au Printemps
64 Blvd Haussman 75009.
Map 6 D4. **Tel** 01 42 82 50 00.

BHV
52–64 Rue de Rivoli 75004.
Map 13 B3. **Tel** 01 42 74 90 00.

Le Bon Marché
24 Rue de Sèvres 75007.
Map 11 C5. **Tel** 01 44 39 80 00.

Bookstall, Vanves market *(see p339)*

FNAC
Forum des Halles, 1 Rue Pierre Lescot 75001. **Map** 13 A2.
Tel 0825 020 020.
74 Ave des Champs-Elysées 75008.
Map 4 F5. **Tel** 0825 020 020.

FNAC Digitale
77–81 Blvd St-Germain 75006.
Map 13 A5. **Tel** 0825 020 020.

Galeries Lafayette
40 Blvd Haussmann 75009.
Map 6 E4. **Tel** 01 42 82 34 56.

Virgin Megastore
52–60 Ave des Champs-Elysées 75008. **Map** 4 F5.
Tel 01 49 53 50 00.

Paris's Best: Shops and Markets

By turns ultra-conservative and wackily avant-garde, Paris is a treasure trove of quality shops and boutiques. Time-honoured emporia mix with modern precincts in a city that buzzes with life in its inner quarters, not least in the markets. Here you can buy everything from exotic fruit and vegetables to fine china and vintage treasures. Whether you're shopping for handmade shoes, perfectly-cut clothes or traditionally-made cheeses, or simply soaking up the atmosphere, you won't be disappointed.

Place de la Madeleine
Top-class groceries and delicacies are sold on the north side of this square. (See p214.)

THE CENTRE OF PARIS COUTURE

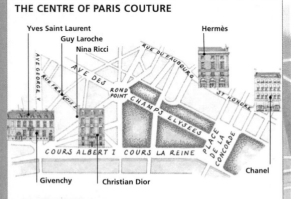

Yves Saint Laurent
Guy Laroche
Nina Ricci
Hermès
RUE DU FAUBOURG
AVE GEORGE V
AVE DES
RUE FRANÇOIS
ROND POINT
ST HONORE
CHAMPS ELYSEES
COURS ALBERT I   COURS LA REINE
PLACE DE LA CONCORDE
Chanel
Givenchy
Christian Dior

Chanel
Coco Chanel (1883–1971) reigned over the fashion world from No. 31 Rue Cambon. The main boutique is in the Avenue Montaigne. (See p325.)

See inset map

Champs-Elysées

R I V E R

Invalides and Eiffel Tower Quarter

Rue de Rivoli
Inexpensive mementos like this Paris snow shaker can be found in the shops on the Rue de Rivoli. (See p130.)

Marché de la Porte de Vanves
This charming and relaxed market sells old books, linen, postcards, china and musical instruments. (Weekends only – see p339.)

Kenzo
The Japanese designer has colourful apparel for men, women and children in his clothes shops. (See p325.)

Cartier

The early Cartier jewellery designs with their beautifully-cut stones are still highly sought after. This shop in the Rue de la Paix sells all the Cartier lines. (See p329.)

Rue de Paradis

Here you can buy porcelain and crystal at reduced prices at the company showrooms. Look out for Lumicristal which stocks Baccarat and Bernardaud. (See pp330–32.)

Passage des Panoramas

This once-prosperous covered arcade is home to the historic Stem print shop. (See p218.)

Opéra Quarter

| 0 kilometres | 1 |
| 0 miles | 0.5 |

Tuileries Quarter

Beaubourg and Les Halles

S E I N E

The Marais

St-Germain-des-Prés

Ile de la Cité

Ile St-Louis

Latin Quarter

Rue des Francs-Bourgeois

Stylish fashion stores (see pp324–5) line this thoroughfare in the Marais.

Luxembourg Quarter

Jardin des Plantes Quarter

Montparnasse

Rue Mouffetard

The market sells cheeses and other quality foods. (See p339.)

Forum des Halles

This modern glass arcade has many shops. (See p109.)

Clothes and Accessories

For many people Paris is synonymous with fashion and Parisian style is the ultimate in chic. More than anywhere else in the world, women in Paris seem to be in tune with current trends and when a new season arrives they rush, as one, to don the look. Though less trend-conscious generally, Parisian men are aware of style and mix and match patterns and colours with élan. Finding the right clothes at the right price means knowing where to shop. For every luxury boutique on the Avenue Montaigne, there are ten young designers' shops waiting to become the next Jean-Paul Gaultier – and hundreds more selling imitations.

HAUTE COUTURE

Paris is the home of *haute couture*. Original *couture* garments, as opposed to imitations and adaptations, are one-off creations, designed by one of the *haute couture* houses listed with the Fédération Française de la Couture. The rules for being classified by the Fédération are fairly strict, and some top brands are not included. Astronomical prices put *haute couture* beyond the reach of all but a few immensely deep pockets, but it's still the lifeblood of the fashion industry providing inspiration for the mass market.

The fashion seasons are launched with the *couture* shows in January and July. Many shows are held in the Carrousel du Louvre *(see p123)*. If you want to see a show, you stand a much better chance of getting a seat at the private *couture* shows (the main shows are for buyers and the press). To do this call the press offices of the *haute couture* houses a month in advance. You can only be sure you have a place when you receive the ticket. Alternatively, telephone the fashion house or, if you're in Paris, try going to the boutique and asking if there's a show – and do remember to dress the part.

Most *couture* houses make *prêt-à-porter* clothes as well – ready-to-wear clothes fitted on a standard model. They're still not cheap, but give you an idea of some of the designer elegance and creativity at a fraction of the cost.

WOMEN'S CLOTHES

The highest concentration of *couture* houses is on the Right Bank. Most are on or near the Rue du Faubourg-St-Honoré and the classier Avenue Montaigne: **Christian Dior**, **Pierre Cardin**, **Chanel**, **Gianni Versace**, **Givenchy**, **Louis Féraud**, **Nina Ricci** and **Yves Saint Laurent**. This is where you will rub shoulders with the rich and famous.

Hermès offers timeless chic. **MaxMara's** Italian elegance is quite popular in France and no one can resist a **Giorgio Armani** suit. **Karl Lagerfeld** has a shop where the latest creations from his own line, Lagerfeld Gallery, are exhibited.

The theatrical **Paco Rabanne** and chic **Prada** have also stuck to the Right Bank, but many other fine fashion houses prefer the Left Bank. Try **Sonia Rykiel** for knitwear, **Junko Shimada** for sporty casuals and **Barbara Bui** for soft, feminine clothes.

Many designers have a Left Bank branch in addition to their Right Bank bastions, and there are many ready-to-wear shops here. For sheer quality there's **Georges Rech**, but don't forget Yves Saint Laurent and **Jil Sander** for their exquisite tailoring. Try Armani's St-Germain temple of fashion, or Prada's affordable boutique, **Miu Miu**, in the Rue St Honoré. **Joseph** has its cult following for well-cut clothes, and **Irié** is the place for reasonably-priced clothes which are trendy but will stand the test of time. Also

in the Saint-Germain-des-Près district, the **Comptoir des Cotonniers** stocks excellent basics, **Maje** has everything from boho chic to stylish cuts, and **Vanessa Bruno** is extremely popular for feminine flair. Simple cuts with quirky details can be found at **Zadig et Voltaire**, which has a following amongst French fashionistas.

Ready-to-wear shops blanket Paris, and in the beautiful Place des Victoires they thrive off shoppers looking to escape the crowds on Rue du Faubourg-St-Honoré. The **Victoire** boutique offers one of the best collections of current designer labels with Michael Klein, Helmut Lang and Thierry Mugler among many others. **Kenzo** is here (its flagship store is near the Pont Neuf), along with fellow Japanese designers **Comme des Garçons**, with its avant-garde, quirky fashion for both sexes, **Claudie Herlot** and **Y-3** just down the street, near Ventilo. The nearby Rue Jean-Jacques-Rousseau has now become one of the city's prime shopping stops.

Moving east to the Rue du Jour, **Agnès B** presents the latest French fashions. There are also many shops selling inexpensive copies of new designs in the centre. **Martin Margiela** carries excellent quality basics with a twist.

The Marais is a haven for up-and-coming designers and is always busy on Saturdays. One of the best streets is the Rue des Rosiers, which includes the wonderful **Zadig et Voltaire**, **L'Eclaireur** and a branch of **Tehen** for clothes. **Nina Jacob** is on the neighbouring Rue des Francs-Bourgeois, and daring designer **Azzedine Alaïa's** shop is just around the corner. **Abou d'Abi Bazar** stocks a range of designers, and Japanese company **Muji** sells stylishly-simple staple garments and accessories.

The Bastille area has trendy boutiques, as well as some more established names. Designer **Jean-Paul Gaultier**

DIRECTORY

WOMEN'S CLOTHES

Abou d'Abi Bazar
124 Rue Vielle du Temple
75003. **Map** 13 C3.
Tel 01 42 71 13 26.

Agnès B
2–19 Rue du Jour 75001.
Map 13 A1.
Tel 01 45 08 56 56
www.agnesb.com
One of several branches.

Azzedine Alaïa
7 Rue de Moussy 75004.
Map 13 C3.
Tel 01 42 72 19 19.

Barbara Bui
23 Rue Etienne-Marcel
75001. **Map** 13 A1.
Tel 01 40 26 43 65.
www.barbarabui.com
One of several branches.

Chanel
42 Ave Montaigne
75008.
Map 5 A5.
Tel 01 47 23 47 12.
www.chanel.com
One of several branches.

Christian Dior
30 Ave Montaigne
75008.
Map 10 F1.
Tel 01 40 73 73 73.
www.dior.com

Claudie Pierlot
1 Pl des Victoires 75002.
Map 12 F1.
Tel 01 44 82 55 38.
www.claudie-pierlot.com
One of three branches.

Colette
213 Rue St-Honoré
75001.
Map 12 D1.
Tel 01 55 35 33 90.
www.colette.fr

Comme des Garçons
54 Rue du Faubourg
St-Honoré 75008.
Map 4 E3.
Tel 01 53 30 27 27.

Comptoir des Cotonniers
33 Rue des Francs
Bourgeois 75004.
Map 13 C3.
Tel 01 42 76 95 33.

L'Eclaireur
3 ter Rue des Rosiers
75004. **Map** 13 C3.
Tel 01 48 87 10 22.

Eres
2 Rue Tronchet 75008.
Map 5 C5.
Tel 01 47 42 28 82.
One of several branches.

Gaëlle Barré
17 Rue Keller 75011.
Map 14 F4.
Tel 01 43 14 63 02.
www.gaellebarre.com

Georges Rech
54 Rue Bonaparte 75006.
Map 12 E3.
Tel 01 43 26 84 11.
www.georges-rech.fr
One of several branches.

Giorgio Armani
18 Ave Montaigne 75008.
Map 10 F1.
Tel 01 42 61 55 09.
www.giorgioarmani.com

Givenchy
3 Ave Georges V 75008.
Map 4 E5.
Tel 01 44 31 50 00.
www.givenchy.com

H&M
15 Rue du Commerce
75015. **Map** 10 E5.
Tel 01 40 57 24 60.
One of several branches.

Hermès
24 Rue du Faubourg-St-
Honoré 75008.
Map 5 C5.
Tel 01 40 17 46 00.
www.hermes.com
One of several branches.

Irié
8 Rue du Pré-aux-Clercs
75007. **Map** 12 D3.
Tel 01 42 61 18 28.

Isabel Marant
16 Rue de Charonne
Tel 01 49 29 71 55.
www.isabelmarant.tm.fr

Jay Ahr
2 Rue du 29 Juillet 75001.
Map 12 D1.
Tel 01 42 96 95 23.

Jean-Paul Gaultier
6 Rue Vivienne 75002.
Map 12 F1.
Tel 01 42 86 05 05.
One of several branches.

Jil Sander
56 Ave Montaigne
75008. **Map** 10 F1.
Tel 01 44 95 06 70.

Joseph
147 Blvd St-Germain
75006. **Map** 12 E4.
Tel 01 55 42 77 55.

Junko Shimada
13 Rue St-Florentin
75008. **Map** 11 C1.
Tel 01 42 60 94 12.
One of two branches.

Kenzo
3 Pl des Victoires 75001.
Map 12 F1.
Tel 01 40 39 72 03.
One of several branches.

Kookaï
82 Rue Reaumur 75002.
Map 13 B1.
Tel 01 45 08 93 69.
www.kookai.fr
One of several branches.

La City
141 Rue de Rennes
75006. **Map** 16 D1.
Tel 01 45 44 71 18.
www.lacity.fr
One of several branches.

Les Petites
10 Rue du Four 75006.
Map 13 A1.
Tel 01 55 42 98 78.
www.lespetites.fr

Louis Féraud
90 Rue du Faubourg-St-
Honoré 75008. **Map** 4 E3.
Tel 01 44 71 03 86.
www.feraud.com

Mac Douglas
9 Rue de Sèvres 75006.
Map 12 D4.
Tel 01 45 48 14 09.
One of several branches.

Maje
42 Rue du Four 75006.
Map 12 E4.
Tel 01 42 68 68 60.
www.maje-paris.fr

Mango
6 Blvd des Capucines
75009. **Map** 6 E5.
Tel 01 53 30 82 70.
One of several branches.

Martin Margiela
25 bis Rue de
Montpensier 75001.
Map 12 E1.
Tel 01 40 15 07 55.

MaxMara
31 Ave Montaigne
75008. **Map** 5 A5.
Tel 01 47 20 61 13.
One of several branches.

Miu Miu
219 Rue St Honoré
75001. **Map** 5 C5.
Tel 01 58 62 53 20.
www.miumiu.com

Muji
47 Rue des Francs-
Bourgeois 75004.
Map 14 D3.
Tel 01 49 96 41 41.

Nina Jacob
23 Rue des Francs-
Bourgeois 75004.
Map 14 D3.
Tel 01 42 77 41 20.

Nina Ricci
39 Ave Montaigne
75008. **Map** 10 F1.
Tel 01 40 88 67 60.
www.ninaricci.fr

Pierre Cardin
27 Ave de Marigny
75008. **Map** 5 B5.
Tel 01 42 66 68 98.
www.pierrecardin.com

Prada
10 Ave Montaigne
75008. **Map** 3C5.
Tel 01 53 23 99 40.

Promod
60 Rue Caumartin 75009.
Map 6 D4.
Tel 01 45 26 01 11.
One of several branches.

Ragtime
23 Rue de l'Echaudé
75006. **Map** 12 E4.
Tel 01 56 24 00 36.

Sinéquanone
16 Rue du Four 75006.
Map 12 E4.
Tel 01 56 24 27 74.
One of several branches.

Sonia Rykiel
175 Blvd St-Germain
75006. **Map** 12 D4.
Tel 01 49 54 60 60.
www.soniarykiel.com
One of several branches.

Stella Cadente
93 Quai de Valmy 75010.
Map 13 C4.
Tel 01 42 09 66 60.
www.stella-cadente.com
One of two branches.

has a boutique in the Rue du Faubourg St-Antoine. His "senior" and "junior" collections reflect price and attitude. **Isabel Marant's** boutique is renowned for its originality, and **Gaëlle Barré** is a stylist with a fast-growing reputation. *The* swimsuit store is **Eres**, while for leather, it's **Mac Douglas**.

Young designers' clothes are found at **Colette**, **Stella Cadente** and **Jay Ahr** (where you will find great evening dresses), while **Zucca** now has several boutiques. For fabulous, if somewhat pricey, clothes from the 1920s to the 1950s, try **Ragtime**.

Not all Parisians have pocketbooks that allow them to shop on the Avenue Montaigne, but those on smaller budgets still manage to look chic in clothes from high street stores. There are many large chain stores here which have branches in other European cities. Chain stores tend to stock each store differently, depending on the desires and buying patterns of the local clientele. Because of this it is possible to find quintessentially French fashion in large chains such as **Zara**, particularly at the branches on Rue de Rennes and near the Opera.

Mighty Swedish retailer **H&M** has an exciting concept store for young fashion in Paris's 15th arrondissement and stocks designs by Sonia Rykiel in some of its larger shops. French high street stores are also numerous. Well-known names such as **Kookaï** and **Mango** stock fresh and funky items. **Sinéquanone** and **LA City**, on the other hand, are rather classic in their designs, while **Promod** is a very cheap store for fun merchandise.

CHILDREN'S CLOTHES

Lots of options for children exist in various styles and many price ranges. Many top designers of adult clothes also have boutiques for children. These include **Kenzo**, **Baby Dior**, **Agnès B**, **Sonia Rykiel** and **Teddy's**.

Ready-to-wear shops such as **Jacadi** and **Du Pareil au Même** are serviceable and wide-ranging; **Tartine et Chocolat** offer delectable classics with a contemporary twist. **Bonpoint** stocks adorably chic clothing for mini-Parisians. **Petit Bateau** is coveted as much by grown-ups as it is by children. The inevitable has finally happened – children now have their own concept store in **Bonton**, which stocks baby toiletries, stylish clothing, toys and furniture for children's rooms.

For little feet, **Froment-Leroyer** probably offers the best all-round classics. **Six Pieds Trois Pouces** has a vast choice of styles.

MEN'S CLOTHES

Men's fashions are a mix of bespoke tailoring and ready-to-wear, with menswear collections by the top designers every bit as coveted as their feminine counterparts.

On the Right Bank, there's **Giorgio Armani**, **Pierre Cardin**, **Kenzo**, **Lanvin** (also good for accessories) and **Yves Saint Laurent**. On the Left Bank, **Michel Axael** and **Jean-Charles de Castelbajac** are known for their ties and **Francesco Smalto's** elegant creations are worn by some of the world's leading movie stars. **Y-3's** clothes (designed by Yohji Yamamoto) are for those who are intent on making a serious fashion statement, while **Gianni Versace** offers classic, suave Italian style. **APC**, **Paul Smith** and **Ron Orb** garments are rather more contemporary, and **Olivier Strelli**, **Polo by Ralph Lauren** and **Loft Design By** are chic without being overtly trendy, and thus are likely to have a longer shelf-life.

The ultimate in Parisian elegance for men is a suit, custom-made shirt or silk tie from **Charvet**. A trip to the **Place Vendôme** store is a pleasure in itself. Be sure to ask the charming and friendly staff for a tour around their atelier for an insight into how such exquisite creations are crafted. **Madelios** is a

great department store for men which mixes designer and high-street brands.

LIFESTYLE STORES

Since **Colette** first burst on to the Parisian shopping scene in the late 1990s, the fad for lifestyle shops has shown no sign of slowing down. Concept stores tend to be high-end affairs crammed with designer labels, some obscure, some household names, all grouped together to kit you out with everything you could possibly need. From fashionable books to shoes, beauty products, household goods, music and furniture via designer mineral water, handbags, trainers and evening gowns, the one-stop shopping experience provides the ultimate in retail therapy.

Spree in Montmartre mixes fashion, art and design so that you can buy a great outfit and some interesting art at the same time, while **Montaigne Market** brings together the best of *haute couture* and new designers.

VINTAGE AND SECOND-HAND STORES

The vintage craze hit Paris some time back and there are some wonderful shops to plunder for a retro look. The best of the bunch is **Didier Ludot**, where an Aladdin's Cave of chic *haute couture* is elegantly displayed. From vintage Courrèges dresses to excellent condition Chanel suits, this is the place for top of the range retro. The **Depôt-Vente de Buci-Bourbon** is another good place to bargain hunt. A cheaper option and a way to access more recent looks is to head for one of the many second-hand or consignment stores in the city. Chic Parisians discard their outfits with the seasons so it is very easy to pick up some quality items which are normally in top condition from places such as **Réciproque** in Passy or **Alternatives** in the Marais. Sample pieces, sale stock and last season's collection pieces can be found at **Le Mouton à Cinq Pattes**.

DIRECTORY

Vanessa Bruno
25 Rue St-Sulpice 75006.
Map 12 E5.
Tel 01 43 54 41 04.
www.vanessabruno.com

Ventilo
27 bis Rue du Louvre
75002. **Map** 12 F2.
Tel 01 44 76 82 95.
www.ventilo.fr
One of several branches.

Versace
41 Rue François Premier
75008. **Map** 10 F1.
Tel 01 47 42 88 02.
www.versace.com

Victoire
10 Place des Victoires
75002. **Map** 12 F1.
Tel 01 42 61 63 87.
www.victoire-paris.com
One of several branches.

Yohji Yamamoto
25 Rue du Louvre 75001.
Map 12 F1.
Tel 01 45 08 82 45.

Yves Saint Laurent
38 Rue du Faubourg-St-
Honoré 75008. **Map** 5 C5.
Tel 01 42 65 74 59.
www.ysl.com
One of several branches.

Zadig et Voltaire
3 Rue des Rosiers 75004.
Map 13 C3.
Tel 01 44 59 39 06.
One of several branches.

Zara
45 Rue de Rennes 75006.
Map 16 D1. *Tel 01 44 39
03 50.* www.zara.fr
One of several branches.

Zucca
8 Rue St-Roch 75001.
Map 12 E1.
Tel 01 44 58 98 88.

CHILDREN'S CLOTHES

Agnès B
(See p325).

Baby Dior
(See p325 Christian Dior).

Bonpoint
320 Rue St-Honoré
75001.
Map 13 A2.
Tel 01 49 27 94 82.
www.bonpoint.com

Bonton
82 rue de Grenelle
75007. **Map** 10 F3.
Tel 01 44 39 09 20.
www.bonton.fr

Du Pareil au Même
1 Rue St-Denis 75001.
Map 13 A3. *Tel 01 42 36
07 57.* www.dpam.fr

Froment-Leroyer
7 Rue Vavin 75006.
Map 16 E1.
Tel 01 43 54 33 15.
www.froment-leroyer.fr
One of several branches.

Jacadi
17 Rue Tronchet 75008.
Map 5 C5.
Tel 01 42 65 84 98.
www.jacadi.fr

Kenzo
(See p325).

Petit Bateau
116 Ave des Champs
Elysées 75008.
Map 4 E4.
Tel 01 40 74 02 03.
www.petit-bateau.com

**Six Pieds Trois
Pouces**
78 Ave de Wagram
75017. **Map** 4 E2.
Tel 01 46 22 81 64.
One of several branches.

Tartine et Chocolat
84 Rue du Faubourg-St-
Honoré 75008.
Map 5 B5.
Tel 01 45 62 44 04.

Teddy's
38 Rue François-1er
75008. **Map** 10 F1.
Tel 01 47 20 79 79.

MEN'S CLOTHES

APC
38 Rue Madame 75006.
Map 12 E5. *Tel 01 45 48
12 77.* www.apc.fr

Celio
26 Rue du Faubourg
St-Antoine 75012.
Map 14 E4.
Tel 01 43 42 31 68.
One of several branches.

Charvet
28 Place Vendôme 75001.
Map 6 D5.
Tel 01 42 60 30 70.

Francesco Smalto
44 Rue François-1er
75008. **Map** 4 F5.
Tel 01 47 20 70 63.
www.smalto.com

Gianni Versace
41 Rue François Premier
75008. **Map** 10 F1.
Tel 01 47 42 88 02.
www.versace.com

Giorgio Armani
(See p325).

**Jean-Charles de
Castelbajac**
10 Rue de Vauvilliers
75001. *Tel 01 55 34 10
10.* www.jedecastel
bajac.com

Kenzo
(See p325).

Lanvin
22 Rue du Faubourg
St-Honoré 75008.
Map 14 F4.
Tel 01 44 71 31 33.
www.lanvin.com
One of several branches.

Loft Design By
18 Ave Franklin Roosevelt
75008. **Map** 5 A5.
Tel 01 45 61 12 37.
One of several branches.

Michel Axael
44 Rue du Dragon 75006.
Map 12 E4.
Tel 01 42 84 13 86.

Olivier Strelli
7 Blvd Raspail 75007.
Map 12 D4.
Tel 01 45 44 62 21.
www.strelli.be
One of two branches.

Paul Smith
22 Blvd Raspail 75007.
Map 12 D4.
Tel 01 53 63 08 74.

Pierre Cardin
(See p325).

Ron Orb
147 Rue du Temple
75003.
Map 13 B2.
Tel 01 40 28 09 33.

Y-3
47 Rue Etienne
Marcel 75001.
Tel 01 45 08 82 45.

Yves Saint Laurent
6 and 12 Pl St-Sulpice
75006.
Map 12 D4.
Tel 01 43 29 43 00.

LIFESTYLE STORES

Colette
(See p325).

Montaigne Market
57 Ave Montaigne
75008. **Map** 5 A5.
Tel 01 42 56 58 58.
www.montaigne
market.com

Spree
16 Rue de La Vieuville
75018.
Map 6 F1.
Tel 01 42 23 41 40.
www.spree.fr

VINTAGE AND SECOND-HAND STORES

Alternatives
18 Rue du Roi-de-Sicile
75004.
Map 13 C3.
Tel 01 42 78 31 50.

**Depôt-Vente de
Buci-Bourbon**
6 Rue de Bourbon-le-
Château 75006.
Map 12 E4.
Tel 01 46 34 45 05.

Didier Ludot
19-24 Galerie
Montpensier 75001.
Map 12 E1.
Tel 01 42 96 06 56.

**Le Mouton à
Cinq Pattes**
8 Rue St-Placide
75006.
Map 11 C5.
Tel 01 45 48 86 26.
One of several branches.

Réciproque
95 Rue de la Pompe
75016. **Map** 9 A1.
Tel 01 47 04 30 28.

JEWELLERY

Agatha
97 Rue de Rennes 75006.
Map 12 D5.
Tel 01 45 48 92 57.
www.agatha.fr
One of several branches.

JEWELLERY

The *couture* houses probably stock some of the best jewellery and scarves. **Chanel's** jewels are classics while **Hermès** offers elegant designs in natural materials. **Boutique YSL** is a great place for accessories.

Among the main expensive Paris jewellery outlets are **Boucheron**, **Mauboussin** and **Poiray**. They are for the serious jewellery buyer. Other top retailers include **Harry Winston** and **Cartier**. **Dinh Van** has some quirky pieces, whilst **Mikimoto** is a must for pearls and **H Stern** has some innovative designs using semi-precious and precious stones. For a range of more unusual jewellery and accessories, try the **Daniel Swarovski Boutique**, which is owned by the Swarovksi crystal family.

Trends and imitations can be found around the Marais, the Bastille and Les Halles, in that order for quality. Those of note include **Scooter**, where chic young Parisians shop, **Métal Pointu's**, which sells great fantasy jewellery, and **Agatha** for copies of Chanel designs and basics.

Imitations in precious metals are available at **Verlor**, a cheap jeweller where one can find copies of pieces by top jewellers using genuine stones. Another reasonably priced Parisian jeweller is **Pietra Dura**, where stunning, hand-made pieces, which incorporate semi-precious stones, can be found at affordable prices.

SHOES, BAGS AND BELTS

Fair trade trainers (organic cotton and natural Amazonian rubber) by Veja can be found in **Le Bon Marché**. Go to **Repetto** for cult pumps in a host of colours, or **Sidonie Larizzi** who will make up shoes from one of numerous leather swatches. Current favourites with the fashion set include **Michel Perry**, **Bruno Frisoni** and **Robert Clergerie**. **Christian Louboutin** and **Rodolphe Ménudier** are mainstays for sexy stilettos.

Carel stocks smart basics, **Cosmo Paris** and Vivaldi sell trendy models and **Jonak** is a must for good imitations of designer footwear. **Bowen** has a selection of traditional men's shoes and **Fenestrier** creates chic versions of classics, although **Berluti** is the last word in elegance for many Parisian men.

Beautifully made leather goods can be found at **Longchamp**, **Gucci** and **Hermès**, who still make special orders in their Paris workshops. For ladies' hand-bags, nothing beats **Chanel** or **Dior** at the top end of the scale, although **Goyard** comes close. Mid-range bags from **Furla** are a great compromise, as are the colourful bags from **Karine Dupont**. Fabric bags from **Jamin Puech**, **Vanessa Bruno** or **Hervé Chapelier** are a feature in every chic Parisian closet. For a great range of shoes, accessories and bags at reasonable prices, **Lollipops** boutiques can be found across Paris.

HATS

One of Paris's favourite milliners is **Marie Mercié**. **Anthony Peto** now creates men's hats at her old shop in Rue Tiquetonne. For quirky creations in wool try **Grevi** who sell matching scarves and gloves.

LINGERIE

For a delightful selection of beautiful, modern lingerie go to **Fifi Chachnil**, whose shop is filled with colourful underwear. **La Boîte à Bas** sells fine French stockings, whereas **Princesse Tam Tam** offers trendy, quality items at reasonable prices, whilst divine designer underwear can be found at cult store **Sabbia Rosa**. The ultimate in magnificent Parisian lingerie can be bought off the peg or made to order at **Cadolle**, the store which invented the bra. For a more raunchy number, try **Yoba** on the Rue du Marché St-Honoré.

SIZE CHART

For Australian sizes follow the British and American conversions.

Children's clothing

French	2–3	4–5	6–7	8–9	10–11	12	14	14+ (years)
British	2–3	4–5	6–7	8–9	10–11	12	14	14+ (years)
American	2–3	4–5	6–6x	7–8	10–11	12	14	16 (size)

Children's shoes

French	24	25½	27	28	29	30	32	33	34
British	7	8	9	10	11	12	13	1	2
American	7½	8½	9½	10½	11½	12½	13½	1½	2½

Women's dresses coats and skirts

French	34	36	38	40	42	44	46
British	6	8	10	12	14	16	18
American	2	4	6	8	10	12	14

Women's blouses and sweaters

French	81	84	87	90	93	96	99 (cms)
British	31	32	34	36	38	40	42 (inches)
American	6	8	10	12	14	16	18 (size)

Women's shoes

French	36	37	38	39	40	41
British	3	4	5	6	7	8
American	5	6	7	8	9	10

Men's suits

French	44	46	48	50	52	54	56	58
British	34	36	38	40	42	44	46	48
American	34	36	38	40	42	44	46	48

Men's shirts

French	36	38	39	41	42	43	44	45
British	14	15	15½	16	16½	17	17½	18
American	14	15	15½	16	16½	17	17½	18

Men's shoes

French	39	40	41	42	43	44	45	46
British	6	7	7½	8	9	10	11	12
American	7	7½	8	8½	9½	10½	11	11½

DIRECTORY

Boucheron
26 Pl Vendôme 75001.
Map 6 D5.
Tel 01 42 61 58 16.
www.boucheron.com
One of several branches.

Boutique YSL
38 Rue du Faubourg-St-
Honoré 75008. **Map** 5
C5. *Tel 01 42 65 74 59.*

Cartier
13 Rue de la Paix 75002.
Map 6 D5. *Tel 01 58 18
23 00.* www.cartier.fr
One of several branches.

Chanel
(See p325).

**Daniel Swarovski
Boutique**
52 Rue Bonaparte 75006.
Map 12 E3. *Tel 01 56 24
15 60.* www.daniel-
swarovski.com

Dinh Van
16 Rue de la Paix 75002.
Map 6 D5.
Tel 01 42 61 74 49.
www.dinhvan.com
One of several branches.

H Stern
3 Rue Castiglione 75001.
Map 12 D1. *Tel 01 42 60
22 27.* www.hstern.net
One of several branches.

Harry Winston
29 Ave Montaigne
75008. **Map** 10 F1.
Tel 01 47 20 03 09.
www.harrywinston.com

Mauboussin
20 Pl Vendôme 75001.
Map 6 D5.
Tel 01 44 55 10 00.
www.mauboussin.com

Métal Pointu's
2 Rue du Marché St-
Honoré 75001. **Map** 12
D1. *Tel 01 42 60 01 42.*
www.metalpointus.com

Mikimoto
8 Pl Vendôme 75001.
Map 6 D5.
Tel 01 42 60 33 55.
www.mikimoto.fr

Pietra Dura
6 Rue de Ponthieu 75008.
Map 5 A5.
Tel 01 45 63 18 18.

Poiray
1 Rue de la Paix 75002.
Map 6 D5.
Tel 01 42 61 70 58.
www.poiray.com

Scooter
10 Rue de Turbigo 75001.
Map 13 A1.
Tel 01 45 08 50 54.
One of several branches.

Verlor
57 Rue de Rivoli 75001.
Map 13 A1.
Tel 01 40 41 03 26.

SHOES, BAGS
AND BELTS

Berluti
26 Rue Marbeuf 75008.
Map 4 F5. *Tel 01 53 93
97 97.* www.berluti.com

Bowen
46 Rue Pierre Charon
75008.
Map 4 F5.
Tel 01 47 20 45 90.

Bruno Frisoni
34 Rue de Grenelle
75007. **Map** 12 D4.
Tel 01 42 84 12 30.

Carel
4 Rue Tronchet 75008.
Map 6 D4.
Tel 01 43 66 21 58.
One of several branches.

Christian Louboutin
38-40 Rue de Grenelle
75007.
Map 10 F3.
Tel 01 42 22 33 07.

Cosmo Paris
25 Rue du Four 75006.
Map 12 E4.
Tel 01 56 24 15 49.

Fenestrier
23 Rue du Cherche-Midi
75006. **Map** 12 D5.
Tel 01 42 22 66 02.
www.jfenestrier.com

Furla
8 Rue de Sèvres 75006.
Map 11 C5.
Tel 01 40 49 06 44.
www.furla.com
One of several branches.

Goyard
233 Rue St-Honoré
75001. **Map** 5 C5.
Tel 01 42 60 57 04.
www.goyard.com

Gucci
23 Rue Royale 75001.
Map 5 C5.
Tel 01 44 94 14 70.
www.gucci.com

Hermès
(See p325).

Hervé Chapelier
1bis Rue du Vieux-
Colombier 75006.
Map 12 D4.
Tel 01 44 07 06 50.

Jamin Puech
61 Rue de Hauteville
75010. **Map** 7 B4.
Tel 01 40 22 08 32.

Jonak
70 Rue de Rennes 75006.
Map 16 D1.
Tel 01 45 48 27 11.

Karine Dupont
16 Rue du Cherche-Midi
75006.
Map 12 D4.
Tel 01 42 84 06 30.

Le Bon Marché
24 Rue de Sevres
75007.
Map 11 C5.
Tel 01 44 39 80 00.

Lollipops
60 Rue Tiquetonne
75002.
Map 13 A1.
Tel 01 42 33 15 72.
www.lollipops.fr

Longchamp
21 Rue du Vieux
Colombier 75006.
Map 12 D4.
Tel 01 42 22 74 75.
www.longchamp.com

Michel Perry
42 Rue de Grenelle
75007. **Map** 10 F3.
Tel 01 42 84 12 45.

Repetto
22 Rue de la Paix 75002.
Map 6 D5.
Tel 01 44 71 83 12.

Robert Clergerie
5 Rue du Cherche-Midi
75006. **Map** 12 D1.
Tel 01 45 48 75 47.

Rodolphe Ménudier
14 Rue de Castiglione
75001. **Map** 12 D1.
Tel 01 42 60 86 27.

Vanessa Bruno
(See p327).

Vivaldi
38 Rue de Rivoli 75001.
Map 13 A2.
Tel 01 44 54 08 56.

HATS

Anthony Peto
56 Rue Tiquetonne
75002.
Map 13 A1.
Tel 01 40 26 60 68.

Grevi
1 Place Alphonse-Deville
75006. **Map** 14 D3.
Tel 01 42 22 02 49.
www.grevi.com

Marie Mercié
23 Rue St-Sulpice 75006.
Map 12 E4.
Tel 01 43 26 45 83.

LINGERIE

La Boîte à Bas
27 Rue Boissy-d'Anglas
75008. **Map** 5 C5.
Tel 01 42 66 26 85.

Cadolle
4 Rue Cambon 75001.
Map 6 D5.
Tel 01 42 60 94 22.

Fifi Chachnil
68 Rue Jean-Jacques
Rousseau 75001.
Map 12 F2.
Tel 01 42 21 19 93.

Princesse Tam Tam
5 Rue Montmartre
75001.
Map 13 A1.
Tel 01 45 08 50 69.

Sabbia Rosa
73 Rue des Sts-Pères
75006. **Map** 12 D4.
Tel 01 45 48 88 37.

Yoba
11 Rue du Marché
St-Honoré 75001.
Map 12 D1.
Tel 01 40 41 04 06.

Gifts and Souvenirs

Paris has a wealth of stylish gifts and typical souvenirs, from designer accessories and perfume to French foods and Eiffel Tower paperweights. Shops on the Rue de Rivoli and around major tourist attractions such as Nôtre Dame or Sacré Coeur offer a range of cheap holiday trinkets. **Les Drapeaux de France** sells historic uniformed and costumed figurines. For upscale mementoes, try quality reproductions of artwork and jewellery in museum boutiques – **Le Musée du Louvre**, **Musée d'Orsay**, **Les Arts Decoratifs** or **Musée Carnavalet**.

GIFTS

Au Printemps has excellent own-brand accessories, especially ladies' handbags. The luxury floor is ideal for window-shopping or high-end purchases such as Tiffany jewellery or Cartier watches. It also stocks small, reasonably-priced items.

For those looking to take home gastronomic tasters, the famed food hall at **Le Bon Marché**, La Grande Epicerie, offers anything and everything you might need for a gourmet feast or quick snack.

Galeries Lafayette now boasts the world's biggest lingerie department.

PERFUME AND COSMETICS

Many shops advertise discounted perfume and cosmetics. Some even offer duty-free perfume to shoppers from outside the EU, with discounts on the marked prices when you show your passport. They include **Eiffel Shopping** near the Eiffel Tower. The **Sephora** chain has a big selection, or try the department stores for a range of designers' perfumes. In particular, the beauty department at **Au Printemps** is one of Europe's biggest with one of the world's largest perfume selections. It stocks many beauty brands that are hard to find elsewhere.

If you fancy stepping back in time, **Detaille 1905** is the place for you. This old-fashioned perfumery filled to the brim with fragrant goodies personifies Belle Epoque style and charm. The shop's own range of six main fragrances for women and for men is still made from original recipes.

Parfums Caron also has many scents created over 100 years ago, which are unavailable elsewhere, so this is the place to find exclusive presents that you will almost certainly decide to keep for yourself. Beautifully packaged perfumes made from natural essences are available from **Annick Goutal**. **Guerlain** has the ultimate in beauty care, while the elegant shops of **L'Artisan Parfumeur** specialize in exquisitely packaged scents that evoke specific memories. They have also reissued favourites from the past, including perfume made to exactly the same formula as one that was worn at the court of Versailles. **Frédéric Malle** is another big name in top-of-the-range scent. Exclusive perfumes can also be found in the beautiful surroundings of the **Salons du Palais Royal**, an upscale Shiseido store. Serge Lutens, the company's creative director and a renowned parfumier, creates exquisite and exotic scents which can only be bought in this particular store.

Paris is also home to several *haute* cosmetics designers. One of the most renowned is Terry de Gunzberg, whose store **By Terry** stocks fantastic products. Personalize your gift by having a message inscribed on the sleek, silver packaging.

HOUSEHOLD GOODS

Though certain items are obviously rather delicate to carry home, it is difficult to ignore some of the world's most elegant tableware, found in Paris's chic shops. If you are wary of loading up your holdall with breakable pieces, many shops will arrange to ship crockery overseas.

Luxury household goods can be found on the Rue Royale, where many of the best shops are located. They sell items such as rustic china and reproduction and modern silverware. **Lalique's** Art Nouveau and Art Deco glass sculptures are collected all over the world. Impeccable silverware including fine photograph frames and even chopsticks comes from **Christofle**.

For a great variety of porcelain and crystal, try **La Cristallerie Paradis**, which stocks Baccarat, Daum and Limoges crystal, or go to **Baccarat** itself. Baccarat also has a boutique on the Place de la Madeleine. The interior designer **Pierre Frey** has a showroom displaying fabrics which have been made into a fabulous array of cushions, bedspreads and tablecloths. Excellent quality bed linen can also be found at **Yves Delorme**.

La Chaise Longue has a selection of well-designed *objets*, along with fun gift ideas. **Ekobo** sells stylish, ethically- and ecologically-produced tableware and decorative items. **DOM** and **Muskhane** stock hip, ethnic accessories for funky flats. The extensive interior design store at **Galeries Lafayette** has everything a proud home-owner could need from fancy mops to cutting-edge three-piece suites. **Sentou** stores are full of chic designer pieces for Parisian living. Sentou Raspail, on the Left Bank, offers the store's complete range while Sentou Marais focuses on lighting and furniture.

Kitchen equipment which can't be beaten, including copper pans, comes from **E. Dehillerin**. A must-have item in many Parisian homes is a scented candle from **Diptyque**. *Figuier* is their most popular fragrance.

The basement at **BHV** *(see p321)* is full of all sorts of tools and equipment for doing up your house and sprucing up the garden.

BOOKS, MAGAZINES AND NEWSPAPERS

Many English and American publications can be found at large magazine stands or at some of the bookshops listed. If French is no obstacle the weeklies *Pariscope, L'Officiel des Spectacles* and *Télérama*'s Paris supplement *Sortir* have the most comprehensive listings for the city.

The *International Herald Tribune*, an English-language daily newspaper, is published in Paris and contains good American news coverage. The *Paris Voice* webzine and the bi-weekly FUSAC *(France–USA Contacts* small ads magazine) are also published in English.

Some of the large department stores have a book section *(see* Department Stores *p321)*. There is a large branch of **WHSmith** and **Galignani** was the first English bookshop to be established in Europe in 1801. The **San Francisco Book Company** offers English language books at good prices and **Shakespeare & Co** is a Left Bank legend facing Notre Dame. The American-influenced **Village Voice** has a good literary and intellectual selection of new books, while the **Abbey Bookshop** does the same for second-hand books. **Tea and Tattered Pages** is a British second hand bookshop. French-language bookshops include **La Hune**, specializing in art, design, architecture, photography, fashion and cinema; **Gibert Joseph**, selling general and educational books; and **Le Divan** which has social science, psychology, literature and poetry sections. The **Red Wheelbarrow Bookstore** sells a wide range of French–English bilingual books set in France as well as a great selection of classics translated from French. **I Love My Blender** on Rue du Temple is dedicated to English language authors and sells wonderful gifts.

FLOWERS

Some Parisian florists such as **Pascal Mutel** are very well known, so be sure to buy one of their signature vases. **Bouquets Passionnement** and **Monceau Fleurs** offer a good selection at reasonable prices; and **Mille Feuilles** is the place to go to in the Marais. *(See* also Specialist Shops *p332)*. Stunning silk flowers can be found at **Hervé Gambs**, whose chic store is brimming over with beautiful artifical blooms.

SPECIALIST SHOPS

For cigars, **A La Civette** is perhaps Paris's most beautiful tobacconist. It is also probably the most devoted to its wares and has humidified shop windows to keep its merchandise in top condition. Go to **A L'Olivier** in the Rue de Rivoli for a wonderful selection of exotic oils and vinegar. Or, if honey is your favourite condiment, try **La Maison du Miel** where you can buy all sorts of fine honeys, including varieties made from lavender and acacia flowers. You can also buy refreshing beeswax soap and a variety of candles here.

Mariage Frères has become a cult favourite for its 350 varieties of tea; it also sells a number of teapots and its tea shop serves up many tempting treats *(see p318)*.

Couture fabrics can be purchased from a range at **Wolff et Descourtis**. For an unusual gift of traditional French card games or tarot cards, go to **Jeux Descartes**.

One of the world's most famous and delightful toyshops is **Au Nain Bleu**, while the name **Cassegrain** is synonymous with high-quality stationery and paper products. **Calligrane** sells a tempting range of high-quality desk accessories and paper products.

Hidden away down an atmospheric passage, **Pep's** repairs all broken umbrellas and parasols in France's only brolly hospital.

For the ultimate in eccentric shopping visit **Deyrolle**, Paris's famous taxidermist. Where else could you find the right gift for the person who has everything.

DIRECTORY

Eiffel Shopping
9 Ave de Suffren 75007.
Map 10 D3.
Tel 01 45 66 55 30.

Frédéric Malle
21 Rue du Mont Thabor
75001. **Map** 12 D1.
Tel 01 42 22 77 22.

Guerlain
68 Ave des Champs-
Elysées 75008. **Map** 4 F5.
Tel 01 45 62 52 57.
www.guerlain.com
One of several branches.

Parfums Caron
34 Ave Montaigne
75008. **Map** 10 F1.
Tel 01 47 23 40 82.

**Salons du Palais
Royal Shiseido**
142 Galerie de Valois
75001. **Map** 12 F1.
Tel 01 49 27 09 09.

Sephora
70 Ave des Champs-
Elysées 75008.
Map 11 B1. *Tel 01 53 93
22 50.* **www**.sephora.fr
One of several branches.

HOUSEHOLD
GOODS

Baccarat
11 Pl de la Madeleine
75008. **Map** 5 C5.
Tel 01 42 65 36 26.
www.baccarat.com
(See also p201).

La Chaise Longue
30 Rue Croix-des-Petits-
Champs 75001. **Map** 12
F1. *Tel 01 42 96 32 14.*
One of several branches.

Christofle
24 Rue de la Paix 75002.
Map 6 D5.
Tel 01 42 65 62 43.
www.christofle.com
One of several branches.

Diptyque
34 Bld St Germain 75006.
Map 13 B5.
Tel 01 43 26 77 44.
www.diptyqueparis.com

DOM
21 Rue Ste-Croix de la
Bretonnerie 75004.
Map 13 B3.
Tel 01 42 71 08 00.

E. Dehillerin
18 Rue Coquillière 75001.
Map 12 F1.
Tel 01 42 36 53 13.
www.e-dehillerin.com

Ekobo
4 Rue Hérold, 75001.
Map 12 F1.
Tel 01 45 08 47 43.

**La Cristallerie
Paradis**
17 bis Rue de Paradis
75010. **Map** 7 B4.
Tel 01 48 24 72 15.

Lalique
11 Rue Royale 75008.
Map 5 C5.
Tel 01 53 05 12 81.
www.cristallalique.fr

Muskhane
3 Rue Pastourelle 75003.
Map 13 C2.
Tel 01 42 71 07 00.

Pierre Frey
47 Rue des Petits Champs
75001. **Map** 5 C5.
Tel 01 44 77 36 00.
www.pierrefrey.com

Point à la Ligne
67 Ave Victor Hugo
75116. **Map** 3 B5.
Tel 01 45 00 87 01.

Sentou
26 Blvd Raspail 75007.
Map 12 D4.
Tel 01 45 49 00 05.
29 Rue François Miron
75004. **Map** 13 C3.
Tel 01 42 78 50 60.

Yves Delorme
8 Rue Vavin 75006.
Map 16 D1.
Tel 01 44 07 23 14.

BOOKS,
MAGAZINES AND
NEWSPAPERS

Abbey Bookshop
29 Rue de la Parcheminerie
75005. **Map** 13 A4.
Tel 01 46 33 16 24.

Le Divan
203 Rue de la Convention
75015. **Map** 12 E3.
Tel 01 53 68 90 68.

Galignani
224 Rue de Rivoli 75001.
Map 13 A2.
Tel 01 42 60 76 07.

Gibert Joseph
26 Blvd St-Michel 75006.
Map 12 F5.
Tel 01 44 41 88 88.

La Hune
170 Blvd St-Germain
75006. **Map** 12 D4.
Tel 01 45 48 35 85.

I Love My Blender
36 Rue du Temple 75004.
Map 13 C2.
Tel 01 42 77 50 32.
www.ilovemyblender.fr

**The Red
Wheelbarrow
Bookstore**
22 Rue St-Paul 75004.
Map 14 D4. *Tel 01 48 04
75 08.* **www**.thered
wheelbarrow.com

**San Francisco Book
Company**
17 Rue M le Prince
75006. **Map** 12 F5.
Tel 01 43 29 15 70.

Shakespeare & Co
37 Rue de la Bûcherie
75005. **Map** 13 A4.
Tel 01 43 25 40 93.

**Tea and Tattered
Pages**
24 Rue Mayet 75006.
Map 15 B1.
Tel 01 40 65 94 35.

Village Voice
6 Rue Princesse 75006.
Map 12 E4. *Tel 01 46 33
36 47.* **www**.villagevoice
bookshop.com

WHSmith
248 Rue de Rivoli 75001.
Map 11 C1.
Tel 01 44 77 88 99.

FLOWERS

**Bouquets
Passionnement**
53 Ave Kléber 75016.
Map 9 C1.
Tel 01 47 20 87 09.

Hervé Gambs
60 Blvd Beaumarchais
75011. **Map** 14 E3.
Tel 02 41 62 68 68.

Monceau Fleurs
84 Blvd Raspail 75006.
Map 12 D4. *Tel 01 45 48
70 10.* **www**.monceau
fleurs.com

Pascal Mutel
6 Carrefour de l'Odéon
75006. **Map** 12 F4.
Tel 01 43 26 02 56.
www.pascalmutel.com

SPECIALIST SHOPS

A La Civette
157 Rue St-Honoré
75001. **Map** 12 F2.
Tel 01 42 96 04 99.

A L'Olivier
23 Rue de Rivoli 75004.
Map 13 C3. *Tel 01 48 04
86 59.* **www**.alolivier.com

Au Nain Bleu
5 Blvd Malesherbes
75008. **Map** 5 B3.
Tel 01 42 65 20 00.
www.aunainbleu.com
One of several branches.

Calligrane
6 Rue du Pont-Louis-
Philippe 75004. **Map** 13
B4. *Tel 01 48 04 09 00.*

Cassegrain
190 Blvd Haussmann
75008. **Map** 5 A4.
Tel 01 42 60 20 08.
www.cassegrain.fr

Deyrolle
46 Rue du Bac 75007.
Map 12 D3.
Tel 01 42 22 30 07.

Jeux Descartes
52 Rue des Écoles 75005.
Map 13 A5.
Tel 01 43 26 79 83.
One of three branches.

La Maison du Miel
24 Rue Vignon 75009.
Map 6 D5.
Tel 01 47 42 26 70.
www.maisondumiel.com

Mariage Frères
30 Rue du Bourg-Tibourg
75004. **Map** 13 C3.
Tel 01 42 72 28 11.
www.mariagefreres.com
One of several branches.

Pep's
223 Rue St Martin 75003.
Map 8 E4.
Tel 01 42 78 11 67.
www.peps-paris.com.fr

Wolff et Descourtis
18 Galerie Vivienne
75002. **Map** 12 F1.
Tel 01 42 61 80 84.

Food and Drink

Paris is as famous for food as it is for fashion. Gastronomic treats include *foie gras*, cold meats from the *charcuterie*, cheese and wine. Certain streets are so overflowing with food shops that you can put together a picnic for 20 in no time: try the Rue Montorgueil *(see p339)*. The Rue Rambuteau, running either side of the Pompidou Centre, has a marvellous row of fishmongers, cheese delicatessens and shops selling prepared foods. *(See also What to Eat and Drink in Paris pp296–9* and Cafés, Tea Salons and Bars *pp316–19.)*

BREAD AND CAKES

There is a vast range of breads and pastries in France's capital. The *baguette* is often translated as "French bread"; a *bâtard* is similar but thicker, while a *ficelle* is thinner. A *fougasse* is a crusty, flat loaf made from *baguette* dough, often filled with onions, cheese, herbs or spices. Since most French bread contains no fat it goes stale quickly: the sooner you eat it, the better. The French would never eat day-old bread so be sure to be up in time to make it to the bakery for breakfast!

Croissants can be bought *ordinaire* or *au beurre* – the latter is flakier and more buttery. *Pain au chocolat* is a chocolate-filled pastry eaten for breakfast and *chausson aux pommes* is filled with apples. There are also pear, plum and rhubarb variations. A *pain aux raisins* is a bread-like wheel filled with custard and raisins.

Poilâne sells perhaps the only bread in Paris known by the name of its baker (the late Lionel, brother of Max) and his hearty wholewheat bread is tremendously popular, with freshly baked loaves being jetted around the world to satisfy the cravings of certain film stars. There are always big queues at the weekend and around 4pm when a fresh batch comes out of the oven.

Many think **Ganachaud** bakes the best bread in Paris. Thirty different kinds, including ingredients such as walnuts and fruit, are made in the old-fashioned ovens.

Although **Les Panetons** is part of a larger chain, it is one of the best of its kind with a broad range of breads. Favourites here include five-grain bread, sesame rolls and *mouchoir aux pommes*, a variation on the traditional *chausson*.

It is very important to remember that every Parisian has a favourite neighbourhood bakery, so when you are buying bread locally simply plump for the shop with the longest queues.

Many of the Jewish delicatessens have the best ryes and the only pumpernickels in town. One of the best known is **Sacha Finkelsztajn**.

Le Moulin de la Vierge uses a wood fire to bake organic breads and rich pound cakes. **Boulangerie de l'Ouest** is second only to **Max Poilâne** in the Montparnasse area with *baguettes*, *fougasses*, cakes and pastries. **Pâtisserie Secco** sells a good selection of filled *baguettes*, salads and excellent cakes. **Pierre Hermé** is to cakes what Chanel is to fashion, while **Ladurée** macaroons are legendary.

CHOCOLATE

Like all food in France, chocolate is to be savoured. **Christian Constant's** low-sugar creations are made with pure cocoa and are known to connoisseurs. **Dalloyau** makes all types of chocolate and is not too expensive (it's also known for its pâtisserie and cold meats). **Fauchon** is world famous for its luxury food products. Its chocolates are excellent, as is the pâtisserie. **Lenôtre** makes classic truffles and pralines. Robert Linxe at **La Maison du Chocolat** is

constantly inventing fresh, rich chocolates with mouth-watering exotic ingredients. **Richart** boasts beautifully presented and hugely-expensive chocolates, which are usually coated with dark chocolate or liqueur-filled. **Debauve & Gallais** are best known for their wonderful and delicious glacé chestnut treats *(marron glacés)*.

CHARCUTERIE AND FOIE GRAS

Charcuteries often sell cheese, snails, truffles, smoked salmon, caviar and wine as well as cold meats. **Fauchon** has a good grocery, as does the department store **Le Bon Marché**. **Hédiard** is a luxury shop similar to Fauchon, and **Maison de la Truffe** sells *foie gras* and cured salami sausages as well as truffles. For Beluga caviar, Georgian tea and Russian vodka goto **Petrossian**.

The Lyon and Auvergne regions of France are the best known for their *charcuterie*. Examples can be bought from **C G Traiteur**. **Aux Vrais Produits d'Auvergne** has a number of outlets where you can stock up on dried and fresh sausages and delicious Cantal cheese (rather like Cheddar). **Pou** is a sparklingly clean and popular shop selling *pâté en croute* (pâté baked in pastry), *boudins* (black and white puddings), Lyonnais sausages, ham and *foie gras*. Just off the Champs-Elysées, **Vignon** has superb *foie gras* and Lyonnais sausages as well as popular prepared foods.

Together with truffles and *foie gras*, with the ultimate in gourmet food, from cheaper *paté de foie gras* to the more expensive whole liver itself. Though most specialist food shops sell *foie gras*, you can be sure of quality at **Comtesse du Barry**, which has six outlets in Paris. **Divay** is relatively inexpensive and will ship overseas. **Labeyrie** has a range of beautifully-packaged *foie gras* suitable for giving as presents.

CHEESE

Although Camembert is undoubtedly a favourite, there is an overwhelming range of cheeses available.

A friendly *fromager* will help you choose. **Marie-Anne Cantin** is one of the leading figures in the fight to protect traditional production methods, and her fine cheeses are available at the shop that she inherited from her father. Some say that **Alléosse** is the best cheese delicatessen in Paris. It is an Aladdin's cave of cheeses made according to traditional methods and matured in the shop's own cellars. **Crèmerie Quatrehomme** sells farm-made cheeses, many of which are in danger of becoming extinct; these include a rare and delicious truffle Brie (when in season). **Le Jardin Fromager** is one of the best shops in Paris for all types of cheese – the *chèvre* (goat's cheese) is particularly good, and outside on the pavement the daily specials are offered at remarkably reasonable prices. **Barthelemy** in the Rue de Grenelle has a truly exceptional Roquefort. **Androuet** is a Parisian institution with several branches across the city. Try a pungent Munster or a really ripe Brie. A charming cheese shop on the bustling Rue Montorgeuil market street, **La Fermette**, offers a dazzling array of dairy products, which the helpful and friendly staff will happily vacuum-pack for the journey home. This is imperative when bringing cheese through customs, so don't forget to ask your *fromager* to wrap it for you. Well-heeled locals queue in the street to buy oozing *livarot* and sharp *chèvre* from **La Fromagerie d'Auteuil**.

WINE

The chain store which has practically cornered the every-day tippling market is **Nicolas** – there's a branch in every neighbourhood with a range of wines to suit all pockets. As a rule, the sales-people are knowledgeable

and helpful. Try the charming **Legrand Filles et Fils** (*see p319*) for a carefully chosen selection. **Caves Taillevent** on the Rue du Faubourg-St-Honoré is worth a sightseeing tour. It is an enormous, overwhelming cellar with some of the most expensive wine. **Cave Péret** on the Rue Daguerre has a vast selection of wines and can offer personal advice to help you with your purchase. The beautiful **Ryst-Dupeyron**, in the St-Germain quarter, displays whiskies, wines, ports, and Monsieur Ryst's own Armagnac. He will even personalize a bottle for that special occasion.

Other great wine stores include **Lavinia** (*see p319*), which is the largest in Europe, and **Renaud Michel** at Nation, whose small boutique is well stocked and well connected. The staff in **Les Caves Augé** are also very knowledgeable and friendly.

CHAMPAGNE

Fabulous fizz can be found at most wine stores, but some know their bubbles better than others. The **Nicolas** chain, mentioned above, frequently has great offers on well-known brands so this is a good place to come and stock up on your favourite famous tipple. **La Cave des Martyrs** on the Rue des Martyrs is a friendly and well-stocked wine shop with charming staff to help you with your selection. The **Repaire de Bacchus** on the Rue d'Auteuil is a good place to go to for hard-to-find vintages. The *sommelier* here is very knowledgeable and able to provide excellent alternative advice if your preferred brand is out of stock. **Legrand Filles et Fils**, on the Rue de la Banque, is one of the few shops in Paris to stock Salon, a rare high-end champagne. They also sell champagne by Jacques Selosse which is little-known but well-loved by champagne connoisseurs. **Les Caves du Panthéon** on the Rue Saint Jacques, is a small but lovely wine shop which has a

particularly interesting selection of champagnes. Close by is **Ex Cellar France**, a corner wine-shop which is distinguished both by its charming and helpful staff and also by its frequent deals on champagne. The climate-controlled section of **Hédiard** at Place de la Madeleine is a good place to find rare, fine sparkling wines. **Caprices de l'Instant** is a fashionable wine store which stocks good quality champagne including bottles by some lesser-known producers. A stroll along the Boulevard St-Germain can be enhanced with a visit to **La Maison des Millésimes**, a wonderful store carrying excellent vintages of household-name champagnes.

OYSTERS

The ultimate aphrodisac for some, a slippery sea creature for others, there is no doubt that the once humble oyster can cause heated debate. In Paris, the argument tends to be over the best place to purchase the gourmet mollusc, with every seafood fan worth his platter claiming a favourite spot. It is, of course, important to get it right. A deciding factor for some is the grace with which your fishmonger will agree to open them for you. In general, a polite request will be honoured, although sometimes you may have to wait a while before being presented with a platter perfect for a picnic. The fishmonger on the Rue Cler market street, **La Sablaise Poissonnerie**, has an excellent reputation as does the **Poissonnerie du Dôme** in the city's 14th arrondissement. Over in the traditionally rough-and-ready area around the Rue Oberkampf, you can find excellent oysters at the **Poissonnerie Lacroix**. If you prefer to eat your oysters on the spot then head to an *huitrerie* (oyster bar) such as **L'Ecume Saint-Honoré** near chic Rue St-Honoré, where you can tuck into your oysters and a wide range of other shellfish straight away at the few tables tucked into the corner of the store.

DIRECTORY

BREAD AND CAKES

Boulangerie de l'Ouest
4 Pl Constantin Brancusi
75014. **Map** 15 C3.
Tel 01 43 21 76 18.

Ganachaud
226 Rue des Pyrénées
75020.
Tel 01 43 58 42 62.

Max Poilâne
87 Rue Brancion 75015.
Tel 01 48 28 45 90.

Le Moulin de la Vierge
105 Rue Vercingétorix
75014. **Map** 15 A4.
Tel 01 45 43 09 84.
One of several branches.

Les Panetons
113 Rue Mouffetard
75005. **Map** 17 B2.
Tel 01 47 07 12 08.

Pâtisserie Secco
20 Rue Jean-Nicot 75007.
Map 10 F2.
Tel 01 43 17 35 20.

Pierre Hermé
72 Rue Bonaparte 75006.
Map 12 E4.
Tel 01 43 54 47 77.

Poilâne
8 Rue du Cherche-Midi
75006.
Map 12 D4.
Tel 01 45 48 42 59.

Sacha Finkelsztajn
27 Rue des Rosiers
75004. **Map** 13 C3.
Tel 01 42 72 78 91.
www.laboutiquejaune.fr

CHOCOLATE

Christian Constant
37 Rue d'Assas 75006.
Map 16 E1.
Tel 01 53 63 15 15.

Dalloyau
101 Rue du Faubourg-
St-Honoré 75008.
Map 5 B5.
Tel 01 42 99 90 00.
One of several branches.

Debauve & Gallais
30 Rue des Saints-Pères
75007.
Map 12 D4.
Tel 01 45 48 54 67.
One of two branches.

Fauchon
26 Pl de la Madeleine
75008. **Map** 5 C5.
Tel 01 70 39 38 00.
www.fauchon.com

Lenôtre
36 Ave de la Motte
Picquet 75007. **Map** 10
F4. *Tel* 01 45 55 71 25.
One of several branches.

La Maison du Chocolat
225 Rue du Faubourg-St-
Honoré 75008. **Map** 4 E3.
Tel 01 42 27 39 44.

Richart
258 Blvd St-Germain
75007. **Map** 11 C2.
Tel 01 45 55 66 00.

CHARCUTERIE AND FOIE GRAS

C G Traiteur
58 Rue des Martyrs
75009. **Map** 6 F2.
Tel 01 48 78 96 45.

Comtesse du Barry
1 Rue de Sèvres 75006.
Map 12 D4. *Tel* 01 45 48
32 04. www.comtesse
dubarry.com
One of several branches.

Divay
4 Rue Bayen 75017. **Map**
4 D2. *Tel* 01 43 80 16 97.

Fauchon
26 Pl de la Madeleine
75008. **Map** 5 C5.
Tel 01 70 39 38 00.

Hédiard
21 Pl de la Madeleine
75008. **Map** 5 C5.
Tel 01 43 12 88 88.

Labeyrie
11 Rue d'Auteuil 75016.
Tel 01 42 24 17 62.

Maison de la Truffe
19 Pl de la Madeleine
75008. **Map** 5 C5.
Tel 01 42 65 53 22.

Petrossian
18 Blvd Latour-Maubourg
75007. **Map** 11 A2.
Tel 01 44 11 32 22.

Pou
16 Ave des Ternes 75017.
Map 4 D3.
Tel 01 43 80 19 24.

Vignon
14 Rue Marbeuf 75008.
Map 4 F5.
Tel 01 47 20 24 26.

CHEESE

Alléosse
13 Rue Poncelet 75017.
Map 4 E3.
Tel 01 46 22 50 45.

Androuët
134 Rue Mouffetard
75005. **Map** 17 B1.
Tel 01 45 87 85 05.
www.androuet.com

Barthelemy
51 Rue de Grenelle
75007. **Map** 12 D4.
Tel 01 45 48 56 75.

Crèmerie Quatrehomme
62 Rue de Sèvres 75007.
Map 11 C5.
Tel 01 47 34 33 45.

La Fermette
86 Rue Montorgueil
75002. **Map** 13 A1.
Tel 01 42 36 70 96.

La Fromagerie d'Auteuil
58 Rue d'Auteuil 75016.
Tel 01 45 25 07 10.

Le Jardin Fromager
53 Rue Oberkampf
75011. **Map** 14 E1.
Tel 01 48 05 19 96.

Marie-Anne Cantin
12 Rue du Champ-de-
Mars 75007. **Map** 10 F3.
Tel 01 45 50 43 94.

WINE

Cave Péret
6 Rue Daguerre 75014.
Map 16 D4.
Tel 01 43 22 08 64.

Les Caves Augé
116 Blvd Haussman
75008. **Map** 5 C1.
Tel 01 45 22 16 97.

Caves Taillevent
199 Rue du Faubourg-
St-Honoré 75008. **Map** 4
F3. *Tel* 01 45 61 14 09.

Nicolas
35 Blvd Malesherbes
75008. **Map** 5 C5.
Tel 01 42 65 00 85.
www.nicolas.com

Renaud Michel
12 Pl de la Nation 75012.
Map 9 A3.
Tel 01 43 07 98 93.

Ryst-Dupeyron
79 Rue du Bac 75007.
Map 12 D3.
Tel 01 45 48 80 93.

CHAMPAGNE

Caprices de l'Instant
12 Rue Jacques Coeur
75004. **Map** 14 E4.
Tel 01 40 27 89 00.

La Cave des Martyrs
39 Rue des Martyrs
75009. **Map** 6 F3.
Tel 01 40 16 80 27.

Les Caves du Panthéon
174 Rue St Jacques
75005. **Map** 13 A5.
Tel 01 46 33 90 35.

Ex Cellar France
25 Rue des Ecoles 75005.
Map 13 A5.
Tel 01 43 26 99 43.

Hédiard
21 Place de la Madeleine
75008. **Map** 5 C5.
Tel 01 43 12 88 88.

La Maison des Millésimes
137 Boulevard St-Germain
75006. **Map** 12 F4.
Tel 01 40 46 80 01.

Repaire de Bacchus
1 Rue de Maistre 75018.
Tel 01 46 06 80 84.

OYSTERS

L'Ecume Saint-Honoré
6 Rue du Marché St-
Honoré 75001. **Map** 12
D1. *Tel* 01 42 61 93 87.

Poissonnerie du Dôme
4 Rue Delambre 75014.
Map 16 D2.
Tel 01 43 35 23 95.

Poissonnerie Lacroix
44 Rue Oberkampf
75011. **Map** 14 E1.
Tel 01 47 00 93 13.

La Sablaise
28 Rue Cler 75007. **Map**
10 F3. *Tel* 01 45 51 61 78.

Art and Antiques

In Paris you can buy art and antiques either from shops and galleries with established reputations, or from flea markets and avant-garde galleries. Many of the prestigious antiques shops and galleries are located around the Rue du Faubourg-St-Honoré and are worth a visit even if you can't afford to buy. On the Left Bank is Le Carré Rive Gauche, an organization of 30 antiques dealers. *Objets d'art* over 50 years old, worth more than a given amount (values vary for all categories of art object), will require a *Certificat pour un bien culturel* to be exported anywhere in the world (provided by the vendor), plus a *licence d'exportation* for non-EU countries. Seek professional advice from the large antique shops.

EXPORTING

The Ministry of Culture designates *objets d'art*. Export licences are available from the **Comité National des Conseillers du Commerce Extérieur de la France**. The **Centre des Renseignements des Douanes** has a booklet, *Bulletin Officiel des Douanes*, with all the details.

MODERN CRAFTS AND FURNITURE

One of the best places for furniture and *objets d'art* is **Sentou**, where you can find objects and textiles, as well as furniture by contemporary designers. Another essential venue is the showroom of the Italian designer, **Giulio Cappellini**. **Le Viaduc des Arts** *(see pp270–71)* is a railway viaduct, each arch of which has been transformed into a shop front and workshop space. A great place for contemporary metal-work, tapestry, sculpture, ceramics and much more.

ANTIQUES AND OBJETS D'ART

If you wish to buy antiques, you might like to stroll around the areas that boast many galleries – in Le Carré Rive Gauche around Quai Malaquais, try **L'Arc en Seine** and **Anne-Sophie Duval** for Art Nouveau and Art Deco. Rue Jacob is still one of the best places to seek beautiful objects, antique or modern. Close to the Louvre, the **Louvre des Antiquaires** *(see p120)* sells expensive, quality furniture. On the Rue du Faubourg-St-Honoré you will find **Didier Aaron**, expert on furniture from the 17th and 18th centuries. **Village St-Paul** between the Quai des Célestins, the Rue Saint Paul and the Rue Charlemagne, is the most charming group of antiques shops and is also open on Sundays.

La Calinière has a superb range of *objets d'art* and old lighting fixtures. Glassware from the 19th century to the 1960s is sold at **Verreglass**. **Le Village Suisse** in the south of the city also groups many art and antiques dealers.

REPRODUCTIONS, POSTERS AND PRINTS

A beautiful, contemporary art gallery called **Artcurial** on the Place des Champs-Elysées has one of the best selections of international art periodicals, books and prints. On the Boulevard Saint Germain, **La Hune** is a popular bookshop, particularly for art publications. The museum bookshops, especially those in the Palais de Tokyo *(see p203)*, Louvre *(see p123)*, Musée d'Orsay *(see p145)* and Pompidou Centre *(see p111)* are good places to buy art books, posters and postcards.

Galerie Documents on the Rue de Seine sells original antique posters. Or leaf through the second-hand book stalls along the banks of the Seine.

ART GALLERIES

Established art galleries are located on or around the Avenue Montaigne. The **Louise Leiris** gallery on Rue de Téhran was founded in 1920 by D H Kahnweiler, the dealer who "discovered" both Georges Braque and Pablo Picasso.

Artcurial Gallery, located on the ground floor of the Hôtel Dassault, holds regular exhibitions and specializes in limited editions of contemporary sculpture, photography, prints and multiples. **Galerie Lelong** is devoted to contemporary artists.

On the Left Bank **Adrien Maeght** has a tremendous stock of paintings at prices to suit most budgets; he also publishes fine art books. **Galerie 1900–2000** specializes in works by Surrealist and Dada artists, and **Galerie Jeanne Bucher** represents post-war Abstraction with artists like Nicolas de Staël and Vieira da Silva. **Dina Vierny** is a bastion of Modernism, founded by sculptor Aristide Maillol's famous model of the same name. **Rue Louise-Weiss** has become an area for cutting-edge creativity and innovation known as "Scène Est", including the popular **Air de Paris** gallery. In the Marais try **Yvon Lambert**, **Galerie Templon** – specializing in American art, **Galerie Sit Down** and **Galerie du Jour Agnès B**. In the Bastille, try **Lavignes-Bastille** and **L et M Durand-Dessert**, also a fashionable place to buy catalogues on new artists, if not their actual works.

AUCTIONS AND AUCTION HOUSES

The great Paris auction centre, in operation since 1858, is **Drouot-Richelieu** *(see p218)*. Bidding can be intimidating since most of it is done by dealers. Beware of the auctioneer's high-speed patter. *La Gazette de L'Hôtel Drouot* tells you what auctions are coming up when.

Drouot-Richelieu has its own auction catalogue as well. The house only accepts cash and French cheques, but there is an exchange desk on site. A 10–15 per cent commission to the house is charged, so add it on to any price you hear. You may view from 11am to 6pm on the day before the sale, and from 11am to noon on the morning of the sale. Items considered not good enough for the

main house are sold at **Drouot-Nord**. Here auctions take place from 9am to noon and viewing is just 5 minutes before the sales begin. The most prestigious auctions are held at **Drouot-Montaigne**.

The **Crédit Municipal** holds around 12 auctions a month, and almost all the items on sale are small objects and furs off-loaded by rich Parisians. The rules follow

those at Drouot. Information can also be found in *La Gazette de L'Hôtel Drouot.*

Service des Domaines sells all sorts of odds and ends, and here you can still find bargains. Many of the wares come from bailiffs and from Customs and Excise *(see p366)* confis-cations. Viewing is from 10am to 11.30am on the day of the sale in St-Maurice, southeast of the city.

DIRECTORY

EXPORTING

Centre des Renseignements des Douanes
Tel 08 11 20 44 44.
www.douane.gouv.fr

Comité National des Conseillers du Commerce Extérieur de la France
22 Ave Franklin Roosevelt 75008. **Map** 5 A4.
Tel 01 53 83 92 92.
www.cnccef.org

MODERN CRAFTS AND FURNITURE

Cappellini
4 Rue des Rosiers 75004.
Map 13 C3.
Tel 01 42 78 39 39.
www.cappellini.it

Sentou
26 Blvd Raspail 75007.
Map 12 D4.
Tel 01 45 49 00 05.

Le Viaduc des Arts
Ave Daumesnil 750012.
Map 14 F5.
Tel 01 43 40 75 75.
This comprises a series of shops on the Avenue.

ANTIQUES AND OBJETS D'ART

Anne-Sophie Duval
5 Quai Malaquais 75006.
Map 12 F3.
Tel 01 43 54 51 16.
www.annesophie duval.com

L'Arc en Seine
31 Rue de Seine 75006.
Map 12 E3.
Tel 01 43 29 11 02.

La Calinière
68 Rue Vieille-du-Temple 75003. **Map** 13 C3.
Tel 01 42 77 40 46.

Didier Aaron
118 Rue du Faubourg-St-Honoré 75008.
Map 5 C5.
Tel 01 47 42 47 34.
www.didieraaron-cie.com

Louvre des Antiquaires
2 Pl du Palais Royal 75001. **Map** 12 E2.
Tel 01 42 97 27 27.

Verreglass
32 Rue de Charonne 75011. **Map** 14 F4.
Tel 01 48 05 78 43.

Village St-Paul
Between the Quai des Célestins, the Rue St-Paul and the Rue Charlemagne 75004. **Map** 13 C4.

Le Village Suisse
78 Ave de Suffren 75015.
Map 10 E4. www.le villagesuissparis.com

REPRODUCTIONS, POSTERS, PRINTS

Artcurial Gallery
7 Rond Point des Champs-Elysées 75008.
Map 5 A5.
Tel 01 42 99 16 16.

Galerie Documents
53 Rue de Seine 75006.
Map 12 E4.
Tel 01 43 54 50 68.

La Hune
170 Blvd St-Germain 75006.
Map 12 D4.
Tel 01 45 48 35 85.

ART GALLERIES

Adrien Maeght
42 Rue du Bac 75007.
Map 12 D3.
Tel 01 45 48 45 15.

Air de Paris
32 Rue Louise-Weiss 75013. **Map** 18 E4.
Tel 01 44 23 02 77.

Dina Vierny
36 Rue Jacob 75006.
Map 12 E3.
Tel 01 42 60 23 18.
www.galeriedina vierny.com

Galerie 1900–2000
8 Rue Bonaparte 75006.
Map 12 E3.
Tel 01 43 25 84 20.

Galerie Jeanne Bucher
53 Rue de Seine 75006.
Map 12 E4.
Tel 01 44 41 69 65.

Galerie du Jour Agnès B
44 Rue Quincampoix 75004.
Map 13 B2.
Tel 01 44 54 55 90.

Galerie Lelong
13 Rue de Téhéran 75008. **Map** 5 A3.
Tel 01 45 63 13 19.

Galerie Sit Down
4 Rue Ste-Anastase 75003.
Map 14 D2.
Tel 01 42 78 08 07.

Galerie Templon
30 Rue Beaubourg 75003. **Map** 13 B1.
Tel 01 42 72 14 10.

L et M Durand-Dessert
28 Rue de Lappe 75011.
Map 14 F4.
Tel 01 48 06 92 23.

Lavignes-Bastille
27 Rue de Charonne 75011. **Map** 14 F4.
Tel 01 47 00 88 18.

Louise Leiris
47 Rue de Monceau 75008. **Map** 5 A3.
Tel 01 45 63 28 85.

Yvon Lambert
108 Rue Vieille-du-Temple 75003. **Map** 14 D2.
Tel 01 42 71 09 33.

AUCTION HOUSES

Crédit Municipal
55 Rue des Francs-Bourgeois 75004.
Map 13 C3.
Tel 01 44 61 64 00.
www.creditmunicipal.fr

Drouot-Montaigne
15 Ave Montaigne 75008.
Map 10 F1.
Tel 01 48 00 20 80.
www.drouot.fr

Drouot-Nord
64 Rue Doudeauville 75018.
Tel 01 48 00 20 99.

Drouot-Richelieu
9 Rue Drouot 75009.
Map 6 F4.
Tel 01 48 00 20 20.

Service des Domaines
Tel 01 45 11 62 62.

Markets

For eye-catching displays of wonderful food and a lively atmosphere, there is no better place to shop than a Paris market. There are large covered food markets; markets where stalls change regularly; and permanent street markets with a mixture of shops and stalls which are open on a daily basis. Each has its own personality reflecting the area in which it is located. A list of some of the more famous markets, with approximate opening times, follows. For a complete list of markets contact the Paris Office du Tourisme *(see p280)*. And while you're enjoying browsing round the stalls remember to keep an eye on your purse. Bargaining is not automatic, but you might be able to negotiate near closing time.

FRUIT AND VEGETABLE MARKETS

The French treat food with the kind of reverence usually reserved for religion. Many still shop on a daily basis to be sure of buying the freshest produce possible, so food markets tend to be busy. The majority of fruit and vegetable markets are open from around 8am to 1pm and from 4pm to 7pm Tuesday to Saturday, and from 9am to 1pm Sunday.

Buy produce loose rather than in boxes, but keep a close eye on what the stallholder puts in your bag. Most outdoor stalls prefer to serve you rather than allow you to handle the produce yourself, but don't be afraid to point to the individual fruit and vegetables of your choice. Your connoisseurship will be respected. A little language is useful for specifying *pas trop mûr* (not too ripe), or *pour manger ce soir* (to be eaten tonight). If you go to the same market every day you'll become familiar to the stall holders and will be less likely to be fobbed off with the occasional "reject" fruit or vegetable. You will also get to know the stalls worth buying from and the produce worth buying. Seasonal fruit and vegetables are, of course, usually a good buy, tending to be fresher and cheaper than at other times of the year. Finally, it is best to shop at markets early in the day when the food is freshest and the queues are shortest.

FLEA MARKETS

It's often said that you can no longer find bargains at the Paris flea markets. Though this may be true, it's still worth going to one for the sheer fun of browsing. And bear in mind that the price quoted is not the one that you are expected to pay – it is generally assumed that you will bargain. Most flea markets are located on the city's boundaries. Whether you pick up any real bargains has as much to do with luck as with judgement, and may depend on whether the seller knows the true value of their goods. The biggest, busiest and most famous market, incorporating several smaller specialist ones, is the Marché aux Puces de St-Ouen. Be sure to keep your eye on your wallet, as pickpockets frequent these markets.

SPECIALIST MARKETS

Try the Marché aux Fleurs Madeleine, the Marché aux Fleurs on the Ile de la Cité *(see p81)* or the Marché aux Fleurs Ternes in the Champs-Elysées district for fresh flowers. On the Ile de la Cité on Sundays the Marché aux Oiseaux bird market replaces the flower market. Stamp collectors will enjoy the permanent Marché aux Timbres where you can also buy old postcards. In Montmartre the Marché St-Pierre, famous for cheap fabrics, is patronized by professional designers.

Marché d'Aligre

(See p235.)
Built in 1779, this lively covered market is one of the cheapest in the city. Here traders hawk ingredients such as North African olives, groundnuts and hot peppers and there are even a few halal butchers. The noise reaches a crescendo at weekends when the cries of the market boys mingle with those of militants of all political persuasions as the latter petition and protest in the Place d'Aligre. The stalls on the square sell mostly second-hand clothes and bric-à-brac. This is a trendy, bohemian area of town with few tourists and many Parisians.

Rue Cler

(See p190.)
This high-class, pedestrianized food market is patronized mainly by the politicians and captains of industry who live and work in the vicinity, so it's good for people-spotting! The produce is excellent – there's a Breton delicatessen and some good *fromageries*.

Marché Enfant Rouges

39 Rue de Bretagne 75003. **Map** 14 D2. Ⓜ *Temple, Filles-du-Calvaire.* Ⓒ *8.30am–1pm, 4–7.30pm Tue–Sat (to 8pm Fri, Sat); 8.30am–2pm Sun.*
This long-established, charming fruit and vegetable market on the Rue de Bretagne is part covered, part outdoors and dates from 1620. The produce is famous for its freshness, and there are cheap eateries too. On Sunday mornings there are sometimes street performers and accordionists.

Marché aux Fleurs Madeleine

Pl de la Madeleine 75008. **Map** 5 C5. Ⓜ *Madeleine.* Ⓒ *8am–7.30pm Mon–Sat.*

Marché aux Fleurs Ternes

Pl des Ternes 75017. **Map** 4 E3. Ⓜ *Ternes.* Ⓒ *8am–7.30pm Tue–Sun.*

Marché St-Pierre

Pl St-Pierre 75018. **Map** 6 F1. Ⓜ *Anvers.* Ⓒ *2–7pm Mon, 9am–7pm Tue–Sat.*

Marché aux Timbres

Cour Marigny 75008. **Map** 5 B5. Ⓜ *Champs-Elysées.* Ⓒ *9am–7pm Thu, Sat, Sun & public hols.*

Marché Joinville

Corner of Rue Jomard and Rue de Joinville 75019. **M** *Crimée.*
🕐 *7am–2.30pm Thu & Sun.*
This lively canalside market is known for its cheap fruit and vegetables. It is situated on the Canal d'Ourcq, near the Parc de la Villette, and is always teeming with shoppers.

Marché St Germain

4–6 Rue Lobineau 75006. **Map** 12 E4. **M** *Mabillon.* 🕐 *8am–1pm, 4–8pm Tue–Fri; 8am–1.30pm, 3.30–8pm Sat; 8am–1.30pm Sun.*
St-Germain is one of the few covered markets left in Paris and has been enhanced by renovation. Here you can buy Italian, Mexican, Greek, Asian and organic produce and other goods.

Rue de Lévis

Blvd des Batignolles 75017. **Map** 5 B2. **M** *Villiers.* 🕐 *8am–1pm, 4–7pm Tue–Sat; 9am–2pm Sun.*
Rue de Lévis is a bustling, popular food market near the Parc Monceau with a number of good pâtisseries, an excellent cheese delicatessen and a *charcuterie* which is known for its savoury pies. The part of the street that leads to Rue Legendre sells haberdashery and fabrics. The shops on this pedestrianized street also have stalls outside selling their wares.

Rue Montorgueil

75001 & 75002. **Map** 13 A1. **M** *Les Halles.* 🕐 *usually 9am–7pm Tue–Sun.*
The Rue Montorgueil is what remains of the old Les Halles market. The street has been repaved and restored to its former glory. Here you can buy expensive, exotic fruit and vegetables like green bananas and yams from the market gardeners' stalls. You can also sample the delicious offerings from the delicatessens or from the Stohrer pastry shop.

Rue Mouffetard

(See p166.)
Rue Mouffetard is one of the oldest market streets in Paris. Although it has become touristy and somewhat overpriced, it's still a charming winding street full of quality food products. It's worth queuing for the freshly-made bread at Les Panetons bakery at No. 113 *(see pp333–5)*. There is also a lively African market down the nearby side street of Rue Daubenton.

Rue Poncelet

75017. **Map** 4 E3. **M** *Ternes.*
🕐 *8am–noon, 4–7.30pm Tue–Sat; 8am–12.30pm Sun.*
The Rue Poncelet food market is situated away from the main tourist areas of Paris but is worth visiting for its authentic French atmosphere. Choose from the many bakeries, pâtisseries and *charcuteries* or enjoy authentic Auvergne specialties from Aux Fermes d'Auvergne.

Marché de la Porte de Vanves

Ave Georges-Lafenestre & Ave Marc-Sangnier 75014. **M** *Porte-de-Vanves.* 🕐 *7am–7.30pm Sat & Sun.*
Porte de Vanves is a small market selling good-quality bric-à-brac and junk as well as some second-hand furniture. It's best to get to the market early on Saturday morning for the best choice of wares. Artists exhibit nearby in the Place des Artistes.

Marché Président-Wilson

Situated in Ave du Président-Wilson, between Pl d'Iéna & Rue Debrousse 75016. **Map** 10 D1. **M** *Alma-Marceau.* 🕐 *7am–2.30pm Wed, 7am–3pm Sat.*
This very chic food market on Avenue Président-Wilson is close to the Musée d'Art Moderne and the Palais Galliera fashion museum. It has become important because there are no other food shops nearby. It is best for meat.

Marché aux Puces de Montreuil

Porte de Montreuil, 93 Montreuil 75020. **M** *Porte-de-Montreuil.* 🕐 *7am–7.30pm Mon, Sat & Sun.*
Go early to the Porte de Montreuil flea market, where you'll have a better chance of picking up a bargain. The substantial second-hand clothes section attracts many young people. There's also a wide variety of items including used bicycles, bric-à-brac and an exotic spices stand.

Marché aux Puces de St-Ouen

(See p233.)
This is the best known, the most crowded and the most expensive of all the flea markets, situated on the northern outskirts of the city. Here you'll find a range of markets, locals dealing from their car boots and a number of extremely large buildings packed with stalls. Some of them are very upmarket, others

sell junk. The flea market is a 10–15-minute walk from Clignancourt metro – don't be put off by the somewhat sleazy Marché Malik which you have to pass through on your way from the metro. A *Guide des Puces* (guide to the flea markets) can be obtained from the information kiosk in the Marché Biron on the Rue des Rosiers. The more exclusive markets will take credit cards and arrange for goods to be shipped home. New stock arrives on Friday, the day when professionals come from all over the world to sweep up the best buys.

Among the markets here the Marché Jules Vallès is good for turn-of-the-19th century *objets d'art.* Marché Paul-Bert is more expensive, but charming. Items on sale include furniture, books and prints. Both markets deal in second-hand goods rather than antiques.

In a different league, Marché Biron sells elegant, expensive antique furniture of very high quality. Marché Vernaison is the oldest and biggest market, good for collectables such as jewellery as well as lamps and clothes. No information about the Marché aux Puces is complete without mentioning Chez Louisette in the Vernaison market. This café is always full of locals enjoying the home cooking and the well-intentioned renditions of Edith Piaf songs. Marché Cambo is a fairly small market with beautifully-displayed antique furniture. Marché Serpette is popular with the dealers: everything sold here is in mint condition.

Marché Raspail

Situated on Blvd Raspail between Rue du Cherche-Midi & Rue de Rennes 75006. **Map** 12 D5. **M** *Rennes.* 🕐 *7am–2.30pm Tue, Fri; 9am–3pm Sun.*
The Raspail market sells typical French groceries as well as Portuguese produce on Tuesdays and Fridays. But Sunday is the day for which it's famous, when health-conscious Parisians turn up in droves for the organically-grown produce. Marché Raspail is not a cheap market, but it is very good.

Rue de Seine and Rue de Buci

75006. **Map** 12 E4. **M** *Odéon.* 🕐 *8am–1pm, 4–7pm Tue–Sat; 9am–1pm Sun.*
The stalls here are expensive and crowded but sell quality fruit and vegetables. There are also a large florist's and two excellent pâtisseries.

ENTERTAINMENT IN PARIS

Whether you prefer classical drama or cabaret, showgirls or ballet, opera or jazz, cinema or dancing the night away, Paris has it all. Free entertainment is aplenty as well, from the street performers outside the Pompidou Centre to musicians busking in the metro. Parisians themselves enjoy strolling along the boulevards or sitting at a pavement café, and nursing a drink. Of course, for the ultimate "oh-la-la!" experience, showgirls await you at celebrated cabarets while bright young things pose in nightclubs. For fans of spectator sports there is tennis, the Tour de France, horse racing, football or rugby. Recreation centres and gyms cater to the more active, while the municipal swimming pools delight waterbabies. You can also catch a game of *boules* (or *pétanque*) in Paris's squares and parks.

PRACTICAL INFORMATION

For the visitor in Paris there is no shortage of information about what's on offer.

The **Office du Tourisme** near the Tuileries and Opera is the city's main tourism distribution point for leaflets and schedules of events. It has a recorded information telephone service giving details of free concerts and exhibitions along with information on transport to the venues. Its website is also extremely useful. Your hotel reception desk or concierge should also be able to help you with any such information. They usually keep a wide range of brochures and leaflets for guests, and will generally be more than happy to make reservations for you.

Ballerina of the Ballet de l'Opéra

BOOKING TICKETS

Depending on the event, tickets can be bought at the door, but for blockbuster concerts it is necessary to book well in advance. For most major events, including some classical music concerts and museum shows, tickets can be purchased online or at the **FNAC** chain or **Virgin Megastore**. For popular events book well ahead, Parisians can be very quick off the mark for hot tickets. However, for theatre, opera and dance performances, you can often buy inexpensive tickets at the last minute. If the tickets are marked *sans visibilité* you will be able to see the stage only partially, or perhaps not at all. Often, obliging ushers

Nightclubbing in Paris

will put you in a better seat, depending on availability, but don't forget to tip.

Theatre box offices are open daily from approximately 11am–7pm. Most box offices accept credit card bookings made by phone or in person, but you may have to arrive early to pick up your tickets if you booked by telephone, as they may be sold to someone else at the last minute. If you

LISTINGS MAGAZINES

Paris has several good listings magazines. Among them are *Pariscope* and *L'Officiel des Spectacles*. They are published every Wednesday. *Le Figaro* has a good listings section on Wednesdays. *Télerama*, France's leading culture and listings weekly, has a Paris supplement called *Sortir*. For English listings, see the webzine *Paris Voice* at www.parisvoice.com.

Concert at Opéra National de Paris Garnier *(see p348)*

The Odéon Théâtre de l'Europe, a major theatre venue sometimes staging plays in English

are really keen and can't get hold of tickets, you can always turn up at the box office just before the performance in case there are unclaimed or returned tickets.

TICKET TOUTS

If you must have a ticket to a sold-out performance, do as the French do: stand at the entrance with a sign that says *cherche une place (or deux,* etc). Many people have an extra ticket to sell. Often the people selling the extra tickets are doing so because a person in their party cannot come and they will simply sell the ticket on at face value. It is fine to buy these tickets, but do watch out for touts and be sure you don't buy a counterfeit or overpriced ticket.

Pétanque players

CUT-PRICE TICKETS

Half-price tickets to current plays are sold on the day of performance at **Kiosque Théâtre**. Credit cards are not accepted and a small commission is charged per ticket. There is a booth on the Place de la Madeleine *(see p216)*, open 12.30–8pm, Tuesday–Saturday, 12.30–4pm Sunday, and on the Parvis de la Gare Montparnasse, which is open 12.30–8pm Tuesday–Saturday, 12.30–4pm Sunday. A third booth located on Place des Ternes is open 12.30–8pm, Tuesday–Saturday, 12.30–4pm Sunday. The *kiosque* is a Parisian institution and often has passes for the season's top shows.

DISABLED VISITORS' FACILITIES

Where facilities do exist, they are either very good or dreadful. Many venues have wheelchair space, but always phone in advance to make sure it's properly equipped. As far as public transport is concerned, the metro, with its long stairways, is completely inaccessible to wheelchairs. Some bus lines are equipped with ramps to make them accessible to wheelchairs; check with the city's transport authority, the RATP, to find out which lines have facilities.

USEFUL ADDRESSES

FNAC
Forum des Halles, 1 Rue Pierre-Lescot 75001. **Map** 13 A2. *Tel* 0825 020 020.

The Grand Rex cinema *(see p354)*

FNAC
26 Ave des Ternes 75017.
Map 4 D3. *Tel* 0825 020 020.

G7 Taxis
Tel 01 47 39 47 39

Office du Tourisme
25 Rue des Pyramides 75001.
Map 12 E1. *Tel* 08 92 68 30 00.
www.parisinfo.com

Taxis Bleus
Tel 08 91 70 10 10.

Virgin Megastore
52–60 Ave des Champs-Elysées 75008. **Map** 4 F5.
Tel 01 49 53 50 00.

Theatre

From the grandeur of the Comédie Française to slap-stick farce and avant-garde drama, theatre is flourishing in Paris and the suburbs – the training ground for the best young actors and directors. The city also has a long tradition of playing host to visiting companies, and it attracts many foreign productions, often in the original languages.

There are theatres scattered throughout the city and the theatre season runs from September to July; national theatres close during August but many commercial ones stay open. For complete listings of what's on read *Pariscope* or *L'Officiel des Spectacles (see p340)*.

NATIONAL THEATRES

Founded in 1680 by royal decree, the **Comédie Française** *(see p120)*, with its strict conventions regarding the style of acting and interpretation, is the bastion of French theatre. Its aim is to keep classical drama in the public eye and also to perform works by the best modern playwrights.

The Comédie Française (inextricably linked in the national consciousness to Molière) is the oldest national theatre in the world and one of the few institutions of France's *ancien-régime* to have survived the Revolution. It settled into its present home after players occupied the Palais-Royal during the Revolution. The traditionally-styled red velvet auditorium has a vast stage equipped with the latest technology.

The majority of the repertoire is classical, dominated by Corneille, Racine and Molière, followed by second strings Marivaux, Alfred de Musset and Victor Hugo. The company also performs modern plays by French and foreign playwrights.

The **Odéon Théâtre de l'Europe**, also known as the Théâtre National de l'Odéon *(see p140)*, was at one time the second theatre of the Comédie Française. It now has two sites and specializes in performing plays from other countries in their original languages.

Next door the **Petit Odéon** is a studio space specializing in new plays.

The **Théâtre National de Chaillot** is a huge under-ground auditorium in the Art Deco Palais de Chaillot *(see p200)*. It stages experimental and contemporary theatre, lively dance productions and, occasionally, musical revues.

The **Théâtre National de la Colline** has two performance spaces and specializes in contemporary dramas.

FURTHER AFIELD

A thriving multi-theatre complex in the Bois de Vincennes, the **Cartoucherie** houses five separate avant-garde theatres, including the internationally famous **Théâtre du Soleil**.

INDEPENDENT THEATRES

Among the most important of the serious independents are the **Comédie des Champs-Elysées**, the **Hébertot** and the **Atelier**, which aims to be experimental. Other notable venues include the **Théâtre Marigny**, for excellent modern French drama, the **Montparnasse** and the **Théâtre Antoine** which pioneered the use of realism on stage. The **Madeleine** maintains consistently high standards and the **Huchette** specializes in Ionesco plays. The British director Peter Brook has a loyal following at the **Bouffes-du-Nord**.

For over a hundred years the **Palais Royal** has been the temple of risqué farce. With fewer French Feydeau-style farce writers these days, translations of British and American sex comedies are filling the gap. Other notable venues include the **Bouffes-Parisiens**, **La Bruyère**, the **Michel** and the **St-Georges**.

The **Théâtre du Gymnase** presents popular one-man comedy shows.

CAFE-THEATRES AND CHANSONNIERS

There is a long tradition of entertainment in cafés, but the café-theatres of today have nothing in common with the "café-concerts" of the late 19th century. These modern entertainments have originated because young actors and new playwrights could not find work, while drama students were unable to pay to hire established theatres. Don't be surprised if there is an element of audience participation, or alternatively, in small venues, if the actors can sometimes seem a little too close for comfort. This form of theatre is now so popular in Paris that one can often see posters advertising classes for café-theatre or notices inviting people to join small troupes. Café-theatres rose to prominence during the 1960s and 70s, when unknowns such as Coluche, Gérard Depardieu and Miou-Miou made their debut at the **Café de la Gare** before going on to success on the screen, so who knows who you might see at your local café.

Good venues for seeing new talent include the **Théâtre d'Edgar** and **Le Point Virgule**, while **Cabaret Michou** is an old-fashioned spot which is very popular and tends to specialize in broad caricature. Traditional *chansonniers* – cabarets where ballads, folk songs and humour abound – include **Au Lapin Agile** *(see p225)*, in the heart of Montmartre. Political satire is on offer at the **Caveau de la République** and the **Deux Anes**, also in Montmartre. Another form of café entertainment that often veers towards the theatrical is the *café-philosophique*. These are philosophical discussions or debates, held on topics such as justice, war and love, in which skilled orators take to the floor to declaim their positions. Audience participation is encouraged. Such events are held in many locations, including at **Les Editeurs**. Although debates take place in French, English language events also exist: play readings are a regular feature at the **Café de Flore**.

CHILDREN'S THEATRE

Some Paris theatres, such as the **Théâtre du Gymnase**, the **Porte St-Martin** and the **Café d'Edgar**, have children's matinées on Wednesdays and weekends. In the city parks there are several tiny puppet theatres *(marionnettes)*, which are sure to delight children and adults alike. *(See* Independent Theatres *p344.)* The **Lido** also has an occasional children's season with shows at 2pm and 4pm (call for details).

OPEN-AIR THEATRE

During the summer, weather permitting, open-air performances of Shakespeare and classic French plays are held in the Shakespeare Garden in the Bois de Boulogne. There are also occasional performances in the Tuileries and in Montmartre as part of Paris's summer festival; check listings magazines for these events.

ENGLISH-LANGUAGE THEATRE IN PARIS

The Improfessionals (improvo) and Mondays @ 7 are Paris-based companies who perform in English (details in listings magazines). There are also several English-language poetry societies which host poetry and play readings, the best is the Live Poets Society. **Kilometre Zero** is an interesting English-language arts collective that performs plays, publishes a magazine and hosts open-mike recital evenings. **La Java** puts on excellent stand-up comedy acts in English each month, courtesy of Anything Matters. Peter Brook occasionally puts on Shakespeare plays at the

Bouffes-du-Nord. A historic venue, it is much-loved by expatriates and plays host to some of the finest comic talent on the circuit at the moment.

STREET THEATRE

Street theatre thrives during the summer. Jugglers, mime artists, fire-eaters and musicians can be seen in tourist areas such as the Pompidou Centre *(see pp110–11)*, St-Germain-des-Prés and Les Halles.

CABARET

The music hall revue is the entertainment form most associated with late 19th-century Paris. It evokes images of bohemian artists and absinthe-induced debauchery. Today, most of the girls are likely to be non-French and the audience is made up mainly of foreign businessmen and tour groups.

When it comes to picking a cabaret the rule of thumb is simple: the better-known places are the best. Lesser-known shows resemble nothing so much as Grade-B strip shows. All the cabarets listed here *(see p344)* guarantee topless women sporting outrageous feather- and sequin-encrusted headpieces, an assortment of vaudeville acts and, depending on your point of view, a spectacularly entertaining evening or an exercise in high kitsch.

The **Lido** is the most Las Vegas-like of the cabarets and stars the legendary Bluebell Girls. The **Folies-Bergères** is renowned for lively entertainment. It is the oldest music hall in Paris and probably the most famous in the world.

The **Crazy Horse** features some of the more risqué costumes and performances, and dancers with names such as Betty Buttocks, Fila Volcana and Nouka Bazooka. It has been transformed from its Wild West bar-room into a jewel-box theatre with a champagne bucket fastened to each seat. Here, the lowly striptease of burlesque shows has been refined into a vehicle for comedy sketches

and international beauties. **Paradis Latin** is the most "French" of all the city's cabaret shows. It has variety acts with remarkable special effects and scenery in a beautiful, old Left Bank theatre, partly designed by Gustave Eiffel.

The **Bobin'O** offers a commercial show that is inspired by all of Paris' cabarets. The **Moulin Rouge** *(see p228)*, once the haunt of Toulouse-Lautrec, is the birthplace of the cancan. Today, the Moulin Rouge is less extravagant than the screen version portrayed in the famous film, but cabaret fans can still be certain of an evening of glamour, glitz and good times. Outrageously camp, transvestite parodies of these showgirl reviews can be seen at **Cabaret Michou**.

BOOKING TICKETS

Tickets can be bought at the box office, by telephone or through ticket agencies. Box offices are open daily from about 11am–7pm; some accept credit card bookings by telephone or in person. Most tickets can also be bought online, via either theatre websites or Internet ticket agencies.

TICKET PRICES

Ticket prices generally range from €7–€30 for the national theatres and €8–€38 for the independents. Reduced-price tickets and student stand-bys are available in some theatres 15 minutes before curtain-up. For cabaret, expect to pay from €23–€60; €68–€105 with dinner.

The **Kiosque Théâtre** offers half-price tickets on the day-of-performance: credit cards are not accepted and a small commission is charged for each ticket. There are booths in three locations *(see p341)*.

DRESS

These days, evening clothes are only worn to gala events at the Opéra National de Paris Garnier, the Comédie Française or the premiere of an up-market play.

DIRECTORY

NATIONAL THEATRES

Comédie Française
Salle Richelieu, 1 Pl Colette 75001. **Map** 12 E1. *Tel 08 25 10 16 80.*
www.comedie-francaise.fr

Odéon Théâtre de l'Europe
Ateliers Berthier, 8 Blvd Berthier 75017. **Map** 12 F5. *Tel 01 44 85 40 40.*
Théâtre de l'Odéon, Pl de l'Odéon 75006. **Map** 12 F4.
www.theatre-odeon.fr

Théâtre National de Chaillot
Pl du Trocadéro 75016. **Map** 9 C2.
Tel 01 53 65 31 00.
www.theatre-chaillot.fr

Théâtre National de la Colline
15 Rue Malte-Brun 75020. *Tel 01 44 62 52 52.* www.colline.fr

FURTHER AFIELD

Cartoucherie
Route du Champ-de-Manoeuvre 75012.
www.theatre-du-soleil.fr

Théâtre de l'Aquarium
Tel 01 43 74 99 61.

Théâtre de l'Epée de Bois
Bois de Vincennes.
Tel 01 48 08 39 74.

Théâtre de la Tempête
Tel 01 43 28 36 36.

Théâtre du Chaudron
Tel 01 43 28 97 04.

Théâtre du Soleil
Tel 01 43 74 24 08.

INDEPENDENT THEATRES

Bouffes-du-Nord
37 bis Blvd de la Chapelle 75010.
Map 7 C1.
Tel 01 46 07 34 50.
www.bouffesdunord.com

Bouffes-Parisiens
4 Rue Monsigny 75002.
Map 6 E5.
Tel 01 42 96 92 42.
www.bouffes parisiens.com

La Bruyère
5 Rue La Bruyère 75009.
Map 6 E3.
Tel 01 48 74 76 99.

Comédie des Champs-Elysées
15 Ave Montaigne 75008. **Map** 10 F1.
Tel 01 53 23 99 19.
www.comediedes champselysees.com

Gaiéte Montparnasse
26 Rue de la Gaiéte 75014. **Map** 15 C2.
Tel 01 43 20 60 56.

Hébertot
78 bis Blvd des Batignolles 75017. **Map** 5 B2.
Tel 01 43 87 23 23.

Madeleine
19 Rue de Surène 75008.
Map 5 C5.
Tel 01 42 65 07 09.

Marigny
7 Ave de Marigny 75008.
Map 5 A5.
Tel 0892 222 333.

Michel
38 Rue des Mathurins 75008. **Map** 5 C4.
Tel 01 42 65 35 02.

Montparnasse
31 Rue de la Gaîté 75014. **Map** 15 C2.
Tel 01 43 22 77 74.

Palais Royal
38 Rue Montpensier 75001. **Map** 12 E1.
Tel 01 42 97 40 00.

Porte St-Martin
16 Blvd St-Martin 75010.
Map 7 C5.
Tel 01 42 08 00 32.

St-Georges
51 Rue St-Georges 75009. **Map** 6 E3.
Tel 01 48 78 63 47.

Théâtre Antoine
14 Blvd de Strasbourg 75010. **Map** 7 B5.
Tel 01 42 08 77 71 & 01 42 08 76 58.

Théâtre de l'Atelier
Pl Charles Dullin 75018.
Map 6 F2.
Tel 01 46 06 49 24.
www.theatre-atelier.com

Théâtre du Gymnase
38 Blvd Bonne-Nouvelle 75010. **Map** 7 A5.
Tel 01 42 46 79 79.
www.theatredu gymnase.com

Théâtre de la Huchette
23 Rue de la Huchette 75005.
Map 13 A4.
Tel 01 43 26 38 99.

Théâtre Sudden
14 bis Rue Sainte-Isaure 75018.
Map 2 F4.
Tel 01 42 62 35 00.
www.suddentheatre.fr

CAFE-THEATRES AND CHANSONNIERS

Au Lapin Agile
22 Rue des Saules 75018.
Map 2 F5.
Tel 01 46 06 85 87.
www.au-lapin-agile.com

Cabaret Michou
80 Rue des Martyrs 75018. **Map** 6 F3.
Tel 01 46 06 16 04.
www.michou.com

Café de la Gare
41 Rue du Temple 75004. **Map** 13 B2.
Tel 01 42 78 52 51.

Caveau de la République
23 Place République 75003. **Map** 8 D5.
Tel 01 42 78 44 45.
www.caveau.fr

Deux Anes
100 Blvd de Clichy 75018. **Map** 6 D1.
Tel 01 46 06 10 26.

La Java
105 Rue du Faubourg du Temple 75010.
Map 8 E5.
Tel 01 53 19 98 88.
www.anything matters.com

Le Point Virgule
7 Rue St-Croix-de-la-Bretonnerie 75004.
Map 13 C3.
Tel 01 42 78 67 03.

Les Editeurs
Carrefour de l'Odéon 75006.
Map 12 F4.
Tel 01 43 26 67 76.

Théâtre d'Edgar
58 Blvd Edgar-Quinet 75014.
Map 16 D2.
Tel 01 42 79 97 97.

CABARET

Bobin'O
14–20 Rue de la Gaîté 75014. **Map** 15 C3.
Tel 08 20 00 90 00.
www.bobino.fr

Crazy Horse
12 Ave George V 75008.
Map 10 E1.
Tel 01 47 23 32 32.
www.lecrazyhorse paris.com

Folies-Bergères
32 Rue Richer 75009.
Map 7 A4.
Tel 0892 681 650.
www.foliesbergere.com

Lido
116 bis Ave des Champs-Elysées 75008.
Map 4 E4.
Tel 01 40 76 56 10
www.lido.fr

Moulin Rouge
82 Blvd de Clichy 75018.
Map 6 E1.
Tel 01 53 09 82 82.
www.moulinrouge.fr

Paradis Latin
28 Rue du Cardinal Lemoine 75005.
Map 13 B5.
Tel 01 43 25 28 28.

Classical Music

The music scene in Paris is busy and exciting, with many first-class venues offering an excellent range of opera, and classical and contemporary music productions. There are also numerous concerts in churches (some of which are free) and many music festivals, particularly during the summer months.

Information about what's on is listed in *Pariscope* and *L'Officiel des Spectacles*. A free monthly listing of musical events is given out at most concert halls. Also, try the Office du Tourisme in the Rue des Pyramides *(see pp340–41)* for details of many free and open-air classical music performances.

running the Salle Pleyel, the Cité de la Musique also operates other venues at Parc de la Villette. These concert halls present a varied programme of music from all periods, genres and cultures.

The **Théâtre du Châtelet** has become one of the city's principal venues for all kinds of concerts, opera and dance. The high-quality programme includes opera classics from Mozart's *Così fan tutte* to Verdi's *La Traviata*, and more modern works, such as Boessman's *Contes d'Hiver*, and occasional concerts by international opera stars. Great attention is also devoted to 20th-century music here, and throughout the season there are lunchtime concerts and recitals in the foyer.

The beautiful Art Deco **Théâtre des Champs-Elysées** is a celebrated classical music venue which also produces some opera and dance. Radio-France is part-owner of the theatre, and its Orchestre National de France gives concerts here, as do many touring orchestras and soloists. The Orchestre des Champs-Elysées, directed by Philippe Herreweghe, is in residence here, and gives period-instrument performances.

Radio-France is the biggest single concert organizer in Paris, with a musical force that includes two major symphony orchestras: the Orchestre National de France and the Orchestre Philharmonique. Many of its concerts are given in Paris's other concert halls, but the **Maison de Radio-France** has a large hall and several smaller studios that are used for concerts and broadcasts open to the public *(see p202, Maison de Radio France)*.

The **Cité de la Musique** is a massive cultural centre devoted entirely to music – of all genres and from all eras. Classical music features heavily on its programme, with lots of chamber music and recitals, as well as more ambitious orchestral concerts.

OPERA

Opera lovers will find themselves well catered for, with many productions mounted at the Bastille and the beautifully renovated **Opéra National de Paris Garnier**. Opera is also an important part of the programming at the Théâtre du Châtelet, as well as being produced intermittently by a variety of small organizations, and there are occasional large-scale lavish productions at the **Palais Omnisports de Bercy** or POB *(see p359)*.

The Opéra de Paris's ultra-modern home is the **Opéra National de Paris Bastille** *(see p98)*, where performances make full use of the house's mind-boggling array of high-tech stage mechanisms. There are 2,700 seats, all with a good view of the stage, and the accoustics are excellent.

Productions feature classic and modern operas, and interpretations are often avant-garde: past examples include Philippe Mamoury's *K...*; Bob Wilson's production of *The Magic Flute*, done in the style of Japanese Noh; Messiaen's *St Francis of Assisi*, with video screens and neon added to bring the story up to date. On Thursday lunchtimes they also offer free concerts, lectures and films as part of an occasional programme known as *Casse-Croûte à l'Opéra*.

There are also occasional dance performances, when the Bastille plays host to the ballet company from the Opéra National de Paris Garnier *(see p217)*. The house includes two smaller spaces, the **Auditorium** (500 seats) and the **Studio** (200 seats) for smaller-scale events connected to the current productions on the main stages here and at the Opera Garnier.

The **Opéra Comique** (also known as the Salle Favart), directed by Jérôme Deschamps, no longer has opera, but stages a wide range of eccentric, lightweight productions, including some popular music-hall-style work and operetta.

North of the city centre, at St Denis, the **Stade de France** hosts occasional opera spectaculars. Past productions have included Verdi's *Aïda*, directed by Charles Roubaud, as well as Bizet's *Carmen* and *Nabucco* by Verdi.

CONCERTS

Paris is the home of three major symphony orchestras, and a good half-dozen other orchestras; it is also a major venue for touring European and American orchestras. Chamber music is also flourishing, either as part of the programming of the major venues, or in smaller halls and churches.

The **Salle Pleyel** is Paris's principal concert hall. After extensive renovation, it is now owned by the state-run Cité de la Musique and houses the Orchestre de Paris, directed by Christoph Eschenbach, as well as Radio France's Philharmonic Orchestra, led by Myung-Whun Chung. The Salle Pleyel has optimal acoustics for the classical and contemporary orchestra repertoire. In addition to

The **Auditorium du Louvre** was built as part of the Grand Louvre project *(see pp122–9)* and it is used mostly for chamber, piano and vocal recitals. The Musée d'Orsay's *(see p144–7)* **Auditorium du Musée d'Orsay** is a medium-sized auditorium, with an active concert programme. Concerts are usually held once or twice a week, and prices vary.

Other museums often hold concerts as part of an exhibition theme – such as troubadours at the Musée National du Moyen Age *(see p154–7)* – so do check the listings magazines.

Musique à la Sorbonne is a concert series in the **Grand Amphithéâtre de la Sorbonne** and the **Amphithéâtre Richelieu de la Sorbonne**. Productions have included a Slavonic music festival, featuring the works of East European composers.

Occasionally concerts are given in the **Conservatoire d'Art Dramatique**, where Beethoven was introduced to Paris audiences in 1828 and where Hector Berlioz's major work, *La Symphonie Fantastique*, was first performed. Otherwise, it's not usually open to public.

CONTEMPORARY MUSIC

Contemporary music in Paris has a high profile and is definitely alive and kicking. Although no longer at the head of any orchestra, Pierre Boulez is still a major figure in the capital's contemporary music scene. Jonathan Nott now directs the experimental Ensemble InterContemporain, which is lavishly supported by the French state in its home at the Cité de la Musique *(see pp234–5)*. **IRCAM**, founded by Pierre Boulez *(see p108)*, is a major centre for ground-breaking new musical forms. It organizes a programme of new music performances, talks and an annual festival in June.

Other bright stars among the many talented composers include Pascal Dusapin, Philippe Fénelon, George Benjamin and Philippe

Manoury, as well as Georges Aperghis, who specializes in musical theatre.

The fabulously designed **Cité de la Musique** complex at Parc de la Villette includes both a spectacularly domed *salle de concerts* surrounded by a glass-roofed arcade, and the **Conservatoire National de Musique** with its opera theatre and two small concert halls. The Chamber Orchestra of Europe plays regularly here. Both venues are used for regular performances, including jazz, ethnic and contemporary music, as well as *chanson* and Early Music.

For details either phone the venue concerned or consult the listings magazines. For those interested in contemporary music, the quarterly magazine *Résonance* is published by IRCAM at the Pompidou Centre.

FESTIVALS

Some of the most important music festivals are the result of the work of the **Festival d'Automne à Paris**, which acts as a behind-the-scenes stimulator, commissioning new works, subsidizing others and in general enlivening the Parisian musical, dance and theatrical scene from September to December.

The **Festival St-Denis** running throughout June and July holds concerts, with an emphasis on choral works. Most performances are given in the Basilique St-Denis.

Musique Baroque au Château de Versailles, from around the middle of March to the middle of June, is an offshoot of the Baroque Music Centre, founded in Versailles in 1988. Operas, concerts, recitals, chamber music, dance and theatre are on offer in the fabulous surroundings of Versailles *(see pp248–53)*.

Other interesting festivals include the Chopin festival, held in the Orangerie in the Bois de Boulogne from mid-June to mid-July, and the Quartier 25 d'Eté festival, which host a series of outdoor classical music concerts. For tickets, it is

usually necessary to go to the theatre box office or venue concerned, though some festivals may run an advance online or postal booking service.

CHURCHES

Music is everywhere in Paris's churches, in the form of classical concerts, organ recitals or religious services. The most outstanding churches which hold regular concerts include **La Madeleine** *(see p216)*, **St-Germain-des-Prés** *(see p138)*, **St-Julien-le-Pauvre** *(see p152)* and **St-Roch** *(see p121)*. Music is also performed in the **Eglise des Billettes**, **St-Sulpice** *(see p172)*, **St-Gervais–St-Protais** *(see p99)*, **Notre-Dame** *(see pp82–5)*, **St-Louis-en-l'Ile** *(see p87)* and **Sainte-Chapelle** *(see pp88–9)*.

A great proportion, but not all, of these concerts are free. If you have any difficulty contacting the church in question, try the Office du Tourisme for information *(see pp340–41)*.

EARLY MUSIC

A number of early-music ensembles have taken up residence in Paris. The Chapelle Royale gives a concert series at the **Théâtre des Champs-Elysées** with programmes ranging from Renaissance vocal music to Mozart. Their enchanting sacred music concerts (look out for Bach cantatas) take place at **Notre-Dame-des-Blancs-Manteaux** *(see p102)*.

Baroque opera is more the domain of Les Arts Florissants, founded and directed by American-born William Christie, who perform French and Italian operas from Rossi to Rameau, and Les Musiciens du Louvre, directed by Marc Minkowski. Both companies perform regularly at the Théâtre du Châtelet and the Opera National Garnier. The **Théâtre de la Ville** is also an excellent venue in which to hear Baroque chamber music, as is the pretty **Eglise Saint-Germain l'Auxerrois**.

BOOKING TICKETS

For tickets, it's always best to deal directly with the relevant box office. Booking tickets at the main venues is possible online or by post up to two months before the performance and by telephone two weeks to a month in advance. If you want a good seat, it's best to book in advance as tickets tend to sell quickly. Last-minute tickets may also be available at the box office, and certain venues, such as the Opéra National de Paris Bastille, keep some tickets for the cheaper seats aside for the purpose. Ticket agents, notably in the **FNAC** stores *(see p341)*, and a good hotel concierge can also help. These agencies accept credit card bookings – a useful service as not all venues are guaranteed to accept them.

Half-price tickets on the day of performance can be bought at one of three **Kiosque Théâtre** *(see p341)*, located at Place de la Madeleine, the Parvis de la Gare Montparnasse and Place des Ternes. However, these agencies usually only deal for performances taking place at private theatres.

Note, however, that many theatres and concert halls may be closed during the holiday season in August, so inquire first to avoid disappointment.

TICKET PRICES

Ticket prices can range from €8–€85 for the Opéra de Paris Bastille and the principal classical music venues, and from €5–€25 for the smaller halls and concerts in churches around the city, such as Sainte-Chapelle.

DIRECTORY

CLASSICAL MUSIC VENUES

Amphithéâtre Richelieu de la Sorbonne
17 Rue de la Sorbonne 75005. **Map** 12 F5.
Tel 01 42 62 71 71.

Auditorium
See Opéra National de Paris Bastille.

Auditorium du Louvre
Musée du Louvre, Rue de Rivoli 75001.
Map 12 E2.
Tel 01 40 20 55 00.

Auditorium du Musée d'Orsay
102 Rue de Lille 75007.
Map 12 D2.
Tel 01 40 49 49 66.

Centre de Musique Baroque de Versailles
22 Ave de Paris, Versailles.
Tel 01 39 20 78 10.

Cité de la Musique
Parc de La Villette, 221 Ave Jean-Jaurès 75019.
Tel 01 44 84 44 84.
www.cite-musique.fr

Conservatoire d'Art Dramatique
2 bis Rue du Conservatoire 75009.
Map 7 A4.
Tel 01 42 46 12 91.

Eglise des Billettes
24 Rue des Archives 75004. **Map** 13 C2.
Tel 01 42 72 38 79.

Eglise de la Madeleine
Pl de la Madeleine 75008.
Map 5 C5.
Tel 01 42 50 96 18.

Eglise St-Germain l'Auxerrois
2 Place du Louvre 75001.
Map 12 F2.
Tel 01 42 60 13 96.

Festival d'Automne
156 Rue de Rivoli 75001.
Map 12 F2.
Tel 01 53 45 17 00.

Festival Chopin
Orangerie de Bagatelle
Bois de Boulogne 75016.
Map 3 A4.
Tel 01 45 00 22 19.

Grand Amphithéâtre de la Sorbonne
45 Rue des Ecoles 75005.
Map 13 A5.
Tel 01 42 62 71 71.

IRCAM
1 Pl Igor Stravinsky 75004.
Map 13 B2.
Tel 01 44 78 48 43.

Maison Radio-France
116 Ave du Président-Kennedy 75016.
Map 9 B4.
Tel 01 42 20 42 20.

Notre-Dame
Pl du Parvis-Notre-Dame 75004.
Map 13 A4.
Tel 01 42 34 56 10.

Notre-Dame-des-Blancs-Manteaux
12 Rue des Blancs-Manteaux 75004.
Map 13 C3.
Tel 01 42 72 09 37.

Opéra Comique
(Salle Favart) 5 Rue Favart 75002. **Map** 6 F5.
Tel 08 25 01 01 23.

Opéra National de Paris Bastille
120 Rue de Lyon 75012.
Map 14 E4.
Tel 08 92 89 90 90.
www.operadeparis.fr

Opéra National de Paris Garnier
Place de l'Opéra 75009.
Map 6 E4.
Tel 08 92 89 90 90.
www.operadeparis.fr

Pompidou Centre
19 Rue Beaubourg 75004. **Map** 13 B2.
Tel 01 44 78 12 33.

Quartier d'Eté Festival
Various venues.
Tel 01 44 94 98 00.

Sainte-Chapelle
4 Blvd du Palais. **Map** 13 A3. *Tel* 01 53 40 60 80.

St-Germain-des-Prés
Pl St-Germain-des-Prés 75006. **Map** 12 E4.
Tel 01 55 42 81 33.

St-Gervais–St-Protais
Pl St-Gervais 75004.
Map 13 B3.
Tel 01 48 87 32 02.

St-Julien-le-Pauvre
1 Rue St-Julien-le-Pauvre 75005. **Map** 13 A4.
Tel 01 42 26 00 00.

St-Louis-en-l'Ile
19 bis Rue St-Louis-en-l'Ile 75004. **Map** 13 C5.
Tel 01 46 34 11 60.

St-Roch
296 Rue St-Honoré 75001. **Map** 12 D1.
Tel 01 42 44 13 20.

St-Sulpice
Pl St-Sulpice 75006.
Map 12 E4.
Tel 01 46 33 21 78.

Salle Pleyel
252 Rue du Faubourg St-Honoré 75008.
Map 4 E3. *Tel* 01 42 56 13 13. **www**.sallepleyel.fr

Stade de France
La Plaine St-Denis 93210.
Tel 08 92 70 09 00.
www.stadedefrance.com

Studio
See Opéra National de Paris Bastille.

Théâtre de la Ville
2 Pl du Châtelet 75004.
Map 13 A3.
Tel 01 42 74 22 77.

Théâtre des Champs-Élysées
15 Ave Montaigne 75008. **Map** 10 F1.
Tel 01 49 52 50 50.

Théâtre du Châtelet
1 Pl du Châtelet 75001.
Map 13 A3.
Tel 01 40 28 28 40.

Dance

When it comes to dance, Paris is more a cultural crossroads than a cultural centre. Due to a deliberate government policy of decentralization, many of the top French dance companies are based in the provinces, although they frequently visit the capital. In addition, the greatest dance companies from all over the world perform here. Paris has a well-deserved reputation as a centre of excellence for modern and experimental dance, and has numerous workshops and places in which to learn its many forms.

CLASSICAL BALLET

The opulent **Opéra National de Paris Garnier** *(see p217)* is the home of the Ballet de l'Opéra de Paris which enjoys a reputation as one of the world's best classical dance companies.

Since the **Opéra National de Paris Bastille** opened in 1989, the Opéra National de Paris Garnier has been used almost exclusively for dance. Extensively restored both inside and out, it is one of the largest theatres in Europe, with performance space for 450 artists and a seating capacity of 2,200.

Modern dance companies such as the Martha Graham Company, Paul Taylor, Merce Cunningham, Alvin Ailey, Jerome Robbins and Roland Petit's Ballet de Marseille also regularly perform here. The Opéra National de Paris Garnier also shares operatic productions with the Opéra National de Paris Bastille.

MODERN DANCE

The **Théâtre de la Ville** (once run by Sarah Bernhardt) has become one of Paris's most important venues for modern dance. Through performances at the Théâtre de la Ville, modern choreographers such as Jean-Claude Gallotta, Regine Chopinot, Maguy Marin and Anne Teresa de Keersmaeker have gained international recognition. Here you may also see troupes such as Pina Bausch's Wuppertal Dance Theatre, whose tormented, existential choreography may not be to everyone's taste, but is popular with Parisian audiences.

Music performances also run throughout the season and include chamber music, recitals, world music and jazz.

The **Maison des Arts et de la Culture de Créteil** presents some of the most interesting dance works in Paris. It is located in the modern, concrete, mid-20th-century Paris suburb of Créteil, south east of the city. Under artistic director Didier Fusillier, dance at MAC is part of an ambitious programme of avant-garde theatre, installations and performance as showcased at its annual festival EXIT, which is held in March. Acclaimed French choreographer Maguy Marin was MAC's resident dance guru for some years.

Set amid the opulent *couture* shops and embassies, the elegant Art Deco **Théâtre des Champs-Élysées** has 1,900 seats. It is frequented by an upmarket audience who watch major international companies perform here. It was here that Nijinsky first danced Stravinsky's iconoclastic *The Rite of Spring*, which led to rioting among the audience.

The theatre is more famous as a classical music venue, but visitors have included the Dance Theatre of Harlem and London's Royal Ballet, plus a strong Russian presence, notably the St Petersburg Ballet Theatre.

The lovely old **Théâtre du Châtelet** is a renowned opera and classical music venue, but it is also host to international contemporary dance companies such as the Tokyo Ballet and the Birmingham Royal Ballet.

Experimental dance companies perform in the

Théâtre de la Bastille, where innovative theatre is also staged. Many directors and companies start here, then go on to international fame.

The **Centre National de la Danse** in Pantin, a northeastern suburb of Paris, is France's national *conservatoire*. It hosts workshops, talks and performances, from classical ballet to experimental dance.

EVENTS LISTINGS

To find out what's on, read the inexpensive weekly entertainment guides *Pariscope* and *L'Officiel des Spectacles*. Posters advertising dance performances are widely displayed in the metro and on the streets, especially on the green advertisement columns, the *colonnes Morris*.

TICKET PRICES

Expect to pay €10–€100 for tickets to the Opéra de Paris Garnier (€5–€60 for a ballet), €6–€75 for the Théâtre des Champs-Élysées, and anything from €9–€30 for other venues.

DANCE VENUES

Centre National de la Danse
1 Rue Victor Hugo 93507 Pantin.
Tel 01 41 83 98 98.

Maison des Arts et de la Culture de Créteil
Pl Salvador Allende 94000 Créteil.
Tel 01 45 13 19 19.

Opéra National de Paris Bastille
See p98.

Opéra National de Paris Garnier
See pp216–7.

Théâtre de la Bastille
76 Rue de la Roquette 75011.
Map 14 F3.
Tel 01 43 57 42 14.

Théâtre de la Ville
See p334.

Théâtre des Champs-Elysées
See p334.

Théâtre du Châtelet
See p334.

Rock, Jazz and World Music

Music lovers will find every imaginable form of music in Paris and its environs, from international pop stars in major venues to buskers of varying degrees of talent on the streets and in the metro. There's a huge variety of styles on offer, with reggae, hip-hop, world music, blues, folk, rock and jazz – Paris is said to be second only to New York in the number of jazz clubs and jazz recordings made here and there is always an excellent selection of bands and solo performers.

On the summer solstice (21 June) each year, the Fête de la Musique takes place. The whole city parties all night, with everything from huge outdoor stages and top bands to one-man buskers or accordionists playing traditional French songs invading Paris's streets, squares and cafés.

For complete listings of what's happening, buy *Pariscope* (published every Wednesday) at any kiosk. For jazz fans there's the monthly *Jazz* magazine for schedules and in-depth reviews.

MAJOR VENUES

The top international acts are often at the enormous arenas: **Palais Omnisports** at Bercy, **Stade de France** at St-Denis or the **Zénith**. Other venues such as the legendary *chanson* centre of the universe, the **Olympia**, or the **Grand Rex** (also a cinema), offer a more traditional concert-hall atmosphere. They host everyone from bewigged and cosmetically enhanced iconic first ladies of country to acid jazz stars. (*See* Directories *p350 & p359*).

ROCK AND POP

Until recently, Paris's indigenous rock groups (Les Négresses Vertes, the hit fusion band of the nineties and noughties, are probably the best-known) drew foreign attention precisely because they were French. For too long, Paris pop meant Johnny Hallyday and insipid covers of US and UK hits, or Serge Gainsbourg and his distinctive, decadent style. Paris rock traditionally (and deservedly) attracted either patronizing praise or outright mockery.

That is no longer the case. The international success of the groups Daft Punk and Air and the contribution to the music scene of producer, songwriter and musician Bertrand Burgalat led to a growth in confidence in the local music scene. The phrase "French Touch" often describes hip producers, writers or singers, now in demand all over the world. Banlieue- (suburb-) based rap, rai and reggae no longer sound like French versions of imported forms, instead they now have their own identity.

There is no shortage of gigs. The latest bands usually play at **La Cigale** and its downstairs den of din, **La Boule Noire**, the **Divan du Monde** and the **Elysée-Montmartre**, while the **Bataclan** and the **Rex** club are the best places for R&B. The **Olympia** is the city's most famous rock venue, attracting top acts. Many nightclubs also double up as live music venues (*see pp351–3*).

JAZZ

Paris is still jazz-crazy. Many American musicians have made the French capital their home because of its receptive atmosphere. All styles, from free-form to Dixieland and swing, and even hip-hop-jazz crossover, are on offer. Clubs range from quasi-concert halls to piano bars and pub-like venues. One of the most popular places, though not the most comfortable, is the **New Morning**. It's hot and the table service can be a little erratic, but all the great jazz musicians continue to perform here, as they have in the past. Arrive early to ensure a good seat. **Le Duc des Lombards** is a lively jazz club in Les Halles, which also features salsa.

Many jazz clubs are also cafés, bars or restaurants. The latter includes the intimate **Autour de Midi... et Minuit** in Montmartre, with its vaulted "cave". Dining might not be a requirement, but it's always wise to check first.

Other hotspots are **Le Petit Journal Montparnasse** for modern jazz, **Le Petit Journal St-Michel** for Dixieland. A trendy crowd is drawn to **La Bellevilloise's** Sunday jazz brunches in Ménilmontant. **Caveau de la Huchette** looks like the archetypal jazz joint, but today it favours swing and big-band music, and is popular with students. The **Caveau des Oubliettes** has a growing reputation for cutting-edge jazz.

For a change, try the local talent at small, friendly bars such as the less expensive **Bistrot d'Eustache** and super cool **La Flèche d'Or**, set in an old railway station. The **Jazz Club Etoile** in the Méridien hotel is a well-respected venue which features Sunday jazz brunch. On the other side of town, the **Trabendo** has an intriguing mix of up-and-comers and down-and-outers. Although the **Sunset** is primarily known for jazz, it also includes blues nights on its programme.

Paris has two international jazz festivals in summer: the Paris Jazz Festival (*see p63*) and Jazz à la Villette in July. The Paris Jazz Festival is the mainstay of the summer calendar, and Jazz à la Villette offers films on jazz, debates and discussions and *boeufs* (jam sessions).

WORLD MUSIC

With its large populations from West Africa, the Maghreb, the Antilles and Latin America, Paris is a natural centre for world music. The **Chapelle des Lombards** has played host to top acts; it also has jazz, salsa and Brazilian music. **Aux Trois Mailletz** is a medieval cellar with everything from blues to tango and rock and roll covers, while **Kibélé** is a great place for North African sounds. Many jazz clubs intersperse their programmes with ethnic music. These include **New Morning**, which also has shows with South American artists, and **Baiser Salé**, for popular acts including Makossa, Kassav, Malavoi and Manu Dibango.

World music in a stunning setting can be found at the Institut du Monde Arabe, a wonderful architectural feat (see p164) which draws stars from the Arab music world to its concert hall.

TICKET PRICES

Prices at jazz clubs can be steep, and there may be a cover charge of over €15 at the door, which usually includes the first drink. If there is no cover charge, the drinks will be expensive and at least one must be bought.

Tickets can be bought online or from FNAC outlets and Virgin Megastore (see p341), or directly from venue box offices and at the door of the clubs themselves.

DIRECTORY

MAJOR VENUES

Grand Rex
1 Blvd Poissonnière
75002. **Map** 7 A5.
Tel 08 92 68 05 96.

Olympia
28 Blvd des Capucines
75009. **Map** 6 D5.
Tel 08 92 68 33 68.
www.olympiahall.com

Palais Omnisports de Paris-Bercy
8 Blvd de Bercy 75012.
Map 18 F2.
Tel 08 92 39 01 00.
www.bercy.fr

Zénith
211 Ave de Jean-Jaurès
75019.
Tel 08 90 71 02 07.
www.le-zenith.com/paris

ROCK AND POP

Bataclan
50 Blvd Voltaire
75011.
Map 14 E1.
Tel 01 43 14 00 30.

La Cigale/ La Boule Noire
120 Blvd Rochechouart
75018. **Map** 6 F2.
Tel 01 49 25 81 75.

Divan du Monde
75 Rue des Martyrs
75018. **Map** 6 F2.
Tel 01 40 05 06 99.

Elysée-Montmartre
72 Blvd Rochechouart
75018. **Map** 6 F2.
Tel 01 44 92 45 36.
www.elyseemont martre.com

Rex Club
5 Blvd Poissonnière
75002.
Map 7 A5.
Tel 01 42 36 10 96.

JAZZ

Autour De Midi... et Minuit
11 Rue Lepic 75018.
Map 6 E1.
Tel 01 55 79 16 48.

Baiser Salé
58 Rue des Lombards
75001.
Map 13 A2.
Tel 01 42 33 37 71.

Bellevilloise
19 Rue Boyer 75020.
Tel 01 46 36 07 07.
www.labellevilloise.com

Bistrot d'Eustache
37 Rue Berger, Carré des Halles 75001.
Map 13 A2.
Tel 01 40 26 23 20.

Caveau de la Huchette
5 Rue de la Huchette
75005.
Map 13 A4.
Tel 01 43 26 65 05.

Caveau des Oubliettes
52 Rue Galande
75005.
Map 13 A4.
Tel 01 46 34 23 09.

Le Duc des Lombards
42 Rue des Lombards
75001.
Map 13 A2.
Tel 01 42 33 22 88.

La Flèche d'Or
102bis Rue de Bagnolet
75020.
Tel 01 44 64 01 02.

La Grande Halle de la Villette
211 Ave Jean-Jaurès
75019.
Map 8 F1.
Tel 01 40 03 75 75.

Jazz Club Etoile
Hôtel Méridien,
81 Blvd Gouvion-St-Cyr
75017.
Map 3 C3.
Tel 01 40 68 30 42.
www.jazzclub-paris.com

New Morning
7–9 Rue des Petites-Écuries
75010.
Map 7 B4.
Tel 01 45 23 51 41.

Paris Jazz Festival
Parc Floral Bois de Vincennes 75012.

Le Petit Journal Montparnasse
13 Rue du Commandant-Mouchotte
75014.
Map 15 C2.
Tel 01 43 21 56 70.

Le Petit Journal St-Michel
71 Blvd St-Michel
75005.
Map 16 F1.
Tel 01 43 26 28 59.

Sunset
60 Rue des Lombards
75001. **Map** 13 A2.
Tel 01 40 26 46 60.
www.sunset-sunside. com

Trabendo
211 Ave Jean-Jaurès
75019.
Map 8 F1.
Tel 01 42 01 12 12.

WORLD MUSIC

Aux Trois Mailletz
56 Rue Galande
75005.
Map 13 A4.
Tel 01 43 54 42 94.

Baiser Salé
(See Jazz).

Chapelle des Lombards
19 Rue de Lappe
75011. **Map** 14 F4.
Tel 01 43 57 24 24.

Institut du Monde Arabe
(See p164).

Kibélé
12 Rue de l'Echiquier
75010. **Map** 7 B5.
Tel 01 48 24 57 74.

New Morning
7 Rue des Petites-Ecuries
75010.
Map 7 B4.
Tel 01 45 23 51 41.

Nightclubs

The club scene in Paris is now somewhat under siege as government legislation on noise levels hampers establishments' *modus operandi*. The city council is waging war on noise pollution and whilst this suits those with neighbours who possess large stereos, it's bad news for people who like to dance till dawn. They carry on regardless, albeit with fewer decibels, and you will still find every type of sound (and a great deal of creativity) on the club scene. There are clubs to suit every taste and it's worth noting that bouncers often treat foreign would-be entrants preferentially, so be sure to stand proud, ditch the attempts at French and speak English when you get near the door. The English website www.gogoparis.com reviews some of the capital's trendiest establishments. Alternatively, read the posters at the Bastille metro station or listen to Radio NOVA 101.5 FM, which gives details of the night's best raves. Flyers advertising what's on at which clubs can be found on café, bar and shop counters. Popular nighttime options for the more mature set include social dancing and visits to suave piano bars. If you're wondering about what to wear, the smart side of the smart-casual approach is usually the safest bet. Attire for nightclubs varies; for upscale venues be sure to put your designer-labelled best foot forward, whilst more relaxed ones will accept an urban look, but generally, tracksuits, jeans and trainers are definite no-nos.

MAINSTREAM

A vast yet convivial venue, **Le Bataclan** is a showcase for current bands. After the show on Saturday nights, it becomes one of the best nightclubs in Paris, legendary for its varied mouth-watering choice of funk, soul and new jack swing.

Barrio Latino occupies three floors of a building designed by Gustav Eiffel. It combines Latin music with great cocktails and tapas served from trolleys by roaming staff. Dancers can perfect their moves at the Sunday salsa classes. The expensive **Le Baron** attracts a select crowd, and plays host to ultra-fashionable party producers. Linked to the **Alcazar**, which is a fashionable Terence Conran bar and restaurant very popular with a pre-club crowd, **WAGG** just next door is a wonderful spot for some uninhibited dancing. WAGG is unpretentious although the door staff are discriminating, and the disco and soul

played in the stone cellars make for a great night out. **Les Bains-Douches**, a former Turkish bath, may have lost some of its glitterati appeal but it is still a place to go to see and be seen. Its upstairs restaurant, now serving Thai food, is a popular place for private dinner parties. This is the place to be, so book a table for dinner if you're concerned about gaining entry and getting a much-coveted seat. The dance floor is tiny and music is mainly house, with 1970s and 1980s disco on Mondays, and R&B on Wednesdays. Gay night is *Café con Leche* on Sundays. Legendary promoters and Parisian nightowls David and Cathy Guetta left Les Bains a while ago and took some of their regulars with them, but the club is still a flash place to be and there is always the possibility of spotting a film star. A mix of ages and trends frequent the **Rex Club**. Despite the essentially conservative nature of the clientele, the music on

different nights ranges from glam rock and house to "exotique" – funk, reggae and world music. Sounds are mainly rock and roll at the smart and non-ageist **Zed Club**. The vast **La Machine** caters to mainstream tastes most nights, with rock, house, groove and dance music each occupying a different floor.

EXCLUSIVE

If you aren't rich, beautiful and at least super-hip (if not actually on the celebrity "A" list), gaining entry to Paris's more exclusive clubs will be difficult. If you are, be prepared for a degree of humiliation and snooty service all the same. **Castel's** is a strictly private club and the happy few who make it, dine in one of two restaurants before heading down to the dance floor.

Regine's is mostly full of besuited executives and wealthy foreigners who dine and dance to the easy-listening music. However, it is enjoying something of a renaissance, especially on ladies nights (Thursday), when a trained physiognomist picks out the best looking women for a girls-own session complete with a male strip show. Predictably, when the doors open to men later, it becomes one of Paris's top nightspots for seeing and being seen.

The wood-panelled, cosy **Ritz Club** in the legendary Ritz hotel is open only to members and hotel guests, though the chic and elegant are welcome. The ambience is upmarket and the music is easy listening. A younger, glamorous set have begun to make the Ritz Club their home, attracted, no doubt, by its old-fashioned star quality.

Le World Place is one of the city's hippest places to see and be seen in. The smooth and stylish decor sets off the expensive tans sported by the jetsetters, supermodels and film stars who come here. Booking a table at the expensive, but decent, Lobster Café restaurant is a good way to ensure access. Equally posh, **Le VIP** is populated by wannabes attracted by the name. Private parties are often held here, so it's a good idea to call ahead.

Showcase is a hot venue on Paris's night-scene with over 3,000 sq metres (32,000 sq feet) of space below the Pont Alexandre III. It triples as a bar, nightclub and concert hall. Another extremely upscale spot is **L'Etoile** situated near the Arc de Triomphe. Be prepared to make the effort to look your best (and most-solvent) to get in here.

The most popular of the posh clubs and the most laid-back and friendly once you're inside, is **Le Cab** (formerly known as Cabaret). The interior has been redesigned by Ora Ito, and today, anybody who's anybody comes here to dance like crazy or lay back and take it all in on one of the sumptuous mattresses in the chillout area.

TRENDY

MadaM is known for its late-night sessions and beautiful, moneyed crowds. The music is very French, with lots of electro and disco, and the decor is sylish, with a members' club atmosphere.

An ultra-hip young crowd come to enjoy cocktails and sushi at the glam rock styled **Bound** lounge and restaurant near the Champs-Elysées. Bound's terrace is a big draw in warmer weather. For a top dancing night out, try the fortnightly "Bal" with live big band at the **Elysée Montmartre**.

Paris's trendy clubs seem to have a longer shelf-life than those in some other cities and another hip venue that's still going strong is **Le Gibus** which offers different dance styles throughout the week. Check the flyers to pick your own style of party. The **Batofar**, the scarlet lighthouse ship moored on the Seine in the 13th arrondissement, is now a

mainstay of the Paris club scene. The music here varies from underground techno to reggae depending on the night of the week, but the crowd are always friendly and relaxed. In the summer, try not to miss their wonderfully chilled-out afternoon sessions on the quayside.

The **Nouveau Casino** behind the ever trendy Café Charbon (see p319) in Oberkampf pulls in an eclectic crowd for events varying from dub to air-guitar competitions. **Le Social Club** has made an impressive mark on the Paris club scene with both its mixed programming and excellent live music agenda.

Old-timer **La Flèche d'Or** also offers an eclectic array of concerts, DJ nights and concept evenings. Whilst if it's just a large dance floor that's needed, then **Mix Club** should suffice.

WORLD MUSIC

Le Cabaret Sauvage entertains a chic crowd under a big-top. Its eclectic programme includes jazz, African sounds and drum 'n' bass. **Le Casbah** is exclusive, jazzy and one of the best established venues on the Paris club scene. Its African-Middle Eastern decor has always been a magnet for models and trendies who, in between dances, do a little nocturnal shopping in the club's downstairs boutique. Le Casbah is at present deservedly enjoying something of a renaissance of its former "chicest of the chic" reputation.

If your nervous system responds favourably to the heaving rhythms and throbbing beat of authentic Latin music, you should head for **La Java**, which combines glorious sounds with the quaint appeal of a Belleville dance hall. **Barrio Latino** definitely is the place to go for salsa with soul. Spread out over four floors, it has a restaurant on the second floor, while the other three are given over to dancing.

La Bellevilloise often has eclectic world music (see p350). Other lively world music and rock nights are held at **Satellit' Café** and **La Maroquinerie** which attract big stars. The latter also houses a restaurant and literary café.

GAY AND LESBIAN

The gay scene in Paris is thriving. **Le Queen** boasts a great line-up of DJs. Monday is disco night, Friday and Saturday are garage and soul and the rest of the week is drum and bass and house. Some of the raunchier events are men-only. Girls should go with pretty boys. Some nights at **La Machine** draw in a gay crowd. **Le Champmeslé**, one of the most venerable fixtures of Paris's ever more upfront and confident lesbian scene, continues to evolve and attract a new clientele. **Le Tango** is a converted dance hall that features a wacky crowd, Madonna and accordian music.

For a pre-club venue, lesbian bar **Le Troisième Lieu** is the hippest and busiest. **Le Day Off** is a favourite haunt for afterwork drinks. Scream is the gay night at the **Elysée Montmartre**. **Le Club 18** is the oldest gay club in the city. A young and beautiful crowd come here for the fun music and very laid-back atmosphere. It's a small venue so it's packed at weekends, when the admission fee includes a drink. Entry is usually free on weeknights.

ADMISSION CHARGES

Some clubs are strictly private, others have a more generous admission policy. Prices can range from €12 to €15 or €30, or more, and may be higher after midnight and on weekends. But quite often there are concessions for women.

In general, one drink (une consommation) is included in the club's entry price; thereafter it can become an extremely expensive evening.

DIRECTORY

DISCO AND CLUB VENUES

Alcazar
62 Rue Mazarine 75006.
Map 12 F4.
Tel 01 53 10 19 99.
www.alcazar.fr

Les Bains-Douches
7 Rue du Bourg-
L'Abbé 75003.
Map 13 B1.
Tel 01 53 01 40 60.
www.lesbains
douches.net

Le Baron
6 Ave Marceau 75008.
Map 10 E1.
Tel 01 47 20 04 01.
www.clublebaron.com

Barrio Latino
46-48 Rue du Faubourg
Saint Antoine 75012.
Map 14 F4.
Tel 01 55 78 84 75.

Le Bataclan
50 blvd Voltaire
75011.
Map 13 E1.
Tel 01 43 14 00 30.
www.le-bataclan.com

Batofar
Moored opposite 11
Quai Francois Mauriac
75013.
Tel 09 71 25 50 61.
www.batofar.org

Bound
49–51 Ave George V
75008.
Map 4 E5.
Tel 01 53 67 84 60.
www.buddha-bar.com

Le Cab
2 Pl de Palais Royal
75001.
Map 12 E1.
Tel 01 58 62 56 25.
www.cabaret.fr

Castel's
15 Rue Princesse
75006.
Map 12 E4.
Tel 01 40 51 52 80.

Le Duplex
2 Bis Avenue Foch
75116.
Map 4 D4.
Tel 01 45 00 45 00.
www.leduplex.fr

Elysée Montmartre
72 Blvd Rochechouart
75018.
Map 6 F2.
Tel 01 44 92 45 36.
www.elysee
montmartre.com

L'Etoile
12 Rue de Presbourg
75016.
Map 4 D4.
Tel 01 45 00 78 70.
www.letoileparis.com

La Flèche d'Or
102 bis Rue de Bagnolet
75002.
Tel 01 44 64 01 02.
www.flechedor.fr

Le Gibus
18 Rue du Faubourg-du-
Temple 75011.
Map 8 E15.
Tel 01 47 00 78 88.
www.gibus.fr

Hammam Club
94 Rue d'Amsterdam
75009.
Map 6 D2.
Tel 01 55 07 80 00.
www.hammanclub.com

La Machine
90 Blvd de Clichy
75018. **Map** 4 E4.
Tel 01 53 41 88 88.
www.lamachinedu
moulinrouge.com

MadaM
128 Rue de la Boétie
75008.
Map 4 F5.
Tel 01 58 76 02 11.
www.madam.fr

Mix Club
24 Rue de l'Arrivée
75015.
Map 15 C1.
Tel 01 56 80 37 37.

Nouveau Casino
109 Rue Oberkampf
75011.
Map 14 E1.
Tel 01 43 57 57 40.

Les Planches
40 Rue Colisée 75008.
Map 5 A4.
Tel 01 42 25 11 68.

Red Light
34 Rue du Départ 75015.
Map 15 C2.
Tel 01 42 79 94 53.
www.enfer.fr

Regine's
49–51 Rue Ponthieu
75008.
Map 5 A5.
Tel 01 43 59 21 13.

Rex Club
5 Blvd Poissonnière
75002.
Map 7 A5.
Tel 01 42 36 10 96.

Ritz Club
Hôtel Ritz, 15 Pl
Vendôme 75001.
Map 6 D5.
Tel 01 43 16 30 30.
www.ritzparis.com

Showcase
Port des Champs-Elysées
75008.
Map 11 A1.
Tel 01 45 61 25 43.

Le Social Club
142 rue Montmartre
75002.
Map 13 A1.
Tel 01 40 28 05 55.

Le Tango
13 Rue Au Maire 75003.
Map 13 C1.
Tel 01 42 72 17 78.

Le World Place
32–34 Rue du Marbeuf
75008. **Map** 4 F5.
Tel 01 56 88 36 36.
www.worldplace-
paris.com

VIP
76 Ave des Champs-
Elysées 75008.
Map 4 E4.
Tel 01 56 69 16 66.

WAGG
62 Rue Mazarine
75006. **Map** 12 F4.
Tel 01 55 42 22 00.

Zed Club
2 Rue des Anglais 75005.
Map 13 A5.
Tel 01 43 54 93 78.

WORLD MUSIC

Cabaret Sauvage
59 Blvd Macdonald
75019.
Tel 01 42 09 03 09.

Le Casbah
18-20 Rue de la Forge-
Royale 75011.
Tel 01 43 71 04 39.

La Java
105 Rue du Faubourg-du-
Temple 75010.
Map 8 E5.
Tel 01 42 02 20 52.

La Maroquinerie
23 Rue Boyer 75020.
Map 15 B4.
Tel 01 40 33 35 05.

Satellit Café
44 Rue Folie Méricourt
75011. **Map** 14 E1.
Tel 01 47 00 48 87.

GAY AND LESBIAN VENUES

La Champmeslé
4 Rue Chabanais 75002.
Map 12 E1.
Tel 01 42 96 85 20.

Le Club 18
18 Rue de Beaujolais
75001.
Map 12 F1.
Tel 01 42 97 52 13.

Le Day Off
10 Rue de l'Islay 75008.
Map 5 C4.
Tel 01 45 22 87 90.

Le Queen
102 Ave des Champs-
Elysées 75008.
Map 4 E4.
Tel 01 53 89 08 90.

Le Troisième Lieu
62 Rue Quincampoix
75004.
Map 13 B2.
Tel 01 48 04 85 64.

Cinema

Paris can justifiably claim to be one of the world's capitals of film appreciation. With more than 370 screens within the city limits, distributed among over 100 cinemas and multiplexes, a fabulous cornucopia of films are screened, both brand-new and classic. American movies share the limelight with home-grown dramas and comedies, and virtually every filmmaking industry in the world has found a niche in the city's art houses. Cinemas change their programmes on Wednesdays. The cheapest practical guides to what's on are *Pariscope* and *L'Officiel des Spectacles (see p340)* with complete cinema listings and timetables for some 300 films. Films shown in subtitled original language versions are coded "VO" *(version originale)*; dubbed films are coded "VF" *(version française)*. The Fête du Cinéma is held for one week in late June/July. The system is that you pay full price for one film, after which a special card gives access to unlimited films at just €3 a ticket, for the duration of the festival.

MOVEMENTS IN CINEMA

Paris was the cradle of the cinematograph over 100 years ago, when Auguste and Louis Lumière invented the early film projector. Their screening of *L'Arrivée d'un Train en Gare de la Ciotat* (Arrival of a Train at la Ciotat Station) in Paris in 1895 is considered by many to mark the birth of the medium. The French reverence for film as a true art form is based on a theory of one of the world's first film critics, Ricciotto Canudo, an Italian intellectual living in France, who dubbed cinematography "the Seventh Art" in 1922. The title holds true even today. The city was of course also the incubator of that very Parisian vanguard movement, the New Wave, when film directors such as Claude Chabrol, François Truffaut, Jean-Luc Godard and Eric Rohmer in the late 1950s and early 60s revolutionized the way films were made and perceived. The exploration of existential themes, the use of long tracking shots and the rejection of studios for outside locations are some of the characteristics of New Wave film. In 2001, the success of *Amélie Poulain* revitalized the Parisian filmmaking scene; many of its locations are easy to spot as you walk around town. The same is true of *The Da Vinci Code*, also featuring *Amélie* star Audrey Tautou.

CINEMA ZONES

Most Paris cinemas are concentrated in several cinema belts, which enjoy the added appeal of nearby restaurants and shops.

The Champs-Elysées remains the densest cinema strip in town, where you can see the latest Hollywood smash hit or French *auteur* triumph, as well as some classic reissues, in subtitled original language versions. Cinemas in the Grands Boulevards, in the vicinity of the Opéra de Paris Garnier, show films in both subtitled and dubbed versions. Boulevard de Clichy is home to two Pathé multiplexes with a total of 12 screens showing current dubbed, French and VO releases. A major hub of Right Bank cinema activity is in the Forum des Halles shopping mall.

The Left Bank, historically associated with the city's intellectual life, remains the centre of the art and repertory cinemas. Yet, it has equally as many of the latest blockbusters. Since the 1980s, many cinemas in the Latin Quarter have closed down and the main centre for Left Bank theatres is now the Odéon-St-Germain-des-Prés area. The Rue Champollion is an exception. It has enjoyed a revival as a mini-district for art and repertory films.

Further to the south, Montparnasse remains a lively district for new films in both dubbed and subtitled prints.

BIG SCREENS AND PICTURE PALACES

Among surviving landmark cinemas are two Grands Boulevards venues, the 2,800-seat **Le Grand Rex** with its Baroque decor, and the **Max Linder Panorama**, which was refurbished by a group of independent film buffs in the 1980s for both popular and art film programming.

The massive 14-screen **MK2 Bibliothèque** cinema (plus bar, shops and exhibition space), has opened up in the revitalised 13th arrondissement and just across the river, the **Bercy Village** cinema complex is well worth a visit too.

In the Cité des Sciences et de l'Industrie at La Villette, scientific films are shown at **La Géode** *(see p237)*. This has a hemispheric screen (once the world's largest) and an "omnimax" projector which uses 70-mm film shot horizontally to project an image which is nine times larger than the standard 35-mm print. Along the Canal St-Martin, **MK2**'s twin cinema complexes – **Quai de la Loire** and **Quai de la Seine** – are linked by a canal boat.

REVIVAL AND REPERTORY HOUSES

Each week, more than 150 titles representing the best of world cinema can be seen. For old Hollywood films, the independent **Grand Action** mini-chain can't be beaten. Other active and thoughtful repertory and reissue venues include the excellent **Reflets Médicis** screens in the Rue Champollion and the **Pagode**. The latter is particularly striking; the Oriental pagoda was constructed in 1895.

Studio 28 in Montmartre is a lovely old movie house with lights in the theatre designed by Jean Cocteau and a charming garden bar full of fairy lights and kitsch cut-outs of old film stars. Opened in the 1920s, Studio 28 claims to be the first ever avant-garde cinema and once played host to film greats such as Luis Buñuel and Abel Gance. They screen everything from the latest releases through to Fellini festivals and documentary shows. There are at least ten films screened here each week, including art-house classics and pre-releases. The cinema also holds regular debates with well-known directors and actors. Another Parisian institution, **Studio Galande** has shown the *Rocky Horror Picture Show* to costumed movie-goers every Friday night for over 20 years.

CINÉMATHÈQUE FRANÇAISE

The private "school" of the New Wave generation, this famous film archive and repertory cinema was created by Henri Langlois in 1936 *(see p200)*. It has lost its monopoly on classic film screenings, but it is still a must for cinephiles in search of that rare film no longer in theatrical circulation or, perhaps, recently restored or rescued. The association is now housed at 51 Rue de Bercy in a wonderfully futuristic-looking building designed by Frank Gehry. The sail-like façade has given the building its nickname: "dancer revealing her tutu". The film library has more than 18,000 digitalized movies, and there are enough exhibitions, projections, lectures and workshops to satisfy the appetite of any film enthusiast. For those interested in the building's architecture there are tours on the first Sunday of each month.

NON-THEATRICAL VENUES

In addition to the Cinémathèque Française, film programmes and festivals are integral parts of two highly popular Paris cultural institutions, the Musée d'Orsay *(see pp144–5)* and the Pompidou Centre *(see pp110–11)* with its two screening rooms. The Musée d'Orsay regularly schedules film programmes to complement current art exhibitions and is usually restricted to silent films. The Pompidou Centre organizes vast month-long retrospectives, devoted to national film industries and on occasion to some of the major companies.

Finally, the **Forum des Images** *(see p109)* in the heart of Les Halles is a hi-tech film and video library with a vast selection of films and documentaries featuring the city of Paris from the late 19th century to the present day. The archives here are amazing and include newsreels and advertisements featuring Paris alongside the feature films and documentaries. The Forum has three cinemas, all of which run daily screenings of feature films. One ticket allows the visitor access to both the video library and to the cinema screenings. The screenings are frequently grouped according to theme or director, making it possible to spend several hours enjoying a mini-retrospective. See website for details.

TICKET PRICES

Expect to pay around €9 at first-run venues or even more for films of unusual length or special media attention. However, exhibitors practise a wide array of collective discount incentives, including cut-rate admissions for students, the unemployed, the elderly, old soldiers and large families. Wednesday is discount day for everybody at some cinemas – prices are slashed to as low as €4.

France's three exhibition giants, Gaumont, UGC and MK2, also sell special discount cards and accept credit card reservations for their flagship houses, while repertory houses issue "fidelity" cards.

FILMS WITH STRONG IMAGES OF PARIS

Historical Paris (studio-made)

An Italian Straw Hat
(René Clair, 1927)

Sous les toits de Paris
(René Clair, 1930)

Les Misérables
(Raymond Bernard, 1934)

Hôtel du Nord
(Marcel Carné, 1937)

Les Enfants du Paradis
(Marcel Carné, 1945)

Casque d'Or
(Jacques Becker, 1952)

La Traversée de Paris
(Claude Autant-Lara, 1956)

Playtime
(Jacques Tati, 1967)

New Wave Paris (location-made)

Breathless
(Jean-Luc Godard, 1959)

Les 400 coups
(François Truffaut, 1959)

Documentary Paris

Paris 1900
(Nicole Vedrès, 1948)

La Seine a rencontré Paris
(Joris Ivans, 1957)

Paris as seen by Hollywood

Seventh Heaven
(Frank Borzage, 1927)

Camille
(George Cukor, 1936)

An American in Paris
(Vincente Minnelli, 1951)

Gigi
(Vincente Minnelli, 1958)

Irma La Douce
(Billy Wilder, 1963)

Paris when it Sizzles
(Richard Quine, 1964)

Frantic
(Roman Polanski, 1988)

French Kiss
(Lawrence Kasdan, 1995)

The Ninth Gate
(Roman Polanski, 1999)

Moulin Rouge
(Baz Luhrmann, 2001)

The Bourne Identity
(Doug Liman, 2002)

Before Sunset
(Richard Linklater, 2004)

The Da Vinci Code
(Ron Howard, 2006)

Cinema Festivals

Film festivals are a way of life for Parisian movie buffs. There are several major events each year and lots of small themed festivals happening at any given time around the city. The annual Paris Film Festival, held at the end of March, may be dwarfed by its glitzier sister in Cannes, but the capital's version is a far friendlier event for the public to attend – and there are still more than enough opportunities to spot celebrities.

OPEN AIR FESTIVALS

There are several outdoor cinema festivals throughout the summer, including the Festival Silhouette which shows short films in the lovely Buttes Chaumont (*see p234*), the Cinéma au Clair de Lune festival which has projections of films at Parisian sites which are relevant to the movie and Le Cinéma en Plein Air which draws crowds to a lawn in La Villette (*see pp236-7*), where a giant inflatable screen shows old and contemporary classics. This is one of the summer's most popular events so be sure to get there early and don't forget to take a hamper full of goodies to nibble on throughout the movie.

INDOOR FESTIVALS

During the annual Paris Film Festival, over 100 films are shown at the Gaumont Marignon on the Champs-Elysées. The city's gay and lesbian film festival at the Forum des Images usually takes place in November. Paris Tout Court is an impressive short film festival held at the Arlequin in St-Germain which also stages lectures and meetings with renowned directors and artists. Other film festivals include the L'Etrange festival which shows weird and wonderful offbeat films from around the world to enthusiastic audiences.

DIRECTORY

CINEMAS

Action Ecoles
23 Rue des Ecoles 75005.
Map 13 A5.
Tel 08 92 680 591.

Arlequin
76 Rue de Rennes 75006.
Map 12 E4.
Tel 01 45 44 28 80.

Le Balzac
1 Rue Balzac 75008.
Map 4 E4.
Tel 01 45 61 10 60.

Centre Georges Pompidou
19 Rue Beaubourg 75004.
Map 13 B2.

Le Champo
51 Rue des Ecoles 75005.
Map 13 A5.
Tel 01 43 54 51 60.

Cinémathèque Française
51 Rue de Bercy 75013.
Tel 01 71 19 33 33.
www.cinemateque.fr

Cinema Studio Galande
42 Rue Galande 75005.
Map 13 A4.
Tel 08 92 68 06 24.

Cine Sorbonne
9 Rue Champollion 75005.
Map 13 A5.
Tel 01 43 26 70 38.

Forum des Images
Porte St-Eustache,
Forum des Halles 75001.
Map 13 A2.
Tel 01 44 76 63 00.
www.forumdesimages.fr

Gaumont Marignan
27 Ave Champs-Elysées 75008.
Map 5 A5.
Tel 08 92 69 66 96.

La Géode
26 Ave Corentin-Cariou 75019.
Tel 08 92 68 45 40.
www.lageode.fr

Grand Action
Action Rive Gauche,
5 Rue des Ecoles 75005.
Map 13 B5.
Tel 01 43 54 47 62.

Le Grand Rex
1 Blvd Poissonnière 75002.
Map 7 A5.
Tel 08 92 68 05 96.

Latina
20 Rue du Temple 75004.
Map 7 C2.
Tel 01 42 78 47 86.

Lucernaire
53 Rue Notre-Dame-des-Champs 75006.
Map 16 E2.
Tel 01 45 44 57 34.

Max Linder Panorama
24 Blvd Poissonnière 75009. **Map** 7 A5.
Tel 08 92 68 00 31.

Majestic Bastille
4 Blvd Richard Lenoir 75011. **Map** 14 E4.
Tel 01 47 00 02 48.

MK2 Beaubourg
50 Rue Rambuteau 75003.
Map 7 B2.
Tel 08 92 69 84 84.

MK2 Bibliothèque
128-162 Ave de France 75013. **Map** 18 F4.
Tel 08 92 69 84 84.

MK2 Quai de la Seine/Quai de la Loire
75019. **Map** 8 F1.
Tel 08 92 69 84 84.

Odeon Christine
4 Rue Christine 75006.
Map 12 F4.
Tel 01 43 25 85 78.

Pagode
57 bis Rue de Babylone 75007. **Map** 11 C4.
Tel 01 45 55 48 48.

Racine Odeon
6 Rue de l'Ecole de Médecine 75006.
Map 12 F4.
Tel 01 46 33 43 71.

Reflets Médicis
3-7 Rue Champollion 75005.
Map 12 F5.
Tel 01 46 33 25 97.

St-Andre des Arts
30 Rue St Andre des Arts 75006.
Map 12 F4.
Tel 01 43 26 48 18.

Studio 28
10 Rue Tholozé 75018.
Map 6 E1.
Tel 01 46 06 36 07.

UGC Ciné Cité Bercy
2 Cour St-Emilion 75012.
Tel 08 92 700 000.

UGC Cine-Cite les Halles
7 Place de la Rotonde 75001.
Map 7 A2.
Tel 08 92 70 00 00.

Sport and Fitness

There is no end of sporting activities in Paris. Certain events such as the Roland Garros tennis tournament and the Tour de France bicycle race are national institutions. The only drawback is that many of the facilities are on the outskirts of the city.

For details regarding all sporting events in and around Paris contact Paris's tourist office. The weekly entertainment guides *L'Officiel des Spectacles*, *Pariscope* and the Wednesday edition of *Le Figaro* also have good listings of the week's sporting events *(see p340)*. For in-depth sports coverage there is the daily paper *L'Equipe*. See also *Children's Paris* on page 362.

OUTDOOR SPORTS

The annual Tour de France bicycle race finishes in July in Paris to city-wide frenzy, when the French president awards the coveted *maillot jaune* (yellow jersey) to the winner. For over twenty years now the final stage of the tour has taken place over several laps of a circuit taking in the Louvre, the quais along the Seine and the Champs-Elysées. Finding a spot to watch can be extremely tough, it's best to hunt down your space several hours before the riders are expected.

For those brave enough to cycle through the city traffic, bikes may be hired throughout Paris, including at **Vélo Paris** in Montmartre and at around 1,500 locations across the city with the self-service **Vélib'** scheme. The first 30 minutes are free, after which there are additional charges: at a rate of €1 for the next 30 minutes, €2 for another 30 minutes and thereafter at €4 for every additional 30 minutes. Regular users can buy a one- or seven-day card.

The **Fédération Française de Cyclotourisme** in the Rue Louis Bertrand provides information on over 300 cycling clubs around Paris. Things are gradually improving for those who favour pedal power: the city council shuts down some of the quaysides on Sundays and national holidays to allow cyclists freewheeling next to the Seine and the Canal St-Martin. The city has also undertaken a programme of expansion for its cycle lanes *(pistes cyclables)*, and Parisian drivers are becoming more respectful of cyclists as more people turn to travelling on two wheels. Those who can't wait for the quais along the Seine to be closed on Sundays should head over to the Bois de Vincennes or the Bois de Boulogne for a leisurely bike ride through the woods. The more ambitious can pick up a copy of the free Paris à Vélo map from a tourist office to find details of all the city's cycle lanes. If you'd prefer to take an organized cycle tour through the city, there are several organizations who run fun trips. **Fat Tire Bike Tours** in the Rue Edgar Faure are expensive but have daily trips in spring and summer in which knowledgeable guides shepherd cyclists around the streets whilst imparting interesting information on the city's landmarks. Their partner, **City Segway Tours**, offers guided tours on electric Segway scooters (over 12s only). **Paris à Vélo c'est Sympa!** runs multi-lingual tours to offbeat parts of the city.

Roller bladers can enjoy parades through the city on Friday nights. The police close off boulevards around the city allowing thousands of skate fans to join the trip every week. The parade usually starts at Place de la Bastille at 10pm, but you can join the route at any point if the whole circuit seems a little much. Contact www.pari-roller.com for details of the route. Beginners can enjoy free tuition prior to the departure of the parade if they arrive at the start point at 8pm. There are many good outlets in the city for rollerblade rental. The parade's website provides useful links to recommended outlets. As a safety precaution the trip is cancelled if the weather is inclement and the roads are wet.

Parisians enjoy Sunday afternoon boating in the Bois de Vincennes *(see p235)*, the Bois de Boulogne *(see p254)* and the Parc des Buttes-Chaumont *(see p234)*. Just queue up to hire a boat.

All the golf courses are outside Paris. Many are private clubs, but some will admit non-members – for further information contact the **Fédération Française du Golf** in the Rue Anatole-France. Otherwise try the **Golf de Chevry, Golf de Villeray, Golf de St-Quentin en Yvelines** or the **Golf de Villennes**. Expect to pay at least €25 each time you want to play.

You can go horse-riding in both the Bois de Boulogne and the Bois de Vincennes. For details, contact the **Comité Departemental d'Equitation de Paris** in the Rue Laugier.

Tennis can be played at municipal courts such as the **Tennis Luxembourg** in the Jardin du Luxembourg. Courts are available every day on a first-come first-served basis. **Tennis de la Faluère** in the Bois de Vincennes has some of the better courts, but these must be booked at least 24 hours in advance.

INDOOR SPORTS

There are plenty of gyms in Paris which you can use with a day pass. Expect to pay €20 or more, depending on the facilities.

Club Med Gym is a well-equipped, popular chain of gyms with more than twenty sites in Paris and the suburbs. Good choices include the branches in Rue de Berri and Rue de Rennes. **Club Jean de Beauvais** in the Rue Jean de Beauvais, is a state-of-the-art gym with personalized fitness programmes. The **Ken Club** on Avenue President Kennedy is an upmarket gym complete with pool and sauna in the chic 16th arrondissement. Its proximity to France's public radio HQ means French media personalities are often to be found there working out on their lunch break. In theory the **Ritz Gym**, which has the finest indoor swimming pool in Paris, is for guests or members only, but if the hotel is not too full you can buy a day pass.

Skating is a cheap pastime and can be enjoyed year-round at the **Patinoire d'Asnières-sur-Seine** on Boulevard Pierre de Coubertin. Winter-only rinks include one at the Hôtel de Ville.

Squash can be played at **Squash Club Quartier Latin** in the Rue de Pontoise, where options also include billiards, gym and a sauna. Other good clubs include the **Squash Montmartre** and the **Jeu de Paume et de Squash**.

SPECTATOR SPORTS

A day out at the races is a chance to see the rich in all their finery. The world-famous Prix de l'Arc de Triomphe is held at the **Hippodrome de Longchamp** in the Bois de Boulogne on the first Sunday in October. More flat racing takes place at the **Hippodrome de St-Cloud** and **Maisons-Laffitte**, which are a short drive west of Paris. For steeple-chasing go to the **Hippodrome d'Auteuil** in the Bois de Boulogne. The **Hippodrome de Vincennes** on Route de la Ferne hosts the trotting races. For detailed information on all of these, consult **France Galop** by phone or check their website.

The 24-hour car race at Le Mans, 185 km (115 miles) southwest of Paris, is one of the best-known road races in the world. It takes place every year in mid-June. Contact the **Automobile Club de l'Ouest** for details. The **Palais Omnisports de Paris-Bercy** sports stadium in Boulevard Bercy is the venue for a vast

range of events, including the BNP Paribas Masters tennis tournament, cycle trials, showjumping, world-class martial arts demonstrations, tournaments in everything from figure skating to handball and major rock concerts.

Parc des Princes can hold 50,000 people. It is home to the main Paris football team, Paris St-Germain.

The colossal **Stade de France** is a major venue for football, rugby and music concerts. Sports fans can go on a behind the scenes tour.

The **Stade Roland Garros** in Avenue Gordon-Bennett is famous for its international tennis tournament. From late May to mid-June everyone lives and breathes tennis. Business meetings are transferred from the conference room to the stadium. Apply for tickets several months ahead. Don't miss a trip to the stadium's excellent museum of tennis featuring everything from prototype rackets to a Bjorn Bjorg headband. Also, be sure to book a table at one of the swanky restaurants here, which are transformed into a place to see and be seen during the tournament. Tennis fans should also be sure to catch the mens' masters series at the Palais Omnisports de Paris Bercy in November and the womens' Open Gaz de France tournament, which takes place at the **Stade Pierre de Coubertin** on Avenue Georges Lafont, in March.

SWIMMING

There is a massive aquatic fun park, known as **Aquaboulevard**, in south Paris (*see p362*). Besides an exotic artificial beach, swimming pools, water toboggans and rapids, there are tennis and squash courts, golf, bowling, table tennis, billiards, a gym, bars and shops.

Of the many municipal swimming pools, one of the best is the **Piscine des Halles** in Place de la Rotonde, with an Olympic-sized swimming pool in the underground shopping complex. For a lovely 1930s mosaic decor with two levels

of private changing cabins, a whirlpool, sauna and water jets, go to the **Piscine Pontoise-Quartier Latin**. This complex also has a small gym overlooking the pool, where fitness fans can pump a little iron before taking a dip. The **Piscine Henry de Montherlant** is part of a municipal sports complex that includes tennis courts and a gym. The beautiful Art Nouveau pool in the Butte aux Cailles (*see pp272-3*) is a treat for serious swimmers and sunbathers. A decent-sized indoor pool is perfect for laps whilst the two outdoor swimming areas are great for lounging. The villagey atmosphere of the surrounding area only serves to reinforce the feeling of relaxing on holiday miles away from the city. The **Piscine Josephine Baker** near the Bibliothèque F. Mitterand is a pleasing addition which floats on the Seine. In the summer the rooftop terrace is a good spot for sunbathing.

Some of the smarter hotels and gyms also have their own pools. It is possible to buy a day pass to the chic **Sofitel Paris Club Med Gym** in the Rue Louis Armand and have access to their 15-metre pool. Similarly at the **Novotel Tour Eiffel**, non-guests are welcomed to their health club and pool which has a retractable roof for swimming under the sun in spring and summer. It is important to note that all municipal pools and some private ones insist that bathers wear swimming caps and that male swimmers wear swimming trunks rather than baggy shorts.

MISCELLANEOUS

Baseball, fencing, jogging in the parks, volleyball, windsurfing at La Villette (*see pp236–9*) and bowling are just some of the other sporting activities that can be enjoyed during your stay.

Fishing on the Seine (with the appropriate permits) is fast becoming a popular pastime with Parisians. The Seine is home to a variety of freshwater fish.

DIRECTORY

OUTDOOR SPORTS

Comité Départemental d'Equitation de Paris
69 Rue Laugier 75017.
Tel 01 42 12 03 43.

Fat Tire Bike Tours & City Segway Tours
24 Rue Edgar Faure 75015. **Map** 10 D4.
Tel 01 56 58 10 54.
www.fattirebiketours.com/paris
www.citysegway tours.com

Fédération Française de Cyclotourisme
12 Rue Louis Bertrand 94200, Ivry-sur-Seine.
Tel 01 56 20 88 88.
www.ffct.org

Fédération Française du Golf
68 Rue Anatole France, 92300 Levallois Perret.
Tel 01 41 49 77 00.
www.ffgolf.org

France Galop
Tel 01 49 10 20 30.
www.france-galop.com

Golf de Chevry
91190 Gif-sur-Yvette.
Tel 01 60 12 40 33.

Golf de St-Quentin en Yvelines
78190 Trappes.
Tel 01 30 50 86 40.

Golf de Villennes
Route d'Orgeval, 78670 Villennes-sur-Seine.
Tel 01 39 08 18 18.

Golf de Villeray
91380 St-Pierre du Perray.
Tel 01 60 75 17 47.
www.bluegreen.com

Paris à Vélo c'est Sympa!
37 Blvd Bourdon 75004.
Map 14 E4.
Tel 01 48 87 60 01.

Paris Tourist Office
Tel 08 92 68 30 00.

Tennis de la Faluère Route de la Pyramide
Bois de Vincennes 75012.
Tel 01 43 74 40 93.

Tennis Luxembourg Jardins du Luxembourg
Blvd St-Michel 75006.
Map 12 E5.
Tel 01 43 25 79 18.

Vélib'
www.velib.paris.fr

Vélo Paris
44 Rue d'Orsel 75018.
Map 6 F2.
Tel 01 42 64 97 39.

INDOOR SPORTS

Club Jean de Beauvais
5 Rue Jean de Beauvais 75005.
Map 13 A5.
Tel 01 46 33 16 80.

Club Med Gym
26 Rue de Berri 75008.
Map 4 F4.
Tel 01 43 59 04 58.
149 Rue de Rennes 75006.
Map 15 C1.
Tel 01 45 44 24 35.
www.clubmedgym.com

Jeu de Paume et de Squash
7 Ter Rue Lauriston 75116. **Map** 4 D4.
Tel 01 47 27 46 86.

Ken Club
100 Ave President Kennedy 75016.
Tel 01 46 47 41 41.

Patinoire d'Asnières-sur-Seine
Blvd Pierre de Coubertin, 92600 Asnières.
Tel 01 47 99 96 06.

Ritz Gym
Ritz Hotel, Pl Vendôme 75001. **Map** 6 D5.
Tel 01 43 16 30 30.

Squash Club Quartier Latin
19 Rue de Pontoise 75005. **Map** 13 B5.
Tel 01 55 42 7788.

Squash Montmartre
14 Rue Achille-Martinet 75018.
Map 2 E4.
Tel 01 42 55 38 30.

SPECTATOR SPORTS

Automobile Club de l'Ouest
Tel 02 43 40 24 24.
www.lemans.org

Hippodrome d'Auteuil
Bois de Boulogne 75016.
Tel 01 42 88 85 30.

Hippodrome de Longchamp
Bois de Boulogne 75016.
Tel 01 44 30 75 00.

Hippodrome Maisons-Laffitte
1 Ave de la Pelouze, 78600 Maisons-Laffitte.
Tel 01 39 12 81 70.

Hippodrome de St-Cloud
1 Rue de Camp Canadien, 92210 St-Cloud.
Tel 01 47 71 69 26.

Hippodrome de Vincennes
2 Route de la Ferme, 75012 Vincennes.
Tel 01 49 77 17 17.

Palais Omnisports de Paris-Bercy
8 Blvd Bercy 75012.
Map 18 F2.
Tel 01 43 07 53 58.

Parc des Princes
24 Rue du Commandant-Guilbaud 75016.
Tel 32 75 (French only).

Stade de France
93210 La Plaine St-Denis.
Tel 08 92 70 09 00.
www.stadedefrance.com

Stade Pierre de Coubertin
82 Ave Georges Lafont 75016.
Tel 01 45 27 79 12.

Stade Roland Garros
2 Ave Gordon-Bennett 75016.
Tel 01 47 43 48 00.
www.fft.fr

SWIMMING

Aquaboulevard
4 Rue Louis-Armand 75015.
Tel 01 40 60 10 00.

Novotel Tour Eiffel
61 Quai de Grenelle 75015. **Map** 9 B5.
Tel 01 40 58 20 00.

Piscine Butte-aux-Cailles
5 Pl Paul-Verlaine 75013.
Map 17 A5.
Tel 01 45 89 60 05.

Piscine des Amiraux
6 Rue Hermann Lachapelle 75018.
Tel 01 46 06 46 47.

Piscine des Halles
10 Pl de la Rotonde, Niveau 3, Entrance Porte St Eustache, Les Halles 75001. **Map** 13 A2.
Tel 01 42 36 98 44.

Piscine Henry de Montherlant
32 Blvd de Lannes 75016.
Tel 01 40 72 28 30.

Piscine Josephine Baker
Quai François Mauriac 75013.
Tel 01 56 61 96 50.

Piscine Pontoise-Quartier Latin
19 Rue de Pontoise 75005.
Map 13 B5.
Tel 01 55 42 77 88.

Piscine St Germain
12 Rue Lobineau 75006.
Map 12 E4.
Tel 01 56 81 25 40.

Piscine Saint-Merri
16 Rue de Renard 75004.
Map 13 B3.
Tel 01 42 72 29 45.

Sofitel Paris Club Med Gym
8 Rue Louis Armand 75015.
Tel 01 45 54 79 00.

CHILDREN'S PARIS

It's never too early to instil a lifelong taste for this magical city in your children. Scaling the dizzy heights of the Eiffel Tower *(see pp194–5)*, boating down the Seine *(see pp72–3)* or a visit to Notre-Dame *(see pp82–5)* are fun at any age, and with children in tow you will see old haunts through new eyes. The historic parks are probably best appreciated by older children and adults, but everyone will love the technological wizardry of the Disneyland Resort Paris *(see pp242–5)*. During the summer, funfairs, circuses and all sorts of impromptu events are staged in gardens and parks, notably in the Bois de Boulogne *(see pp254–5)*. Or, take children to an entertainment centre, museum, adventure playground, or zoo, or to a show at one of the café theatres.

La Cité des Enfants at La Villette

PRACTICAL ADVICE

Paris welcomes young families in hotels *(see p278)* and most restaurants *(see p295)*. Many sights and attractions offer child reductions, while infants under three or four enter free. Children under 18 are admitted free of charge to all state-run museums throughout the year. Ask at the Office du Tourisme *(see p280)* for full details of child reductions, or check in the weekly entertainment guides such as *Pariscope, L'Officiel des Spectacles* and *Paris Mômes*.

A lot of the children's activities are geared to end-of-school times, including Wednesday afternoons when French children have time off. For information on museum workshops, contact the museums individually.

Babychou and **Kidizen** are specialist babysitting organizations in the city. They also offer a wide range of other services, including hiring out cots, strollers and other equipment.

MUSEUMS

Top of the museum list for children is undoubtedly the **Cité des Sciences et de l'Industrie** *(see pp236–9)* at Parc de la Villette. Hands-on activities and frequently changing exhibitions illuminate many aspects of science and modern technology in this immense complex. There are sections for children called La Cité des Enfants and Techno Cité. In central Paris, the Palais de la Découverte, within the Grand Palais *(see p208)*, is an old-fashioned but lively science museum where staff entertain the children by adopting the role of mad inventors.

The Louvre *(see pp122–9)* organizes thematic art trails around the museum for all ages, as well as special sessions designed to introduce children to various aspects of art. It is possible to download art trails from the website. The Musée D'Orsay *(see pp144–5)* has a variety of fun, interactive museum tours for children aged 5 to 12 to enjoy while The Galerie des Enfants at the Pompidou Centre *(see pp110–13)* also offers special sessions with a focus on modern art.

Other enjoyable museums for children include the Musée de la Marine *(see p201)* and the Musée de la Poupée *(see p114)*. The former covers the history of the French maritime tradition and includes scale models of some of France's finest battleships, dreadnoughts and submarines. The latter displays a collection of hand-made dolls dating from the mid-19th century, and also offers doll-making classes for both adults and children.

USEFUL CONTACTS

Babychou Services
Tel 01 43 13 33 23.
www.babychou.com

Kidizen
Tel 01 40 26 24 59.
www.kidizen.fr

The Café d'Edgar theatre

The Guignol marionnettes

PARKS, ZOOS AND ADVENTURE PLAYGROUNDS

The best children's park within Paris is the Jardin d'Acclimatation in the Bois de Boulogne *(see pp254–5)*, with a children's theatre, a circus, a pony club, a mini railway and boats, and the Musée en Herbe, a museum

Pony rides, Jardin d'Acclimatation

created especially for children offering entertaining educational activities.

Out of town at Elancourt, **France Miniature** recreates France on a small scale, with fascinating mini monuments.

The Bois de Vincennes *(see p235)* has simple amusements for children in the inexpensive Parc Floral. It also has the largest funfair in France, open from Palm Sunday through to the end of May. Perhaps the most appealing zoo is the small Ménagerie in the Jardin des Plantes *(see p164)*.

ENTERTAINMENT CENTRES

There are many supervised children's activity centres in Paris. The Atelier des Enfants in the Pompidou Centre *(see pp110–11)* has a workshop on Wednesday and Saturday afternoons from 2.30 to 4pm. The medium of instruction is French but the circuses, mime-shows, marionnettes and craft or museum workshops focus on actions rather than words.

Several café-theatres, including Café d'Edgar *(see p343)* and Abricadabra at the Antipode

Paris Miniature

Barge on the Canal de L'Ourcq offer children's shows with mime, dance or music. The most spectacular cinematic experience is in La Géode at the Cité des Sciences et de l'Industrie (see p237). The cinema **Le Saint Lambert** specializes in children's films and comic strips in French, though most films for children will not have English subtitles. Cinema tickets are cheaper on Wednesdays, with no child reductions at weekends.

Une Journée au Cirque offers children a day's entertainment when they can meet the animals, put on clown make-up or practise tightrope walking. Shows are in the afternoon, after lunch with the *artistes*.

The Guignol marionnette puppet shows are a summer tradition. Guignol himself is a far gentler character than the traditional English Mr Punch. Most of the main parks hold Guignol shows in summer on Wednesday afternoons and at weekends. Consult the entertainment guides such as *Pariscope, L'Officiel des Spectacles* and *Paris Mômes*.

ADDRESSES

Une Journée au Cirque
115 Blvd Charles de Gaulle, 92390 Ville-neuve-la-Garenne. **Tel** 01 47 99 40 40. **www**.journeeocirque.com

France Miniature
25 Route du Mesnil, 78990 Elancourt. **Tel** 01 30 16 16 30. **www**.franceminiature.com

Le Saint Lambert
6 Rue Peclet 75015.
Tel 08 92 68 96 99.

Circus acrobats training at Une Journée au Cirque

Fireworks over Sleeping Beauty Castle, Disneyland Resort Paris

Old-fashioned fairground carousels are situated near Sacré-Coeur (*see pp226–7*) and Forum des Halles (*see p109*). A great way of inspiring interest in the city's history, and great fun too, is a boat trip. Several companies compete (*see pp72–3*) from different departure points, and pass a host of waterfront sites including Notre-Dame, the Louvre and the Musée d'Orsay. Boats departing from La Villette travel along the Paris canal system. Radio-controlled model boats are popular on the ponds of the Jardin du Luxembourg (*see p172*). Or, take the family boating on the lakes of the Bois de Boulogne (*see pp254–5*) or the Bois de Vincennes (*see p235*). Riding is also popular in these parks (*see p357 Directory*).

THEME PARKS

The two parks of Disneyland Resort Paris (*see pp242–5*) are the biggest and most spectacular of the Paris theme parks. Seven hotels, each with a different, imaginative theme, and a campsite provide on-site accommodation. The complex also includes a golf course, shops and restaurants.

Parc Asterix is a French theme park centring around the legendary world of Asterix the Gaul. Here six themed "worlds" feature gladiators, slave auctions and rides among the many attractions. The park is situated 38 km (24 miles) northeast of Paris. Take the RER line B to Charles de Gaulle Airport then the shuttle bus to Parc Asterix.

SPORTS AND RECREATION

The giant waterpark **Aqua-boulevard** is one of the best places to take energetic youngsters. Also good is the indoor pool at **Forum des Halles**. The weekly entertainment guide *Pariscope* lists the swimming pools in and around Paris. Remember that it is compulsory to wear a swimming cap. Accomplished roller-skaters and skate-boarders practise outside the Palais de Chaillot (*see p200*). On Sundays, in summer, the roads along the Seine (between Châtelet and Bercy) are closed to traffic. Bikers and rollerbladers descend en masse. Disneyland Resort Paris (*see pp242–5*) has ice-skating rinks and a range of other sports facilities.

Donald Duck

ADDRESSES

Aquaboulevard
4 Rue Louis Armand 75015.
Tel 01 40 60 10 00. ◯ 9am–9pm Mon–Fri, 8am–9pm Sat, Sun.

La Piscine des Halles
Forum des Halles, 10 Pl de la Rotonde, Les Halles 75001. **Map** 12 F2. ***Tel*** 01 42 36 98 44. ◯ 11.30am–10pm Mon, Tue, Thu, Fri; 7–8.15am, 10am–11pm Wed; 9am–7pm Sat, Sun.

Parc Asterix
BP8 Plailly 60128. 📠 08 26 30 10 40. ◯ Apr–mid-Oct: 10am–6pm Mon–Fri, 9.30am–7pm w/e & hols. **www**.parcasterix.fr

Apache
56 Rue du Commerce 75015.
Map 10 E5. ***Tel*** 01 40 43 10 04.
One of several branches.

CHILDREN'S SHOPS

There is no shortage of chic children's fashion in Paris. A good place to start is the Rue du Jour in Beaubourg and Les Halles which has a number of children's boutiques. The city has many appealing toy shops such as Au Nain Bleu (*see p331*) or the branches of Apache (*see Addresses*), but, like the clothes shops, they can be prohibitively expensive. (*See also p326*.)

**Toy characters from *Tintin*,
the popular comic book series**

Roller-skaters near the Eiffel Tower

Carousel near Sacré-Coeur

STREET LIFE AND MARKETS

Outside the Pompidou Centre (see pp110–11) street entertainers draw the crowds on sunny afternoons. Musicians, conjurors, fire-eaters and artists of all kinds perform here. In Montmartre there is a tradition of street-painting, predominantly in the Place du Tertre (see p224) where

Model boats for hire in the Jardin du Luxembourg

someone will always be willing to draw your child's portrait. It's also fun to take the funicular up the hill to Sacré-Coeur (see pp226–7), then walk down through the pretty streets.

Parisian markets are colourful and animated. Try taking children to the Marché aux Fleurs on the Ile de la Cité (see p81) or to the food markets on the Rue Mouffetard, in the Jardin des Plantes Quarter (see p166 and p339), or the Rue de Buci in St-Germain-des Prés. The biggest flea market, Marché aux Puces de St-Ouen, is at weekends (see p233 and p339).

Alternatively take children to the quiet Ile de la Cité or Ile St-Louis on the Seine.

VIEWPOINTS AND SIGHTSEEING

Top of the sightseeing list for children is a trip up the Eiffel Tower (see pp194–5). On a clear day spectacular views over Paris will enable you to point out a number of sights, and at night the city is magically lit up. Lifts run until 11pm and queues are much shorter in the evenings. If you are pushing a baby buggy, bear in mind that the ascent is in three stages, using two separate lifts.

Other interesting sights for children include Sacré-Coeur (see pp226–7) with its ovoid dome – the second highest point in Paris after the Eiffel Tower – and Notre-Dame cathedral (see pp82–3) on the Ile de la Cité. Children will enjoy feeding the pigeons in the cathedral square, visiting the gargoyles on the West Front and listening to you recount the story of the hunchback of Notre-Dame. There are incomparable views from the towers. Children and adults alike will appreciate the enchanting Sainte-Chapelle (see pp88–9), also on the Ile de la Cité. Children under the age of 18 almost always go free.

Contrast ancient and modern Paris with a visit to the Pompidou Centre (see pp110–13) and enjoy a ride on the caterpillar-like escalators outside, or go to the café on the roof terrace for the views. There is also the 56-storey Montparnasse Tower (see p178) with some spectacular telescopic views from the top terrace; and there is the huge arch at La Défense (see p255) which has lifts to exhibition platforms where visitors can overlook the whole complex.

OTHER INTERESTS

Children are quick to see the funny side of unusual spectacles. Les Egouts, Paris's sewers, offer a short tour of the city's sewerage system

Escalators at the Pompidou Centre

(see p190). Display boards in several languages explain the processes.

The Catacombes (see p179) are a long series of quarry tunnels built in Roman times, and lined with ancient skulls in the 18th century.

On the Ile de la Cité is the Conciergerie (see p81), a turreted prison where many hapless aristocrats spent their final days. The Grévin waxworks are in Boulevard Montmartre (see p218). The museum's Revolution rooms will especially appeal to older children, with gruesome scenes and grisly sound effects, demonstrating the reality of social upheaval.

EMERGENCIES

Enfance et Partage is a free 24-hour child help-line (also for adults). One of Paris's largest children's hospitals is **Hôpital Necker**.

Enfance et Partage *Tel* 08 00 05 12 34. **www**.enfance-et-partage.org

Hôpital Necker 149 Rue de Sèvres 75015. **Map** 15 B1. *Tel* 01 44 49 40 00. **www**.aphp.fr

A young visitor to Paris

SURVIVAL
GUIDE

PRACTICAL INFORMATION

Paris offers a vast wealth of things to see and do. A little forward planning can save time and inconvenience. Make use of tourist offices and ring in advance to confirm a sight is open and is not closed for refurbishment or holidays. Guided tours are often the best way to see the essential sights while you get your bearings (see p383). Buying a *Paris Pass* will give you unlimited access to the city's many attractions, and cuts down on time spent in queues (see p367). If you're on a tight budget, admission prices are sometimes lower at certain times of day, or on Sundays. Beware that some shops and museums are closed all day on Monday. Card-carrying students and senior travellers can obtain discounts on some tickets and admissions (see p368). Purchase a *carnet* or travel pass to economize and simplify travel on the metro and buses (see pp382 & 384–7).

PARIS
Convention
and Visitors Bureau
Tourist Office logo

VISAS AND PASSPORTS

France is part of the Schengen common European border treaty, which means that travellers moving from one Schengen country to another are not subject to border controls. Schengen residents need only to show an identity card when entering France. Visitors from the UK, Ireland, the US, Canada, Australia and New Zealand need to show a full passport. Tourists from these countries may stay in France without a visa for 90 days within a continuous 180-day period. For more information and to check visa requirements, visitors should consult the website of their embassy in France.

TAX-FREE GOODS AND CUSTOMS INFORMATION

Visitors resident outside the EU can reclaim the sales tax (TVA, or VAT) they pay on French goods if they spend more than €175 in the same shop in one day and take the goods out of France (see p320). *Détaxe* receipts can be issued on purchase to reclaim the tax paid (this is usually 12 per cent). The documents need to be endorsed at a *détaxe* office (located at airports) on exiting the EU within three months of purchase, then posted in the provided envelope. There are some goods on which a rebate cannot be claimed including food and drink, medicines, tobacco, cars and motorbikes. The **Centre des Renseignements des Douanes** provides full information about this.

In general, all personal goods, including cars and bicycles, may be imported to France if they are obviously for personal use and not for sale. There are no restrictions on the quantities of duty-paid and VAT-paid goods that can be taken from one EU country to another, as long as they are for personal use. Visitors under the age of 17 are not allowed to import duty-paid tobacco or alcohol into France. Duty-free purchases of liquids carried by travellers arriving in Paris from a non-EU country and connecting directly onto another flight will be confiscated at security check.

The maximum value of currency that can be brought into or taken out of France is €10,000. Sums in excess of this must be declared to the customs authority.

TOURIST INFORMATION

The main tourist office in Paris, the **Office du Tourisme et des Congrès de Paris**, is near the Jardin des Tuileries (see p130). It will have the latest maps, information and brochures, and can provide comprehensive information about events in the city.

There are other tourist offices at Place du Tertre in **Montmartre**, at the **Gare du Nord**, **Gare de l'Est** and **Gare de Lyon**, at **Anvers** metro station and at the **Paris Expo** exhibition centre at Porte de Versailles during trade fairs. There are also summer-only kiosks at sights such as Notre Dame and the Hôtel de Ville.

ADMISSION CHARGES

An admission fee is usually charged, or a donation expected, at museums. The entrance fee to some national and municipal museums is

Le Musée d'Orsay, where entry is free on the first Sunday of the month

◁ River view of Pont Neuf and the Ile de la Cité

waived on the first Sunday of each month for their permanent collections. Some museums reduce their rates for an evening visit (for example, the entrance fee to the Louvre is reduced after 6pm on Wednesday and Friday, when the museum stays open until 10pm). Visitors under 18 years of age and European passport holders aged 18–26 years are usually admitted free to museums, and there are sometimes discounts for students and seniors who have ID showing their date of birth.

The *Paris Pass* gives the bearer unlimited access to over 60 of the city's attractions for 2, 4 or 6 days, without having to queue (temporary exhibitions are not included). It also offers unlimited travel on the metro, buses and RER within central Paris, and a ticket for a hop-on hop-off bus tour. The pass must be bought in advance through the website (www.parispass. com) and is either posted (allow time for delivery) or can be collected in Paris (see website for details).

OPENING HOURS

Most of the city's museums and monuments open from 10am to 6pm. Municipal museums, such as those run by the city of Paris, are usually closed on Monday. The national museums are closed on Tuesday, except Versailles and the Musée d'Orsay, which are closed on Monday. Most ticket counters close 30–45 minutes before the official closing time. To avoid queues and packed museums take advantage of the *nocturnes* (late-night opening) that many of the major museums offer or visit on weekday mornings.

Most Paris shops and businesses are open from 9am to 7pm. Some close for an hour or two from around 1pm. Smaller food shops tend to open earlier, around 7am, and take a longer midday break. Most businesses are closed on Sunday, but

Kiosque Théâtre booking kiosk

Sunday trading is allowed in tourist areas. Many shops close on Monday.

LISTINGS AND TICKETS

The main listings magazines, available at all newsagents, are *Pariscope* and *L'Officiel des Spectacles (see p340)*. Each Wednesday they publish full information on the week's theatre, cinema and exhibits, as well as on cabarets, dinner clubs and some restaurants. FNAC ticket agencies take bookings for all entertainment venues, including temporary museum shows. There are FNAC branches throughout Paris. For further details call one of their branches *(see p341)*. For booking the theatre only, the Kiosque Théâtre sells same-day tickets at 50 per cent discount. There are kiosks at Place de la Madeleine and the Parvis de la Gare Montparnasse *(see p341)*.

DIRECTORY

CUSTOMS INFORMATION

Centre des Renseignements des Douanes
Tel 08 11 20 44 44.
◖ 8.30am–6pm Mon–Fri. **www**.douane.gouv.fr

TOURIST INFORMATION

Office du Tourisme et des Congrès de Paris
25 Rue des Pyramides 75001. **Map** 12 E1.
◖10am–7pm daily (from 11am Sun & public holidays; from 9am daily Jun–Oct)
www.parisinfo.com

Anvers
72 Blvd Rochechouart 75018. **Map** 7 A2.
◖10am–6pm daily.

Gare de l'Est
Pl du 11 Novembre 1918, 75010. **Map** 18 F1.
◖ 8am–7pm Mon–Sat.

Gare de Lyon
20 Blvd Diderot 75012. **Map** 18 F1.
◖ 8am–6pm Mon–Sat.

Gare du Nord
18 Rue de Dunkerque 75010. **Map** 7 B2.
◖ 8am–6pm daily.

Montmartre
21 Pl du Tertre 75018. **Map** 6 F1.
◖10am–7pm daily.

Paris Expo
1 Pl Porte de Versailles 75015. ◖11am–7pm during trade fairs.

FRENCH TOURIST OFFICES ABROAD

Australia
Level 13, 25 Bligh St, Sydney NSW 2000.
Tel 02 9231 5244.
www.au.franceguide.com

Canada
1800 Ave McGill College, Suite 1010, Montréal, Quebec H3A 3J9.
Tel 514 288 2026.
www.franceguide.com

United Kingdom
Lincoln House, 300 High Holborn, London WC1V 7JH.
Tel 0906 8244 123 (within UK).
www.uk.franceguide.com

United States
info.us@franceguide.com
www.us.franceguide.com

EMBASSIES

Australia
4 Rue Jean Rey 75015.
Map 10 D3.
Tel 01 40 59 33 00.
www.france.embassy. gov.au

Canada
35 Ave Montaigne 75008.
Map 10 F1.
Tel 01 44 43 29 00.
www.amb-canada.fr

Great Britain
35 Rue du Faubourg St-Honoré 75008.
Map 5 C5. *Tel 01 44 51 31 00.* http://ukinfrance. fco.gov.uk/en

Ireland (Eire)
12 Ave Foch 75016. **Map** 3 B4. *Tel 01 44 17 67 50.*
www.embassyofireland.fr

New Zealand
7ter Rue Léonard de Vinci 75016. **Map** 3 C5. *Tel 01 45 01 43 43.* **www**. nzembassy.com/france

USA
Ave Gabriel 75008.
Map 5 B5. *Tel 01 43 12 22 22.* http://france. usembassy.gov

TRAVELLERS WITH SPECIAL NEEDS

Services for people with special needs are improving in Paris. Most pavements are contoured to allow wheelchairs an easier passage, and restaurants, hotels and museums are adapting their facilities. There is, for example, wheelchair access to the first and second floor of the Eiffel Tower, at a reduced tariff, while the Louvre and Musée d'Orsay are free to disabled visitors and their escorts.

Increasingly, sights are sporting the *Tourisme & Handicap* label denoting that they are accessible to people with physical, mental, hearing and visual impediments. The Office du Tourisme et des Congrès *(see p367)* has a guide (*Les Sites Labellisés "Tourisme & Handicap" à Paris et en Ile-de-France*) listing these. The association **J'Accede** has details (in French) of accessible museums, hotels, bars, restaurants and cinemas in Paris and other French cities.

Metro stations and bus routes accessible to travellers with limited mobility are marked with a wheelchair symbol on their maps. The RATP's **Infomobi** website details all their accessible public transport and stations. Paris's international train stations have lifts, ramps, courtesy wheelchairs, signs in Braille, and a magnetic loop at ticket counters for the hearing impaired. **Accès Plus** is a free service to greet and accompany disabled travellers on their journey. **Les Compagnons du Voyage** will provide an escort for persons with limited mobility on any form of public transport, for a fee.

Some Paris taxi companies (such as G7, *see p389*), have vehicles suited to travellers with limited mobility; taxis are bound by law to assist disabled travellers.

For further up-to-date informaton on public facilities for the disabled contact the **GIHP**.

Tourisme & Handicap sign

STUDENT TRAVELLERS

Students with valid ID cards benefit from discounts of 25–50 per cent at theatres, museums, cinemas and many public monuments. An ISIC card (International Student ID card) may be bought from the main travel agencies and the **CIDJ**. The **BVJ** has two reasonably priced hostels in Paris *(see p279)*.

SENIOR TRAVELLERS

Some museums and monuments, theatres and independent cinemas offer reductions for visitors aged over 60. Théâtre du Chatelet *(see p347)* for example, offers discounted tickets 15 minutes before showtime to over-65s. Expect to be asked for ID, such as a passport, to prove your date of birth. Canal tour operators **Canauxrama** and **Paris Canal** offer reduced tariffs. Over-60s are eligible for a 25 per cent discount from state railway **SNCF** on off-peak travel. Check their website for details.

The Eiffel Tower, a wheelchair-accessible attraction

ETIQUETTE AND SMOKING

Etiquette (*la politesse*) is everything to Parisians. On entering a shop or cafe, you're expected to say *"bonjour Madame"* or *"bonjour Monsieur"* to staff, and when leaving to say *"au revoir"*. Be sure to add *"s'il vous plaît"* (please) when ordering something, and *"pardon"* if you accidentally bump someone.

The French shake hands on meeting someone for the first time, and when greeting workmates or acquaintances. Friends and colleagues who know each other well usually greet each other with a kiss on each cheek. If you are unsure, wait to see if they proffer a hand or a cheek.

Smoking is prohibited in all public places, but is allowed on restaurant, café and pub terraces, as long as they are not enclosed.

PUBLIC CONVENIENCES

Automated, self-cleaning toilets can be found across the city. They have been upgraded to be larger than previously, wheelchair-usable and free. Children under 10 are not allowed into these toilets on their own because the automated cleaning function can be a danger to small children. There are also more than 30 free public toilet facilities in Paris; locations are listed on the **Mairie de Paris** website.

PARIS TIME

Paris is 1 hour ahead of Greenwich Mean Time (GMT) or British Summer Time (BST). New York is 6 hours behind Paris, Los Angeles is 9 hours behind and Auckland is 11 hours ahead. France observes Daylight Saving in summer; clocks are put forward by 1 hour on the last weekend in March and put back by 1 hour on the last weekend in October. The French use the 24-hour clock.

ELECTRICAL ADAPTORS

The voltage in France is 220 volts. Plugs have two small round pins; heavier-duty appliances have two large round pins. Better hotels offer built-in adaptors for shavers only or will lend you an adaptor. Adaptors can also be bought at department stores, such as BHV (see p321).

CONVERSION CHART

Imperial to Metric
1 inch = 2.54 centimetres
1 foot = 30 centimetres
1 mile = 1.6 kilometres
1 ounce = 28 grams
1 pound = 454 grams
1 pint = 0.6 litre
1 gallon = 4.6 litres

Metric to Imperial
1 millimetre = 0.04 inch
1 centimetre = 0.4 inch
1 metre = 3 feet 3 inches
1 kilometre = 0.6 mile
1 gram = 0.04 ounce
1 kilogram = 2.2 pounds
1 litre = 1.8 pints

RESPONSIBLE TOURISM

A great green wave has been quietly rolling over Paris. Compost boxes are appearing on tiny apartment balconies,

organic markets are thriving, recycling bins are popping up in public transport stations, hotels use eco-friendly products and skincare devotees are scooping up chemical-free creams by the potful.

Paris has over 400 parks and gardens to help the city breathe, and sustainable development is a priority. "*Eco-quartiers*" are emerging, an example of which is the Rungis development in the 13th arrondissement, which has solar panels powering hot water and electricity and where 50 per cent of water on the roof is collected for

Fresh produce at one of Paris's organic markets

gardens, recycling is prevalent and priority is given to pedestrians, cyclists and public transport. Even the Eiffel Tower is eco-alert – its power is 100 per cent renewable. The addition of solar panels on some shop roofs in 2011 will further reduce energy consumption.

An increasing number of Paris hotels, such as **Hotel Garvarni**, are sporting the *European Ecolabel* or the *Clef Verte* (Green Key), as a mark of their commitment to efficient energy and water consumption, waste separation and reduction in chemical use.

Organic, or "*bio*", cafés and restaurants are flourishing, including **97 Bio**, which also has take-home baskets of fresh organic vegetables; **Phyto Bar**, with its macrobiotic food and grocery store; and **Le Petit Bazaar**, which sells fair trade coffee and recycled toys.

There are weekly organic markets at Boulevard Raspail, Place Brancusi and Boulevard Batignolles. Organic supermarkets, such as Naturalia and Biocoop, can be found across the city. **Le Marché des Gastronomes** is an independent store selling organic and fair trade produce.

DIRECTORY

Personal Security and Health

Paris is as safe or as dangerous as you make it – common sense is usually sufficient to keep you out of trouble. If you fall sick during your visit, pharmacists are an excellent source of advice. In France, pharmacists can diagnose many health problems and suggest appropriate treatment. For more serious medical help, someone at the emergency numbers in the box below will be able to deal with most enquiries. There are many specialist services available, including a general advice line for English-speakers in crisis and a phoneline for psychiatric help.

French pharmacy sign

Emergency button at metro stations

EMERGENCY NUMBERS

SAMU (ambulance)
Tel 15 (freecall); 112 from a mobile.

Police
Tel 17 (freecall).

Sapeurs-Pompiers (fire department)
Tel 18 (freecall).

SOS – all services (from a mobile)
Tel 112 (freecall).

SOS Médecins (doctor, house calls)
Tel 36 24.
www.sosmedecins-france.fr

SOS Dentaire (dentist)
Tel 01 43 37 51 00.

Burn Specialists
Hôpital Cochin 75014.
Tel 01 58 41 41 41.

SOS Help (English-language crisis line)
Tel 01 46 21 46 46.

SOS Psychiatrie (for psychiatric help)
Tel 01 47 07 24 24.

Sexual Disease Screening
Tel 01 40 78 26 00.

POLICE

As Paris is one of the most visited capitals in the world, the police are no strangers to dealing with tourists. If you need assistance, look for bilingual officers sporting a badge identifying the languages they speak. Thefts, assaults, loss of property and missing persons must be reported in person at the nearest police station; central police stations (*Commissariat de Police*) within the 20 arrondissements are open 24 hours a day, 7 days a week. Bilingual officers are usually available, but if not there is a software programme called SAVE (*Système d'Accueil des Victimes Etrangères*) available in 20 languages, which allows tourists to record their complaint in their own language. For lost or stolen passports call your embassy or consulate (*see p367*).

WHAT TO BE AWARE OF

Paris is, on the whole, a safe city. The centre, in particular, experiences little violent crime. Muggings and brawls do occur, but they are rare compared to many other world capitals. However, do try to avoid poorly lit or isolated places. Beware of pickpockets, especially on the metro and on buses during the rush hour and in major tourist areas. Keep all valuables securely concealed and if you carry a handbag or case, never let it out of your sight. Take only as much cash as you think you will need and remember that most places accept credit cards. Travellers' cheques are a safe method of carrying large sums of money.

When travelling late at night, avoid long transfers in metro stations, such as Châtelet-Les-Halles and

Parisian fireman　　Policewoman　　Policeman

Typical Paris police car

Paris fire engine

Paris ambulance

Montparnasse. Generally, areas around RER train stations tend to attract groups of youths from outlying areas who come to Paris for entertainment and may become unruly. The last RER trains to and from outlying areas should also be avoided.

Make sure you insure your possessions before arrival. On sightseeing or entertainment trips do not carry valuables with you. You should never leave luggage unattended in metro or train stations because it could cause a bomb scare.

IN AN EMERGENCY

The telephone number for police is 17 and for an ambulance it is 15. In the event of an emergency in the metro, call the station agent by using the yellow telephone marked *Chef de Station* on all metro and RER platforms, or go to the ticket booth at the entrance. Most metro stations have emergency buttons and train carriages have alarm pulls.

The RAPT is continually upgrading security and has some 7,000 video cameras in stations and on trains, as well as 17,300 in the rail and bus network. Transport police patrol stations, and a small team of police officers survey the network electronically.

Visitors should be vigilant in heavy tourist areas for pickpockets and not let themselves be distracted. Caution should be exercised in the Les Halles area at night and at weekends.

In the case of a medical emergency, call **SAMU** (ambulance) or the **Sapeurs-Pompiers** (fire department). Fire department ambulances are often the quickest to arrive at an emergency. First-aid and emergency treatment is provided at all fire stations.

If you have been the victim of a physical assault, the police will ask that you undergo an examination at the medical-legal emergency unit near Notre Dame.

HOSPITALS AND PHARMACIES

All EU nationals holding a European Health Insurance Card (EHIC) are entitled to use the French national health service. Patients must pay for all treatments and can then reclaim most of the cost from the health authorities. The process may be lengthy and travellers should therefore consider purchasing private travel insurance. Non-EU nationals must have full private medical insurance while in France and pay for services, claiming their costs back in full from their insurance company.

Hospitals with casualty departments are shown on the Street Finder maps (*see pp390–423*). For English-language visitors, there are two private hospitals with bilingual staff and doctors: the **American Hospital of Paris** and the **Franco-Britannique Hospital**. The **Centre Médical Europe** is an inexpensive private clinic, which also has a dental practice.

There are many pharmacies throughout the city, and a short list is provided opposite. Pharmacies are indicated by a green cross on the shop front.

DIRECTORY

MEDICAL CENTRES

American Hospital of Paris
63 Blvd Victor-Hugo 92200, Neuilly-sur-Seine.
Map 1 A3. *Tel* 01 46 41 25 25.
Private hospital. Enquire about insurance and costs.

Centre Médical Europe
44 Rue d'Amsterdam 75009.
Map 6 D3. *Tel* 01 42 81 93 33.
🕐 *8am–8pm Mon–Sat.*
Private clinic. Appointments, or walk-in.

Franco-Britannique Hospital
3 Rue Barbès 92300, Levallois-Perret. **Map** 7 A1.
Tel 01 46 39 22 22.
Private hospital.

PHARMACIES

British and American Pharmacy
1 Rue Auber 75009. **Map** 6 D4.
Tel 01 42 65 88 29.
🕐 *8.30am–8.30pm Mon–Fri, 10am–8pm Sat.*

Pharmacie Anglo-Americaine
37 Ave Marceau 75016.
Map 10 E1.
Tel 01 47 20 57 37.
🕐 *8.30am–7.30pm Mon–Fri, 9am–5pm Sat.*

Pharmacie Bader
12 Blvd St-Michel 75005.
Map 12 F5.
Tel 01 43 26 92 66.
🕐 *9am–9pm Mon–Sat, 11am–9pm Sun.*

Pharmacie des Halles
10 Blvd Sebastopol 75004.
Map 13 A3.
Tel 01 42 72 03 23.
🕐 *9am–midnight Mon–Sat, 9am–10pm Sun.*

Pharmacie Les Champs
84 Ave des Champs-Elysées 75008.
Map 4 F5.
Tel 01 45 62 02 41.
🕐 *24 hours daily.*

Banking and Local Currency

Visitors to Paris will find that the banks usually offer them the best rates of exchange. Privately owned bureaux de change, on the other hand, have variable rates, and care should be taken to check small print details relating to commission and minimum charges before any transaction is completed.

Société Générale bank

BANKS AND BUREAUX DE CHANGE

Most banks will exchange foreign currency and traveller's cheques. Make sure you have ID with you. The main French banks are BNP Paribas, Société Générale, Crédit Agricole and Crédit Mutuel (CIC). Banks generally offer the best exchange rates but the commission rates vary.

Private bureaux de change offer poorer exchange rates than banks. Central Paris non-bank exchanges are usually open 9am–6pm Mon–Sat, and are found along the Champs-Elysées, around the Opéra and near some tourist attractions and monuments. They are also at all main railway stations, where they are generally open 8am–9pm daily. Airport exchange offices tend to open 7am–11pm daily. Private exchange offices can also be found in some hotels and shops.

CREDIT AND DEBIT CARDS

Major credit cards such as Visa and MasterCard, and debit cards such as Switch, Maestro and Cirrus, are widely accepted by most businesses. Most banks have ATMs (outside or in an indoor area) which accept these cards. This is the quickest and easiest way of obtaining money in local currency, although a small charge for this service will be

deducted from your account. Many French businesses do not accept American Express credit cards.

French credit and debit cards operate on a chip-and-PIN system, so you will need to know your PIN *(code personnel)* for making purchases in shops. If you have a card that does not use chip-and-PIN technology you should ask that your card be swiped in the magnetic reader.

Be sure to notify your bank and credit card providers before you leave for France. Some banks forbid foreign transactions for security reasons unless they have been notified ahead of time.

Credit and debit card reader

WIRING MONEY

Money can be transferred via companies such as Western Union or MoneyGram, or bank to bank. **Banque Postale**, the post office bank, is an agent for Western Union. A transfer can be made online at Western Union or Banque Postale using a credit card, or by going to a main Banque Postale office. Depending on opening hours, the money can be picked up 10–15 minutes after it is wired. Make sure you have ID when you collect the funds and, if available, the transfer reference number. Charges are paid by the sender. **MoneyGram** has its own

offices in Paris. For a bank transfer, you will need the French IBAN number, SWIFT/BIC code, bank name and address and name of the account holder. Often, the money is transferred to the main bank, then on to the relevant branch and can take 2–5 business days to arrive in the French account.

DIRECTORY

FOREIGN BANKS

American Express
11 Rue Scribe 75009. **Map** 6 D5.

Barclays
6 Rond-Point des Champs-Elysées 75008. **Map** 4 D4.

HSBC
117 Ave des Champs-Elysées 75008. **Map** 5 C5.

BUREAUX DE CHANGE

Le Comptoir des Tuileries
27 Rue de l'Arbre Sec 75001. **Map** 12 F2.

Global Change
134 Blvd St-Germain 75006. **Map** 12 F4.

49 Ave de l'Opéra 75002. **Map** 6 E5.

Travelex
45 Ave de l'Opéra 75001. **Map** 6 E5.

Gare du Nord (opposite Eurostar arrivals). **Map** 7 B2.

LOST CARDS AND TRAVELLER'S CHEQUES

American Express
Tel 01 47 77 70 00 (cards).
Tel 08 00 90 86 00 (cheques).

MasterCard
Tel 08 00 90 13 88 (cards).

Visa
Tel 08 00 90 11 79 (cards).

WIRING MONEY

Banque Postale (Western Union)
11 Rue des Sèvres 75006. **Map** 15 B1.
www.labanquepostale.fr

MoneyGram
29 Bld de la Chapelle 75010. **Map** 7 C1.
www.moneygram.com

THE EURO

The euro (€) is the common currency of the European Union (EU). It went into general circulation on 1 January 2002, initially for 12 participating countries. France was one of those 12 countries.

EU members using the euro as sole official currency are known as the eurozone. Several EU members have opted out of joining this common currency. Euro notes are identical throughout the eurozone countries, each one including designs of fictional architectural structures and monuments. The coins, however, have one side identical (the value side), and one side with a unique image. Both notes and coins are exchangeable in all of the participating eurozone countries.

Bank Notes
Euro bank notes have seven denominations. The €5 note (grey in colour) is the smallest, followed by the €10 note (pink), €20 note (blue), €50 note (orange), €100 note (green), €200 note (yellow) and €500 note (purple).

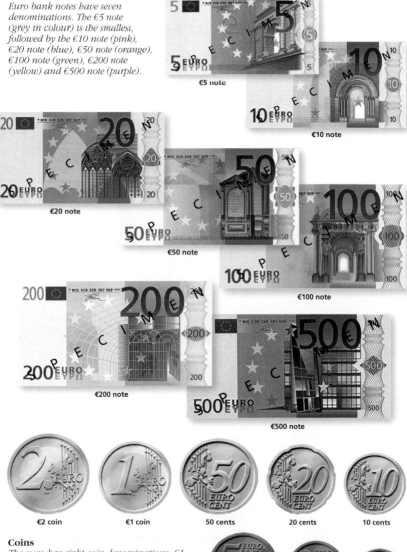

€5 note

€10 note

€20 note

€50 note

€100 note

€200 note

€500 note

€2 coin

€1 coin

50 cents

20 cents

10 cents

Coins
The euro has eight coin denominations: €1 and €2; 50 cents, 20 cents, 10 cents, 5 cents, 2 cents and 1 cent. The €1 and €2 coins are both silver and gold in colour. The 50-, 20- and 10-cent coins are gold. The 5-, 2- and 1-cent coins are bronze.

5 cents

2 cents

1 cent

Communications and Media

LA POSTE
Post office sign

The main French telecommunications agency is France Télécom. The postal service is La Poste. Both work efficiently. Public telephones are located in most public places and usually require a phonecard *(télécarte)*. Post offices have "hot stations" for customer information, and automatic vending machines for stamps and weighing packages. There are numerous post offices *(bureaux de poste)*, identified by the blue-on-yellow La Poste sign, scattered around the city. Foreign-language newspapers can be bought at newsagents throughout Paris, and some TV channels and radio stations broadcast foreign-language programmes.

FRENCH TELEPHONE NUMBERS

Telephone numbers in France have ten digits. The first two digits indicate the region: 01 and 09 are for Paris and the Ile de France; 02 for the northwest; 03 for the north-east; 04 for the southeast; 05 for the southwest. French mobile numbers begin with 06, 07 and 08 indicates a special rate number. Toll-free numbers *(numéro vert)* begin with 0800. For useful telephone numbers and codes please see the box below.

PUBLIC TELEPHONES

Paris has a large number of public telephones. To use one, you need a phonecard *(télécarte)*, although some do accept credit cards. Sold in *tabacs*, post offices, France Télécom agencies and some newsagents, there are two kinds of *télécartes* – smart cards, available in 50 or 120 telephone units, which you simply insert in the phone, and code cards for which you tap in a code. For international calls, the International Telephone Card provides good value for money. If using a credit card, you will receive credit for calls up to €15. When the limit is reached, the call is cut off. Most telephone boxes can also receive calls – the box number is displayed above the phone unit.

MOBILE TELEPHONES

In order to use your mobile phone in France, it must be compatible with the European-standard dual-band GSM 900 or 1800 MHz frequencies. Contact your provider before leaving home to check your phone's compatibility.

Alert your network before travelling so that they can set your phone to allow "roaming". If you don't do this, your phone may not work. Always check roaming charges with your service provider before travelling, as making and receiving calls can be very expensive. Some companies offer "packages" for foreign calls which can work out better value for money.

If your phone is GSM and unlocked, you can insert a local SIM card into it, which can be obtained in Paris from one of the main local providers such as **Orange**, **Bouygues Télécom** or **SFR** and topped up as required. This way you get a French phone number and pay normal, local mobile rates.

INTERNET ACCESS

Internet access is widely available in Paris. There are a huge number of Internet cafés. Public libraries also provide Internet access. There are many free Wi-Fi spots around the city, including in parks, gardens and town halls. Thanks to the *Pass Paris-Wi-Fi*, a free wireless broadband service set up by the Paris City Council (Mairie de Paris), you can connect instantly to the Internet by selecting the option "*Paris wi-fi 2h*" with your navigator. The Mairie de Paris has a list of 260 free Wi-Fi sites (*Localisation des points Wi-Fi*) on their website (www.paris.fr), while www.cafes-wifi.com lists cafés with Wi-Fi Internet access.

Using the Internet in a library

USEFUL TELEPHONE NUMBERS AND CODES

- **To call the police**, dial 17; **for an ambulance**, 15.

- **Directory enquiries**, dial 118 712.

- **International directory enquiries**, for all countries, dial 118 700.

- **To make direct international calls**, dial 00 followed by the country code, area code (omit the initial 0) and the number.

- **To make a reverse charge call (PCV)**, dial 0800 99 00 followed by the country code.

- Country telephone codes: **Australia**: 61; **Canada** and **USA**: 1; **Eire**: 353; **New Zealand**: 64; **UK**: 44.

- **Low-rate period**: 7pm–8am Mon–Fri, all day Sun and public holidays.

- **To telephone France from your home country**, dial: from the UK 00 33; from the US 011 33; from Australia: 00 11 33. Omit the first 0 of the French area code.

Many hotels offer Wi-Fi connections, but these are rarely free. There are pay-for-service Internet kiosks and Wi-Fi hotspots at Charles de Gaulle and Orly airports. Wi-Fi cards are available from bookstores in the terminals or you can purchase a session ahead of time on the Paris airports site (www.adp.fr).

POSTAL SERVICES

The postal service in France is fast and usually reliable. Postage stamps *(timbres)* can be bought at post offices and are sold individually or in *carnets* of ten. They can be bought either at a post office counter or vending machine. Post offices also have self-service machines on which you can weigh letters and parcels, both domestic and international, which will then dispense the appropriate stamp. There are eight different price zones for international mail. Alternatively, you can buy stamps online and print them at home, or they can be bought at *tabacs*. Post offices also sell phonecards, and will cash or send international money orders. They usually open 8am–7pm Mon–Fri and 9am–1pm Sat. Be prepared for long queues during peak times (early morning, lunch time and early evening).

For *poste restante* (mail holding), the sender should write the recipient's name in block letters, then "Poste Restante", followed by the address of the Paris-Louvre post office *(see Directory)*.

Further information on all mail services is provided on the **La Poste** website.

Parisian letter box

POSTCODES

The first three digits of Paris postcodes (750 or 751) indicate Paris; the last two numbers indicate the arrondissement (district) number. Paris's arrondissements are numbered from 1 to 20 *(see p390)*. The postcode of the first arrondissement is 75001.

TV AND RADIO

The French TV channels are *TF1* and *France 2*, both with a lightweight mix; *France 3*, with documentaries, debate and classic films; *5e* ("*La Cinquième*") with discussion programmes; the Franco-German high-culture *ARTE*, specializing in arts, classical music and films; and *M6* airing mainly music, reality TV shows and commercial series. Cable and satellite channels include CNN, Sky, a variety of BBC channels and the English- and French-language news channel *France 24*. *BBC Radio 4* can be picked up during the day, while *BBC World Service* broadcasts at night. *Radio France International* (738 AM), along with live broadcasting in French and English, gives daily news in English on their website (www.rfi.fr).

NEWSPAPERS AND MAGAZINES

British and other European newspapers can be bought on the day of publication at newsagents *(maisons de la presse)* or newsstands *(kiosques)* throughout the city. These include European or international editions, such as *Financial Times Europe*, the *Guardian International*, *The Weekly Telegraph*, *USA Today*, *The Economist* and *The International Herald Tribune*.

The main French national dailies are – from right to left

A *kiosque* selling newspapers and magazines

on the political spectrum – *Le Figaro*, *Le Monde*, *Libération* and *L'Humanité*. The weeklies include the satirical *Le Canard Enchaîné*, news magazines *Le Nouvel Observateur*, *Marianne* and *L'Express*, as well as listings magazines *(see p367)*.

DIRECTORY

MOBILE TELEPHONES

Bouygues Télécom
Tel 3106.
www.bouyguestelecom.fr

Orange
Tel 09 69 36 39 00 *(English speaking).*
www.orange.com

SFR
Tel 1026 *(from a landline phone in France).*
www.sfr.com

INTERNET ACCESS

Cyber Cube
5 Rue Mignon, 75006.
Map 12 F4. *Tel* 01 53 10 30 50.
9 Rue d'Odessa, 75014.
Map 15 C2. *Tel* 01 56 80 08 00.
www.cybercube.fr

Milk
13 Rue Soufflot, 75005.
Map 17 B1. *Tel* 01 43 54 55 55.
www.milklub.com/v3/

POSTAL SERVICES

La Poste
www.laposte.fr

Paris-Champs Elysées
71 Ave des Champs Elysées
75008. **Map** 4 F5. *Tel* 3631.

Paris-Forum des Halles
1 Rue Pierre Lescot, Forum des Halles, 75001.
Map 13 A2. *Tel* 3631.

Paris-Louvre
52 Rue de Louvre 75001.
Map 12 F1. *Tel* 3631.

COURIERS

Chronopost
Tel 08 25 80 18 01.
www.chronopost.fr

DHL
Tel 08 20 20 25 25.
www.dhl.fr

FedEx
Tel 08 20 12 38 00.

GETTING TO PARIS

Paris is a major hub of European air, road and rail travel. Direct flights from all over the world serve the French capital's two main international airports. Paris is also at the centre of France's vast internal rail network and of Europe's high-speed train network,

Boeing 737 passenger jet

with regular, fast Eurostar services under the Channel from London, Thalys from Brussels, Amsterdam and Cologne, and TGVs from Marseille and Geneva, as well as many other cities. Motorways *(autoroutes)* converge on Paris from all directions, including the UK via the Eurotunnel.

ARRIVING BY AIR

Paris is served by nearly all international airlines. It has two major airports, Charles de Gaulle (CDG) and Orly (ORY), and one secondary airport, Beauvais.

The main airlines with regular flights between the UK and Paris are **British Airways**, **bmi** and **Air France**, along with low-cost carriers **easyJet**, **bmibaby**, **Flybe** and **Jet2**. From the United States there are regular flights direct to Paris, mainly on **American Airlines**, **United**, **Delta** and Air France. From Canada, **Air Canada** and Air France fly direct to Paris.

Qantas provides flights to Paris from Australia and New Zealand. **Air Austral** has flights from Australia via Réunion. **Emirates** and **Etihad Airways** fly from Australia via the Middle East, while **Cathay Pacific**, **Thai Airways** and **Singapore Air** fly from Asia.

Ryanair flies from Dublin, Shannon and Glasgow, and **Wizz Air** from parts of Eastern Europe to Beauvais airport.

For contact details of all these airlines, see page 377.

TICKETS AND FARES

The peak summer season in Paris is from July to September. Airline fares are at their highest at this time. Different airlines may have slightly varying high summer season periods. Generally, airlines offer their lowest fares to passengers booking on the Internet via their websites. It often pays to book far in advance. However, last-minute deals are sometimes available. Addresses of some discount agencies in Paris are listed on page 379. These agencies offer flights to Paris at competitive prices. Travel reservation Internet companies such as Expedia book airline tickets at discounted prices.

CHARLES DE GAULLE (CDG) AIRPORT

Paris's main airport, Charles de Gaulle (also known as Roissy), lies 30 km (19 miles) north of the city. It has two main terminals, CDG1 and CDG2, and a charter flight terminal, T3. A free CDGVAL shuttle train connects the three terminals.

Charles de Gaulle airport RER station

Buses, trains and taxis all run to central Paris from Charles de Gaulle airport. **Air France Buses** operates two bus services from both CDG1 and CDG2: one goes to Porte Maillot and Charles de Gaulle-Etoile (running about every 12 minutes, with a journey time of about 40 minutes); the other runs to the Gare de Lyon and Montparnasse TGV train station every 30 minutes, with a journey time of about 50 minutes.

The **RATP Roissybus** serves all three terminals, and departs every 20 minutes from 6am until 11pm for L'Opéra, taking about 50 minutes.

Airport Shuttle provides a door-to-door private transfer service in a minibus between Charles de Gaulle, Orly and Beauvais airports and individual hotels. It costs €40 per person, or €21–5 each for two or more people. Book at least 48 hours ahead, then call them after landing to confirm your journey. They also drop off at the Arc de Triomphe for €18 per person.

Disneyland Paris runs the VEA shuttle bus service from 8.30am until 7.45pm daily (until 10pm Friday and 9.30pm Sunday) every 30–45 minutes from CDG1 and CDG2.

Access to central Paris by train is from **RER** stations (Line B) at CDG1 and CDG2.

Waiting area at Charles de Gaulle airport

RER trains leave regularly every 5–15 minutes and take 40 minutes to Gare du Nord and 45 minutes to Châtelet-Les-Halles, and then continue to several other major stations including Luxembourg, St-Michel and Port Royal.

Taxis take 25–45 minutes to the centre of Paris and cost €45–55. Queues for taxis can be long.

ORLY AIRPORT (ORY)

Paris's other main airport, Orly, is located 15 km (9 miles) south of the capital. It has two terminals, Orly Sud and Orly Ouest.

Travellers arriving at Orly can take a bus, train or taxi to central Paris. The buses are run by **Air France Buses** and **RATP Orlybus**. Air France buses take about 30 minutes to reach the city centre, stopping at Les Invalides and Gare de Montparnasse. The Orlybus runs every 12–20 minutes and takes

Orlyval train leaving Orly Airport

about 25 minutes to reach the city centre at Denfert-Rochereau. The shuttle Jet Bus service takes travellers from the airport to Villejuif-Louis Aragon metro station every 15–20 minutes.

A shuttle bus service (VEA) links the airport with Disneyland Resort Paris. It runs every 45 minutes between 8.30am and 7.30pm.

Orlyrail bus service links the airport with **RER** Line C at Pont de Rungis. Trains leave from here every 15 minutes

(every 30 minutes after 9pm), taking 25 minutes to reach the Gare d'Austerlitz. An automatic train, ORLYVAL, links the airport with RER Line B at Antony station, from where trains leave every 4–8 minutes for Châtelet-les-Halles.

Taxis to the city centre take about 25–45 minutes and cost €25–30.

BEAUVAIS AIRPORT

Beauvais airport serves mainly budget airlines. It is 70 km (44 miles) from Paris. A shuttle bus service operates between Beauvais and Porte-Maillot – buses leave 20 minutes after a flight has landed. Tickets are available in the arrivals lounge, or at the sales points outside. Trains run from Beauvais station to Gare du Nord, but the station is a 15-minute taxi-ride from the airport, and the train journey takes 75 minutes into Paris. Taxis take 1–1½ hours and cost about €100–130.

DIRECTORY

MAIN AIRLINES SERVING PARIS

Air Austral
Tel 0825 013 012 (France).
www.air-austral.com

Air Canada
Tel 01 888 247 2262 (Canada), 0825 880 881 (France).
www.aircanada.ca

Air France
Tel 0820 320 820 (France).
www.airfrance.fr

American Airlines
Tel 01 800 433 7300 (USA), 08 26 46 09 50 (France). www.aa.com

bmi
Tel 0844 8484 888 (UK), +44 1332 648 181 (overseas).
www.flybmi.com

bmibaby
Tel 0905 8282 828 (UK).
www.flybmi.com

British Airways
Tel 0844 493 0787 (UK), 0825 825 400 (France).
www.ba.com

Cathay Pacific
www.cathaypacific.com

Delta
Tel 01 800 241 4141 (USA), 08 92 70 26 09 (France).
www.delta.com

easyJet
Tel 0871 244 2366 (UK), 0826 103 320 (France).
www.easyjet.com

Emirates
www.emirates.com

Etihad Airways
www.etihadairways.com

Flybe
www.flybe.com

Jet2
Tel 0871 226 1737 (UK), +44 203 031 8103 (overseas).
www.jet2.com

Qantas
www.qantas.com

Ryanair
Tel 0871 246 0000 (UK), 0892 780 210 (France).
www.ryanair.com

Singapore Air
www.singaporeair.com

Thai Airways
Tel 01 800 426 5204 (USA).
www.thaiairways.fr

United
Tel 01 800 864 8331 (USA), 0810 72 72 72 (France).
www.united.com

Wizz Air
http//wizzair.com

AIRPORT TRANSFER INFORMATION

Air France Buses
Tel 08 92 35 08 20.
www.cars-airfrance.com

Airport Shuttle
Tel 01 53 39 18 18.
www.parishuttle.fr

RATP Roissybus/ Orlybus
Tel 3246 (information).
www.ratp.fr

RER Trains
Tel 3246.

CDG AIRPORT HOTELS

Holiday Inn
Tel 01 34 29 30 00.
www.ichotelsgroup.com

Ibis
Tel 01 49 19 19 19.
www.ibishotel.com

Novotel
Tel 01 49 19 27 27.
www.novotel.com

Sheraton
Tel 01 49 19 70 70.
www.starwoodhotels.com

ORLY AIRPORT HOTELS

Hilton Hotel
Tel 01 45 12 45 12.
www.hilton.com

Ibis
Tel 01 56 70 50 50.
www.accorhotels.com

Mercure
Tel 01 49 75 15 50.
www. mercure.com

ARRIVING BY RAIL

Eurostar trains travel directly from central London (St Pancras), Ashford and Ebbsfleet (both in Kent) to central Paris (Gare du Nord) in 2 hours and 15 minutes. There are up to 24 departures daily. Other high-speed services into Paris include Thalys trains from Brussels, Amsterdam and Cologne, and **TGVs** from throughout France. Pre-booking is essential. **Rail Europe** offers a comprehensive information and booking service for these and other trains throughout Europe.

As the railway hub of France and the Continent, Paris has six major international railway stations operated by the French state railways, known as **SNCF** *(see p388)*. The Gare de Lyon (Map 18 F1) is the city's main station, serving the south of France, the Alps, Italy and Switzerland. The Gare de l'Est (Map 7 C3) serves eastern France, Austria, Switzerland and Germany. Trains from Britain, Holland, Belgium, Scandinavia and northeast France arrive at the Gare du Nord (Map 7 B3). Trains from some Channel ports and Normandy arrive at the Gare St-Lazare (Map 5 C3). The termini for trains from Spain, as well as from the Brittany ports, are the Gare Montparnasse (Map 15 C2)

and Gare d'Austerlitz (Map 18 D2). Trains from south-west France arrive at Gare d'Austerlitz. Other main stations are: Gare de Bercy; Massy-Palaiseau; Marne-la-Vallée for Disneyland Resort Paris; and Aéroport Charles-de-Gaulle.

There is a tourist office at the Gare de Lyon where accommodation can be booked *(see p367)*. All the railway stations are served by city buses, the metro and RER trains. Directional signs show where to make connections.

Gare du Nord station concourse

EUROTUNNEL

Travellers coming to Paris from Britain by road will need to cross the English Channel. The simplest and most popular way to do so is on the vehicle-carrying train shuttles which travel through the Channel Tunnel. Operated by **Eurotunnel**, these run between the terminals at Folkestone and Calais.

Passengers are directed onto the trains and remain with their vehicle, though they may get out of their car and walk about inside the train during the journey.

The journey through the Tunnel takes about 30 minutes and is unaffected by sea conditions. Trains depart every 15–30 minutes, depending on demand. The Tunnel terminal has direct motorway access on both the English and the French side.

ARRIVING BY SEA

Ship and catamaran car ferry companies operate across the Channel each day. On the short Dover–Calais route alone, there are up to 100 crossings per day, including those run by **SeaFrance** and **P&O**, which offer fast frequent services taking 90 minutes to cross the Channel. **Transmanche Ferries**, part of Corsica Ferries, runs a route between Newhaven and Dieppe, which takes nearly 4 hours. **Norfolkline** operates a 2-hour crossing between Dover and Dunkerque.

Two companies ply the longer western routes across the Channel. **Brittany Ferries** crossings from Plymouth to Roscoff take up to 8 hours, and from Poole to Cherbourg they take 4¼ hours on a conventional

Main entrance of the Gare du Nord, one of the busiest train stations in Europe

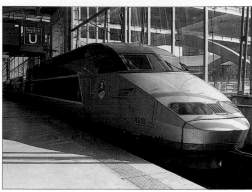
A high-speed TGV train

THE TGV

Trains à Grande Vitesse, or TGV high-speed trains, travel at speeds up to 300 km/h (186mph). Paris is the nucleus for the TGV network and it is possible to connect from the Eurostar to other TGVs serving 150 destinations in France as well as Switzerland, Germany and Northern Europe. All of France's major cities can be reached by TGV and the number of stations is growing all the time, making this an ever-more convenient form of transport *(see pp380–81)*.

ferry, or 3 hours on the *Condor Vitesse* (fast ferry). From Portsmouth, Brittany Ferries take 6 hours to travel to Caen, and 11 hours overnight to St Malo. **LD Lines** runs ferries from Portsmouth to Le Havre in 5½ hours. Driving to Paris from Cherbourg takes 4–5 hours; from Dieppe or Le Havre, about 2½–3 hours; and from Calais, 2 hours.

ARRIVING BY ROAD

The main coach operator to Paris is **Eurolines**, based at the Gare Routière Internationale above the Galleini metro station in eastern Paris. Its coaches travel from Belgium, Holland, Ireland, Germany, Scandinavia, the UK, Italy

and Portugal. The Eurolines terminus in London is the centrally located Victoria Coach Station, from where there are between three and five departures for Paris each day, depending on the season. The journey from London to Paris takes between 8 and 9 hours.

Paris is an oval-shaped city. It is surrounded by an outer ring road called the Boulevard Périphérique. All motorways leading to the capital link in to the Périphérique, which separates the city from the suburbs. Each former city gate, called a *porte*, now corresponds to an exit from (or entrance to) the Périphérique. Arriving motorists should take time to check their destination address and consult a map

of central Paris to find the closest corresponding *porte*. For example, a motorist who wants to get to the Arc de Triomphe should exit at Porte Maillot.

For the uninitiated, driving to the centre of Paris in heavy traffic and then parking can be a difficult experience *(see p389)*, which is why public transport is a more appealing option *(see pp382–8)*.

A long-haul international Eurolines coach

DIRECTORY

ARRIVING BY RAIL

Eurostar
Tel 08432 186 186 (UK).
www.eurostar.com

Rail Europe
www.raileurope.com

SNCF
Tel 3635. www.sncf.com
or www.voyages-sncf.com

TGV
www.tgv-europe.com

ARRIVING BY SEA

Brittany Ferries
Tel 0871 244 0744 (UK).
www.brittany-ferries.co.uk

LD Lines
Tel 0844 576 88 36 (UK).
www.ldlines.com

Norfolkline
Tel 0844 847 5042 (UK).
www.norfolkline.com

P&O
Tel 08716 642 121 (UK).
www.poferries.com

SeaFrance
Tel 03 21 17 70 26.
www.seafrance.com

Transmanche Ferries
Tel 0825 304 304 (France),
0800 917 1201 (UK).

ARRIVING BY ROAD

Eurolines
Ave de Général de Gaulle, Bagnolet, Paris.
Tel 0892 899 091.

Victoria Coach Station, London SW1.
Tel 0870 5808 080.
www.eurolines.com

Eurotunnel
Tel 0844 335 3535 (UK),
0810 630 304 (France).
www.eurotunnel.com

Traffic Reports around Paris
www.sytadin.tm.fr

DISCOUNT TRAVEL AGENCIES

Carlson Wagonlit
Tel 0826 824 826.
www.carlsonwagonlit
voyages.fr

Directours
Tel 01 45 62 62 62.
www.directours.com

Jet Tours
Tel 08 20 83 08 80.
www.jettours.com

Nouvelles Frontières
Tel 0825 000 747.
www.nouvelles-
frontieres.fr

Arriving in Paris

This map depicts the bus and rail services between the two main airports and the city. It shows the ferry–rail links from the UK, the main railway links from other parts of France and Europe, and the long-haul coach services from other European countries. It also shows the main city railway and coach termini, the airport shuttle connections and the airport bus and rail stops. The frequency of services and journey times from the airport are provided, as are the approximate times of rail journeys from other cities. Metro and RER line connections to other parts of Paris are indicated at the termini and route stops.

⚓ CALAIS
*Ferry and Eurotunnel links with Dover and Folkestone. Eurostar train London–Paris **Gare du Nord** (2 hrs 15 mins) passes through here on the way to St Pancras and Ashford from Paris. **SNCF** train to **Gare du Nord** (1 hr 30 mins–3 hrs 30 mins).*

⚓ LE HAVRE
Ferry links with Portsmouth. **SNCF** *train to* **Gare St-Lazare** *(2 hrs 10 mins).*

⚓ DIEPPE
Ferry links with Newhaven (summer). **SNCF** *train to* **Gare St-Lazare** *(2 hrs 20 mins).*

⚓ CAEN
Ferry links with Portsmouth. **SNCF** *train to* **Gare St-Lazare** *(1 hr 50 mins).*

⚓ CHERBOURG
Ferry links with Portsmouth and Poole. **SNCF** *train to* **Gare St-Lazare** *(3 hrs).*

GARE ST-LAZARE
Rouen (1 hr 30 mins).

GARE MONTPARNASSE
Bordeaux *(3 hrs 30 mins)*
Brest *(4 hrs 30 mins)*
Lisbon *(19 hrs 40 mins)*
Madrid *(12 hrs 25 mins)*
Nantes *(2 hrs 15 mins)*
Rennes *(2 hrs 15 mins)*

Porte Maillot
Ⓜ ①
RER Ⓐ Ⓒ

Charles de Gaulle-Etoile
Ⓜ ① ② ⑥
RER Ⓐ

Champs-Elysées

Chaillot Quarter

Gare St-Laz
Ⓜ ③ ⑫

Invalides
Ⓜ ⑧ ⑬
RER Ⓒ

Invalides and Eiffel Tower Quarter

Montparnasse

Gare Montparnasse
Ⓜ ④ ⑥ ⑫ ⑬ ⑭

Porte de Orléans
Ⓜ ④

KEY

▬▬	SNCF see pp378–9
▬▬	Coaches see p379
▬▬	Roissybus see p377
▬▬	Air France bus see p377
▬▬	RER B see p377
▬▬	Orlyrail see p377
▬▬	Orlyval see p377
▬▬	Orlybus see p377
▬▬	Jet Bus see p377
Ⓜ	Metro station
RER	RER station

0 kilometres 1
0 miles 0.5

GARE TGV DE MASSY-PALAISEAU
Bordeaux *(3 hrs 30 mins)*
Lille *(1 hr 50 mins)*
London *(4 hrs 15 mins)*
Lyon *(2 hrs 10 mins)*
Nantes *(2 hrs 30 mins)*
Rennes *(2 hrs 10 mins)*

Antony
RER Ⓑ

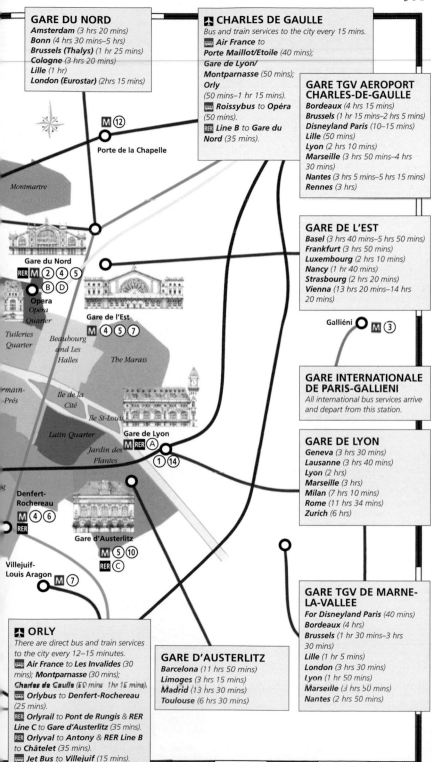

GARE DU NORD
Amsterdam (3 hrs 20 mins)
Bonn (4 hrs 30 mins–5 hrs)
Brussels (Thalys) (1 hr 25 mins)
Cologne (3 hrs 20 mins)
Lille (1 hr)
London (Eurostar) (2hrs 15 mins)

CHARLES DE GAULLE
Bus and train services to the city every 15 mins.
Air France to
Porte Maillot/Etoile (40 mins);
Gare de Lyon/
Montparnasse (50 mins);
Orly
(50 mins–1 hr 15 mins).
Roissybus to *Opéra*
(50 mins).
Line B to *Gare du*
Nord (35 mins).

GARE TGV AEROPORT CHARLES-DE-GAULLE
Bordeaux (4 hrs 15 mins)
Brussels (1 hr 15 mins–2 hrs 5 mins)
Disneyland Paris (10–15 mins)
Lille (50 mins)
Lyon (2 hrs 10 mins)
Marseille (3 hrs 50 mins–4 hrs 30 mins)
Nantes (3 hrs 5 mins–5 hrs 15 mins)
Rennes (3 hrs)

GARE DE L'EST
Basel (3 hrs 40 mins–5 hrs 50 mins)
Frankfurt (3 hrs 50 mins)
Luxembourg (2 hrs 10 mins)
Nancy (1 hr 40 mins)
Strasbourg (2 hrs 20 mins)
Vienna (13 hrs 20 mins–14 hrs 20 mins)

GARE INTERNATIONALE DE PARIS-GALLIENI
All international bus services arrive and depart from this station.

GARE DE LYON
Geneva (3 hrs 30 mins)
Lausanne (3 hrs 40 mins)
Lyon (2 hrs)
Marseille (3 hrs)
Milan (7 hrs 10 mins)
Rome (11 hrs 34 mins)
Zurich (6 hrs)

GARE TGV DE MARNE-LA-VALLEE
For Disneyland Paris (40 mins)
Bordeaux (4 hrs)
Brussels (1 hr 30 mins–3 hrs 30 mins)
Lille (1 hr 5 mins)
London (3 hrs 30 mins)
Lyon (1 hr 50 mins)
Marseille (3 hrs 50 mins)
Nantes (2 hrs 50 mins)

ORLY
There are direct bus and train services to the city every 12–15 minutes.
Air France to *Les Invalides* (30 mins); *Montparnasse* (30 mins);
Charles de Gaulle (50 mins–1 hr 15 mins).
Orlybus to *Denfert-Rochereau* (25 mins).
Orlyrail to *Pont de Rungis* & *RER Line C* to *Gare d'Austerlitz* (35 mins).
Orlyval to *Antony* & *RER Line B* to *Châtelet* (35 mins).
Jet Bus to *Villejuif* (15 mins).

GARE D'AUSTERLITZ
Barcelona (11 hrs 50 mins)
Limoges (3 hrs 15 mins)
Madrid (13 hrs 30 mins)
Toulouse (6 hrs 30 mins)

Porte de la Chapelle
Montmartre
Gare du Nord
Opéra
Opéra Quarter
Tuileries Quarter
Beaubourg and Les Halles
Gare de l'Est
The Marais
Galliéni
-main--Prés
Ile de la Cité
Ile St-Louis
Latin Quarter
Gare de Lyon
Jardin des Plantes
Denfert-Rochereau
Gare d'Austerlitz
Villejuif-Louis Aragon

GETTING AROUND PARIS

Central Paris is compact. The best way to get around is to walk. Cycling and rollerblading are also popular with Parisians and tourists alike. Public transport is very efficient. The metro, RER train and bus system operated by the RATP makes getting around Paris cheap and easy, and the city authorities are working on green travel initiatives. The city is divided into six travel zones: zones 1 and 2 correspond to the centre and zones 3, 4, 5 and 6 to the suburbs and the airport. Some suburbs are served by a tramway. River boats make for a scenic mode of transport. Driving a car in the city centre can be an unpleasant experience. Traffic is often heavy, there are many one-way streets and parking is notoriously difficult and expensive.

GREEN TRAVEL

Paris has one of the world's most efficient and dependable public transport systems and city authorities are keen to make the capital more environmentally friendly. Residents and visitors alike are encouraged to swap cars for bicycles, and to strap on rollerblades or walking shoes as busy thoroughfares shut down to traffic at weekends as part of the *Paris-Respire* (Paris Breathes) initiative. The Mairie de Paris (Paris City Council) is enlarging footpaths, declaring more streets pedestrian-only, increasing bike lanes and planting trees in an effort to cut down on parking spaces and wean Parisians off cars. Around 55 per cent of city dwellers don't own a car.

In a bid to reduce carbon dioxide emissions by 22,000 tons a year and in order to improve traffic congestion, the Mairie is making 3,000 electric cars *(Auto-libs)* available for Parisians to pick up and drop off at rental stands throughout the city.

An eco-friendly Vélo taxi

The RATP is testing buses that run on second-generation bio-fuels and plans to gradually introduce vehicles equipped with hybrid electric-thermic engines in an effort to reduce fuel consumption along with noise and air pollution. The electric tramway is punctual, silent, and super green – for every three trees removed during its construction, four new ones were planted.

On the Paris metro, the MF01 trains running on some lines have been designed to recover two-thirds of all energy lost during braking operations. In addition, a proportion of the water building up in the underground network is returned to nature instead of down city drains, and recycling bins have been placed in RER and a number of metro stations.

Taxis G7 has introduced hybrid cars to their fleet and is putting drivers through eco-training courses while Taxis Bleus is promoting the use of biofuels, hybrid engines, particle filters and better driving techniques to reduce fuel consumption. Verture has a fleet composed entirely of hybrid vehicles, and offsets its carbon dioxide via an association that funds sustainable development *(see p389)*.

To estimate your carbon footprint, click onto the *ecocomparateur* on the SNCF website *(see p379)*. This helps you work out how much carbon dioxide your trip produces according to your transport method.

Vélo taxis are electrically assisted tricycle rickshaws that are slower than traditional taxis, but are adept at zipping in and out of traffic.

The introduction of the free **Vélib'** self-service bike hire system has spawned a new generation of street-savvy cyclists.

TICKETS AND TRAVEL PASSES

Tickets can be purchased at all main metro and RER stations, at the airports and several tourist offices. Individual tickets are relatively cheap and you can buy a block of ten *(carnet)* for ease. The *Paris Visite* pass for one, two, three or five days includes discounted entry to some sights, but is comparatively expensive unless you intend to travel extensively. To get a *Passe Navigo Découverte*, you do not need to be a resident of Paris but you will need a passport photo and to pay €5. A *Passe Navigo* requires a Paris address. It has replaced all travel cards. Visitors can also buy a one-day Mobilis card, valid for travel on most public transport.

Paris Visite pass

Mobilis card

Navigo travel card

Navigo Découverte pass

WALKING IN PARIS

One of the best and easiest ways of getting around central Paris is to walk. Australian, British, Irish and New Zealand visitors need to remember that cars drive on the right-hand side of the road. There are many two-stage road crossings where pedestrians wait on an island in the centre of the road before proceeding. These are marked *piétons traversez en deux temps*.

CYCLING IN PARIS

Paris is well equipped for cyclists. It's reasonably flat, manageably small, has many backstreets where car traffic is restricted, and more than 370 km (230 miles) of cycle lanes *(pistes cyclables)*. Parisian motorists are increasingly respectful of cyclists as more and more of their fellow citizens turn to two wheels.

Vélib', a self-service bike scheme, offers both residents and visitors the cheapest way of getting around the city. Bike stands are located every 300 m (330 yds) and payment is by credit card at the access terminals, which operate in eight different languages. See page 357 for rates.

Bicycles (apart from Vélibs) may be taken on SNCF trains, and suburban stations also rent bicycles. There are bicycle shops throughout Paris, and many also organize guided tours by bike.

Bikes for hire by residents or tourists, at a Vélib' bike stand

TRAVELLING BY BOAT

Paris's main river-boat shuttle service, the **Batobus**, runs every 15–30 minutes, with stops at eight of the city's most famous attractions – Eiffel Tower, Musée d'Orsay, St-Germain des Près, Louvre, Hôtel de Ville, Champs Elysées, Jardin des Plantes, and Notre Dame. Tickets can be bought at Batobus stops, RATP and tourist offices. The service shuts down annually from early January to early February *(see pp72–3).*

Paris Vision tour bus

GUIDED TOURS

Double-decker bus tours with commentaries in English, Italian, Japanese and German are organized by **France Tourisme**, **Cityrama** and **Paris Vision**. The tours begin from the city centre and take about 2 hours. They pass the main sights but do not stop at all of them. **Les Cars Rouges** runs bus tours stopping at many of the sights in Paris. Each ticket is valid for 2 days and allows you to hop on or off at any of the stops.

Bike tours are run by a number of companies. **Paris Charms and Secrets** runs 4-hour tours in English on electric bikes departing from Place Vendôme. **Paris Bike Tour** departs from the Marais, **Paris à Velo C'est Sympa!** leaves from near the Bastille, while **Bike About Tours** starts from close to the Hôtel de Ville.

Paris Walks conducts daily tours in English, including a "Chocolate Walk" and a "Fashion Walk". The **Comité Départemental de la Randonée Pédestre de Paris** runs free thematic walks in French.

More information on guided tours is available at the Office du Tourisme *(see p366).*

DIRECTORY

RIVER BOATS

Batobus
Port de la Bourdonnais 75001.
Map 10 D2. **Tel** 08 25 05 0101.
www.batobus.com

BUS TOUR OPERATORS

Cityrama
2 Place des Pyramides 75001.
Map 12 E1. **Tel** 01 44 55 61 00.
www.pariscityrama.com

France Tourisme
33 Quai des Grands Augustins
75006. **Map** 12 F4.
Tel 01 53 10 35 35.
www.francetourisme.fr

Les Cars Rouges
17 Quai de Grenelle 75015.
Map 9 C4. **Tel** 01 53 95 39 53.
www.carsrouges.com

Paris Vision
214 Rue de Rivoli 75001.
Map 12 D1. **Tel** 01 42 60 30 01.
www.parisvision.com

BICYCLE HIRE & TOURS

Bike About Tours
Vinci Car Park, 4 Rue de Lobau
75004. **Map** 13 B3.
Tel 06 18 80 84 92.
www.bikeabouttours.com

Paris à Vélo C'est Sympa!
22 Rue Alphonse Baudin 75011.
Map 14 E2. **Tel** 01 48 87 60 01.
www.parisvelosympa.com

Paris Bike Tour
38 Rue de Saintonge 75003.
Map 14 D2. **Tel** 01 42 74 22 14.
www.parisbiketour.net

Paris Charms and Secrets
106 Rue Vielle du Temple, 75003.
Map 14 D2.
Tel 01 42 29 00 00.
www.parischarmssecrets.com

Vélib'
www.velib.paris.fr

WALKING TOURS

Comité Départemental de la Randonée Pédestre de Paris
35 Rue Piat 75020.
Tel 01 46 36 95 70.
www.rando-paris.org

Paris Walks
12 Passage Meunier 9320-St
Denis. **Map** 17 B5.
Tel 01 48 09 21 40.
www.paris-walks.com

Travelling by Metro and RER

The RATP (Paris transport company) operates 14 main metro lines, referred to by their number and terminus names, which criss-cross Paris and its suburbs. There are also two minor lines – 3b (Gambetta–Porte de Lilas) and 7b (Louis Blanc–Pré St Gervais). The metro is often the fastest and cheapest way to get across the capital, as there are hundreds of stations *(see map on inside back cover)*.

RATP logo

Metro stations are easily identified by their logo, a large circled "M", and some by their Art Nouveau entrances. The metro and RER (Paris rail network) systems operate in much the same way. The trains run from 4.45am to between 12.40am and 1.30am (1 hour later on weekends).

Art Nouveau metro sign

Modern metro sign

Reading the Metro Map

Metro and RER lines are shown in various colours on the metro map. Metro lines are identified by a number, which is located on the map at either end of a line. Some metro stations serve only one line, others serve more than one. There are stations sharing both metro and RER lines and some are linked to one another by inter-connecting passages.

RER and metro station serving the same lines

Metro and RER stations with inter-connecting passage

Metro line

Metro station serving one line

Metro station serving two lines

② Metro line identification number

USING THE RER

The RER is a system of commuter trains which travel underground in central Paris and above ground in outlying areas. Metro tickets and passes are valid on it. There are five lines, known by their letters: A, B, C, D and E. Each line forks. For example, Line C has six forks, labelled C1, C2 etc. All RER trains bear names (for example, ALEX or VERA) to make it easier to read RER timetables in the station halls and on platforms. Digital panels on all RER platforms indicate train name, direction of travel (terminus) and upcoming stations. RER stations are identified by a large circled logo. The main city stations are: Charles de Gaulle-Etoile, Châtelet-Les-Halles, Gare de Lyon, Nation, St-Michel-Notre-Dame, Auber-Haussmann St-Lazare and the Gare du Nord-Magenta.

The RER and metro systems overlap in central Paris. It is

often quicker to take an RER train to a station served by both, as in the case of La Défense and Nation. However, getting into the RER stations, which are often linked to the metro by a maze of corridors, can be very time-consuming.

The RER is particularly useful for getting to Paris airports and to many of the outlying towns and tourist attractions. Line B serves Charles de Gaulle airport and Orly airport; Line A goes to Disneyland Resort Paris; and Line C runs to Versailles and Orly airport.

RER logo

BUYING A TICKET

Ordinary metro and RER tickets can be bought either singly or as a *carnet* of ten, from ticket booths or ticket machines in the booking halls (carry some €1 and €2 coins). The useful **Paris Visite** bus, metro and RER pass *(see p382)* is widely available, and you can also buy it in advance at certain travel agencies and rail ticket agents abroad (e.g. Rail Europe in London). There is also the **Passe Navigo Découverte** *(see p382)* which requires a passport photo. One metro ticket entitles you to travel anywhere on the metro, and on RER trains in central Paris. RER trips outside the centre (such as to airports) require special tickets. Fares to suburbs and nearby towns vary. Consult the fare charts posted in RER stations. You must retain your ticket during the trip, as regular inspections are made and you can be fined for not having a ticket.

MAKING A JOURNEY BY METRO

1 To determine which metro line to take, travellers should first find their destination on a metro map. (Maps can be found inside stations and also on the inside back cover of this book.) Trace the metro line by following the colour coding and the number of the line. At the end of the line you will see the number of the terminus – remember this, as it will help you to find the correct train.

Insert the train ticket in the first slot.

Remove the ticket from the second slot.

2 Metro tickets are sold at all stations. These are equipped with coin-operated automatic machines. One metro ticket allows the bearer travel for one journey, including any transfers on the metro system, and on RER trains in central Paris.

3 To enter the platform area, insert the metro ticket, with the magnetic strip facing down, into the first barrier slot. Remove the ticket from the second slot, then walk through. Alternatively, swipe your *Passe Navigo Découverte* over the reader in the barrier.

← DIRECTION
Ⓜ ① CHÂTEAU DE VINCENNES

GARE DE LYON
REUILLY-DIDEROT
NATIO J
PORTE DE VINCENNES
SAINT-MANDÉ-TOURELLE
BÉRAULT
CHÂTEAU DE VINCENNES

4 At the entrance to each station platform, and in the station corridors, there are lists of upcoming stations corresponding to a given terminus. Terminus names are also indicated on the platform and should be checked before boarding the train.

DIRECTION
Ⓜ ①
CHÂTEAU DE VINCENNES

5 To change lines, get off at the appropriate transfer station and follow the *correspondance* (connections) signs on the platform indicating the appropriate direction.

6 There is a release button which you press to open the metro doors. Before the doors open and close, a single tone will sound.

7 Inside the trains are charts of the line being served by the train. The station stops are plotted on the chart, so travellers can track their journeys.

← SORTIE

8 The "Sortie" sign indicates the way out. At all metro exits there are neighbourhood maps.

Travelling by Bus

The bus is an excellent way to see the great sights of Paris. The bus system is run by the RATP, which also runs the metro, so you can use the same tickets for both. There are more than 200 bus lines in greater Paris and over 3,500 buses in daily circulation at rush hour. Buses can be the fastest way to travel short distances, especially now that there are more bus-only lanes. However, during peak hours buses may get caught in heavy traffic and are often crowded. Visitors should check the times for the first and last buses as they vary widely, depending on the line. Night buses run throughout the night.

Ticket-cancelling machine

Cancelling a Bus Ticket
Insert the ticket into the machine in the direction of the arrow, then withdraw it.

Bus stop sign

Night bus sign

Bus stop

Bus Stop Signs
Signs at bus stops display route numbers. A white background indicates a service every day all year; a black one means no service on Sundays or public holidays.

TICKETS AND PASSES

A single bus ticket entitles the bearer to a single journey on a single line. If you want to make a change, you'll need another ticket. (Exceptions to this rule are the buses Balabus, Noctambus, Orlybus and Roissybus, and lines 221, 297, 299, 350 and 351.) Children under four travel for free, and those aged between four and ten may travel at half price.

Bus-only tickets are purchased from the bus driver and must be cancelled to be valid. To do this, insert the ticket into the cancelling machine inside the bus. Hold on to your ticket until the end of the journey; inspectors do make random checks and are empowered to levy on-the-spot fines if you cannot produce a valid cancelled ticket for your journey.

You can also purchase a *carnet* of ten tickets, each of them valid for a single bus,

metro or RER journey. However, a carnet cannot be purchased on buses, and can only be bought at metro stations.

Travel passes are a good idea if you are planning a number of journeys during your stay. For a set fee, you can enjoy unlimited travel on Paris buses with a *Paris Visite* pass *(see p382)*. Never cancel these as it will render them invalid. They should be shown to the bus driver whenever you board a bus, and to a ticket inspector on request. If you have a *Passe Navigo Découverte (see p382)*, swipe it across the card-reading machine as you board the bus.

USING THE BUSES

Bus stops and shelters are identified by the number shields of the buses that stop at them, and by the distinctive RATP logo. Route maps at bus stops indicate transfers and nearby metro and RER stops. Bus stops also display timetables, and show first and last buses. Neighbourhood maps are also displayed at most bus shelters.

Most buses must be flagged down. Some models have multiple doors which must be opened by pressing a red button inside the bus to exit, or outside the bus to enter.

Paris's Buses
Passengers can identify the route and destination of a bus from the information on the panels at the front. It's possible to enter some buses from the middle door; there's a button on the exterior of the bus.

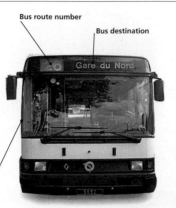

Bus route number

Bus destination

Gare du Nord

Passengers enter the bus at the front door

Bus front displaying information

All buses have buttons and bells to signal for a stop. Some buses do not go all the way to their terminus, in which case there will be a slash through the name of the destination on the front panel.

All of central Paris's 60 bus routes are equipped to allow wheelchair access; this means that at least 70 per cent of stops on the route are accessible; suitable stops are designated by a wheelchair symbol on the bus route sign. All buses have some seats reserved for disabled and elderly persons. These seats are identified by a sign and must be given up on request.

NIGHT AND SUMMER BUSES

There are 47 night bus lines, called Noctilien, serving Paris and its suburbs (from 12:30am–5:30am Monday to Thursday and 1am–5.30am Friday and Saturday). The network is laid out around the five major transfer stations of Gare de Lyon, Gare de l'Est, St Lazare, Montparnasse and Châtelet. The terminus for most lines is Châtelet, at Avenue Victoria or Rue St-Martin. Noctilien

stops are identified by a letter "N" set in a white circle on a blue background. Noctilien buses must be flagged down. Travel passes are valid, as are normal metro tickets, which must be cancelled on board. Travellers may buy tickets on board the bus. See www. noctilien.fr for more details.

In summer, the RATP also operates buses in the Bois de Vincennes and Bois de Boulogne, and the Balabus which stops at major tourist sites. **RATP Information** has useful details about these and the best ways to get around.

RATP Information
54 Quai de la Rapée 75012. *Tel 32 46*. **www**.ratp.fr

TRAMWAY

There are three RATP tramways operating in Paris – T1 (Gare de St Denis–Noisy le Sec), T2 (La Défense–Porte de Versailles) and T3 (Pont du Garigliano–Porte d'Ivry), and the network is expected to grow. T3, dubbed the *Tramway des Maréchaux* as it follows the wide boulevards named after military marshals, is handy for exploring the outer reaches of the 13th, 14th and 15th arrondissements. The T4 (Aulnay-sous-Bois–Bondy) is run by SNCF and is a tram-train line.

RATP metro and public bus tickets are valid for use on tramways.

Passengers embarking at an RATP tram stop

USEFUL BUS ROUTES

Here is a selection of some of the most useful bus routes around the centre of Paris, taking in some of the great sights of the city. The routes show the major bus stops, and locations of some of the notable sights.

KEY
- ■ Major sight
- ▬ Bus route
- ○ Bus stop *(selected stops only)*
- **Balabus** Balabus (Apr–Sep)

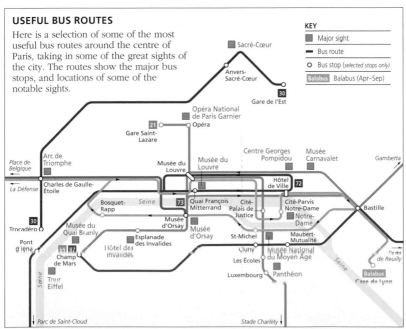

Using SNCF Trains

The French state railway, Société Nationale des
Chemins de Fer (SNCF), has two services in
Paris: the *Banlieue* suburban service and the
Grandes Lignes, or long-distance service.
The suburban services all operate within
the five-zone network *(see p382)*. The
long-distance services operate throughout
France. These services allow visitors to
travel to parts of France close to Paris in a
day round trip. The TGV high-speed service
is particularly useful for such journeys, as it is
capable of travelling about twice as fast as
standard trains *(see pp378–9)*.

Gare de l'Est railway
station in 1920

RAILWAY STATIONS

France has always been known
for the punctuality of its trains,
and has maintained a high
level of investment in the
state-owned rail system, SNCF.

As the railway hub of
France, Paris boasts six major
international railway stations
operated by the SNCF: the
Gare du Nord, Gare de
l'Est, Gare de Lyon, Gare
d'Austerlitz, Gare St-Lazare and
Gare Montparnasse *(see p378)*.

All the main train stations
have long-distance and
suburban destinations. Some
of the main suburban locations,
such as Versailles and Chantilly,
are served by both long-
distance and suburban trains.

Stations have departures
and arrivals boards showing
the train number, departure
and arrival times, delay,
platform number, place of
departure and main stops en
route. For those with heavy
luggage, there are trolleys,
requiring a €1 coin (refunded
when the trolley is returned).
See the SNCF website for
further information *(see p379)*.

TICKETS

Tickets to suburban
destinations can be purchased
at automatic machines
located inside station halls
(the machines give change;
most also take credit cards).
You can also buy tickets at
the ticket counters. These
are marked with panels
indicating the kind of tickets
(billets) sold: *Banlieue* for
suburban tickets, *Grandes
Lignes* for mainline tickets
and *Internationale* for
international tickets. Fare
rates vary according to the
type of train.

For all trains that can be
booked online through the
SNCF or Rail Europe websites,
there are two or three basic
fare rates for each class. The
cheapest tickets are called
PREMs, which are advance-
purchase fares that cannot be
altered after payment; weekend
and last-minute specials are
also offered as *PREMs*.
On some trains, fares are
cheaper at off-peak times
(périodes bleus). Peak times
(périodes blanches) are from
5am until 10am on Monday
and from 3pm until 8pm on
Friday and Sunday.

Composteur Machine
The composteur *machines are
located in station halls and at
the head of each platform.
Tickets and reservations must
be inserted face up.*

A time-punched ticket

SNCF sells several travel cards
that give fare reductions of
around 50 per cent, including
the *Carte 12–25* for young
people, *Carte Senior* for
people over 60 years of age,
Carte Escapades for frequent
travellers and *Carte Enfant +*
for parents with small
children. Further details of
fares are available on the
SNCF website *(see p379)*.

Before boarding a train,
travellers must remember to
time-punch *(composter)* their
tickets and reservations in a
composteur machine. Beware
that inspectors do check
travellers' tickets and anyone
who fails to time-punch their
ticket can be fined.

A double-decker Banlieue train

SUBURBAN TRAINS

Suburban lines are found at
all main Paris train stations
and are clearly marked
Banlieue. Tickets for city
transport cannot be used on
Banlieue trains, with the
exception of some RER tickets
to stations with both SNCF
and RER lines. Several tourist
destinations are served by
Banlieue trains, including
Chantilly, Chartres, Giverny
and Versailles *(see pp248–53)*.
For further destinations, look at
the SNCF website *(see p379)*.

Travelling by Car

Although driving and parking can be difficult in central Paris, a hire car might be useful for visiting outlying areas. Taxis are a more expensive way of getting around than trains or buses, but can be an advantage late at night when the metro has stopped running. There are about 800 taxi ranks (*station de taxis*) throughout Paris.

DRIVING

To hire a car, a valid driving licence, passport and proof of insurance are required (most firms also require one major credit card). International driving licences are not needed for short-term visitors (up to 90 days) from the EU, North America, Australia and New Zealand.

Cars drive on the right-hand side and must yield to traffic merging from the right, even on thoroughfares, unless marked by a *priorité* sign, which indicates right of way. Cars on a roundabout usually have right of way, though the Arc de Triomphe is a hair-raising exception as cars give way to traffic on the right.

PARKING

Parking in Paris is difficult and expensive. Never park where there are *Parking (Stationnement) Interdit* signs. Park only in areas with a large "P" or a *Parking Payant* sign on the pavement or road, and pay at the *horodateur* (parking metre). Buy a *carte de stationnement* (€10 or €30 from a *tabac*) to use in the metre, and place the parking ticket so that it is

clearly visible through the windscreen. Parking meters (*horodateurs*) operate from 9am until 7pm Monday to Friday. Unless otherwise indicated, parking is free on Saturday, Sunday, public holidays and in nominated areas in August.

Illuminated sign on a taxi

TAXIS

There are over 15,000 taxis operating in central Paris, yet there never seem to be enough to meet demand, particularly during rush hours and on Friday and Saturday nights. The city is expected to have 20,000 taxis by 2012.

Taxis can be hailed in the street, but not within 50 m (55 yards) of a taxi rank. Since ranks always take priority over street stops, the easiest way to get a cab is to find a rank and join the queue. Ranks are located at many busy cross-roads, at main metro and RER stations, hospitals, train stations and airports. An illuminated white light on the taxi roof shows that it is available. A small light lit below means that the taxi is occupied. If the white light is covered the taxi is off duty. Taxis on their last run can refuse to take passengers.

The meter should have a specified initial amount showing at the rank, or when it is hailed. If you order a taxi, the metre will show the charge from where the driver started his journey to collect you. Initial charges for radio taxis vary widely, depending

on the distance the taxi covers to arrive at the pick-up point. Payment by cheque is not accepted but many vehicles take credit cards.

Rates vary according to the city area and the time of day. Rate A, in the city centre, is charged per kilometre. The higher rate B applies in the city centre on Sundays, holidays and at night (7pm–7am), or daytime in the suburbs or airports. The highest rate, C, applies to the suburbs and airports at night. Taxis charge for each piece of luggage, and for a fourth passenger. Drivers expect fares to be "rounded up".

DIRECTORY

CAR HIRE AGENCIES

Car hire agencies abound in Paris. Here is a list of major firms with agencies at Charles de Gaulle and Orly airports, main railway stations and city-centre locations. Call for information and reservations.

Avis
Tel 0820 05 05 05.

Budget
Tel 0825 003 564.

Europcar
Tel 0825 358 358.

Hertz
Tel 0825 861 861.

National Citer
Tel 0825 161 212.

Sixt
Tel 0820 007 498.

TAXIS AND CAR SERVICES

Neocab
Tel 08100 47336. Environmentally friendly cab service with free Wi-Fi and TV. http://neo-cab.com (Bookings can be made online).

Les Taxis Bleus
Tel 08 91 70 10 10.
www.taxis-bleus.com
(Bookings can be made online).

Taxis G7
Tel 01 47 39 47 39, 01 47 39 00 91 (special needs). www.taxisg7.fr (Bookings can be made online).

Urban Driver
Tel 0825 625 100. Motorcycle taxi service. www.urban-driver.com (Bookings can be made online).

No entry sign

INTERDIT SUR TOUTE LA LONGUEUR DE LA VOIE

AXE ROUGE

Parking Interdit (no parking)

Tow-away zone ETC ETC

30

Speed limit sign in km

STREET FINDER

The map references given with all sights, hotels, restaurants, shops and entertainment venues described in this book refer to the maps in this section (see How the Map References Work *opposite*). A complete index of street names and all the places of interest marked on the maps can be found on the following pages. The key map shows the area of Paris covered by the *Street Finder*, with the arrondissement numbers for each district. The maps include not only the sightseeing areas (which are colour-coded), but the whole of central Paris with all the districts important for hotels, restaurants, shopping and entertainment venues. The symbols used to represent sights and features on the *Street Finder* maps are listed opposite.

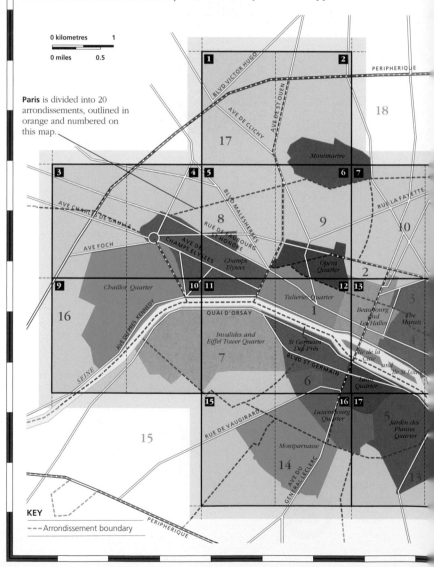

0 kilometres 1

0 miles 0.5

Paris is divided into 20 arrondissements, outlined in orange and numbered on this map.

KEY

--- Arrondissement boundary

HOW THE MAP REFERENCES WORK

The **first figure** tells you which *Street Finder* map to turn to.

Hôtel de Ville ⑲

4 P de l'Hôtel-de-Ville 75004.
Map 13 B3. **Tel** *01 42 76 50 49.*
Ⓜ *Hôtel de Ville.* ⬭ *groups: by arrangement.* ⬤ *public hols, official functions* ♿ 🏳

The **letter and number** give the grid reference. Letters go across the map's top and bottom; figures on its sides.

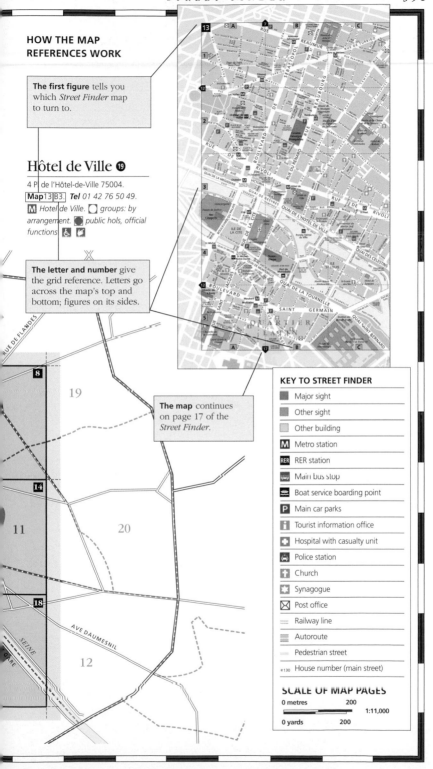

The **map** continues on page 17 of the *Street Finder.*

KEY TO STREET FINDER

⬛	Major sight
⬛	Other sight
⬜	Other building
Ⓜ	Metro station
RER	RER station
🚌	Main bus stop
🚤	Boat service boarding point
P	Main car parks
ℹ️	Tourist information office
✚	Hospital with casualty unit
🚓	Police station
✝	Church
✡	Synagogue
⊠	Post office
—	Railway line
▬	Autoroute
—	Pedestrian street
«130	House number (main street)

SCALE OF MAP PAGES

0 metres	200	
		1:11,000
0 yards	200	

Street Finder Index

Each place name is followed by its arrondissement number, and then by its Street Finder reference.

Each place name is followed by its arrondissement number, and then by its Street Finder reference.

Each place name is followed by its arrondissement number, and then by its Street Finder reference.

Each place name is followed by its arrondissement number, and then by its Street Finder reference.

Each place name is followed by its arrondissement number, and then by its Street Finder reference.

Each place name is followed by its arrondissement number, and then by its Street Finder reference.

Each place name is followed by its arrondissement number, and then by its Street Finder reference.

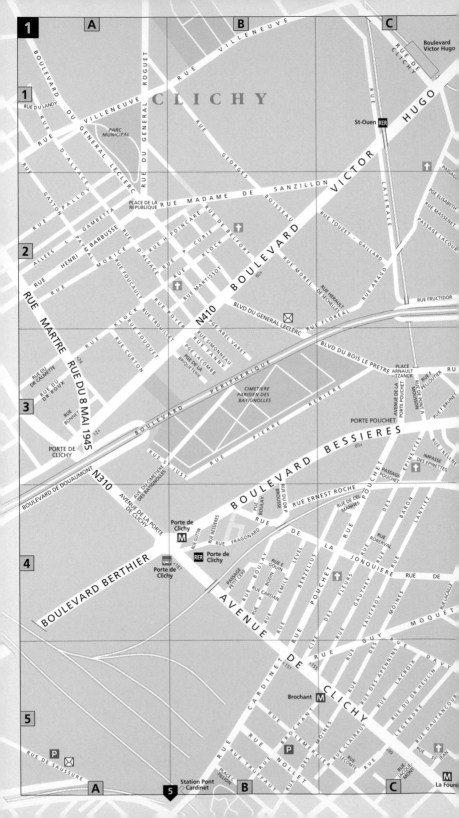

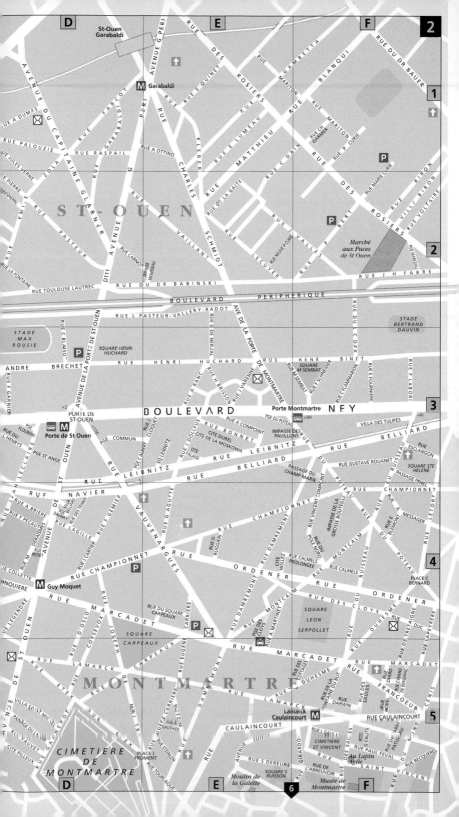

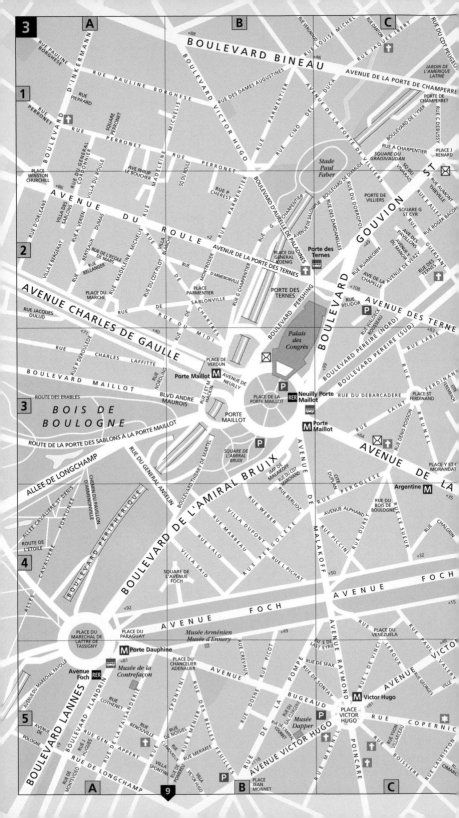

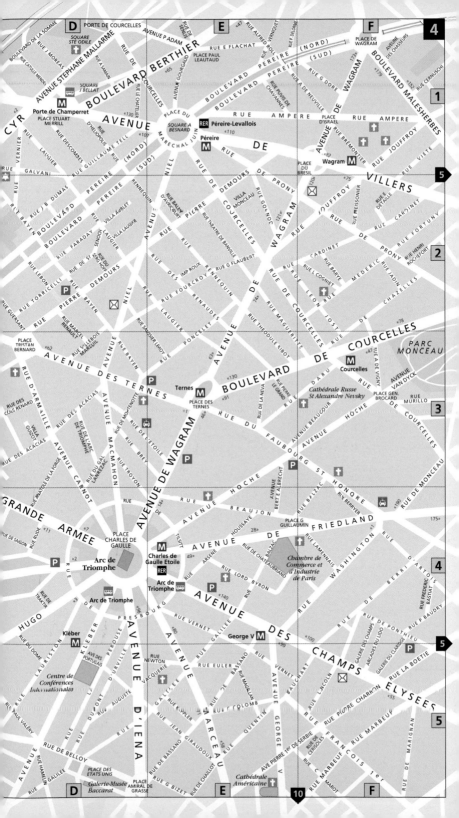

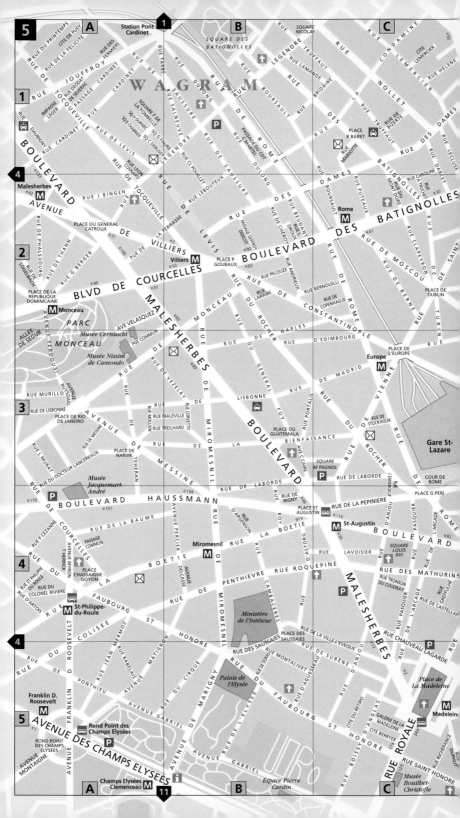

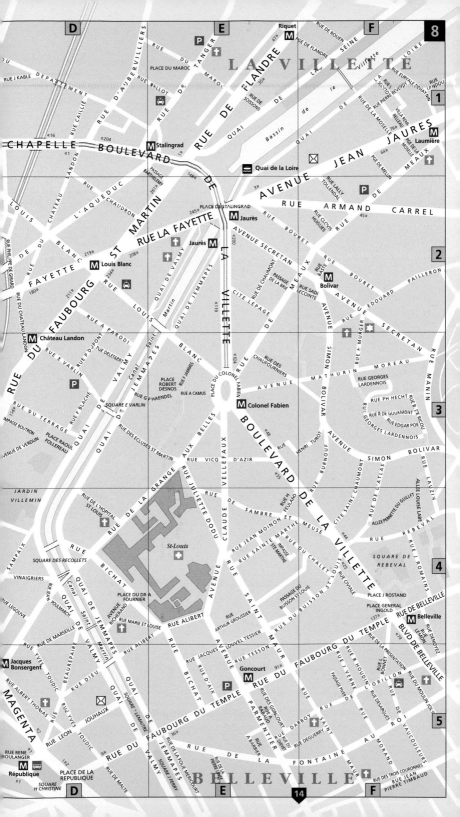

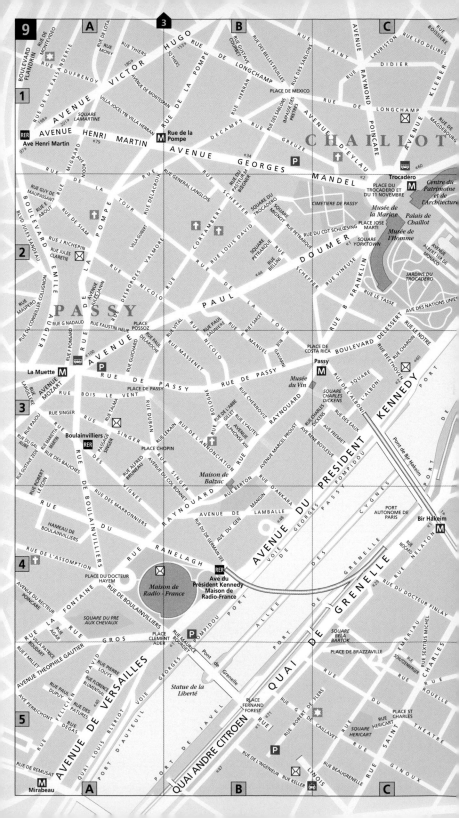

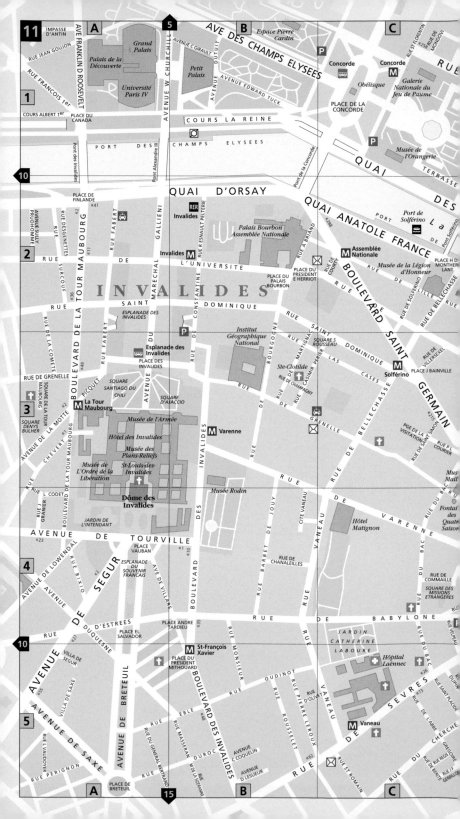

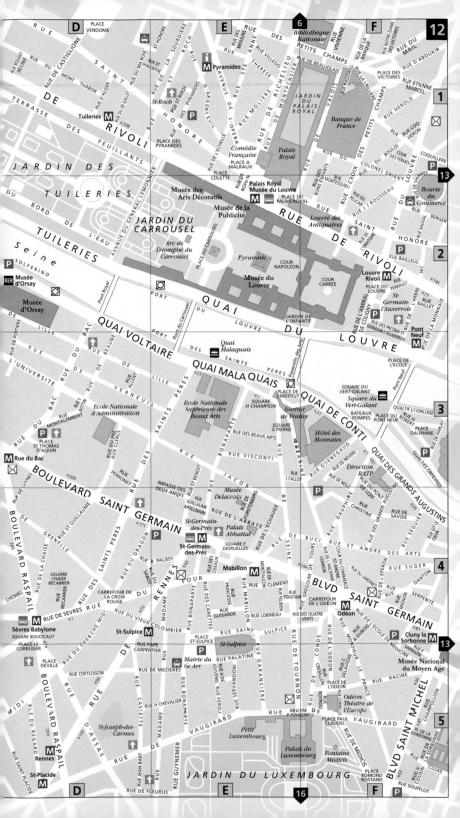

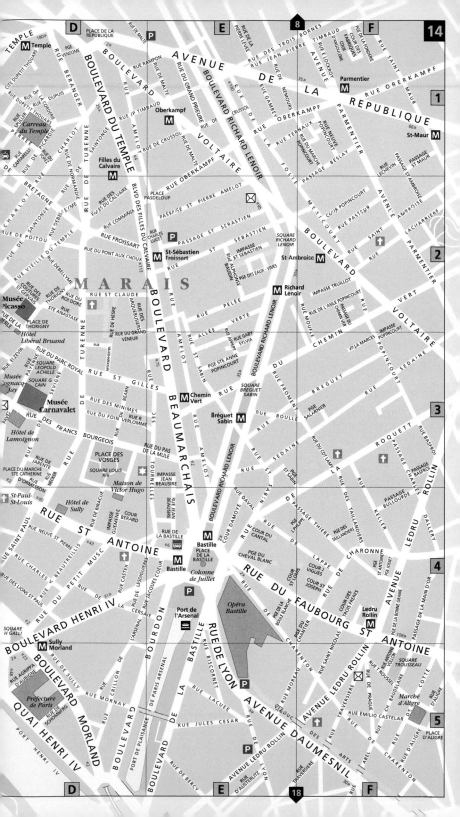

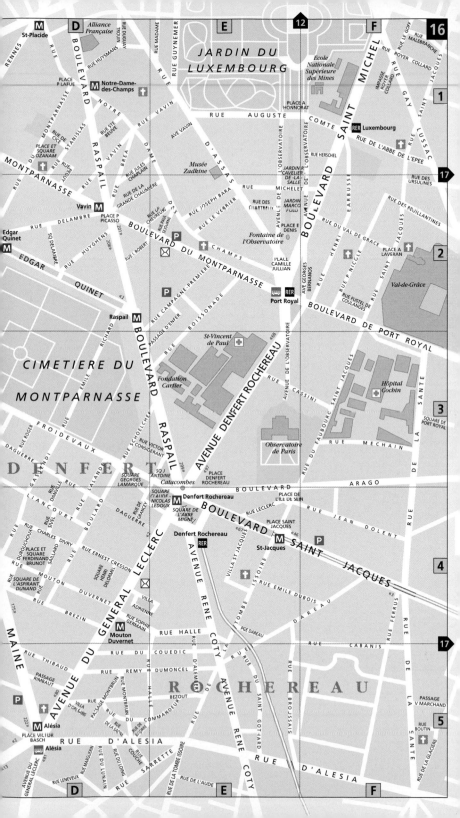

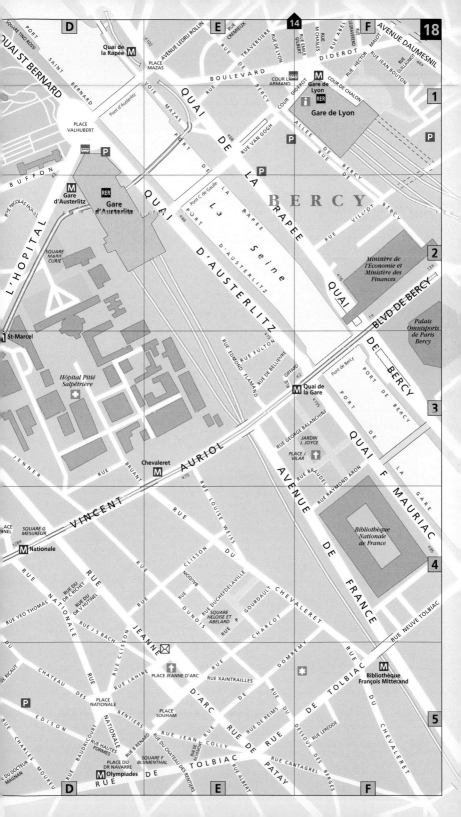

General Index

Acknowledgments

Dorling Kindersley would like to thank the many people whose help and assistance contributed to the preparation of this book.

Main Contributor
Alan Tillier has lived in all the main areas of Paris for 25 years, during which time he has been Paris correspondent for several journals including *Newsweek, The Times* and the *International Herald Tribune*. He is the author of several *Herald Tribune* guides for business travellers to Europe.

Contributors
Lenny Borger, Karen Burshtein, Thomas Quinn Curtiss, David Downie, Fiona Dunlop, Heidi Ellison, Alexandre Lazareff, Robert Noah, Andrew Sanger, Martha Rose Shulman, David Stevens, Ian Williams, Jude Welton.

Dorling Kindersley wishes to thank the following editors and researchers at Websters International Publishers: Sandy Carr, Siobhan Bremner, Valeria Fabbri, Gemma Hancock, Sara Harper, Annie Hubert, Celia Woolfrey.

Additional Photography
Marta Bescos, Anna Brooke, Rough Guides/James McConnachie, Andy Crawford, Michael Crockett, Lucy Davies, Mike Dunning, Philip Gatward, Steve Gorton, Alison Harris, Andrew Holligan, Chas Howson, Britta Jaschinski, Dave King, Ranald MacKechnie, Oliver Knight, Michael Lin, Eric Meacher, Neil Mersh, Ian O'Leary, Stephen Oliver, Poppy, Susannah Price, Tim Ridley, Philippe Sebert, Sheillee Shah, Steve Shott, Peter Wilson, Steven Wooster.

Additional Illustrations
John Fox, Nick Gibbard, David Harris, Kevin Jones Associates, John Woodcock.

Cartography
Andrew Heritage, James Mills-Hicks, Suresh Kumar, Alok Pathak, John Plumer, Chez Picthall (DK Cartography). Advanced Illustration (Cheshire), Contour Publishing (Derby), Euromap Limited (Berkshire). Street Finder maps: ERA-Maptec Ltd (Dublin) adapted with permission from original survey and mapping by Shobunsha (Japan).

Cartographic Research
Roger Bullen, Tony Chambers, Paul Dempsey, Ruth Duxbury, Ailsa Heritage, Margeret Hynes, Jayne Parsons, Donna Rispoli, Andrew Thompson.

Design and Editorial
Managing Editor Douglas Amrine
Managing Art Editor Geoff Manders
Senior Editor Georgina Matthews
Series Design Consultant Peter Luff
Editorial Director David Lamb
Art Director Anne-Marie Bulat

Production Controller Hilary Stephens
Picture Research Naomi Peck
Production Controller Hilary Stephens
Proofreader Stewart Wild
DTP Designer Andy Wilkinson
Design and Editorial Assistance Janet Abbott, Emma Ainsworth, Vandana Bhagra, Sonal Bhatt, Hilary Bird, Anna Brooke, Vanessa Courtier, Maggie Crowley, Lisa Davidson, Simon Davis, Guy Dimond, Nicola Erdpresser, Elizabeth Eyre, Simon Farbrother, Fay Franklin, Anna Freiberger, Rhiannon Furber, Eric Gibory, Amy Harrison, Lilly Heise, Paul Hines, Fiona Holman, Gail Jones, Laura Jones, Nancy Jones, Stephen Knowlden, Maite Lantaron, Chris Lascelles, Delphine Lawrance, Jude Ledger, Carly Madden, Nicola Malone, Sam Merrell, Rebecca Milner, Fiona Morgan, Lyn Parry, Shirin Patel, Pure Content, Rada Radojicic, Pamposh Raina, Philippa Richmond, Louise Rogers, Ellen Root, Philippe Rouin, Sands Publishing Solutions, Meredith Smith, Andrew Szudek, Alka Thakur, Roseen Teare, Dora Whitaker.

Special Assistance
Miranda Dewer at Bridgeman Art Library, Editions Gallimard, Lindsay Hunt, Emma Hutton at Cooling Brown, Janet Todd at DACS.

Photographic Reference
Musée Carnavalet, Thomas d'Hoste.

Photography Permissions
Dorling Kindersley would like to thank the following for their kind permission to photograph at their establishments: Aéroports de Paris, Basilique du Sacré-Coeur de Montmartre, Beauvilliers, Benoit, Bibliothèque Historique de la Ville de Paris, Bibliothèque Polonaise, Bofinger, Brasserie Lipp, Café de Flore, Caisse Nationale des Monuments Historiques et des Sites, Les Catacombes, Centre National d'Art et de Culture Georges Pompidou, Chartier, Chiberta, La Cité des Sciences et de l'Industrie and L'EPPV, La Coupole, Les Deux Magots, Fondation Cousteau, Le Grand Colbert, Hôtel Atala, Hôtel Liberal Bruand, Hôtel Meurice, Hôtel Relais Christine, Kenzo, Lucas-Carton, La Madeleine, Mariage Frères, Memorial de la Shoah, Thierry Mugler, Musée Armenien de France, Musée de l'Art Juif, Musée Bourdelle, Musée du Cabinet des Medailles, Musée Carnavalet, Musée Cernuschi: Ville de Paris, Musée du Cinema Henri Langlois, Musée Cognacq-Jay, Musée de Cristal de Baccarat, Musée d'Ennery, Musée Grévin, Musée Jacquemart-André, Musée de la Musique Méchanique, Musée National des Châteaux de Malmaison et Bois-Préau, Collections du Musée National de la Légion d'Honneur, Musée National du Moyen Age-Thermes de Cluny, Musée de Notre-Dame de Paris, Musée de l'Opéra, Musée de l'Ordre de la Libération, Musée d'Orsay, Musée de la Préfecture de la Police, Musée de Radio France, Musée Ro-din, Musée des Transports Urbains, Musée du Vin, Musée Zadkine, Notre-Dame du Travail, A l'Olivier, Palais de la Découverte, Palais de Luxembourg, Pharamond, Pied de

Cochon, Lionel Poilaêne, St Germain-des-Prés, St Louis en l'Ile, St Médard, St Merry, St Paul–St-Louis, St-Roch, St-Sulpice, La Société Nouvelle d'Exploitation de La Tour Eiffel, La Tour Montparnasse, Unesco, and all the other museums, churches, hotels, restaurants, shops, galleries and sights too numerous to thank individually.

Picture Credits

a-above.; b-below/bottom; c-centre; f-far; l-left; r-right; t-top.

Works of art have been reproduced with the permission of the following copyright holders: © ADAGP/SPADEM, Paris and DACS, London 2011: 44cl; © ADAGP, Paris and DACS, London 2011: 61br, 61tr, 105tc, 107cb, 109b, 111tc, 111cb, 112bl, 112t, 112br, 113bl, 113br, 119c, 120b, 179tl, 180bc, 181cr, 211tc; © DACS 2011: 38tl, 45cr, 50br, 55cr, 57tl, 100t, 100br, 100clb, 100cl, 100ca, 101t, 101ca, 101cr, 101bl, 104, 107cra, 113c, 137tl, 178cl, 178ca, 208br.

Christo–The Pont Neuf wrapped, Paris, 1975-85: 40cla; © Christo 1985, by kind permission of the artist. Photos achieved with the assistance of the EPPV and the CSI pp 234-9; Courtesy of Erben Otto Dix: 110bl; Photos of Disneyland ® Paris: 242tr, 243bl, 243cr, 362t. The characters, architectural works and trademarks are the property of The Walt Disney Company. All rights reserved; Fondation Le Corbusier: 59t, 254b; Courtesy of The Estate of Joan Mitchell: 113t; © Henry Moore Foundation 1993: 191b. Reproduced by kind permission of the Henry Moore Foundation; Beth Lipkin: 241t; Courtesy of the Maison Victor Hugo, Ville de Paris: 95cl; Courtesy of the Musée d'Art Naïf Max Fourny Paris: 223b, 225b; Musée Carnavalet: 214b; Musée de L'Histoire Contemporaine (BDIC), Paris: 210br; Musée de L'Orangerie: 130tr; Musée du Louvre: 125br, 128c; Musée National des Châteaux de Malmaison et Bois-Préau: 255cr; Musée Marmottan: 58c, 58cb, 59c, 60tl, 131tr; Musée de la Mode et du Costume Palais Galliera: 57br; Musée de Montmartre, Paris: 223t; Musée des Monuments Français: 199tc, 200cr; Musée National de la Légion d'Honneur: 32bc, 143bl; Musée de la Ville de Paris: Musée du Petit Palais: 54cl, 207cb; © Sundancer: 362bl.

The Publishers are grateful to the following individuals, companies and picture libraries for permission to reproduce their photographs:

A Curious Group of Hotels/L'Hotel: 283tr; Académie de la Grande Chaumière: 177tc; ADP: 377b; Agence Républic: 382, 382br; Alamy: Tibor Bognar 115tr; Christel Broque 201cra; Bertrand Collet 269cl; Directphoto.org 372tl; Glenn Harper 212tl; Image State 270br; A la Poste 375c; Jack Sullivan 371cra; Justin Kase Zfivez 371tr; Allsport UK; Sean Botterill 41br; A21vey & Towers: 378bl; The Ancient Art and Architecture Collection: 22clb; James Austin: 88t.

Banque de France: 133t; Nelly Bariand: 165c; Bateaux Parisiens: 72crb; Gérard Boullay: 84tl, 84tr, 84bl, 84br, 85t, 85cra, 85crb, 85br, 85bl; Bridgeman Art Library,

London: (detail) 21br, 22cr, 23cl, 30cr–31cl, (detail) 35br; British Library, London (detail) 18br, (detail) 23bl, (detail) 24tl, (detail) 31tl; B N, Paris 19bl, (detail) 23tc, (detail) 23cr; Château de Versailles, France 19tr, 19bc, (detail) 19br, (detail) 30br, (detail) 155b; Christie's, London 8–9, (detail) 24cb, 34cla, 36tl, 44c; Delomosne, London 32clb; Giraudon 16, (detail) 26bl, (detail) 26clb, (detail) 27br, (detail) 30bl, (detail) 30cla, (detail) 31bl, 33cb, 58br, (detail) 60bl, 60ca, 60c; Lauros– Giraudon 23tr; Louvre, Paris 56t, 60br, 61bl, 61tl; Roy Miles Gallery 27tr; Musée de L'Armée, Paris (detail) 83br; Musée Condé, Chantilly (detail) 4tr, 18bl, 19tcl, (detail) 19tcr, (detail) 19c, (detail) 22tl, (detail) 26bc; Musée Crozatier, Le Puy en Velay, France (detail) 25bl; Musée Gustave Moreau, Paris 56b, 233c; Musee National d'Art Moderne, Centre Pompidou, Paris 111c; National Gallery (detail) 29tl, (detail) 44b; Musée de la Ville de Paris, Musée Carnavalet (detail) 30bc, (detail) 31tr, 31crb, 97t. CineAqua: 200bl. Collection Painton Cowen 40cla; Palais de Tokyo, Paris 59b; Temples Newsham House, Leeds 25cr; Uffizi Gallery, Florence (detail) 24br; © British Museum: 31tc.

Camping International Maisons Laffitte: 281br; Cité de la Musique: Eric Mahondieu 237br; Cité des Sciences et de l'Industrie: Sophie Chivet 239br; Michel Lamoureux 238cb, 238b, 239tl, 239tr, 238c; NASA/ESA 238tr; Sylvain Sonnet 238 clb; Natacha Soury 238tl; Michel Viard 239tl; Cliché Photothèque des Musées de la Ville de Paris – © DACS 2011: 21ca, 21crb, 28cr–29cl, 96tr; courtesy of Poilâne: 321bl; Collections du Mobilier National-Cliché du Mobilier National: 167cr; Corbis: Burnstein Collection 229b; Jose Fuste Raga 376bl; Ray Juno 10cl; Richard List 11cl; Sylvain Saustier 268b; Tom Craig: 273t, 273br.

R Doisneau: Rapho 143t.

Espace Montmartre: 222bl; Eurolines: 379crb; European Commission 371; Mary Evans Picture Library: 38bl, 81br, 89tl, 94b, 130b, 141cl, 191c, 194cr, 195crb, 211b, 226bl, 247br, 251t, 253b, 388t.

Four Seasons Hotel George V: 277bl; France Miniature: Stefan Meyer 361tr.

Getty Images: AFP/Pierre Verdy 106clb; Fred Dufour 192clb; Giraudon: (detail) 22bl, (detail) 23crb; Lauros– Giraudon (detail) 33bl; Musée de la Ville de Paris Musée Carnavalet (detail) 213t; Le Grand Véfour: 293t; Philippe Guignard: 193br.

Roland Halbe: 192tr; La Halle Saint Pierre 225bc; Robert Harding Picture Library: 22br, 26tl, 29ca, 29br, 36cla, 38tl, 41tl, 45cr, 65br, 240cb, 381cr; B M 27ca; B N 191tr, 210bc; Biblioteco Reale, Turin 127t; Bulloz 210cb; P Craven 380b; R Francis 82clb; I Griffiths 376t; H Josse 210br, Musée National des Châteaux de Malmaison et Bois-Préau 33tc; Musée de Versailles 26cl; R Poinot 361b; P Tetrel 251crb; Explorer 12bl; F. Chazot 341b; Girard 65c; P Gleizes 62bl; F Jalain 378b; J Moatti 340bl, 340cl; Walter Rawlings 43bc; A Wolf 123br, 123tl; Alison Harris: Musée de

Montparnasse 179cl; Le Village Royale 132tl; Hemispheres Images: Bertrand Gardel 92cl; John Heseltine Photography: 174; Hôtel de L'Abbaye: 283bc; Hôtel de Crillon: 282crb; Hôtel Duc de Saint Simon: 282br; Hôtel du Jeu de Paume: 283crb; Hotels Paris Rive Gauche/Hôtel des Grands Hommes: 278br; Hulton Getty: 45cl, 101br, 181tc, 233bl, 234c; Charles Hewitt 40clb; Lancaster 181tc.

© IGN Paris 1990 Authorisation N° 90–2067: 13b; Institut du Monde Arabe: Georges Fessey 165tr; InterContinental Hotels Group: 215crb, 283tl.

The Kobal Collection: 44t, 140b; Columbia Pictures 181br; Société Générale de Films 38tc; Les Films du Carrosse 109cl; Kong: Patricia Bailer 10b.

The Lebrecht Collection: 229br; François Lequeux 194cl; Leonardo Media Ltd.: 279br, 279cl, 279tl, 282cl, 283cra.

Magnum: Bruno Barbey 64b; Philippe Halsmann 45b; Le Meurice: Peter Hebeisen 278tl; Les Abeilles: 272br; Ministère de L'Economie et des Finances: 371c; Ministère de L'Intérieur SGAP de Paris: 370b; © photo Musée de L'Armée, Paris: 189cr; Musée des Arts Décoratifs, Paris: L Sully Jaulmes 54t, Cabinet (1922-1923) Jacques-Emile Ruhlmann 57tr; Musée Bouilhet-Christofle: 132t; Musée Cantonal des Beaux-Arts, Lausanne: 115b; Musée Carnavalet: Dac Karin Maucotel 97b; Musée d'Art et d'Histoire du Judaïsme/Christophe Fouin 103br; Musée National de L'Histoire Naturelle: D Serrette 167cl; © Musée de L'Homme, Paris: D Ponsard 198cb, 201c; © Photo Musée de la Marine, Paris: 32bl, 196cl; Musée National d'Art Moderne – Centre Georges Pompidou, Paris: 61tr, 110br, 110bl, 111t, 111cb, 112t, 112bl, 112br, 113t, 113c, 113bl, 113br; Musée des Plans-Reliefs: 186crb; Musée de la Poste: 179tl; Musée du Quai Branly: Patrick Gries/Bruno Descoings 54cb, 192br.

The Odéon-Théâtre de L'Europe: 341t.

Palais de Tokyo: Michael Lin 203cr; Paris Convention & Visitors Bureau: Marc Bertrand 222br, 383bl; Nicky Bouwmeester 160; Fabian Charaffi 375bc; Amélie Dupont 55tr,162cla, 203cr, 323bl, 382ca; David Lefranc 366br, 368bl; Alain Potignon 369c, 375crb; © Paris Tourist Office: Catherine Balet 270cl; David Lefranc 268c, 269t, 269br, 270tr, 271t, 271br, 272cl, 272bl; Paris Vision & Cityrama: 383ca; Photolibrary: F1 Online/Widmann Widmann 372c; Photononstop/Jean-Marc Romain 371cr; Philippe Perdereau: 132b, 133b; Popperfoto: 229bl; La Poste: 374tl; Le Pre Verre: 292cr.

Paul Raferty: 246b; RATP: 382br, 385ca, 385cb, 387cr; RATP.SG/G.I.E. Totheme 54; 386; Redferns: W Gottlieb 38clb; © Photo Réunion des Musées Nationaux: Grand Trianon 26crb; Musée Guimet 202tr; Musée du Louvre 27cb, (detail) 32cr–33cl, 55tl, 123bl, 124t, 124cl, 124b, 125t, 125c, 126c, 126bl, 126br, 127b, 128t, 128b, 129t, 129c; Musée Nationaux d'Art Moderne 111crb; Musée Picasso 55cr, 100t, 100c, 100cl, 100clb, 100br, 101bl, 101cr, 101ca, 101t; Roger-Viollet: (detail) 24clb, (detail) 39bl, (detail) 194bc, (detail) 211t; Ann Ronan Picture Library: 173cr; Philippe Ruault: Fondation Cartier 179bl; Plaza Athénée: 277tr.

Photo Scala, Florence: Musée du Quai Branly/Patrick Gries/Valérie Torre 193cr,/Patrick Gries/Bruno Descoings 193c; Sealink Plc: 378cl; Senderens: Roberto Frankenberg 294bl; Sipapress: 224c; SNCF – Service Presse Voyages France Europe: 388bl; CAV/Christophe Recoura 378b; CAV/Jean-Marc Fabbro 378ca; /French railways 376cra; Frank Spooner Pictures: F Reglain 64ca; P Renault 64c; SuperStock: Hemis.fr 109tl; Sygma: 35crb, 240cl; F Poincet 40tl; Keystone 40bc, 241cra; J Langevin 41br; Keler 41crb; J Van Hasselt 41tr; P. Habans 62c; A Gyori 63cr; P Vauthey 65bl; Y Forestier 188t; Sunset Blvd 241br; Water Carone 340t.

Tallandier: 25cb, 25tl, 28cl, 28clb, 28bl, 29bl, 30tl, 31cr, 31ca, 32tl, 32cb, 32br, 38cla, 39ca, 39br, 40cb, 52cla; B N 28br, 32crb, 38bc; Brigaud 39crb; Brimeur 34bl; Charmet 36cb; Dubout 17b, 20br, 24ca, 25br, 26br, 30c, 33cr, 33tr, 34br, 35bl, 36clb, 36bl, 36br, 37bl, 37br, 37clb, 37tl, 38crb; Josse 20cla, 20tc, 20c, 20clb, 21tl, 36bc; Josse-B N 20bl; Joubert 38c; Tildier 37ca; Vigne 34clb; Tourisme & Handicaps: 368tr; Le Train Bleu: 295t.

Vedettes de Paris: 72cl, 72clb; Vidéothèque de Paris: Hoi Pham Dinh 106lb; Agence Vu: Didier Lefèvre 340cr.

Front Endpaper: John Heseltine Photography br. © DACS 2011: cra; Paris Convention & Visitors Bureau: Nicky Bouwmeester br. Back endpaper: RATP CML Agence Cartographique.

Map Cover - Corbis: Rudy Sulgan.

Jacket:
Front - Corbis: Rudy Sulgan.
Back - AWL Images: Dan Bannister bl; Dorling Kindersley: Max Alexander clb; Rough Guides/James McConnachie tl, cla.
Spine - Corbis: Rudy Sulgan t.

SPECIAL EDITIONS OF DK TRAVEL GUIDES

DK Travel Guides can be purchased in bulk quantities at discounted prices for use in promotions or as premiums. We are also able to offer special editions and personalized jackets, corporate imprints, and excerpts from all of our books, tailored specifically to meet your own needs.

To find out more, please contact:
(in the United States) SpecialSales@dk.com
(in the UK) travelspecialsales@uk.dk.com
(in Canada) DK Special Sales at general@tourmaline.ca
(in Australia)
business.development@pearson.com.au

Phrase Book

In Emergency

Help!	Au secours!	oh sekoor
Stop!	Arrêtez!	aret-ay
Call a doctor!	Appelez un médecin!	apuh-lay uñ medsañ
Call an ambulance!	Appelez une ambulance!	apuh-lay oon oñboo-loñs
Call the police!	Appelez la police!	apuh-lay lah poh-lees
Call the fire brigade!	Appelez les pompiers!	apuh-lay leh poñ-peeyay
Where is the nearest telephone?	Où est le téléphone le plus proche?	oo ay luh teblehfon luh ploo prosh
Where is the nearest hospital?	Où est l'hôpital le plus proche?	oo ay l'opeetal luh ploo prosh

Communication Essentials

Yes	Oui	wee
No	Non	noñ
Please	S'il vous plaît	seel voo play
Thank you	Merci	mer-see
Excuse me	Excusez-moi	exkoo-zay mwah
Hello	Bonjour	boñzhoor
Goodbye	Au revoir	oh rub-vwar
Good night	Bonsoir	boñ-swar
Morning	Le matin	matañ
Afternoon	L'après-midi	l'apreh-meedee
Evening	Le soir	swar
Yesterday	Hier	eeyehr
Today	Aujourd'hui	oh-zhoor-dwee
Tomorrow	Demain	dubmañ
Here	Ici	ee-see
There	Là	lah
What?	Quoi, quel, quelle?	kwah, kel, kel
When?	Quand?	koñ
Why?	Pourquoi?	poor-kwah
Where?	Où?	oo

Useful Phrases

How are you?	Comment allez-vous?	kom-moñ talay voo
Very well, thank you.	Très bien, merci.	treh byañ, mer-see
Pleased to meet you.	Enchanté de faire votre connaissance.	oñshoñ-tay dub febr votr kon-ay-sans
See you soon.	A bientôt.	byañ-toh
That's fine	C'est bon	say bon
Where is/are...?	Où est/sont...?	ooay/soñ
How far is it to...?	Combien de kilometres d'ici à...?	kom-byañ dub keelo-metr d'ee-see ah
Which way to...?	Quelle est la direction pour...?	kel ay lah deer-ek-syoñ poor
Do you speak English?	Parlez-vous anglais?	par-lay voo oñg-lay
I don't understand.	Je ne comprends pas.	zhuh nuh kom-proñ pah
Could you speak slowly please?	Pouvez-vous parler moins vite s'il vous plaît?	poo-vay voo par-lay mwañ veet seel voo play
I'm sorry.	Excusez-moi.	exkoo-zay mwah

Useful Words

big	grand	groñ
small	petit	puh-tee
hot	chaud	show
cold	froid	frwah
good	bon/bien	boñ/byañ
bad	mauvais	mob-veh
enough	assez	assay
well	bien	byañ
open	ouvert	oo-ver
closed	fermé	fer-meh
left	gauche	gohsh
right	droite	drwabt
straight on	tout droite	too drwabt
near	près	preh
far	loin	lwañ
up	en haut	oñ ob
down	en bas	oñ bah
early	de bonne heure	dub bon urr
late	en retard	oñ rub-tar
entrance	l'entrée	l'on-tray
exit	la sortie	sor-tee
toilet	les toilettes, le WC	twab-let, vay-see
free, unoccupied	libre	leebr
free, no charge	gratuit	grah-twee

Making a Telephone Call

I'd like to place a long-distance call.	Je voudrais faire un appel á l'étranger.	zhuh voo-dreh febr uñ apel a laytroñ-zhay
I'd like to make a reverse charge call.	Je voudrais faire une communication en PCV.	zhuh voo-dreh febr oon komoonikab-syoñ oñ peb-seb-veh
I'll try again later.	Je rappelerai plus tard.	zhub rapel-eray ploo tar
Can I leave a message?	Est-ce que je peux laisser un message?	es-keh zhub pub leh-say uñ mehsazb
Hold on.	Ne quittez pas, s'il vous plaît.	nub kee-tay pab seel voo play
Could you speak up a little please?	Pouvez-vous parler un peu plus fort?	poo-vay voo par-lay uñ pub ploo for
local call	la communication locale	komoonikab-syoñ low-kal

Shopping

How much does this cost?	C'est combien s'il vous plaît?	say kom-byañ seel voo play
I would like ...	je voudrais...	zhub voo-dray
Do you have?	Est-ce que vous avez?	es-kub voo zavay
I'm just looking.	Je regarde seulement.	zhub rubgar sublmoñ
Do you take credit cards?	Est-ce que vous acceptez les cartes de crédit?	es-kub voo zaksept-ay leb kart dub kreb-dee
Do you take travellers' cheques?	Est-ce que vous acceptez les cheques de voyages?	es-kub voo zaksept-ay leb shek dub vwayazb
What time do you open?	A quelle heure vous êtes-ouvert?	ab kel urr voo zet oo-ver
What time do you close?	A quelle heure vous êtes fermé?	ab kel urr voo zet fer-may
This one.	Celui-ci.	subl-wee-see
That one.	Celui-là.	subl-wee-lah
expensive	cher	shebr
cheap	pas cher, bon marché	pah shebr, boñ mar-shay
size, clothes	la taille	tye
size, shoes	la pointure	pwañ-tur
white	blanc	bloñ
black	noir	nwabr
red	rouge	roozh
yellow	jaune	zhobwn
green	vert	vehr
blue	bleu	bluh

Types of Shop

antique shop	le magasin d'antiquités	maga-zañ d'oñteekee-tay
bakery	la boulangerie	booloñ-zhuree
bank	la banque	boñk
book shop	la librairie	lee-brebree
butcher	la boucherie	boo-shebree
cake shop	la pâtisserie	patee-sree
cheese shop	la fromagerie	fromazb-ree
chemist	la pharmacie	farmab-see
dairy	la crémerie	krem-ree
department store	le grand magasin	groñ maga-zañ
delicatessen	la charcuterie	sharkoot-ree
fishmonger	la poissonnerie	pwasson-ree
gift shop	le magasin de cadeaux	maga-zañ dub kadob
greengrocer	le marchand de légumes	mar-sboñ dub lay-goom
grocery	l'alimentation	alee-moñta-syoñ
hairdresser	le coiffeur	kwafubr
market	le marché	marsb-ay
newsagent	le magasin de journaux	maga-zañ dub zboor-no
post office	la poste, le bureau de poste, le PTT	pobst, boorob dub pobst, peb-teb-teb
shoe shop	le magasin de chaussures	maga-zañ dub sbow-soor
supermarket	le supermarché	soo pebr-marsbay
tobacconist	le tabac	tabab
travel agent	l'agence de voyages	l'azboñs dub vwayazb

Sightseeing

abbey	l'abbaye	l'abay-ee
art gallery	la galerie d'art	galer-ree dart
bus station	la gare routière	gabr roo-tee-yebr

cathedral	la cathédrale	katay-dral
church	l'église	l'aygleez
garden	le jardin	zhar-dañ
library	la bibliothèque	beebleeo-tek
museum	le musée	moo-zay
railway station	la gare (SNCF)	gahr (es-en-say-ef)
tourist	les renseignements	roñsayn-moñ
information	touristiques, le	toorees-teek, sandee-
office	syndicat d'initiative	ka d'eenee-syateev
town hall	l'hôtel de ville	l'obtel dub veel
closed for	fermeture	febrmeb-tur
public holiday	jour férié	zhoor febree-ay

Staying in a Hotel

Do you have a	Est-ce que vous	es-kub voo-zavay
vacant room?	avez une chambre?	oon sbambr
double room,	la chambre à deux	sbambr ab dub
with double bed	personnes, avec	pebr-son avek un
	un grand lit	groñ lee
twin room	la chambre à	sbambr ab
	deux lits	dub lee
single room	la chambre à	sbambr ab
	une personne	oon pebr-son
room with a	la chambre avec	sbambr avek
bath, shower	salle de bains,	sal dub bañ,
	une douche	oon doosb
porter	le garçon	gar-soñ
key	la clef	klay
I have a	J'ai fait une	zhay fay oon
reservation.	réservation.	rayzebrva-syoñ

Eating Out

Have you	Avez-vous une	avay-voo oon
got a table?	table de libre?	tabbl dub leebr
I want to	Je voudrais	zhub voo-dray
reserve	réserver	rayzebr-vay
a table.	une table.	oon tabbl
The bill	L'addition s'il	l'adee-syoñ seel
please.	vous plaît.	voo play
I am a	Je suis	zhub swee
vegetarian.	végétarien.	vezhay-tebryañ
Waitress/	Madame,	mab-dam,
waiter	Mademoiselle/	mab-demwabzel/
	Monsieur	mub-syub
menu	le menu, la carte	men-oo, kart
fixed-price	le menu à	men-oo ab
menu	prix fixe	pree feeks
cover charge	le couvert	koo-vebr
wine list	la carte des vins	kart-deb vañ
glass	le verre	vebr
bottle	la bouteille	boo-tay
knife	le couteau	koo-tob
fork	la fourchette	for-sbet
spoon	la cuillère	kwee-yebr
breakfast	le petit	pub-tee
	déjeuner	deb-zhub-nay
lunch	le déjeuner	deb-zhub-nay
dinner	le dîner	dee-nay
main course	le plat principal	plab prañsee-pal
starter, first	l'entrée, le hors	l'oñ-tray, or-
course	d'oeuvre	dubvr
dish of the day	le plat du jour	plab doo zhoor
wine bar	le bar à vin	bar ab vañ
café	le café	ka-fay
rare	saignant	say-noñ
medium	à point	ab pwañ
well done	bien cuit	byañ kwee

Menu Decoder

apple	la pomme	pom
baked	cuit au four	kweet ob foor
banana	la banane	banan
beef	le boeuf	bubf
beer, draught	la bière, bière	bee-yebr, bee-yebr
beer	à la pression	ab lab pres-syoñ
boiled	bouilli	boo-yee
bread	le pain	pan
butter	le beurre	burr
cake	le gâteau	gab-tob
cheese	le fromage	from-azb
chicken	le poulet	poo-lay
chips	les frites	freet
chocolate	le chocolat	sboko-lab
cocktail	le cocktail	cocktail
coffee	le café	kab-fay
dessert	le dessert	deb-ser
dry	sec	sek
duck	le canard	kanar

egg	l'oeuf	l'uf
fish	le poisson	pwab-ssoñ
fresh fruit	le fruit frais	frwee freb
garlic	l'ail	l'eye
grilled	grillé	gree-yay
ham	le jambon	zboñ-boñ
ice, ice cream	la glace	glas
lamb	l'agneau	l'anyob
lemon	le citron	see-troñ
lobster	le homard	omahr
meat	la viande	vee-yand
milk	le lait	leb
mineral water	l'eau minérale	l'ob meeney-ral
mustard	la moutarde	moo-tard
oil	l'huile	l'weel
olives	les olives	leb zoleev
onions	les oignons	leb zonyoñ
orange	l'orange	l'oroñzb
fresh orange juice	l'orange pressée	l'oroñzb press-eb
fresh lemon juice	le citron pressé	see-troñ press-eb
pepper	le poivre	pwavr
poached	poché	posb-ay
pork	le porc	por
potatoes	les pommes de terre	pom-dub tebr
prawns	les crevettes	krub-vet
rice	le riz	ree
roast	rôti	row-tee
roll	le petit pain	pub-tee pañ
salt	le sel	sel
sauce	la sauce	sobs
sausage, fresh	la saucisse	sobsees
seafood	les fruits de mer	frwee dub mer
shellfish	les crustaces	kroos-tas
snails	les escargots	leb zes-kar-gob
soup	la soupe, le potage	soop, pob-tazb
steak	le bifteck, le steack	beef-tek, stek
sugar	le sucre	sookr
tea	le thé	tay
toast	pain grillé	pan greeyay
vegetables	les légumes	lay-goom
vinegar	le vinaigre	veenaygr
water	l'eau	l'ob
red wine	le vin rouge	vañ roozb
white wine	le vin blanc	vañ bloñ

Numbers

0	zéro	zeb-rob
1	un, une	uñ, oon
2	deux	dub
3	trois	trwab
4	quatre	katr
5	cinq	sañk
6	six	sees
7	sept	set
8	huit	weet
9	neuf	nerf
10	dix	dees
11	onze	oñz
12	douze	dooz
13	treize	trebz
14	quatorze	katorz
15	quinze	kañz
16	seize	sebz
17	dix-sept	dees-set
18	dix-huit	dees-weet
19	dix-neuf	dees-nerf
20	vingt	vañ
30	trente	tront
40	quarante	karoñt
50	cinquante	sañkoñt
60	soixante	swasoñt
70	soixante-dix	swasoñt-dees
80	quatre-vingts	katr-vañ
90	quatre-vingt-dix	katr-vañ-dees
100	cent	soñ
1,000	mille	meel

Time

one minute	une minute	oon mee-noot
one hour	une heure	oon urr
half an hour	une demi-heure	oon dub-mee urr
Monday	lundi	luñ-dee
Tuesday	mardi	mar-dee
Wednesday	mercredi	mebrkrub-dee
Thursday	jeudi	zhub-dee
Friday	vendredi	voñdrub-dee
Saturday	samedi	sam-dee
Sunday	dimanche	dee-moñsb

Paris Metro and Regional Express Railway (RER)

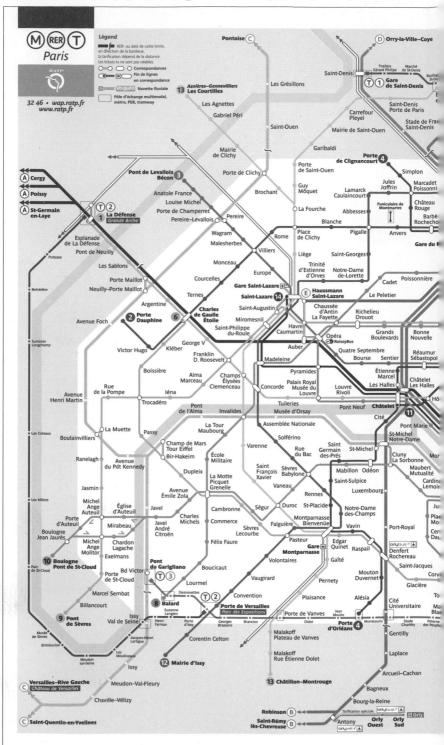